OXFORD MONOGRAPHS IN INTERNATIONAL HUMANITARIAN AND CRIMINAL LAW

International Law and the Investigation of Transnational Crimes

OXFORD MONOGRAPHS IN INTERNATIONAL HUMANITARIAN AND CRIMINAL LAW

This series emerged through the vision of the late Antonio Cassese. Since then the series has published original and innovative works on challenging issues in international humanitarian law and international criminal justice, primarily by emerging authors. Given the ever-growing intersection of these areas with other fields of international law such as the jus ad bellum, and disciplines such as criminology, sociology, and history, the scope of the series also incorporates these perspectives. Fresh approaches and new ideas for improving conceptual and practical challenges are welcomed. The series editors encourage submissions from around the world, and will consider edited collections, although the primary focus is on authored works.

ALSO PUBLISHED IN THIS SERIES

The Arms Trade and International Criminal Law
Reframing Accountability for Complicit Weapon Suppliers
Tomas Hamilton

International Criminal Tribunals and Domestic Accountability
In the Court's Shadow
Patryk I. Labuda

The Morality of the Laws of War
War, Law, and Murder
Marcela Prieto Rudolphy

Accountability for Mass Starvation
Testing the Limits of the Law
Edited by Bridget Conley, Alex de Waal, Catriona Murdoch, and Wayne Jordash KC

The Defence of Mistake of Law in International Criminal Law
A Study on Ignorance and Blame
Antonio Coco

The Use of Force against Individuals in War under International Law
A Social Ontological Approach
Ka Lok Yip

International Law and the Investigation of Transnational Crimes

YURIKA ISHII, PHD
Professor, Sophia University, Japan

OXFORD
UNIVERSITY PRESS

OXFORD
UNIVERSITY PRESS

Great Clarendon Street, Oxford, OX2 6DP,
United Kingdom

Oxford University Press is a department of the University of Oxford.
It furthers the University's objective of excellence in research, scholarship,
and education by publishing worldwide. Oxford is a registered trade mark of
Oxford University Press in the UK and in certain other countries.

Published in the United States of America by Oxford University Press
198 Madison Avenue, New York, NY 10016, United States of America.

British Library Cataloguing in Publication Data
Data available

Library of Congress Control Number: 2025942405

ISBN 9780198957058

DOI: 10.1093/9780198957089.001.0001

Printed and bound by
CPI Group (UK) Ltd., Croydon, CR0 4YY

MIX
Paper | Supporting
responsible forestry
FSC
www.fsc.org
FSC® C013604

The manufacturer's authorised representative in the EU for product safety is
Oxford University Press España S.A. of Parque Empresarial San Fernando de Henares,
Avenida de Castilla, 2 – 28830 Madrid (www.oup.es/en or product.safety@oup.com).
OUP España S.A. also acts as importer into Spain of products made by the manufacturer.

Series Editors preface

The book *International Law and the Investigation of Transnational Crimes* by Yurika Ishii is a wide-ranging study which explores in depth the mechanisms and structures of an area of law that deals with the reaction of States to crimes which require for their punishment a very significant measure of international cooperation. Even though these crimes do not represent a threat to the values protected by the international community as a whole (contrary to the so-called core crimes, ie aggression, war crimes, crimes against humanity, and genocide), the fact that States share an interest in their prosecution makes them particularly relevant for shedding light on the functioning of inter-State cooperation.

The author clarifies in this regard that despite the originally domestic nature of these categories of crimes, the need for cooperation among States represents the distinctive trait that binds them together. In other words, we are here in an area where there is a horizontal rather than a vertical articulation of the relationships between international law and the prosecuting or investigating authorities, as well as a strong societal interest in suppressing these offences. This is not necessarily linked to the interests of the international community but rather to the common interest of two or more States, based on a certain dose of reciprocity.

The book skilfully maps the entire area of transnational criminal law, offering a definition, appropriately differentiating it from international criminal law, and illustrating the evolving role of individuals in this area of law. The author presents various categories of transnational crimes, ranging from corruption to tax offences, from security fraud to the violation of competition laws, reasoning on the various specific cooperation mechanisms which have been devised for the investigation (and prosecution) of these offences.

The book is divided into three parts and thirteen chapters, including introduction and conclusion. Part I sets the stage by analysing the State-centric structure of transnational criminal law and delving into the obligations to suppress various transnational crimes. It addresses the complexities arising from conflicts of prescriptive and enforcement jurisdiction. Part II focuses on investigations covering a broad range of offences (from violations of competition laws and economic sanction laws to securities and tax frauds, foreign bribery, and terrorism). Part III examines direct cooperation with foreign private entities, emphasizing the importance of such horizontal collaboration in combating transnational crime, exploring the direct cooperation between governments and private entities in collecting information for criminal investigations, and focusing on how such mechanisms are structured and the legal implications involved. This cooperation becomes complex when the private entities are foreign and when they are subject to conflicting legal requirements in their home countries. The key issue is the data protection and privacy legislation. While widespread agreement exists on the necessity of addressing and preventing serious crimes such as terrorism, the approach to privacy varies considerably across jurisdictions. This divergence raises fundamental questions about how governments may rely on private entities to aid in law enforcement efforts.

The conclusion summarizes the essential findings of the book and highlights the significance of international cooperation achieved through mechanisms beyond traditional mutual legal assistance treaties. In particular, it emphasizes how various types of agreements and frameworks have played a role in facilitating cross-border cooperation and addressing complex transnational challenges. The book also underscores how effective resolution of global issues requires collaboration and coordination among nations. Finally, emphasis is also placed on the role of human rights standards and how the requirement of protecting such rights influences transnational cooperation.

This book is an important addition to the series that broadens the scope of the reflection on the inter-State dimensions of international criminal law so as to address not only the so-called core crimes (ie aggression, genocide, crimes against humanity, and war crimes) but also the wider area of 'transnational crimes'. Crimes that are normally more closely linked to the protection of interests relevant for States at domestic level, but which entail common efforts for their prosecution, require enhanced cooperation and respect for human rights standards. The lessons drawn in this area of law can possibly offer new perspectives for the development of a concerted effort by States in areas in which cooperation and mutual legal assistance for the enforcement of criminal law are required.

We are hopeful that this book will be of interest to all those involved in the area of the studies of transnational criminal law, international criminal law, and more broadly the law of inter-State cooperation in criminal matters.

The Editors

Acknowledgements

This book is based on my PhD dissertation, written in Japanese and accepted by the University of Tokyo, Graduate Schools for Law and Politics, in 2011. It was published as a book *Ekkyo Hanzai no Kokusaiteki Kisei* in Japanese by Yuhikaku in 2017 and was awarded the 51st Adachi Mineichiro Award. The manuscript of this volume is based on the concepts and materials used in the doctoral research. However, I have rewritten the entire manuscript in English for this publication and updated the information. This book includes the most recent research findings, especially on direct cooperation with financial institutions and communication service providers. This book does not cover information that became available after December 2024. The research was funded by the Japan Society for the Promotion of Science Grants-in-Aid for Scientific Research (KAKENHI) 22830135, 21K01173, and 22K18255. The views expressed in this book are my own and do not represent the institutions or groups to which I belong or have previously belonged.

This project would not have been possible without the tangible and intangible support of experts, friends, and colleagues. The faculty staff at the University of Tokyo during my time in Hongo from 2003 to 2010, Professor NAKATANI Kazuhiro, my supervisor, patiently supported this research. Professors ONUMA Yasuaki, IWASAWA Yuji, OKUWAKI Naoya, NAKAGAWA Junji, KOTERA Akira, and TERAYA Koji, guided me along the path of international law studies.

The foundation of this study was shaped by numerous conversations, collaborations, and moments of shared inquiry over the years. I am grateful for the insights gained through exchanges with friends, colleagues, and professors at the University of Tokyo and Cornell Law School, in various research groups, and through my engagement with the Japanese Society of International Law, the American Society of International Law, the European Society of International Law, and the Association Internationale de Droit Pénal.

My time at the Max Planck Institute for Comparative Public Law and International Law in Heidelberg in 2008 and 2010, the Max Planck Institute for the Study of Crime, Security and Law in Freiburg in 2011, and Harvard Law School from 2014 to 2015 provided valuable opportunities to reflect, share ideas, and advance this research.

I also deepened my understanding through study groups at the Ministry of Foreign Affairs, the Ministry of Justice, and the National Police Agency of Japan. Discussions with practising attorneys and scholars in related fields—particularly in constitutional law, criminal procedure, and information law—offered perspectives that significantly influenced this work.

I am thankful for the support of librarians at the University of Tokyo, the Max Planck Institutes in Heidelberg and Freiburg, and Harvard University. The Peace Palace Library's database has been an essential tool in my daily research. I also appreciate the assistance of the faculty, administrative, and library staff at the National Defense Academy of Japan, from 2010 to March 2025. Sophia University has offered me the environment to finalize this book since April of this year.

Robert Cavooris, Kezia Johnson, Victoriya Sherly, and the editorial staff of the Oxford University Press and Newgen Knowledgeworks helped me finalize this publication.

Yuki, my husband, has been my steadfast support throughout this journey, standing by me every step of the way. Marika, our ten-year-old daughter, has filled my life with energy and comfort. My parents gave me the strength to begin my studies in international law, and my parents-in-law have provided indispensable support to continue.

Although this book challenges the State-centric perspective often found in international legal studies, it is ultimately driven by my trust in the States. Even in a deeply interconnected world, I believe that governments remain essential in protecting individuals and ensuring our safety. Article 97 of the Constitution of Japan expresses that '[t]he fundamental human rights by this Constitution guaranteed to the people of Japan are fruits of the age-old struggle of man to be free; they have survived the many exacting tests for durability and are conferred upon this and future generations in trust, to be held for all time inviolate'. Our rights are not merely legal guarantees—they are a legacy forged through struggle and passed down through the hard work of building communities, institutions, and governments. States have an important role to play as a force for good in this regard. Of course, States may also assume the role of oppressor, curtailing fundamental rights. It is incumbent upon us to safeguard against such encroachments. As Article 12 cautions, '[t]he freedoms and rights . . . shall be maintained by the constant endeavour of the people, who shall refrain from any abuse of these freedoms and rights.' We can hold onto freedom and privacy while ensuring our shared security. It is not an easy balance, but it is possible and worth striving for. I am grateful for the environment I grew up in and the people I encountered that helped me maintain my faith in this principle.

YI
April 2025

Contents

Table of Cases

INTERNATIONAL COURTS AND TRIBUNALS

Permanent Court of International Justice

International Court of Justice

European Court of Justice, Court of Justice of the European Union

European Court of Human Rights

Inter-American Court of Human Rights

NATIONAL COURTS

Belgium

Canada

France

Germany

Japan

New Zealand

Singapore

Switzerland

United Kingdom

United States

Table of National and Regional Legislation

CANADA

CAYMAN ISLANDS

CHINA

DENMARK

EUROPEAN UNION

FINLAND

FRANCE

GERMANY

INDIA

SAUDI ARABIA

SEYCHELLES

SINGAPORE

SOUTH AFRICA

SPAIN

SWEDEN

SWITZERLAND

THAILAND

UNITED KINGDOM

UNITED STATES

UNION OF SOVIET SOCIALIST REPUBLICS (USSR) (SEE RUSSIA AFTER 8 DECEMBER 1991)

URUGUAY

VIETNAM

VIRGIN ISLANDS

ZAIRE

Table of Treaties

Abbreviations

AAT	Australian Administrative Tribunal, Australia
ABA	American Bar Association
AI	artificial intelligence
ALJ	administrative law judge, the United States
AMF	Autorité des Marchés Financiers, France
AML/CFT	anti-money laundering and combating the financing of terrorism
APA	advance pricing arrangement
APEC	Asia-Pacific Economic Cooperation
API	Advance Passenger Information
APL	American Presidential Lines, LLC
BCBS	Basel Committee on Banking Supervision
BCSC	British Columbia Securities Commission, Canada
BfV	*Bundesamt für Verfassungsschutz* (Federal Office for the Protection of the Constitution), Germany
BSI	Banca della Svizzera Italiana
CARF	Crypto-Asset Reporting Framework
CBPR	Cross-Border Privacy Rules
CCPCJ	Commission on Crime Prevention and Justice
CDD	customer due diligence
CFTC	Commodity Futures Trading Commission, the United States
CIA	Central Intelligence Agency, the United States
CJEU	Court of Justice of the European Union, the European Union
CLOUD Act	Clarifying Lawful Overseas Use of Data Act, the United States
COB	Commission des Opérations de Bourse, France
CoE	Council of Europe
CRS	common reporting standard
DGSI	*Direction générale de la Sécurité intérieure* (General Directorate for Internal Security), France
DHS	Department of Homeland Security
DLT	distributed ledger technology
DNA	deoxyribonucleic acid
DOC	Department of Commerce, the United States
DOJ	Department of Justice, the United States
DPA	deferred prosecution agreement
DPP	data protection and privacy
EC	European Commission
EC	European Community
ECHR	European Convention on Human Rights
ECJ	European Court of Justice, the European Union

ECOSOC	United Nations Economic and Social Council
ECtHR	European Court of Human Rights
EDPB	European Data Protection Board, the European Union
EDPS	European Data Protection Supervisor, the European Union
EEA	European Economic Area
EEC	European Economic Community
EUROPOL	European Union Agency for Law Enforcement Cooperation, the European Union
FATCA	Foreign Account Tax Compliance Act, the United States
FATF	Financial Action Task Force
FBI	Federal Bureau of Investigation, the United States
FCPA	Foreign Corrupt Practices Act, the United States
FFI	foreign financial institution
FinCEN	Financial Crimes Enforcement Network, the United States
FINMA	Financial Market Supervisory Authority, Switzerland
FISA	Foreign Intelligence Surveillance Act, the United States
FIU	financial intelligence unit
FNCB	First National Community Bank
FOIA	Freedom of Information Act, the United States
FSA	Financial Services Authority, the United Kingdom
FSF	Financial Stability Forum
FTC	Federal Trade Commission, the United States
G8	Group of Eight
G7	Group of Seven
G20	Group of Twenty
GDPR	General Data Protection Regulation, the European Union
GLBA	Gramm–Leach–Bliley Act, the United States
GMM	Global Mofy Metaverse
GPS	global positioning system
GS Corp	Global Securities Corporation
HSI	Homeland Security Investigations, the United States
HSPD-6	Homeland Security Presidential Directive 6, the United States
IATA	International Air Transport Association
ICAO	International Civil Aviation Organization
ICC	International Criminal Court
ICCPR	International Covenant on Civil and Political Rights
ICJ	International Court of Justice
ICPO	International Criminal Police Organization
ICSFT	International Convention for the Suppression of the Financing of Terrorism
IEC	International Electrotechnical Commission
IET	Interest Equalization Tax, the United States
IGA	intergovernmental agreement
IMF	International Monetary Fund
IOSCO	International Organization of Securities Commissions

IPO	International Production Order, Australia
IPO Act	Telecommunications Legislation Amendment (International Production Orders) Act, Australia
IRS	Internal Revenue Service, the United States
ISO	International Organization for Standardization
IT	information technology
JFTC	Japanese Fair Trade Commission, Japan
JIT	joint investigation team
KFTC	Korean Fair Trade Commission, the Republic of Korea
KSA	Kingdom of Saudi Arabia
LED	Law Enforcement Directive, the European Union
MACMA	Mutual Assistance in Criminal Matters Act, the New Zealand
MLAT	mutual legal assistance treaty
MLR 2017	Money Laundering, Terrorist Financing and Transfer of Funds (Information on the Payer) Regulations, the United Kingdom
MLR 2019	Money Laundering and Terrorist Financing (Amendment) Regulations 2019, the United Kingdom
MMOU	International Organization of Securities Commissions' Multilateral Memorandum of Understanding
MOU	memorandum of understanding
MPF	Ministério Público Federal, Brazil
MRI	Marc Rich International
NCA	National Crime Agency, the United Kingdom
NPA	non-prosecution agreement
NSA	National Security Agency, the United States
NSL	national security letter, the United States
OECD	Organisation for Economic Co-operation and Development
OEEC	Organization for European Economic Cooperation
PATRIOT Act	Uniting and Strengthening America by Providing Appropriate Tools Required to Intercept and Obstruct Terrorism Act, the United States
PCIJ	Permanent Court of International Justice
PCSC Agreement	Preventing and Combating Serious Crime Agreement
PNR	passenger name record
QI	Qualified Intermediary, the United States
RICO Act	Racketeer Influenced and Corrupt Organizations Act, the United States
RTZ	Rio Tinto Zinc Corporations
SAR	suspicious activity report
SCA	Stored Communications Act, the United States
SEC	Securities and Exchange Commission, the United States
SFBC	Swiss Federal Banking Commission, Switzerland
SFO	Serious Fraud Office, the United Kingdom
SIS	Schengen Information System
SOX Act	Public Company Accounting Reform and Investor Protection Act, the United States

SWIFT	Society for Worldwide Interbank Financial Telecommunications
TFEU	Treaty on the Functioning of the European Union
TFTP	Terrorist Financing Tracking Program
TIEA	tax information exchange agreement
TSDB	Terrorist Screening Database, the United States
UNCAC	United Nations Convention against Corruption
UNCTAD	United Nations Conference on Trade and Development
UNODC	United Nations Office on Drugs and Crime
UNTOC	United Nations Convention against Transnational Organized Crime
USSR	Union of Soviet Socialist Republics
UWO	Unexplained Wealth Order, the United Kingdom
VCLT	Vienna Convention on the Law of Treaties
VIAG	Vetco International AG
WCO	World Customs Organization
WTO	World Trade Organization

Abbreviations for Reporters and Journals

[Note] Sources in the tables of treaties and legislation are cited in full, except for the following standard reporters and journals.

AS	Amtliche Sammulung der Bundesgesetze und Verordnugen der schweizerischen Eidgenossenschaft (Switzerland)
BGBl	Bundesgesetsblatt (Austria, Germany)
BOE	Diario oficial Boletín Oficial del Estado (Spain)
CETS	Council of Europe Treaty Series (Council of Europe)
CTS	Clive Parry (ed), *The Consolidated Treaty Series* (Oceana Publications, 1969–1981)
ECR	European Court of Justice Report
ETS	European Treaty Series (the Council of Europe)
ICJ Report	International Court of Justice Report
JO	Journal officiel de la République française (France)
KAV	Hein's KAV Series
LNTS	League of Nations, Treaty Series
NRG Martens	Georg Friedrich von Martens (ed.), *Nouveau recueil général de traités* (Dieterich, 1843–1875; 2e sér, 1826–1910; 3e sér, 1908–1926)
OJ	Official Journal (the European Union)
Pub L	Public Law (the United States)
Stat	Statute at Large (the United States)
Stb	Staatblad van het Koninkrijk der Nederlanden (the Netherlands)
TIAS	Treaties and Other International Acts Series (the United States)
UNTS	United Nations, Treaty Series
UST	United States Treaties and Other International Agreements (the United States)

PART I

INVESTIGATION OF TRANSNATIONAL CRIMES THROUGH INTER-STATE COOPERATION

1

Introduction

Unconventional Investigations of Transnational Crimes

1. Transnational Criminal Law and Public International Law

Obtaining information and evidence abroad is the main challenge in combating transnational crime. The growing interconnectedness and interdependence of countries and societies across borders form the broader societal context underlying this difficulty. The perpetrators are exploiting the opportunities of globalization and trade liberalization. Offences are typically committed in an organized manner and often involve legitimate activities through multinational corporations and financial institutions. The rapid advancement of communication technology has significantly contributed to both the spread and investigation of crimes. Criminal networks can easily coordinate their activities across borders and conduct illegal financial transactions. As a result, the evidence scatters across multiple countries in most cases.

States have developed various international and unilateral mechanisms to investigate unlawful acts to overcome this hurdle. As a result, transnational criminal law consists of a complex web of domestic laws, informal intergovernmental arrangements, bilateral, regional, and multilateral treaties. States use unilateral law enforcement, administrative cooperation, and direct cooperation methods to detect and prevent unlawful conduct and obtain evidence for criminal proceedings. As they track illicit activities through bank accounts, transportation information, and communications data, the role of private sectors expanded as an indispensable part of the investigations. Financial institutions are the gatekeeper as they screen transactions and redirect suspicious matters to the competent authorities. Communication service providers must store, disclose, and submit communication data when required for an investigation.

Contrary to the reality concerning the regulation of transnational crimes, most treatises retain the State-centric feature of international law studies. A conventional explanation of obtaining evidence in another State is the following.[1] A State

[1] John David McClean, *International Co-Operation in Civil and Criminal Matters* (3rd edn, OUP 2012) 153; Darryl Robinson, Sergey Vasiliev, Elies van Sliedregt and Valerie Oosterveld, *An Introduction to International Criminal Law and Procedure* (5th edn, CUP 2024) 69, 89. It is noted that the updated version of the latter treatises extensively covers the advanced form of State cooperation with respect to national proceedings.

International Law and the Investigation of Transnational Crimes. Yurika Ishii, Oxford University Press.
 DOI: 10.1093/9780198957089.003.0001

may not exercise its jurisdiction within another State's territory without the latter's consent. Therefore, the former State must rely on the mutual legal assistance of the latter State. It may be successful when there is a mutual legal assistance treaty (MLAT) or an ad hoc cooperation, including the request under the letters rogatory. An MLAT typically obliges State parties to go through an expedited process. However, the treaty usually does not require the State parties to amend its substantive criminal laws. It only obligates both parties to cooperate if it does not conflict with their primary policies. In addition, an MLAT requires the judicial review of the requested State, which assures the legality of the evidence before the Court of the requesting State. Alternatively, it may not be successful when there is no such treaty, or the latter State is not cooperative.

Such a simple approach no longer suffices to explain the intricacies involved. A thorough analysis is necessary on the intersection between international law and investigation of transnational crimes.

1.1 Working Definition of Transnational Crimes

The working definition of transnational crimes in this book is crimes that are prescribed under domestic laws of each State but require internationally institutionalized regulation. This book contends that the concept of 'transnational crimes' emerged out of the necessity of international cooperation. The offences include terrorism, transnational organized crimes, and white-collar crimes, such as securities law violations and tax offences.[2]

The term 'regulation' encompasses not only the procedural aspects of combating transnational crimes and relevant international agreements but also extends to cover substantive criminal and administrative laws, along with preventive measures implemented in each State. The term 'international regulation' means the regulation among more than one State. In international legal studies, the necessity for international regulation is often equated with whether the matter is of international concern and has universal or general implication. However, most transnational crimes do not fall into this category. States criminalize certain acts because of their national interests. As these regulations become more prevalent, States often willingly cooperate with other States' regulations for mutual convenience and benefit.

Other scholars adopt different descriptions of transnational crimes. Neil Boister explained the concept as 'a set of crimes that have actual or potential transboundary effects or transboundary moral impact'.[3] In this context, transnational criminal

[2] Nikos Passas, 'Globalization, Criminogenic Asymmetries, and Economic Crime' (1999) 1 European Journal of Law Reform 399, 400.

[3] Neil Boister, *An Introduction to Transnational Criminal Law* (OUP 2018).

law means 'the suppression by international law through domestic penal law of criminal activities that have actual or potential transboundary effects or moral impact'.[4] Neil Boister, Sabine Gless, and Florian Jessberger, in their book in 2021, characterized that the law can be defined as '(a) horizontal international obligations between States to criminalize and cooperate, and (b) the vertical application of criminal law and procedures by those States to individuals to meet these international obligations'.[5]

The variance in definitions does not result in a significant divergence in essence. This book does not specifically address crimes that do not necessitate institutionalized cooperation. Its definition is therefore more confined. However, its analytical scope is more comprehensive as it includes domestic administrative laws such as competition law, securities law, and tax law. While this book focuses on the procedural aspect of the law, the research findings can be used to examine other substantive areas of the law. For example, the analysis could be extended to areas of economic sanctions law, intellectual property law, and environmental law. In addition, the cross-border investigations explored in this book are also used to inspect conventional crimes that have transnational implications, such as online scam.

It is noted that police cooperation plays an important role in practice, where the agencies exchange information during criminal investigations. Such cooperation takes place both on a bilateral level and through organizations including the International Criminal Police Organization (ICPO) and the European Union Agency for Law Enforcement Cooperation (EUROPOL), which are primarily responsible for facilitating the exchange of information between member States.[6] The ICPO has a database for sharing information on suspects' fingerprints, deoxyribonucleic acid (DNA) information, stolen vehicles, artwork, and passports, which is frequently used in the early stages of an investigation. However, members of these organizations cannot request that other States take coercive measures. The participation and collaboration among police agencies are generally done on a voluntary basis. The focus of this book is the mechanisms that ensure enforceability among participating States, and therefore it would not deal with the police cooperation as an independent subject.

[4] ibid.

[5] Neil Boister, Sabine Gless, and Florian Jessberger, 'Introduction' in Neil Boister, Sabine Gless, and Florian Jeßberger (eds), *Histories of Transnational Criminal Law* (OUP 2021) 3.

[6] For the significance of the police cooperation, see Saskia Hufnagel and Carole McCartney, 'Police Cooperation against Transnational Criminals' in Neil Boister and Robert J Currie (eds), *Routledge Handbook of Transnational Criminal Law* (Routledge 2014) 107; Saskia Hufnagel and Carole McCartney, 'Introduction' in Saskia Hufnagel and Carole McCartney (eds), *Trust in International Police and Justice Cooperation* (Hart Publishing 2017) 1; Frank G Madsen, 'Policing Transnational Organised Crime—The International Perspective' in Pierre Hauck and Sven Peterke (eds), *International Law and Transnational Organised Crime* (OUP 2016) 494.

1.2 Distinction between International and Transnational Crimes

It is necessary to distinguish transnational and international criminal law at this stage. International crimes are offences of which elements are defined under international law and implemented through international mechanisms. They include core crimes such as genocide, war crimes, crimes against humanity, and crimes of aggression. With the increase in the number of international or mixed criminal tribunals since the 1990s and the establishment of the International Criminal Court (ICC), their investigation has become a major topic of legal studies in this field.[7] However, the investigation of international crimes by international organizations is beyond the scope of this volume, as it requires a different set of considerations.[8]

Contrary to international crimes, transnational crimes are defined and implemented through domestic laws. M Cherif Bassiouni explained international criminal law based on direct and indirect enforcement mechanisms.[9] The former refers to the international judicial institutions, such as the ICC, that investigate, prosecute, adjudicate, and enforce their sanctions.[10] The latter refers to the national incorporation of internationally prohibited conduct through criminalizing such conduct in domestic criminal laws, prosecuting persons within State jurisdiction, and punishing those found guilty per national sanctions.[11]

Transnational crimes are solely governed under the indirect enforcement mechanism. Its nature, elements, and investigative procedure are solely based on domestic laws. The multilateral conventions, if any, only provide the minimum standard. Most developed States implement more rigorous regulations and require their like-minded countries to do the same. There are institutionalized mechanisms of judicial and administrative cooperation to that effect.

[7] Statute of the International Criminal Court (adopted on 17 July 1998, entered into force on 1 July 2002) 2187 UNTS 90.

[8] It is noted that the Ljubljana–The Hague Convention on Mutual Legal Assistance oblige member States to mutually assist other States concerning specific crimes of genocide, crimes against humanity, war crimes, and other international crimes as defined in the treaty. It is designed to facilitate close mutual legal assistance and includes provisions on joint investigation, digital information exchange, video conferencing, and specific investigation techniques. Ljubljana–The Hague Convention on International Cooperation in the Investigation and Prosecution of the Crime of Genocide, Crimes against Humanity, War Crimes and Other International Crimes (adopted on 26 May 2023) <https://www.gov.si/assets/ministrstva/MZEZ/projekti/MLA-pobuda/The-Ljubljana-The-Hague-MLA-Convention.pdf>. All websites were last accessed on 31 March 2025.

[9] M Cherif Bassiouni, 'The Modalities of International Cooperation in Penal Matters' in M Cherif Bassiouni (ed), *International Criminal Law, Volume 2: Multilateral and Bilateral Enforcement Mechanisms* (Brill 2008) 3; M Cherif Bassiouni, *Introduction to International Criminal Law* (Martinus Nijhoff Publishers 2012).

[10] Bassiouni, 'The Modalities of International Cooperation in Penal Matters' (n 9) 3.

[11] ibid.

1.3 Historical Development of Transnational Criminal Law

The nature of transnational crimes varies to a significant extent. What they have in common, however, is that they are committed against the backdrop of globalization or the increased interconnection and interaction of people, goods, and capitals of different jurisdictions. These crimes are done across borders in an organized, repetitive, and continuous manner, making ad hoc cooperation insufficient.

The concept of transnational crimes only emerged in the 1970s from the demands for inter-State coordination. It was notwithstanding the fact that the phenomena are nothing new that an unlawful act constitutes a crime in more than one State.[12]

The first occasion that the term 'transnational crimes' was used in an official document of an international organization was at the Fifth United Nations Congress on the Prevention of Crime and the Treatment of Offenders in 1975.[13] The term identified certain criminal phenomena transcending State borders, transgressing the laws of several States.[14] However, as Gerhard Mueller, who drafted the report of the Congress, pointed out, the term was of criminology, rather than that of law.[15]

Since the early 1970s, researchers in international relations studies, mainly in the United States, theorized 'transnational relations'. Robert Keohane and Joseph Nye explained that inter-subject relations where at least one of the parties is not State became equally important as inter-State relations against the background of the economic globalization started by the deregulation in the United States and the United Kingdom.[16] The phenomena that brought about in the society of the developed countries and posed threats against national security became the subject of analysis of international relations and domestic and comparative laws.[17]

[12] Henri Donnedieu de Vabres, *Introduction à l'étude Du Droit Pénal International: Essai d'histoire et de Critique Sur La Compétence Criminelle Dans Les Rapports Avec l'étranger* (Sirey 1922) 102.

[13] Department of Economic and Social Affairs, Fifth United Nations Congress on the Prevention of Crime and the Treatment of Offenders, A/CONF.56/10 No 3. 76. IV. 2.

[14] ibid. The report lists the following offences as transnational crimes: crime as business, organized crime, white-collar crime and corruption, offences involving works of art and other cultural property, criminality associated with alcoholism and drug abuse, violence of transnational and comparative international significance, and criminality associated with migration and flight from national disasters and hostilities.

[15] Gerhard OW Mueller, 'Transnational Crime: Definitions and Concepts' in Dimitri Vlassis and Phil Williams (eds), *Combating Transnational Crime: Concepts, Activities and Responses* (Routledge 2001) 13. For Mueller's role in the Congress, see also Mangai Natarajan, 'Gerhard Mueller's Role in Developing the Concept of Transnational Crime for the United Nations' in Neil Boister, Sabine Gless, and Florian Jeßberger (eds), *Histories of Transnational Criminal Law* (1st edn, OUP 2021) 70.

[16] Robert O Keohane and Joseph S Nye, *Transnational Relations and World Politics* (Harvard UP 1972) 13.

[17] For instance, see Peter Lupsha, 'Transnational Organized Crime versus the Nation-State' (1996) 2 Transnational Organized Crime 21; Alex P Schmid, 'The Links between Transnational Organized Crime and Terrorist Crimes' (1996) 2 Transnational Organized Crime 40; RM Mackenzie Simon, 'Transnational Crime, Local Denial' (2007) 34 Social Justice 111; Margaret E Beare, *Encyclopedia of Transnational Crime and Justice* (Sage Publishing 2012); Michael G Findley, Daniel L Nielson, and

The definition of 'transnational crimes' used in various international organizations reflected the conceptualization of these originally non-legal studies. In 1995, the United Nations designated eighteen categories of transnational crimes, considered criminological concepts, as the cross-border movement of people, finance, and goods brought about.[18]

Among transnational crimes, economic crimes such as financial crimes and corporate offences are typically provided in administrative and economic laws in domestic laws. States began to regulate these crimes against the background of the deregulation of finance in the 1970s and the increase of multinational corporations. These policies emerged against the backdrop of neoliberalism, where States started to loosen the regulation against the economy, encourage competition within the markets, and strengthen the security of the privatization of assets.[19] The movement of industry and capital across the border was facilitated by a combination of tax policies, subsidiaries, and monetary control, resulting in effective deregulation.

On the other hand, States began to strengthen the sanction against activities that harmed this economic order. Before this transformation, there were often cases where a violation of an administrative or economic law did end up in criminal punishment. To implement the regulation effectively, States started to amend the laws to introduce economic crimes, including white-collar crimes.[20]

The economic criminal laws became necessary because the demand emerged to punish the acts that harm the social interests of each State. The key component facilitating economic crimes is trade liberalization. While it promoted globalization, it allowed criminal organizations to take advantage of increased economic transactions via free trade agreements and bilateral investment treaties. As Bruce Zagaris puts it, these treaties did not provide for comprehensive enforcement mechanisms.[21] In addition, since these economic crimes were not harmonized, offenders used the gap between the States to conduct unlawful activities. As Nikos Passas pointed out, this gap created 'criminogenic asymmetries', which refers to structural discrepancies, mismatches, and inequalities in the realm of economy, law, politics, and culture.[22] They fuel the demand for illegal goods and services by

Jason Campbell Sharman, *Global Shell Games: Experiments in Transnational Relations, Crime, and Terrorism* (CUP 2014).

[18] United Nations, Fourth United Nations Survey of Crime Trends and Operations of Criminal Justice Systems, UN Doc A/CONF. 169/15/Add. 1, 4 April 1995, para 9.

[19] David Harvey, *A Brief History of Neoliberalism* (OUP 2005) 3.

[20] Bruce Zagaris, *International White Collar Crime* (2nd edn, CUP 2015). See also Valsamis Mitsilegas, 'Transnational Criminal Law and the Global Rule of Law' in Giuliana Ziccardi Capaldo (ed), *The Global Community Yearbook of International Law and Jurisprudence 2016*, vol 1 (OUP 2017). Valsamis Mitsilegas describes that States have adopted many regulatory measures to counter transnational crimes.

[21] Zagaris (n 20) 2.

[22] Passas (n 2) 402.

incentivizing people and organizations to engage in illegal practices and reducing authorities' ability to control crimes.[23]

Furthermore, the elements of organized crimes and terrorism overlap with natural crimes, such as murder and fraud, that are punishable under the criminal law. However, a distinct category of organized crimes is necessary because of the mode of their commission. The offenders disrupt the social order by various means including instilling fear among residents and bribing local officials. Similarly, terrorism is penalized for its non-discriminatory nature against citizens or political intention.

In the 1970s, the increasing accessibility of air travel to the public led to a growing need for States to collaborate due to the rise in cross-border transportation. With the expansion of internet usage in the 1990s, communication among offenders became significantly more accessible, posing new challenges for law enforcement agencies. The development of such technology is making new responses necessary.

In summary, transnational criminal law represents a negative side effect of globalization. The context and nature of these issues differ significantly, both quantitatively and qualitatively, from those recognized by international lawyers in the nineteenth century.

2. Types of Transnational Crimes in International Law

From the standpoint of public international law, this book categorizes transnational crimes into the following three groups according to the nature of the international obligations imposed on States to suppress the offence.

2.1 Crimes Not Requiring Criminalization under International Law

The first group of transnational crimes is one for which international law does not define the elements of the crimes, and for which there is no international legal obligation for states to regulate them. Nonetheless, various cooperation mechanisms exist based on both legally binding and non-binding instruments.

A key aspect of information exchange for this type of crime is an intergovernmental agreement that obliges cooperation in exchanging information beyond criminal cooperation, for example, enforcement cooperation of competition laws, tax laws, or security laws. The Convention on Mutual Administrative Assistance in Tax Matters of 1988 and bilateral tax information exchange agreements (TIEAs)

[23] ibid.

oblige State parties to exchange information. They are not necessarily done for criminal investigations, but the information obtained through these processes may be used in criminal proceedings. They commonly exclude the principles of double criminality or speciality, which have been the core principles in criminal cooperation since the nineteenth century.

The implementation of these agreements may be done through regulatory networks of financial authorities such as the Basel Committee on Banking Supervision, the International Organization of Securities Commissions (IOSCO), and the International Association of Insurance Supervisors.[24] The authorities cooperate within the mandate of their national laws. In practice, information exchanged through these networks rarely becomes evidence of criminal proceedings. However, at least the information is used to monitor unusual and illegal activities. Furthermore, officials may participate in informal information exchanges if such engagement does not contradict their obligations to maintain confidentiality.

These networks originated from efforts to consolidate conflicts that arose due to unilateral law enforcement actions aimed at gathering information without the cooperation of other States. Before the 2010s, the United States was the sole country that brought about such conflicts by exercising its long-arm jurisdiction. Unilateral law enforcement concerning corporate crimes, organized crimes, and terrorism is done without obtaining the consent of the territorial State where the information or the evidence is located. The validity of unilateral law enforcement under international law has been vigorously disputed since the 1950s. While the academic dispute ended, the practice persists to this day, albeit more refined and sophisticated. The measures are taken under criminal and administrative proceedings.

Such means have been intensified after the 9/11 terrorist attacks of 2001 and the global financial crisis of 2008. In theory, a State alleging that such an exercise of jurisdiction is excessive may diplomatically protest the prosecuting State and establish a blocking statute prohibiting the corporation from disclosing the information. Yet, in practice, there is an increasing number of direct cooperation, where a State would agree with another State that the latter requires a corporation of the former to submit their materials directly. Examples are the executive agreements established by the US Clarifying Lawful Overseas Use of Data (CLOUD) Act.[25] Such a unilateral law enforcement measures may trigger the creation of cooperation mechanisms.

[24] For the characteristics of the regulatory networks that are not based on the treaties, see Kal Raustiala, 'The Architecture of International Cooperation: Transgovernmental Networks and the Future of International Law' (2002) 43 Virginia Journal of International Law 1; Benedict Kingsbury, Nico Krisch, and Richard B Stewart, 'The Emergence of Global Administrative Law' (2005) 68 Law and Contemporary Problems 15.

[25] Clarifying Lawful Overseas Use of Data Act (CLOUD Act), Pub L No 115-141 132 Stat 1210 (2018). The United States concluded executive agreements with the United Kingdom and Australia. See Chapter 12, Section 5.2.

2.2 Crimes with Shared Interests in Criminalization and Cooperation among States

The second category is transnational crimes that are common to domestic laws. Some multilateral treaties define the elements of these crimes and oblige State parties to cooperate to suppress these crimes. They standardize the requirements for what constitutes an offence in the national laws of each country and facilitate judicial assistance.[26] Important instruments include the Drug Convention of 1988,[27] the United Nations Convention against Transnational Organized Crimes of 2000,[28] three Protocols thereto,[29] and the United Nations Convention against Corruption (UNCAC) of 2003.[30] The United Nations Office on Drugs and Crime was founded in 1997 to offer practical and technical assistance through various programmes and network of field offices and to inform member States the latest trends of the crimes covered by these treaties. A significant milestone in this regard is the adoption of the UN Cybercrime Convention in December 2024.[31] The Convention reflects advancements in investigative techniques and establishes detailed mechanisms. However, its acceptance by interested States remains uncertain at the time of writing.

Certain transnational crimes are defined within non-criminal cooperation instruments, which require member States to criminalize conduct that compromises their objectives. For instance, the Convention on International Trade in Endangered Species of Wild Fauna and Flora regulates international trade in

[26] The International Court of Justice addressed that the definition of offences and related legal rules and procedures to implement the United Nations Convention against Transnational Organized Crime (UNTOC) was 'a matter for the domestic law of the prosecuting State . . . [T]he Convention helps to co-ordinate but does not direct the actions of States parties in the exercise of their domestic jurisdiction'. *Immunities and Criminal Proceedings (Equatorial Guinea v France)* Preliminary Objections (Judgment) [2018] ICJ Rep 292, para 114.

[27] United Nations Convention against Illicit Traffic in Narcotic Drugs and Psychotropic Substances (adopted on 20 December 1988, entered into force on 11 November 1990) 1582 UNTS 95 (Drug Convention).

[28] United Nations Convention against Transnational Organized Crime (adopted on 15 November 2000, entered into force on 29 September 2003) 2225 UNTS 209.

[29] Protocol against the Smuggling of Migrants by Land, Sea and Air, supplementing the United Nations Convention against Transnational Organized Crime (adopted on 15 November 2000, entered into force on 28 January 2004) 2241 UNTS 507; Protocol to Prevent, Suppress and Punish Trafficking in Persons, Especially Women and Children, supplementing the United Nations Convention against Transnational Organized Crime (adopted on 15 November 2000, entered into force on 25 December 2003) 2237 UNTS 319; Protocol against the Illicit Manufacturing of and Trafficking in Firearms, Their Parts and Components and Ammunition, supplementing the United Nations Convention against Transnational Organized Crime (adopted on 11 July 2001, entered into force on 3 July 2005) 2326 UNTS 208.

[30] United Nations Convention against Corruption (adopted on 31 October 2003, entered into force on 14 December 2005) 2349 UNTS 41 (UNCAC).

[31] United Nations Convention against Cybercrime (adopted on 24 December 2024) A/RES/79/243, Annex.

plants and animals to ensure their survival is not threatened.[32] Member States must prohibit trade in specimens that contravene its provisions and must penalize trade in, or possession of, such specimens.[33] Yet, the Convention leaves the nature of penalties to the discretion of each State, resulting in varying approaches, ranging from fines to imprisonment. Another example is the Trade-Related Aspects of Intellectual Property Rights Agreement, under which criminal procedures and penalties are mandatory only for wilful trademark counterfeiting and copyright piracy on a commercial scale.[34] Members may choose to apply criminal procedures in other cases of intellectual property infringement but are not obligated to do so. These treaties do not provide a framework for international cooperation on criminal matters, and enforcement is primarily handled by domestic law enforcement, customs, and border control agencies. Nevertheless, they promote the criminalization of conduct that addresses issues of international concern.

2.3 Crimes Requiring Obligatory Enforcement and Cooperation among States

The third is transnational crimes that harm the collective interests protected under international law. There are also multilateral treaties that define the elements of these crimes and oblige State parties to implement them in each State. Examples include a series of anti-terrorism conventions concluded in the early 1970s, the Hostage Convention of 1979, and the Convention against Torture and Other Cruel, Inhuman or Degrading Treatment or Punishment of 1984. These conventions provide *aut dedere aut judicaire* principle, compelling the member States to exercise their jurisdiction.

The difference between the second and third categories is whether the international community recognizes interests that should be secured by international law because the benefit of combating the said crime cannot be reduced to an individual State's concern.[35]

Much has been written on these treaties. Yet, less attention has been paid regarding the regulation of these crimes and the interconnection between the treaties and other domestic crimes. The regulatory networks created concerning the crimes that belong to the first category may be used to combat crimes that belong to the second and third categories and vice versa. For instance, the anti-money

[32] Convention on International Trade in Endangered Species of Wild Fauna and Flora (adopted on 3 March 1973, entered into force on 1 July 1975) 993 UNTS 243. Its scope is limited to international trade and species affected by such trade (ibid art 1).

[33] ibid art 8.

[34] Agreement on Trade-Related Aspects of Intellectual Property Rights (adopted on 15 April 1994, entered into force on 1 January 1995) 1869 UNTS 299, art 61.

[35] Naoya Okuwaki, 'Kokusaihō Kara Mita Kokusai Keiji Kyōryoku No Gendaiteki Tenkai' (2003) 278 Hogaku Kyoushitsu 4.

laundering and combating the financing of terrorism (AML/CFT) regimes, developed after the 9/11 terrorist attacks of 2001 through Financial Action Task Force (FATF), are the backbone of suppressing financial crimes, organized crimes and terrorism. Laws on different crimes are interconnected with each other in practice.

3. Questions of This Research

3.1 State-Centrism of International Cooperation on Criminal Matters

The central statement of this book is that the structure of the public international law studies characterized by State centrism and distinctions based on different fields of law, such as treaties on civil, criminal, and administrative matters, are no longer suitable for comprehending the reality of the suppression of transnational crimes.

The critical question arises concerning the legitimacy of these mechanisms concerning individuals, including natural persons and legal entities subject to investigation. The regulations of transnational crimes are far more sophisticated and intrusive to the private realm than the long-standing mutual assistance. The impact of regulating transnational crimes is immense against the individuals' and corporations' rights and interests, including the right to privacy. However, the individuals affected by international cooperation procedures have little room to claim their rights. Three examples are illustrative.

First, treaties concerning cooperation on criminal matters establish principles to balance sovereignty and the necessity for cooperation. These principles include reciprocity, double criminality, and speciality. While they impact the status of individuals involved, they are not intended to confer specific rights to those individuals.[36] Both in case laws of domestic courts of each State and in academic literature, it is denied that persons may invoke these principles to object against the requested State's decision to comply with the request.[37] When one of the State parties contravened the principles, the other party may pursue the State responsibility. However, such a violation hardly affects the validity of the procedure.

Second, while international human rights law rules apply to such bilateral cooperation, these rules only exert a limited influence on conditioning or restricting the latter procedural aspects. For instance, the International Covenant on Civil and

[36] John Dugard and Christine van den Wyngaert, 'Reconciling Extradition with Human Rights' (1998) 92 American Journal of International Law 187; M Cherif Bassiouni, 'An Appraisal of the Growth and Developing Trends of International Criminal Law' (1974) 45 Revue International de Droit Penal 405. See also Ian Brownlie, *Principles of Public International Law* (OUP 2008) 318.

[37] For instance, John Hawley, in his work of 1893 exploring the US jurisprudence concerning extradition cases, made the point. John G Hawley, *The Law and Practice of International Extradition between the United States and Those Foreign Countries with Which It Has Treaties of Extradition* (Callaghan and Company 1893) 35.

Political Rights provides a series of rights that the suspect would enjoy throughout the criminal proceeding.[38] However, this instrument obliges the State parties to respect those rights within a single jurisdiction. It is basically for the forum to decide whether and to what extent these rules are applicable when criminal proceedings are conducted in multiple jurisdictions.[39]

Third, in general, international cooperation mechanisms are used solely by the law enforcement authorities and prosecutors, not the defendants. In some legal jurisdictions, the defendants may use the evidence that is advantageous among the materials obtained from the cooperation. However, they are generally not entitled to request the materials. There may be cases where the defendant may rely on civil procedures, but there is no guarantee for such an attempt.

The most acute issue in international regulation of transnational crime is the conflict between the necessity to deal with transnational crime and the rights of individuals, including the right to due process and the right to privacy. Whether measures taken are legitimate, if not illegal, has been disputed, particularly after the end of the Cold War when the States started to expand and deepen the regulations of transnational crimes. On what condition can the taking of evidence and information for the regulation of transnational crimes be legitimate under the laws of the territorial State, the prosecuting State, and international law? How would these regulations affect the previous legal studies concerning the mutual legal assistance? These are the core questions that persist throughout this book.

As the scope of transnational criminal law expands, the cooperation between law enforcement authorities and private sectors, including financial institutions, communication service providers, and corporations, has been essential. However, the concept of public–private partnership has not been well explored in international criminal law studies. Lawyers in the compliance sector often take it for granted that institutions follow the government's instruction without looking at a broader picture of the burden-sharing among the stakeholders. It is necessary to shed light on such an aspect in the context of international law enforcement cooperation.

The 'law' concerned here is primarily the domestic laws of each State. However, one cannot overlook the fact that the application and enforcement of those laws beyond national borders affect the legal order of other States and that of the international society. The problem is not limited to the jurisdictional basis of transnational criminal law. Even if the State concerned agrees to the investigation of another State, the rights of the individuals and legal entities in it remain. The

[38] International Covenant on Civil and Political Rights (adopted on 16 December 1966, entered into force on 23 March 1976) 999 UNTS 171.

[39] See Chapter 3, Section 3. See also Albin Eser, 'Basic Issues' in Edward Martin Wise (ed), *Criminal Science in a Global Society: Essays in Honor of Gerhard O.W. Mueller* (FB Rothman 1994) 3; Neil Boister, 'Further Reflections on the Concept of Transnational Criminal Law' (2015) 6 Transnational Legal Theory 9.

ultimate concern of this book is whether their rights and legitimate interests would be secured. Based on these perspectives, this book not only focuses on the issues that constrain the rights of individuals but also considers the problems of the principles of individual rights to deal with transnational crimes. As Ronald Dworkin put it as a critique of positivism, studies on transnational criminal laws must also consider principles—a standard that is to be observed 'not because it will advance or secure an economic, political, or social situation deemed desirable, but because it is a requirement of justice or fairness or some other dimension of morality'.[40]

The demands for fair competition and market transparency that transnational criminal law seek to protect are becoming more widely accepted. Still, there are persistent concerns that these regulations may excessively limit the privacy and freedom of economic activities of individuals and corporations. Furthermore, when domestic laws and regulations are directed at particular foreign entities or corporations for security or geopolitical reasons, the call for equity should be given consideration.

This potential conflict among different principles has been common in the history of international criminal law. Henri Donnedieu de Vabres pointed out that it continuously contained a tension between the desire for universal peace and the need to secure its national interest in his treatise published in 1928.[41] However, the situation diverges from what a scholar of the inter-war period had illustrated. Rather than grappling with a conflict between peace in the international community and the interests of each State, transnational criminal law now confronts the challenge of balancing the interests of global society and the rights of individuals.

3.2 Dynamisms of the Regulations of Transnational Crimes

This State-centric structure of mutual legal assistance in criminal matters stems from methodology in international legal studies. Positivism has been its mainstream that laws are created according to the will of the State, which is a decentralized authority in the international society that lacks a centralized system. Consequently, the subject of international law has been the States, and individuals have remained to be an object or the beneficiaries of international legal interests.

Lassa Oppenheim explicitly denied such a status of private individuals under international law. Oppenheim, in his treatise in 1905, excluded natural law to uphold positive international law, and stated that the rights and obligations of the law of nations are exclusively those of nations.[42] For Oppenheim, individuals were

[40] Ronald M Dworkin, 'The Model of Rules' (1967) 35 The University of Chicago Law Review 14, 23.
[41] Henri Donnedieu de Vabres, *Les Principes Modernes Du Droit Pénal International* (Librairie du Recueil Sirey 1928) 10.
[42] Lassa Oppenheim, *International Law: A Treatise* (Longmans, Green and Co 1905) 16.

only 'objects' of the law of nations.[43] In those rare instances where States conferred certain privileges on individuals through international treaties, such individuals did not thereby acquire 'international rights'. Rather, the treaties imposed an obligation only on the State to give effect to those privileges through its domestic law. Although such treaties mostly speak of rights that individuals should have as derived from the treaties themselves, this is nothing more than an inaccuracy of language.[44] The idea was widely shared in the international legal studies. Scholars such as John Westlake[45] and William Hall,[46] who influenced jurisprudence in the nineteenth century and the early twentieth century, also claimed that there was no room for private individuals to object to the implementation of the treaty.

As long as this idea is maintained, when a State goes too far when regulating transnational crimes—for instance, violating another State's sovereignty or infringing individual rights—the problem only arises vis-à-vis the victim States. When the interested States consent to the regulation, there will be no further legal problems. The problems that this book deals with would never surface.

However, there have been a series of objections against such a State-centric understanding of international law as it does not reflect the realities of international society. To begin with, Oppenheim's positivist interpretation, which perceives law solely as a system of rules, has faced criticism from multiple angles since the 1930s, when the concept of legal realism gained prominence and found advocates in the United States.[47]

In the context of international legal studies, Philip Jessup pioneered the 'transnational law' field to overcome this nature.[48] Jessup defined the term 'transnational' 'to include all law which regulates actions or events that transcend national frontiers'.[49] Jessup criticized the idea that international law cannot confer rights or impose duties directly on an individual because the individual is not a subject but an object of international law. According to his perspective, it did not reflect the reality of international society.[50]

International lawyers at the time, including Myres S McDougal[51] and later Wolfgang Friedman,[52] supported his claim. For example, McDougal, who led the

[43] ibid 341.
[44] ibid 343.
[45] John Westlake, *International Law* (CUP 1910) 1–3.
[46] William Edward Hall, *A Treatise on International Law* (Clarendon Press 1884) 51.
[47] Felix S Cohen, 'Transcendental Nonsense and the Functional Approach' (1935) 35 Columbia Law Review 809.
[48] Philip Caryl Jessup, *Transnational Law* (Yale UP 1956) 1. Jessup already pointed out the limits of the State-centric notion of public international law at Philip Caryl Jessup, *A Modern Law of Nations: An Introduction* (Macmillan Company 1948) 16.
[49] Jessup, *Transnational Law* (n 48) 2.
[50] ibid 7.
[51] Myres S McDougal, 'International Law, Power, and Policy: A Contemporary Conception' (1953) 82 Recueil des Cours 133.
[52] Wolfgang Friedmann, *The Changing Structure of International Law* (Stevens 1964) 60.

New Haven School, pointed out the limitations of considering international law as a set of rules and claimed that law should be understood as a decision process for the allocation of power and authority.[53]

Rosalyn Higgins, who was influenced by the New Haven School, opposed against the concept of 'subjects and objects of international law'.[54] She argued that 'international law is not to be understood as a set of "rules". . . . [I]ts norms are not fixed indefinitely and thus wholly responsive to the needs of the system.'[55] The dichotomy of subjects and objects has neither credible reality nor functional purpose. By characterizing international law as 'a particular decision-making process', Higgins claimed that individuals are 'participants', along with States, international organizations, multilateral corporations, and private non-governmental groups.[56]

In a different context, ONUMA Yasuaki emphasized the diverse societal function of international law in a more general context. In his words, '[i]deas and phenomena pertinent to international law require analyses and evaluations of various things, including its diverse functions in different forums'.[57] He accordingly endorsed the concept of 'participant of international law', which was 'a notion more functional and dynamic' than the dichotomy of subjects and objects.[58] Onuma highlighted that the realization of international law was not done only through reciprocal relations of the States and judicial institutions, and international law was limited to not only norms of adjudication but also norms of conduct, and non-governmental organizations, experts, and media played significant roles in formulating the international legal process.[59] There are numerous other writings asserting that the State-centric nature of international law should be rectified.[60]

Observing the reality of transnational crime regulations, the interest of the subjects closely aligns with their rights when considering the structure and function of rights in the analysis. The approach that is based on the static interpretation is not capable of grasping this resemblance. Measures taken against transnational crime under domestic laws are not necessarily characterized as the 'application of the law' but rather the 'realization of the law', which involves natural persons and corporations. The regulation is not designed solely for criminal prosecution. It also encompasses gathering essential information to detect and prevent offences.

[53] McDougal (n 51) 143.

[54] Rosalyn Higgins, *International Trade Law and the Avoidance, Containment and Resolution of Disputes: General Course on Public International Law* (Martinus Nijhoff 1991) 80.

[55] ibid 81.

[56] ibid.

[57] ONUMA Yasuaki, *International Law in a Transcivilizational World* (CUP 2017) 187.

[58] ibid.

[59] ibid 244.

[60] See, for instance, Thomas M Franck, *The Power of Legitimacy among Nations* (OUP 1990) 5; Eric Stein, 'International Integration and Democracy: No Love at First Sight' (2001) 95 American Journal of International Law 489, 490; Jutta Brunnée and Stephen J Toope, *Legitimacy and Legality in International Law: An Interactional Account* (CUP 2010) 15; Kate Parlett, *The Individual in the International Legal System: Continuity and Change in International Law* (CUP 2011).

The sanctions extend beyond criminal penalties to encompass negative responses within social norms, which may not be enforceable through the courts. In this regard, domestic regulations embrace a dynamic approach, serving multiple functions beyond criminal prosecution.

In the context of transnational crime regulations, the interests of legal subjects closely align with their rights when analysing the structure and function of those rights. It encompasses gathering essential information to detect and prevent offences. The sanctions extend beyond criminal penalties to encompass negative responses within social norms, which may not be enforceable through the courts. Measures taken against crimes under domestic laws are not necessarily characterized as the 'application of the law' but rather the 'realization of the law'. A static interpretation fails to accurately capture this alignment.

The argument of this book is not to claim that an alternative paradigm to State-centrism has been introduced into the regulation of transnational crime. While the increasing impact of non-State actors on international relations is undisputed, the legal status, rights, and obligations of non-State actors are governed by domestic laws. However, this gap between the State-centric approach of international legal studies and the domestic laws governing cross-border crimes may lead to a consequence that the rights and interests of individuals may not be appropriately protected by States under which the individuals are subject to. The gap must be addressed in the international legal studies.

In addition, there has been criticism regarding the inclination to perceive the criminal justice system as a system tied to the State. It is too narrow to conceptualize the transnational criminal law as a matter of criminal law. It aligns with the fact that distinct concepts of organized crime and economic crime arose from sociological necessity.[61] Ely Aaronson and Gregory Sheffer argue that it is essential to understand how 'processes of transnational legal ordering catalyze the construction and flow of legal norms that reconfigure the relationship among international, regional, national, and local sites of criminal justice norm making and practice'.[62]

Mikkel Jarele Christensen and Neil Boister advocate for the need to characterize the concept of transnational criminal justice as 'a space in which the law is shaped by politics and different social dynamics and such as those that play out between different types of professionals' in seeking how these structures are best conceptualized.[63] It is based on their understanding that the transnational criminal law

[61] Edwin Sutherland, who defined the concept of white-collar crime, was a sociologist and criminologists. Edwin Hardin Sutherland, *White Collar Crime* (Dryden Press 1949).

[62] Ely Aaronson and Gregory Shaffer, 'The Transnational Legal Ordering of Criminal Justice' in Gregory Shaffer and Ely Aaronson (eds), *Transnational Legal Ordering of Criminal Justice* (CUP 2021) 4. See also Gregory Shaffer, 'Transnational Legal Ordering and State Change' in Gregory C Shaffer (ed), *Transnational Legal Ordering and State Change* (1st edn, CUP 2012).

[63] Mikkel Jarle Christensen and Neil Boister, 'New Perspectives on the Structure of Transnational Criminal Justice' in Mikkel Jarle Christensen and Neil Boister (eds), *New Perspectives on the Structure of Transnational Criminal Justice* (Brill 2018) 4.

describes 'the legal technologies constructed or reconfigured to provide the framework for criminalisation, harmonisation and cooperation targeting specific forms of criminal behavior'.[64]

These concepts of transnational criminal justice support the principles of fairness and equity, aiming to safeguard the interests of both individuals and corporations, even when these interests are not formally recognized as rights. The question remains as to the current State of the law regarding their implementation in criminal justice.

3.3 Unconventional Investigations of Transnational Crimes

In this context, the focus of this book is on the significant and indispensable role of unconventional investigative methods in combating transnational crimes. It examines three key aspects of recent developments in the investigation of such crimes.

The first aspect is the development of various mechanisms by law enforcement agencies to effectively gather information in response to the complexities of modern transnational crimes.[65] In addition, some States extend its jurisdictional arms in law enforcement through obtaining a 'consent' from individuals and corporations and cross-border search through internet. The existing law is not sufficient to protect human rights, most importantly the right to fair trial, because of the territory-based and decentralized nature of international human rights law and State law in most jurisdictions.

The second aspect involves obtaining information and evidence related to criminal offences through administrative measures and informal collaboration. States have the option to gather information via administrative collaboration, which may involve informal arrangements rather than being strictly bound by a formal treaty. These cooperative mechanisms began to flourish only following the end of the Cold War. They do not incorporate the principles found in a typical MLAT, such as the requirement of double criminality and exceptions for political or fiscal offences. In most cases, the provision of information does not undergo court scrutiny. The decision of whether to provide the information to a foreign counterpart rests with the head of the administration.

Administrative agreements conventionally stipulate that the evidence cannot be utilized in criminal proceedings without the providing State's consent. Nevertheless, a recent trend indicates the omission of such language, with the discretion now resting with the receiving State. The information shared via

[64] ibid.

[65] Although it is beyond the scope of this book, the author previously examined the limits and significance of territoriality in the context of cross-border cyberspace investigations. Yurika Ishii, 'Limits of State Jurisdiction in Cyberspace: The Legality of the Cross-Border Remote Access and the Use of Policeware' (2025) 67 Japanese Yearbook of International Law 26.

administrative cooperation falls short of establishing the commission of a crime. Consequently, the State may find itself reliant on established cooperative avenues for criminal affairs to acquire additional essential information. Still, the administrative mechanism has proven indispensable in countering transnational crimes, driven by two significant shifts in the landscape in major developed countries. One is the heightened intrusiveness of administrative investigations attributed to the broadening jurisdiction of the governments. These investigations encompass a wide array of economic offences, including breaches of competition regulations, securities fraud, and tax evasion. These investigations play a central role in detecting criminal activities. The other is that a majority of developed nations have revised their legislation concerning, for example, securities law and tax law, enabling prosecutors to utilize evidence obtained by administrative institutions for criminal proceedings.

The third aspect concerns direct collaboration with private entities, focusing on two key areas, namely AML/CFT regulations and digital investigations. For the prevention and detection of money laundering, financial institutions are mandated to retain and share financial data with governmental authorities. In the context of the digital investigation, communication service providers play a pivotal role, including major platform operators, such as Google, Amazon, Meta (formerly Facebook), and Alphabet. Issues under international law arise when States must require foreign entities to comply with their laws.

By exploring these three aspects, this book will make a case for the consent-based investigation of transnational crimes. States used to be reluctant to cooperate in criminal matters, particularly for sensitive crimes such as political crimes. However, administrative cooperation and direct cooperation have the potential to overcome such boundaries. It is imperative to track the evolution of these mechanisms and their potential impact on the field of international legal studies.

It is noted that a legally operative 'consent' includes both recognition and acquiescence. Recognition means a positive acknowledgement, even in an implied or tacit manner. Acquiescence means an omission to protest a situation where a right to protest existed and its exercise was called for. This book does not differentiate between the two concepts, as distinguishing them is impractical and does not affect the outcome in this context.

4. Methodology

This book's methodology follows the positivist doctrine, as it understands that international law is a system of principles and rules. The tasks of this book are to clarify the legal rules governing each transnational crime and the conditions for its application through demonstration. Since the regulations are tailored to the specific characteristics of each offence, understanding the context in which these rules were introduced is essential for proper legal interpretation.

International law is a product of a dynamic process of claim and counterclaim, assertion and reaction, by governments as representatives of States and other international actors.[66] Therefore, the book gives weight to the process of articulating and assessing what occurs when rights or interests are engaged.[67] Deconstructing international legal arguments seems necessary to clarify historically conditioned 'codes' or 'conceptual schemes'.[68] Such a clarification regarding transnational criminal law is the main task of this volume.

While research on transnational offences from the standpoint of international law has been mostly a description of the status of treaties, this book aims to clarify the legal structure of those regulations by picturing the dynamism of the interaction between domestic and international laws. It systematically reviews the limits and significance of the executive jurisdiction of States, the rights and obligations of States under various cooperation mechanisms concerning transnational crimes, and the structure of such arrangements. It will lead to clarifying the extent of the individual's rights and an alternative explanation concerning the structure of transnational criminal law instead of the classical account illustrated in the beginning.

The following perspectives will be considered when analysing the current State of international regulations on transnational crime.

The first point is the difference between conventional mutual legal assistance on criminal matters—letters of rogatory and MLAT—and cooperation on transnational crimes. The history and the nature of the former is examined in this chapter. The latter has been developed to overcome the former's limits so that their structures and characteristics will be the focus of the analysis.

The second is the relations between unilateral law enforcement—the measures done without the territorial State's consent where the materials are located—and the bilateral cooperation mechanisms, including non-binding arrangements. As will be examined in Part II, bilateral cooperation mechanisms have been developed to overcome the limits of unilateral law enforcement.

The third is the relations with international cooperation and the rights and status of the individuals. No general principle secures individuals' rights and position when multiple States are involved in a criminal process. However, there are limited cases and practices to overcome the deficiency. Furthermore, as will be

[66] James Crawford, *Chance, Order, Change: The Course of International Law* (Martinus Nijhoff 2014) 20.
[67] ibid.
[68] ibid 13.

discussed in Part II, there are State practices to secure financial privacy, specifically securing the financial information or the transfer of the information to other States.

5. Structure of the Book

This book is divided into three parts and thirteen chapters, including this introduction and the conclusion. Part I sets the stage by analysing the State-centric structure of transnational criminal law and delving into the obligations to suppress various transnational crimes. It addresses the complexities arising from conflicts of prescriptive and enforcement jurisdiction. It then examines the evolving status of individuals within the framework of transnational criminal law. Part II shifts the focus to investigations conducted through non-criminal cooperation, revealing how various transnational crimes have been addressed through such means. Chapters cover a range of offences, from violations of competition laws and economic sanction laws to securities and tax frauds, foreign bribery, and terrorism. Part III examines direct cooperation with foreign private entities, emphasizing the importance of collaboration in combating transnational crime. Key topics include AML regulations and the involvement of communication service providers in the fight against criminal activities.

The following explains this structure in detail. Part I, Chapter 2, starts by examining why international legal studies maintain the State-centric structure when it deals with transnational crimes. It traces the history of States' reluctance to cooperate on criminal matters. It also explores why reciprocity has been the core principle of the letters of rogatory and MLATs. Then, it explores that States failed to codify a universal mutual legal assistance treaty under the auspice of the League of Nations. Post–World War II saw the increase and development of the MLATs, but it did not overcome the conventional structure of international law.

It also looks into substantive obligations to suppress certain transnational crimes, such as drug trafficking, organized crimes, and terrorism. It was generally established after the Cold War ended to enhance cooperation multilaterally. The important point in this context is that a few States agreed on enhanced regulations on a bilateral or regional basis.

Chapter 3 investigates the status of individuals in transnational criminal law. The first section will discuss the intrusive nature of the investigation of organized crimes in recent years. Then, it explores the significance and limitations of international human rights law, particularly focusing on the de-centrality of this legal framework and the evolution of privacy rights under international law through the European Court of Human Rights. General principles of transnational criminal law are discussed to provide a broader context for understanding the legal standards concerning safeguarding defendants' rights. The latter section will examine how courts in different jurisdictions have addressed the admissibility of evidence unlawfully obtained abroad. While the forum court generally applies the law of the forum State, there are variations in the reasoning and its implications.

Chapters 4 and 5 examine how States have expanded their prescriptive and enforcement jurisdiction in response to the evolving demands of cross-border evidence gathering. It is noted that the concept of jurisdiction encompasses the obligations of States, including the duty to protect public interests, such as national security, and the rights of individuals.

Chapter 4 examines the development of theories of prescriptive jurisdiction. It focuses on the legal conflicts that arise when States assert jurisdiction beyond their borders, often leading to disputes with the affected States. These conflicts highlight the tension between one State's territorial sovereignty and another's extraterritorial legislative actions. The chapter also examines how these jurisdictional claims have influenced international relations by necessitating compromises.

Chapter 5 shifts the focus to the practice of States obtaining evidence from individuals and corporations with their consent. The most important practice in this context is using non-prosecution or deferred prosecution agreements, which allow companies to comply with government requests without facing criminal charges.

Part II examines cases involving investigations through intergovernmental cooperation, beyond MLATs and other forms of criminal cooperation. The main argument of this part is that non-criminal cooperation is crucial for investigating transnational crimes.

There are common patterns in establishing such cooperative frameworks: (1) harmonization of domestic laws among developed States, (2) establishment of law enforcement agencies tasked with implementing economic laws and authorized to investigate criminal cases, and (3) mandates for these agencies to share information with their counterparts in other States. A significant international issue is the process in which the United States attempted to expand its jurisdiction, leading to resistance from other States, which is dealt with in Chapter 4. The interconnectedness of the global economy has driven a shift towards prioritizing cooperation in suppressing offences that impacts cross-border transactions. Jurisdictional conflicts have become less frequent as countries recognize the need for a unified approach. The pathways of cooperation vary depending on the area, necessitating separate examinations. The issue of due process and the right to a fair trial is a widely recognized concern. It is an essential pillar of the rule of law. However, international law lacks established standards, resulting in each State and jurisdiction implementing its own policies. This part will conduct an examination of various cases and materials related to each field.

Part II addresses sanctions for violations of competition, securities, and tax laws, selected for their significant impact on global markets and international relations. These areas often involve administrative sanctions, which can be imposed more leniently than criminal penalties. Additionally, it covers foreign bribery and terrorism, with a particular focus on non-criminal investigations. While there is extensive literature on these crimes in international criminal law studies, this book focuses on whether and to what extent States use information and data obtained through administrative procedures in criminal proceedings to combat these offences.

Chapter 6 explores the violations of competition law, which set the earliest cases of jurisdictional conflict. It explores the nature of the disputes, exploring the US unilateral law enforcement practices, civil and criminal jurisdictions, and the use of subpoenas to foreign subsidiaries concerning the criminal sanction against violations of competition laws. It also tracks the European States' enactment of blocking statutes. It further examines the challenges in harmonizing competition laws and the lack of progress in achieving a uniform global framework. The significance and limitations of cooperation mechanisms among competition authorities are thoroughly analysed, specifically emphasizing the concept of positive comity. Different cooperation mechanisms are outlined, including negative comity agreements, positive comity agreements, and enforcement cooperation.

Chapter 7 deals with securities fraud. It first explores the jurisdictional conflict and the harmonization of securities laws. It delves into the practices of the United States and other States, examining how conflicts can arise when enforcing securities laws across different jurisdictions. Collecting information through subpoenas and the waiver-by-conduct doctrine are highlighted as key aspects of cooperation and conflict resolution. It also evaluates the limits and significance of conventional judicial assistance, mainly focusing on legal assistance treaties on civil and commercial matters. In addition, cooperation mechanisms between financial regulatory authorities take centre stage in the discussion. The historical development of such mechanisms is explored, and the mandate of these authorities is analysed. Different authorizations for providing information to other States under various conditions, such as more lenient conditions than MLAT or on the same conditions, are examined. The prohibition of exchanging information for criminal investigations and the summary of these mechanisms are also discussed. The chapter further explores bilateral administrative cooperation between financial authorities for criminal investigations and the IOSCO Multilateral Memorandum of Understanding.

Chapter 8 deals with tax fraud. It highlights the role of offshore markets and bank secrecy in facilitating tax evasion. It explores the creation and proliferation of offshore markets, focusing on bank secrecy practices in countries like Switzerland and various Caribbean nations. Multilayered information exchange networks in the context of tax fraud investigations are thoroughly examined. The historical development of such networks and the emergence of model treaties are discussed. The increase in information exchange mechanisms, including the Convention on Mutual Assistance in Tax Administration and Enforcement and TIEA, is also analysed. Obtaining evidence from financial institutions is another critical aspect explored in the chapter. The US jurisdictional arms, such as Qualified Intermediaries and the Foreign Account Tax Compliance Act, are analysed in this context. The chapter also discusses the role of the Organisation for Economic Co-operation and Development (OECD) Global Forum in addressing tax fraud.

Chapter 9 deals with foreign bribery. It delves into the jurisdictional arms used for investigating foreign corruption, with a particular focus on the US Foreign Corrupt Practices Act. Then, it examines multilateral conventions related to combatting foreign bribery. The OECD Anti-Bribery Convention and the UNCAC are discussed, shedding light on their significance in addressing this issue. State practice in combatting foreign bribery is thoroughly analysed. The approaches taken by the United States and the United Kingdom are highlighted, emphasizing their efforts in addressing this issue. However, the lack of cross-border investigation in other States and regions is also discussed, indicating potential challenges in tackling the crime. Informal and enhanced international cooperation are important aspects of the chapter. It explores how informal cooperation with corporations and incentivization of reporting can play a role in combatting foreign bribery effectively.

Chapter 10 examines the investigation of terrorism, analysing the constitutional framework, anti-terrorism legislation, and foreign intelligence and surveillance practices. Notably, the US National Security Agency's surveillance activities and the privacy frameworks between the European Union and the United States, including the Privacy Framework of 2000, the Privacy Shield of 2016, and Data Privacy Framework of 2022, are scrutinized. Collection of transportation information, including airline passenger name record data, biometrics, and biogenetic information, are thoroughly examined.

Part III explores the direct cooperation between governments and private entities in collecting information for criminal investigations, focusing on how such mechanisms are structured and the legal implications involved. This cooperation becomes complex when the private entities are foreign and when they are subject to conflicting legal requirements in their home countries. The key issues are data protection and privacy legislations. While widespread agreement exists on the necessity of addressing and preventing serious crimes such as terrorism, the approach to privacy varies considerably across jurisdictions. This divergence raises fundamental questions about how governments may rely on private entities to aid in law enforcement efforts.

Chapter 11 deals with AML/CFT regulations. Its evolution in the United States, organized offences' criminalization, and EU law's development are explored. The role of the FATF and self-regulations by financial institutions are also discussed, along with efforts to harmonize national legislation of non-member States of FATF. The chapter discusses the Society for Worldwide Interbank Financial Telecommunications (SWIFT) programme and gatekeeper regulations concerning information sharing. The chapter also delves into the impact of AML/CFT regulations on individual rights. It explores how AML/CFT measures, such as the SWIFT programme and gatekeeper regulations, may impose restrictions on individual rights.

Chapter 12 examines the direct cooperation with communication service providers. The chapter analyses the jurisdictional scope, considering its implications for users' human rights. The extension of jurisdictional scope is examined, particularly through national legislation and bilateral exchange agreements, including the US data access agreements and the Second Additional Protocol of the Cybercrime Convention. The basis of these agreements and their impact on cross-border communication service providers are discussed. It highlights the evolving conflicts and challenges in the digital age. It delves into personal information protection, data legislation, and decryption issues that contribute to this new form of legal conflict. Human rights protection is a significant consideration in the chapter. It explores the right to a fair trial and the emergence of digital human rights in the context of communication service providers.

The conclusion in Chapter 13 summarizes the essential findings and insights presented throughout its chapters. It highlights several important aspects that have been explored in the preceding discussions. First, it underscores the significance of international cooperation achieved through mechanisms beyond traditional MLATs, as this book demonstrates how various types of agreements and frameworks have played a role in facilitating cross-border cooperation and addressing complex transnational challenges. Second, it recognizes the evolving practices of unilateral law enforcement practices and the changing nature of the jurisdictional principles. It acknowledges that while States may take unilateral actions, effective resolution of the situation often requires collaboration and coordination among nations. Third, it reflects on the impact of privacy and human rights standards on the rights and obligations of States in the context of mutual assistance. It highlights how these standards have influenced how States cooperate, exchange information, and address cross-border legal challenges while respecting individual rights. It reinforces the idea that while States may navigate their unique legal systems and priorities, collaboration remains essential for effectively tackling transnational crimes and ensuring justice across borders.

2
The State-Centric Structure of Transnational Criminal Law

1. Introduction

The starting point of this book was the criticism of the State-centric structure of international legal studies. Information exchange arrangements on economic and white-collar crimes developed primarily after the end of the Cold War, when the number of transnational crimes increased and the modality of unlawful conduct became complex. However, States did not replace pre-existing information exchange mechanisms with a *de novo* arrangement. They amended the previous practice to adapt effectively to transnational crimes. Earlier means, including letters of rogatory, are still good today and remain the last resort when no other means are available. In this sense, the recent mechanisms are not conceptually distinct from the previous forms of international cooperation.

It is essential to comprehend the mechanisms supporting the State-centric structure of international cooperation. A key initial step in this process involves a detailed analysis of the historical context and the rationale behind previously employed mechanisms. This chapter provides an account of the history and the theoretical background of such an understanding and the limits of mutual legal assistance treaties (MLATs) in investigating contemporary transnational crimes. Chapter 3 then discusses the implications of the intrusive nature of the investigative techniques developed for organized crimes and the relevance and limits of international human rights law.

Section 2 provides a detailed analysis of the reasons behind the State-centric nature of mutual legal assistance mechanisms in criminal matters, namely the challenges associated with their establishment and the importance of the principle of reciprocity. It then considers the background behind the absence of a multilateral treaty in contrast to the civil law domain. Section 3 tracks post–World War II developments where States agreed to enter into multilateral conventions that compel them to suppress specific crimes. These conventions impose only a minimal obligation for judicial assistance, as they maintain the State-centric structure developed through mutual legal assistance treaties. Section 4 points out that States opt to create bilateral and regional treaties to effectively address and combat these crimes.

International Law and the Investigation of Transnational Crimes. Yurika Ishii, Oxford University Press.
 DOI: 10.1093/9780198957089.003.0002

2. Reciprocal Mutual Legal Assistance on Criminal Matters

2.1 Letters Rogatory

Modern international cooperation on criminal matters, including mutual legal assistance, dates back to the early nineteenth century.[1] They took the form of requisition proceedings, which include the exchange of search and arrest warrants, court records, interrogation protocols, evidence, transfer of witnesses and suspects, or extradition requests.[2] Research on legal assistance in criminal matters appears in the works of criminal lawyers in Great Britain and France,[3] where States established letters of rogatory under their domestic laws,[4] and in the works of German lawyers up to the nineteenth century, where cooperation among principalities and free imperial cities was a crucial task. In addition, there was a research conducted in the 1870s to the 1880s through the International Law Association on the taking of evidence for foreign courts.[5] Cooperation is performed on natural offences in practice. Before the Industrial Revolution, regulatory laws were under-developed, and where they exist, they did not provide criminal sanctions.

In the early twentieth century, States and academics sought to standardize international criminal cooperation. A draft convention was prepared and adopted by the Committee of Experts for the Progressive Codification of International Law led by Walther Adrian Schücking and Giulio Diena.[6] Harvard Law School International Law Research subsequently prepared and adopted a draft convention on judicial

[1] For the history of the criminal cooperation, see generally Maurice Travers, 4 *Le Droit Pénal International et Sa Mise En Œuvre En Temps de Paix et En Temps de Guerre* (Sirey 1920) 1; Ferdinand Von Martitz, 2 *Internationale Rechtshilfe in Strafsachen: Beiträge Zur Theorie Des Positiven Völkerrechts Der Gegenwart* (H Haessel 1897).

[2] For an overview of the early development in Europe, see Karl Härter, 'Norms, Procedures and Practices of Transnational Criminal Law in 18th and Early 19th-Century Europe' in Neil Boister, Sabine Gless, and Florian Jeßberger (eds), *Histories of Transnational Criminal Law* (OUP 2021) 18.

[3] Julien Bregeault, *De l'audition En Matière Criminelle Des Témoins Résidant En Pays Étranger* (E Thorin 1878); Maurice Travers, *L'entr'aide Répressive Internationale et La Loi Française Du 10 Mars 1927* (Librairie du Recueil Sirey 1928).

[4] Johann Vesque von Püttlingen, *Handbuch Des in Österreich-Ungarn Geltenden Internationalen Privatrechtes Mit Besonderer Berücksichtigung Des Staats-Und Völkerrechtes* (W Braumüller 1878); Friedrich Meili, *Lehrbuch Des Internationalen Strafrechts Und Strafprozessrechts* (Art Institut O Füssli 1910); Martitz (n 1).

[5] Henry Diedrich Jencken, 'The Taking of Evidence for Foreign Courts' in International Law Association (ed), *Report of the Sixth Annual Conference Held at Frankfort-on-the-Main, 20–23 August, 1878* (William Clowes and Sons, Ltd 1878) 92; Sherston Baker, 'The Taking of Evidence for Foreign Tribunals' in International Law Association (ed), *Report of the Eighth Annual Conference, Held at Berne, August 24th–27th, 1880* (William Clowes and Sons, Ltd 1880) 160; Jacopo Baisini, 'The Taking of Evidence for Foreign Courts' in International Law Association (ed), *Report of the Fifteenth Conference Held at Genoa, October 5th–10th, 1892* (Wyman and Sons, Ltd 1892) 79.

[6] Committee of Experts of League of Nations, 'Draft Convention Prepared by the Committee of Experts for the Progressive Codification of International Law (A.15.1928.V)' (1928) 22 American Journal of International Law Special Supplement 46.

assistance in 1939 ('Harvard Draft').[7] Their efforts were never materialized into an actual treaty. However, the debates of this period became the basis for legal studies after the end of World War II. This section examines these debates to determine the meaning and limitations of cooperation in criminal matters.

Contemporary judicial assistance on criminal matters started after modern States established criminal procedural laws.[8] Sporadic practices and provisions concerning the service of documents contained in consular treaties existed in the eighteenth century.[9] However, systemic cooperation based on treaties started only in the mid-nineteenth century. Evidence was initially gathered by letters rogatory through diplomatic or consular channels from the judicial authorities of the requesting State to their counterparts in the requested State.[10] It was the pillar of criminal cooperation until the mid-twentieth century.[11] For instance, the research of Maurice Travers, published in 1928, shows that the letters rogatory was the most relied procedure for the criminal cooperation. There were approximately 800 requests from 1920 to 1925 in France and 200 to 350 in Switzerland.[12] Another report published by American Bar Association (ABA) shows that it was used proactively in the 1950s.[13]

The mechanism was codified in criminal procedural laws in States such as Italy in 1866[14] and Spain in 1881.[15] States, including Britain in 1870,[16] Belgium in 1869,[17] the Netherlands in 1869,[18] and Brazil in 1892,[19] introduced this mechanism

[7] Harvard Law School International Law Research, 'Judicial Assistance' (1939) 33 American Journal of International Law Supplement 11; Harvard Law School International Law Research, 'Draft Convention on Judicial Assistance' (1939) 33 American Journal of International Law Supplement 86.

[8] The practice of judicial assistance has existed since ancient times. Harvard Law School International Law Research, 'Judicial Assistance' (n 7) 26. Examples illustrated in this report included a Greek inscription dating from the first or second century BC.

[9] ibid 27. See, eg, Declaration Between Baden and Italy Relative to the Communication of Judicial Acts and the Execution of Commissions Rogatory, 23 January 1868, 136 CTS 485.

[10] Vienna Convention on Consular Relations (adopted on 24 April 1963, entered into force on 19 March 1967, 596 UNTS 261, art 5(j).

[11] Neil Boister, *An Introduction to Transnational Criminal Law* (OUP 2018) 312. See also Philip F Sutherland, 'The Use of the Letter of Request (or Letter Rogatory) for the Purpose of Obtaining Evidence for Proceedings in England and Abroad' (1982) 31 International and Comparative Law Quarterly 784.

[12] Travers (n 3) 4.

[13] American Bar Association Section of International and Comparative Law, 'Report of the Committee on International Judicial Cooperation' [1956] Proceedings (American Bar Association Section of International and Comparative Law) 93. See also Michael Abbell, 'Obtaining Evidence in the U.S. in Criminal Cases through Use of Compulsory Process' in Richard D Atkins (ed), *The Alleged Transnational Criminal: The Second Biennial International Criminal Law Seminar* (Martinus Nijhoff Publishers 1995) 294.

[14] Codice di procedura penal del regno d'Italia, art 854, *reproduced in* Ferdinand Monier, *Des Commissions Rogatoires En Droit International* (Impr H Jouve 1909), 214.

[15] Ley de Enjuiciamiento Criminal, Gaceta de 17 de Septiembre de 1882, Artículos 193–94, *reproduced in* Monier (n 14) 250.

[16] Extradition Act of 1870, 33 & 34 vict cap 52, Extradition Act of 1873, 36 & 37 vict cap 60.

[17] Loi sur l'organisation judiciaire, promulguée le 18 juin 1869, art 139.

[18] Wet van 16 Juli 1869, Stbl No 139.

[19] Brazilian Law of No 221, 20 November 1894.

in extradition laws. Japan enacted a law providing procedures for letters rogatory on civil and criminal cases in 1905.[20] The United States exceptionally refused to employ this mechanism because of the defendant's constitutional right to confront the witnesses.[21]

When international lawyers tried to unify judicial assistance after the 1870s through the inter-war period, they started to refer to the civil letters rogatory as a model. The systemic use of the letters rogatory on civil matters began in Britain and continental Europe in the mid-nineteenth century.[22] In 1896, the Hague Conference on Private International Law adopted a Convention relating to Civil Procedure.[23] The premise for this development was that the mutual assistance in civil and commercial matters, which governed relations between private individuals, would not be hindered by differences in the civil and commercial laws of States or their application to foreign nationals.

Experts at the time generally accepted the idea of analogy to transplanting established judicial assistance mechanisms on civil matters into criminal procedures, although they were aware of the difference between the two areas. It was a procedural law, and there was no reason to distinguish civil and criminal matters based on substantive arguments. For instance, Paul Johann Anselm Feuerbach, in 1812, supported assistance on civil and criminal matters unless there was a restriction in the treaty.[24] Johann Vesque von Puttlingen affirmed the judicial assistance on criminal matters in his treatise on private laws in 1860.[25] Furthermore, Friedlich Meili, in a discussion about whether there was an obligation for judicial assistance for the justice of international society in the absence of a treaty, refers to judicial assistance.[26] These scholars and diplomats seem to have based their arguments on the dualism of domestic and international law. The international legal obligation and its domestic implementation were separate matters. They did not pay close attention to the tension between judicial assistance and sovereignty.

In the Harvard Draft on judicial assistance, the experts assimilated assistance in criminal and civil proceedings. They employed the same methods to obtain evidence but modified certain details to ensure the protection of the rights of

[20] Act on Mutual Assistance on Letters Rogatory by Foreign Courts, Act No 63 of 13 March 1905.

[21] Constitution of the United States, Amd art 6. The principle and the exceptions are provided in Federal Rules of Criminal Procedures, Rule 15.

[22] An Act to provide for taking Evidence in Her Majesty's Dominions in relation to Civil and Commercial Matters pending before Foreign Tribunals, 29 July 1856, 19 & 20 vict cap 113, in *The Statutes of the United Kingdom of Great Britain and Ireland* (1856) 619; Loi sur l'organisation judiciaire, 18 juin 1869, *Codes Bruylant* (1869) I, 889; Civilprozeßordnung, *Deutsches Reichsgesetzblatt*, Nr 6, S 83, 30 Januar 1877, Artikle 331; Loi du 7 julliet 1896 apportant des modifications au code de procedure civile, *Annuaire de législation étrangère* (1896) 521. See Monier (n 14) 20.

[23] Convention du 14 novembre 1896 relative à la procédure civile (adopted on 14 November 1896, entered into force 23 May 1899) 183 CTS 470.

[24] Paul Johann Anselm Feuerbach, *Lehrbuch Des Gemeinen in Deutschland Gültigen Peinlichen Rechts* (GF Heyer 1812) 307.

[25] Vesque von Püttlingen (n 4) 279.

[26] Meili (n 4) 361.

individuals affected by the procedure.[27] The draft mentioned that '[i]n matters of procedure, simplicity is a prime requisite, and there is no reason for evolving two separate systems',[28] referring to States which treated the two subjects as the same.

Extradition mechanisms developed during the same period. Scholars have debated whether the principles of double criminality, speciality, and non-extradition of political offenders should apply. In practice, treaties limited the scope of judicial assistance to the offences subject to extradition treaties.[29] Alternatively, treaties allowed the requested party to refuse judicial assistance when the offences were not subject to extradition treaties.[30]

However, on a theoretical level, there was no reason to limit judicial assistance as a part of extradition law. Schücking, the special rapporteur of the 1928 Draft Convention at the Hague Conference, concluded that the two were independent procedures.[31] Even after the attempt at codification failed, as explained in Section 3 below, most of the scholarly arguments supported this view. Those who affirmed the assimilation of judicial assistance in civil and criminal matters endorsed this position. The others emphasized the difference between judicial assistance and extradition. For instance, Maurice Travers denied whether the extradition rules applied to the letters rogatory.[32] Extradition was usually disadvantageous for the offender, especially when the domestic court rendered the sentence. Conversely, judicial assistance might benefit the individual. Refusing the request to submit material would put an innocent offender at risk of being convicted.[33]

[27] Harvard Law School International Law Research, 'Judicial Assistance' (n 7) 91.

[28] ibid.

[29] Among the list of judicial assistance treaties attached to the Draft Convention to the Hague Conference, the treaties that were not extradition treaties were: Italy–San Marino, Convention of Friendship and Good Relations (adopted on 28 June 1897) reprinted in 2 Martens, 3rd, 794; Columbia–Ecuador Treaty of Friendship, Commerce and Navigation (adopted on 10 August 1905) reprinted in Martens, 3rd, 856; Paraguay–Uruguay, Convention for the Purpose of Simplifying and Facilitating Procedure by Way of Letters Rogatory (adopted on 28 February 1915) 15 LNTS 393; Latvia–Norway, Treaty of Commerce and Navigation (adopted on 14 August 1924) 36 LNTS 924; Poland–Czechoslovakia, Treaty concerning Judicial Assistance (adopted on 6 March 1925) reprinted in Legal Gazette of the Polish Republic 1926, no 14/80; Poland–Austria, Treaty concerning Judicial Assistance (adopted on 19 March 1924) reprinted in Legal Gazette of the Polish Republic 1926, no 84/467 and Austria BGBl no 226/1926; Austria–Italy, Treaty on Judicial Cooperation in Penal Matters (adopted on 6 April 1922) Austria BGBl no 6/1925.

[30] France–Spain, Treaty (adopted on 14 December 1877) reprinted in 12 Recueil des traités de la France 65 (Alexandre Jehan Henry Clercq, Jules de Clercq 1881) art 13; Estonia–Finland, Treaty (adopted on 2 January 1925) art 15, 43 LNTS 1044, 12; Romania–Hungary, Treaty (adopted on 16 April 1924) art 20, 42 LNTS 1038, 146; Finland–Latvia, Treaty (adopted on 7 June 1924) art 15, 38 LNTS 990, 344; Estonia–Latvia, Treaty (adopted on 12 July 1921) art 14, 37 LNTS 964, 424; Latvia–Lithuania, Treaty (adopted on 12 July 1921) art 14, 25 LNTS 620, 312; France–Denmark, *Traité d'extradition franco-danois* (adopted on 28 March 1877) art 13, reprinted in 12 Recueil des traités de la France 7 (Alexandre Jehan Henry Clercq, Jules de Clercq 1881); Switzerland–Uruguay, *Traité d'extradition entre la Suisse et la République de l'Uruguay* (adopted on 27 February 1923, entered into force on 15 July 1927), reprinted in (1927) 43 Recueil officiel du droit fédéral 135. See the list of treaties in the Draft Convention.

[31] Committee of Experts of League of Nations (n 6) 32.

[32] Travers (n 1) 175.

[33] ibid.

2.2 Concerns Inherent to Judicial Assistance on Criminal Matters

While States and experts generally accepted the assimilation of judicial assistance in civil and criminal matters, some aspects were intrinsic to judicial assistance in criminal cases. The mutual legal assistance would conflict with the sovereignty of the requested State. Therefore, there was a consensus that the criteria for this process should be stricter compared to those for civil matters.

2.2.1 Penal Law *Tabu*

States have equal sovereignty, and no State is superior to any other State. The exercise of criminal jurisdiction is the fundamental power of a State. Therefore, States are cautious regarding the application of another State's criminal law within its domain. As a result, they exclude other States' personal or *in rem* criminal jurisdiction in their domestic courts. Domestic courts tended to resist the recognition and application of other States' public laws, regardless of the existence of friendly relations, shared legal traditions, or the reasonableness of the measures in question. Andreas Lowenfeld named this the penal law *tabu* in his Hague Academy in 1979.[34] His primary focus was on securities or competition laws, but he referred to penal law cases as the most classic examples.

Scholars advocating for international cooperation in criminal matters were acutely aware of States' reluctance to enhance such collaboration. Ferdinand Monier, who extensively studied the practice of letters rogatory in criminal cases, argued that their implementation would not infringe upon the sovereignty of the requested State. However, he acknowledged that reciprocal agreements were essential for the effective collection of evidence. Unlike judicial assistance in civil matters, Monier emphasized that criminal judicial cooperation needed to be approached cautiously to avoid conflicting with the policies and sensitivities tied to the sovereignty of the requested States.[35]

2.2.2 Grounds for Rejection

The penal law *tabu* influenced the scope of the refusal grounds of the requests. The Harvard Draft provided the most comprehensive basis for refusal. It offered that a letter rogatory shall be executed unless (1) 'execution is impossible on account of absence of the person whose evidence is required, or on account of inability to locate such person, or for any similar reason',[36] or (2) 'the government of the State or execution considers that execution of the request would be contrary to the public

[34] Andreas F Lowenfeld, *Public Law in the International Arena: Conflict of Laws, International Law, and Some Suggestions for Their Interaction* (Martinus Nijhoff 1979) 417.

[35] Monier (n 14) 4–8.

[36] Harvard Law School International Law Research, 'Draft Convention on Judicial Assistance' (n 7) art 4(8)(a).

interests'.[37] Furthermore, execution of a letter rogatory may be refused 'in so far as the evidence sought would be patently irrelevant to the proceeding in the State of origin, or in so far as the taking of the evidence sought would violate a privilege accorded by the law of the State of execution'.[38] In the case of judicial assistance on criminal matters, they included the following additional grounds: (1) if the proceeding in the State of origin dealt with a political offence, (2) the person sought was a national of the requested State, (3) the forum State conducted the investigation in absentia, and (4) the double criminality was not satisfied.

There was not much disagreement on the political offence. The Harvard Draft provided that if the proceeding in the State of origin deals with such an offence, the execution of a request 'may' be refused.[39] The authors commented that the aversion to assisting other States ran through this field. Extradition treaties almost universally provide that there should be no extradition for such offences.[40]

Some treaties provided a nationality clause, but most scholars did not support this concept. For instance, Julien Bregeault criticized this clause because it excessively protects nationals at the expense of justice.[41]

The absence of a defendant was recognized as grounds for refusal because it would limit the defendant's right to confront the witness. This right to confrontation was one of the obstacles to developing judicial assistance.[42] The Harvard Draft also stated that this right would not pose a hurdle because, although the court before the proceeding might exclude the evidence, it would not be grounds for refusing the request for assistance.

The mandatory double criminality requirement, that the court must refuse the request if the conduct is punishable in both the requested and forum States, was not endorsed in State practices and academia. On the other hand, an optional clause, that the court may refuse the request, did not face much opposition.[43]

2.2.3 Paths of Judicial Assistance

The path of the request, in a sense, is a technical issue.[44] It depends on the status of the judicial assistance within the requested State. However, it has been important in theory and practice in developing mutual assistance mechanisms. Treaties in the early twentieth century were not consistent in this regard. Some treaties specified

[37] ibid art 4(8)(b).
[38] ibid art 4(9).
[39] ibid art 6(2)(b).
[40] Harvard Law School International Law Research, 'Judicial Assistance' (n 7) 93.
[41] Bregeault (n 3) 12.
[42] US Constitution, amend VI. See John David McClean, *International Co-Operation in Civil and Criminal Matters* (OUP 2012) 148. See also Section 4.2.
[43] Harvard Law School International Law Research, 'Judicial Assistance' (n 7) 97.
[44] Committee of Experts of League of Nations (n 6) 27.

only cooperation between the judicial authorities[45] or those that referred to the domestic systems of the State parties.[46]

The Committee of Experts at the Hague Conference in 1928 noted that there were three main paths of communication: between (1) the ministries of foreign affairs of the State parties, (2) the judicial authorities, and (3) the ministry of foreign affairs of the requesting State and the judicial authority of the requested State. One question was whether the foreign ministry of the requested State should be involved. It would be more efficient if the process did not go through the institution. On the other hand, some States and academics felt that this was necessary because it was a matter of international relations. Bregeault stated that the communication of letters rogatory between judges, without the intervention of the governmental authority, might restrict the sovereignty of the requested State.[47] The Draft Convention of 1928 provided that States should go through diplomatic channels unless the State parties agreed on a special arrangement.[48]

Another issue was whether the process had to go through judicial review by the courts. The Harvard Draft of 1939 explicitly stated that the 'tribunal' included not only a judicial authority but also an administrative authority.[49] The report conceded that State practices mostly involved courts in judicial assistance, and the inclusion of certain administrative authorities in the term 'tribunal' marks an important departure from many treaties.[50]

The argument remained as to whether the process had to whether the process should be channelled through the foreign office or the courts, as mutual legal assistance could impinge on sovereignty, although it would be more time-consuming and costly.

2.2.4 Lack of Obligation under General International Law

Lastly, there was broad agreement that, in the absence of a binding treaty, no legal obligation to cooperate existed. This issue arose primarily in the context of extraditing fugitives, which was the main form of cooperation at the time. For instance, Oppenheim stated that no universal rule of customary international law commands extradition, noting that States had always upheld their competence to grant asylum to foreign individuals as an inference from their territorial supremacy.[51]

[45] Italy–Panama (adopted on 7 August 1930) 140 LNTS 241; Paraguay–Uruguay (adopted on 28 February 1915) art 1, 15 LNTS 199; German–Turkish (adopted on 3 September 1930) art 1, 133 LNTS 334, reprinted in 29 American Journal of International Law, Supplement 323; Great Britain–Yugoslavia (adopted on 27 February 1936, entered into force on 18 August 1937) 28 (1937) arts 2 and 7, Treaty Series 1.

[46] French–USSR (signed on 11 August 1936) art 1, 176 LNTS 365.

[47] Bregeault (n 3) 9.

[48] Committee of Experts of League of Nations (n 6) 28.

[49] Harvard Law School International Law Research, 'Draft Convention on Judicial Assistance' (n 7) art 1(d), 15. The comments stated that 'the term "tribunal" as here used includes all courts and a limited number of administrative agencies'. ibid 36.

[50] Committee of Experts of League of Nations (n 6) 36.

[51] Lassa Oppenheim, *International Law: A Treatise* (Longmans, Green and Co 1905) 383.

Some scholars claimed otherwise at the end of the nineteenth century. For instance, Edward Clarke claimed that States were obliged to surrender the offender based on moral obligation.[52] Similarly, Francis Wharton stated that it was an obligation to extrude a fugitive for justice.[53] However, neither went so far as to prescribe that the duty was legal. Furthermore, Robert Phillimore distinguished the obligation to extradite based on general law and extradition treaties and claimed that the former was not established on positive law.[54] He cited Hugo Grotius, as he claimed that States were obliged to deny asylum against fugitives and had to transfer the offender to the place where he or she committed the offence but accepted that States did not endorse this view.[55] It is noted that his understanding of Grotius was not accurate, because Grotius did not envisage States sovereignty when he made this argument.[56]

In summary, by the end of World War II, there was a consensus among scholars that (1) the assimilation of judicial assistance from civil and criminal matters was generally acceptable, (2) the principles of extradition treaties were not considered to apply to judicial assistance on the taking of evidence, and (3) there was no obligation to assist other States when there was no treaty.

2.2.5 Reciprocity

(1) Tension between Reciprocity in Judicial Assistance and Universalism

Reciprocity is the backbone of mutual legal assistance in criminal matters. It is generally defined as 'the status of a relationship between two or more States under which a certain conduct by one party is in one way or another juridically dependent upon that of the other party'.[57] It is 'a basic phenomenon of social interaction and consequently a guiding principle behind the formation and application of the law'.[58] The principle is widely adopted in bilateral treaties to make the other party comply with the agreement because international society lacks a central mechanism to enforce the treaty obligation.[59]

[52] Edward Clarke, *A Treatise upon the Law of Extradition* (Stevens and Haynes 1888) 14.

[53] Francis Wharton, *A Treatise on the Conflict of Laws, or, Private International Law Including a Comparative View of Anglo-American, Roman, German, and French Jurisprudence* (Kay and Brothers 1872) 597.

[54] Robert Phillimore, *Commentaries upon International Law*, vol 1 (T & JW Johnson 1854) 437.

[55] ibid.

[56] For the interpretation of Grotius's chapter, see Terumi Furukawa, 'Punishment' in ONUMA Yasuaki (ed), *A Normative Approach to War: Peace, War, and Justice in Hugo Grotius* (Clarendon Press 1993) 221.

[57] Bruno Simma, 'Reciprocity' in Rüdiger Wolfrum (ed), *Max Planck Encyclopedia of Public Internation Law* (online edn, OUP 2008) para 2.

[58] ibid para 1.

[59] Arianna Whelan argues against the perception that reciprocity is opposed to the communitarian interests or a way of denoting reactions to unfriendly or wrongful conduct. Instead, she claims that it can serve the realization of community interests. Arianna Whelan, *Reciprocity in Public International Law* (CUP 2023) 43.

This principle was incorporated into multilateral treaties and domestic laws that implemented letters of rogatory and other forms of judicial assistance from the beginning. It is therefore necessary to examine the significance and limitations of this principle in the context of judicial assistance.

Reciprocity is not a legal requirement.[60] According to this principle, when a State decides whether to provide judicial assistance or extradite a fugitive, it can consider political elements such as relations with the requesting State.[61] The reciprocity became incorporated into judicial assistance mechanisms to secure the independence of the States. Maurice Travers criticized the inclusion of the principle, arguing that while it held some significance, it lacked both logical and practical necessity and was inconsistent with the spirit of the League of Nations.[62] He noted that preserving reciprocity was inappropriate because it represented distrust among States.[63] On the other hand, Wolfgang Mettgenberg, who extensively researched the State practices and theories of the nineteenth century, claimed that the requirements of reciprocity are not so strict as to seriously hinder the development of international legal assistance.[64] He also pointed out that reciprocity contributes to the uniformity of the extradition system and promotes the development of a harmonized legal framework.[65] This uniformity encourages States to expand and refine their legal assistance relationships. In addition, the principle serves as a strong safeguard even for weaker contracting parties. Reciprocity continues to function to maintain equitable relations among States and to prevent imbalances and discontent.[66]

The debates on the scope of reciprocity had practical aspects in the early twentieth century when States started to enact domestic laws on judicial assistance to foreign States. A major issue in early practice was whether a State should assist the counterparty even if there was no reciprocity, namely that the requesting State may not provide the same assistance. There were States that did not require reciprocity as a condition for implementing the request for criminal cooperation. For instance, Great Britain's Extradition Law of 1870 did not provide this principle. The legislation enjoyed general support within Britain.[67] In 1877, the Royal Commission on Extradition commented that it was to the benefit of the requested State not to give

[60] Institut de droit international, Session d'Oxford, 'Extradition', Projet de rèsolutions, 9 septembre 1880, para 5, 2 Annuaire de l'Institut de droit international (1880) 99.

[61] Institut de droit international, Session d'Oxford, Rapports par Charles Brocher, Louis Renault et Caspar Bluntchli, 2 Annuaire de l' Institut de droit international (1880) 60–130.

[62] Travers (n 1) 388.

[63] ibid; Travers (n 3) 6.

[64] Wolfgang Mettgenberg, 'Die Reziprozität Im Deutschen Auslieferungsrecht' (1909) 25 Archiv für öffentliches Recht 1, 133–37.

[65] ibid 138–39.

[66] ibid.

[67] Extradition Act 1870, 33 & 34 vict c 52.

freedom to the fugitive, especially because he might commit another crime.[68] No State would want to be a safe haven for a person who would do harm to another State. Therefore, there would be no case law preventing the extradition of fugitives even in the absence of full reciprocity.[69] In his 1910 work, Francis Taylor Pigott cited this report to claim that there was no reason to refrain from cooperating with other States because it would be not only for the benefit of the requesting State but also for the requested State to implement the request.[70]

Neither did France's extradition act of 1927 require reciprocity.[71] Donnedieu de Vabres stressed that assisting other States in criminal matters would serve the universal suppression of criminals. Extradition laws should not be based on the policy of transactions and bargaining expressed in the reciprocity clause.[72] He thus believed in a universal convention of extradition, which was based on justice, not on reciprocity, because the common obligation and interests of States existed to suppress fugitives.

In his treatise of 1928, Donnedieu de Vabres explained three stages of the development of extradition based on his thorough examination of State practices.[73] The first was the contractual stage, where the two governments assisted each other on a reciprocal basis under bilateral agreements. The agreements would reflect various elements of geographical, social, and political situations. The second was where the States enacted national legislation that uniformly provided the measures for the procedure, although the assistance was still based on reciprocity. In the third stage, bilateral agreements and national legislation were integrated into a general treaty, obliging the States to cooperate without a reciprocal basis to realize universal interest. France's extradition law of 1927 was situated in the second stage.[74]

In summary, while reciprocity was commonly provided in bilateral agreements, States took different approaches concerning the scope and meaning of this principle. Whether it had to be necessarily relied upon in the domestic law of the requested States.

[68] Great Britain, Royal Commission on Extradition, *Report of the Commissioners, Presented to Both Houses of Parliament by Command of Her Majesty* (1878), 24 Parliamentary Papers 907 (17 August 1877).

[69] ibid.

[70] Francis Taylor Piggott, *Extradition: A Treatise on the Law Relating to Fugitive Offenders* (Butterworth 1910) 18.

[71] Loi du 10 mars 1927 relative à l'extradition des étrangers, *Journal Officiel* du 11 mars 1927.

[72] Henri Donnedieu de Vabres, 'De La Reciprocité En Matière d'extradition d'après La Loi Francais Du 10 Mars 1927 et Le Nouveau Projet Allemand' (1928) 35 Revue générale de droit international public 333, 570.

[73] Henri Donnedieu de Vabres, *Les Principes Modernes Du Droit Pénal International* (Librairie du Recueil Sirey 1928) 248–52.

[74] Donnedieu de Vabres (n 72) 570.

(2) ICJ, *Certain Questions of Mutual Assistance in Criminal Matters* (2008)

The International Court of Justice (ICJ)'s case in 2008 between Djibouti and France was the one that showed the limits of the reciprocity principle.[75] The facts are as follows. France and Djibouti concluded the Treaty of Friendship and Cooperation in 1977 (the 1977 Convention) and the Convention on Mutual Assistance in Criminal Matters in 1986 (the 1986 Convention). Article 1 of the 1986 Convention provided that the two States engage in judicial assistance as widely as possible based on reciprocity ('*s'accorder mutuellement*'). Article 2(c) of the 1986 Convention provided that judicial assistance may be refused if the requested State considers that execution of the request is likely to impair its sovereignty, security, *ordre public*, or other essential interests. Article 17 of the 1986 Convention provided that reasons shall be given for any refusal of judicial assistance.

On 19 October 1995, the charred body of a French judge and technical advisor to the Djiboutian Ministry of Justice, Bernard Borrel, was found in Djibouti. Both Djibouti and France commenced judicial investigations into the cause of his death. In 2004, the investigating judge in Djibouti issued a letter rogatory addressed to the French judicial authorities in accordance with the 1986 Convention, requesting the transmission of the French file on the case. The French authorities informed Djibouti that they were 'not in a position to comply' with the request for the execution of the letters rogatory without giving further reasons for their refusal. In 2006, Djibouti applied to the ICJ to inquire whether France failed to comply with its international obligations under Article 17 because it did not give Djibouti the reasons for its refusal.

On the merits, the ICJ dealt with Djibouti's claim that France had violated obligations of cooperation arising out of the 1977 Treaty. In the end, the Court found that this convention was not directly concerned with mutual assistance in criminal matters. Then, the Court examined whether it still had a legal impact.

The Court held that a general clause of friendship and cooperation inserted in a treaty of friendship could influence not only the interpretation of other provisions of the same treaty but also of different treaties, in this case, the 1986 Convention, in accordance with Article 31(3)(c) of the Vienna Convention on the Law of Treaties (VCLT), a provision the Court reasserted to reflect customary international law. The ICJ, however, rejected Djibouti's farther-reaching contention that a serious violation of the 1986 Treaty would at the same time constitute a breach of the Treaty of Friendship, noting that the bearing the Treaty of Friendship has on the interpretation of the 1986 Convention 'is as far as the relationship between the two instruments can be explained in legal terms'.[76]

[75] *Certain Questions of Mutual Assistance in Criminal Matters (Djibouti v France)* (Judgment) [2008] ICJ Rep 177.

[76] ibid para 114.

On the basis of the obligation of the 1986 Convention, Djibouti made the following three claims: (1) Article 1 places France under an obligation to execute the international letter rogatory; (2) France undertook to carry this out in January 2005, and it failed to perform this undertaking; and (3) as a subsidiary argument, France breached the obligation in question when it gave Djibouti notice of its refusal to execute the letter rogatory.[77]

The first point, the obligation to execute the letter rogatory, was based on Article 1, which stipulated the obligation to execute the international letter rogatory. France did not dispute that Djibouti fully executed the letters rogatory issued by French judicial authorities, but it maintained that requests for mutual assistance must be assessed case by case.[78] In its view, its dispute with Djibouti was over the execution of a specific letter rogatory, and no issue of reciprocity could arise in regard to it.[79] The Court supported France's view, stating that 'the Convention nowhere provides that the granting of assistance by one State in respect of one matter imposes on the other State the obligation to do likewise when assistance is requested of it in turn'.[80] Accordingly, the Court considered that Djibouti could not rely on the principle of reciprocity in seeking execution of the international letter rogatory it submitted to the French judicial authorities.

Regarding the obligation to execute the letter rogatory set out in Article 3(1) of the 1986 Convention, the Court observed that the obligation to execute international letters rogatory laid down in Article 3 was to be realized in accordance with the procedural law of the requested State, that is, France in this case. Thus, 'the ultimate treatment of a request for mutual assistance in criminal matters clearly depends on the decision by the competent national authorities, following the procedure established in the law of the requested State'.[81] While it must, of course, ensure that the procedure is put in motion, the State does not thereby guarantee the outcome, in the sense of the transmission of the file requested in the letter rogatory.[82]

Second, regarding the alleged undertaking by France to execute the international letter rogatory requested by Djibouti, the Court considered that, by virtue of its content and the factual and legal circumstances surrounding it, the letter of 27 January 2005 does not, by itself, entail a legal undertaking by France to execute the international letter rogatory transmitted to it by Djibouti on 3 November 2004.[83]

On the third point, France's refusal to execute the international letter rogatory, the Court first considered whether France's refusal fell within the scope of Article

[77] ibid para 115.
[78] ibid para 117.
[79] ibid.
[80] ibid para 119.
[81] ibid para 123.
[82] ibid.
[83] ibid paras 125–30.

2(c). It found that the terms of Article 2 provided a State to which a request for assistance had been made with considerable discretion. However, this exercise of discretion was still subject to the obligation of good faith codified in Article 26 of the VCLT.[84] As to whether the decision of the competent authority was made in good faith, the Court recalled that the judge who made the decision stated the grounds for her decision to refuse the request for mutual assistance, explaining why transmission of the file was considered to be 'contrary to the essential interests of France', in that the file contained declassified 'defence secret' documents, together with information and witness statements regarding another case in progress.[85] The Court found that the reasons given by Judge Clément fell within the scope of Article 2(c).

Then, the Court considered whether, as Djibouti contended, a violation of Article 17 precluded reliance on Article 2(c), which might otherwise be available. The Court first interpreted that Articles 2 and 17 were 'in a sense linked',[86] as 'Article 2 refers to possible exceptions to the granting of mutual assistance and Article 17 to the duty to give reasons for the invocation of such exceptions in refusing mutual assistance'.[87]

In the end, however, the Court considered that no legal inference was to be drawn from the arrangement of the text of the Convention. On one hand, the Court observed that there was a certain relationship between Articles 2 and 17 in the sense that the reasons that may justify refusals of mutual assistance, which are to be given under Article 17, include the grounds specified in Article 2.[88] At the same time, Articles 2 and 17 provided for distinct obligations, and the terms of the Convention do not suggest that recourse to Article 2 was dependent upon compliance with Article 17.[89] According to this analysis, the Court thus found that France violated its obligation to Djibouti under Article 17. However, it also determined that France was entitled to rely upon Article 2(c) and that, consequently, Article 1 had not been breached.[90] It also determined that this finding constituted appropriate satisfaction to Djibouti.[91]

The disposition that determined the violation of Article 17 was affirmed unanimously. However, there are opinions regarding the Court's interpretation of the principle of reciprocity. In particular, ad hoc judge Abdulqawi Yusuf contended that the aim of the expression 'the widest measure' was the fullest and most open cooperation.[92] Judge Abdul Koroma also criticized the same part of the

[84] ibid para 145.
[85] ibid para 147.
[86] ibid para 153.
[87] ibid.
[88] ibid para 156.
[89] ibid.
[90] ibid.
[91] ibid para 204.
[92] Separate Opinion of ad hoc Judge Yusuf, [2008] ICJ Rep 293, para 11. He claimed that '[w]hile a State party may refuse to comply with a request for mutual assistance in criminal matters, such a refusal may only be exceptional, and must, in any event, be based on proper grounds. This was not so in the present case. Without reciprocity and mutual cooperation, the Convention would no longer be

judgment.[93] He argued that due account must have been taken of principles of equality and mutual respect, which formed the basis of the relationship between the two countries.[94] Furthermore, he noted that the Court was reluctant to engage squarely with the issue when it stated that the concept of reciprocity invoked by Djibouti did not require France to act similarly.[95] Judge Kenneth Keith, in his declaration, criticized the fact that the French judge did not have proper regard for the Convention in failing to expressly address those two alternative methods of affording Djibouti the widest measure of judicial assistance in terms of Article 1 while protecting the interests stated in Article 2(c).[96]

A broader interpretation of the principle of reciprocity might have led the Court to a different conclusion. However, it should be confirmed that all the judges, except for ad hoc Judge Yusuf, did not find that France had breached the substantive obligation of the 1986 Convention. In other words, even if there was a procedural error in the French court, this did not constitute a breach of the Convention, and Djibouti was not entitled to request the evidence. The Court's assessment is consistent with the conclusion in the previous section that the principle of reciprocity imposes certain limits on the promotion of mutual legal assistance in criminal matters.

3. The Failure of the Codification of a Universal Mutual Legal Assistance Treaty in the Inter-War Period

While the laws on cooperation on criminal matters were by no means uniform at the end of the nineteenth century, the inter-war period saw an effort aimed at codification because judicial assistance would serve as a peaceful settlement. There were no serious academic objections. For instance, Meili, the representative of Switzerland at the Hague Conference on Private International Law, stated that the best method would be to unify the main principles as in the Hague Conventions on private laws rather than concluding bilateral conventions.[97]

a convention for mutual assistance but merely an instrument to assist one of the parties. It would be devoid of all meaning and would answer the purpose for which it was concluded for one of the parties only, i.e., France' (ibid). Therefore, 'the necessity for both parties to comply with the fundamental and reciprocal duty "to afford each other the widest measure of mutual assistance" is at the very heart of the Convention' (ibid). Djibouti was entitled to demand execution of the letter rogatory submitted to the French judicial authorities based on the principle of reciprocity stated in Article 1(1) of the 1986 Convention since it had itself afforded France the widest measure of mutual assistance by executing the three letters rogatory requested by the French authorities.

93 Separate Opinion of Judge Koroma, [2008] ICJ Rep 252.
94 ibid 254, para 7.
95 ibid para 10. See also *Djibouti v France* (n 75) para 119.
96 Declaration of Kenneth J Keith, [2008] ICJ Rep 252. See also Kenneth J Keith, 'The International Court of Justice and Criminal Justice' (2010) 59 International and Comparative Law Quarterly 895, 909.
97 Meili (n 4) 349–67. This statement was cited in Committee of Experts of League of Nations (n 6) 52.

In 1927, the Committee of Experts for the Progressive Codification of International Law issued questionnaires for communicating judicial and extra-judicial acts and letters rogatory in penal matters.[98] However, its effort did not bear fruit. This section will briefly overview the process and the discussion.

In 1924, the General Assembly of the League of Nations established the Committee of Experts to research issues ripe for codification, and the eighth questionnaire was an issue on the present topic. The Committee then inquired of the member States whether it was possible to establish, employing a general convention, provisions on this matter. In 1927, it received replies from eighteen of fifty-five countries. Twelve countries replied affirmatively, and the rest replied that this topic was unsuitable for codification.[99] Among the former group, which replied affirmatively, some countries fully supported the plan, such as Estonia[100] and Germany,[101] and countries that stated a more cautious approach, such as Hungary,[102] Poland,[103] Austria,[104] Finland,[105] and Sweden[106] required double criminality to be incorporated in the draft.

The reasons for negative replies varied. Britain stated that judicial assistance on criminal matters did not suit a general convention, and bilateral treaties would suffice when necessary.[107] Similarly, Australia replied that it would be dealt with in a bilateral treaty.[108] South Africa did not provide a specific reason but answered that a general treaty would be impossible, although it was desirable.[109] The United States did not concede the constitutional right of the defendant to confront witnesses. It stated that a treaty on judicial assistance on criminal matters was useful among geographically close States, but there was no need for a general treaty. The United States was suspicious of collecting evidence for other States' criminal procedures because criminal law was local, and the comity of the nations would not cover it. Because of the lack of uniform support, the Committee concluded that it was not possible to codify customary international law.

Schücking and Diena affirmed the theoretical possibility for the codification in their report.[110] Based on a thorough examination of State practices and the academic literature, they came to an affirmative conclusion because 'in the matter

[98] Committee of Experts of League of Nations (n 6) 46.
[99] League of Nations, A15 1928 V (1928) Annex I, 8, reproduced in Shabtai Rosenne, *League of Nations Committee of Experts for the Progressive Codification of International Law (1925–1928)*, vol 2 (Oceana Publications 1972).
[100] ibid Annex III, 89.
[101] ibid 69.
[102] ibid 71.
[103] ibid.
[104] ibid.
[105] ibid.
[106] ibid.
[107] ibid.
[108] ibid 63.
[109] ibid 81.
[110] Committee of Experts of League of Nations (n 6) 47.

of international judicial cooperation in penal cases there is already in existence a large body of legal principles relating to many important questions which are commonly accepted and have found expression in a large number of inter-State treaties'.[111] They also mentioned that it was not only possible but desirable 'since international solidarity is bound to be strengthened if the present inter-State agreements is merged in a collective agreement which would be tantamount to the establishment of a worldwide law'.[112]

However, their report was not supported by States. It was not until 1959 that the European Convention on Mutual Assistance in Criminal Matters,[113] the first unified multilateral convention that stipulated uniform rules, was adopted. There exists no universal treaty tantamount to the Hague Convention on Judicial Assistance on Civil and Commercial Matters of 1896 to this date.

The limits of Schücking and Diena's ideas seem to be the following. First, the cooperation the draft considered was to construct a mechanism of judicial cooperation regardless of differences in the substantive criminal laws and policies of each States. This approach worked in cooperation on civil and commercial matters, presumably because there are fewer conflicts with these private practices and public policies of foreign States. However, it was and has been the conventional practice that State parties negotiate and conclude an agreement on criminal matters only when the policies of the counterpart do not differ in a significant manner so that the cooperation would not conflict with the basic policy of the party. The exception to political offence or double criminality is the one that takes both substantive and procedural laws into account. Therefore, there was a practical constraint to separate the two sets of laws.

Second, the communication of judicial matters that was expected in the report was solely done with the mutual consent of the relevant States. It did not consider that one of the State parties unilaterally collects information based on, for example, the consolidation of multinational corporations.

An external factor in the failure of codification may have been the lack of practical need on the part of States. The International Criminal Police Organization (ICPO) was established in 1923 to strengthen police cooperation. Cooperation through the ICPO does not have the same effect as cooperation through a treaty because it does not have the effect of enforcing the law. However, this inconvenience was mitigated, as the voluntary use of the mechanism increased after World War II.[114]

111 ibid 89.
112 ibid 90.
113 European Convention on Mutual Assistance in Criminal Matters, ETS No 030.
114 For the development of the police cooperation, see Saskia Hufnagel and Carole McCartney, 'Police Cooperation against Transnational Criminals' in Neil Boister and Robert J Currie (eds), *Routledge Handbook of Transnational Criminal Law* (Routledge 2014) 107.

4. The Development of Mutual Legal Assistance Treaties after the End of World War II

4.1 Intra-Regional Efforts

After the end of World War II, international cooperation on criminal matters was based on bilateral or regional treaties. These practices did not differ much from the conventional letters rogatory on the following two points. First, these treaties provided that mutual assistance would be decided after the judicial review of courts or judicial authorities of the State parties. Reciprocity was the core principle, although its exact meaning was not uniform, as the previous section discussed. Second, there was no coordination of laws through these treaties, which meant that the taking of evidence was done solely based on the territory where the measures took place, and there was no room for considering the laws of the forum.

The European Convention on Mutual Assistance in Criminal Matters, the first multilateral convention on this matter, was drafted by the Council of Europe (CoE) in 1953 and adopted in 1959. It broadly provides cooperation on criminal matters, but the taking of evidence is based primarily on the letters rogatory. Because the CoE adopted a policy to exclude controversial offences from the scope of mutual cooperation,[115] the grounds for refusal in this convention were quite broad.[116] On the other hand, it did not codify the principle of double criminality. The CoE explained that mutual assistance was different from extradition, and if the former was done independently from the latter, then there would be no constraint on the freedom of the individual.

Other regional treaties included the Inter-American Convention on Letters Rogatory of 1976[117] and the Inter-American Convention on Mutual Assistance in Criminal Matters of 1992.[118] The latter specifically obliges member States to mutually assist other member States in criminal matters. However, the scope of the grounds for refusal is quite broad.[119] It also retained its State-centric character, as it provided that '[t]his convention applies solely to the provision of mutual assistance among State parties. Its provisions shall not create any right on the part of any private person to obtain or exclude any evidence or to impede the execution of any request for assistance.'[120]

[115] 1969 Explanatory Report on the European Convention on Mutual Assistance in Criminal Matters, reproduced in William C Gilmore, *Mutual Assistance in Criminal and Business Regulatory Matters* (CUP 1995) 38.

[116] European Convention on Mutual Assistance in Criminal Matters, art 2.

[117] Inter-American Convention on Letters Rogatory (adopted on 30 January 1975, entered into force on 16 January 1976) OASTS No 43.

[118] Inter-American Convention on Mutual Assistance in Criminal Matters (adopted on 23 May 1992, entered into force on 14 April 1996) A-55.

[119] ibid art 9.

[120] ibid art 2.

There were practices where mutual assistance was provided on the basis of a political association. After decolonization, such frameworks were established between the former suzerain State and the colonies. During colonization, it was customary for cooperation in criminal matters to occur within the framework of the internal laws of the empire. After the independence of the colonies, the new States had to choose between enacting a new law or accepting the law as it was to continue cooperating with the former suzerain or between colonies. On the other hand, since the colonies did not have the authority to conclude treaties before their independence, similar frameworks of cooperation were not established with the colonies and States outside the empire.

The Commonwealth Scheme relating to Mutual Assistance in Criminal Matters of 1986 is the most prominent example that inherited the cooperation mechanism among former British colonies.[121] This is an instrument that the member States of the Commonwealth agreed on. It was criticized for the fact that the framework would not be able to secure reciprocity, so a treaty was preferable. However, not all the members had the laws to fully implement the framework. Neither had they sufficient human resources. The States agreed that it should have only an advisory effect.[122]

This framework adopted a mechanism for the establishment of a central authority in each member State and for communication between these authorities. Its characteristics were to be based on mutual trust among the political community. When it was requested, it provided mutual assistance without scrutinizing the substantive jurisdiction of the requesting States. Furthermore, the framework provided for a wide range of methods, not only the taking of testimony but also the obtaining and preservation of electronic data, the transmission of communications, and electronic searches. On the other hand, the grounds for refusal were quite broad and included a lack of dual criminality, political offences, military offences, and the risk of double jeopardy.

In contrast, the Communauté française established in 1946 did not create an equivalent framework for cooperation in criminal matters. This association halted its function in 1960 because more than half of the former colonies chose to leave, but it formally existed until the French Constitution was amended in 1995. There were cases where the treaty of amity was concluded, which also included provisions on the mutual assistance of criminal cooperation.

[121] 'Commonwealth Scheme Relating to Mutual Assistance in Criminal Matters within the Commonwealth' (1986) 12 Commonwealth Law Bulletin 1118. The Scheme was updated in 1990, 2002, and 2005.

[122] For the discussion, see McClean (n 42) 177; Patrick L Robinson, 'The Commonwealth Scheme Relating to the Rendition of Fugitive Offenders: A Critical Appraisal of Some Essential Elements' (1984) 33 International and Comparative Law Quarterly 614.

4.2 The United States

The United States led the creation of the network of the bilateral judicial assistance, mainly with the countries with which it has had close political or geographical relationships. As noted in the previous section, the United States did not endorse a general multilateral convention on this topic because it was restricted by its Constitution. However, it started to conclude bilateral treaties out of necessity to obtain evidence from abroad in the mid-1930s.[123] Its content aimed to strengthen conventional methods on the following points.

First, the agreements commonly provided a wide range of cooperation. The State party may request every sort of information related to an investigation. In practice, not only the information for the identification of the suspect but also the bank account, the location of the individuals other than the suspect, and the record for communication were included. Second, the grounds for refusal were limited. Political offence exceptions and bank secrecy were excluded from these grounds. This point will be discussed in Part II. Third, the path of cooperation was simplified. The agreements generally provided that the authority may directly request cooperation from its counterpart without judicial review of ministries of foreign affairs and courts. It should be noted that in 1981, the ABA issued a recommendation that the authority should not take an administrative action associated with the potential conflict of law or the significant difference of policies without prior notification and consultation with the Department of State and, when appropriate, with the government of a foreign State.[124] The Department of Justice (DOJ) clarified its policy to consult with the Department of State in such a case.[125]

MLATs have been concluded between countries other than the United States. Furthermore, the United Nations Office on Drugs and Crime (UNODC) published a manual on mutual legal assistance to promote its proliferation.[126] However, there are limits to the MLAT, as it still takes time and money compared with unilateral law enforcement or other informal cooperation.

Another development was the enactment of laws on cooperation in each State. Before the 1970s, when the regulations began, only a limited number of States had specific domestic laws to implement cooperation.[127] Instead, common practice was that the codes of the criminal procedure provided clauses that their judicial

[123] McClean (n 42) 61. In addition, US case law concerning the Confrontation Clause, the Sixth Amendment of the US Constitution, has evolved in step with technological advancements. See *US v Abu Ali*, 528 F 3d 210 (4th Cir 2008). See also McClean (n 42) 151.

[124] American Bar Association Recommendation, Report No 101, 12 August 1981.

[125] See Part II, Chapters 4 and 5.

[126] UNODC, *Manual on Mutual Legal Assistance and Extradition* (United Nations 2012).

[127] As far as the present author researched, besides the United States and Europe (the member States of European Convention on Mutual Cooperation on Penal Matters), Burundi and Zaire (current Zimbabwe) retained its extradition law issued when they were under colonization by Belgium (Décret du 12 avril 1886 relatif à l'extradition [1886] Bulletin official 22, reprinted in Conseil colonial, Belgium, *Compte rendu des séance*).

authority would cooperate with foreign authority in general. In such cases, the courts and the judicial authorities could refuse the requests, and indeed, there were few such cases.[128]

Some States started to loosen the requirements under domestic laws to allow judicial authorities to cooperate with other States more closely. For instance, the law of Switzerland in 1981 generally requires the satisfaction of the reciprocity.[129] However, the law provides that authorities may cooperate even when reciprocity was not satisfied, when there was such a need from the nature of the crime, when it served the interests of the defendant, or when it was beneficial to investigate a crime done against nationals of the country.[130] Austria provided that when reciprocity was not satisfied, the minister of justice should be consulted.[131] However, these movements were performed in a specific context in a limited number of countries.

One of the most important practices is the United States reforms following the 9/11 terrorist attacks in 2001. The ensuing investigation revealed that the compartmentalization of government agencies contributed to the United States' inability to prevent the terrorist attack. Congress passed the Homeland Security Act of 2002. The act created the Department of Homeland Security, which merged the US Customs Service (formerly part of the Treasury Department) and the Immigration and Naturalization Service (formerly part of the DOJ) into the Offices of Investigations, Intelligence and International Affairs within the Immigration and Customs Enforcement. In 2010, the division was integrated into the Homeland Security Investigations (HSI), which is the primary federal law enforcement organization to counter transnational threats, including drug cartels and money laundering syndicates.[132]

The US government launched Transnational Criminal Investigative Units programmes in 2011 under the umbrella of the HSI to train and closely coordinate with foreign law enforcement officials for investigation of individuals engaged with transnational criminal activities. The units 'targets, collect evidence, share intelligence, and facilitate the prosecution of transnational criminal organizations' through both the US and foreign judicial systems.[133]

[128] For instance, Union of Soviet Socialist Republics' (USSR) 1924 criminal law provided such a clause. However, at the time of inter-war period, it did not conclude any agreement on cooperation on criminal matters except with the exchange of letters with the United States; and Taracouzio commented that there was not much to learn from the practices of the USSR. See TA Taracouzio, 'International Cooperation of the USSR in Legal Matters' (1937) 31 American Journal of International Law 55.

[129] Federal Act on International Mutual Assistance in Criminal Matters, AS 1982 846, art 8(1).

[130] ibid art 8(2).

[131] Auslieferungs- und Rechtshilfegesetz (ARHG), vom 4 Dezember 1979, BGBl Nr 529/1979, art 3(3).

[132] For the development of the HSI, see its website, Homeland Security Investigations, History <https://www.dhs.gov/hsi/history>. All websites were last accessed on 31 March 2025.

[133] 'Transnational Criminal Investigative Units (TCIUs)', <https://www.dhs.gov/hsi/task-forces/tciu>. According to the website, the programme 'has more than 600 vetted and trained foreign law

4.3 The European Union

Another notable development is the judicial cooperation in the European Union since the 2000s.[134] Criminal cooperation remains primarily within the competence of the member States. However, intraregional cooperation in addressing drug and organized crime is closely tied to the principle of freedom of movement within the European Union, which the Schengen Agreement of 1985 and its subsequent amendments in 1990 stipulated.[135] Cooperation among countries within Schengen area encompasses unique aspects, such as exchanging personal data, including deoxyribonucleic acid information, between police agencies.[136] Although not directly related to the European Union, the Schengen Agreement was later incorporated into the EU framework through an annexe to the 1999 Amsterdam Treaty. All EU member States, except for Ireland and the United Kingdom, must implement Schengen-related legislation, thereby abolishing border checks among the member States.

The Maastricht Treaty of 1992 provided limited policy cooperation in justice and home affairs.[137] The Amsterdam Treaty of 1997 established police and judicial cooperation on criminal matters as the third pillar of the European Union, alongside the other two pillars of economic and foreign policy cooperation.[138] This led to the introduction of various legal instruments to foster collaboration in criminal justice and the development of the European Union's concept of a 'free, safe, and just space'.[139]

enforcement officers in 16 locations across North, Central and South America, the Caribbean, the Middle East, and Asia'.

[134] See Gerhard OW Mueller, 'Transnational Crime: Definitions and Concepts' in Dimitri Vlassis and Phil Williams (eds), *Combating Transnational Crime: Concepts, Activities and Responses* (Routledge 2001) 13; Cyrille Fijnaut, 'Transnational Organized Crime and Institutional Reform in the European Union: The Case of Judicial Cooperation' in Phil Williams and Dimitri Vlassis (eds), *Combating Transnational Crime: Concepts, Activities and Responses* (Routledge 2001) 276; Frank Madsen, 'The Historical Evolution of the International Cooperation against Transnational Organised Crime: An Overview' in Pierre Hauck and Sven Peterke (eds), *International Law and Transnational Organised Crime* (OUP 2016) 3.

[135] Convention implementing the Schengen Agreement of 14 June 1985 [2000] OJ L239/19, arts 92–119. The database (Schengen Information System (SIS)) registers the names and pseudonyms of suspects, their physical characteristics, date and place of birth, gender, and nationality. The data entered into the SIS is checked by an independent supervisory authority in each country to ensure that it does not contravene data protection regulations. Since 2013 a new system (SIS II) has been established, which is based on the SIS database (SIS II).

[136] Hufnagel and McCartney (n 114); Saskia Hufnagel, 'Policing and Prosecution of Transnational Crime' in Valsamis Mitsilegas, Saskia Hufnagel, and Anton Moiseienko (eds), *Research Handbook on Transnational Crime* (Edward Elgar Publishing 2019) 32.

[137] European Union, Treaty on the European Union (Consolidated Version), Treaty of Maastricht [1992] OJ C325/5, art K.

[138] European Union, Treaty on the European Union (Consolidated Version), Treaty of Amsterdam (2 October 1997) Protocol (No 2) integrating the Schengen Aquis into the Framework of the European Union, art 1.

[139] Treaty of Amsterdam, arts 29–42.

While mutual criminal assistance between EU member States had already been established through the European Convention on Mutual Assistance in Criminal Matters of 1959 and other treaties, a new Mutual Criminal Assistance Convention was concluded in 2000.[140] Its membership is limited to EU Member States, and it is designed in line with the Schengen Agreement and the EU treaties. The Convention explicitly addresses assistance in particular law enforcement methods, such as video calls and telephone interrogations, controlled deliveries, and undercover investigations, with the primary objective of combating drug, organized, and terrorist crime within the European Union.[141]

The Convention provides for assistance to be provided per the modalities and procedures of the requesting State, anticipating joint investigations by the authorities.[142] However, compliance with such modalities and procedures must not contravene fundamental principles of the territorial State, and any non-compliance must be promptly communicated to the requesting State.[143]

Additionally, the Convention allows for joint investigations to be carried out by the member States, such as undercover investigations.[144] The implementation of such investigations is determined on a case-by-case basis by the competent authorities of the requesting State. The duration, clear conditions, and legal status of the officials involved are determined by the national laws and procedures of the receiving State. Cooperation among relevant States is also required to prepare, supervise, and coordinate for officials' safety.

As a result of increasing cases in which the law enforcement authorities of one country enter the territory of another country to carry out law enforcement actions, the agreements emphasize that the implementation of the law should be in line with the legislation of the requested country. Some national laws, such as the UK Regulation of Investigatory Powers Act 2000, allow searches outside the country, such as wiretapping and the use of confidential human sources abroad by investigative agencies, as long as they comply with local law.[145]

A notable feature is that the European Union incorporated the principle of mutual recognition of judicial decisions of the member States.[146] The implementing

[140] Convention established by the Council in accordance with Article 34 of the Treaty on the European Union the Convention on Mutual Assistance in Criminal Matters between the Member States of the European Union [2000] OJ C197/3. The 1959 instrument is the Convention on Mutual Assistance in Criminal Matters between the Member States of the European Union (adopted on 20 April 1959, entered into force on 12 June 1962) arts 10–11, ETS No 30.

[141] ibid arts 8–16. Verena Murschetz, *European Police Cooperation in the Future Legal Framework of the European Union* (Brill 2010).

[142] Convention on Mutual Assistance in Criminal Matters of 2000 (n 140) art 4(3).

[143] ibid art 4(1).

[144] ibid art 13. See also European Union, Council Resolution of 26 February 2010 on a Model Agreement for setting up a Joint Investigation Team (JIT) [2010] OJ C70/01.

[145] Regulation of Investigatory Powers Act 2000, c 23, s 27(3).

[146] While it is beyond the scope of this chapter, the European Union has adopted other mutual recognition mechanisms including the European Arrest Warrant framework. Council Framework Decision 2002/584/JHA on the European arrest warrant and the surrender procedures between Member States [2002] OJ L190/1.

State is obliged to recognize and ensure execution of the request of the other State, unless there is a ground for an exception as provided under the EU law. Under the European Investigation Order Directive of 2014, a judicial decision issued in or validated by the judicial authority in one EU member State provides for investigative measures to be carried out in another member State to collect or use evidence in criminal matters.[147] The Directive harmonized the procedural laws among States and provides law enforcement officers with a single standard form for obtaining evidence. It sets rigorous timelines and establishes limited grounds for refusal by the executing State.

5. Multilateral Treaties to Suppress Transnational Crimes

5.1 A Brief Overview of the Historical Development

The multilateral treaties to suppress certain transnational crimes typically include a provision for judicial assistance. In the late nineteenth century, some European States and the United States concluded treaties to address certain harmful conducts. Examples include treaties to suppress the slave or trade, illegal fishing, and the protection of submarine cables.[148] However, comparable treaties at the global level were not established until the 1960s, when States agreed to cooperate in suppressing transnational crimes involving multiple States. It started with the regulation of the aerial hijacking and later with illicit cross-border transactions such as drug smuggling and other organized crimes.

In 1971, the Commission on the Prevention and Control of Crime was established under the United Nations Economic and Social Council as the primary international body for organized crime control within the United Nations. Subsequently, the Fifth United Nations Congress on the Prevention of Crime and Treatment of Offenders, which commenced in 1975, further emphasized the need for international cooperation on organized crime.

The end of the Cold War brought to light the issue of organized crime in developing countries, which the United States and the European Commission (EC) had previously overlooked as an international security concern. In particular,

[147] Directive 2014/41/EU of the European Parliament and of the Council regarding the European Investigation Order in criminal matters [2014] OJ L130/1. It was introduced in 2017. The Directive does not apply in Denmark and Ireland.

[148] For instance, see International Convention for Regulating the Police of the North Sea Fisheries outside Territorial Waters (signed on 6 May 1882, entered into force on 15 May 1884), 9 *Martens NRG 2e* 556; Convention internationale pour la protection des câbles sous-marins (adopted on 14 March 1884, entered into effect on 1 May 1888) Treaty Series 380; International Convention for the Suppression of the White Slave Traffic (signed on 4 May 1910, entered into force on 14 August 1951) 211 CTS 45; International Opium Convention (signed on 23 January 1912) 8 LNTS 187; International Convention for the Suppression of the Traffic in Women and Children (adopted on 30 September 1921, entered into force on 15 June 1922) 9 LNTS 415.

the United States recognized that effectively controlling organized crime was imperative in combating drug trafficking.[149] Furthermore, with the advancement of European unification, the fight against organized crime became a prominent agenda item in the EC and the CoE.[150] In the late 1990s, the European Union prioritized the battle against organized crime, conducting empirical analyses based on police information and developing harmonized legislation and judicial cooperation through organizations such as the European Union Agency for Law Enforcement Cooperation and the European Justice Organization.[151]

Under the auspices of the United Nations, efforts were made to draft a convention to prevent organized crime.[152] Formal negotiations for the Convention commenced in 1996 through the UN Commission on Crime Prevention and Justice (CCPCJ), established in 1992.

During this period, the Group of Eight (G8) member States led the formulation of the Convention's content. At the G8 Naples Summit in June 1994, the G8 adopted the Naples Declaration and Global Plan of Action against Transnational Organized Crime, proposing the conclusion of a Convention for the Prevention of Transnational Organized Crime to the UN CCPCJ. In 1995, the G8 established a group of experts known as the Lyon Group, comprising enforcement officials, criminal justice officials, and diplomats from G8 countries. The Lyon Group was tasked with critically examining the existing system of international cooperation, identifying deficiencies, and proposing measures for better coordination in the fight against organized crime.[153] The Lyon Group played a pivotal role in coordinating the views of G8 countries and influencing the drafting of the Convention by submitting their consolidated perspectives to the Crime Prevention and Justice Committee.

The recognition of the necessity for such a convention emerged within the United Nations, culminating in the decision to initiate negotiations for a convention at the UN General Assembly in February 1996. Subsequently, in January 1999, a Special Committee on the Drafting of the Convention was established to coordinate efforts, leading to the adoption of the United Nations Convention against Transnational Organized Crime (UNTOC) by the UN General Assembly in November 2000. The Convention entered into force in September 2003.

[149] US White House Office, *A National Security Strategy of Engagement and Enlargement* (White House 1996) 25.

[150] Commission of the European Communities, 'Communication from the Commission to the Council and the European Parliament: Developing a Strategic Concept on Tackling Organised Crime' COM (2005) 232 final, 2 June 2005; Council of the European Union, 'Action Plan to Combat Organised Crime' [1997] OJ C251/1.

[151] European Union Agency for Criminal Justice Cooperation, 'Special Investigate Measures' <https://www.eurojust.europa.eu/judicial-cooperation/instruments/special-investigative-measures>.

[152] John David McClean, *Transnational Organized Crime: A Commentary on the UN Convention and Its Protocol* (OUP 2007) 4.

[153] P8 Senior Experts Group on Transnational Organised Crime, 40 Recommendations to Combat Transnational Organised Crime (1996).

5.2 Prototypes of Judicial Cooperation in Multilateral Treaties

It is important to distinguish between treaties that require member States to exercise enforcement jurisdiction in accordance with the principle of *aut dedere aut judicare* and those that merely require them to establish prescriptive jurisdiction in respect of defined offences.[154] However, the mechanisms for judicial assistance are common among these multilateral treaties. In the author's observation, the Drug Convention of 1988 provides a prototype of judicial cooperation through multilateral conventions, because it was designed to address the limits of the MLATs as described in Section 2 and to resolve disparities in national laws among countries.

First, the convention identifies a wide range of forms of mutual assistance, such as providing legal assistance in investigations, prosecutions, and judicial proceedings for offences defined according to the Convention's standards.[155] Mutual assistance may include obtaining statements, serving judicial documents, conducting searches and seizures, providing information and evidence, and identifying or tracing proceeds, property, and objects for evidence.[156] These are illustrative examples, and State parties may also provide other forms of legal assistance as allowed by their national law.

Second, the convention designates a central authority responsible for implementing mutual assistance and establishes channels of communication between competent bodies to facilitate the prompt exchange of information on crime. The exchanged information may include other criminal activities if deemed appropriate by the home State. The treaty streamlines the process by designating a central authority for examination, thus omitting the involvement of the ministries of foreign affairs and courts.[157]

Third, the convention provides limited grounds for refusing a request for assistance.[158] These include situations where the request is not made in accordance with the provisions of the Convention; where the requested State determines that implementing the request would jeopardize its sovereignty, security, public order, or other vital interests;[159] where ongoing investigations, prosecutions, or judicial proceedings are related to similar offences; where the requested State is prohibited by its national law from taking the requested measures;[160] or where accepting the request would violate the mutual assistance legislation of the receiving State party. However, they do not include the principles of double criminality or the exclusion

[154] For this distinction, see Chapter 1, Sections 2.2 and 2.3.
[155] Drug Convention, art 7(1).
[156] ibid art 7(2).
[157] ibid art 7(11).
[158] ibid art 7(15)(a).
[159] ibid art 7(15)(b).
[160] ibid art 7(15)(c).

of political offences.[161] The convention requires member States to criminalize certain activities to overcome gaps in domestic laws.

Furthermore, the convention explicitly provides that refusal to assist cannot be based solely on bank secrecy, recognizing the need to obtain records related to drug trafficking and money laundering, which are often carried out in conjunction with drug trafficking.[162] While similar provisions have been introduced in bilateral treaties, the Drug Convention is the first multilateral treaty to establish such provisions, reflecting a unified agreement on criteria for addressing these offences.

The UNTOC,[163] its protocols concerning human trafficking,[164] migrants smuggling,[165] trafficking of firearms,[166] and United Nations Convention against Corruption[167] also provide detailed and specifically designed procedures to exchange information among member States. They are modelled after the Drug Convention, but they also include several important provisions to enhance the cooperation.

The UNTOC introduced specific provisions for joint investigations and special investigative techniques, which include controlled deliveries and electronic surveillance, undercover operations, and financial investigations.[168] The instrument provides rules concerning the establishment of criminal records[169] and particular measures to combat money laundering and corruption.[170] It is also noted that the UNODC facilitate capacity building through various programs.

The United Nations Convention against Cybercrime, which the UN General Assembly adopted in December 2024, is the latest notable development. While there are the CoE's Cybercrime Convention of 2001 and the Second Protocol of 2021, the UN Convention against Cybercrime is the first multilateral instrument that is open to all the UN member States. It obliges States to enhance the investigative cooperation and sets forth the procedures on the provisions of electronic evidence, which reflects the latest development of information technology.[171] However, given the opposition from major information technology corporations,

[161] ibid art 7(15)(d).
[162] ibid art 7(5).
[163] UNTOC, art 18. The instrument also outlines specific measures to combat money laundering and corruption and provisions for the freezing and confiscation of assets. For the significance of this convention, see also Neil Boister, 'The UN Convention against Transnational Organised Crime 2000' in Pierre Hauck and Sven Peterke, *International Law and Transnational Organised Crime* (OUP 2016) 126.
[164] Human Trafficking Protocol, art 10.
[165] Migrants Smuggling Protocol, art 10.
[166] Firearms Protocol, art 12.
[167] United Nations Convention against Corruption, arts 43 and 46.
[168] UNTOC, arts 19–20.
[169] ibid art 22.
[170] ibid arts 7 and 9.
[171] United Nations Convention against Cybercrime (adopted on 24 December 2024, not yet in force) UNGA Res 79/460 (2024) UN Doc A/RES/79/460, art 40.

it remains uncertain to what extent the convention will secure ratification from Member States and whether it will function effectively as designed.

5.3 ICJ, *Application of the ICSFT and of the International Convention on the Elimination of All Forms of Racial Discrimination* (2024)

These multilateral treaties may be the foundation of international cooperation even among hostile States. The ICJ acknowledged this characteristic in its interpretation of the International Convention for the Suppression of the Financing of Terrorism (ICSFT) in the 2024 judgment.[172]

The case involved allegations of terrorist activities, including the Russia-backed forces' downing of MH17 in eastern Ukraine, following Russia's occupation of the area in 2014. Ukraine brought proceedings under the ICSFT, claiming that Russia failed to prevent and suppress terrorism financing in eastern Ukraine.

The Court upheld Russia's violation of Article 9(1) of the ICSFT. The clause provides that '[u]pon receiving information that a person who has committed or who is alleged to have committed an offence set forth in [the Convention] may be present in its territory, the State Party concerned shall take such measures as may be necessary under its domestic law to investigate the facts contained in the information'.[173]

The Court considered the evidentiary threshold for a State's obligation to investigate alleged terrorism financing under Article 9. This threshold is relatively low, requiring only credible information that an alleged offender may be present in the State's territory.[174] Investigations aim to establish whether a crime occurred, even if initial details are vague. However, unsubstantiated claims do not trigger this obligation.[175] States must conduct meaningful investigations following their legal procedures and cooperate with other States, aligning with the ICSFT's goal of enhancing international collaboration in preventing and suppressing terrorism financing.

In the view of the Court, the notes verbales by the Ukraine contained sufficiently detailed allegations to give rise to an obligation by Russia to undertake investigations. The Court also considered the amount of time that elapsed before the Russia responded to Ukraine's request. It also added that, to the extent Russia

[172] ICJ, *Application of the International Convention for the Suppression of the Financing of Terrorism and of the International Convention on the Elimination of All Forms of Racial Discrimination (Ukraine v Russian Federation)* (Judgment, 31 January 2024) <https://www.icj-cij.org/case/166/judgments>. In addition to the claims concerning the ICSFT, Ukraine claimed Russia's violation of the International Convention on the Elimination of All Forms of Racial Discrimination, which this chapter will not deal with.

[173] ICSFT, art (1)9.

[174] ICJ (n 172) para 103.

[175] ibid para 104.

encountered difficulties ascertaining the location or identity of the individuals named in Ukrainian communications, Russia was required to seek to specify to Ukraine what further information may have been required.[176]

There are limits in the multilateral treaty mechanisms. Ukraine lost the claims on other provisions, because it could not provide sufficient evidence to trigger the procedures as provided in the instrument. However, the ICJ notably held that a relatively low standard of evidence is sufficient to initiate judicial cooperation procedures. This decision underscores the Court's approach to balancing effective enforcement with procedural safeguards in international judicial cooperation.

6. Concluding Remarks

Examining mutual legal assistance in criminal matters within the State-centric structure of transnational criminal law underscores both its complexity and the challenges of achieving close cooperation between States. Despite the development of mutual assistance treaties since the World War II, significant hurdles remain, including issues related to penal law *tabu*, grounds for refusal, and the lack of obligation under general international law. The developments described in Section 4 underscore the need to go beyond strict intergovernmental relations in judicial cooperation between States. Nevertheless, as these mechanisms are not sufficient to collect information on transnational crime, States have begun to either unilaterally collect information across borders or to use administrative mechanisms, as will be explored in the following chapters.

[176] ibid para 110.

3

Rights of Natural and Legal Persons in Transnational Criminal Law

1. Introduction

This chapter aims to explore the limits of transnational criminal law from the perspective of international human rights law. Investigating transnational crimes involves many intrusive measures that may conflict with human rights norms. Each State has its constitutional systems in place to oversee and balance the actions of law enforcement agencies, although the degree of effectiveness can differ.

A difficulty arises when these restrictions do not directly apply because the investigation is undertaken across national borders. This chapter mainly deals with the remedies available to individuals where the authority concerned has taken an illegal measure beyond the jurisdiction of the forum State of the criminal trial. The main issues are whether the individual can challenge the illegality during the criminal proceedings and whether the court should declare the evidence inadmissible. The question concerns the obligation of the forum State in exercising its jurisdiction to protect the right to a fair trial. Fundamental principles such as legality, proportionality, and due process are the cornerstone for safeguarding this right. The exclusionary rule, which mandates the court to exclude evidence obtained in contravention of the constitution, criminal procedural law, and relevant legal provisions, stems from these principles. Other human rights issues, such as information and digital and financial privacy, will be dealt with in Parts II and III of this book.

Section 2 outlines the enhanced forms of investigation techniques and the blurred line between criminal procedure and intelligence operations and between civil, administrative, and criminal investigations. Section 3 points out the limits of international law in protecting targeted individuals. Section 4 examines the legal standards for the right to a fair trial when the investigation takes place across borders. Section 5 overviews how these principles would affect the rights of legal persons.

International Law and the Investigation of Transnational Crimes. Yurika Ishii, Oxford University Press.
 DOI: 10.1093/9780198957089.003.0003

2. Intrusive Nature of the Investigation of Transnational Crimes

2.1 Challenges in the Cross-Border Investigation

Investigating transnational crime is challenging for several reasons.[1] One is due to the advanced and complex nature of the technologies involved. The offenders hide their identities, communicate anonymously, and easily move money across borders to prevent law enforcement from tracing and apprehending them. The groups buy and sell mobile phones and bank accounts. They use encryption and anonymization technologies, including dark webs, for illicit transactions and communications. They also use cryptocurrency for transactions, where no third party serve as a gatekeeper. In addition, they often generate income through legitimate means and intertwine lawful and unlawful activities, making it difficult to trace their actions.

Another factor is its global dimension. Organized crime syndicates have networks in multiple countries. The perpetrators can easily move personnel, money, and contraband across borders. Furthermore, such groups often seek to infiltrate and corrupt law enforcement agencies, political institutions, and even the judiciary. It creates a significant barrier to practical international cooperation.

For these reasons, investigating transnational crimes demands significant human power, technology, and funding resources. Many governments have developed intrusive and specific investigative methods to overcome these obstacles. Such methods have been standardized across countries. This section briefly outlines the enhanced investigative techniques and the rationale behind utilizing these advanced measures.

2.2 Enhanced Forms of Investigation

Conventional investigation techniques include undercover operations, phone tapping, and room bugging. In addition, biometric information technology has advanced, which utilizes data unique to an individual, such as deoxyribonucleic acid (DNA), retina, and voices.[2] The importance of these means remains as of today.

[1] For general observations relevant to the present section, see Neil Boister and Robert J Currie, *Routledge Handbook of Transnational Criminal Law* (Routledge 2015); Tom Obokata, *Transnational Organised Crime in International Law* (Hart Publisher 2010). The difficulties vary across jurisdictions, but this section does not aim to explore them in depth. It is noted, however, that research specific to countries or types of crime has primarily been conducted within the field of criminology. See also research reports on specific crimes issued by the United Nations Office on Drugs and Crime (UNODC), available at its website, UNODC, 'Resources: Data and Analysis' <https://www.unodc.org/unodc/en/data-and-analysis/index.html>. All websites were last accessed on 31 March 2025.

[2] UNODC, *Current Practices in Electronic Surveillance in the Investigation of Serious and Organized Crime* (United Nations Publication 2009) 3.

However, the central point in the present context is that human activities can be traced using digital technology. Such means include audio and visual surveillance, as well as the tracking and monitoring of communication data.[3] Vehicle registration numbers are captured by cameras from all passing vehicles, allowing movements across transport networks to be traced. These enable police authorities to employ electronic surveillance and facilitate the collection of information that would otherwise be unobtainable. In addition, the use of artificial intelligence has significantly enhanced detection and analysis of the data, as it enables systems to identify patterns and detect anomalies that would be difficult or time-consuming for humans.

Among these techniques, targeted surveillance involves the monitoring and analysing of specific individuals by intercepting both digital and physical activities. Examples of these efforts include communication interception, which entails gathering records of the target's communications, such as phone calls or emails. Another example is global positioning system (GPS) location tracking, which uses GPS devices installed on a target's vehicle and devices to monitor, record, and analyse their movement patterns. Similarly, service usage history is often reviewed to gather insights into the target's patterns across various digital services. These activities frequently involve collecting data directly from communication service providers.

On the other hand, mass surveillance, which is the monitoring of an entire population or a substantial part of the population, relies on large-scale data collection and analysis. In addition to targeted surveillance, examples include geofence warrants, where authorities request data from location-based servers within a specified area to identify potential suspects or gather evidence.

In recent years, the advancements in neurotechnology have sparked concerns.[4] Neurotechnology refers to tools and techniques that interact directly with the brain and nervous system to monitor, influence, or enhance cognitive and neural functions. Platform operators may use this technology to capture and maintain users' attention.[5] Its potential impact on criminal investigations is significant, as it could improve lie detection and enable memory retrieval, thereby affecting witness testimonies and the collection of evidence.

[3] Audio monitoring encompasses the detection and analysis of Voice over Internet Protocol communications, a technology commonly used for international calls. Visual surveillance involves the use of CCTV systems, which are deployed in both public and private settings to capture video footage. Facial recognition technology further enhances surveillance by capturing images and cross-referencing them with databases to identify or verify individuals, thereby confirming their identity and location.

[4] United Nations Human Rights Council, *Impact, Opportunities and Challenges of Neurotechnology with Regard to the Promotion and Protection of All Human Rights* (2024) A/HRC/57/61.

[5] See Nita A Farahany, *The Battle for Your Brain: Defending the Right to Think Freely in the Age of Neurotechnology* (1st edn, St Martin's Press 2023).

2.3 Limits of the Conventional Distinctions

Addressing organized crime presents at least two significant challenges concerning due process and the protection of human rights. The subsequent sections explore the distinctions between criminal investigation and intelligence surveillance and the overlap among criminal, civil, and administrative procedures.

2.3.1 Distinction between Criminal Investigation and Intelligence Surveillance

(1) Government Intelligence Surveillance

The boundary between criminal proceedings and intelligence surveillance has become increasingly blurred in many jurisdictions to effectively address the threats of organized crimes, as described in Section 2.1. Several countries permit the coercive collection of data for national security purposes, which will be discussed in Chapter 10, Section 2. Governments collect information through cyber defence measures as part of their efforts to address serious cybercrimes and cyberattacks, although the measures are typically limited to metadata collection.[6] In such cases, information may be exchanged between intelligence agencies and law enforcement, particularly in matters related to organized crime and terrorism.

The concern is that such intrusive investigations could potentially circumvent constitutional restraints on law enforcement authorities. Criminal procedures are under rigorous scrutiny in most jurisdictions. It usually takes place under the oversight of a court or an independent body from the law enforcement authorities and is ordinarily subject to the principles of necessity and proportionality. The police have limited powers for intelligence gathering but are authorized to use repressive measures if they have a warrant issued by a court. On the other hand, information gathering by intelligence services is usually conducted without such oversight. Many States conduct surveillance operations, including espionage activities or intrusion into a system, under the direction of a military or a national security agency. However, they are not supposed to infringe on the constitutional rights of their people.

After World War II, States separated the administrative and judicial police to address concerns over the close cooperation between police and intelligence services under fascist regimes. Since the 1990s, however, intelligence services have increasingly been employed to address organized crime and terrorist offences. This shift reflects the complexity of investigating such crimes and the emphasis on

[6] Metadata is data that provides information about other data. Concerning the communication data, it refers to information about the communication process, such as the sender and recipient addresses or numbers, time stamps, IP addresses, or the location of data. It does not include the content data, which is the information conveyed through the communication.

prevention, aiming to thwart criminal activities before they occur rather than responding after the fact.

Following the 9/11 terrorist attacks of 2001, many countries legalized mass surveillance and other intelligence operations under domestic law.[7] In addition, governments often require telecommunications providers and private companies to store, disclose, and submit customer information in bulk, even without specific criminal charges. While such operations may necessitate legal authorization or oversight by an independent body, the level of scrutiny is generally much lower than that applied in criminal proceedings. The issue gained widespread attention when Edward Snowden, a former US National Security Agency contractor, exposed a secret US government programme that collected communication records from service providers.[8]

Chapter 10 will detail the legal issues arising from mass surveillance, including its implications for privacy and civil liberties. The point at this stage is that contemporary approaches to the investigation of transnational crime rely, at least in part, on both targeted surveillance and mass surveillance.

(2) Private Sector Intelligence Surveillance

Another important trend is that private intelligence agencies and corporations play a growing role in gathering information for governments and preparing evidence for criminal prosecutions.

There are several roles that these private companies play in actively collecting information for intelligence purposes. First is the intelligence operations. Companies would primarily rely on open-source data but may also engage in more intrusive, on-the-ground activities.[9] The government can outsource activities previously carried out by national security agencies to private companies.

Second is the monitoring of cyber data. Private intelligence firms provide advanced tools for processing and analysing large datasets, enabling governments to identify and respond to cyber threats in real time. They can monitor internet traffic, social media platforms, and other digital ecosystems for potential risks.

Third is forensic analysis, which involves using data to investigate and uncover criminal or security-related activities. Private firms can conduct forensic examinations into financial crimes, cyber intrusions, and data breaches. They can also provide expertise in analysing physical and digital evidence.

Fourth is risk assessment. Firms and think-tanks can provide corporations and governments with in-depth intelligence on geopolitical developments, security risks, and market conditions. Such intelligence helps mitigate risks for

[7] See collected papers in Fred H Cate and James X Dempsey, *Bulk Collection: Systematic Government Access to Private-Sector Data* (OUP 2017).

[8] Edward Snowden, *Permanent Record: A Memoir of a Reluctant Whistleblower* (Macmillan 2019).

[9] Patrick R Keefe, 'Privatized Spying: The Emerging Intelligence Industry' in Loch K Johnson (ed), *The Oxford Handbook of National Security Intelligence* (OUP 2010) 296.

governments and multinational corporations operating in politically unstable regions.

Private intelligence agencies and corporations are not bound by the same rigorous administrative constraints, oversight mechanisms, or bureaucratic processes that govern public institutions. They can operate with a degree of flexibility that is not afforded to government entities. While their activities must remain within the bounds of the law, such as respecting privacy rights and avoiding actions that constitute legal violations, the absence of government accountability structures can enable them to engage in resource collection and intelligence activities with fewer procedural limitations.

2.3.2 Distinction between Civil, Administrative, and Criminal Procedures

In investigating transnational crimes, government authorities employ various procedures beyond criminal proceedings, such as civil and administrative actions. States mandated administrative agencies, such as competition, securities, and tax authorities, to investigate misconduct and allowed the judicial branch to use the information and evidence obtained in the process in the criminal proceedings afterwards. As described in Part II, they often acquire evidence from transaction and tax records.

In many countries, administrative law and criminal law constitute two sets of legal frameworks, each with objectives and purposes. Administrative law primarily focuses on regulating and overseeing government agencies and their interactions with the public and often prioritizes procedural efficiency and regulatory compliance. They employ simplified evidentiary rules and procedural safeguards, though protecting basic rights such as the right to appeal. On the other hand, criminal procedures are formalized and adjudicated by judicial courts. They provide procedural safeguards to ensure fairness, including the presumption of innocence, the right to a defence, the right to remain silent, protections against self-incrimination, and stringent evidentiary standards. Consequently, the protections afforded to defendants under criminal law, such as the right to a fair trial, are not equivalently established in administrative law.

When administrative law is used to probe organized crimes, it may bypass procedural safeguards inherent in criminal procedures. On the other hand, due to the complexity of organized crimes, relying on these systems to detect and identify illegal activities is often necessary.

In practice, the United States was the first to enact comprehensive legislation in the form of the Racketeer Influenced and Corrupt Organizations (RICO) Act in 1970.[10] These offences encompass using profits obtained from repeated criminal activities to set up or run an enterprise, acquiring benefits from an enterprise

[10] Racketeer Influenced and Corrupt Organizations Act, Title IX, Pub L No 91-452, 84 Stat 941 (1970); 18 USC 1961. The RICO Act outlined major organized crimes; 18 USC 1962(a)–(d).

through illegal activities, and participating in the activities of an enterprise using gains obtained through illicit means. The RICO Act was unique because the instrument allows for relief through civil and criminal proceedings.[11] The Attorney General has the authority to institute civil proceedings to prevent and restrain violations of the RICO Act, including seeking remedies such as injunctive relief, divestment, dissolution of enterprises, or other equitable relief.[12] The burden of proof is generally lower than that of criminal proceedings. Additionally, in civil proceedings brought by the US Department of Justice, the Court may close the proceedings if it deems it appropriate to protect the rights of affected individuals. The RICO Act also includes a punitive damages system, allowing the Court to impose sanctions on individuals without relying on criminal proceedings.

Countries enacted domestic legislation or amended their penal laws specifically targeting organized crime since the 1980s.[13] For example, Italy has passed a robust anti-mafia law, the Rognoni-La Torre Law of 1982, against the influence of the mafia.[14] In addition, the country amended the penal code to combat mafia-like associations, which include intimidation and seeking illicit economic gain.[15] Japan, which also suffered from *boryokudan* or *yakuza* groups, organized crime syndicates, enacted the Act on Prevention of Unjust Acts by Organized Crime Group Members in 1991.[16] The Philippines first enacted the Dangerous Drugs Act of 1972 to address syndicates and organized crime groups in areas of drug trafficking.[17] It replaced the act with the Comprehensive Dangerous Drugs Act 2002, which provides comprehensive measures to suppress organized crimes involving illegal drug transactions.[18] Australia,[19] Canada,[20] South Africa,[21] the United Kingdom,[22] and other developed countries followed suit. While they separate administrative penal procedures from criminal justice, the collaboration between administrative

[11] 18 USC 1967; US Department of Justice, 'Overview of the Law Enforcement Strategy to Combat International Organised Crime' (April 2008) <https://www.justice.gov/sites/default/files/criminal-icitap/legacy/2015/04/23/04-23-08combat-intl-crime-overview.pdf>.

[12] 18 USC 1964(b).

[13] For case studies on national legislations, see Felia Allum and Stan Gilmour (eds), *The Routledge Handbook of Transnational Organized Crime* (2nd edn, Routledge 2022) chs 4–9; Kathrin Strobel, *Organized Crime and International Criminal Law: History, Lex Lata, and Developments de Lege Ferenda* (Brill/Nijhoff 2021).

[14] Legge 13 settembre 1982, n 646, GU n 253 del 14-09-1982. The text is available online at <https://www.normattiva.it/uri-res/N2Ls?urn:nir:stato:legge:1982-09-13;646>. The law was enacted to counter the Camorra, one of the largest Mafia-type associations in Italy.

[15] Codice Penale, art 416-bis.

[16] Act No 77 of 1991.

[17] Republic Act No 6425. The text is available at <https://lawphil.net/statutes/repacts/ra1972/ra_6425_1972.html>.

[18] Republic Act No 9165. The text is available at <https://lawphil.net/statutes/repacts/ra2002/ra_9165_2002.html>.

[19] Criminal Code Act 1995, s 390.

[20] Criminal Code, RSC, 1985, c C-46, s 467.1(1).

[21] Prevention of Organized Crime Act, No 121 of 1998.

[22] Proceeds of Crime Act 2002, c 29; Serious Crime Act 2007, c 27.

and criminal branches in suppressing organized crime developed through such practice.

3. State-Centric Character of Mutual Legal Assistance on Criminal Matters and Limits of International Human Rights Law

3.1 Limits of the Substantive Rights under the Criminal Procedural Law

International human rights law provides limited protection for individuals targeted by enhanced investigations of transnational crimes, both in substantive guarantees and procedural safeguards. Numerous international and regional instruments impose obligations on member States to respect and ensure human rights. These obligations extend to the conduct of State authorities, including in the realm of transnational criminal investigations. At the international level, an array of courts, bodies, and mechanisms is responsible for monitoring and enforcing compliance with human rights law. These institutions play a pivotal role in shaping the development of transnational criminal law by addressing human rights concerns and setting legal standards.[23]

Nevertheless, in the context of cross-border investigations, the protective capacity of international human rights law can prove inadequate. The most pertinent right in the present context is the right to a fair trial. The right has been codified in various international human rights treaties. The International Covenant on Civil and Political Rights (ICCPR) Article 14(1) provides that '[i]n determining any criminal charge against him, or of his rights and obligations in a suit at law, everyone shall be entitled to a fair and public hearing by a competent, independent and impartial tribunal established by law'. The principle stipulates procedural fairness and 'contains guarantees that States parties must respect, regardless of their legal traditions and their domestic law'.[24] The interpretation of this provision, as clarified through national practices and the work of the Human Rights Committee, is well established.

[23] For a comprehensive overview of international human rights law in the context of the implementation of transnational criminal law, and in particular the United Nations Convention against Transnational Organized Crime (UNTOC), see Serena Forlati and United Nations Office on Drugs and Crime, 'The United Nations Convention against Transnational Organized Crime and International Human Rights Law' (2022) UNODC Issue Paper <https://www.unodc.org/documents/organized-crime/tools_and_publications/21-01901_Human_Rights_eBook.pdf>.

[24] Human Rights Committee, General Comment No 32, *Article 14: Right to Equality before Courts and Tribunals and to a Fair Trial*, UN Doc CCPR/C/GC/32 (23 August 2007) <https://www.refworld.org/legal/general/hrc/2007/en/52583>.

Specific rules under the provision include equality before the courts,[25] the right to a fair and public hearing by the courts,[26] the presumption of innocence,[27] the right of defence,[28] the right to criminal compensation[29] and the principle of *non bis in idem*.[30] Furthermore, the principle of due process prohibits unreasonable or arbitrary searches and seizures, as well as the use of improperly obtained self-incriminatory statements.

The exclusionary rule bars courts from admitting evidence that has been unlawfully obtained, either to deter government authorities from conducting investigations improperly or to safeguard the defendant's substantive rights. However, the contents of the exclusionary rule vary from a jurisdiction to another.[31] In addition, some of the special investigative methods discussed in Section 2 do not strictly fall under this rule. First, the rule does not apply to the civil and administrative hearings. Second, some jurisdictions allow for an exception known as the independent source doctrine. In other words, evidence originally obtained through an unlawful search or seizure may later be admissible if the evidence is subsequently obtained through a lawful means. It may include an expanded version of this doctrine, where a search and seizure can be valid if it is based on a partially tainted warrant if the remaining untainted information provides enough probable cause to justify its authorization.

The issue lies in the rule's assumption that law enforcement authorities and the court operate within the same State. It fails to account for situations where they belong to different countries. While the court remains obligated to ensure a fair trial, it must additionally assess whether and to what extent it should consider the measures undertaken by law enforcement authorities operating in a foreign territory or belonging to another jurisdiction.[32]

[25] ICCPR, art 14(1).
[26] ibid art 14(1).
[27] ibid art 14(3).
[28] ibid art 14(3)(a)–(g).
[29] ibid art 14(4).
[30] ibid art 14(5).
[31] See collected articles in Stephen C Thaman (ed), *Exclusionary Rules in Comparative Law* (Springer 2013); Sabine Gless and Thomas Richter, 'Introduction' in Sabine Gless and Thomas Richter (eds), *Do Exclusionary Rules Ensure a Fair Trial?* (Springer 2019). This edited volume by Sabine Gless and Thomas Richter includes country reports on Germany, Switzerland, China, Taiwan, Singapore, and the United States. These reports, along with discussions on the rationale behind exclusionary rules, legal practices, and potential alternatives, examine whether and under what circumstances exclusionary rules can effectively protect human rights in criminal proceedings.
[32] Stefano Ruggeri's edited volume addresses this issue directly by examining domestic legal systems from various regions in the context of obtaining evidence from abroad. Stefano Ruggeri, *Transnational Inquiries and the Protection of Fundamental Rights in Criminal Proceedings: A Study in Memory of Vittorio Grevi and Giovanni Tranchina* (Springer 2012). In addition, a comparative study led by Martin Böse, Maria Bröcker, and Anne Schneider explores the legal issues that arise in the context of transnational criminal proceedings based on comparative studies and examines responsibilities of requesting and requested States. Martin Böse, Maria Bröcker, and Anne Schneider, *Judicial Protection in Transnational Criminal Proceedings* (Springer 2021).

3.2 De-Centrality of International Human Rights Law

The mechanisms for mutual legal assistance on criminal matters are primarily State-centric, as described in Chapter 2. They are for coordinating rights and obligations among States. The opportunity for individuals to challenge a violation of their rights is limited when States take evidence and information for a criminal procedure. While the 1970s saw a vast increase in international cooperation on criminal matters and an expansion of the human rights catalogue, the relevance of the two fields of law had not been paid attention.[33]

Since its inception, the purpose and objectives of establishing such a mechanism have been exclusively to obtain evidence from other States. Protection of the rights of private individuals was often out of the scope of the discussion. There are principles employed in most mutual legal assistance treaties (MLATs), such as dual criminality and non-extradition of political offenders, that reflectively affect the status of individuals. However, they are to enable States to agree with specific measures. When the law enforcement authorities breach these principles, the accused is often not entitled to challenge.[34] The 1960s saw a significant development of international human rights law, including the adoption of the International Covenant on Economic, Social and Cultural Rights[35] and the ICCPR.[36] However, the discipline of international human rights law itself is based on the decentralized nature of international society and has inherent limitations in dealing with cross-border crimes.

There are a few situations where this de-centric nature of international human rights law becomes an issue. The first is when an accused person seeks redress in the country of jurisdiction for evidence collected in breach of the law of the place where the evidence is located. The rule that evidence collected by law enforcement officials in violation of the law may not be used for fact-finding in a criminal trial is commonly recognized within the criminal procedure of each country.[37] This rule is also derived from the fair trial principle in international human rights law. However, the courts are not obliged to consider illegal acts committed by a foreign authority in other countries.

[33] M Cherif Bassiouni, 'An Appraisal of the Growth and Developing Trends of International Criminal Law' (1974) 45 Revue International de Droit Penal 405. M. Cherif Bassiouni was one of the earliest scholars to have criticized the separation of international criminal law and international human rights law. See also Robert J Currie, 'The Protection of Human Rights and the Suppression of Transnational Crime' in Neil Boister and Robert J Currie (eds), *Routledge Handbook of Transnational Criminal Law* (Routledge 2015) 27.

[34] See Chapter 1, Section 3.1, and Chapter 2, Section 2.2. See also Ivan Anthony Shearer, *Extradition in International Law* (Manchester UP 1971) 150.

[35] International Covenant on Economic, Social and Cultural Rights (16 December 1966) 993 UNTS 3.

[36] International Covenant on Civil and Political Rights (adopted on 16 December 1966, entered into force on 3 January 1976) 999 UNTS 171.

[37] Thaman (n 31).

Second, the question arises whether *res judicata* applies when a person who has been criminally punished in another country is subject to criminal prosecution for the same factual situation. In other words, when an individual is prosecuted in a country, whether they could be tried in another country arises. The ICCPR provides that '[n]o one shall be liable to be tried or punished again for an offence for which he has already been finally convicted or acquitted per each country's law and penal procedure'.[38] It does not prohibit States from imposing criminal sanctions on the same person for the same act. The Human Rights Committee has explicitly stated that the provision 'does not guarantee ne bis in idem with respect to the national jurisdictions of two or more States'.[39]

Third, there are cases where there is evidence of the case in another country, and the accused needs that evidence. In this case, the significance of the equality of arms becomes an issue. The principle assumes that the proceedings are completed within one country and does not envisage cases where criminal assistance between several countries enters the proceedings. The prosecution can request assistance because it has evidence in another country and can use information databases, such as those between police agencies, which the accused cannot access. There is also an exchange of relevant information between authorities, including reports, interview transcripts, and other records. Still, the accused cannot access this information unless it is to be used as evidence. The growing amount of information obtained through such informal cooperation is sometimes said to be problematic because of the increasing asymmetry between the two parties.[40]

It is noted that there are regional human rights treaties where individuals may seek redress for human rights violations in courts such as the European Court of Human Rights (ECtHR), the Inter-American Court of Human Rights, and the African Court on Human and Peoples' Rights.[41] As the following part will explore, several cases concern the violation of human rights in cross-border law enforcement.

[38] ICCPR, art 14(7).

[39] Human Rights Committee (n 24) para 57. The Committee added in the same paragraph that '[t]his understanding should not, however, undermine efforts by States to prevent retrial for the same criminal offence through international conventions'. See also *ARJ v Australia* Communication No 692/1996, para 6.4; *AP v Italy* Communication No 204/1986, para 7.3.

[40] Sabine Gless and John AE Vervaele, 'Law Should Govern: Aspiring General Principles for Transnational Criminal Justice' (2013) 9 Utrecht Law Review 1.

[41] African Charter on Human and Peoples' Rights (adopted on 27 June 1981, entered into force on 21 October 1986) OAU Doc CAB/LEG/67/3 rev 5, (1982) 21 ILM 58. See also African Commission on Human and Peoples' Rights, *Principles and Guidelines on the Right to a Fair Trial and Legal Assistance in Africa* (May 2003) DOC/OS(XXX) 247.

3.3 Criminal Justice Cooperation and International Human Rights Law

3.3.1 States' Obligations under International Human Rights Law

Efforts that emerged to overcome this divergence between criminal justice cooperation and international human rights law began at the end of the 1990s. At an early stage, scholars explored how international human rights law could constrain or guide criminal justice cooperation in extradition cases. The impetus for this movement was the *Soering* case of 1989 before the ECtHR[42] and a series of subsequent judgments and recommendations from human rights bodies.[43] The approach aimed to strike a balance between the goals of crime suppression and the protection of human rights.[44]

Respect for human rights in criminal justice cooperation was also the theme of the International Criminal Law Association Congress in 1999.[45] The participants extensively discuss the investigation of organized crime and international cooperation.[46] The declaration adopted at the conference affirmed that the rule of law must be maintained even when dealing with organized crime. This resolution is significant and merits detailed explanation.

The Instrument provides that efforts involving active investigations, which may substantially impact fundamental rights, must be undertaken per statutory provisions and with due regard for human rights. States involved in criminal justice cooperation have obligations under human rights treaties. It is the responsibility of the States concerned to ensure the rights of the individual, either the accused or the victim.[47] Other means of obtaining evidence must be exhausted before resorting to special investigations. Such investigative methods should be permitted only in serious cases and with prior approval from a judge or carried out under judicial control.

For searches that infringe on an individual's right to privacy, the law must permit them and be authorized and supervised by a judicial body. In addition, investigations based on obtaining information in confidence from individuals within the

[42] *Soering v the United Kingdom* App No 14038/88 (Judgment) (ECtHR, 7 July 1989).

[43] See, eg, *Chitat Ng v Canada* Communication No 469/1991, UN Doc CCPR/C/49/D/469/1991 (1994); *Roger Judge v Canada* Communication No 829/1998, UN Doc CCPR/C/78/D/829/1998 (2003).

[44] John Dugard and Christine van den Wyngaert, 'Reconciling Extradition with Human Rights' (1998) 92 American Journal of International Law 187; Neil Boister, 'Human Rights Protection in the Suppression Conventions' (2002) 2 Human Rights Law Review 199, 203.

[45] Association Internationale de Droit Penal, 'XVIth International Congress of Penal Law (Budapest, 5–11 September 1999)' in Jose Luis de la Cuesta (ed), *Association Internationale de Droit Penal, Resolutions of the Congresses (1926–2004)* (2007) 154.

[46] XVIth International Congress of Penal Law (Budapest, 5–11 September 1999, Congress International Association of Penal Law, *Résolutions des Congrès de l'association internationale de droit pénal, 1926–2004* (Erès 2009) 148, s III, para 1.

[47] Association Internationale de Droit Penal (n 45) 154, s E, para 2.

organization, known as 'pentiti', were not considered advisable due to issues of legitimacy and equality before the law. However, if used, such measures must be legal and subject to judicial control.

Convictions must not be based solely on the person's testimony but also require proof of a serious offence, and the person's anonymity should not be guaranteed. The minimum rights guaranteed to individuals involved in international criminal proceedings in the requesting State must include the right to obtain evidence abroad and be informed of the exchange of evidence in their case.[48] It also provides for individuals to have smooth access to international forums for the remedy of human rights violation.[49] The principles and approaches set out in this resolution became the foundational ones.

3.3.2 Applying International Human Rights Law in Cross-Border Investigations

A question arises as to how international human rights law offers a mechanism for remedy in a cross-border investigation scenario. It is necessary to look at the source of the law because human rights treaties differ in their scope of application. The ICCPR provides that '[e]ach State Party to the present Covenant undertakes to respect and to ensure to all individuals within its territory and subject to its jurisdiction the rights recognised in the present Covenant'.[50] The International Court of Justice and the Human Rights Committee stated that the obligation under this Convention would extend extraterritorially if the individual is under the jurisdiction of the State.[51] However, States have offered a range of positions concerning the extraterritorial application of the covenant and their stances are far from consistent. On the other hand, the European Convention on Human Rights (ECHR) sets out the broadest human rights obligations, explicitly stating that the obligations of States Parties are 'to all persons within their jurisdiction'.[52] Yet, the meaning of the term 'within their jurisdiction' is disputed through various cases.

There is a wealth of scholarship articulating the meaning of jurisdiction in relation to the extraterritorial application of human rights law, though it is not confined to the context of cross-border investigations. Most notably, Marko Milanovic offer significant contributions to the discourse on the extraterritorial application of human rights law. He supports an approach that distinguishes between a State's

[48] ibid 154, s E, para 3.

[49] ibid 154, s E, para 4.

[50] ICCPR, art 2(1).

[51] International Court of Justice, *Legal Consequences of the Construction of a Wall in the Occupied Palestinian Territory* (Advisory Opinion, 9 July 2004) [2004] ICJ Reports 136 para 109; Human Rights Committee, General Comment 31, *Nature of the General Legal Obligation on the States Parties to the Covenant*, UN Doc CCPR/C/21/Rev.1/Add.13 (2004) para 10.

[52] European Convention on Human Rights (adopted on 4 November 1950, entered into force on 3 September 1953) 213 UNTS 222, art 1. See also Martin Böse, 'Judicial Protection in International and EU Law' in Martin Böse, Maria Bröcker, and Anne Schneider (eds), *Judicial Protection in Transnational Criminal Proceedings* (Springer 2021) 395.

negative obligations, such as to refrain from violating rights, and positive obligations, which ensure that rights are protected, suggesting that negative obligations should apply extraterritorially without territorial limitations, while positive obligations may require a State's control over a territory to be effectively fulfilled.[53]

Lea Raible develops a theory asserting that States owe human rights obligations to individuals outside their territories when they exercise significant power over them. She argues that the concept of jurisdiction in human rights law should be linked to the nature of human rights themselves, which aim to guarantee dignity and equality. Raible introduces the idea of political power, suggesting that a State has human rights obligations towards individuals abroad when it possesses the capacity to guarantee their equality concerning protected human activities.[54] This perspective sets a high threshold for establishing extraterritorial obligations, emphasizing the importance of State institutions in securing individual moral status.

While the construction of their arguments varies, a couple of commonalities warrant consideration. First, the concept of jurisdiction under international law entails both the rights and obligations of the State. Jurisdiction is not a discretionary privilege that a State may choose to exercise; rather, it imposes a binding duty that the State cannot abdicate. Second, the obligation of States to uphold human rights stems from the inherent and universal nature of these rights. Human rights are not determined by geography, nationality, or political boundaries. They are fundamental entitlements that belong to every individual, irrespective of their location. These theoretical foundations contribute to a broader understanding of the role of human rights law in the context of criminal justice cooperation.

4. The Legal Standards of the Protection of the Defendants

4.1 A General Overview

There are several theoretical grounds regarding the defendant's rights when more than two States were involved in the criminal procedure and when the State, other than the forum State, violated the defendant's rights.

On the one hand, there is an approach to discounting the illegality of the measures taken abroad by the authorities of a State other than the forum State. However, this approach remains a minority. Most courts support the exclusionary rule in

[53] Marco Milanovic, *Extraterritorial Application of Human Rights Treaties: Law, Principles, and Policy* (OUP 2013). He articulates three models of extraterritorial application, namely the spatial model, the personal model, and positive and negative obligations. See also Marco Milanovic, Thomas Gammeltoft-Hansen, and Jens Vedsted-Hansen, 'Extraterritoriality and Human Rights: Prospects and Challenges' in Thomas Gammeltoft-Hansen and Jens Vedsted-Hansen (eds), *Human Rights and the Dark Side of Globalisation* (1st edn, Routledge 2016) 61.

[54] Lea Raible, *Human Rights Unbound: A Theory of Extraterritoriality* (1st edn, OUP 2020) 210.

such a case. It is against the principle of fairness to disregard the violation of human rights solely because it was taken in a foreign territory. General principles of transnational criminal law should apply.

The methods of discipline can generally be organized into three categories.[55] The first approach is that the legality of an act should be determined in the light of the law of the State in which enforcement takes place and that its effect should also be produced in the State of the forum (*locus regit actum*). The second approach is that the effect of the act should be determined in the light of the law of the forum State (*forum regit actum*). The third view emphasizes the nature of the rights of the private person infringed and the approach that the infringement must be found not to be wrongful under the law of the enforcing State and the law of the forum State.

There seems to be a consensus that the courts shall respect the defendant's right to a fair trial, including the exclusionary principle and the equality of arms.[56] Whether the law-enforcing State has legitimate jurisdiction is a matter of due process.[57] However, the review standards differ from one State to another. In addition, there are certain rights that only some States protect, such as the attorney–client privilege and certain rights of privacy.[58] It matters which State's rules and standards, either the forum State or the law-enforcing State, would apply.

4.2 Review Standards of Domestic Courts

4.2.1 Silver Platter Doctrine and Its Limits

There is an approach that the exclusionary principle would not apply or affect the criminal procedure in the present setting. There are two main justifications for this doctrine. First, based on the principle of sovereign equality, other States' legitimate exercise of jurisdiction must be respected. Therefore, courts must accept the results of judicial cooperation, even if procedural defects exist under the forum State's law. This preference for implementing cooperation is explained as

[55] Lorna Harris, *Mutual Assistance in Criminal Matters: International Co-Operation in the Investigation and Prosecution of Crime* (Sweet & Maxwell 2000); Alun Jones, *Jones and Doobay on Extradition and Mutual Assistance* (Anand Doobay and Alun Jones eds, Sweet & Maxwell 2005); Clive Harfield, *Covert Investigation* (OUP 2008) 164. See also JIMG Jahae and others, 'Criminal Evidence Obtained Abroad—How to Assess the Legality of Obtaining It' in CM Breur and others (eds), *New Trends in Criminal Investigation and Evidence* (Intersentia 2000) 351.

[56] Sabine Gless, 'Transnational Cooperation in Criminal Matters and the Guarantee of a Fair Trial: Approaches to a General Principle' (2013) 9 Utrecht Law Review 90, 91. See Human Rights Committee (n 24) para 13.

[57] Anna Petrig, 'The Expansion of Swiss Criminal Jurisdiction in Light of International Law' (2013) 9 Utrecht Law Review 34; Sabine Gless, 'Bird's-Eye View and Worm's-Eye View: Towards a Defendant-Based Approach in Transnational Criminal Law' (2015) 6 Transnational Legal Theory 117, 122.

[58] Gless and Vervaele (n 40) 122; Neil Boister, 'Further Reflections on the Concept of Transnational Criminal Law' (2015) 6 Transnational Legal Theory 9.

conducive to the conduct of justice and friendly diplomatic relations.[59] It is also sometimes explained that, from the perspective of the separation of powers, courts do not have the power to review the illegality of acts committed in foreign territory.[60] Second, even if there has been a breach of domestic law in a foreign country, the accused should not enjoy the benefit of protection in the domestic law of the requested country and, therefore, should not be allowed to rely on the domestic law of that foreign country where the breach took place.[61] In both terms, the view is based on a State-centric approach.

The US courts have adopted this view under the name of the Silver Platter Doctrine, under which neither the Fourth Amendment prohibition on unlawful search and seizure nor the judicially established exclusionary rule apply to the evidence obtained by illegal searches by foreign officials in a place beyond the US jurisdiction.[62] Only if the measures taken are so extreme as to shock the conscience, or if the US involvement in the search is substantial so as to covert the investigation to a joint operation with the United States, will the court remove the evidence. The 'silver platter' is a metaphor for the judicial authorities receiving evidence from the investigating authorities without effort.

The original significance of this jurisprudence is that evidence illegally obtained by State police without compliance with due process will not be excluded in a federal court as long as the federal police officers did not participate in and request the search and seizure.[63] In the context of the relationship between federal and State police, this principle was rejected by the Supreme Court in 1960 because allowing such a principle would give State police an incentive to breach due process.[64] However, it has been turned around and used as a legal principle that even evidence gathered by authorities in an area outside their jurisdiction is not excluded. It means that the doctrine can be applied to allow admissibility of evidence when authorities carry out law enforcement in the territory of another State.

Under the US federal law, the Fourth Amendment to the Constitution, a due process clause, governs the unlawful law enforcement of investigative agencies. It provides that '[t]he right of the people to be secure in their persons, houses, papers,

[59] Dugard and van den Wyngaert (n 44) 189.

[60] Aukje AH Van Hoek and Michiel JJP Luchtman, 'Transnational Cooperation in Criminal Matters and the Safeguarding of Human Rights' (2005) 1 Utrecht Law Review 1, 2.

[61] Jahae and others (n 55) 354.

[62] For this doctrine, see Bruce Zagaris, *International White Collar Crime: Cases and Materials* (CUP 2010) 272. See also Christopher L Blakesley, 'National Reports: United States of America' in Albin Eser, Otto Lagodny, and Christopher L Blakesley (eds), *The Individual as Subject of International Cooperation in Criminal Matters* (Nomos 2002) 605; Stephen C Thaman, 'Report on USA' in Stefano Ruggeri (ed), *Transnational Inquiries and the Protection of Fundamental Rights in Criminal Proceedings* (Springer 2012) 509; Harry S Chandler, 'Searches South of the Border Admission of Evidence Seized by Foreign Officials' (1967) 53 Cornell Law Review 886. For the latest development, see David C Gray, Meagan Cooper, and David McAloon, 'The Supreme Court's Contemporary Silver Platter Doctrine' (2012) 91 Texas Law Review 7.

[63] *Lustig v United States* (1949) 69 S Ct 1372.

[64] *Elkins v United States* (1960) 364 US 206.

and effects, against unreasonable searches and seizures, shall not be violated, and no Warrants shall issue, but upon probable cause, supported by oath or affirmation, and particularly describing the place to be searched and the persons or things to be seized'.[65]

However, the US federal courts have held that the Fourth Amendment and the exclusionary principle are independent. In *United States v Verdugo-Urquidez*, the Supreme Court held that the drafting history of the Amendment showed that 'its purpose was to protect the people of the US against arbitrary action by their government, and not to restrain the Federal Government's actions against aliens outside United States territory'.[66] There was no indication that the Amendment would 'apply to United States activities directed against aliens in foreign territory or international waters'.[67] The Supreme Court was concerned because the rule would apply 'not only to law enforcement operations abroad but also to other foreign operations—such as armed forces actions—which might result in "searches and seizures"'.[68] The Court added that '[m]embers of the Executive and Legislative Branches would be plunged into a sea of uncertainty as to what might be reasonable in the way of searches and seizures conducted abroad'.[69] The political branches must impose such restrictions. Thus, the issue centred on whether to exclude the evidence due to the malicious conduct of the US authorities involved, rather than the nature of the violated rights.[70]

There is an issue where the authority takes measures in collaboration with foreign authorities. The question is whether it is sufficient to do so per the law of the country of implementation.

In *United States v Barona*, the Drug Enforcement Administration officials investigated the defendant for her role in an international cocaine-trafficking conspiracy by requesting wiretaps in Denmark.[71] Denmark granted the requests, using the wiretap records of both the US and foreign nationals. The defendant argued the Danish wiretaps violated her rights under the Fourth Amendment because the US court did not issue the warrant, and the court should exclude the record. The Ninth Circuit Court admitted the evidence, holding that there was no violation of the Fourth Amendment if the authorities complied with the law of the enforcing State, in this case, Danish law.

[65] US Constitution amend IV.

[66] *United States v Verdugo-Urquidez* (1990) 494 US 259, 266. See also Gray, Cooper, and McAloon (n 62) 9. The proposition is that neither the Fourth Amendment nor the judicially created exclusionary rule applies to acts of foreign officials. See also *United States v LaChapelle*, 869 F 2d 488, 489 (9th Cir 1989; *United States v Maher*645 F 2d 780, 782 (9th Cir 1981).

[67] *Verdugo-Urquidez* (n 66) 266.

[68] ibid 273.

[69] ibid.

[70] Gray, Cooper, and McAloon (n 62) 9; William C Heffernan, 'The Fourth Amendment Exclusionary Rule as a Constitutional Remedy' (2000) 29 Annual Review of Criminal Procedure 799, 825.

[71] *United States v Barona*, 56 F 3d 1087 (9th Cir 1995).

The court held that two limited exceptions would apply. The first occurs 'if the circumstances of the foreign search and seizure are so extreme that they "shock the [judicial] conscience", [so that] a federal appellate court in the exercise of its supervisory powers can require exclusion of the evidence'.[72] It is to preserve the integrity of the criminal justice system. The second exception applies when the US agents' participation in the investigation is so substantial that the action is a joint venture between the US and foreign officials; that a violation of foreign law occurred, making the search unreasonable; and that the United States did not rely in good faith upon the foreign officials' representations that their law was being complied with.[73] These cases show that the court, while admitting the non-applicability of the Fourth Amendment, counts the nature of the right infringed and the extent of the violation.

4.2.2 The Law of the Enforcing State

There is an approach that the court should decide on the admissibility based on the law of the enforcing State. In such a case, two instances can be envisaged. One is where the implementing country has taken measures in breach of its laws and provided evidence or information to the court-place country through criminal justice cooperation. The other is where the authorities of the forum State have taken illegal measures in a foreign country.

It is possible to support the applicability of the law of the enforcing State in either case. In the former scenario, one may argue that the effect of a measure taken in the implementing State should be transferred directly to the forum State. In the latter setting, one would contend that it is unbalanced for evidence to be excluded in the country of implementation concerned but not in the country of the jurisdiction where it was illegally collected, and the court should exclude evidence to sanction the law enforcement authorities that committed unlawful acts.

The resolution of the International Criminal Law Association Congress in 1999 declared that evidence obtained in violation of the law of the country of implementation or without the approval of the competent authorities of the country of implementation must be excluded if the law of the forum State provides that it should be excluded in similar circumstances within the country.[74] This should not be understood as endorsing this view, as it makes conformity with the law of the country of implementation a necessary condition but makes the criteria of the law of the place of jurisdiction a sufficient condition for exclusion.[75] However, any court hardly support this approach in practice because it is an attempt to determine the

[72] ibid.
[73] ibid.
[74] Association Internationale de Droit Penal (n 45) 140.
[75] See contra Jahae and others (n 55) n 22.

admissibility of the evidence of a criminal case by reference to the law of another country, which may refute the penal law *tabu*.

4.2.3 The Law of the Forum State

Most of the domestic courts assess the evidence in light of the law of the forum State. While the nature of the rights of the accused will vary from country to country, the exclusion principle will be understood as part of the constitutional due process of law principle. The exclusionary principle is to guarantee the defendant's rights rather than a sanction against the law enforcement authority. It follows that cooperation with law enforcement authorities will be required in advance, as evidence will be excluded in the absence of coordination.[76]

In practice, the MLAT may include a provision on joint investigation that provides for the modalities and procedures of the law of the forum State to be followed. For example, the US–EU MLAT provides that the legal standard required to obtain the measure in that State is the standard applicable to its domestic investigative activities.[77] There is also a relatively large number of national precedents that take this view.[78] The types of case law can be divided into those in which the illegality of measures taken by foreign authorities is in dispute and those in which the illegality of measures taken by the home authorities is in dispute.

(1) Measures Taken by Foreign Authorities

In many instances, the legality of the measures taken by foreign authorities is often reviewed in light of the forum State's law. The following are the sporadic examples that emerged after the 1980s. In a case in Germany in 1987, a Dutch pretrial judge interrogated an informant in the Netherlands at the request of the German authorities.[79] The authorities did not inform the defendant and his defence counsel of this investigation, and the defence counsel could not cross-examine them. The issue before the court was the admissibility of the interrogation affidavits. The Supreme Court held that, as a matter of principle, the defence counsel was entitled to be present at the time of the interrogation under German law. As a general rule, interrogations in a foreign country are based solely on the law of the country in which the interrogation was conducted. However, the requested judge should respect German law as far as possible. They must avoid violating German law unless it is justified by foreign law. The defendant should have been informed at the appropriate time that the interrogation would take place. As this was not done, his right

[76] ibid.

[77] Agreement on mutual legal assistance between the European Union and the United States of America [2003] OJ L181/34. Article 5(4) provides that where the joint investigation team requires investigative measures to be taken in one of the States setting up the team, the legal standard required to obtain the measure in that State shall be the standard applicable to its domestic investigative activities.

[78] Chantal Joubert, *Judicial Control of Foreign Evidence in Comparative Perspective* (Rozenberg Publishers 2005) 138; Jahae and others (n 55) 360.

[79] BGH 5. Strafsenat, 11 March 1987.

of defence was unduly restricted. The fact that being notified would have delayed the proceedings was not a defence. The court excluded the evidence.

In a case in the Netherlands in 1999, a Turkish resident in the Netherlands was charged with allegedly attempting to illegally import heroin from Turkey to the Netherlands.[80] The Dutch authority obtained the evidence partly through the European Convention on Mutual Legal Assistance. The defendant disputed the admissibility. It was because the evidence was obtained through entrapment conducted without the authorization of the Turkish authorities, which was highly likely to be a breach of Turkish law. In addition, persons whose calls are intercepted must be so notified promptly under Turkish law, which did not take place in this case. The Dutch Supreme Court did not decide based on Turkish law but rejected the admissibility of the evidence in light of Dutch law.

Furthermore, Japan's Supreme Court addressed the admissibility of evidence obtained through plea bargaining in the United States in 1995 in a case concerning the *Lockheed* affair.[81] The issue was whether depositions taken under the US criminal procedure was admissible. Japan's Code of Criminal Procedure does not incorporate a plea bargain procedure similar to the US procedure, where immunity removes a witness's privilege against self-incrimination, compelling testimony to prosecute others. The Court held it inadmissible. It stated that criminal proceedings must adhere to the principles of fairness, public welfare, and protection of individual rights as outlined in the law. Furthermore, the Court ruled that evidence obtained through international judicial cooperation must conform to Japanese evidentiary standards.[82]

These trends show that States evaluate under the forum State's law and decide the admissibility of the evidence.

(2) *Measures Taken by the Forum State's Authority*

There are cases where the defendant challenges the legality of measures taken by the forum State's authority in a foreign territory. In a case in Germany in 1996, the defendant was found guilty of smuggling illegal drugs into Swiss territory.[83] The defendant challenged the admissibility of statements of a witness under oath obtained by Swiss officers at the request of the assistance. The issue was that the interrogation did not comply with German law. The German Supreme Court held that, in the case of the execution of a request for international mutual assistance, the law of the place where the execution took place must be followed. However, it also held that German judges are bound by the law, and therefore, the illegality

[80] HR nr.109.075 (1999).

[81] Supreme Court, Showa 62(a) 1351, 49(2) *Keishu* 1 (1995).

[82] It is noteworthy that international human rights law has shaped the courts' practice. For the effect of international law in domestic laws, particularly Japanese law, in general, see Yuji Iwasawa, *International Law, Human Rights, and Japanese Law* (Clarendon Press 1998) 28.

[83] BGH 3. Strafsenat, 24 June 1996, 3 StR 609/95. See also Joubert (n 78) 138.

of the evidence is determined according to the forum State's law. In this case, it was held that the authority collected the evidence in violation of German law, and therefore, it cannot be used for fact-finding. The Supreme Court reversed the case to the Court of Appeal.

In a case in France in 1992, a preliminary judge went to Spain to question one of the suspects during the investigation phase of an attempted robbery murder. This interrogation was conducted without the consent of the local authorities and did not follow the prescribed procedures required to obtain a statement.[84] *Cour d'appel* did not accept the defendant's argument that the court should dismiss the evidence because 'there is no law prohibiting the preliminary judge from travelling and putting his observations and opinions on paper' and held that the report containing his opinions had no value as an affidavit, but merely as information.[85] Cour de Cassation reversed this decision, holding it is always an investigation when an investigator conducts the interrogation.[86] If the magistrate had conducted the proceedings in accordance with the 1969 French–Spanish Criminal Mutual Assistance Convention, then he should not have been able to conduct a simultaneous investigation without crossing his jurisdiction.[87] The court partly excluded the evidence on the grounds that it was in breach of French law.[88]

In a case in Canada in 1998, the court decision on whether the defendant shall be extradited to the United States on suspicion of murder in Canadian territory and was arrested in the United States under US legal procedures.[89] However, the defendant had no defence counsel when Canadian officials questioned him in the United States because the court did not appoint any lawyer. The accused moved to exclude the evidence because it was a violation of his constitutionally guaranteed right to request counsel.[90] The issue before the court was whether the court should decide the admissibility based on Canadian law because the interrogation took place in the territory of the United States. The question then arose as to whether the Supreme Court of Canada found that the Canadian Constitution applied because Canadian authorities are expected to comply with the Constitution and the Code of Criminal Procedure outside Canadian territory. The violation of this procedure took place to disrupt the accused at a time when he was particularly vulnerable. Therefore, the degree of unlawfulness was high. The court excluded the evidence because the forum country's law regulates conduct outside the law enforcement officer's territory and that the way the evidence was collected was malicious.[91]

[84] Code de procédure pénale, arts 106–107.
[85] Cour d'appel d'Aix-en-Provence, du 23 janvier 1992, 91-83.243.
[86] Cour de Cassation, Chambre criminelle, du 20 août 1992, 92-82.
[87] Joubert (n 78) 137.
[88] ibid.
[89] *R v Cook* [1998] 2 SCR 597.
[90] Constitution Act 1982, being sch B to the Canada Act 1982 (UK), c 11, art 10(b).
[91] Although the evidence excluded in this case was not damaging to the accused, it was still not admissible. See also Joubert (n 78) 137.

A series of cases before New Zealand courts from 2012 to 2014, involving co-operation between New Zealand and the US authorities, presents an intriguing variation of this scenario.[92] The case concerns an extradition request from the United States to render Kim Dotcom, a German, Hong Kong, and Finnish national living in New Zealand, for charges of racketeering, copyright infringement, and money laundering under the US law relating to the activities of his file-sharing website Megaupload.[93] New Zealand authorities carried out an investigation based on the Mutual Assistance in Criminal Matters Act (MACMA) of 1992.[94] However, there were several procedural flaws in the search and seizure under New Zealand law. One of the issues was the legality of the provision by the New Zealand police of copies of digital files to the US authority, the Federal Bureau of Investigation (FBI). It was revealed that the FBI sent the copied hard drives to the United States without formal authorization from New Zealand authorities. The High Court held that the procedure was unlawful because it was in violation of the MACMA.[95] It also quashed the evidence and ruled that further items seized would not be handed over to the US authorities.[96] The seized devices would be cloned and stripped of irrelevant personal material for future disclosure. It is noted that the Court of Appeals reinstated the warrants,[97] which was upheld by the Supreme Court.[98] Yet, the key point is that New Zealand courts adhered to their own laws and did not consider US law or the original plan to send the material to the United States for forensic examination when evaluating the legality of the search and seizure.[99]

In summary, the standards of the human rights protection in a cross-border investigation case differ across countries, and the lack of uniformity makes it difficult to conclude that common rules have been established under international law.

4.2.4 Common Principles of Law: The Human Centric Approach

In the mid-1990s, the status of individuals in public international law came under scrutiny. The studies criticized the State-centric approach, which deemed persons

[92] See generally Neil Boister, 'Law Enforcement Cooperation between New Zealand and the United States: Serving the Internet "Pirate" Kim Dotcom Up on a "Silver Platter"?' in Saskia Hufnagel and Carole McCarthy (eds), *Trust in International Police and Justice Cooperation* (Hart Publishing 2017) 193.

[93] ibid.

[94] Mutual Assistance in Criminal Matters Act 1992, No 86. Although New Zealand and the United States do not have an MLAT, both countries are parties to the UNTOC, which obligates New Zealand to assist the United States in investigating organized crimes.

[95] *Dotcom v Attorney General* [2012] 3 NZLR 115, para 144.

[96] ibid para 145. See also Boister (n 92) 201–12.

[97] *Attorney-General v Dotcom* [2014] NZCA 19, [2014] 2 NZLR 629.

[98] *Dotcom v Attorney-General* [2014] NZSC 199, [2015] 1 NZLR 745.

[99] There was another round of request from the United States for the original devices for evidentiary purposes in 2016. In 2022, the Deputy Solicitor-General made a decision under the MACMA to direct the police to send the original devices to the United States. The defendant sought judicial review of that determination, which was not successful. *Dotcom v Attorney General* [2024] NZSC 150. In 2024, the Minister of Justice finally signed the extradition order, although at the time of writing, the extradition has not been taken place.

as the objects of the law and gave no standing to claim the remedies for human rights violations.

Albin Eser was the pioneer in seeking common norms of human rights protection in criminal procedural law in different countries to overcome the decentralized nature of human rights law. Eser highlighted the differences between the inquisitorial and adversarial systems as a manifestation of the decentralized nature of transnational criminal law. Yet, he argued that there was a common goal for the demand for truth-finding. The actual consequences do not differ among the legal systems.[100] Eser based his argument on the comparative law study by Eser, Otto Lagodny, Christopher Blakesley, and others. They surveyed how human rights were guaranteed in the legislation of several European countries, including Germany, Finland, Italy, the Netherlands, and the United States, at workshops in 1995 and 1997. They published the research results in 2002.[101]

Towards the end of the 2000s, there was a movement to clarify the general principles of transboundary criminal law, overcome the limitations mentioned above in international human rights law, and guarantee the substantial rights of the accused.[102] A series of studies have been published that attempt to empirically clarify the position of certain procedural principles in different countries from the perspective of domestic criminal procedural law.[103] One of the backgrounds of this trend was the rapid development of criminal justice cooperation within the European Union since the 2000s.[104]

An alternative approach to the State-centric one is to decide the application of human rights norms in light of the nature of the defendant's rights that authorities violated. A criterion is whether allowing the measure would amount to a 'flagrant denial of justice'. This phrase is from the *Soering* case before the ECtHR in 1989.[105] The petitioner, in this case, was arrested in the United Kingdom, where he had fled after murdering in the United States, and extradition was requested under the extradition treaty. The case concerned whether extradition would violate Article 6

[100] Albin Eser, 'Common Goals and Different Ways in International Criminal Law: Reflections from a European Perspective' (1990) 31 Harvard International Law Journal 117; Albin Eser, 'Collection and Evaluation of Evidence in Comparative Perspective' (1997) 31 Israel Law Review 429.

[101] Otto Lagodny, 'Comparative Study' in Albin Eser, Otto Lagodny, and Christopher L Blakesley (eds), *The Individual as Subject of International Cooperation in Criminal Matters: A Comparative Study* (Nomos Verlagsgesellschaft 2002) 695.

[102] As mentioned above, there have been attempts to do so since the end of the 1990s, for example, in the International Criminal Law Association. The research examining human rights principles in view of the special characteristics of transnational criminal law have been published in (2013) 9(4) Utrecht Law Review and (2015) 6(1) Transnational Legal Theory, various papers included in the special issue of World Conference on New Trends in Criminal Investigation and Evidence, *New Trends in Criminal Investigation and Evidence* (CM Breur and others eds, Intersentia 2000); Ruggeri (n 32); Boister and Currie (n 1). In addition, Robert Currie elaborated on the development of human rights norms in suppressing transnational crime in the Routledge Handbook in 2015. Currie (n 33).

[103] See Ruggeri (n 32) and Böse, Bröcker, and Schneider (n 32).

[104] Helmut Satzger, *International and European Criminal Law* (2nd edn, Hart Publishing 2017).

[105] *Soering* (n 42).

of the ECHR, which provides the right to life. The ECtHR held that where a person subject to extradition may face a flagrant denial of justice, the requested State must avoid it.[106] In subsequent cases, such a denial included the denial of the right of defence or deliberate and systematic denial of the right to appoint an attorney.[107]

In the *Drozd and Janousek* case before the ECtHR in 1992, the applicants complained that they had not received a fair trial before *Tribunal de Corts*, the highest criminal court in the Principality of Andorra, and that they had been imprisoned in France after being convicted by that court.[108] The procedure did not meet the prescribed requirements of French law. They regarded France and Spain as responsible for the conduct of the Andorran authorities. The ECtHR held that, as the Convention did not require contracting parties to impose its standards on third States or territories, France was not obliged to verify whether the proceedings that resulted in the applicants' conviction were compatible with all the requirements of Article 6. To require such a review would also thwart the current trend, in principle in the interests of those concerned, to strengthening international cooperation in the administration of justice. Contracting States were obliged, however, to refuse their cooperation if it emerged that the conviction was the result of a flagrant denial of justice.

Although the current setting to decide the admissibility of the evidence may differ from the *Soering* and other human rights cases, several scholars, such as Albin Eser, pursued this approach based on international human rights law. Developing this argument, Stephen Saltzburg pointed out that there is a normative hierarchy of private rights. There are norms where a departure from the procedure would violate the accused's fundamental rights. The idea is that the evidence should be excluded.[109] He points out that the Convention against Torture and Other Cruel, Inhuman or Degrading Treatment or Punishment provides that 'any statement which is established to have been made as a result of torture shall not be invoked as evidence in any proceedings'.[110] However, in this view, cases in which the illegality of the measures taken becomes an issue are limited to extreme cases, such as where the authority tortured the defendant. It has a limited scope in practice, where relatively minor violations of the procedural law are at issue.

Furthermore, there is a view that evidence should be excluded unless it is found to be admissible, both under the law of the territory State or under the law of the

[106] ibid, para 113.

[107] Guide on Article 6: Right to Fair Trial (Criminal Limb) 53, <http://www.echr.coe.int/Documents/Guide_Art_6_criminal_ENG.pdf>. See, eg, *Al-Moayad v Germany* App No 35865/03 (ECtHR, 2 February 2007) para 101.

[108] *Drozd and Janousek v France and Spain* App No 12747/87 (Admissibility and Merits) (ECtHR, 26 June 1992).

[109] Stephen A Saltzburg, 'The Reach of the Bill of Rights Beyond the Terra Firma of the United States' (1979) 20 Virginia Journal of International Law 742, 775.

[110] Convention against Torture and Other Cruel, Inhuman or Degrading Treatment or Punishment (adopted on 10 December 1984, entered into force on 26 June 1987) 1465 UNTS 85, art 15.

forum State. In other words, it requires double admissibility of evidence and sets the higher standards.[111] It goes further into its substance and tries to determine whether the collection of evidence was fair.

Sabine Gless suggests that where there is a 'flagrant denial of justice' in the collection of evidence or assistance from the perspective of the forum State, even if this is in line with the implementing State's law, the court should exclude the evidence.[112] Gless emphasizes the importance of the fundamental principles derived from this individual-based approach to transnational criminal law. The objective is to carry out justice through cross-border law enforcement, balancing different interests, including, among other things, the interests of affected individuals.

Gless notes that cross-border criminal law includes not only national criminal laws but also non-binding standards issued by international organizations, which leads to the pluralism of cross-border criminal law and the conflict of national laws.[113] She then advocates overcoming the State-centric nature of transboundary criminal law and introducing a binding cooperative framework to guarantee the rights of the accused across borders. This is because, without such a framework, private individuals would be left without guarantees, as States have different responsibilities for human rights guarantees. For example, Gless points to the lack of settled rules on the allocation of jurisdiction concerning the prosecution of the accused and that strictly defining them is necessary for the protection of the accused.[114] While there are two approaches to their security, one in which each country resolves the issue individually and the other in which a common, unified framework is sought, the former is not sufficient to guarantee the rights of the accused. It is, therefore, necessary to adopt the latter approach.

The general principles of transnational criminal law that Gless highlights include legal certainty. Its purpose is to protect individuals affected by cross-border criminal law on a multi-country basis.[115] The common principles should be modified in the light of these transnational aspects, not merely by identifying the principle but also by clarifying which country is responsible for its prosecution. For example, if the principle of the law of one case against another is modified from the perspective of protecting the interests of the accused with an orientation towards legal clarity, not only the prevention of double prosecution but also parallel prosecution must be prevented.

There are empirical studies to support this claim. Chantal Joubert, in her 2004 study examining implementation in Canada, Germany, France, and the

[111] Christopher Gane and Mark Mackarel, 'Admissibility of Evidence Obtained from Abroad into Criminal Proceedings: The Interpretation of Mutual Legal Assistance Treaties and Use of Evidence Irregularly Obtained' (1996) 4 European Journal of Crime Criminal Law and Criminal Justice 98.

[112] Gless (n 56); Gless and Vervaele (n 40).

[113] Gless (n 57) 127.

[114] ibid 130.

[115] ibid 131.

Netherlands and in international tribunals from a comparative law perspective, notes that, depending on the specific case, whether to adopt the tribunal-place-country principle or the implementation-place-country principle varies depending on the individual case.[116] While it was difficult to extract a common legal principle from State practice, it found a broad trend in court cases to balance the rights of the defendant and the necessity to impose sanctions on the authorities. In addition, an edited book by Gless and Thomas Richter surveyed whether using exclusionary rules can effectively protect human rights in criminal proceedings.[117]

It is noted that the development of the European Union's high standard of the protection of individuals and its unique criminal justice cooperation mechanism contributed to transnational criminal legal studies. The organization created novel inter-State cooperation frameworks. Much debate has been raised from the perspective of guaranteeing individual rights about the nature of EU law, which significantly modifies or even eliminates the traditional principle of mutual criminal justice assistance and establishes an obligation of cooperation between Member States. However, this approach relies on mutual trust in the foundations of EU law and seeks to apply it to the regulation of transnational crimes. Aukje van Hoek suggests that where criminal mutual assistance treaties have been concluded, such treaty relations imply that there is already sufficient knowledge of the legal and social situation within the partner country and, therefore, an examination of the illegality of individual cases is unnecessary.[118] Furthermore, he argues that in Europe, there is no need to verify the human rights guarantees of other Member States, as the ECHR already ensures the protection of human rights.[119]

Therefore, applying the EU standard to the domain of public international law would be inappropriate, as the two frameworks operate under different principles and levels of integration. As discussed in the previous section, there appears to be no binding obligation on States to adhere to the high standards equivalent to the EU law, as State practice varies and no consensus has been reached.

5. Protection of the Rights of the Legal Persons

Another issue concerns corporations' rights as opposed to those of natural persons. Corporations are subjected to harsh penalties for violating administrative regulations, which Part II will describe. A question emerges whether corporations

[116] Joubert (n 78) 153.
[117] Gless and Richter (n 31).
[118] Van Hoek and Luchtman (n 60) 2.
[119] ibid 3. See also Thomas Weigend, 'Defense Rights in European Legal Systems under the Influence of the European Court of Human Rights,' in Darryl Brown, Jenia Iontcheva Turner, Bettina Weisser (eds), *The Oxford Handbook of Criminal Process* (OUP 2019) 164. It is noted that the development of international human rights law in regional courts and tribunals is beyond the scope of this book.

enjoy human rights under international human rights law. There are several different approaches, and the regional courts are not consistent on this issue.[120]

Adopting the 'humanist tradition' involves deriving rights from intrinsic human qualities such as dignity, freedom, and equality. This perspective leads to the view that limits the rights of corporations, as they are artificial entities that lack these fundamental human attributes. In addition, according to this position, corporations do not have direct access to human rights protection mechanisms established by international or regional human rights bodies. These mechanisms are designed primarily to protect the rights of natural persons, ensuring that the unique human qualities at the core of human rights are upheld.

The Inter-American Human Rights Court upheld this approach in an advisory opinion issued in 2016.[121] The Court unanimously held that legal entities are not holders of rights provided under the American Convention on Human Rights, based the interpretation of the Convention, in accordance with the natural sense of the terms used and taking into account the context and its object and purpose.

On the other hand, there is an approach that recognizes human rights to corporations because it views the legal construct of a corporation as having a separate legal personality and deserving of fundamental rights protection. The European Court of Justice (ECJ), and later the Court of Justice of the European Union, upheld their rights under the ECHR. It looked at the corporate form as defined by domestic law and assumed that corporations enjoy a range of human rights, such as procedural rights, the prohibition of discrimination, peaceful enjoyment of possession, and freedom of expression.

In particular, the ECJ addresses that safeguarding fundamental rights for corporations is essential for maintaining a fair and just legal system. By equating corporations with human beings in terms of their rights and protection under the law, the ECJ adheres to the political concept of liberalism, which emphasizes the importance of protecting individual rights and freedoms, including those of corporations. This perspective is justified by the recognition that corporations are key stakeholders in economic integration. They contribute significantly to economic growth, employment, and improved living standards. The Court regards corporations as individuals in an economic context, thereby including them as subjects of protection under the general principles of community law. Consequently, granting human rights to corporations is viewed as necessary to ensure the effective functioning of the rule of law.[122]

[120] Patricia Wiater, 'Fundamental Rights of Corporations as International Human Rights: The Perspective of Regional Economic Courts' (2023) 23 Human Rights Law Review <https://doi.org/10.1093/hrlr/ngad025>.

[121] Advisory Opinion OC-22/16, IACtHR Series A22(2016) [Spanish], translated in (2017) 3 International Labor Rights Case Law 29. See also Diego Mejía-Lemos, 'Advisory Opinion OC-22/16' (2017) 111 American Journal of International Law 1000.

[122] For the objectives of the community law, see Case 29/69 *Erich Stauder v City of Ulm* [1969] ECR 419; Case 11/70 *Internationale Handelsgesellschaft mbH v Einfuhr- und Vorratsstelle für Getreide*

In summary, there is no unified international legal rule governing the rights of legal persons at this stage. Their recognition and protection vary based on national laws and regional human rights conventions.

6. Concluding Remarks

The State practice demonstrated that there is only a minimum protection of individuals in case of cross-border investigation. National courts may offer protection according to each State's domestic law, but they are far from unified. Consequently, the problems Bassiouni identified in his 1974 article have yet to be resolved. However, there are scholarly attempts to seek appropriate measures based on not only the law of the country of jurisdiction but also the law of the country of implementation and international law. The following chapters will demonstrate how such efforts resonate with actual State practice.

und Futtermittel [1970] ECR 1125, 1134. For the rights of corporations, see Joined Cases 46/87 and 227/88 *Hoechst v Commission* [1989] ECR 2859, para 19. The judgment has been cited in subsequent judgments.

4
Jurisdictional Conflicts and Their Convergence

1. Introduction

The international cooperation on criminal matters theorized up to the 1930s envisaged inter-State relations among comparable criminal justice systems, as Chapter 2 addressed. On the contrary, international regulations on transnational crimes are often designed to overcome asymmetrical relations between States. As this book advocates for a consent-based mechanism in investigating transnational crimes, Chapters 4 and 5 deal with issues concerning jurisdiction, considering the changing patterns of authority over natural and legal persons' activities. This chapter focuses on the consent of States, while Chapter 5 addresses the consent of individuals.

In general, a State must be able to identify a sufficient nexus between itself and the object of its assertion of jurisdiction. The primary reason why international law determines the bases of jurisdiction is to secure the independence and sovereign equality of States.[1] There are bases of prescriptive jurisdiction that have been identified in various studies,[2] which include territory, nationality, ship and aircraft registration, and protective and passive personality principles, among others.

States agreed to establish extended prescriptive jurisdiction under multilateral treaties to suppress certain serious crimes.[3] For instance, the United Nations Convention against Transnational Organized Crime (UNTOC) obligates State parties to establish territorial or flag jurisdiction over the offences defined in the Convention.[4] They are also allowed to establish jurisdiction based on their

[1] *The SS Lotus (France v Turkey)* PCIJ Rep Series A No 10 (7 September 1927) 18–19.

[2] Harvard Research in International Law, 'Draft Convention on Jurisdiction with Respect to Crime in Harvard Research in International Law "Jurisdiction with Respect to Crime"' (1935) 29 American Journal of International Law, Supplement 439, 439–42. See also Kenneth Gallant, *International Criminal Jurisdiction* (OUP 2022) 141.

[3] For the development of criminal jurisdiction jurisprudence to suppress serious crimes, see Cedric Ryngaert, *Jurisdiction in International Law* (OUP 2015); Gallant (n 2) 149, 529; Micheál Ó Floinn and others, 'Introduction' in Micheál Ó Floinn and others (eds), *Transformations in Criminal Jurisdiction* (Hart Publishing 2023) 1.

[4] United Nations Convention against Transnational Organized Crime [UNTOC] (adopted on 15 November 2000, entered into force on 29 September 2003) 2225 UNTS 209, art 15(1).

International Law and the Investigation of Transnational Crimes. Yurika Ishii, Oxford University Press.
 DOI: 10.1093/9780198957089.003.0004

nationality and habitual residence or if the offence is done outside of the State with a view to the commission of a serious crime within the territory.[5] However, since States generally cannot arrest and search individuals within another State's territory without the latter's consent, their effectiveness is diminished when dealing with offenders outside their borders.

In practice, States have extended their jurisdictional reach by enforcing laws against legal entities, a fundamental aspect of investigating transnational crimes. While Part II will explore individual fields of law, this chapter addresses the mechanisms of such law enforcement of the investigating State.

For an extended period after World War II ended, the United States was the only nation to implement measures to gather information and evidence on the connections between American and foreign companies. Until deregulation and liberalization in Europe and Japan in the 1980s, the United States was the single country with large multinational corporations. Since the 1950s, the rise in US exports led to a corresponding rise in intra-firm trade, namely trade between different branches and subsidiaries of the same corporation group. It is less expensive than a trade between two separate legal entities. However, companies in other countries have not followed suit. The main reasons were regulatory barriers such as restrictions on foreign investment, constraints on currency exchange, or protectionist trade policies in other countries. In addition, many countries did not have the economic resources to support the development of multinationals. Therefore, most of the analysis in this chapter concerns the US practice. In this chapter, the term 'foreign company' means a company incorporated under the law of a country other than the United States unless otherwise specified.

The US authorities often used subpoena *duces tecum* to compel foreign companies to produce documents and other evidence to the US courts.[6] The prosecutor requests the issuance of a subpoena in grand jury proceedings, obtains a warrant issued by the court, fills in its subpoena column themself, and serves it on the subpoenaed person. Compared to search and seizure warrants, subpoenas do not require probable cause for their issuance and are frequently used in favour of the plaintiff or the prosecutor.

When the United States has substantive jurisdiction over a case, individuals and corporations are not immune from the obligation to comply with subpoenas under the US law. However, when such measures conflict with foreign laws, they often provoke resistance from other States, leading to disputes where courts or authorities contest their jurisdiction over a particular case or matter (*Justizkonflikt*). The extent of prescriptive jurisdiction mirrors the fundamental interests the law seeks

[5] ibid art 15(2).

[6] Federal Rules of Criminal Procedure, r 17(c). For the problems of this mechanism from the international law point of view, see Frederick Alexander Mann, 'The Doctrine of International Jurisdiction Revisited after Twenty Years' (1984) 186 Recueil des Cours 9, 47.

to safeguard. Jurisdictional rules change according to evolving social and technological factors and shifting political preferences.[7] Therefore, it is essential to track the transformation of the basis of the jurisdictional rules to ascertain the permissible scope of the application of the law.

This chapter first examines the justification for indirect law enforcement (Section 2). Then, it discusses how mutual legal assistance treaties (MLATs) relate to unilateral measures (Section 3) and examines how disputes converged against the background of globalization (Section 4). In light of these developments, it explores the contemporary basis of prescriptive jurisdiction under international law (Section 5).

2. Prescriptive Jurisdiction under the US Law

2.1 Jurisdictional Basis

This section starts with an observation that the United States has acknowledged an extensive scope of prescriptive jurisdiction. Under its jurisprudence, there is an established rule of the presumption against extraterritoriality, which serves to evade unintended conflicts with the laws of other States.[8] However, in some cases, Congress explicitly authorizes the court to exercise its jurisdiction in a cross-border case. In other cases, the court overrules the presumption by interpreting statutory rules.

The US courts interpret the scope of the application of law to avoid unreasonable interference with the sovereign authority of other States.[9] Reasonableness is a principle of statutory construction, not a discretionary authority permitting the courts to decline the application of the US law. The American Law Institute addressed that '[w]hen the intent of Congress to apply a particular provision is clear, a court must apply that provision even if doing so would interfere with the sovereign authority of other states'.[10] Furthermore, '[i]nterference with the sovereign authority of foreign states may be reasonable if the application of federal law would serve the legitimate interests of the United States'.[11]

As a matter of the US domestic law, there is the comity doctrine, which means that courts respect the laws and judicial decisions of other jurisdictions, not as a matter of obligation but out of deference and mutual respect.[12] It is also upheld in

[7] Cedric Ryngaert, 'International Jurisdiction Law' in Austen Parrish and Cedric Ryngaert (eds), *Research Handbook on Extraterritoriality in International Law* (Edward Elgar Publishing 2023) 13.

[8] American Law Institute, *Restatement of the Law, Fourth, The Foreign Relations Law of the United States* (American Law Institute Publishers 2018) s 405.

[9] ibid.

[10] ibid.

[11] ibid.

[12] ibid s 403. See also Joel R Paul, 'The Transformation of International Comity' (2008) 71 Law & Contemporary Problems 19.

the *Fourth Restatement of the Foreign Relations Law* of 2018 that a court should decline to exercise jurisdiction in deference to the laws and interests of another foreign country.[13] In some cases, a statute may list the factors for the court to consider, such as the Clarifying Lawful Overseas Use of Data (CLOUD) Act.[14]

The United States has established various mechanisms to authorize the US law enforcement authorities to compel private corporations to store, disclose, and submit documents, data, and other materials while they operate in a foreign State. The basis of prescriptive jurisdiction varies. It is mostly based on territorial jurisdiction, where the operation affects US territory, or on personal jurisdiction, where the company is part of a group that includes entities with the US nationality.[15]

In its *Fourth Restatement*, the American Law Institute adopted the view that '[c]ustomary international law permits exercises of prescriptive jurisdiction if there is a genuine connection between the subject of the regulation and the state seeking to regulate'.[16] According to the Reporter's note, '[t]his usually takes the form of a specific connection between the state and the subject being regulated',[17] such as territoriality or nationality. However, '[i]nternational law is also not static, so new bases of prescriptive jurisdiction may be recognized'.[18]

It also points out that '[i]nternational law recognizes no hierarchy of bases of prescriptive jurisdiction and contains no rules for assigning priority to competing jurisdictional claims'.[19] Therefore, '[t]here is no general international-law rule that requires one form of prescriptive jurisdiction to give way to another, even if one basis is less common or more controversial than another'.[20]

The *Fourth Restatement*'s approach was a departure from the *Third Restatement of the Foreign Relations Law* of 1987, which rested on the reasonableness test, which Section 2.3 below describes.[21] In other words, it did not support the contention

[13] American Law Institute (n 8) s 403.

[14] The Clarifying Lawful Overseas Use of Data Act, Pub L No 115-141, 132 Stat 1213 (2018) s 103. The elements that courts consider in a comity analysis under the CLOUD Act are: the investigative interests of the US governmental entity seeking disclosure; the interests of the qualifying foreign government (the counterparty of the data access agreement) in preventing the disclosure; the likelihood, extent, and nature of penalties faced by the provider or its employees due to conflicting legal requirements; the location, nationality, and connection of the subscriber or customer to the US or the foreign government requesting the data; the provider's ties to and presence within the United States; the importance of the requested information to the investigation; the likelihood of timely and effective access to the information through less harmful alternatives; and if requested on behalf of a foreign authority, the investigative interests of that authority. For the specific analysis on the access to the foreign service providers, see Chapter 12, Section 2.2.1(1).

[15] Mann (n 6); Ryngaert (n 3) 143. See also Darryl Brown, 'Extraterritorial Ambit through Offence Definitions, Technology and Economic Power' in Micheál Ó Floinn and others (eds), *Transformations in Criminal Jurisdiction* (Hart Publishing 2023) 75.

[16] American Law Institute (n 8) s 407.

[17] ibid Comment, para c.

[18] ibid s 407.

[19] ibid Comment, para d.

[20] ibid.

[21] American Law Institute, *Restatement of the Law, Third, The Foreign Relations Law of the United States* (American Law Institute Publishers 1987) ss 402–403.

that international law obliges States to assess the reasonableness of exercising prescriptive jurisdiction on a case-by-case basis because State practice does not substantiate the existence of such a requirement.[22] Similarly, international law does not mandate that a State with a legitimate basis for asserting prescriptive jurisdiction must refrain from doing so merely because another State has a stronger interest in exercising jurisdiction.[23]

2.2 The Doctrine of the Unity of Enterprise

The United States frequently exercises personal jurisdiction to order a foreign subsidiary to produce documents and materials. A foreign subsidiary is a company organized under foreign law and primarily controlled or owned by the US citizens, including companies organized under the US law. The US Department of Justice (DOJ) has used the doctrine of the unity of enterprise to justify the order. It is a principle that multiple entities with a common ownership, management, or control should be considered to have unity.

This doctrine is often used in franchise arrangements or other contractual relationships between companies to apply labour, bankruptcy, and tax laws. The basic objective is to prevent the company's circumvention of regulations by creating a subsidiary. Some scholars acknowledge that a country should have the power to obtain the information if it is outside its jurisdiction but the group that controls the information is present within its territory. In the words of Robert Y Jennings, there is 'no reason in general principle' why the country should not order an alien, subjection to its *in personam*, 'to produce documents relevant to a case in which he is a party, no matter where he may choose to keep those documents'.[24]

On the other hand, some scholars opposed using this jurisprudence as a justification for extraterritorial application because a foreign company is a legal entity separate and distinct from a US company. Derek W Bowett questioned its validity because 'the defendant corporation is neither national nor a resident in the true sense: the corporate separation is disregarded to treat the residence of the affiliate as if it were the residence of the defendant'.[25] The essential inquiry for Bowett was to see 'whether the foreign corporation is doing business within the United States,

[22] American Law Institute (n 8) s 407, Reporter's n 6. For the analysis of the reasonable test in the Third and Fourth Restatements, see Hannah L Buxbaum and Ralf Michaels, 'Reasonableness as a Limitation on the Extraterritorial Application of U.S. Law: From 403 to 405 (via 404)' in Paul B Stephan and Sarah H Cleveland (eds), *The Restatement and Beyond* (OUP 2020) 283.

[23] American Law Institute (n 8) s 407, Reporter's note 6.

[24] Robert Y Jennings, 'Extraterritorial Jurisdiction and the United States Antitrust Laws' (1957) 33 British Year Book of International Law 146, 171.

[25] Derek W Bowett, 'Jurisdiction: Changing Patterns of Authority over Activities and Resources' (1983) 53 British Year Book of International Law 1, 9.

. . . so the answer may well turn on the decree of control exercised by the foreign parent.'[26]

The International Court of Justice before the case concerning the Barcelona Traction held that '[t]he concept and structure of the company are founded on and determined by a firm distinction between the separate entity of the company and of the shareholder, each with a distinct set of rights.'[27] This part can be interpreted that, in the words of Fredrick Alexander Mann, 'as a matter of international law parent and subsidiary are each subject to the exclusive jurisdiction of their respective sovereigns. They cannot be identified.'[28]

2.3 The Significance of the Balancing of Interests Test

In response to this criticism that the US extraterritorial jurisdiction was excessive, the courts started to limit its jurisdiction based on the balancing-of-interests doctrine as described above. It was first formulated in the American Law Institute's *Second Restatement of the Foreign Relations Law* in 1965.[29] When two States require inconsistent conduct upon a person, they are required 'to consider, in good faith, moderating the exercise of its enforcement jurisdiction.'[30] Relevant factors listed were

> (a) vital national interests of each of the states, (b) the extent and the nature of the hardship that inconsistent enforcement actions would impose upon the person, (c) the extent to which the required conduct is to take place in the territory of the other state, (d) the nationality of the person, and (e) the extent to which enforcement by the action of either state can reasonably be expected to achieve compliance with the rule prescribed by that state.[31]

However, this formula allows the court to favour the forum State. In early cases in the late 1950s and early 1960s, the US courts refused to enforce subpoenas when compliance would violate foreign law, based on a balancing of interests.[32] However, most of the cases afterwards endorsed the enforcement of the order.[33]

[26] ibid.

[27] Case concerning the *Barcelona Traction, Light and Power Co., Ltd (Belgium v Spain)* [1970] ICJ Rep 4, para 41.

[28] Mann (n 6) 56.

[29] American Law Institute, *Restatement of the Law, Second, The Foreign Relations Law of the United States* (American Law Institute Publishers 1965) s 40.

[30] ibid.

[31] ibid.

[32] *Chase Manhattan Bank* 297 F 2d 611 (2d Cir 1962); *Ings v Ferguson* 282 F 2d 149 (2d Cir 1960); *First National Bank of New York v Internal Revenue Service* 271 F 2d 616 (2d Cir 1959), cert denied 361 US 948 (1960).

[33] Mann (n 6) 51.

Issues arose when the entity from which the information was sought was under an obligation not to disclose the information in the country in which it is located. An early leading case in which the US courts considered whether they could still compel disclosure in such cases was the *Societe International* of 1958.[34] In this case, the court's order that the target company produce documents led to a serious diplomatic conflict between the United States and the home State, Switzerland. Similarly, in the 1968 *First National Community Bank (FNCB)* case, the German pharmaceutical company Boehringer Sohn AG became the subject of civil proceedings in the United States for violating US civil antitrust laws. The Second Circuit Court ordered the German branch of the US-based FNCB to produce the company's bank transaction records in the Federal Republic of Germany.[35] It held the production of the documents on the basis that, under the balance-of-interest analysis, the benefits to the United States of applying competition law outweighed the disadvantages to Germany and the German branch of FNCB. Germany protested against this decision. From the 1960s to the 1980s, the increase in unilateral US enforcement led to intense jurisdictional conflicts between the United States and the rest of the world as US transnational corporations expanded.[36]

The *Third Restatement* elaborated on the approach and specifically stated the rules concerning the jurisdiction over foreign corporations.[37] The basic rule is that a State may exercise jurisdiction 'to prescribe for limited purposes with respect to activities of foreign branches of corporations organised under its laws'.[38] A State may not ordinarily regulate the activities of corporations organized under the laws of a foreign State on the basis that they are owned or controlled by nationals of the regulating State. However, 'it may not be unreasonable for a State to exercise jurisdiction for limited purposes' with respect to certain activities of affiliated foreign entities.[39] Such conducts include uniform accounting, disclosure to investors, or preparation of consolidated tax returns of multinational enterprises by direction to the parent corporations. In addition, 'by direction to either the parent or the subsidiary in exceptional cases, depending on all relevant factors, including the extent to which (i) the regulation is essential to the implementation of a program to further a major national interest of the state exercising jurisdiction; (ii) the national

[34] *Societe Internationale Pour Participations Industrielles et Commerciales, SA v Rogers* (1958) 357 US 197.

[35] *In re First National City Bank* 285 F Supp 845 (SDNY 1968); *United States v First National City Bank* 396 F 2d 897 (2d Cir 1968). See also Rolf Stürner, 'Die Gerichte Und Behörden Der U.S.A. Und Die Beweisaufnahme in Deutschland' (1982) 81 Zeitschrift für Vergleichende Rechtswissenschaft 159.

[36] Peter Schlosser, *Der Justizkonflikt Zwischen Den USA Und Europa* (De Gruyter 1985); Peter Schlosser, 'Jurisdiction and International Judicial and Administrative Co-Operation' (2000) 284 Recueil des Cours 9; Rolf Stürner, 'Der Justizkonflikt Zwischen U.S.A. Und Europa' in Walther J Habscheid, Rolf Stürner, and Dieter G Lange (eds), *Der Justizkonflikt mit den Vereinigten Staaten von Amerika* (Gieseking-Verlag 1986).

[37] American Law Institute (n 21) s 414.

[38] ibid s 414(1)(a).

[39] ibid.

program of which the regulation is a part can be carried out effectively only if it is also applied to foreign subsidiaries; (iii) the regulation conflicts or is likely to conflict with the law or policy of the state where the subsidiary is established'.[40]

Its commentary note explains the distinction between transnational activities of a branch or subsidiary related to international transactions, such as export and import, foreign exchange and credits, and transborder investment on the one hand, and local activities [such as industrial and labour relations, health and safety practices, or conduct related to preservation or control of the local environment] on the other.[41] It also recognized that 'orders issued directly to a foreign corporation are regarded as particularly intrusive and can be justified only by clearly showing necessity'.[42]

It also specifies a situation when a command by a parent State may conflict with a clearly expressed State policy under whose law the subsidiary is organized.[43] 'If that State is also the state in whose territory the activity regulated is to be carried out or precluded, exercising jurisdiction on the basis of intercorporate affiliation may be unreasonable. A State may not ordinarily require a corporation (or similar entity) to do a conduct outside its territory that is prohibited by the State under whose law the corporation is organized or forbid the corporation to do an act outside its territory that is required by the State under whose law the corporation is organized.[44]

2.4 Conflict of Laws and Public Law

International lawyers criticized the balance-of-interests approach, as will be discussed in detail in the following chapters. While such disapproval is comprehensible, it is noted that this approach came out of the conflict of laws jurisprudence in US legal studies. The transformation from a formal application of law to a balancing-of-interests approach aligns with the jurisprudence of conflict laws.

Joseph Story, one of the pioneers of conflict law jurisprudence in the United States,[45] emphasized legal stability, predictability, simplicity and uniformity of results at the end of the nineteenth century.[46] The American Law Institute adopted

[40] ibid s 414(1)(b).

[41] ibid s 414, Comment, para c.

[42] ibid Comment, para c.

[43] ibid Comment, para d.

[44] ibid Comment, para d.

[45] He has been regarded to have introduced the theory of comity in the US law. Yet, Kurt Nadelmann criticized this view, stating that the US courts relied on the Dutch theory of comity long before Story's work. Kurt H Nadelmann, 'Joseph Story's Contribution to American Conflicts Law: A Comment' (1961) 5 The American Journal of Legal History 230.

[46] Joseph Story, *Commentaries on the Conflict of Laws, Foreign and Domestic* (Little Brown 1834).

the principle that the law should be determined by a connection, such as the place of the tort or the contract, in the *First Restatement on Conflict of Laws* of 1934.[47]

However, in the first half of the twentieth century, with the rise of legal realism, conflict law scholarship advocated determining the governing law by focusing on the correct outcome in a particular case. David F Cavers was an early critic of strict adherence to the choice of governing law rule, which fails to consider the content of the substantive law of the country or State involved in the case and the legal objectives it seeks to achieve.[48] The governing law must be determined not by the mechanical application of legal rules but to achieve an equitable result. Indeed, courts sometimes seek to depart from applying this rule by using the doctrines of remittitur or public policy, thereby undermining predictability.[49] Cavers presented a choice-of-law framework made through a balancing of interests.

Brainerd Currie also argued that the specific checks and balances in a case should be examined, the content of the law in question and the consequences of its application should be compared, and these consequences should be assessed by considering which laws are associated with which checks and balances in terms of fairness to litigants and the social policy that the conflicting law seeks to achieve.[50] Based on the understanding that laws are designed to achieve certain legal objectives or policies, Currie clarified that even when a case formally appears to be subject to multiple laws, there can be two types of conflicts: genuine and spurious. He argued that the role of the judiciary is to consider the purpose of the law whose application is concerning the specific circumstances of the case in question, taking into account the governing interest to determine this.

The governing interest approach can be positioned as a direct influence of this discussion of conflict jurisprudence, which had contract and tort laws in mind, on considering the application of public law as well. For example, Harold G Maier, while noting that the balance of interests between private and public laws differs in detail, argues that choice of law is about deciding which State or national law is most appropriate to apply and, in response, which political group has the strongest influence on the outcome of the case.[51] In this sense, any choice of law

[47] American Law Institute, *Restatement of the Law of Conflict of Laws* (American Law Institute Publishers 1934). For the development and transformation of the American Law Institute's Restatements in US Foreign Relations Law, see Sarah H Cleveland and Paul B Stephan, 'Introduction: The Roles of the Restatements in US Foreign Relations Law' in Paul B Stephan and Sarah H Cleveland (eds), *The Restatement and Beyond: The Past, Present, and Future of US Foreign Relations Law* (OUP 2020) 1.

[48] David F Cavers, 'A Critique of the Choice-of-Law Problem' (1933) 47 Harvard Law Review 173.

[49] ibid 200.

[50] Brainerd Currie, 'The Constitution and the Choice of Law: Governmental Interests and the Judicial Function' (1958) 26 The University of Chicago Law Review 9.

[51] Harold G Maier, 'Extraterritorial Jurisdiction at a Crossroads: An Intersection between Public and Private International Law' (1982) 76 American Journal of International Law 280; Harold G Maier, 'Interest Balancing and Extraterritorial Jurisdiction' (1983) 31 American Journal of Comparative Law 579.

in the modern era involves an attempt to identify and balance the interests of the various political groups involved in the case.

The approach not to artificially distinguish legal structures is maintained in the *Fourth Restatement*, which states that 'the public-private distinction in international law lacks a clear conceptual basis because different legal systems draw the line in different places'.[52] It asserts that the customary international law rules apply to 'assertions of public and private law, and to exercises of criminal and civil jurisdiction, but they permit a wide variety of solutions to conflict-of-laws problems'.[53] The criticism arose, however, because the US courts used this approach to emerge out of the private law context in deciding on public law cases that have international impacts.

3. Mutual Legal Assistance Treaties and Unilateral Law Enforcement

One of the issues has been whether a court should refrain from ordering the production and submission of materials when a MLAT exists between the forum State and the State affected by unilateral law enforcement measures. The prevailing view maintains that the US courts retain the discretion to issue such orders, as MLATs and production orders constitute distinct and independent legal processes.[54] The court is not obligated to prioritize the treaty over unilateral measures.[55]

There used to be a conflicting view on this issue.[56] The object and purpose of an MLAT are to promote cooperation between States while at the same time protecting the territorial sovereignty of the parties. Unilateral law enforcement is unacceptable for them, as it would undermine such aims and objectives. Rolf Stürner, for example, points out that if one party to a treaty were to rely on procedures other than those provided for in the treaty to obtain information from the other party, the standards and procedures for information exchange in the treaty would become meaningless.[57]

However, in *Societe Nationale Industrielle Aerospatiale v District Court*, the US Supreme Court held that a treaty is not exclusive and does not prevent a court from issuing a production order.[58] The plaintiff sued Societe Nationale Industrielle Aerospatiale, a French State-owned company that manufactured aircraft and

[52] American Law Institute (n 8) Comment, para d.
[53] ibid.
[54] Andreas F Lowenfeld, 'Sovereignty, Jurisdiction, and Reasonableness: A Reply to AV Lowe' (1981) 75 American Journal of International Law 629.
[55] *United States v Bank of Nova Scotia* 691 F 2d 1384, 1390 (11th Cir 1982).
[56] Stürner (n 36).
[57] ibid 31.
[58] *Societe Nationale Industrielle Aerospatiale v District Court* (1987) 482 US 522. It is noted that the Societe Nationale Industrielle Aerospatiale went into liquidation in 2000.

space rockets, for damages arising from a collision involving an aircraft built and sold by the company. The defendant agreed to discovery. Thereafter, when the plaintiffs continued to make discovery requests under the Federal Rules of Civil Procedure, the defendants argued that because they were located in France and the discovery requests had to be conducted in French territory, only the Hague Evidence Collection Convention should govern the process.[59] The Convention establishes procedures for the judicial authorities of one contracting State to request evidence in the territory of another contracting State in civil cases, to which the United States and France, the relevant States in the case, were parties.

The Supreme Court rejected the claim. First, the Hague Convention on Civil Procedure does not establish an exclusive or mandatory procedure for obtaining documents or information in the territory of a foreign State party to the Convention.[60] The wording of the Convention and the history of its proposal and ratification by the United States supported the conclusion that the Convention is to establish an optional procedure for obtaining evidence in a foreign country. The Convention used permissive language and did not oblige States parties to amend their national laws or use specific procedures. The Convention did not distinguish between evidence located abroad and the one under the jurisdiction of the parties. Therefore, when requesting evidence located in the territory of a State party to the Convention, it was not obligatory to first rely on the Convention.[61]

Second, it was one means of evidence gathering that was not obligatory to follow the procedures set out in the Convention but could be followed where it enabled evidence to be collected and adopted selectively by the courts.[62]

Third, in all cases, the comity did not require US litigants to rely on Convention procedures before commencing discovery under the Federal Rules. Convention proceedings were time-consuming, expensive, and less evidential than direct reliance on Federal Rules. In this context, the concept of comity must be determined after a more specific analysis of the respective interests of the foreign State and the requesting State rather than by a blanket rule that the State must first rely on the treaty. The decision to rely on a treaty must consider three factors: the specific facts of the case, the sovereign interests of the State, and the likelihood that it will be found to be effective in using the procedures of the treaty.[63]

Societe Nationale was a civil law case in which the defendant consented to jurisdiction but opposed the discovery. However, the DOJ came to rely on this case in a procedure to issue a subpoena. Under the US domestic law, the enforcement of

[59] Convention on the Taking of Evidence Abroad in Civil or Commercial Matters (adopted on 18 March 1970, entered into force on 7 October 1972) 847 UNTS 231.
[60] 482 US 533.
[61] ibid.
[62] ibid 540.
[63] ibid 541.

federal laws is generally in the form of claims by government authorities against private parties under the Federal Rules of Civil Procedure.

One of the earliest cases in which the tension between unilateral law enforcement and mutual assistance treaties became an issue was the *Vetco* case in 1981. The issue was the relationship between the information exchange provisions of the US–Swiss tax treaty and law enforcement.[64] Vetco was a US corporation engaged in manufacturing and selling electrical appliances and had a Swiss-registered subsidiary. In 1981, the Internal Revenue Service (IRS) issued a subpoena ordering Vetco in the United States to produce documents relating to tax information in possession of its wholly owned Swiss subsidiary, Vetco International AG (VIAG), in Switzerland. The IRS requested the documents per the information exchange provisions in the US–Swiss tax treaty concluded in 1972. The submission of such documents by VIAG could violate Article 273 of the Swiss Criminal Code, which prohibits the submission of documents to foreign authorities to protect business secrets. However, the court allowed the warrant to be issued based on the balance-of-interest analysis and ordered Vetco to comply.

In the *Marc Rich SA* case in 1983, the court did not even go through the balancing of the interests test. Marc Rich, a US national, founded Marc Rich SA in 1974 as a Swiss-registered commodity trading company. The company had a wholly owned subsidiary in Switzerland, Marc Rich International (MRI).[65] MRI had a branch office in the United States. Rich traded in crude oil and petroleum products and made profits during the oil crises of 1973 and 1979 but failed to declare them to the IRS.

In 1980, the IRS opened an investigation into the company's founder on suspicion of tax fraud. The Second Circuit Court of Appeal granted an application in the US District Court for a subpoena against the US branch of MRI for the comprehensive production of documents relating to the 1980 and 1981 oil transactions in possession of MRI's parent company.[66]

Marc Rich SA objected against the court's jurisdiction because the order was made against a foreign parent company with its branch office in the United States. It also contended that the submission may constitute a violation of Article 273 of the Swiss Criminal Code, which prohibits disclosure of a trade secret to foreign authorities.[67]

However, the court affirmed jurisdiction without even balancing the interests, stating that the corporation is subject to the US jurisdiction. Where 'the territorial

[64] *United States v Vetco Inc* 644 F 2d 1324 (9th Cir 1981), cert denied 454 US 1098 (1981). For a critical assessment of the case, see Mann (n 6) 59.

[65] The company was renamed Glencore and merged with Xstrata in 2013.

[66] *Matter of Marc Rich & Co v Attorney General* 707 F 2d 663 (2nd Cir 1983), cert denied, 463 US 1215 (1983).

[67] Swiss Criminal Code (Schweizerisches Strafgesetzbuch (StGB) vom 21. Dezember 1937) art 273 criminalizes industrial espionage.

principle is applicable, the Government may punish a defendant in the same manner as if it were present in the jurisdiction when the detrimental effects occurred.'[68] In the court's words,

> [i]t would be strange ... if the United States could punish a foreign corporation for violating its criminal laws upon a theory that the corporation was constructively present in the country at the time the violation occurred, but a federal grand jury could not investigate to ascertain the probability that a crime had taken place.[69]

The court imposed a fine of USD 50,000 per day for contempt of court, taking into account the financial benefit the company would have gained from the tax fraud.

The Swiss government protested that the submission of such documents could violate Swiss criminal law and, therefore, confiscate the relevant documents located in Switzerland. The matter should be resolved through the channels of private criminal law assistance between the United States and Switzerland. In response, the court ruled that this constituted contempt of court and granted sanctions, including freezing Rich's bank accounts in the United States. In 1984, Mark Rich entered into plea bargaining with the IRS, but the settlement amounted to USD 150 million, and the fine for contempt of court reached USD 21 million.[70]

The US courts maintained the position that even in the presence of an MLAT, evidence could be ordered to be produced by subpoena with penalties.[71] It led to the enactment of blocking statutes by other States, and the dispute was brought to a standstill.

4. Convergence of the Jurisdictional Conflicts

In response to the protests from foreign governments, the United States took various measures since the 1980s to avoid international disputes arising from conflicts of jurisdiction.

First, the United States led the effort to standardize regulations governing various corporate activities. This was the case in many economic laws, including antitrust laws, securities laws, and other financial laws. Important examples in the context of the suppression of transnational crimes include the anti-money laundering effort, which Chapter 13 will address. In some cases, other countries, in addition to the European Community and later the European Union, drove the lawmaking process.

68 *Marc Rich & Co v United States*, 707 F 2d 663, 666 (2nd Cir 1983).
69 ibid.
70 For an analysis of this case, see Mann (n 6) 53.
71 *In re Sealed Case*, 832 F 2d 1268 (DC Cir 1987).

Second, the DOJ employed internal rules requiring a cautious approach to the use of subpoenas. When collecting evidence from outside the region, prosecutors should consult the Office of International Affairs of the DOJ in advance to avoid conflicts with the country where the evidence is located.[72] The office advises the prosecutor of the relationship with the country where the evidence is located,[73] the proceedings in which the evidence will be used,[74] the proceedings other than those for which it was requested in which it may be used,[75] what assistance is required,[76] the period of time required,[77] and the statute of limitations for prosecution,[78] among other considerations, before giving advice.

Third, the United States tightened the regulation on corporations doing business in the United States. Failure to make proper disclosure to law enforcement authorities can result in the suspension of transactions with the US financial institutions and the loss of access to dollar clearing. As a result, foreign companies under the US jurisdiction came to provide information in accordance with those regulations and did not protest ex parte law enforcement. Furthermore, when the government brings charges against corporations, the agencies increasingly use plea deals, deferred prosecution agreements, and non-prosecution agreements, which will be discussed in Chapter 5.

As a result, conflicts between the United States and other governments over its excessive exercise of jurisdiction have decreased. This reduction in disputes has, in turn, led to a corresponding decline in assertions that bilateral agreements on mutual legal assistance obstruct the enforcement of domestic laws. As Part II will explain, these measures laid the foundation for consent-based investigations of transnational crimes.

5. Concluding Remarks

Unilateral law enforcement by the United States, which once caused judicial friction, is gradually being refined and, in many cases, with the consent of the State concerned. In doing so, it has also come to rely on jurisdictional grounds that are not disputed by other States. For example, as Part II will discuss, reliance on the

[72] US DOJ, *Criminal Resource Manual*, s 267 <https://www.justice.gov/archives/jm/criminal-resource-manual>; US DOJ, *Justice Manual*, Title 9, ch 9-13.510, 'Obtaining Evidence Abroad—General Considerations' <https://www.justice.gov/jm/title-9-criminal>.

[73] US DOJ, *Criminal Resource Manual*, s 268. Cooperation with the State concerned depends on the clear fact that the evidence is located.

[74] ibid s 269.

[75] ibid.

[76] ibid s 270.

[77] ibid s 271.

[78] ibid s 272.

effects principle as a jurisdictional basis for competition law can no longer be criticized as it is.

Today, it is widely recognized that a State has the authority to enforce its laws over legal entities incorporated within its jurisdiction.[79] Incorporation is typically based on the entity's registered office or statutory seat. Alternatively, the actual residence or head office model considers the principal office located within the territory. The issuance of corporate securities on a national stock market can also establish a sufficient connection to justify the State's legal authority. Furthermore, a corporation's business activities within the State may serve as a basis for law enforcement jurisdiction.

This chapter primarily examined US laws and policies, as they were the most influential, particularly before other regions and States followed suit in expanding the scope of jurisdiction. However, the challenge lies in how international legal jurisprudence addresses this issue, a topic that has been extensively explored in the literature. The key issues, as outlined in this chapter, are the jurisdictional basis that justifies the application and enforcement of the law and the rules governing concurrent jurisdiction. The following chapters in Part II will delve into this question, considering specific laws and practices.

[79] For the latest analysis, see Vincenzo Mongillo, 'The Jurisdictional Reach of Corporate Criminal Offences in a Globalised Economy: Effectiveness and Guarantees "Taken Seriously"' in Micheál Ó Floinn and others (eds), *Transformations in Criminal Jurisdiction* (Hart Publishing 2023) 90.

5

Consents of Individuals and Private Entities in a Foreign Territory

1. Introduction

A State holds exclusive authority over criminal investigations within its territory. There is no disagreement that when a police officer physically comes in and collects materials without the consent of the State, that would constitute a violation of sovereignty. This rule stems from the concept of territorial sovereignty, which is fundamental to allocating jurisdiction. In the *Lotus* case, the Permanent Court of International Justice (PCIJ) held in its *obitur* that 'it may not exercise its power (*la puissance*) in any form in the territory of another State'.[1] It continued that, in this sense, 'jurisdiction is certainly territorial'.[2]

The judgment is significant, as it holds guiding principles for the State to establish and exercise its jurisdiction. However, its broad scope renders it unsuitable for deriving the rules for specific measures.[3] One of the reasons for the complexity is that the concept of 'territory', which is the primary basis of jurisdictions, has different meanings, which the PCIJ did not distinguish. Territory is not only a geographical and physical concept but also a legal construct denoting control and authority delimited based on a certain space.[4] Therefore, the scope of territorial principles is flexible and adaptable. Concerning enforcement jurisdiction, there is a general agreement that not all actions by one State within the territory of another

[1] *SS Lotus (France v Turkey)* (Judgment) PCIJ Series A No 10 (1927) 18.

[2] ibid.

[3] It is noted the *obitur* has been heavily criticized as it no longer reflects current State of law. See, for instance, Frederick Alexander Mann, 'The Doctrine of Jurisdiction in International Law' (1964) 111 Recueil des Cours 1, 35; Cedric Ryngaert, *Jurisdiction in International Law* (OUP 2015) 55. With regard to the logical flaws in the judgment concerning the prescriptive jurisdiction, see Alejandro Chehtman, 'The Presumption against Extraterritorial Criminal Jurisdiction' in Micheál Ó Floinn and others (eds), *Transformations in Criminal Jurisdiction: Extraterritoriality and Enforcement* (Hart Publishing 2023) 18. It is noted that Akio Morita, by contrast, reassesses the significance of '*liberté*' as this judgment referred, in light of the historical development of prescriptive jurisdiction in the post-World War II period. Akio Morita, 'Theoretical Analysis of Conflicting Approaches on State Jurisdiction—Focusing on "Liberté" and "Basic Positions"' (2024) 67 Japanese Yearbook of International Law 126.

[4] Hannah L Buxbaum, 'Territory, Territoriality, and the Resolution of Jurisdictional Conflict' (2009) 57 The American Journal of Comparative Law 631, 635. Although it falls outside the scope of this chapter, the limitations of the concept of territoriality become evident in the context of cross-border investigations in cyberspace. See Yurika Ishii, 'Limits of State Jurisdiction in Cyberspace: The Legality of the Cross-Border Remote Access and the Use of Policeware' (2025) 67 Japanese Yearbook of International Law 26.

International Law and the Investigation of Transnational Crimes. Yurika Ishii, Oxford University Press.
 DOI: 10.1093/9780198957089.003.0005

are illegal.[5] Such an act violates sovereignty if it infringes upon the territorial State's public authority.[6] As articulated by Michael Akehurst, '[t]he act is illegal only if it represents a usurpation of the sovereign powers of the local State, either because of the nature of the act or because of the purpose for which the act is done'.[7] Whether an action qualifies as a violation of the sovereignty of another State has been extensively debated, reflecting varied viewpoints on what constitutes law enforcement. The characterization of investigations by officials, or in a broader term, the exercise of public authority, varies, depending on the constitutions of each State.

In addition, a legal problem occurs because, in the words of Robert Jennings and Arthur Watts, '[t]he exercise of jurisdiction may impinge upon the interests of other states'.[8] In other words, '[w]hat one state may see as the exercise of its sovereign rights of jurisdiction another State may see as an infringement of its sovereign rights of territorial or personal authority'.[9] The reaction of the affected States matters in assessing the legality of the action.

Investigating transnational crimes entails employing diverse measures that have cross-border ramifications for other States. The investigating State may argue that its action does not infringe on the sovereignty of the territorial State, as it is not 'enforcing' its law.[10] This chapter discusses scenarios wherein the executing State depends on the 'consent' of individuals, including both natural and legal persons, for criminal investigations. Section 2 analyses gathering information and evidence through the voluntary cooperation of individuals within a foreign territory. Section 3 delves into agreements made with law enforcement agencies and corporations, encompassing topics such as deferred prosecution agreements (DPAs).

[5] Michael Akehurst, 'Jurisdiction in International Law' (1972) 46 British Year Book of International Law 145, 146.

[6] Robert Jennings and Arthur Watts, *Oppenheim's International Law* (9th edn, Longman 1992) 18. In a case before the International Court of Justice (ICJ), Nicaragua claimed that the deltas created by sediment eroded from the road are 'physical invasions, incursions by Costa Rica into Nicaragua's sovereign territory . . . through the agency of sediment' and that their presence constitutes 'trespass' into Nicaragua's territory. The Court stated that '[t]here is no evidence that Costa Rica exercised any authority on Nicaragua's territory or carried out any activity therein', and denied Colombia's violation of territorial sovereignty. *Construction of a Road in Costa Rica along the San Juan River (Nicaragua v Costa Rica)* (Judgment, 16 December 2015) [2015] ICJ Rep 665, 738, para 223.

[7] Akehurst (n 5) 146.

[8] Jennings and Watts (n 6) 457.

[9] ibid.

[10] Although it is beyond the scope of this book, States take different approaches to the international service of process in civil and commercial matters, reflecting the divergence of the concept of law enforcement. Some countries, such as the United States, claim that it is a mere notification and not an act of enforcement. Others, including Japan, claim that it is an exercise of State jurisdiction. The issue is relevant when a State attempts to effect service by airmail or email and the defendant claims that the service is not valid. The 1965 Convention on the Service Abroad of Judicial and Extrajudicial Documents in Civil or Commercial Matters, Article 10, provides that the convention shall not interfere with the freedom to send judicial documents, by postal channels, directly to persons abroad, provided the State of destination does not object.

2. Collection of Information and Evidence with a Voluntary Cooperation of Individuals

2.1 Informal Inquiries in a Foreign Territory

The issue of this section is the legality of a situation where a police officer or other public figures contact via a telephone call, email, or physically visit another country in their personal capacity to gather information from an individual based on their voluntary cooperation. An issue arises because the concept of the 'enforcement jurisdiction' is not uniform among States.

The United States is distinct for its unique approach to collecting information abroad. Voluntary cooperation of an individual is not characterized as law enforcement, as long as the investigator reveals his or her identity and the inquiry is not coercive.[11] Only when the official asserts the governmental authority does the inquiry become an act of State. Coerciveness is the central aspect of this concept. The American Law Institute's *Fourth Restatement of the Foreign Relations Law* of 2018 characterizes enforcement jurisdiction as a State's measures 'to induce or compel compliance or punish noncompliance with its laws or regulations'.[12]

The US Department of Justice (DOJ)'s *Criminal Resource Manual* provides guidance on obtaining evidence outside the country.[13] It explains that such measures involve considerations 'unfamiliar to many American prosecutors', which include the possible violation of the sovereignty of other States.[14] The Manual warns that

> [t]he other nation may regard an effort by an American investigator or prosecutor to investigate a crime or gather evidence within its borders as a violation of sovereignty. Even such seemingly innocuous acts as a telephone call, a letter, or an unauthorized visit to a witness overseas may fall within this stricture.[15]

The text of the Manual indicates that the DOJ does not consider it against the law to conduct such measures.[16]

On the contrary, many countries would consider that the legal grounds, purpose, and mode of the measures count. When it has an authoritative nature, such

[11] For the US perspective, see Michael Abbell, *Obtaining Evidence Abroad in Criminal Cases 2010* (Brill 2010) 13.

[12] American Law Institute, *Restatement of the Law, Fourth, The Foreign Relations Law of the United States* (American Law Institute Publishers 2018) s 432.

[13] US DOJ, *Criminal Resource Manual*, s 267 <https://www.justice.gov/archives/jm/criminal-resource-manual-267-obtaining-evidence-abroad-general-considerations>. All websites were last accessed on 31 March 2025.

[14] ibid.

[15] ibid.

[16] Prosecutors are advised to consider various factors, including location of the evidence, its intended use, type of assistance needed, and time required. ibid ss 268–71.

as when the government monopolizes the measures, the action is considered law enforcement.

Albin Eser articulates major disparities between the United States and Germany. In his words, the US criminal procedure is based on the adversarial system and is governed by certain rules of evidence.[17] An American judge is not an investigator but an 'arbitrator' between the prosecutor and the accused.[18] The search for material justice and material truth requires adherence to procedural rules designed to ensure an area of freedom from State power.[19] Eser also points out that the prosecutors have broad discretion in the American legal system, which is odd to the Europeans. To the American observer, continental criminal procedure retains the appearance of an inquisition, where the judge finds the facts and assesses the evidence.[20] Prosecution is mandatory, lest the objective of material justice be frustrated from the outset.[21]

Such an outline does not accurately represent practice, given the convergence of the two traditions, as acknowledged by Eser. The distinction between adversarial and inquisitorial systems is overly simplified, as most countries integrate elements of both. In the United States, criminal procedures are governed by laws that reflect public interests to ensure fairness and integrity of the judicial systems. On the other hand, the European systems integrate discretionary prosecution and the option for defendants to enter guilty pleas. In addition, the United Kingdom is a country with a common law tradition, and it takes a cautious standpoint in enforcing its law outside the territory. However, Eser's argument illustrates that a monolithic understanding of law enforcement is inadequate for addressing the complexities of cross-border criminal investigations. This perspective underscores the necessity for an approach that accounts for the diverse legal procedures of international law enforcement activities.

International disputes seldom arise from informal forms of investigation, such as emails and telephones, which are not intrusive. The territorial States may find such actions problematic and could lodge diplomatic protests against the investigating State. However, States typically refrain from taking further action as long as the individual falls under the prescriptive jurisdiction of the investigating State in compliance with international law. On the other hand, invasive actions can trigger disputes as they may violate sovereignty and the principle of non-interference. The threshold is crossed when government authorities physically enter another State's

[17] Albin Eser, 'Common Goals and Different Ways in International Criminal Law: Reflections from a European Perspective' (1990) 31 Harvard International Law Journal 117, 121.
[18] ibid.
[19] ibid.
[20] ibid.
[21] ibid.

territory and take coercive measures.[22] In practice, however, such a case rarely happens.

2.2 Distinction among Secret Police, Espionage and Investigation

An additional concern arises when these informal investigations become indistinguishable from activities associated with secret police and espionage. The secret police of authoritarian regimes often operate clandestinely on foreign soil, ostensibly in a personal capacity. Their primary objective is to monitor and gather intelligence on individuals suspected of violating the laws of their home country.

It is widely accepted that espionage itself is not prohibited under international law. The issue of the infringement of jurisdiction does not occur, as such activities are not considered law enforcement. However, if these operations violate the host country's laws, they are subject to sanctions per the local law. It is common for the operatives' home governments to deny any official connection to their activities, thus avoiding direct responsibility for the actions of their agents.

The covert nature of such actions often circumvents due process and, in a broader context, the rule of law. They may lead to abuses, such as the unlawful arrest of the individuals. For instance, in the early 2020s, it was widely reported that China established more than 100 covert police stations in foreign soils to monitor and investigate individuals, including those involved in political activities.[23] The territorial States, including the United States,[24] the Netherlands,[25] Japan,[26] and the

[22] Examples include the Israeli Mossad's capture of Adolf Eichmann in Argentine in 1960 and the US Drug Enforcement Administration's abduction of a drug dealer Humberto Álvarez-Machaín in Mexico in 1990. In both instances, the States from which the individuals were abducted vehemently condemned the actions of the abducting States.

[23] A non-governmental organization based in Madrid, Safeguard Defenders, published a report, citing cases of Chinese nationals being coerced into returning to China from the EU member States. Laura Harth, and Yenting Chen, *Chasing Fox Hunt: Tracing the PRC's Forced Return Operations around the Globe* (Safeguard Defenders 2022).

[24] US DOJ, 'Two Arrested for Operating Illegal Overseas Police Station of the Chinese Government' (17 April 2023) <https://www.justice.gov/opa/pr/two-arrested-operating-illegal-overseas-police-station-chinese-government>.

[25] The Dutch government did not explicitly confirm the existence of the offices. However, the spokeswoman for the Dutch foreign ministry expressed that such an operation would be illegal. Isabella Kwai and Emma Bubola, 'Dutch Are Investigating Reported Illegal Chinese Police Stations' *The New York Times* (26 October 2022) <https://www.nytimes.com/2022/10/26/world/europe/china-police-netherlands.html>.

[26] The Japanese government stated in the House of Councillors that, during an investigation into a fraud case involving two Chinese women reported to the police in February 2024, the police conducted a search of the office of the Japan Community Federation of Fuzhou, a general incorporated association linked to the case. The investigation revealed that the association had facilitated the renewal of Chinese driving licences for at least dozens of individuals. Japan also lodged a diplomatic protest, emphasizing that any activities infringing on Japan's sovereignty are absolutely unacceptable. Response to an Inquiry No 28, the 216th Diet, House of Councillors, 27 June 2023.

United Kingdom,[27] have conducted searches of their sites and stated that such operations within their territories are unacceptable, as they infringe upon their sovereignty. The Chinese government denies any knowledge of such operations.

There is no established boundary between informal investigations and secretive or unauthorized investigations under international law. Nevertheless, as long as it is an exercise of State authority, it would constitute violation of the sovereignty of the foreign State. Moreover, the practices of secret police would contravene the principles of criminal procedural law established under domestic laws, including legality, transparency, and accountability, while raising significant concerns under international human rights law.

3. Use of Agreements with Corporations

A much more significant method of obtaining consent is through the government's agreements with corporations.[28] The use of agreements with individuals and corporations sharply increased in the late 2000s in the United States.[29] As discussed in Chapter 4, the United States has mechanisms that allow law enforcement authorities to require private corporations to store, disclose, and submit information even when operating in a foreign State. This practice has led to significant conflicts with other States. In response, the United States has started using agreements with corporations. This section examines the structure and issues of these agreements from an international law perspective.

3.1 Investigation Based on the Consents of the Corporations

The primary tools are categorized as (1) plea agreements and (2) DPAs or non-prosecution agreements (NPAs). This section starts with an overview of the essential characteristics of each agreement.

A plea agreement is concluded between the prosecutor and a criminal defendant, wherein the defendant admits guilt to the offence in exchange for concessions from the prosecutor.[30] The agreement involves the defendant's commitment

[27] The UK security minister said China has closed its reported police service stations at sites across Britain, and that an investigation did not reveal any illegal activity by the Chinese State at these sites. Reuters, 'China Has Closed Unofficial "Police Stations" in Britain, UK Minister Says' *The Guardian* (7 June 2023) <https://www.theguardian.com/world/2023/jun/07/china-has-closed-unofficial-police-stations-in-britain-uk-minister-says>.

[28] Materials covered by Section 3 were partially published in Yurika Ishii, 'On Law Enforcement through Agreements between the US Regulatory Authorities and Foreign Corporations' in Dominik Brodowski and others (eds), *Regulating Corporate Criminal Liability* (Springer 2014) 237–48.

[29] Brandon L Garrett, 'Globalized Corporate Prosecutions' (2011) 97 Virginia Law Review 1775.

[30] Federal Rules of Criminal Procedure, r 11. See also Joel Samaha, *Criminal Procedure* (West 2010) 461.

to cooperate in the investigation. When a corporation is a party, this often entails payment of criminal fines, forfeiture of assets, and implementation of compliance and ethics programmes. While commonly utilized in cases involving individuals to avoid lengthy trials, corporations are hesitant to enter such agreements due to the associated criminal conviction, which brings reputational risks, potential debarment, and delisting from stock exchanges.[31]

The prosecutors have been using DPAs more actively since the early 2000s.[32] A DPA is also a negotiated agreement whereby the prosecutor defers the prosecution in exchange for a corporation's actions. Criminal charges are filed to the court, but they are to be subsequently dismissed when the corporation fulfils its obligation under the agreement.[33] In the case of NPAs, no criminal charges are filed.[34] This pretrial diversion is authorized under the Speedy Trial Act of 1974.[35] The DOJ officially encouraged its use through General Attorney's memorandums in 1999.[36] It is noted that a DPA does not prevent criminal prosecutions against the senior officers or employees of the corporation who are accountable for the offence.

While the terms and conditions of DPAs and NPAs vary based on the offence's nature or the corporation's size, it generally requires the corporation to admit the wrongful act in a written statement, which is to be published on the internet. It accompanies the payment of restitution, which is as expensive as an ordinary criminal fine.[37] In addition, the corporation is obliged to cooperate with the authority's investigation. It may involve providing documents and inquiries to its employees as evidence of wrongdoing.

By the terms of the agreements, the corporation is obliged to make reforms according to the instruction of the regulatory authority. It must submit a reform plan and establish an independent monitor to oversee compliance for a certain

[31] Geraldine Szott Moohr, 'Prosecutorial Power in an Adversarial System: Lessons from Current White Collar Cases and the Inquisitorial Model' (2004) 8 Buffalo Criminal Law Review 165; Garrett (n 29) 1776.

[32] Ved P Nanda, 'Corporate Criminal Liability in the United States' in Mark Pieth and Radha Ivory (eds), *Corporate Criminal Liability: Emergence, Convergence, and Risk* (2011) 71; Brandon L Garrett, 'Structural Reform Prosecution' (2007) 93 Virginia Law Review 853, 888.

[33] US DOJ Office of the Deputy Attorney General, 'Memorandum from Mark Filip: Principles of Federal Prosecution of Business Organizations, August 28, 2008' (2008) <https://www.justice.gov/sites/default/files/dag/legacy/2008/11/03/dag-memo-08282008.pdf>.

[34] ibid.

[35] Speedy Trial Act, Pub L No 93-619, 88 Stat 2080 (1974) 18 USC 3161 (h)(2).

[36] US DOJ Office of the Deputy Attorney General, 'Memorandum from Eric Holder: Bringing Criminal Charges against Corporations' (16 June 1999) http://www.justice.gov/criminal/fraud/documents/reports/1999/charging-corps.PDF. The policy was continued by the succeeding administration, albeit with some detailed differences. See US DOJ Office of the Deputy Attorney General, 'Memorandum from Paul J. Mcnulty: Principles of Federal Prosecution of Business Organization' (2007) <https://www.justice.gov/sites/default/files/dag/legacy/2007/07/05/mcnulty_memo.pdf>; US DOJ Office of the Deputy Attorney General (n 33). See also Nanda (n 32) 80.

[37] Lawrence D Finder, Ryan D McConnell, and Scott L Mitchell, 'Betting the Corporation: Compliance or Defiance?' (2009) 28 Corporate Counsel Review 1, 16; Ellen S Podgor, *White Collar Crime* (Nancy J King, Jerold H Israel, and Peter J Henning eds, West 2013) 1524; Nanda (n 32) 80.

period.[38] Its appointment is, in general, subject to the consent of the authority. The corporation bears the expenses for the reform and monitoring processes. The monitor reviews and evaluates the effectiveness of the company's internal controls, record-keeping, and policies or procedures relating to compliance. The monitor also submits periodic reports to the DOJ. The report may be a trigger to restart the investigation process if the DOJ finds the corporation's failure to fulfil its obligation, and it may also be used as criminal evidence in the future if the corporation conducts another offence.

These tools are indispensable because corporate crimes involve complex organizational structures and sophisticated financial transactions. Without companies' voluntarily sharing information and cooperating with investigations, law enforcement authorities face significant hurdles in obtaining the essential materials needed for criminal inquiries.[39]

These 'agreements' are not, of course, based on free will between equal parties. Plea agreements are, by definition, a part of the criminal procedure. DPAs form sanctions against the corporation for its criminally liable conduct. They are still a type of 'sanction' because the targeted companies must pay large fines and admit and disclose the facts on which the criminal charges are based.[40] Implementing these agreements is an act of *jus imperii*, which only a State may be entitled to undertake.

This trend towards seeking the cooperation of targeted companies in criminal proceedings has become more pronounced since the end of the 1990s. The background to this trend is that there has been growing concern that the prosecution of companies could have a negative impact not only on the company but also on small- and medium-sized enterprises that have business relationships. The interests of employees and shareholders who are not involved in the crime are harmed.[41] Unlike in the case of natural persons, when pursuing criminal liability of a company, it becomes necessary to prevent bankruptcy, protect the employment of employees not involved in the crime, and ensure that the company fulfils its corporate social responsibility.[42]

[38] US DOJ Deputy Attorney General, 'Memorandum from Craig S. Morford: Selection and Use of Monitors in Deferred Prosecution Agreements and Non-Prosecution Agreements with Corporations' (7 March 2008) <https://www.justice.gov/sites/default/files/dag/legacy/2008/03/20/morford-useofmonitorsmemo-03072008.pdf>.

[39] Garrett (n 29) 1788.

[40] The relevance of such criminal justice is debated in Julie R O'Sullivan, 'How Prosecutors Apply the "Federal Prosecutions of Corporations" Charging Policy in the Era of Deferred Prosecutions and What That Means for the Purposes of the Federal Criminal Sanction' (2014) 51 American Criminal Law Review 29; Gerard E Lynch, 'The Role of Criminal Law in Policing Corporate Misconduct' (1997) 60 Law and Contemporary Problems 23.

[41] Garrett (n 29).

[42] Brandon L Garrett, *Too Big to Jail: How Prosecutors Compromise with Corporations* (Harvard UP 2016).

The flaw of criminal prosecution of corporations became evident in the *Enron* case in 2002. Enron Corporation, an energy company based in the United States, filed for bankruptcy in 2001 after its widespread accounting fraud and corruption were revealed. The repercussions for its employees were profound. Over 20,000 Enron employees, innocent of wrongdoing, suddenly found themselves without jobs. Furthermore, many had placed their retirement funds in Enron stock, only to see its value plummet thereafter. The scandal led to enacting the Sarbanes-Oxley Act of 2002, which aimed to enhance transparency in corporate governance and accounting practices and prevent corporate fraud. Against this background, how companies are sanctioned has also been reformed in light of these requirements. Enforcement is designed to encourage compliance within the company, change its culture and increase transparency while minimizing the negative impact on innocent employees.

The Principles for the Federal Prosecution of Commercial Organizations set the criteria for prosecutors to determine when to initiate a criminal prosecution.[43] It is incorporated into the DOJ's decision criteria that companies cooperate with investigations, for example, by providing relevant information and taking restorative measures, for example, by implementing legal compliance programmes.[44] The Securities and Exchange Commission (SEC) similarly focuses on a company's cooperation, such as self-reporting and collaborating with authorities' investigations, in deciding whether to file a lawsuit.[45]

The degree of cooperation of companies is considered not only at the preliminary stage of prosecution but also at the sentencing stage. In 1984, the Sentencing Reform Act passed.[46] It established the Sentencing Commission and adopted the Sentencing Guidelines.[47] Although the guidelines are amended annually, Chapter VIII of the guidelines, which sets out the sentencing guidelines for companies and other entities, has, since coming into force in 1991, implemented effective legal compliance and ethics programmes by companies ground for sentence reduction when companies are also criminally liable for offences committed by their employees.[48] The criteria for a programme to be deemed effective are also set out in the guidelines, which require companies to develop a corporate code of conduct to

[43] US Attorney's Manual, Title 9, ch 9-27.000, 'Principles of Federal Prosecution of Business Organizations' <https://www.justice.gov/jm/jm-9-28000-principles-federal-prosecution-business-organizations>.

[44] Criminal Division of the US DOJ and Enforcement Division of the US SEC, *A Resource Guide to the US Foreign Corrupt Practices Act* (2012) 99 <https://www.justice.gov/criminal/criminal-fraud/file/1292051/dl>.

[45] Security Exchange Commission, 'Report of Investigation Pursuant to Section 21(a) of the Securities Exchange Act of 1934 and Commission Statement on the Relationship of Cooperation to Agency Enforcement Division (Seaboard Report)' (2001) <http://www.sec.gov/litigation/investreport/34-44969.htm>.

[46] Sentencing Reform ActPub L No 98-473, 98 Stat 2032 (1984) 18 USC 3551.

[47] United States Sentencing Commission, *Guidelines Manual* (November 2014) s 3E1.1.

[48] ibid s 8C2.5(f).

prevent crime before it occurs and to systematically take the necessary measures to implement a legal compliance programme.[49]

Furthermore, if the company does not have such a programme, it may be required to develop one and submit it to a judge as part of the sanctions against the company.[50] It is also frequently required to establish an independent monitor[51] when probation is required, whether through criminal penalties, plea bargaining, or DPAs, which are discussed in Section 3.2.[52] The company concerned bears the cost of establishing the monitor, but the monitor conducts an independent investigation and submits a report to the DOJ. The reports are used to detect crimes in the future.

3.2 Legality of Indirect Law Enforcement against Foreign Corporations

When any of the above-described agreements impose a certain obligation under the US law on a corporation established in a foreign country, its implementation may be indirect law enforcement. Fredrick Alexander Mann defined this term as 'a state's enforcing its rights in its territory exclusively or primarily to bring about an act or omission in foreign territory, in order indirectly to enforce its jurisdiction abroad'.[53] States rely on indirect law enforcement on many occasions as a regulation of multinational corporations under the theory of the unity of enterprise, which was described in Chapter 4, Section 2.2.[54] However, it may conflict with the fundamental principle of territorial sovereignty, in particular when law enforcement coerces the person or corporation to act in violation of the law of the local State, which is the State where the corporation is incorporated.

Moreover, unilateral law enforcement may be regarded as a circumvention of conventional judicial assistance between the United States and the local State. In general, when one State wants to acquire evidence located in another State, the former needs to make a request to the latter to the effect.[55] It is a lengthy and cumbersome process, as discussed in Chapter 2, Section 2.2, but it serves as a mechanism to protect the sovereignty of the territorial State, as it can refuse assistance if fulfilling the request would be contrary to its public interest. The use of de facto agreements allows the requesting State to skip these formal processes.

49 ibid. Criminal Division of the US DOJ and Enforcement Division of the US SEC (n 44) 99.

50 *Guideline Manual* (n 47) s 8D1.4(c)(1).

51 ibid s 8D1.1.

52 Criminal Division of the US DOJ and Enforcement Division of the US SEC (n 44) 116.

53 Frederick Alexander Mann, 'The Doctrine of International Jurisdiction Revisited after Twenty Years' (1984) 186 Recueil des Cours 9, 47; Mann (n 3) 131.

54 Gunnar Hedlund and John H Dunning, *Organization of Transnational Corporations* (Routledge 1993) 52.

55 John David McClean, *International Co-Operation in Civil and Criminal Matters* (OUP 2012) 169.

The agreements between the authorities and the foreign corporations are used as enforcement tools in other fields than criminal law. An important example is foreign financial institution (FFI) agreements under the Foreign Account Tax Compliance Act. Plea agreements and DPAs are, in a broad sense, a part of the sanction for what the corporation did. In contrast, the primary purpose of FFI agreements is to prevent and detect the occurrence of tax offences.[56] It is an agreement whereby an FFI reports to the Internal Revenue Service (IRS) information about financial accounts held by US taxpayers or by foreign entities in which US taxpayers hold a substantial ownership interest.

There are views that criticize the justification of the US unilateral actions since the time of jurisdictional conflict, as described in Chapter 4. For example, Astrid Stadler argued that both regulatory authorities' requiring private individuals to cooperate with the investigation and the court's coercing the individuals to comply with the court order is tantamount to infringement of the sovereignty of the local State.[57] In the same vein, Rolf Stürner questioned the investigation based on the 'voluntary will' of the parties.[58] While he concedes that such a voluntary discovery is not prohibited in continental Europe because the result of the investigation could be used in a formal judicial process, it is hard to characterize the act as not an act of *jus imperii*. Stürner argues against these practices because 'the actual and purported infringement of sovereignty' is not allowed.[59]

The consent of a private individual or company cannot, in theory, remedy a breach of sovereignty. In practice, however, many States do not claim that the use of such agreements is illegal, provided that the investigation remains within certain limits, such as that law enforcement officials do not physically enter the territory of the foreign State. This pragmatic stance allows for cooperation between States and private entities in cross-border investigations.

Criticisms arise partly from the underlying differences in domestic legal systems, which were described in Section 2.[60] For instance, in numerous States, privacy laws restrict State authorities from gathering personal information except through specific procedures. The United States lacks such protection, so 'if authorities want an employee's e-mail, for example, a cooperating company may produce that e-mail without any subpoena and without providing any notice to the

[56] Foreign Account Tax Compliance Act, Pub L No 111-147, 124 Stat 71 (2010), 26 USC 1471–1474, 26 USC 6038D.

[57] Astrid Stadler, 3 *Der Schutz Des Unternehmensgeheimnisses Im Deutschen Und U.S.-Amerikanischen Zivilprozeß Und Im Rechtshilfeverfahren* (Mohr 1989) 1; Ernst C Stiefel, Rolf Stürner, and Astrid Stadler, 'The Enforceability of Excessive US Punitive Damage Awards in Germany' (1991) 39 The American Journal of Comparative Law 779.

[58] Rolf Stürner, 'Die Gerichte Und Behörden Der U.S.A. Und Die Beweisaufnahme in Deutschland' (1982) 81 Zeitschrift für Vergleichende Rechtswissenschaft 159.

[59] ibid 159.

[60] Hague Conference on Private Law, 'Report of the U.S. Delegation to the Eleventh Session of the Hague Conference on Private International Law' (1969) 8 International Legal Materials 785.

employee'.[61] The United States is also flexible in cooperating with private individuals, such as attorneys or corporate monitors, at the stage of a criminal or administrative investigation. Most of the States are not familiar with such measures.

Another limitation is the lack of strict governance in the DPAs and NPAs. The proposed reforms in the agreement often lack specificity. Furthermore, while companies are required to cooperate in investigations, senior executives often evade accountability. Brandon L Garrett's comprehensive research on these practices underscores the necessity for governmental enhancement of corporate law enforcement through the implementation of more rigorous prosecution agreements, judicial oversight, and enhanced transparency.[62]

The environment surrounding the US law enforcement activities has changed since the 2000s. More attention is being paid to the notion of fairness and justice in the global market, by both academics and practitioners. In addition, there is a general recognition that the complexity of corporate crime requires new tools to enable prosecutors to act effectively against the corporation.[63]

3.3 Convergence of the Disputes

Although some have criticized their transparency and legitimacy, it is justified because, given the complexity of corporate activities, the authorities can no longer afford to rely on traditional criminal prosecution. Moreover, these new tools are part of the US effort to promote its own corporate governance standards, which are even stricter than the Organisation for Economic Co-operation and Development (OECD) guidelines. Its aim is to let the corporations enhance their level of compliance by themselves. The Federal Sentencing Guidelines Manual thus provides that the existence of an effective compliance and ethics programme is one of the mitigating factors of corporate punishment.[64]

An important development is seen in economic criminal laws, particularly after the end of the Cold War. States started to criminalize such infringements. The necessity of dealing with transnational crimes came to be recognized so that the US-led other States could establish international frameworks for dealing with transnational corporate crimes.[65] Primary examples are international instruments such as the OECD Convention on Combating Bribery of Foreign Public Officials

[61] Charles F Smith and Brittany D Parling, '"American Imperialism" : A Practitioner's Experience with Extraterritorial Enforcement of the FCPA' [2012] University of Chicago Legal Forum 237, 245.

[62] Garrett (n 32); Garrett (n 42).

[63] William S Laufer, *Corporate Bodies and Guilty Minds: The Failure of Corporate Criminal Liability* (University of Chicago Press 2006) 5.

[64] United States Sentencing Commission, *2011 Federal Sentencing Guidelines Manual* (USSC 2011) s 8B2.1. <https://www.ussc.gov/guidelines/archive/2011-federal-sentencing-guidelines-manual>.

[65] Bruce Zagaris, *International White Collar Crime: Cases and Materials* (CUP 2010) 1; Neil Boister, *An Introduction to Transnational Criminal Law* (OUP 2012) 112.

in International Business Transactions (OECD Bribery Convention),[66] which criminalizes foreign bribery and the United Nations Convention on Transnational Organized Crime,[67] which criminalizes corruption and money laundering among others. Networks of double tax avoidance agreements and the Convention on Mutual Administrative Assistance in Tax Matters have been established to promote information exchange on both civil and criminal matters.[68] OECD has adopted guidelines for multinational enterprises on corporate social responsibilities and governance.[69] These movements created international pressure against States to regulate unlawful economic activities.

It is not that these treaties, regulations, and standards justify indirect law enforcement activities that are otherwise not supported. Nevertheless, they serve as guidelines as to the extent of the judicial cooperation in which States engage. On the one hand, a State may be able to pursue criminal investigations notwithstanding the legal difference between each jurisdiction. It is often the case that the conventions require State parties to harmonize their domestic laws. In the various OECD instruments, as well as in most of the bilateral treaties, it is often provided that banking secrecy does not hinder the gathering of documentary evidence from banks or its being forwarded to the competent authority of the other State in case of certain crimes. Such international cooperation mechanisms prevent States from enacting an equivalent of the blocking statutes of antitrust laws. On the other hand, the requested State may decline the assistance on the grounds that the request is not in accordance with the treaty. For example, it is allowed for the State not to cooperate with a so-called fishing expedition because the request has to be specific, and the information required shall be relevant, at least to a certain extent.[70]

Furthermore, it is notable that many States came to include mechanisms similar to the US's approach in their national legal systems. For instance, the United Kingdom introduced the DPAs under the Crime and Courts Act of 2013 for organizations accused of specific economic crimes, such as fraud, bribery, or money laundering.[71] France introduced the deferred prosecution agreement, the *convention judiciaire d'intérêt public*, as well.[72] It allows the prosecutor to offer a

[66] OECD, Convention on Combating Bribery of Foreign Public Officials in International Business Transactions (adopted on 21 November 1997, entered into force on 15 February 1999) 2802 UNTS 225.

[67] United Nations Convention on Transnational Organized Crime (adopted on 15 November 2000, entry into force on 29 September 2003) 2225 UNTS 209.

[68] Convention on Mutual Administrative Assistance in Tax Matters (adopted on 25 January 1988, entered into force on 1 April 1995) 2323 UNTS 197.

[69] See OECD, *OECD Guidelines for Multinational Enterprises* (OECD Publishing 2011).

[70] See, eg, United States Model Income Tax Convention (15 November 2006) art 26 <http://www.irs.gov/pub/irs-trty/model006.pdf>.

[71] Crime and Courts Act 2013, c 22, s 45, sch 17.

[72] Loi n° 2016-1691 du 9 décembre 2016 relative à la transparence, à la lutte contre la corruption et à la modernisation de la vie économique ('Loi Sapin II'). The scope of the crimes was later expanded to crimes related to environmental matters. Code de procédure pénale, Article 41-1-3, amended by La loi n°2020-1672 du 24 décembre 2020 relative au parquet européen, Article 292.

legal entity accused of corruption, influence peddling, money laundering, or tax fraud to enter into an agreement so that the entity will cooperate with the investigation and anti-corruption measures, and the prosecutor will drop the prosecution. Against the background was the OECD Bribery Convention and the US and the UK practices.[73] Similarly, Brazil introduced a mechanism of 'leniency agreements' in 2013 under the anti-corruption law.[74] Canada introduced a procedure of 'Remediation Agreements' in 2018 under the Criminal Code to deal with economic crimes, such as fraud and corruption.[75] Singapore adopted DPAs in 2018 in the Criminal Justice Reform Act.[76] Argentina incorporated 'collaboration agreements' under the Criminal Justice Reform Act in 2018.[77] Australia followed suit by introducing DPAs in 2020.[78]

Nonetheless, when the local State claims there is excessive law enforcement by a foreign country, the arguments still centre upon the issue of sovereignty. This observation was confirmed in the *UBS* case, which lasted from 2008 to 2010. UBS, the largest bank in Switzerland, entered into a DPA as the DOJ started a criminal investigation on the grounds that UBS assisted in illegal tax evasion of US citizens. In the written statement, UBS admitted its participation in a scheme to defraud the United States and IRS by actively assisting or facilitating a number of US individual taxpayers in establishing accounts at UBS in a manner designed to conceal the US taxpayer's ownership or beneficial interest in these accounts.[79] The bank agreed to provide the US government with the identities and account information of certain US clients under the supervision of the Swiss Financial Market Supervisory Authority.[80]

However, the IRS found it insufficient to investigate the unlawful tax practices through the bank. Therefore, it went to the Federal District Court and obtained a subpoena to enforce its John Doe summons, that is, a summons issued when the IRS does not know the identity of the person under investigation. In the end, it demanded disclosure of the identity of the US account holders who did not comply with certain procedures, which turned out to be more than 52,000 individuals. The facts that justified the summons were obtained by the DPA. The arguments

[73] For the legislative process, see Légifrance, Loi n° 2016-1691 du 9 décembre 2016 relative à la transparence, à la lutte contre la corruption et à la modernisation de la vie économique <https://www.legifrance.gouv.fr/dossierlegislatif/JORFDOLE000032319792/>.

[74] Lei nº 12.846, de 1º de agosto de 2013 (Lei Anticorrupção), art 16.

[75] Criminal Code, pt XXII.1. See Public Prosecution Service of Canada, 'Deskbook, Guideline of the Director Issued under Section 3(3)(c) of the Director of Public Prosecutions Act' (2020) <https://www.ppsc-sppc.gc.ca/eng/pub/fpsd-sfpg/fps-sfp/tpd/p3/ch21.html>.

[76] Criminal Justice Reform Act 2018, pt VIIA.

[77] Ley nº 27.401, de 8 de noviembre de 2017 (Ley de Responsabilidad Penal de las Empresas).

[78] Crimes Legislation Amendment (Combatting Corporate Crime) Bill 2019, sch 2.

[79] *United States v UBS AG*, Deferred Prosecution Agreement, Case No 0:09-cr-60033-JIC, Document 20, entered on FLSD Docket, 18 February 2009.

[80] ibid para 6.

submitted before the court by DOJ and the Swiss government mirror the discussion described in Section 3.2.[81] It is notable that the DOJ's argument not only relies on the balancing approach as always but also underscores the fact that UBS committed the wrongdoing on US soil. Another characteristic of this case is that there has been cooperation between the governments of the United States and Switzerland. Notwithstanding the federal court's decision that the disclosure of the banking information in this situation is unconstitutional, Switzerland eventually handed over nearly 4,500 clients' dossiers.[82]

The agreements do not alter the fundamental structure of the decentralized system of international society. Nonetheless, they help cushion the impact of unilateral law enforcement actions. The corporations and the local States are more likely to comply with the US law when these tools are used.

States will move towards a more active use of these arrangements. However, unless their enforcement is underpinned by legitimacy and transparency, it will be difficult for the investigating State to obtain the cooperation of the local State. Key issues include whether the criteria for entering into an agreement should be legislated, the conditions under which the existence and details of the agreement may remain confidential, how disclosed information during negotiations can be used, whether corporations should be required to make formal admissions, the need for clear definitions of material breach and its consequences, and the role of judicial approval and supervision. Further adjustments will be required between these States, corporations, and the local State to achieve smooth enforcement of transnational criminal law. Such refined law enforcement has led to the prevention of international disputes.

4. Concluding Remarks

This chapter has explored the critical aspects and inherent limitations of the consent-based system of law enforcement. The State-centric mechanism upholds the notion that State sovereignty cannot be violated, even with the consent of the individual. This theoretical framework emphasizes the sanctity of national borders and the principle of non-interference, which is the cornerstone of international law.

[81] *Amicus Brief of Government of Switzerland*, Case No 09-20423-CIV-GOLD/MCALILEY (filed on 30 April 2009) <https://www.bj.admin.ch/dam/bj/en/data/wirtschaft/fallubs/amicus-response-e.pdf.download.pdf/amicus-response-e.pdf>; US DOJ Deputy Attorney General, 'Memorandum of Law in Support of Petition to Enforce "John Doe" Summons' (30 June 2009) <https://www.taxnotes.com/research/federal/other-documents/other-court-documents/u.s-responds-to-switzerland-on-john-doe-summons/ws4j>. For the UBS affair, see also Chapter 8, Section 4.1.3(2)(b).

[82] Nanda (n 32) 83; Garrett (n 29) 1815.

However, the practice of law enforcement presents a more complex reality. States have increasingly come to rely on the consent of individuals, particularly legal entities, when enforcing their laws. This approach has gained wider acceptance, provided it is carried out within the bounds of legitimate prescriptive jurisdiction. While jurisdictional conflicts persist, as discussed in Part II, such occurrences have become less frequent compared to their peak.

PART II

INVESTIGATIONS OF TRANSNATIONAL CRIMES THROUGH NON-CRIMINAL PROCEDURES

6
Violation of Competition Law

1. Introduction

Competition law or antitrust law is a set of rules and regulations aimed at promoting fair competition in the market and preventing anti-competitive practices by businesses.[1] For this purpose, it generally prohibits corporations from monopolizing the market and prohibits cartels for price-fixing, market allocation, and bid-rigging, among others. The most severe breach of competition law is collusion among competitors to form a cartel.

Competition law usually imposes administrative and criminal sanction against responsible entities and individuals. The administrative sanctions include fines, cease and desist orders, corrective measures, disqualification, compensation to competitors, and consumers. Additional measures include public disclosure of the violation, which would damage the company's reputation, and monitoring and compliance programmes. The severity and type of sanctions and the effectiveness of their enforcement can vary depending on the jurisdiction.

The elements of the competition law differ from one jurisdiction to another. However, in most cases, it suffices to evidence the will of the anti-competitive conduct of other market actors on each participant. For instance, when proving the existence of a cartel, it is not necessary to demonstrate the existence of a formal agreement. Instead, competition authorities look for evidence that shows the voluntary participation of the parties involved.[2] Examples include documents, records of telephone calls, and emails, which show price fixation with competitors. The fluctuation of the market price could be the basis of the assumption of such a behaviour.[3] However, these materials are scattered among multiple companies. Therefore, it is technically challenging to collect the information, particularly when it is a cross-border case.[4]

In theory, one way to collect information and evidence is through the assistance of the State where the corporation resides. However, mutual assistance mechanisms

[1] This book will use the term 'competition law' as a general word, and the term 'antitrust law' to specifically refer to the US law.

[2] Maurice Guerrin and Georgios Kyriazis, 'Cartels: Proof and Procedural Issues' (1992) 16 Fordham International Law Journal 266.

[3] ibid 285.

[4] See Nina Hachigian, 'Essential Mutual Assistance in International Antitrust Enforcement' (1995) 29 International Lawyer 117.

International Law and the Investigation of Transnational Crimes. Yurika Ishii, Oxford University Press.
 DOI: 10.1093/9780198957089.003.0006

for competition law enforcement were not widely established before the 1980s. The Organisation for Economic Co-operation and Development (OECD) noted that the lack of such frameworks was due to the different approaches taken towards competition policy.[5] In addition, many States lack the capability to gather information from large corporations.[6] Companies can easily operate across borders, making it difficult for a single country to effectively examine antitrust violations. A mutual legal assistance treaty (MLAT) on criminal matters, if it exists, only plays a complementary role in the present context.

The primary method for obtaining evidence typically involves unilateral law enforcement by a State or jurisdiction that possesses adequate enforcement resources. As Section 2 highlights in an overview, European countries have had competition laws since the 1950s. However, only the United States,[7] the Federal Republic of Germany,[8] and Sweden[9] had laws allowing their national authority to conduct investigations against foreign corporations at the time. When evidence was not available through the cooperation of the other States, the United States issued subpoenas against foreign corporations, which generated diplomatic tensions and legal disputes.

Against this background, the disputes emerged concerning the difference in the substantive laws and policies that the United States and the other States took. The former endorsed the effects doctrine since 1945, which extends US competition laws to foreign entities when their actions have substantial effects on the US markets. The rest did not recognize such a jurisdictional basis. No other country than the United States enforced its law against foreign corporations when the required materials were located abroad. However, the dispute converged because this gap became minimized after the EU competition policy evolved in the 1990s. The countries with sizable markets started establishing cooperation mechanisms to overcome the issue of jurisdiction.

The key to this development lies in the following paths. First, competition law authorities have been empowered to investigate criminal cases under their own domestic laws. It allows them to go beyond simply identifying anti-competitive behaviour and prosecute companies or individuals who engage in such practices.

Second, these domestic authorities have established channels to share information with their counterparts in other countries. By sharing information,

[5] OECD Committee of Experts on Restrictive Business Practices, *Competition Law Enforcement: International Co-Operation in the Collection of Information* (OECD Publications and Information Center 1984) 39.

[6] ibid 23.

[7] Hart–Scott–Rodino Antitrust Improvements Act, Title II, s 201, Pub L No 94-435, 90 Stat 1390 (1976).

[8] Gesetz gegen Wettbewerbsbeschränkungen (1957) BGBl I Nr 41 1081, s 98(2).

[9] Lag (1956:245) om uppgiftsskyldighet rörande prisoch konkurrensförhållanden, ss 2–3. English translation is available at Maher M Dabbah and Barry E Hawk, *Anti-Cartel Enforcement Worldwide* (CUP 2010).

competition authorities can build a more comprehensive picture of a company's activities and identify potential collusion or other illegal practices that might not be apparent from a purely domestic perspective. This collaboration allows for more coordinated enforcement actions and a stronger global response to anti-competitive behaviour. This cooperation operates with more flexibility than conventional MLATs. Authorities act according to their domestic laws without undergoing judicial review. While such information is usually insufficient to serve as evidence in a criminal trial, it can provide valuable leads that may help uncover and develop a case.

Section 2 highlights the unilateral measures and policies taken by the United States, including the effects doctrine. It also covers the methods used by the United States to gather evidence of potential competition law violations, involving both civil and criminal jurisdictions. It then examines the efforts and progress made in harmonizing competition laws, focusing on the EU enforcement against non-EU corporations, as well as similar measures adopted by other States. This section also discusses the criminalization of competition law violations and the procedures for obtaining necessary materials and information.

Section 3 outlines the various mechanisms of cooperation among international competition authorities, emphasizing the significance and limitations of positive comity. It details the types of cooperation agreements, including negative comity, positive comity, and enforcement cooperation.

Section 4 provides an analysis on the rights to a fair trial for both legal and natural persons within the context of international competition law enforcement. It explores relevant case laws and the potential to protect the rights of both natural and legal persons.

2. Jurisdictional Conflicts and Its Convergence: The Effect Doctrine and the Subpoena to Foreign Subsidiaries

2.1 The Failure of the Efforts for Harmonization of the Competition Laws

The antitrust law was first developed in the United States in the late nineteenth century. The government started to deal with unfair competition in industries such as railroad, oil, and sugar, which directly affected the lives of ordinary citizens.

The earliest antitrust act, namely the Interstate Commerce Act of 1887,[10] was enacted after the Granger movement, where the farmers in the mid-West protested the price-fixing of the railroads. The law marked the beginning of government

[10] Interstate Commerce Act 24 Stat 379, ch 104 (1887).

intervention in regulating anti-competitive business practices. Congress later enacted the Sherman Act of 1890,[11] which was supplemented by the Federal Trade Commission Act[12] and the Clayton Antitrust Act of 1914.[13] These statutes made cartels and monopolization of market criminal offences.

The important turning point was the founding of investigating institutions for the anti-competitive conducts. Initially, the Interstate Commerce Act established the Interstate Commerce Commission to oversee rates and practices of railroads companies.[14] In 1910, the Congress expanded its mandate to monitor practices of telephone, telegraph, and wireless companies.[15]

Afterwards, the Federal Trade Commission Act founded the Federal Trade Commission (FTC). The FTC and the US Department of Justice (DOJ) Antitrust Division are the major organ to enforce the federal antitrust laws as of today. The DOJ can commence an investigation under the Antitrust Civil Process Act,[16] and the FTC can issue a civil investigative demand and subpoena to obtain documents and materials.[17] A corporation may be criminally sanctioned if it does not comply with these orders or requests.[18]

On the other hand, the rest of the countries did not pursue anti-competitive policies. In many European countries, including the Great Britain, France, and Germany, the development of corporate industries took place after the Industrial Revolution.[19] In the late nineteenth century, small corporations tried to avoid competition by engaging in cartels. Governments largely remained on the sidelines. Such actions were prohibited to the extent that they were against public policy under civil law or conflicted with extortion under penal law.

There were attempts to harmonize the anti-competitive policy at the international level. The issue first came up at the World Economic Conference in 1927.[20] However, it failed without any concrete results after the depression of the 1930s and the rise of protectionism.[21]

[11] An Act to Protect Trade and Commerce against Unlawful Restraints and Monopolies, Pub L No 51-647, 26 Stat 209 (1890).

[12] Federal Trade Commission Act, Pub L No 63-203, 38 Stat 717 (1914).

[13] Clayton Antitrust Act, Pub L No 63-212, 38 Stat 730 (1914).

[14] For the history of the Interstate Commerce Commission, see Richard Stone, *The Interstate Commerce Commission and the Railroad Industry: A History of Regulatory Policy* (Praeger 1991). The Commission was abolished in 1995.

[15] Railway Rate Act , Pub L No 61-218, 36 Stat 539 (1910).

[16] Antitrust Civil Process Act, 15 USC 1312 (1964).

[17] 15 USC 49, 57(b)-1(c). It is noted that the FTC is responsible for not only federal antitrust laws but also consumer protection laws such as Telemarketing Sale Rule, Identity Theft Act, and Fair Credit Reporting Act. These laws suppress fraud and deception such as telemarketing fraud and internet scams.

[18] 15 USC 1312.

[19] Jürgen Basedow, *Limits and Control of Competition with a View to International Harmonization* (Kluwer 2002).

[20] League of Nations, *The World Economic Conference, Geneva, May 1927: Final Report* (League of Nations 1927).

[21] Daniel Barbezat, 'Cooperation and Rivalry in the International Steel Cartel, 1926–1933' (1989) 49 Journal of Economic History 435.

West Germany went through a unique path compared with other European countries after the end of World War II. In 1944, the Roosevelt administration planned to abolish cartels under occupied Germany. For the United States, it was a matter of national security to dissolve cartels, which formed its foundation in military industries.[22] The Potsdam Agreement, which the United States, the United Kingdom, and the Union of Soviet Socialist Republics (Soviet Union) signed, stipulated that 'the German economy shall be decentralised to eliminate the present excessive concentration of economic power as exemplified in particular by cartels, syndicates, trusts and other monopolistic arrangements'.[23] The reconstruction of the industries took place after the occupation began by the United Nations. The US legislation influenced the Act against Restraints of Competition (*Gesetz gegen Wettbewerbsbeschränkungen*) of 1957. The law applied to all restrictive conduct outside the territory when the behaviour affected it.[24] However, the interpretation of the term 'to have an effect' (*auswirken*) was controversial on a doctrinal level. The government did not apply the law against a foreign entity.

The United States again tried to harmonize domestic competition laws of industrialized countries through international organizations. This approach lacked the basis for international cooperation because there was little commonality among States' competition policies. The US corporations opposed such an effort that would disadvantage companies' competitiveness. Standardizing norms proved challenging due to the significant divergencies in industry structures across various States.

The first attempt involved regulation through the International Trade Organization. Its constituent instrument stipulated anti-competitive acts and a procedure where the harmed member state may apply for consultation or investigation through the organization.[25] However, the US government considered the draft provisions ineffective and refused to ratify the treaty in the end.[26]

Second, the United Nations Economic and Social Council (ECOSOC) became the forum for negotiating an international convention for harmonization. An ad hoc Committee on Restrictive Business Practices was established in 1951 under the ECOSOC, and a draft was submitted in 1952, reflecting the Havana Charter's provisions.[27] In a move that deviated from the International Trade Organization

[22] For the security concern of the United States, see Corwin D Edwards, *Economic and Political Aspects of International Cartels* (Arno Press 1944) 68. For the historical development, see Tony A Freyer, *Antitrust and Global Capitalism, 1930–2004* (CUP 2006) 53.

[23] The Berlin (Potsdam) Conference, 17 July–2 August 1945, *Protocol of the Proceedings*, 1 August 1945, ch II, s B(12).

[24] Gesetz gegen Wettbewerbsbeschränkungen (27 July 1957) BGBl I S 1081, art 98(2).

[25] Charter for International Trade Organization (adopted on 24 March 1948) UN Doc E/Conf.2/78.

[26] Jürgen Basedow, 'Antitrust or Competition Law, International' in Rüdiger Wolfrum (ed), *Max Planck Encyclopedia of Public International Law* (online edn, OUP 2014).

[27] ECOSOC, *Report of the Ad hoc Committee on Restrictive Business Practices*, Rec 16th Sess Supp No 11 (E/2380, E/AC.37/3, 1953); ECOSOC, *Analysis of Governmental Measures Relating to Restrictive Business Practices*, Rec 16th Sess Supp No 11 A (E/2379, E/Ac.37/2, 1953); ECOSOC, *Text of National*

Charter, the ECOSOC draft distinguished public and private enterprises by providing a rule to protect foreign public enterprises over private enterprises.[28] Member states could file lawsuits on their behalf or for enterprises damaged in their jurisdiction when private entities engaged in anti-competitive activities. In contrast, in the case of public enterprises, member states could file lawsuits only when such activities damaged them.[29]

The US industries vehemently opposed this draft for the following reasons.[30] Because the United States has an industrial structure centred on private companies, the United States would be disadvantaged by a convention that gave public companies an advantage. In addition, while competition laws differed from one State to another, the draft called for measures to eliminate restrictive business practices according to the State's constitution, legal system, and economic organization. This would put companies in countries with stricter competition laws in disadvantageous positions. Furthermore, the investigative institution constituted the members of the ECOSOC and might reflect the intentions of other States to hinder the United States. Lastly, the draft provided for restrictions on the freedom of private enterprise activities and consequently on private property but did not include provisions on procedures to guarantee rights. In response to the opposition of domestic economic organizations, the United States proposed the conference to discontinue the drafting, which terminated the process.[31]

Third, an expert committee on restrictive acts was established at the headquarters of the General Agreement on Tariffs and Trade in 1958. The committee submitted a report to the State parties in 1960.[32] However, the committee could not offer a unified view on whether third-party involvement should be allowed. The State parties adopted the resolution that it was impractical for a State party to impose or investigate any regulation on this type of practice.[33]

In summary, it became clear by the mid-1950s that States could not agree on an international instrument for harmonizing competition policy and facilitating dispute settlements concerning competition law.

Legislation and other Governmental Measures Relating to Restrictive Business Practices, Rec 16th Sess Supp No 11 B (E/2379, Add.2, E/AC.37/2 Add.2, 1953).

28 ECOSOC, Report E/2380 (n 27) 12, Annex II, 'Draft articles of agreement', art 3(1).

29 ibid art 3(2).

30 For the background, see Gilbert H Montague, 'Limitation of What UN Can Do Successfully: The Proposed UN Program on Restrictive Business Practices' (1955) 1 Antitrust Bulletin 441. See also Junji Nakagawa, *International Harmonization of Economic Regulation* (OUP 2011) 188.

31 UN Economic and Social Council (4 April 1955) UN Doc E/2612/Add.2; (31 May 1954) UN Doc E/2612/Add.1.

32 'Restrictive Business Practices, Arrangements for Consultations Report' (2 June 1960) L/1015, BISD 9S/170.

33 'Restrictive Business Practices, Arrangements for Consultations, Decision of the Contracting Parties' (18 November 1960) BISD 9S/29.

2.2 The US Unilateral Law Enforcement

2.2.1 Effects Doctrine

The US courts adopt the presumption against extraterritoriality, which is an interpretive principle whereby courts avoid reading US statutes as applicable on foreign soil without Congress's clear indication.[34] However, the US courts started to apply antitrust laws based on the effects doctrine against the background that it had the largest economy after World War II. It is a principle that allows a country to apply its competition laws to conduct that occurs outside its borders if that conduct has a substantial effect on the country's domestic market. As the doctrine has been the subject of much scholarly attention,[35] this section will provide on a concise overview.

The courts first endorsed the doctrine in *Alcoa* case of 1945.[36] After a series of jurisprudences that elaborated upon the standards,[37] Congress enacted the Foreign Trade Antitrust Improvement Act in 1982, which stipulated that the antitrust laws would not apply unless the conduct in question has a 'direct, substantial, and reasonably foreseeable effect' (1) on trade or commerce that is not trade or commerce with foreign nations or on import trade or import commerce with foreign nations or (2) on export trade or export commerce with foreign nations, which is a person engaged in such trade or commerce in the United States.[38]

While the doctrine of effect was initially controversial, competition laws would be ineffective and meaningless without its recognition. The issue under public international law studies has shifted to testing the reasonableness of such an application. By the end of the 1970s, the resolutions of the International Law Association[39] and the Institut de Droit International endorsed this doctrine as a substantive jurisdictional basis.[40]

2.2.2 Obtaining Evidence on Potential Violation of Competition Laws

The main issue concerning the enforcement of competition law was the obtaining of the evidence, which requires a complex series of operations. There are several ways for US officers to collect information, including court subpoenas, which are compulsory procedures, as well as voluntary cooperation from corporations and

[34] *American Banana Co v United Fruit Co*, 213 US 342 (1909).

[35] For the critical analysis of the effects doctrine, see Robert Y Jennings, 'Extraterritorial Jurisdiction and the United States Antitrust Laws' (1957) 33 British Year Book of International Law 146.

[36] *United States v Alcoa*, 148 F 2d 416, 444 (2d Cir 1945).

[37] *Timberlane Lumber Co v Bank of America*, 549 F 2d 597 (9th Cir 1976); *Mannington Mills Inc v Congoleum Corp*, 595 F 2d 1287, 1296 (3d Cir 1979); *Laker Airways Ltd v Pan American World Airways*, 559 F Supp 1124 (DDC 1983); *Laker Airways v Sabana Belgian World Airways*, 731 F 2d 909 (1984).

[38] Foreign Trade Antitrust Improvement Act, Pub L 97-290 (1982), 15 USC 6a.

[39] International Law Association and International Law Association, 'Extra-Territorial Application of Restrictive Trade Legislation (Including Anti-Trust Legislation)' (1972) 109 Recueil des Cours 139.

[40] Institut de Droit International, *Annuaire de l'institut de droit international*, 57 II (1977) 257.

individuals, and evidence collection through civil procedures. The latter two options include a collection of the deposition, an inquiry through a telephone call or an email, and a visit of the officials for investigation, all of which are performed with the consent of the individuals at the initial stage of the investigation.

The difficulty exists in detecting the existence of anti-competitive behaviours, as described in the Section 1. To counter this challenge, the US DOJ first introduced the Corporate Leniency Program in 1978. It initially did not function well. The US DOJ received 'only one leniency application per year, and the original program did not lead to the detection of a single international cartel'.[41] It was replaced with a more effective mechanism in 1993.[42] The revised programme was designed to provide incentives to cartel members, including foreign entities, to take the initiative to approach the competition authority, confess their participation in a cartel, and aid the competition law enforcers. Such cooperation with whistleblowers is necessary to uncover and collect necessary information on cartels, especially when it comes to the operation across national borders.[43]

2.3 Blocking Statutes

Because the United States applied its antitrust acts and proactive law enforcement measures against foreign corporations requiring them to produce documents, the European countries that refused the effects doctrine started to enact blocking statutes prohibiting its corporations from cooperating with foreign authorities' investigations. Much has been written in the international law literature, and this section provides an overview of the key developments.

This practice began in the 1950s. The Netherlands enacted the Economic Competition Law in 1956 to prohibit corporations within its territory from disclosing information to a foreign authority when the request violated international law or conflicted with Dutch law.[44] In the same period, the United States was trying to develop its shipping industry so that it could compel foreign corporations to comply with its antitrust law. Against this effort, Belgium,[45] Denmark,[46]

[41] Scott D Hammond, 'Cornerstone of an Effective Leniency Program' (22 November 2004) <https://www.justice.gov/archives/atr/speech/cornerstones-effective-leniency-program>.

[42] ibid.

[43] UNCTAD MENA Programme, 'Competition Guidelines: Leniency Programmes' (22 June 2016) <https://unctad.org/system/files/official-document/ditcclp2016d3_en.pdf>.

[44] *Wet Economische Mededinging* (28 June 1956) StBl 1958, 413, s 39.

[45] 'Belgium: Law of 27 March 1969, as amended, and Decree of 6 February concerning the Regulation of Marine and Air Transport', translated and reprinted in Alan Vaughan Lowe, *Extraterritorial Jurisdiction: An Annotated Collection of Legal Materials* (Grotius Publications 1983) 98.

[46] 'Denmark: Act No. 254, of 8 June 1967 on Limitation of Danish Shipowner's Freedom to Give Information to Authorities of Foreign Countries', translated and reprinted in Lowe (n 45) 114.

West Germany,[47] Finland,[48] Norway,[49] Sweden,[50] the United Kingdom,[51] and France[52] each enacted blocking statutes to prevent the entities from disclosing the information to foreign authorities.

For instance, the UK Shipping Contracts and Commercial Documents Act of 1964 was meant to secure the country's jurisdiction against 'encroachment by certain foreign requirements' regarding the production of documents and furnishing of information. If any person in the United Kingdom was required to produce or furnish to any court, tribunal, or authority of a foreign country any commercial document that was not within the territorial jurisdiction of that country or any commercial information needed to comply with documents that were not within that jurisdiction, then that requirement constituted an infringement of the jurisdiction that, under international law, belongs to the United Kingdom, and the Minister of the Crown was authorized to prohibit the individual from complying with the requirements.[53]

In France, the statute was enacted in 1968 in response to the FTC's administrative sanction against a French shipping company for its potential violation of antitrust laws.[54] Initially, the draft of the law limited its scope to the shipping industry. However, in the end, the law was applied to all economic and financial transactions. While the prohibition of disclosure was imposed on private individuals and corporations in the 1968 Act, the same obligation was imposed on the administrative authorities under the amended act in 1990.[55]

This trend was accelerated through a series of cartels concerning uranium production in the latter half of the 1970s.

[47] 'Germany: Law on Federal Duties in Matters Concerning Shipping, 24 May 1965 and Decree No.711 of 14 December 1966 on the Transmission of Shipping Documents to Foreign Authorities', translated and reprinted in Lowe (n 45) 118.

[48] 'Finland: Law Prohibiting a Shipowner in Certain Cases to Produce Documents, 4 January 1968', translated and reprinted in Lowe (n 45) 115.

[49] 'Norway: Act No. 3 of 16 June 1967 Authorizing the King in Council to Prohibit Shipowners to Transmit Information to Authorities of Foreign Countries', translated and reprinted in Lowe (n 45) 128.

[50] 'Sweden: Ordinance Regarding the Prohibition in Certain Cases for Shipowners to Produce Documents concerning the Swedish Shipping Industry, 13 May 1966', translated and reprinted in Lowe (n 45) 134.

[51] Shipping Contracts and Commercial Documents Act 1964, c 87, reprinted in (1964) 3 International Legal Materials 962.

[52] Loi n°68-678 du 26 juillet 1968 relative à la communication de documents et renseignements d'ordre économique, commercial, industriel, financier ou technique à des personnes physiques ou morales étrangères, [1968] Journal Officiel de la Rèpublique Francaise Recueil Dalloz 7267, [1968] Bulletin Lègislatif Dalloz 438.

[53] Shipping Contracts and Commercial Documents Act (n 51) art 2(1).

[54] Loi n° 68-678 (n 52).

[55] Loi n° 80-538 du 16 juillet 1980 relative à la communication de documents et renseignements d'ordre économique, commercial ou technique à des personnes physiques ou morales étrangères, (1980) Journal Officiel de la Rèpublique Francaise Recueil Dalloz 1799; (1980) Bulletin Lègislatif Dalloz 285. See Brigitte Ecolivet Herzog, 'The 1980 French Law on Documents and Information' (1981) 75 American Journal of International Law 382.

This issue of jurisdiction emerged in the Westinghouse Electric Corporation affair. Westinghouse was the leading US manufacturers and sellers of heavy electronics, including nuclear power. In 1976, Westinghouse started civil proceedings in the United States against Rio Tinto Zinc Corporations (RTZ), a UK company, and others, which it considered to have participated in the cartel, for breach of the US antitrust laws.[56] The United Kingdom, Canada, Austria, and South Africa protested against law enforcement in the United States.[57] Furthermore, the House of Lords of the United Kingdom[58] and the Supreme Court of Canada[59] held that the letters rogatory that the United States sent to the corporations violated sovereignty because they infringed with the public policy of each State.

In addition, in this proceeding, the United States issued letters of rogatory under the Hague Convention on the Taking of Evidence Abroad in Civil or Commercial Matters of 1970 to request materials to investigate the cartel case. The UK Court did not allow judicial cooperation of which procedure was provided under the UK Evidence (Proceedings in Other Jurisdictions) Act 1975.[60] The Court looked at 'the content and terms of the letters rogatory' and 'the spirit of the 1975 Act', according to which the requests in the letters were to be treated as requests for evidence for the purposes of 'civil proceedings' brought by the requesting court. The court confirmed that the RTZ companies were entitled to invoke the privilege against the production of documents because, if the documents were produced under the letters rogatory, the RTZ companies would be exposed to a greater risk of the commission initiating proceedings for the recovery of a fine against them than they are at present. The production of the documents could authenticate and corroborate the information already in the commission's possession and provide conclusive evidence of a breach of the ban on cartels by the companies and could lead the commission to decide to take action against the companies. Moreover, the individual witnesses were entitled to invoke the Fifth Amendment privilege against self-incrimination regarding the evidence sought through the letters rogatory. This was because the purpose for which the DOJ sought the evidence did not align with the purposes allowed under the 1975 Act. Specifically, the evidence was

[56] *Westinghouse Electric Corporation v Rio Algom Limited et al* 448 F Supp 1284 (1978); *In Re Uranium Antitrust Litigation* 617 F 2d 1248 (1980). Because of the uranium increase caused by this cartel, the Westinghouse's contract could not be implemented. Thus, the company sued twenty-nine companies, including Rio Tinto, in the US court for triple damage.

[57] Brief for the Government of Australia as Amici Curiae, 617 F 2d 1248 (9th Cir 1979) (No 79-1427); Brief for Government of Canada as Amici Curiae, 473 F Supp 382 (ND Ill 1979) (No 76-C-3830); Brief for the Government of United Kingdom as Amicus Curiae in Support for Petitioners, Aide Memoire of 23 June 1982, reproduced in Lowe (n 45) 156.

[58] *Rio Tinto Corporation and others v Westinghouse Electric Corporation* (1978) 1 ALL ER 434.

[59] Supreme Court of Canada, *Gulf Oil Corporation v Gulf Canada Ltd et al* [1980] 2 SCR 39 (18 March 1980). See Crystal L Witterick, 'Regulation of Competition in the Canada/US Context—Extraterritorial Reach of US Antitrust Law—A Canadian Perspective' (1998) 24 Canada–United States Law Journal 299, 304.

[60] *Rio Tinto Corporation v Westinghouse* (n 58) 459

not sought for civil proceedings as defined by the instrument, and since no criminal proceedings had yet been initiated by the DOJ, it could not have sought the evidence under this procedure. Therefore, enforcing the request would constitute an abuse of process.

This series of cases reinforced the trend of rejecting US law enforcement requests. Australia and Canada took the lead in enacting the blocking statutes immediately after the district court rendered the judgment on the *Westinghouse* case.

Australia's Foreign Proceedings (Prohibition of Certain Evidence) Act of 1976 stipulated that the attorney general impose restrictions when he or she is satisfied with the following. The first is that a foreign tribunal is exercising or proposing or likely to exercise jurisdiction or powers of a kind or in a manner not consistent with international law or comity in proceedings relevant to matters to which the laws or executive powers of the Commonwealth relate.[61] Alternatively, the second is that 'the imposition of the restrictions is desirable for protecting the national interest concerning matters to which the laws or executive powers of the Commonwealth relate'.[62] The attorney general may prohibit, among other things, the production of, or for, a foreign tribunal of documents in Australia and the engagement in any act in Australia that would result in such a production.[63] Furthermore, Australia enacted the Foreign Antitrust Judgments (Restriction of Enforcement) Act in 1979.[64] This law stipulated that triple damage antitrust judgments would not be recognized within Australia and prohibited the production of documents for such proceedings. These blocking statutes were abolished in Australia after bilateral agreement with the United States was reached.[65]

Similarly, Canada prohibited the disclosure of conversations, discussions, and information about meetings to a third party or foreign authorities without the government's consent under the Uranium Information Security Regulations enacted in 1976.[66] Then, after the Seventh Circuit issued the judgment of appeals in 1980, the United Kingdom,[67] France,[68] and New Zealand[69] enacted laws to the same effect.

The enforcement of antitrust law faced difficulties because of the existence of these blocking statutes. A notable example is the *Laker Airways* case. British Airways demanded an injunction against the proceeding in the United States

[61] Foreign Proceedings (Prohibition of Certain Evidence) Act, Act No 121 of 1976, s 4.
[62] ibid.
[63] ibid s 5.
[64] Foreign Antitrust Judgments (Restriction of Enforcement) Act, Act No 13 of 1979.
[65] See Section 2.2.
[66] Uranium Information Security Regulations, Statutory Orders and Regulations 76-644, Public Statutes 1976-2368 (21 September 1976).
[67] Protection of Trading Interests Act 1980, c 11.
[68] Loi n°80-538 du 16 juillet 1980 relative a la communication de documents ou renseignements d'ordre economique commercial ou technique a des personnes physiques ou morales etrangeres, J O 1799. English translation is available at Lowe (n 45) 116. See also Herzog, '(n 55) 382.
[69] Evidence Amendment Act (No 2) 1980, No 27.

brought by Laker Airways, which the UK High Court issued,[70] after the order was issued by the UK Secretary General based on the Protection of Trading Interests Act to prohibit the submission of the documents.[71] The House of Lords overturned the High Court's decision, holding that the injunction's requirements were not satisfied.[72] The case ended with a settlement.

Other examples include the case in which the FTC required Pilkington's subsidiary in the United Kingdom and Nippon Sheet Glass Company of Japan to submit a deposition to investigate their restrictive practices. The United Kingdom protested these proceedings, and Pilkington did not comply with the request.[73] There were similar cases in which a corporation refused to submit such information with the governments' support, with West Germany being an exception.[74]

As described in Section 2.2, the US courts considered a prohibition in the balancing of interest approach.[75] With the exception of a limited number of cases in the early 1950s, the US courts have never denied a foreign party's obligation to produce documents even if there was a blocking statute that prohibits the party to comply with the US court's order. However, against the practical difficulties of enforcement, the FTC and DOJ, rather than the courts, realized the inconvenience of not obtaining the necessary evidence.

2.4 The Harmonization of the Competition Laws

2.4.1 Scope of the Application of Competition Laws

(1) EU's Enforcement of Competition Law to Non-EU Corporations

This stalemate was resolved following the development of the competition policy in the European Community (EC).[76] The Rome Treaty of 1957, which established the European Economic Community (EEC), prohibited anti-competitive measures because it was necessary to secure fair competition among the corporations

[70] *British Airways Board v Laker Airways Ltd* [1983] 3 All ER 404 (CA).

[71] Order, 23 June 1983, cited in ibid.

[72] *British Airways Board v Laker Airways Ltd* [1985] AC 58, 84. See also Lawrence Collins, 'Provisional and Protective Measures in International Litigation' (1992) 234 Recueil des Cours 9.

[73] See *Nippon Sheet Glass Company, Ltd* 55 FR 11256 (27 March 1990).

[74] West Germany established a blocking statute against the antitrust regulations of the shipping industry, but did not enact a comprehensive blocking statute. The government of West Germany did not protest against the subpoena issued against the wholly owned subsidiary of the First National City Bank. See *United States v First National City Bank* 396 F 2d 897 (2nd Cir 1968).

[75] For the analysis of the balancing of interests, see Chapter 4. See also Bruno Zanettin, *Cooperation between Antitrust Agencies at the International Level* (Hart Publishing 2002) 51.

[76] For the practices by the 1980s in Germany, EEC, France, the United Kingdom, Switzerland, Italy, and Australia, in addition to the United States, see Cornelis Canenbley, *Enforcing Antitrust against Foreign Enterprises: Procedural Problems in the Extraterritorial Application of Antitrust Laws* (Kluwer 1981).

for market integration.[77] The development of the competition law in the area started after the European Community was established under the Brussels Treaty of 1965.[78] The European Commission began to govern the competition policy.

The European Community Treaty Articles 81(1) and 82 provided for the competition policy as a mandate of the organization. Article 81(1) prohibits anti-competitive behaviours that may affect trade between EU member States and have as their object or effect the prevention, restriction, or distortion of competition within the internal market. Article 82 prohibits the abuse of a dominant position within the internal market so far as it may affect trade between EU member States. Both articles are succeeded to the Treaty on the Functioning of the European Union (TFEU) Articles 101 and 102. Under the TFEU, the European Commission directly enforces EU competition rules. The directorate general for competition is primarily responsible for the implementation. Each member State also has its mandate to establish its national competition law and the European Commission cooperates with the national competition authorities.

In 2002, the European Union adopted the Regulation No 1/2003 for organizing the enforcement of the competition law.[79] The Regulation provides that the European Commission may by decision impose financial sanction against violation of competition laws.[80] However, such decisions 'shall not be of a criminal law nature'.[81]

The development of the competition law and policies altered the European Community's approach towards law enforcement against foreign entities. While most European countries opposed the excessive exercise of jurisdiction of the United States for the implementation of its antitrust law, the European Commission affirmed the application of the anti-competition law across borders for the following reasons.

The first was the recognition of the single economic entity doctrine. In general, two or more legal entities may be deemed as a single economic unit for competition law, irrespective of their independent legal status.[82] This doctrine affirms the application of the EU competition law to a foreign subsidiary of an EU parent company and a foreign parent company of which the subsidiary is located in the European Union. This is virtually the same as the unity of enterprise doctrine affirmed by US courts.

[77] Treaty establishing the European Economic Community (signed on 25 March 1957, entered into force on 1 January 1958) arts 85 and 86.

[78] Treaty establishing a single Council and a single Commission of the European Communities (signed on 8 April 1965, entered into force on 13 July 1967) [1965] OJ 152/2.

[79] Council Regulation (EC) No 1/2003 of 16 December 2002 on the implementation of the rules on competition laid down in Articles 81 and 82 of the Treaty [2003] OJ L1/1.

[80] Regulation No 1/2003, art 23(1)–(2).

[81] ibid art 23(5).

[82] For the development of this doctrine, see Okeoghene Odudu and David Bailey, 'The Single Economic Entity Doctrine in EU Competition Law' (2014) 51 Common Market Law Review 1721.

The validity of this doctrine was disputed before the *Dyestuffs* case, which occurred when the United Kingdom was not a member of the European Community. Imperial Chemical Industries, a dye business company headquartered in Britain, joined a cartel in Switzerland and implemented it through a subsidiary in the area, which resulted in an increase in the price of aniline dyes in Italy, the Netherlands, Belgium, Luxemburg, and Germany.[83] The Commission decided to impose a fine on Imperial Chemical Industries for violating the EC treaty. The United Kingdom objected to its jurisdiction before the EEC in 1969. The concept of an enterprise entity or reciprocating partnership would contradict established principles because it would disregard the separate personalities of the parent and subsidiary.[84]

However, the European Court of Justice (ECJ) affirmed the EC's jurisdiction against Imperial Chemical Industries.[85] It held that the fact that the subsidiary had a legal personality did not serve to rule out the possibility that its conduct was attributable to the parent company. It could be a case where the subsidiary did not independently determine its market behaviour but essentially followed the instructions the parent company gave. If the subsidiary did not have autonomy in determining its course of conduct on the market, then the prohibition of Article 85(1) of the treaty was inapplicable to the relationship between it and the parent company, with which it forms an economic unity. Since an affiliated group so structured forms an agreement, then the parent company can, under certain circumstances, be held responsible for the subsidiary's actions.[86]

The second reason was the implementation doctrine, whereby the court assesses the extent of the anti-competitive conduct within the European Economic Area (EEA). Agreements, concerted practices, decisions of associations of undertakings, or abuses of dominant position that are conceived abroad by foreign undertakings fall within the EC jurisdiction if they concern or are implemented in the European Union.[87] In the *Wood Pulp* case of 1988, the ECJ held that the cartel upheld the implementation of an agreement concluded between wood pulp companies in the United States, Canada, Norway, Sweden, and Finland violated Article 85 of the Treaty. The court looked at not only the selling of goods but also the imports occupying two-thirds of the market. Generally, this doctrine requires a

[83] Case 48/69, *Imperial Chemical Industries Ltd v Commission of the European Communities*, Judgment of 14 July 1972, ECLI:EU:C:1972:70.

[84] Robert Jenning, in his expert opinion, concluded that the EEC has jurisdiction over Imperial Chemical Industries only to the extent that its conduct within the frontiers of the Community was involved, and where this conduct is a violation of the Community rules of competition and any conduct of Imperial Chemical Industries outside of the Community was beyond the Community's jurisdiction. Jennings (n 35) 159.

[85] Case 48/69 (n 83).

[86] ibid para 134.

[87] OECD, 'Working Party No. 3 on Co-Operation and Enforcement' (2008) DAF/COMP/WP3/WD(2008)93.

more rigorous connection between conduct and territory in the EEA than does the doctrine about the effect of the United States.[88]

The third reason was the qualified effect doctrine, whereby the Commission needs to show that the conduct has had substantial, immediate, and foreseeable effects on the EEA. A 2008 report submitted to the OECD explained that this doctrine is 'closely related to the implementation doctrine but is considered to be more precise and covering more areas of restrictive competition conduct'.[89]

The EU law came close to US jurisprudence concerning its application to foreign corporations. In fact, the European Commission is in a sense more aggressive than the United States to impose obligations under the competition laws. The dispute between British Airlines and Laker Airways was virtually the last case where the issue of sovereignty was squarely disputed.

The European Commission's powers of investigation have steadily expanded since the early 2000s. The methods that the European Commission has relied on are as follows.[90] The first is to require corporations to submit information. A financial sanction will be imposed if the corporation does not comply with the request.[91] The second is to obtain information from a subsidiary or branch residing within the EU territory.[92] When the subsidiary or the branch possesses or controls the information, the entity must comply with the request. If the parent company does not adhere to the submission, then the subsidiary will be penalized.[93] The third is to require the disclosure of information based on the Commission's power of inspection and fact-finding powers. In addition, the European Union introduced leniency programmes in 1996, which allow the Commission to obtain voluntary cooperation from non-EU cooperation effectively.[94]

The Regulation No 1/2003 allowed the Commission to interview people who might have useful information and to record their statements.[95] It also gave the Commission officials the power to request any information relevant to the inspection. The Recital of the Regulation recognized that the concerned parties should have the right to be heard by the Commission.[96] Third parties whose interests

88 Case 89/85, 104/85, 114/85, 116/85, 117/85 and 125–129/85 *A Ahlström Osakeyhtiö v Commission of the European Communities* [1988] ECR 5193.
89 OECD (n 87).
90 International Competition Policy Advisory Committee, 'Final Report to the Attorney General and Assistant Attorney General for Antitrust' (2000) <http://www.justice.gov/atr/icpac/finalreport.html>. All websites were last accessed on 31 March 2025.
91 Council Regulation 17/6228 art 18(3).
92 ibid art 11.
93 ibid art 18. European Commission, 'Dealing with the Commission: Notifications, Complaints, Inspections and Fact Finding Powers under Articles 85 and 86 of the EEC Treaty' (CV-95-96-552-EN-C) (1997).
94 Georgios Kiriazis, 'Jurisdiction and Cooperation Issues in the Investigation of International Cartels' (2001) 2 ABA Advanced International Cartel Workshop 6.
95 Council Regulation (EC) No 1/2003 of 16 December 2002 on the implementation of the rules on competition laid down in Articles 81 and 82 of the Treaty [2003] OJ L1/1, art 19.
96 ibid recital 32.

might be affected by a decision should have the chance to submit their observations beforehand.[97] In addition, the Regulation affirmed the defence rights of the concerned parties, including the right of access to the file, as well as the interests to business secrets and the confidentiality of information exchanged within the network.[98]

Regulation No 773/2004 clarified the power to take statements as follows.[99] When the Commission interviews a person with their consent, it must, at the start of the interview, state the legal basis and purpose of the interview and remind them that participation is voluntary. The Commission must also inform the person of its intention to record the interview.[100] The interview may be conducted by any means, including by telephone or electronic means.[101] The Commission may record the statements made by the persons interviewed in any form.[102] A copy of any recording shall be made available to the person interviewed for approval.[103] As Section 4 will explore, the EU law has developed its regulations to both expand its mandate and to ensure the due process.

(2) States Other Than the United States and the European Union

There were a series of efforts made to harmonize the substantive aspect of competition laws through international organizations such as the OECD[104] and the United Nations Conference on Trade and Development (UNCTAD).[105] There were regional efforts made in the European Union and the Southern Common Market (Mercosur) framework in Latin American countries.[106] The OECD and UNCTAD instruments were legally non-binding, and the Mercosur framework did not come to fruition. In the 1990s, however, most of the States came to be equipped with competition laws against the background of the integration of markets and the increase in multinational corporations.

Because of the harmonization of the competition laws in the United States and the European Union, there were fewer conflicts regarding the substantial parts of

[97] ibid.

[98] ibid.

[99] Commission Regulation (EC) No 773/2004 of 7 April 2004 relating to the conduct of proceedings by the Commission pursuant to Articles 81 and 82 of the EC Treaty [2004] OJ L123/18.

[100] ibid art 3(1).

[101] ibid art 3(2).

[102] ibid art 3(3).

[103] ibid.

[104] OECD, *Declaration on International Investment and Multinational Enterprises*, OECD/LEGAL/0144 <https://legalinstruments.oecd.org/public/doc/241/241.en.pdf>.

[105] United Nations, 'The United Nations Set of Principles and Rules on Competition, The Set of Multilaterally Agreed Equitable Principles and Rules for the Control of Restrictive Business Practices' (2000) TD/RBP/CONF/10/Rev.2.

[106] Inventory of the Competition Policy Agreements, Treaties and Other Arrangements Existing in the Western Hemisphere, submitted by the OAS Trade Unit to the FTAA Working Group on Competition Policies, Common Market of the Southern Cone (MERCOSUR), Protocol of the Defense of Competition <http://www.ftaa-alca.org/Wgroups/WGCP/English/cpa/cpa3_e.asp>.

collecting information and evidence from foreign corporations, such as protests against unilateral law enforcement actions by the other party.

States other than the United States and the European Union are generally cautious in applying their laws against foreign corporations. It is also noted that only States with sizable markets have a reason to exercise their laws based on the effects doctrine. Otherwise, corporations can simply avoid countries that excessively exercise their jurisdiction. However, those non-US and non-EU countries generally came to recognize the equivalent of the effect doctrine.

For instance, the Japanese Supreme Court endorsed the application of Japanese Antimonopoly Law against the case that took place outside of the country in 2019.[107] On the other hand, while the Japanese Fair Trade Commission (JFTC), Japan's competition authority, occasionally investigates foreign corporations that operate in Japan, their approach is based on the territorial principle and does not rely on the unity of enterprise doctrine, as the principle of separation of legal personality is strictly upheld under Japanese corporate law.

China takes a proactive approach against antitrust law, the Antimonopoly Law. Once its 2008 competition law became applicable, the competition authority started to require information against foreign companies in the 2010s.[108] The law applies to conduct and transactions outside China that have or may have an impact on competition within the Chinese market. This includes foreign mergers and acquisitions if they meet specific revenue thresholds within China. The State Administration for Market Regulation enforces these provisions and can impose conditions on international transactions to ensure they do not negatively affect competition in China.

The Korean Fair Trade Commission applies the Monopoly Regulation and Fair Trade Act to foreign entities if their actions have a significant impact on the Korean market. This includes the behaviours of firms located outside Korea that affects competition or consumers within the domestic market.[109] Additionally, the Korean Fair Trade Commission has the authority to review and approve foreign

[107] Supreme Court, 12 December 2019, Case Heisei 28 (Gyo Hi) 233, 71(10) Minshu 1958. The case involved the application of Japan's Antimonopoly Act concerning the imposition of fines on businesses engaged in a cartel for the sale prices of television cathode ray tubes agreed upon outside Japan. The Court upheld the application of the law based on the nature of competition law but did not provide clarity on its assessment from an international law perspective. For Asian countries' passive approach on extraterritorial application of their laws in general, see also Mari Takeuchi, 'Asian Experience with Extraterritoriality' in Austen Parrish and Cedric Ryngaert (eds), *Research Handbook on Extraterritoriality in International Law* (Edward Elgar Publishing 2023) 164.

[108] Antimonopoly Law (issued on 30 August 2007, entered into force on 1 August 2008) <https://www.gov.cn/flfg/2007-08/30/content_732591.htm>. The law was last amended in 2022. See also Michael G Faure and Xinzhu Zhang, 'Towards an Extraterritorial Application of the Chinese Anti-Monopoly Law That Avoids Trade Conflicts' (2013) 45 George Washington International Law Review 101.

[109] Monopoly Regulation and Fair Trade Act, Act No 4198 of 1990, amended by Act No 7315, 31 December 2004, art 2-2. An unofficial translated version by Korea Legislation Research Institute and Korea Law Translation Center is available at <https://elaw.klri.re.kr/eng_service/lawView.do?lang=ENG&hseq=61424>.

mergers and acquisitions if they have potential competitive effects in Korea.[110] While nuanced difference exists, national authorities and courts accepts the effects doctrine in many States and jurisdictions.

It is noted that the World Trade Organization (WTO) played a role in the development of the competition laws. Competition policies, which benefits liberalization by ensuring fair and transparent transactions, affect global trade.[111] It was in 1996 that the WTO Ministerial Conference decided to establish the Working Group on the Interaction between Trade and Competition Policy to study this issue, which all WTO members participated. The issues addressed by this working group are relevant to cross-border criminal sanctions for anti-competitive behaviour. They focused on clarifying key principles, including transparency, non-discrimination, and procedural fairness, as well as modalities for voluntary cooperation. It supported the consensus among countries, including developing States, on the importance of suppressing anti-competitive actions.

2.4.2 Use of Administrative Procedures in Criminal Investigations

States have begun to criminalize serious violations of competition laws, particularly in cases involving cartels. Such sanctions may include fines and imprisonment of individuals responsible for the conduct. In the meantime, civil or administrative sanctions became severe as well. They include substantial fines, divestitures, injunctive relief, and other remedies aimed at restoring competition, deterring future violations, and nurturing the culture to comply with competition laws.

It became common that the law enforcing authorities use the materials obtained from administrative investigation for criminal proceedings.[112] The competition authorities usually have the mandate of criminal investigation, albeit under the supervision of an independent judicial court. This practice arises not only because the same conduct can lead to both administrative and criminal liability but also because antitrust investigations are so complex that regular law enforcement agencies lack the expertise to handle them.

The primary issue lies in the inherent leniency of administrative proceedings compared to criminal proceedings. Administrative investigations typically do not require the court-issued search and seizure warrants. This approach is effective because corporations may prefer to cooperate with law enforcement authorities rather than face criminal prosecution and the potential termination of their business.

[110] ibid art 3.

[111] World Trade Organization, 'Working Group on the Interaction between Trade and Competition Policy (WGTCP)—History, Mandates and Decisions' <https://www.wto.org/english/tratop_e/comp_e/history_e.htm>.

[112] For the problems caused by the overlaps of the proceedings in two fields in general, see Giulia Lasagni, *Banking Supervision and Criminal Investigation* (Springer 2019) 24; Vanessa Franssen and Katalin Ligeti, 'Current Challenges in Economic and Financial Criminal Law in Europe and the US' in Katalin Ligeti and Vanessa Franssen (eds), *Challenges in the Field of Economic and Financial Crime in Europe and the US* (Hart Publishing 2017) 10.

Consequently, employing materials obtained from administrative investigations in criminal proceedings can obscure the distinction between these two legal processes. This practice has the potential to compromise the rights of the targeted corporations and individuals, which will discussed in Section 4.

2.4.3 Harmonization of Investigation Methods

Harmonization occurred also in the procedural realm. Since the 2000s, the European Union, Australia, Japan, and other jurisdictions have developed procedures for obtaining materials and information to enhance their competition laws. One significant development has been the incorporation of leniency programmes designed to incentivize whistleblowers to come forward with information about anti-competitive practices, following the successful model established by the United States. This programme has been instrumental in uncovering and prosecuting numerous high-profile cartels.

The European Union introduced its leniency programme in 1996, which was replaced with a new one in 2002 and 2006. It allowed companies involved in a cartel to receive immunity from fines or a reduction in fines in exchange for providing evidence against other cartel members..[113]

The Republic of Korea implemented a leniency programme in 1997, which was the first in the Asian region. The Korea Fair Trade Commission has successfully used this programme to dismantle cartels in various industries, such as the construction and telecommunications sectors.[114]

Similarly, Japan revised its Antimonopoly Act in 2005 to enhance the enforcement power of the JFTC.[115] The amendment provided the JFTC with criminal investigative power to deal with serious violation of the law and introduced the leniency programme.[116] The JFTC offers immunity or reductions in penalties for companies that voluntarily report their involvement in cartels and cooperate with investigations. This programme has led to significant enforcement actions,

[113] Commission Notice on Immunity from fines and reduction of fines in cartel cases [2006] OJ C298/17; [2016] OJ C144/23.

[114] Monopoly Regulation and Fair Trade Act, Act No 4198 of 1990, amended by Act No 6371 of 2001, art 22-2. See OECD, 'Working Party No. 3 on Co-operation and Enforcement, Roundtable on challenges and co-ordination of leniency programmes—Note by Korea' (2018), DAF/COMP/WP3/WD(2018)7.

[115] Act on Prohibition of Private Monopolization and Maintenance of Fair Trade (Antimonopoly Act), Act No 54 of 1947, revised in 2005. An unofficial translated version is available at Japan Fair Trade Commission's website at <https://www.jftc.go.jp/en/legislation_gls/amended_ama09/index.html>.

[116] For the background of the introduction of the leniency programme, see Steven Van Uytsel, 'The Original Leniency Programme of Japan' in Steven Van Uytsel, Mark Fenwick, and Yoshiteru Uemura (eds), *Leniency in Asian Competition Law* (CUP 2022) 129. Van Uytsel describes that the turning point was when 'the JFTC demonstrated the substantial difference between a leniency programme and plea bargaining and the possibility of introducing a leniency programme without it claiming any discretion'. For further development afterwards, see Steven Van Uytsel and Yoshiteru Uemura, 'Negotiated Leniency in Japan Embedded in Ever-Increasing Sanctions' in Steven Van Uytsel, Mark Fenwick, and Yoshiteru Uemura (eds), *Leniency in Asian Competition Law* (CUP 2022) 159.

including the crackdown on the auto parts cartel in the early 2010s, which involved major international companies and resulted in substantial fines.[117]

The OECD report indicates that over fifty jurisdictions have adopted the programme, with the majority doing so between 2000 and 2010.[118] As these cases illustrate, countries came to adopt elaborated procedures for obtaining information so that competition authorities can detect anti-competitive behaviours.

3. Cooperation Mechanisms among Competition Authorities: The Significance and Limits of Positive Comity

3.1 Types of Cooperation Mechanisms

It has been a recommendation of the OECD since 1967 to establish cooperation mechanisms for enforcing competition laws.[119] However, from the 1970s to the 1980s, the situation shifted in the opposite direction, marked by non-cooperation and antagonism, as described in Section 2. Bilateral agreements became possible only after the convergence of the jurisdictional conflicts.

Subsequently, there has been a noticeable increase in cooperation among different jurisdictions in investigating and enforcing competition laws. Authorities began to collaborate closely by sharing information. The leading case was the US's enactment of the International Antitrust Enforcement Assistance Act, which authorized the Federal Trade Commission and the DOJ to enter into mutual assistance agreements with foreign antitrust authorities.[120] This development was underpinned by the transformation of domestic laws to enable the sharing of such information with foreign authorities.

These mechanisms can be categorized into the following three types: negative comity, positive comity, and enforcement cooperation.[121] Initially, treaties often included provisions for both negative and positive comity. However, in more recent practices, agreements tend to include only positive comity. These comity-based approaches do not mandate cooperation between State parties but provide guidelines for collaboration when both parties opt to engage in law enforcement activities. In contrast, enforcement cooperation, the third type, obliges the third party to collect and provide information within its jurisdiction.

[117] For the latest practice, see OECD, 'Working Party No. 3 on Co-Operation and Enforcement: The Future of Effective Leniency Programmes—Note by Japan' (2023) DAF/COMP/WP3/WD(2023)8.

[118] OECD, 'OECD Competition Trend' (2022) 44 <https://doi.org/10.1787/a9c9f711-en>.

[119] OECD, Council Recommendation Concerning Cooperation between Members Countries on Restrictive Business Practices Affecting International Trade (5 October 1967), reprinted in Lowe (n 45) 243.

[120] International Antitrust Enforcement Assistance Act, Pub L 103-438, 108 Stat 4597 (1994).

[121] See, in general, Zanettin (n 75) 53, 114.

In every instance, there has been no dispute that a treaty does not prevent the State party from enforcing its competition law against a corporation that is subject to the other party. It is often the case that a treaty explicitly provides a provision for this effect. It is noteworthy that, by contrast, the existence of a MLAT has been the subject of debate as to whether it precludes States from resorting to alternative, non-treaty mechanisms for the collection of evidence, as discussed in Chapter 4, Section 4.

In addition, there are cases in which the MLAT provides the obligation for co-operation regarding the violation of competition laws, which are criminally sanctioned. For instance, the Canada–US MLAT of 1985[122] was used in the *Plastics Inc* case[123] and the *Fax Paper Industry* case[124] to collect criminal evidence. However, the reliance on the MLAT is insufficient from the perspective of competition co-operation when it does not cover a hard-core cartel, which constitutes a criminal offence.[125] The following sections will examine the characteristics of three corporation agreements compared to the conventional criminal cooperation.

3.2 The Characteristics of the Agreements

3.2.1 Negative Comity Agreements

The first is the analysis of negative comity agreements. Examples of this type of agreement are the West Germany–US Agreement of 1976,[126] the Australia–US Agreement of 1982,[127] and the Canada–US Memorandum of Understanding (MOU) of 1984.[128] The latter two examples were concluded in response to the blocking statutes enacted to oppose unilateral law enforcement in the Westinghouse case.

For instance, the Australia–US Agreement provided notifications, consultations, and considerations of the important interests of the other States. However, it did not enforce competition without obtaining the explicit consent of the other State. One of the characteristics of the US–Australia Agreement, compared with

[122] US–Canada Treaty on Mutual Legal Assistance in Criminal Matters (signed on 18 March 1985, entered into force on 24 January 1990) Annex.

[123] *United States v Plastics Inc, et al*, US Antitrust Cases (CCH) para 45094, Cases 4070–4073 (1994).

[124] US DOJ, 'Antitrust Division breaks International Price Fixing Conspiracy in Fax Paper Industry' (14 July 1994) No 94-382.

[125] ibid.

[126] Federal Republic of Germany–United States, Agreement relating to Mutual Cooperation regarding Restrictive Business Practices (23 June 1976) 27 UST 1956, reprinted in 4 Trade Reg Rep (CCH) s 13501.

[127] Agreement between the Government of the United States of America and the Government of Australia relating to Cooperation on Antitrust Matters (29 June 1982), 4 Trade Reg Rep s 13502.

[128] Memorandum of Understanding between the Government of the United States of America and the Government of Canada as to Notification, Consultation and Cooperation with Respect to the Application of National Antitrust Laws (9 March 1984), 4 Trade Reg Rep s 13503A, reprinted in (1984) 23 International Legal Materials 275.

a conventional MLAT, is its non-reciprocity. Notifications from Australia to the United States were optional, while notifications from the DOJ or FTC were mandatory when the application of the law would affect the laws of Australia. In the same vein, consultation from Australia to the United States was optional, but the other way around was mandatory. This approach aimed to reflect the interests of the State parties to the agreement.

The Canada–US Agreement was based on the negative comity, but its content was more detailed than that of Australia. Canada had established a blocking statute against the 'excessive' exercise of jurisdiction of the United States, but the need to maintain economic relations was greater. Therefore, in 1959 and 1969, joint statements concerning antitrust matters were adopted, confirming that they would notify each other.[129] The 1984 MOU was based on these statements. First, the MOU provided that the party would notify and consult with the other party when it was aware that law enforcement or the investigation would affect the competition policy of the other party.[130] Furthermore, it required that requests made to private individuals within the other State's territory must be made on a voluntary basis.[131] If such requests were coercive, prior notification and consultation were needed. Such requests had to be performed in a specified manner rather than as a comprehensive request.[132] Nonetheless, the 1984 MOU used the word 'will', instead of 'shall'. Therefore, these obligations were considered non-binding.

3.2.2 Positive Comity Agreements

Positive comity was introduced to further develop cooperation among State parties to avoid conflict more directly. The 1991 EU–US Agreement was, as described in Section 3.2.1 or reviewed, introduced against the background that the competition policy of the European Union matured and that the scope of the jurisdiction that the European Commission exercised became assimilated with that of the United States.[133]

However, the agreement neither required an implementation of an obligation nor an enactment or modification of the domestic law. The competition authorities would render assistance to the authorities of the other party in their enforcement activities, 'to the extent compatible with the assisting party's laws and important interests, and within its reasonable available resources'.[134] Cooperation was to

[129] Joint Statement concerning Cooperation in Antitrust Matters (3 November 1969), reprinted in (1969) 8 International Legal Materials 1305.

[130] US–Canada Memorandum of Understanding (n 128) art 2.

[131] ibid art 8(3).

[132] ibid.

[133] It was not that member States unanimously accepted the agreement. France disputed the authority of the European Union to conclude such an agreement. The ECJ held that the Commission had the mandate to conclude the treaty but it required Council's approval, which was given afterwards. Agreement between the Commission and the United States regarding the application of their competition laws (Judgment, 9 August 1994), Case C-327/91, *French Republic v Commission of the European Communities* [1994] ECR I-3641.

[134] Agreement between the Government of the United States of America and the Commission of the European Communities regarding the application of their competition laws (signed on 23 September 1991, entered into force on 23 September 1991) TIAS 91-923, art 4(1).

be engaged in 'in cases where both parties ha[d] an interest in pursuing enforcement activities' and when 'they agree[d] that it [wa]s in their mutual interest to coordinate their enforcement activities'.[135] It was particularly provided that 'neither party is required to provide information to the other party if disclosure of that information to the requesting party (a) is prohibited by the law of the party possessing the information, or (b) would be incompatible with important interests of the party possessing the information'.[136] Furthermore, among other things, parties agreed to 'maintain, to the fullest extent possible, the confidentiality of any information provided to it confidence by the other party under this agreement'.[137] Because the 1991 agreement was successful, a renewed agreement was concluded in 1998.[138] The cases where a positive combination was used for clarification were noted.[139] The basic structure was retained.

The development is viewed positively because collaborations involving positive comity are on the rise. One possible reason for this increase is the flexibility of the mechanism. The first cooperation between the two authorities after the conclusion of the agreement was the investigation of Microsoft Corporation for its anti-competitive actions, which the Novel Corporation raised to the European Commission. In this case, Microsoft negotiated with the authorities to avoid the division. Furthermore, Microsoft waived its privilege to allow the DOJ and European Commission to exchange information and requested that the two authorities coordinate to expedite the procedure. It is generally understood that positive comity functions effectively.[140]

The same mechanism has been incorporated into other treaties, such as the EU–Canada,[141] Brazil–US,[142] Israel–US,[143] Japan–US,[144] Mexico–US,[145]

135 ibid art 4(2).
136 ibid art 8(1).
137 ibid art 8(2).
138 Agreement between the European Communities and the Government of the United States of America on the application of positive comity principles in the enforcement of their competition laws [1998] OJ L173/28.
139 ibid art 4.
140 Laura E Keegan, 'The 1991 US/EC Competition Agreement: A Glimpse of the Future through the United States v. Microsoft Corp. Window' (1996) 2 Journal of International Legal Studies 149.
141 Agreement between the Government of Canada and the European Communities regarding the application of their competition laws [1999] OJ L175/50.
142 Agreement between the Government of the Federative Republic of Brazil and the Government of the United States of America regarding Cooperation between their Competition Authorities in the Enforcement of their Competition Laws (26 October 1999) <http://www.justice.gov/atr/us-brazil-cooperation-agreement>.
143 Agreement between the Government of the United States of America and the Government of the State of Israel Regarding the Application of Their Competition Laws (15 March 1999) <http://www.justice.gov/atr/agreement-between-government-united-states-america-and-government-state-israel-regarding>.
144 Agreement between the Government of Japan and the Government of the United States of America concerning Cooperation on Anticompetitive Activities (7 October 1999) <http://www.jftc.go.jp/en/int_relations/agreements.files/usagree.pdf>.
145 Agreement between the Government of the United Mexican States and the Government of the United States of America regarding the Application of their Competition Laws (11 July 2000) <http://www.justice.gov/atr/agreement-between-government-united-states-america-and-government-united-mexican-states>.

Canada–Mexico,[146] EU–Japan,[147] Canada–US,[148] Canada–Japan,[149] and EU–India treaties.[150] Positive comity has been widely accepted in State practices.

3.2.3 Enforcement Cooperation

One significant limitation of positive comity agreements is that State parties are unable to request coercive measures, relying instead on voluntary cooperation. Some States prefer enforcement cooperation agreements so that they can secure compliance of the counterparty and enforcement across jurisdictions. These agreements often include provisions for mutual assistance in investigations, exchange of information, and coordinated enforcement actions, aiming to strengthen the effectiveness of international cooperation in regulatory matters.

The France–West Germany Agreement in 1984 was an early example that made it possible for States to request mandatory measures.[151] The signing of the agreement was triggered by a synthetic rubber cartel case in 1980. The case was brought about when Firestone, a French company, sold its rubber section to Bayer, another French company. Bundeskartellamt, a German competition authority, issued an injunction against this deal on grounds that the sale violated German competition law. However, this decision was overturned on appeal and was not enforced because the authorities did not fully consider the limitations of jurisdiction imposed by public international law. The two countries then entered into an agreement and promised to take into account each other's national interests in law enforcement. The agreement stated that a party may request that the authorities of the other party provide information on anti-competitive practices and market conditions in the territory of the other party. However, a request may be refused if it is determined that such information is in violation of the confidentiality provisions; if the requested information affects the sovereignty, security, important economic interests, or public policy of the requested State; or if the State is otherwise unresponsive to the request for information. However, this agreement limited not only

[146] Agreement between the Government of Canada and the Government of the United Mexican States regarding the Application of their Competition Laws (15 November 2001) <http://www.competitionbureau.gc.ca/eic/site/cb-bc.nsf/eng/01594.html>.

[147] Agreement between the European Community and the Government of Japan concerning Cooperation on Anti-competitive Activities [2003] OJ L 183/12.

[148] Agreement between the Government of Canada and the Government of the United States of America on the Application of Positive Comity Principles to the Enforcement of their Competition Laws (5 October 2004) <http://www.competitionbureau.gc.ca/eic/site/cb-bc.nsf/eng/01269.html>.

[149] Agreement between the Government of Canada and the Government of Japan concerning Cooperation on Anticompetitive Activities (6 September 2005) <http://www.competitionbureau.gc.ca/eic/site/cb-bc.nsf/eng/01944.html>.

[150] Memorandum of Understanding (21 November 2013) <http://ec.europa.eu/competition/international/bilateral/india_agreement.pdf>.

[151] Agreement between the Government of the Federal Republic of Germany and the Government of the French Republic Concerning Cooperation on Restrictive Practices (28 May 1984), reprinted in (1987) 26 International Legal Materials 531.

the information that could be requested but also the wide range of grounds for refusal.[152]

More recent enforcement agreements generally stipulate the right of parties to request confidential corporate information. Examples include the US–Australia Agreement in 1997,[153] the Denmark–Iceland–Norway Agreement in 2001,[154] and the Australia–Japan Agreement in 2015.[155] While agreements based on active concession only exchange information, such as public information and the date of an on-site investigation, these enforcement cooperation agreements widen the scope of information to be shared and require the sharing of information seized by the authorities themselves, such as emails and documents in which cartel promises are made among peers or companies instructing employees to conceal information.

The US–Australia Agreement, signed in 1997, obliges both civil and criminal partners to share evidence of competition law enforcement on a reciprocal basis. This agreement was designed to exchange a wide range of information based on an MOU on securities law and futures trading with the MLAT.

In terms of the exchange of information, the requirement of a punitive nature has been removed for both parties, regardless of whether the act in question constitutes a crime in their own countries. However, before presenting evidence to another country, one may consider whether the implementation of the request is in accordance with the public interest of the requested country, and one may reject the request if not.

Procedures for protecting sensitive information are strictly defined. This means that the information must be protected in accordance with the laws of the country in which it is located and that the information must be immediately sent to the regulatory authorities of the other country when it is disclosed to a third party without the authority to do so. However, disclosure is permitted if it is required by national law. In addition, the requested State is required to notify the requesting State of any matter it wishes to respect in implementing the request, such as the privileges of the parties involved, such as attorney-at-law privilege.

[152] Zanettin (n 75) 63; Kurt Markert, 'Merger Control in Western Europe: National and International Aspects' in Oscar Schachter and Robert Hellawell (eds), *Competition in International Business: Law and Policy on Restrictive Practices* (Columbia UP 1981) 332.

[153] US–Australia Agreement on Mutual Antitrust Enforcement Assistance (signed on 27 April 1997, entered into force on 5 November 1999), reprinted in 4 Trade Reg Rep (CCH) s 13502.

[154] Denmark–Iceland–Norway Agreement (signed on 16 March 2001) concerning cooperation in matters of competition. Sweden acceded to the convention in an agreement on amendments (signed on 9 April 2003).

[155] Australia–Japan Cooperation Arrangement, reprinted in Anestis Papadopulos, 'Bilateral Enforcement Cooperation Agreements' in Philip Marsden (ed), *Handbook of Research in Trans-Atlantic Antitrust* (Edward Elgar 2011) 676. See The Japan Fair Trade Commission, 'The Japan Fair Trade Commission Concluded Cooperation Arrangement with the Australian Competition and Consumer Commission' (30 April 2015) <https://www.jftc.go.jp/en/pressreleases/yearly-2015/April/150430.html>.

It is expressly stated in the agreement that this arrangement does not prevent the collection of evidence in any form other than that outlined in the agreement. In other words, it does not preclude the right to rely on other mutual assistance treaties, such as the MLAT, or to require a person in the territory of another country to voluntarily submit evidence. It also imposes an obligation to inform each other's regulators about anti-competitive activities and to inform each other of investigations into such activities that affect the important interests of the other country.

Similarly, the Denmark–Iceland–Norway Agreement concluded in 2001, to which Sweden joined in 2003, provides for the exchange of confidential information as follows. Specifically, after it is stated that the exchange of confidential information is in the common interest of member States, it states that the receiving authority between the exchanging authorities shall be subject to the same confidentiality obligations as the providing authority. The information shall be used only for the purposes specified in the convention, and the provision of the information shall be used only for the purposes identified by the prior consent of the providing party.

The evolution of cross-border competition law enforcement and the imposition of civil and criminal sanctions will be influenced by ongoing technological advancements, shifts in market structures due to digitalization, and changes in regulatory priorities. Although the development of regulations for platform operators, such as the EU Digital Markets Act, is beyond the scope of this book, it may alter the formats of investigations.

These developments have made cross-border practices routine with regard to competition law enforcement. It is also not uncommon for evidence obtained through such cooperation, which takes place within the framework of administrative law, to be used in criminal proceedings.

4. Rights of Legal and Natural Persons

4.1 Protection of Fundamental Rights

The enforcement of competition law has become increasingly stringent. Corporations and individuals may face both administrative and criminal sanctions. In addition, the prosecutors may use information obtained in administrative investigation in a criminal prosecution. There is a call for law enforcement to follow established procedural principles that protect 'rights' of the targets, including due process.[156]

[156] Caron Beaton-Wells argues that the perceived fairness of competition law and its enforcement significantly influences compliance from a normative perspective. Caron Beaton-Wells, 'Substance and Process in Competition Law and Enforcement: Why We Should Care If It's Not Fair' in Paul Nihoul and Tadeusz Skoczny (eds), *Procedural Fairness in Competition Proceedings* (Elgar 2015).

There are a couple of issues in this context. First, the rules concerning the procedural fairness in criminal proceedings include the protection of the right to be heard, the right of defence, the right to protection of business secrets and exchange of confidential information, and the right to judicial review.[157]

On the other hand, as described in Section 2.4, most countries originally mandated competition authorities to conduct investigations on the violation of competition law. They also introduced various procedures to effectively enforce the law. The primary focus of the authorities is on economic considerations of deterring and suppressing cartels and other anti-competitive behaviours. The principles of criminal procedure do not apply until the case reaches the stage of criminal proceedings.

4.2 The State and Regional Practice

4.2.1 Development in the EU Law

There seems to be no internationally established standard concerning the competition law enforcement. This issue has been long underexplored in the field of international human rights law.[158] It is partly due to the limits of this field. While many international human rights conventions ensure the protection of the defendant's rights in criminal proceedings, it does not necessarily extend to non-criminal matters.

At this stage, the protection of the rights of the target is based solely on domestic or regional laws. The EU law has been the model in establishing standards for the protection of these principles. The EU Regulations 1/2003 on the implementation of the competition law addresses the need to 'ensure an effective enforcement of the Community competition rules and at the same time the respect of fundamental rights of defense'.[159] For this purpose, the rule is that the party or the authority alleging an infringement of the competition law, namely the former EC Treaty Articles 81(1) and 82, and now the TFEU Articles 101 and 102, bears the burden of proof. It should be for the undertaking or association of undertakings invoking the benefit of a defence against a finding of an infringement to demonstrate to the required legal standard that the conditions for applying such defence are satisfied.

[157] Lasagni (n 112) 27. The right to be heard includes access to evidence in the case file, participation in oral hearings, and proper justification of anti-competitive charges. The right of defence encompasses the prosecutorial burden of proof beyond reasonable doubt; the privilege against self-incrimination; the right to silence; legal professional privilege; rules on evidence, including the exclusion of illegally obtained materials and the prohibition of hearsay; and guarantees of proportionality in inspections.

[158] ibid; Beaton-Wells (n 156).

[159] Regulation 1/2003, preamble 5.

The established jurisprudence of the ECJ is that 'a concerted practice' means 'a form of coordination between undertakings which knowingly substitutes for the risks of competition practical cooperation between them', without an agreement having been concluded.[160] The criteria of coordination and cooperation must be understood in the light of the concept inherent in the provisions of the Treaty relating to competition, according to which each economic operator must determine independently the policy that they intend to adopt on the market.[161] However, subject to proof to the contrary, which the economic operators concerned must adduce, the presumption must be that the undertakings taking part in the concerted action and remaining active on the market take account of the information exchanged with their competitors for the purposes of determining their conduct on that market.

The ECJ and later the Court of Justice of the European Union (CJEU) adopted the European Court of Human Rights' approach to criminal matters, particularly emphasizing the protection of core fair trial rights in proceedings involving competition law violations.[162]

The landmark case for this development was the 1999 decision in *Hüls AG v Commission*. Chemische Werke Hüls AG was one of the major German petrochemical companies in the 1970s. In 1986, the European Commission decided that the company, among other corporations, engaged in the concerted practice that had anti-competitive effect, under a proceeding under Article 85 of the EEC Treaty. However, the only evidence put forward by the Commission to prove Hüls' participation in the meetings during the period in question was a reply from another company, Imperial Chemical Industries, a British company, to the request for information. In this case, the ECJ acknowledged that given the nature of the infringements and the nature and degree of severity of the ensuing penalties, 'the principle of the presumption of innocence applies to the procedures relating to infringements of the competition rules applicable to undertakings that may result in the imposition of fines or periodic penalty payments'.[163]

The CJEU has consistently reaffirmed this approach, particularly concerning the presumption of innocence and other criminal law principles, including the

[160] Joined Cases 40/73 to 48/73, 50/73, 54/73, 55/73, 56/73, 111/73, 113/73 and 114/73 *Suiker Unie and Others v Commission* [1975] ECR 1663, para 26; Joined Cases C-89/85, C-104/85, C-114/85, C-116/85, C-117/85, and C-125/85 to C-129/85 *Ahlström Osakeyhtiö and Others v Commission* [1993] ECR I-1307, para 63.

[161] *Suiker Unie* (n 156) para 173; Case 172/89 *Züchner* [1981] ECR 2021, para 13; *Ahlström Osakeyhtiö* (n 156) para 63; Case T-35/92 *John Deere Ltd v Commission of the European Communities* [1994] ECR II-957, para 86.

[162] See also Lasagni (n 112) 27.

[163] Case C-199/92 P *Hüls AG v Commission of the European Communities* (8 July 1999) [1999] ECR I-4287,para 150. It also cited the judgments of the European Court of Human Rights, *Öztürk v Germany* (21 February 1984) Series A No 73 and *Lutz v Germany* (25 August 1987) Series A No 123-A. It is also noted that the ECHR is the foundation of this approach and there are cases before the European Court of Human Rights that dealt with competition law. See Cristina Teleki, *Due Process and Fair Trial in EU*

non-retroactivity of penalties. The presumption of innocence stems from the Article 6(2) of the European Convention on Human Rights. The protection of fundamental rights are reaffirmed in the preamble to the Single European Act and in Article F(2) of the Treaty on European Union, and protected in the 'Community legal order'. This requirement ensures that fundamental criminal law protections are maintained even when fines are imposed for violations of competition rules. This understanding was upheld in Montecatini in 1999[164] and Groupe Danone in 2005.[165] Furthermore, in the *Intel* case in 2017, the CJEU held that the Commission must record all the interviews, including informal ones, which it conducted for the purpose of collecting information relating to the subject matter of an investigation.[166]

The ECJ has never affirmed a substantive criminal nature of the sanction under competition law, as Regulation 1/2003 explicitly denies such a character. However, the Court has repeatedly emphasized the importance of maintaining effectiveness of the EU competition law.[167] The principles on which it is based are the same as those used in criminal proceedings.

Scholars have generally supported the Court's approach. For instance, Pieter Van Cleynenbreugel emphasizes that respect for due process values is a fundamental institutional precondition for effective decentralized enforcement of EU competition law.[168] He argues that ensuring procedural fairness and protecting defendants' rights not only upholds justice but also enhances the credibility and effectiveness of competition law enforcement throughout the European Union.

4.2.2 Other State Practice

As the EU law developed, the competition law communities and networks began to focus on due process and the protection of fundamental rights. The importance of procedural fairness and transparency no longer disputed. However, most

Competition Law: The Impact of Article 6 of the European Convention on Human Rights (Brill/Nijhoff 2021) 29–47.

[164] Case C-235/92 P *Montecatini SpA v Commission of the European Communities* [1999] ECR I-04539, ECLI:EU:C:1999:362.

[165] Case T-38/02 *Groupe Danone v Commission of the European Communities* [2005] ECR II-04407, ECLI:EU:T:2005:367

[166] Case C-413/14 P *Intel Corp v European Commission* (6 September 2017), ECLI:EU:C:2017:632, para 91.

[167] Case C-338/00 P *Volkswagen v Commission* (18 September 2003) EU:C:2003:473, paras 96–97; Case T-276/04 *Compagnie maritime belge v Commission* (1 July 2008) EU:T:2008:237, para 66. See Lasagni (n 112) 27–28.

[168] Pieter Van Cleynenbreugel, 'Effectiveness through Fairness? "Due Process" as an Institutional Precondition for Effective Decentralized EU Competition Law Enforcement' in Paul Nihoul and Tadeusz Skoczny (eds), *Procedural Fairness in Competition Proceedings* (Edward Elgar Publishing 2015).

advocates do not demand the same level of rigour in administrative investigations as they do in criminal procedural law.

For example, in 2018, the International Competition Network, an informal network of 141 competition authorities from 129 jurisdictions, adopted Recommended Practices on Investigative Process and established the Framework for Competition Agency Procedures, with agencies from 62 jurisdictions becoming original signatories.[169] Their focus is on the administrative process and does not extend to the protection of rights in criminal procedures.

The OECD formally initiated the promotion of fair procedural rules in competition law in 2010. In 2021, the OECD ministers agreed on the Recommendation on Transparency and Procedural Fairness in Competition Law Enforcement.[170] It is the first instrument that the OECD adopted on due process standards for competition law. It is issued not only to member States but also to non-member States and jurisdictions that adhere to the recommendation. It sets specific principles, which includes impartial judicial review. It requires that the States ensure access to a 'review by an adjudicative body' that is 'independent and separate from the competition authority, of decisions, including intermediate compulsory procedural decisions'.[171] The Recommendation states that authorities should ensure that courts can examine facts, evidence, and the merits of competition law enforcement decisions.[172] They should mandate that all decisions are written based solely on the factual record, and, when applicable, include specifics about findings of fact, legal conclusions, and any sanctions imposed.[173] Efforts should be made to complete reviews within a reasonable timeframe, considering the complexity and nature of each case.[174]

States come to recognize the importance of the due process, procedural fairness, and transparency. However, most of them do not equate the competition law enforcement process with the criminal procedures in terms of the protection of individuals.

[169] International Competition Network, *ICN Guidance on Investigative Process* (September 2018) <https://www.internationalcompetitionnetwork.org/wp-content/uploads/2018/09/AEWG_Guidance_InvestigativeProcess.pdf>.

[170] OECD, 'Transparency and procedural fairness in competition law enforcement' (adopted on 6 October 2021) <https://web-archive.oecd.org/fr/temp/2022-10-06/581245-transparency-and-procedural-fairness-in-competition-law-enforcement.htm>. The seven principles are: (1) transparency and predictability; (2) independence, impartiality, and professionalism; (3) non-discrimination, proportionality, and consistency; (4) timeliness, (5) parties' engagement in enforcement; (6) protection of confidential and privileged information; and (7) impartial judicial review.

[171] OECD Recommendation, principle 7.

[172] ibid principle 7(a).

[173] ibid principle 7(b).

[174] ibid principle 7(c).

5. Concluding Remarks

There has been a significant shift towards more intense intergovernmental cooperation among competition authorities concerning the enforcement of competition law. This shift is driven by the recognition that combating anti-competitive behaviours requires a coordinated cross-border response. Forms of cooperation now include sophisticated law enforcement mechanisms such as leniency programmes, agreements with whistleblowers, information sharing, and joint investigations.

In practice, cross-border antitrust enforcement has focused on detecting and collecting information on international cartels. Civil or administrative sanctions play an important role in deterring anti-competitive behaviours. Additionally, the materials and data collected through civil or administrative investigations can be used for criminal prosecutions. In many jurisdictions, competition authorities have the mandate to pursue criminal prosecutions. Due to the diminishing resistance to proactive approaches, a significant number of States are poised to adopt comparable domestic laws and policies.

7
Securities Frauds

1. Introduction

Securities fraud is an illegal activity prohibited under securities laws. The elements of the offence are complex and vary from one jurisdiction to another. However, they generally include insider trading (trading on the stock exchange to one's advantage through having access to confidential information), broker misrepresentation (brokers' providing false or misleading information about a company's financial status), stock churning, and market manipulation. The regulation aims to protect collective social values, such as the integrity of capital markets, beyond the individual property interests of the direct victims.[1] The offence is considered complete when the offender performs the specified actions. Whether the individual obtains financial gain is irrelevant.

Law enforcement authorities will detect irregular transactions in today's highly interconnected financial environment. There are systems for electronically processing the exchange of data pertaining to transactions by connecting securities firms, self-regulatory bodies, and the government securities and exchange authority. This network allows for the automatic detection of anomalies or suspicious activities. Nevertheless, tracking the information and obtaining necessary materials for criminal proceedings pose challenges, particularly in complex cases. These deals are typically executed through elaborate schemes to cover up fraudulent activities. The perpetrators may use various techniques, including creating false documents, using offshore accounts, and using sophisticated investment vehicles.

Many distinctive features characterize cross-border investigation of securities fraud. First, securities law violations can have both criminal and civil dimensions. Fraud can be prosecuted as a crime but can also constitute a tort, providing grounds for a private party to seek damages. Additionally, such conduct is subject to the State's regulatory measures governing the securities exchange. As the following sections explore, the governments use civil, commercial, or administrative cooperation to collect materials across borders.

[1] Klaus Tiedemann, *Wirtschaftsstrafrecht. Einführung Und Allgemeiner Teil Mit Wichtisten Rechtstexten* (Verlag Franz Vahlen 2014) 87.

International Law and the Investigation of Transnational Crimes. Yurika Ishii, Oxford University Press.
 DOI: 10.1093/9780198957089.003.0007

A noteworthy practice is informal cooperation mechanisms that securities and market authorities employ to collect information. These mechanisms are essentially non-legally binding instruments. However, States have established domestic legislation to enable authorities to exchange information related to securities markets. While the information is generally insufficient to constitute evidence for criminal trials, it can provide a significant lead.

Second, there is not much conflict of prescriptive jurisdiction concerning securities fraud. An individual who purchases securities is subject to the legislation of the jurisdiction based on the location in which the securities exchange is established. Jurisdictional conflict in the context of securities fraud is generally attributed to the exercise of enforcement jurisdiction, namely the implementation of intrusive measures by law enforcement agencies.

Third, the practice concerning the cross-border investigation of securities fraud is not widespread. Over sixty stock exchanges, including numerous regional exchanges, serve specific local markets. However, given that only a few countries boast a global securities exchange, major practices are limited to the United States (with New York Stock Exchange and the Nasdaq Stock Market), Eurozone (with Euronext), Japan (with Tokyo Stock Exchange), the United Kingdom (with London Stock Exchange), China (with Shanghai Stock Exchange, Hong Kong Stock Exchange, and Shenzhen Stock Exchange), and Canada (with Toronto Stock Exchange). Although there have been cross-border mergers and acquisitions among securities exchanges since the 2000s, such transactions have not impacted the allocation of national jurisdiction over subsidiaries, and the home State law continues to apply to securities transactions. Each State has its government authorities that precisely monitor and supervise securities exchanges.

Considering these characteristics, this chapter deals with the cross-border securities fraud investigation. Section 2 examines how the substantive law concerning securities fraud developed in States with significant securities markets. It first deals with the evolution of securities regulations in the United States and observes how other countries followed suit. Then, it looks into the United States' information collection through subpoenas and the development of the 'waiver-by-conduct' doctrine. In addition, Section 2 covers the cooperation of the government authorities with the self-regulatory bodies of the financial industry to ensure that institutions comply with their requirements. Section 3 deals with the limits and the significance of judicial assistance. It reviews treaties facilitating legal assistance in criminal, civil, and commercial legal assistance. It then briefly examines the Convention on Insider Trading. Section 4 tracks the evolution of cooperation among financial regulators. It details the authority of financial regulators to share information, with varying conditions compared to mutual legal assistance treaty (MLAT). Then, it deals with cooperation between financial authorities in criminal investigations and the International Organization of Securities Commissions' (IOSCO) Multilateral Memorandum of Understanding (MMOU). Section 5 deals with the rights of legal and natural persons. While there have been efforts to protect such rights, there has been no significant global standardization of these rights.

2. Jurisdictional Conflict and Harmonization of the Securities Laws

2.1 Harmonization of Substantive Laws

2.1.1 Regulations in the United States

While the securities market first matured in the United Kingdom and continental Europe, the criminal sanction of modern securities law originated in the United. The government started to criminally penalize unlawful conduct in the 1930s against the backdrop of the Great Depression in 1929. Securities regulation used to be a matter for State jurisdictions. However, in 1933, Congress enacted the Securities Exchange Act, and the Securities and Exchange Commission (SEC) was established in 1934 to oversee securities transactions at the federal level.[2]

The SEC's primary objectives are to promote full public disclosure, protect investors against fraudulent and manipulative practices in the market, and monitor corporate takeover actions within the United States. In 1934, securities fraud and market manipulation became offences under the Securities Exchange Act. Section 10(b) provides, among other things, that it is unlawful to use or employ, in connection with the purchase or sale of any securities, any manipulative or deceptive device or contrivance in contravention of securities rules and regulations as the SEC may prescribe as necessary or appropriate in the public interest or for the protection of investors.[3] The 1933 Securities Act section 24 and the Securities and Exchange Act section 32(a) prescribe criminal sanctions, including fines and imprisonment.

In 1942, the SEC issued rule 10(b)-5 under the authority of Securities Exchange Act, which prohibits fraudulent acts, making false statements of material facts, omitting material facts necessary to make other statements not misleading, and engaging in schemes or practices that operate as fraud or deceit.[4]

Insider trading was initially considered tort fraud. However, the Insider Trading Sanctions Act was enacted in 1984, which defined and criminalized the misconduct and integrated the clause into the Securities Exchange Act. In addition, the Insider Trading and Securities Fraud Enforcement Act of 1988 expanded liability

[2] Securities Exchange Act, Pub L No 73-291, 48 Stat 881 (1934), 15 USC 78a.
[3] ibid 15 USC 78j(b).
[4] 17 CFR 240.10b-5.

to entities that fail to prevent insider trading and mandated the implementation of preventive compliance systems.[5]

Since its inception, the SEC has jurisdiction over securities exchanges and other transactions. It initiates litigation under the Federal Rules of Civil Procedure. Nevertheless, if there is evidence of criminal conduct, the SEC will transfer the case to the US Department of Justice (DOJ), which will commence criminal proceedings. Both the Securities Act[6] and the Securities Exchange Act[7] allow the use of evidence acquired through the SEC's administrative procedure in the DOJ's criminal procedure.

Another notable feature of the SEC is the Office of Administrative Law Judges. The Administrative Procedure Act requires the US government agencies to appoint administrative law judges (ALJs).[8] It is an option of consulting this intra-organizational body instead of filing a civil complaint in federal court when considering actions such as securities fraud. ALJs serve as independent adjudicators, prepare an initial decision containing findings of fact and conclusions of law, and determine whether sanctions are warranted. During a proceeding, the ALJ may issue subpoenas, hold conferences with the parties, and rule on motions and the admissibility of evidence. There is no jury, and ALJs may resolve certain proceedings without a live hearing. The initial decision of an ALJ is subject to *de novo* review by the SEC.[9] Decisions of the Commission may be appealed to an appropriate US Court of Appeals.[10]

The United States began requiring foreign entities to submit necessary information and materials, leading to conflicts with other States. The US securities law is based on territorial or personal principles, with little opposition to this practice.[11] It covers both transactions within the country and certain offshore transactions, and parties to such transactions must register with the SEC. The criteria for jurisdiction are outlined in Regulation S, which excludes registration requirements for offerings made outside the United States by both US and foreign issuers.[12] It specifies that the offer or sale must be conducted in an offshore transaction and that no

[5] Insider Trading Sanctions Act, Pub L No 98-376, 98 Stat 1264 (1984); Insider Trading and Securities Fraud Enforcement Act, Pub L No 100-704, 102 Stat 4677 (1988).

[6] 15 USC 77t(b).

[7] 15 USC 78u(d).

[8] Administrative Procedure Act, Pub L No 89–554, 80 Stat 415 (1966), 5 USC 3105. This legislation is in line with the US Constitution art II, s 2, cl 2.

[9] SEC, Rules of Practice, 17 CFR 201.411, 47 FR 610 (1982).

[10] ibid 17 CFR 201.490.

[11] See Daniel L Goelzer and Anne Sullivan, 'Obtaining Evidence for the International Enforcement of the United States Securities Laws' (1990) 16 Brooklyn Journal of International Law 145; Arthur Jr Fleischer, 'Extra-Territorial Application of United States Securities Law' in Cecil J Olmstead (ed), *Extra-territorial Application of Laws and Responses Thereto* (OUP 1989).

[12] SEC Regulation S, Rules Governing Offers and Sales Made Outside the United States Without Registration Under the Securities Act of 1933, 1998, 63 FR 9645 (17 CFR 230.901-905).

'directed selling efforts' may be made by the issuer, distributor, affiliates, or persons acting on their behalf.

It is noted that the US Supreme Court's *Morrison v National Australia Bank* case held a narrow interpretation of the jurisdictional scope of the Securities Exchange Act.[13] The case concerned the National Australia Bank's purchase of a mortgage servicing company in the United States in 1998. The bank announced a significant reduction in the book value of an asset, claiming that it was part of an intentional scheme to defraud committed by the US company. It argued that the fact that the alleged fraud occurred in Florida meant that it should be subject to US securities laws and that section 10(b) of the Securities Exchange Act shall apply. The defendants argued that, since the alleged fraud related to trading in Australian securities, US securities laws did not apply. The majority of the Supreme Court ruled that the plain language of the Securities Exchange Act applies solely to US securities, despite the long-standing practice of the Circuit Courts, which had interpreted the provision to include foreign securities.[14]

2.1.2 Practices of Other States Than the United States

Before the 1970s, most States did not criminalize securities law violations, including insider trading, unless they constituted fraud as defined under criminal law. France's regulatory approach to securities markets sets it apart from the trend of delayed regulation observed in other countries. It was against the background of France's matured securities market, which developed during the Second Imperial Period in the latter half of the nineteenth century. By the late 1960s, the Charles de Gaulle administration recognized the need to regulate the securities market in line with the US approach to attracting foreign investment.[15] France prohibited transactions without appropriate information disclosure in 1967.[16] It subsequently criminalized insider trading in 1970.[17] In addition, the United Kingdom, one of the global financial centres, penalized the misconduct in 1980.[18]

[13] *Robert Morrison v National Australia Bank Ltd* 561 US 247 (2010).

[14] For the analysis of the case, see Lea Brilmayer, 'The New Extraterritoriality: Morrison v. National Australia Bank, Legislative Supremacy, and the Presumption against Extraterritorial Application of American Law' (2010) 40 Southwestern Law Review 655; Genevieve Beyea, 'Morrison v. National Australia Bank and the Future of Extraterritorial Application of the US Securities Laws' (2011) 72 Ohio State Law Journal 537.

[15] Carol Umhoefer and Alain Pietrancosta, 'Le Delit d'Initie: Insider Trading Law in France' (1992) 30 Columbia Journal of Transnational Law 89.

[16] Ordonnance n° 67-833 du 28 septembre 1967, instituant une Commission des opérations de bourse et relative à l'information des porteurs de valeurs mobilières et à la publicité de certaines opérations de bourse, art 10. English translation is available at Dolores M Goeldner, 'France: Ordinance Creating a Stock Exchange Commission' (1968) 7 International Legal Materials 1063.

[17] Loi n°70-1208 du 23 décembre 1970 portant modification de la loi n° 66-537 du 24 juillet 1966 sur les sociétés commerciales et de l'ordonnance n° 67-833 du 28 septembre 1967 instituant l'Autorité des marchés financiers et relative à l'information des porteurs de valeurs mobilières et à la publicité de certaines opérations de bourse, art 10-1.

[18] Companies Act 1980, c 22, ss 68–73, 23 June 1980. See Peter Lee, 'Law and Practice with Respect to Insider Trading and Trading on Market Information in the United Kingdom' (1982) 4 Journal of Comparative Corporate Law and Securities Regulation 389.

In other developed countries, insider trading was prohibited based on trading guidelines adopted by securities exchanges, banks, and industries.[19]

The majority of States with sizable securities markets criminalized securities fraud in the early 1990s, although the specific elements varied. For instance, Japan revised the Securities and Exchange Law in 1988 to penalize such behaviours.[20] It was in response to a diplomatic request from the United States following an incident. In this case, the board members of Tateho Chemical, a Japanese corporation, and the financial institutions that traded with the company sold their shares before announcing a 28-billion-yen loss. However, the board members were not held liable.

Switzerland also amended its criminal code to penalize insider trading in 1988 due to pressure from the United States.[21] However, the regulation of other securities offences fell behind and was not addressed until a comprehensive securities law was enacted in 1995.[22]

The emergence of the need to attract securities investment within the European Community (EC) led to changes in securities law regulation.[23] Securities law is subject to the jurisdiction of each member state under EU law. However, due to the negative impact of insider trading on the internal market, the European Economic Community required member States to establish insider trading offences under national law through Directive 89/592 in 1989.[24] This Directive also included a provision prohibiting governments from refusing legal assistance based on bank secrecy laws.[25] Following harmonizing the securities regulations, Italy criminalized insider trading in 1991[26] and Germany in 1994.[27]

[19] For the comparative analysis of domestic laws concerning securities fraud, see also Edgardo Rotman, *Regulating Fraud Across Borders: Internationalised Criminal Law Protection of Capital Markets* (Hart Publishing 2021) 29.

[20] Securities and Exchange Act, Act No 25 of 1948, art 166. For the context of the amendment, see Winifred Swan, 'The 1988 Japanese Insider Trading Amendments: Will Japan See Results from These Tougher Laws' (1991) 12 University of Pennsylvania Journal of International Business Law 275.

[21] Schweizerisches Strafgesetzbuch vom 21. Dezember 1937, art 161, SR 311.0.

[22] See also Lutz Krauskopf, 'Comments on Switzerland's Insider Trading, Money Laundering, and Banking Secrecy Laws' (1991) 9 International Tax and Business Law 277; Peter Nobel and Beat Braendli, 'Switzerland' in Sandra Booysen and Dora Neo (eds), *Can Banks Still Keep a Secret?: Bank Secrecy in Financial Centres around the World* (CUP 2017) 308–336.

[23] Iris HY Chiu, *Regulatory Convergence in EU Securities Regulation* (Wolters Kluwer Law & Business 2008); Viveca Hostetter, 'Turning Insider Trading Insider out in the European Union' (1999) 30 California Western International Law Journal 175.

[24] Council Directive 89/592/EEC of 13 November 1989 coordinating Regulations on Insider Dealing [1989] OJ L334/30.

[25] ibid art 10(1).

[26] Legge 17 maggio 1991, n. 157, Norme relative all'uso di informazioni riservate nelle operazioni in valori mobiliari e alla Commissione nazionale per le societa' e la borsa, Gazzetta Ufficiale della Repubblica Italiana del 20-5-1991. See Eugenio Ruggiero, 'The Regulation of Insider Trading in Italy' (1996) 22 Brooklyn Journal of International Law 157.

[27] Zweites Finanzmarktforderungsgesetz vom 26. Juli 1994, [1994] BGBl I 1749, Abschnitt 3 (Insider Trading Guideline), reprinted in Adolf Baumbach, Klaus Hopt, and Merkt Hanno, *Handelgesetzbuch: Mit GmbH & Co., Handelsklauseln, Bank- Und Börsenrecht, Transportrecht (Ohne Seerecht)* (CH Beck 1982) No 16. See also Klaus Hopt, 'Insider Trading on the Continent' (1982) 4 Journal of Comparative Corporate Law and Securities Regulations 379; Joseph Blum, 'The Regulation

2.1.3 Relevance with Anti-Money Laundering and Countering Terrorist Financing Regulations

Another important development is the Anti-Money Laundering and Countering Terrorist Financing Regulations, which developed since the end of the 1980s. In 1989, the Financial Action Task Force (FATF), an intergovernmental body, was established to develop and implement a comprehensive framework of regulations at the global level. These regulations require financial institutions to submit suspicious transaction reports, aimed at identifying and preventing money laundering activities. Many authorities and mechanisms established under anti-money laundering (AML) regulations overlap with those under securities regulation, as they both aim an integrated approach to combating financial crimes.

There are three main points. First is common procedures of compliance. In both regulations, financial institutions are required to verify the identities of their customers ('Know Your Customers' principle) to prevent both securities fraud and money laundering. They must monitor the transaction to detect both unusual trading behaviours and potential hiding of the source of the money. Then, they are required to report suspicious transactions to regulatory authorities.

The FATF has identified the risks of money laundering in the securities sector.[28] It outlines how criminals might exploit securities firms and generate illicit funds through fraudulent activities such as insider trading, market manipulation, and securities fraud. The securities industries are required to enforce the FATF recommendations in each State.

Second is the inter-agency information sharing. Although not common in every country, there are several jurisdictions where securities fraud and money laundering authorities share financial information. In the case of the United States, the SEC and Financial Crimes Enforcement Network (FinCEN) concluded an agreement to this effect in 2006.[29] They decided for the routine exchange of examination and enforcement information relating to SEC-regulated firms' compliance with the Bank Secrecy Act, which is a part of the AML regulations. In other words, the Bank Secrecy Act has been the statutory basis for this agreement. According to the press release, their memorandum of understanding (MOU) provides that the

of Insider Trading in Germany: Who's Afraid of Self-Restraint' (1986) 7 Northwestern Journal of International Law & Business 507.

[28] FATF, 'Money Laundering and Terrorist Financing in the Securities Sector' (October 2009) <https://www.fatf-gafi.org/en/publications/Methodsandtrends/Moneylaunderingandterroristfinancinginthesecuritiessector.html>; FATF, 'Risk-Based Approach Guidance for the Securities Sector' (26 October 2018) <www.fatf-gafi.org/publications/fatfrecommendations/documents/rba-securities-sector.html>. All websites were last accessed on 31 March 2025.

[29] SEC and Financial Crimes Enforcement Network, 'SEC and FinCEN Sign Information Sharing Agreement' (21 December 2006) <https://www.fincen.gov/sites/default/files/news_release/20061221.pdf>. The text of the MOU has not been publicly available.

SEC will provide FinCEN with information on a regular basis and FinCEN will provide assistance and analytical reports to the SEC.[30]

Third is public–private cooperation. Securities sectors now coordinate with police agencies and share relevant information to suppress both money laundering and securities frauds. The details concerning the direct cooperation between governments and financial institutions are discussed in Chapter 13. Yet, several examples are worthy of referral at this stage.

The United Kingdom launched a forum, Joint Money Laundering Intelligence Taskforce, in 2015.[31] It started as a pilot project and now it is under National Crime Agency (NCA)'s National Economic Crime Centre since 2018. The Taskforce consists of financial institutions, the Financial Conduct Authority, Cifas, and law enforcement agencies, namely the NCA, the His Majesty's Revenue and Customs, the Serious Fraud Office, the City of London Police, and the Metropolitan Police Service. The aim is to improve intelligence sharing arrangements to support the fight against money laundering and to build on the national leadership provided by the NCA's Economic Crime Command against organized economic and financial crime.

In Japan, the police office, the National Police Agency, the supervisory agency, the Financial Service Agency, and stock exchanges also started to coordinate with each other in the mid-2000s. Their main purpose is to exclude 'antisocial forces' from the financial market, rather than suppressing individual frauds.[32] The cooperation relies on voluntary industry actions rather than statutory obligations. In addition, in April 2010, the Japanese Bankers Association began operating a shared database that consolidates information on antisocial forces. In 2017, it decided to promote cooperation among the government and financial institutions to verify the identity of customers to prevent antisocial groups to utilize financial services. Subsequently, in January 2018, the Deposit Insurance Corporation began connecting to the National Police Agency's database of information on organized crime groups, enabling online inquiries to the National Police Agency.

The development of the AML and combating the financing of terrorism regulations contributed to the suppression of securities fraud and harmonization of

[30] ibid.

[31] UK Home Office and others, 'Anti-Money Laundering Taskforce Unveiled' (25 February 2015) <https://www.gov.uk/government/news/anti-money-laundering-taskforce-unveiled>.

[32] The 'antisocial forces' (Han-shakaiteki Seiryoku) means organized crime groups (Boryokudan), their members, companies affiliated with such groups, and other individuals or groups. See Japan Department of Justice, 'Guideline for Companies to Prevent Damage Caused by Antisocial Forces' (2007) <https://www.moj.go.jp/content/000061957.pdf>. For the development of industry guidelines, see Japan Financial Services Agency, 'Annual Paper' (2017) 108 <https://www.fsa.go.jp/common/paper/29/zentai/08.pdf>. Japan also established a liaison body, the Securities Security Liaison Committee, in 2006. Its members include Financial Service Agency, National Policy Agency, Tokyo Stock Exchange, Osaka Stock Exchange Japan Exchange Group, and Japan Securities Dealers Association. The Metropolitan Police Department, Sapporo Securities Exchange, Nagoya Stock Exchange, and Fukuoka Stock Exchange also established another body for the same purpose.

the law among States. The details of its history and the direct cooperation between governments and financial institutions will be covered in Chapter 11.

2.2 Jurisdictional Conflicts

2.2.1 Collection of Information through Subpoena

As stated in the introduction of this chapter, the conflicts regarding the United States's collection of these materials were not primarily about prescriptive jurisdiction. Instead, the issue lay in the intrusive methods employed by the DOJ and SEC. To investigate securities offences, information and documents are necessary to provide evidence of illegal transactions, such as transaction records, the beneficiary of the asset, the holder of the bank account, the date of the transaction, its amount, and identification of the bank and staff involved.

The Securities and Exchange Act authorizes the SEC to conduct necessary investigations to determine legal violations.[33] The SEC can issue subpoenas for testimony or requests for documents. If subpoenas are issued, the individual subpoenaed must appear at a specified time and place to provide testimony under oath.[34] In cases where the requested records are located overseas, the SEC may transfer the subpoena to the entity's representative within the United States.

Additionally, it may initiate a civil procedure and require compulsory disclosure or discovery.[35] When there is an objection made against the procedure that the United States does not have legitimate jurisdiction, the court may rely on the balancing interest standard that was held in the *Societe Internationale* case, comparing the interest of the United States enforcing the subpoena and the interest of that foreign State not to disclose the information. A hard case occurs when a bank secrecy law in the former State restricts the disclosure of customers' bank information to a third party, including a foreign authority. While the scope of bank information differs from one State to another, the protected information generally includes transaction records.[36]

The limits of the unilateral approach became evident in the *Banca della Svizzera Italiana (BSI)* case from 1981 to 1982.[37] In 1981, BSI, an investment company based in Switzerland, engaged in suspicious trading activities involving options for the stock of St Joe Minerals Corporation, an oil and mineral company

[33] 15 USC 78u(a).
[34] 15 USC 78u(b).
[35] Federal Rule of Civil Procedure, rule 37.
[36] Peter C Honegger, 'Swiss Banking Secrecy' [1990] Butterworths Journal of International Banking and Financial Law 344.
[37] For the facts of the case, see *SEC v Banca Della Svizzera Italiana*, 92 FRD 111 (SDNY 1981), 32 Fed R Serv 2d (Callaghan) 1650.

based in the United States, on the Philadelphia Stock Exchange. This interaction occurred just before a tender offer by a subsidiary of Joseph E Seagram & Sons, Inc. BSI purchased all of St Joe's common stock, resulting in profits of nearly USD 2 million overnight. The SEC launched an investigation and obtained a temporary restraining order requiring BSI to disclose the identities of its principles, but BSI refused to comply, citing Switzerland's Banking Act of 1934.[38] The court threatened contempt sanctions if BSI did not answer the SEC's questions. In the end, BSI obtained a waiver of Swiss confidentiality laws and answered some of the interrogatories. However, it took more than nine months for this information to be disclosed, prompting the SEC to recognize the need to overcome such obstacles.[39]

The US authorities took a step towards introducing rules regarding securities transactions, allowing monitoring of beneficiaries when necessary. In 1984, the SEC implemented the 'waiver-by-conduct doctrine', whereby individuals who purchase or sell securities in US markets through foreign banks were considered to have waived their right to protection from foreign bank secrecy laws.[40] The investors were obliged to disclose the information to the SEC, and the investment banks had to include the provision to this effect in their contracts.

2.2.2 Cooperation with Self-Regulatory Bodies

Another supplemental approach to collecting materials across borders was collaborating with the banking industry's self-regulatory body. In 1982, the SEC entered an MOU with the Swiss Bankers Association (Schweizeriche Bankiervereignigung) to require banks to identify violations of US law when transactions were conducted through Swiss bank accounts.[41] Under this agreement, the SEC, the DOJ, and Swiss

[38] Bankengesetz (1934), SR 952.0.

[39] Frederick Alexander Mann, 'The Doctrine of International Jurisdiction Revisited after Twenty Years' (1984) 186 Recueil des Cours 9, 84.

[40] SEC Release No 21186, 30 July 1984, Federal Securities Law Reporter (CCH) s 86,983. For the analysis of this doctrine from the perspective of the US law, see Brian L Nelson, 'Insider Trading Originating Abroad and "Waiver-by-Conduct"' (1985) 19 The International Lawyer 817; John M Fedders and others, 'Waiver by Conduct—A Possible Response to the Internationalization of the Securities Markets' (1984) 6 Journal of Comparative Business and Capital Market Law 1; John M Fedders, 'Policing Trans-Border Fraud in the United States Securities Markets: The Waiver by Conduct Concept—A Possible Alternative or a Starting Point for Discussions' (1985) 11 Brooklyn Journal of International Law 477.

[41] Agreement XVI of Swiss Banker's Association with regard to the handling of requests for information from the Securities and Exchange Commission of the United States on the subject of misuse of inside information, reprinted in US Congress, *Problems with the SEC's Enforcement of U.S. Securities Laws in Cases Involving Suspicious Trades Originating from Abroad: Hearing Before a Subcommittee of the Committee on Government Operations, House of Representatives, One Hundredth Congress, Second Session, June 6, 1988* (US Government Printing Office 1988) 555. See also Bernhard F Meyer, 'Swiss Banking Secrecy and Its Legal Implications in the United States' (1978) 14 New England Law Review 18.

judicial authorities could request information from a commission appointed by the Association.[42] The bank would then provide a detailed report on the transaction to the SEC, which was, in turn, responsible for freezing the customer's account and informing them of the amount involved. The SEC would identify suspicious transactions and obtain information on material price, volume, or other evidence of insider trading activity.[43] Furthermore, when a securities transaction was conducted through a foreign intermediary, the intermediary had to disclose the identification of the customer. It also had to inform customers of the existence of such an obligation.[44]

The Commission des Opérations de Bourse (COB) cooperated with Swiss Bankers Association to obtain information on such transactions in France. France criminalized insider trading in 1970. The relevant elements of insider trading included the transaction being made by using the status of the profession so that the authority had to prove the identification of the customer and the relevance with the investment company. However, foreign banks could not obtain information on customers' identities. No other country criminalized insider trading at the time, which became an obstacle to cooperating with the MLAT.

Beginning in 1972, the COB established contact with the Swiss Bankers Association to report any transactions suspected of insider trading. By 1975, these reports were communicated directly to the banks. The banks then conducted internal investigations and provided their views to the COB regarding whether the conduct could violate French law without disclosing the customer's identity. The COB also collaborated with other regulatory bodies, including the UK Takeover Panel and the Belgian Banking Commission. However, these bodies did not respond to urgent requests for information or provide information that would lead to the identification of customers. The COB began to reject a takeover bid if the seller or the buyer, who held a certain percentage of the corporation's stock, did not disclose their identity.[45]

A bank secrecy law typically safeguards the details of beneficiaries, and intermediaries such as investment banks are obligated to follow these regulations. However, obtaining consent from the customer during the transaction does not pose any legal concerns. As such, such legislation does not typically result in any international legal issues, as it falls within the jurisdiction of the State where the transaction occurs.[46]

[42] Agreement XVI of Swiss Banker's Association (n 41) art 2.
[43] ibid art 3.
[44] ibid art 4.
[45] Décision générale de la COB relative aux offres publiques d'achat et d'échange en date du 25 juillet 1978, *Journal Officiel* du 13 août 1978, D.2.
[46] Nelson (n 40) 817.

2.2.3 Harmonization through the Basel Committee on Banking Supervision

The elements of jurisdiction were largely harmonized through the Basel Committee on Banking Supervision (BCBS). It is a body whose members comprise central banks and bank supervisors.[47] Its mandates include setting standards for bank regulation and promoting regular cooperation on banking supervisory matters to enhance financial stability.

In 1989, it published the *Core Principles for Effective Banking Supervision*.[48] The instrument includes several guidelines that allow and encourage cross-border governance of the financial institutions. Although it is not legally binding, central banks in major financial jurisdictions adhere to the standard, as non-compliance would hinder their ability to remain active in the global financial market.

First, it recommends that '[t]he licensing authority must have the right to set criteria and reject applications for establishments that do not meet the standards set'.[49] As a minimum, the licensing process must include an assessment of whether the prior approval of the home supervisor should be obtained if the proposed owner or parent is a foreign bank.[50] Second, it states that banking supervisors must 'determine that banks have adequate policies, practices and procedures in place, including strict "know-your-customer" rules, that . . . prevent the bank being used, intentionally or unintentionally, by criminal elements'.[51] Lastly, it requires banking supervisors to practise 'global consolidated supervision over their internationally-active banking organisations', adequately monitoring and applying norms to all aspects of the business conducted by these banking organizations across the globe, primarily at their foreign branches, joint ventures, and subsidiaries.[52] For this purpose, banking supervisors must require the local operations of foreign banks to be conducted to the same high standards as are required of domestic institutions and must have powers to share information needed by the home country supervisors of those banks for the purpose of carrying out consolidated supervision.[53] By encouraging cross-border information collection for banking supervision to promote financial stability, it has also laid the groundwork for law enforcement authorities to access information related to potential criminal conduct.

[47] BCBS was established in 1974 by the central bank governors of the Group of Ten countries, after serious disturbances in international currency and banking markets at the time. As of 2024, it has forty-five members from twenty-eight jurisdictions.

[48] BCBS, *Core Principles for Effective Banking Supervision* (September 1997) <https://www.bis.org/publ/bcbsc102.pdf>.

[49] ibid 15, principle 3.

[50] ibid.

[51] ibid 30, principle 15.

[52] ibid 41, principle 23.

[53] ibid 42, principle 25.

3. Limits and Significance of Judicial Assistance Based on Treaties

3.1 Mutual Legal Assistance Treaties on Criminal Matters

The United States established a network of MLATs, enabling parties to exchange information without going through the judicial process. The United States occasionally used this mechanism to request foreign authorities for evidence of securities offences. However, this process was time-consuming and expensive. Refusal is typically based on double criminality, making it difficult to cooperate on securities offences when the counterparty does not criminalize securities fraud.

This limit became evident in the *Santa Fe* case, over which the Switzerland Federal Court ruled in 1985.[54] Santa Fe International Corporation, an oil company, announced its merger with Kuwait Petroleum in October 1981.[55] Before the announcement, an unidentified customer purchased many shares in the company. This prompted the US DOJ to investigate potential insider trading. The stock purchase involved several Swiss banks, so the DOJ ordered them to identify the buyer through a subpoena. However, the banks refused to provide this information, citing Swiss banking laws. In March 1982, the DOJ requested that the Swiss government disclose the identity of individuals under the MLAT. The Swiss Court rejected this request, stating that the treaty was based on reciprocity and that Switzerland did not criminalize insider trading. Subsequently, due to the severity of the incident, the SEC informed Swiss authorities that it would undertake efforts to identify the buyer.

In Washington DC, there were discussions between the Swiss authorities, Swiss banks, and the SEC to explore ways to obtain the information without the Swiss banks facing prosecution. The SEC requested the Swiss court, relying on section 162 of the Swiss Penal Code.[56] Under this provision, a trade may constitute a crime if carried out by a third party who has obtained classified information. However, it is not a crime if the person properly obtained the information during the duties. In 1984, the Swiss Federal Court upheld the SEC's request, stating that the new request provided sufficient evidence of a violation of section 162 of the Swiss

[54] See 'Swiss Supreme Court in the Santa Fe Case' (1983) 22 International Legal Materials 785; 'Switzerland: Supreme Court Opinion in the Second Sant Fe Case Concerning Judicial Assistance, May 16, 1984' (1985) 24 International Legal Materials 745.

[55] For the facts of this case, see Michael D Mann, Joseph G Mari, and George Lavdas, 'Developments in International Securities Law Enforcement and Regulation' (1995) 29 International Lawyer 729. See also *SEC v Certain Unknown Purchasers of the Common Stock of, and Call Options for the Common Stock of Santa Fe International Corporation*, 817 F 2d 1018 (2d Cir 1987).

[56] Proposed methods included (1) the retrospective application of the 1982 Agreement No 16 between the SEC and the Swiss Bankers Association on the Provision of Information on Insider Trading Crimes, (2) an order to provide information without identifying the person (John Doe Procedure), and (3) the referral to a third-party arbitrator. See Michael D Mann, Joseph G Mari, and George Lavdas, 'International Agreements and Understandings for the Production of Information and Other Mutual Assistance' (1995) 29 International Lawyer 780.

Penal Code and allowed the SEC to obtain the relevant information. However, the purchasers objected to prevent further disclosure, delaying the process by nine months. In February 1986, the SEC and the buyers reached a settlement that involved returning the proceeds and paying a fine.

Strict banking secrecy laws, such as those in Switzerland, are exceptional. However, it became evident that the MLAT is limited in investigating complex transactions subject to multiple jurisdictions.

3.2 Mutual Legal Assistance Treaties on Civil and Commercial Matters

The SEC may use procedures through MLATs on civil and commercial bases because the Securities and Exchange Act is 'both civil and criminal'.[57] In particular, the Hague Convention on Evidence in Civil and Commercial Matters was used to obtain information that may eventually be used in criminal procedures. The treaty did not require harmonizing substantive law, and double criminality was unnecessary. There was debate over whether evidence obtained through this civil procedure could be used in a criminal proceeding. In the end, the affirmative position garnered support in practice. In numerous instances where the matter was contested, courts across various jurisdictions upheld this perspective.

One such case occurred between the United States and Singapore.[58] In 1997, the Neptune Orient Line, a Singapore-based shipping company, announced a merger with California-based American Presidential Lines, LLC (APL), and the SEC suspected of insider trading. Shortly before the announcement, many shares in APL were purchased. The SEC suspected the transaction was insider trading and sought to gather the necessary information by filing a civil suit in the United States. The alleged transactions involved a Swiss bank account and a trading account of a US broker's Singapore subsidiary. The SEC filed a civil suit in the United States, froze the assets acquired through the sale of APL shares, identified the buyer through its parent company, and sought to not only prohibit future violations of securities laws but also return profits from insider trading and impose administrative penalties. The SEC requested that authorities within the Singapore Ministry of Finance help with its investigation in Singapore.

In Singapore, the Evidence Act states that the High Court may grant permission for judicial assistance in collecting evidence if it is assistance in civil matters.[59]

[57] See, eg, Thomas C Newkirk and Ira L Brandriss, 'Speech by SEC Staff: The Advantages of a Dual System: Parallel Streams of Civil and Criminal Enforcement of the U.S. Securities Laws, September 19, 1998' (16th International Symposium on Economic Crime, Jesus College, Cambridge, England, 1998) <https://www.sec.gov/news/speech/speecharchive/1998/spch222.htm>.

[58] *SEC v One Unknown Purchaser of the Call Options of APL Ltd and Ong Congqin Bobby*, 97 Civ 2664 (SDNY 15 April 1997), Litigation Release No 15334.

[59] Evidence Act 1893, c 97.

Two individuals who resided in Singapore challenged the SEC proceedings in Singapore courts, arguing that by nature, the procedure was criminal rather than a civil matter and that it was beyond the competence of the High Court under the law of evidence to assist.[60] The applicants claimed that the financial sanctions were criminal proceedings because they were designed by the SEC to prosecute and impose administrative penalties. However, the court examined whether the evidence collection procedure was civil rather than criminal. The court granted the assistance, stating that it was difficult to determine that the law was criminal without referring to the provisions applicable to a particular situation. Assistance in collecting evidence is different from enforcement of the Securities and Exchange Law.

Similarly, in 1996, the Global Securities Corporation (GS Corp), a securities firm in British Columbia, Canada, disputed the provision of information under an MOU between the British Columbia Securities Commission (BCSC) and the SEC.[61] The case questioned whether the exchange of information on securities offences under the MOU was a matter of State jurisdiction under Canada's Securities Act or a matter of criminal assistance with other countries under federal jurisdiction. Under Canadian law, securities regulations are subject to State jurisdiction. The BCSC signed the MOU with the SEC in 1988, jointly with the Ontario Securities Commission and the Quebec Securities Commission.[62]

In June 1996, the SEC asked the BCSC to produce GS Corp's employee records and securities transactions in the United States. The commission ordered GS Corp to provide information under section 141(1)(b) of the British Columbia Securities Act.[63] This provision authorized the chairman of the BCSC to issue orders to help regulate the securities laws of other jurisdictions. GS Corp, on the other hand, refused to submit such an order, alleging that such an order was beyond the authority of the committee. The issue, in this case, was whether the exchange of information on securities offences was a matter of State jurisdiction under the Securities Act or whether it was a matter of criminal assistance with other countries under federal jurisdiction.

The High Court of British Columbia held that judicial assistance under Article 141(1)(b) of the Act was not related to a tort within a State and, therefore, did not constitute a civil transaction subject to the jurisdiction of a State under the Canadian Constitution.[64] Notwithstanding its *obitur*, cooperation across

[60] *Securities and Exchange Commission v Ong Congqin Bobby and Lum Kwan Sung* [1999] 1 SLR 310.

[61] *Global Securities Corp v British Columbia (Securities Commission)* [2000] 1 SCR 494, 2000 SCC 21.

[62] US SEC, the Ontario Securities Commission, the Commision des Valeurs Moblieres du Quebec, the British Columbia Securities Commission, Memorandum of Understanding concerning Consultation, Cooperation and the Exchange of Information Related to the Supervision of Cross-Border Regulated Entities (signed on 7 January 1988, amended on 10 June 2010) <http://www.sec.gov/about/offices/oia/oia_bilateral/canada.pdf>.

[63] British Columbia Securities Act, RSBC 1996, c 418, s 141(1)(b).

[64] Constitution Act, 1867, 30 & 31 Victoria, c 3, s 92(13).

jurisdictions was necessary and desirable because securities transactions are conducted between multiple jurisdictions due to their nature.

In addition, Canada's Evidence Act allowed a State's high court to request evidence relating to foreign proceedings.[65] However, the court rejected the SEC's request because the entity was not a foreign court that could request evidence, even if the Evidence Act was constitutional.

The Federal Supreme Court upheld the State Supreme Court's ruling, stating that the main purpose of Article 141(1)(b) was to enable the Securities Commission to meet its domestic obligations through mutual cooperation with other securities regulators. Under this provision, the Commission monitors what British Columbia registrants are doing abroad, stabilizing the evaluation of parties to the transaction registered in the State. Therefore, since this provision was part of the securities regulations, it was decided that it was enacted within the State's authority.[66]

Although cases are sporadic, they show a growing practical recognition at the time that civil procedures can be utilized to obtain evidence for investigating securities fraud. These judicial endorsements validated the affirmative position and allowed the law enforcement authorities to explore broader and more flexible alternatives to MLATs.

3.3 Convention on Insider Trading of 1989

Aside from the United States's efforts, the Council of Europe's Convention on Insider Trading of 1989 is a notable practice.[67] The instrument provides for the exchange of information between those responsible at the national level for the surveillance of stock exchange transactions with a view to the rapid identification and discovery of irregular insider trading operations. The drafting process started in 1983, against the need for international cooperation on the regulation of insider trading, which 'often embitters business relationships' and 'presents a challenge for the legislature'.[68] The drafters were aware of the 'deficiencies in international law'.[69]

The scope of the cooperation encompasses the search for those responsible for other irregular transactions that could have an adverse impact on the equal access of all stock market traders to information or the quality of the information provided

[65] Evidence Act, RSC 1985 c C-5.

[66] *Global Securities Corp v British Columbia (Securities Commission)* (n 61) para 44. See also Carlin McGoogan, 'Case Comment: Global Securities Corp. v. British Columbia (Securities Commission)' (2003) 61 University of Toronto Faculty of Law Review 219.

[67] Convention on Insider Trading (ETS No 130) (adopted on 20 April 1989, entered into force on 1 October 1991).

[68] Council of Europe, 'Explanatory Report to the Convention on Insider Trading and the Protocol thereto' (20 April 1989) 1 <https://rm.coe.int/16800cb347>.

[69] ibid.

to investors to ensure honest dealing. The list of misbehaviours includes fraudulent financial operations, the rigging of stock market prices, or the laundering of proceeds of crime. Furthermore, the State parties undertake to afford each other the widest measure of mutual assistance in criminal matters relating to insider trading offences.

Such cooperation is not done as a part of the mutual legal assistance on criminal matters. In contrast, the Convention requires States to provide mutual assistance to other member States through the exchange of information and to facilitate the effective supervision of securities markets. It also mandates the establishment of procedures to determine whether individuals engaged in specific financial transactions on stock markets are insiders.

The Convention sets limits to the use of information. The requesting authority may not use the information supplied for purposes other than those set out in its request.[70] When the requesting authority wishes to use the information supplied for purposes other than those set out in the initial request, it must inform the requested authority in advance. The information supplied may be used before a criminal court only in cases where it could have been obtained via the procedures of the Convention.[71] No authority of the requesting party may use or transmit this information for tax, customs, or currency purposes unless otherwise provided in a declaration by the requested party.[72]

The use of the information in the criminal procedure is based on the consent of the requested party. There is no obligation for a judicial review. It will allow the State parties to cooperate with a more lenient standard than an MLAT. The convention also provides the State's obligation to afford each other 'the widest measure of mutual assistance in criminal matters relating to offences involving insider trading'.[73] However, it is designed to be an independent instrument from the European Convention on Mutual Assistance in Criminal Matters or specific agreements or arrangements on mutual assistance in criminal matters in force between parties.[74]

Although the convention is a noteworthy initiative, only a limited number of States have ratified it. Notably, France and Germany are not members, nor are the United States or Japan.[75] Therefore, the instrument has had a limited impact in practice.

70 Convention on Insider Trading art 8(1).
71 ibid art 8(4).
72 ibid art 8(5).
73 ibid art 12(1).
74 ibid art 12(2).
75 As of 2024, the member States are Cyprus, Czeck Republic, Finland, Luxembourg, Netherlands, Norway, Slovenia, Sweden, and the United Kingdom. As for France and Germany, the EC Directive of 1989 requires member States to coordinate on insider trading. Council Directive 89/592/EEC [1989] OJ L334/30. The Directive was replaced with Directive 2003/6/EC of the European Parliament and of the Council of 28 January 2003 on insider dealing and market manipulation (market abuse) [2003] OJ L96/16.

4. Cooperation among Financial Regulatory Authorities

4.1 Historical Development

To address the gap between the demand for legal assistance and the limitations of the MLAT in criminal or civil matters, the SEC began to establish MOUs with foreign financial regulatory authorities. Such agreements are informal and do not have the status of a treaty. The exchange of information between financial regulatory authorities under these MOUs is authorized by the domestic law of each State, which will be discussed in Section 4.2. Before delving into domestic law, examining the historical development of these MOUs is worthwhile.

The first MOU case was between Switzerland and the United States and was established following the BSI incident.[76] During this time, insider trading was not considered a criminal offence in Switzerland, and as a result, it was not covered by the MLAT agreement between the two countries established in 1977. Nonetheless, insider trading can constitute other crimes, such as fraud, breach of trust, or the disclosure of a trade secret. As a result, the authorities agreed to cooperate in detecting and preventing insider trading to an extent feasible. The agreement was initially to enable State parties to cooperate and complement the MLATs. However, as opportunities for obtaining evidence and information through mutual assistance increased, the SEC recognized that it would be easier to establish conditions for mutual assistance under such informal agreements.

The most significant development was broadening the mandate of financial regulatory authorities within each State. Regulatory authorities, including the SEC, used to lack the authority to assist their counterparts in other States, even when such assistance was necessary. They also lacked the authority to investigate conduct not deemed illegal in their own country. The United States amended its laws to address this defect and encouraged other States to do the same, granting regulatory authorities the necessary mandate to investigate and assist their counterparts. The Securities and Exchange Act was amended to define a 'foreign law enforcement authority' as 'any foreign authority that is empowered under foreign law to detect, investigate or prosecute potential violations of law'.[77] Therefore, foreign counterparts needed to be authorized for the United States to cooperate with foreign regulatory authorities.

The BCBS recommended this approach to promote the exchange of information among financial regulatory authorities.[78] As articulated in Section 2.2.3, it was not necessarily in the context of mutual legal assistance on criminal matters but

[76] Memorandum of Understanding between Switzerland and the United States to Establish Mutually Acceptable Means for Improving International Law Enforcement Cooperation in the Field of Insider Trading, reprinted in (1983) 22 International Legal Materials 1.

[77] Securities and Exchange Act, s 24(f)(4)(B).

[78] BCBS (n 48) 42–43.

aimed to maintain the stability of financial institutions. To this end, it urged the creation of national laws that require received information to be used only for the supervision of financial institutions, kept confidential, and cooperation to be conducted on a reciprocal basis. In its word, '[w]here host country laws pose obstacles to sharing information or cooperating with home country supervisors, host authorities should work to have their laws changed in order to permit effective consolidated supervision by home countries'.[79]

As the next section explores, such legislation has been enacted in Japan, the United Kingdom, Australia, France, Germany, Italy, Spain, India, Singapore, and Hong Kong, which are home to major stock exchanges, allowing financial regulatory authorities to share pertinent information and evidence with competent authorities for financial oversight purposes.

4.2 Mandate of the Authorities

The conditions for cooperation and the admissibility of information in criminal proceedings vary across countries. These laws can be broadly categorized into three groups.

4.2.1 Authorization of Financial Authorities to Provide Information to Other States under More Lenient Conditions

The United States enacted the International Securities Enforcement Cooperation Act of 1990 to authorize the SEC to exchange information that would eventually be used in a criminal proceeding in the counterpart's State under comparably lenient conditions.

The act clarifies the SEC's authority to furnish information to a foreign entity. The Commission may aid in requesting a foreign securities authority if the requesting party States deem it necessary to determine whether any individual has violated, is violating, or is about to violate any laws or regulations related to securities matters that the requesting authority administers or enforces.[80] The Commission may conduct such an investigation as it deems necessary to collect information and evidence pertinent to the request for assistance.[81] Assistance can be provided irrespective of whether the facts described in the request would also amount to a violation of the laws of the United States.[82] When deciding whether to assist a foreign securities authority, the Commission must consider several factors. These factors include whether the requesting authority has agreed to provide

[79] ibid 43.
[80] International Securities Enforcement Cooperation Act, 1990, Pub L No 101-550, 104 Stat 2714 (1990), 15 USC 78u (2).
[81] ibid.
[82] ibid.

reciprocal assistance in securities matters to the Commission and whether complying with the request would not harm the public interest of the United States.[83] The law does not require double criminality.

The act also grants the SEC the authority to use evidence gathered from foreign regulatory authorities to some extent. For example, the law requires that the SEC impose sanctions on brokers or dealers who 'have been convicted within ten years preceding the filing of any application for registration or at any time after that of any felony or misdemeanour or of a substantially equivalent crime by a foreign court of competent jurisdiction'.[84]

However, there has been concern about whether the Act is consistent with the Freedom of Information Act (FOIA), which requires government information to be available to the public. The Securities Exchange Act exempts the SEC from disclosing confidential information obtained from a foreign securities authority to third parties in response to a FOIA request.[85] Additionally, the act gives the Commission the power to safeguard privileged information obtained from a foreign securities authority or law enforcement authority if the authority has determined in good faith and represented to the Commission that the information is privileged. Similarly, Australia enacted the Mutual Assistance in Business Regulation Act 1992, which now allows its regulatory body, Australian Securities and Investments Commission, to exercise compulsory powers to obtain documents, information, or testimony on behalf of foreign securities authorities.[86] The body is also authorized to cooperate with international organizations and foreign regulators, which make requests for assistance under international cooperation agreements including the IOSCO Multilateral Memorandum of Understanding.

4.2.2 Authorization of the Financial Authorities to Provide Information under Strict Conditions

Most States have authorized their financial regulatory authorities to collaborate with foreign regulators under strict conditions and with a consent of the department of justice. For example, Switzerland implemented the Securities Trading Act in 1995, which expanded Swiss Financial Market Supervisory Authority (FINMA)'s authority to cooperate with foreign regulatory authorities. The act permits FINMA to request information and documentation from foreign financial

[83] ibid.

[84] 15 USC 78o (b)(4).

[85] Securities and Exchange Act, s 24(d).

[86] Mutual Assistance in Business Regulation Act, 1992 Act No 25; Australian Securities and Investments Commission Act, 2001 Act No 32; The list of the agreements is available at Australian Securities and Investments Commission, 'Memoranda of understanding and other international agreements' <https://www.asic.gov.au/about-asic/what-we-do/international-activities/international-regulatory-and-enforcement-cooperation/memoranda-of-understanding-and-other-international-agreements/>.

market supervisory authorities, which may be necessary for enforcing the law.[87] However, FINMA can only forward publicly inaccessible information and case-related documents to foreign financial market supervisory authorities if the following two conditions are met: (1) the information is used solely for enforcing regulations governing stock markets, securities trading, and securities traders or is sent to other authorities, courts, or bodies for this purpose; and (2) the applicant authorities are bound by official or professional secrecy, notwithstanding provisions on the public nature of proceedings and the notification of the general public about such proceedings.[88] In the case of transmitting information in criminal matters, an agreement with the Federal Office of Justice is needed, and this agreement should be held for purposes other than enforcing regulations governing securities trading.[89]

The EU member States have also authorized their financial regulatory authorities to collaborate with other States under the same conditions as judicial assistance in criminal matters. The Council Directive 2004/39, which aimed to harmonize the securities laws of member States, included provisions on the exchange of information.[90] The Directive was not intended to prejudice criminal proceedings but contained provisions for exchanging information for administrative procedures. This emphasizes the need for strict professional secrecy to protect particular rights and ensure the smooth transmission of information.[91]

Beyond the minimum standard set by the EU Directive, the legislation of member States varies with each other. For instance, in 1968, France enacted a blocking statute restricting the disclosure of economic, commercial, industrial, financial, or technical documents or information to foreigners or entities, as discussed in Chapter 6, Section 2.3.[92] An exception was made in the 1999 Finance Act on the exchange of information with the French financial supervisory authority, *Autorité des Marchés Financiers* (AMF), and the authorities of member states of the EC or the European Economic Area (EEA).[93] According to the law, a request by the COB, succeeded by the AMF, to conduct an on-site investigation or supervision or to exchange information can be refused if it could threaten France's

[87] Bundesgesetz über die Börsen und den Effektenhandel (Börsengesetz, BEHG) vom 24. März 1995, AS 1997 68 [Federal Act on Stock Exchanges and Securities Trading], art 38(1).

[88] ibid art 38(2).

[89] ibid art 38(6).

[90] Directive 2004/39/EC of the European Parliament and of the Council of 21 April 2004 on markets in financial instruments amending Council Directives 85/611/EEC and 93/6/EEC and Directive 2000/12/EC of the European Parliament and of the Council and repealing Council Directive 93/22/EEC, [2004] OJ L145, preamble, para 63.

[91] See ibid art 54 on professional secrecy.

[92] Loi n° 68-678 du 26 juillet 1968 relative à la communication de documents et renseignements d'ordre économique, commercial, industriel, financier ou technique à des personnes physiques ou morales étrangères, art 1.

[93] Code monétaire et financier, art L621-21, codified by Ordonnance n° 2000-1223 du 14 décembre 2000 (V). This provision was abolished in 2007 by Ordonnance n°2007-544 du 12 avril 2007 relative aux marchés d'instruments financiers.

sovereignty, safety, or public order; if criminal proceedings for the same conduct have already been completed in France; or if sanctions have been imposed by a final and binding judgment for the same crime. Additionally, if the French authorities suspect that a breach of financial law has occurred by an entity within the territory of a member state of the EC or EEA that is not under the supervision of that member state, they must inform the authorities concerned as specifically as possible. Appropriate action must also be taken if the authorities are notified that such violations have been committed under their jurisdiction.

Similarly, Germany's Securities Trading Act of 1998 contains a provision for cooperation with competent authorities in other countries.[94] The law allows the Federal Supervisory Office (*Bundesaufsichtsamt*) to share information necessary for supervising securities markets, credit institutions, financial services, investment companies, insurance undertakings, and administrative or court proceedings related to such regulation. The communication of such information must specify the purpose for which it may be used, and the recipient must be informed that the information, including personal data, may be processed or used only for that purpose. If there is reason to believe that such communication violates a German statute or would be detrimental to the interests of the person concerned, no personal data shall be communicated.[95] If information is received from an authority in another country, it may be disclosed or used only in compliance with the specified purpose. The Federal Supervisory Office may share such information with the supervisory authorities of stock exchanges and market supervision units in compliance with the specified purpose.[96] It should be noted that these provisions are separate from those related to international assistance in criminal matters.[97]

4.2.3 Prohibition of the Exchange of Information for the Purpose of Criminal Investigation

Certain States prohibit their authorities from providing information for criminal investigations. For instance, in Japan, the Financial Instruments and Exchange Law was enacted after consolidating and abolishing the Securities and Exchange Law and other related laws and regulations. This law provides for cooperation in investigations with foreign financial instruments and regulatory authorities.[98] The Prime Minister shall ensure that foreign authorities can cooperate in administrative investigations aimed at enforcing laws and regulations equivalent to those covered by this act. Such requests may involve asking individuals who engage in transactions involving securities or derivative transactions with a counterparty in

[94] Gesetz über den Wertpapierhandel/Wertpapierhandelsgesetz (WpHG) 9 September 1998, BGBl I 2708, art 7(1).
[95] ibid art 7(2).
[96] ibid art 7(3).
[97] ibid art 7(4).
[98] Financial Instruments and Exchange Act, Act No 25 of 1948 [*Kin'yū shōhin torihiki-hō*], art 189(1).

the relevant foreign State or ordering other relevant persons or witnesses to provide helpful reports or materials. However, there are exceptions to this rule, such as the absence of reciprocity, the potential harm to Japan's interests, and the risk of using reports or materials for purposes other than contributing to the performance of duties.[99] It is explicitly stated that appropriate measures will be taken to ensure that the reports or materials submitted are not used in criminal proceedings conducted by a court or judge in a foreign State.[100]

4.2.4 Summary

While there are certain limitations on the use of such information in criminal cases, the emergence of legislation in the United States and EU member States allowing financial authorities to provide information on more relaxed terms than criminal procedures have been a significant shift in intergovernmental collaboration to combat financial crime. These actions also enable authorities to obtain information pertaining to a wider range of illegal activities involving financial institutions, including not only securities fraud but also violations of other laws, such as money laundering regulations and laws concerning economic sanctions.

Because of the harmonization of the domestic laws, the States with major securities markets started to promote a wider range of cooperation both through binding and non-binding legal instruments, which Sections 4.3 and 4.4 will explore.

4.3 Bilateral Administrative Cooperation between Financial Authorities for Criminal Investigation

Following the expansion of the regulatory authority mandates in each State, the financial authorities started to conclude MOUs to facilitate information exchange.[101] Prior to the early 1980s, international cooperation in the implementation of securities laws was ad hoc. The institutionalization of such cooperation took place in the 1980s, including the conclusion of the 1982 US–Switzerland MOU,[102] as well as the 1986 UK–US MOU[103] and Japan–US MOU.[104] The US MOUs include provisions for monitoring cooperation, technical assistance, and enforcement cooperation, including support for obtaining evidence and information.

[99] ibid art 189(2).
[100] ibid art 189(4).
[101] For a list of the MOUs that the SEC concluded, see US SEC, 'Cooperative Arrangements with Foreign Regulators' (22 January 2021) <https://www.sec.gov/about/divisions-offices/office-international-affairs/cooperative-arrangements-foreign-regulators>. For an overview of these practice, see Pamela Jimenez, 'International Securities Enforcement Cooperation Act and Memoranda of Understanding' (1990) 31 Harvard International Law Journal 295.
[102] Swiss–US MOU (n 76).
[103] UK–US MOU, 23 September 1986, available at US SEC (n 101).
[104] Japan–US MOU, 23 May 1986, available at US SEC (n 101).

The contents of the MOUs differ from one another. For example, the Japan–US MOU emphasizes the significance of collaboration between securities regulators and their readiness to work together for monitoring purposes. However, the agreement does not specifically address cooperation on securities fraud.[105]

On the other hand, the UK–US MOU is the most comprehensive agreement, detailing specific actions that the authorities must undertake.[106] The first pillar of an MOU is the exchange of information on both administrative and criminal matters. It permits access to information files held by the authorities and requires parties to give testimony, record statements, and submit documents. The information provided can be used as evidence in criminal proceedings. However, when requesting information, it is essential to provide detailed specifications about the content, purpose, relevant laws and regulations, and relevant individuals of the information. Additionally, the use of the information must be limited to a specific purpose, and confidentiality must be maintained. In certain cases, such as the MOU between the US and Canadian authorities, evidence obtained through the memorandum may be used for purposes other than securities law or futures trading law, provided that the other party is notified and that there is no objection from them.[107]

Second, double criminality is not a requirement under an MOU. As the scope of securities crimes in the United States is wider than that in many other countries, it is often the case that the United States would not be able to prosecute a case if both parties were to be penalized.

Third, when authorities discover a violation of the law of another State, they are allowed to share information with the relevant authorities to the extent permitted by law. This approach is based on the legal principle of positive comity.

It is specified that the authorities retain the power to gather information without relying on the MOU. However, if the information is obtained outside of the MOU, then notification to the authorities of the other country may be necessary. In the event that the authorities discover information that may breach the securities laws of the other State, they may be obligated to notify the party. MOUs may include clauses that do not prohibit a party from collecting evidence outside of an MOU. Nevertheless, such actions must be conducted with prudence, and the other party must be informed beforehand if the information is located within the territory of their jurisdiction. Furthermore, discussions must take place regarding the potential impact of such actions on the interests of the other authority and its government, if requested.

[105] ibid.

[106] UK–US MOU (n 103). The instrument complements, but does not supersede or alter the terms or conditions of existing cooperation frameworks. ibid para 29.

[107] US–Canada MOU (10 June 2010) available at US SEC (n 101) paras 25-26.

Today, the SEC concludes MOUs on enforcement, supervision, data protection, and technical assistance. The counterparts include not only financial authorities but also market participants, markets, and entities in the asset management industries.[108]

Although MOUs lack legally binding effects, they still play a crucial role in promoting international cooperation among regulatory authorities.[109] The absence of court procedures under MOUs enables prompt and flexible cooperation between the authorities. Even if an MLAT is already in place, it is considered easier to reach an agreement under an MOU because the authorities usually require only basic information at the initial stages of the investigation, and the treaty process can be time-consuming and expensive. Moreover, MOUs are expected to discourage unilateral law enforcement actions by the United States, thus promoting multilateral cooperation among authorities.

The confidentiality requirements of MOUs may be strictly adhered to even if they lack legal enforceability. A case in point is the Global Mofy Metaverse (GMM) affair involving abnormal price volatility in the copper market, which came to the attention of the Commodity Futures Trading Commission (CFTC) in the late 1990s.[110] The CFTC obtained information from the UK Financial Services Authority (FSA) under the MOU between the CFTC and the UK FSA and filed a lawsuit in 1999, alleging that the GMM colluded with Sumitomo and others to manipulate copper prices and harm futures markets. When GMM and others sought to disclose information obtained by law enforcement from the FSA, they discovered that law enforcement was unable to disclose some of the information because it was obtained under the condition of confidentiality.[111] An ALJ challenged the FSA's order that law enforcement disclose information, arguing that the agency had abandoned confidentiality when it provided the information. In response, the CFTC reversed the ALJ's decision, refusing to allow the disclosure of information obtained under the MOU with the British FSA to GMM and others. The CFTC assessed that judges' interpretation of the MOU undermined their expectation of confidentiality, which is essential for cooperation between authorities in enforcement.

4.4 International Organization of Securities Commissions Multilateral Memorandum of Understanding

In the meantime, a multilateral mechanism was developed through the IOSCO. In 1974, the United States established the Inter-American Association of Securities

[108] US SEC (n 101).

[109] There has been considerable discussion about the role of non-binding instruments in norm creation. See, for instance, Joost Pauwelyn, Ramses A Wessel, and Jan Wouters, *Informal International Lawmaking* (OUP 2013).

[110] CFTC No 99-11, Commodity Futures Law Reporter 28655, 2001 WL 1167807. See also Michael D Mann and William P Barry, 'Developments in the Internationalization of Securities Enforcement' (2005) 39 International Law 667, 691.

[111] Commission Rule 10.42(b)(2)(v).

Commissions to direct securities regulators in fostering capital markets in Latin America. The policy was amended in 1983 to admit countries outside the Americas, and the name was amended to IOSCO in 1986 at the first annual meeting held in Paris. Since the latter half of the 1980s, various countries have sought to harmonize their domestic laws to overcome barriers to entry for foreign companies caused by differences in accounting standards. These standards served as the basis for securities regulations and were seen as obstacles to fair competition in the securities market and as harmful to foreign investors' interests. IOSCO became a platform for achieving this goal, with an increasing number of member countries and the establishment of financial markets. The organization moved from its original regional focus to a more general one.

A notable feature of the IOSCO is its wide range of membership. The By-Laws provide that the organization consists of (1) ordinary members (governmental regulators), (2) associate members (including supranational governmental regulators, subnational governmental regulators where there are national governmental regulators, among others), and (3) affiliate membership (including self-regulatory organizations, securities exchanges, financial market infrastructures including clearing and settlement agencies, among others).[112]

In 1998, the IOSCO adopted the 'Objectives and Principles of Securities Regulation'.[113] The organization declared three objectives of securities regulation, namely the protection of investors; ensuring that markets are fair, efficient, and transparent; and the reduction of systemic risk. A section on cooperation in regulation with non-foreign counterparts was included. First, the regulator should have the authority to share both public and non-public information.[114] Second, the parties should establish information-sharing mechanisms that outline when and how they will share both public and non-public information.[115] Finally, the regulatory system should provide assistance to foreign regulators who need to inquire about the discharge of their functions and exercise of their powers.[116]

In addition, it adopted Principles for Record Keeping Collection of Information.[117] The instrument mandates that each IOSCO member's jurisdiction must have the authority to obtain information identifying the beneficial owners of companies and bank accounts. Additionally, each IOSCO member should work to ensure that either it or another relevant authority within its jurisdiction has

[112] IOSCO, 'IOSCO By-Laws' (1996) pt 2 <https://www.iosco.org/library/by_laws/pdf/IOSCO-By-Laws-Section-1-English.pdf>.

[113] The latest version was adopted in 2017. IOSCO, 'Objectives and Principles of Securities Regulation' (May 2017) <https://www.iosco.org/library/pubdocs/pdf/IOSCOPD561.pdf>.

[114] ibid principle 11.

[115] ibid principle 12.

[116] ibid principle 13.

[117] Resolution on Principles for Record Keeping, Collection of Information, Enforcement Powers and Mutual Cooperation to Improve the Enforcement of Securities and Futures Laws, passed by the President's Committee, November 1997 <https://www.iosco.org/library/resolutions/pdf/IOSCORES15.pdf>.

the power to access necessary information, including statements and documents, for investigating and prosecuting potential violations of securities and futures regulations.

As articulated in Section 2.2.3, the investigation of securities fraud came to have a close connection with that of money laundering and other organized crimes. The 9/11 terrorist attacks of 2001 triggered concerns regarding potential money laundering via securities transactions, prompting a call for greater information sharing among IOSCO member nations.

In response, the IOSCO adopted an MMOU in 2002 aimed at facilitating cross-border cooperation between securities regulators for the exchange of information and the enforcement of laws.[118] This memorandum enabled regulators to share critical information, including beneficiary identities and transaction records for securities and derivative products held at banks and brokers, to aid in investigations.

The MMOU aims to facilitate complete adherence to the securities laws of each country and specify the extent and procedures of mutual assistance, the use of information, confidentiality, and grounds for denial of such assistance. In cases where information or documentation is requested, the relevant authority may compel the individual or entity to provide it, if it does not violate a bank secrecy law or any other applicable laws. Additionally, when permissible under national laws, the cooperation system may involve compelling sworn testimony on matters related to a request for judicial assistance.

However, the MMOU does not replace the MLAT. The MOU explicitly states that it is not legally binding and does not supersede domestic laws that are already in place. Additionally, the MMOU permits the requested State to decrease mutual assistance and information exchange if there are ongoing criminal proceedings against the individuals who are the subject of such requests. This is the case for both the individuals and the cases in question. However, if the requesting country can demonstrate that it pertains to a separate matter, then it will not be considered a valid reason for refusal.

The IOSCO has issued a series of recommendations on substantive regulation. These recommendations suggest that the principle of reciprocity for mutual legal assistance be reconsidered and that restrictions on the exchange of information due to domestic law be strictly evaluated.[119]

The MMOU also operates on a merit-based system, which involves a review of the legal framework for information exchange cooperation and approval of

[118] Multilateral Memorandum of Understanding Concerning Consultation and Cooperation and the Exchange of Information (MMoU) (IOSCO, May 2002) <https://www.iosco.org/v2/about/?subsection=mmou>.

[119] See Resolution on Enforcement Powers (Presidents' Committee of the International Organization of Securities Commissions, November 1997) <https://www.iosco.org/library/resolutions/pdf/IOSCORES14.pdf>.

the authorities' legal authority to exchange information. When a country applies to sign the MMOU, it must disclose its domestic legal system and the IOSCO Technical Committee is responsible for assessing the country's capacity to implement the MMOU, as specified in Appendix B. IOSCO established a panel of experts to monitor each country's willingness and ability to comply with the MMOU, and it has the authority to exclude countries that fail to meet the standards. Moreover, IOSCO has published the names of countries that have not signed the instrument and has pledged to support them in building their capacity to implement it.

The IOSCO does not rely solely on the exchange of information through the MMOU. After the 2008 financial crisis, cooperation between regulators on information exchange, including regulatory oversight, took place through various channels.

The mutual assistance system has been widely praised, and its practical benefits have been recognized, particularly in cases where evidence is being gathered across multiple countries.[120] The use of IOSCO's MMOU has made it possible for requesting authorities to obtain assistance from foreign authorities under the relevant mutual assistance laws. This has made it less likely that foreign authorities will refuse to provide evidence on the grounds of bank secrecy or other legal barriers than if the requesting authorities were to act unilaterally.

The mechanism is not legally binding and serves only as a means by which to coordinate authority between different regulatory bodies. In certain instances, an individual who has a stake in collecting evidence may challenge legal assistance by authorities in court, claiming that it infringes on their rights. In such cases, the outcome may vary depending on how the courts of the relevant jurisdiction perceive the nature of judicial assistance with respect to securities law, and it cannot be assumed that there is a consistent interpretation.

The sharing of information under this mechanism has certain limitations, particularly with regard to information that is protected by law. This is because the exchange of information is not backed by mandatory measures, which could undermine the legal protections that exist for certain types of information. As a result, there is some uncertainty as to the extent to which the exchange of information under the MMOU can be used to obtain information that is protected by law.

Elsag Bailey case is an illustrative example of the challenges involved in cross-border information sharing.[121] In October 1998, Asea Brown Boveri, a joint

[120] John W Kropf and Neal Cohen, *Guide to U.S. Government Practice on Global Sharing of Personal Information* (2nd edn, American Bar Association, Section of Science & Technology Law 2015) 15–16. The authors comments that 'the MMOU has significantly enhanced the U.S. Securities and Exchange Commission's enforcement program by increasing and expediting the SEC's ability to obtain information from a growing number of jurisdictions worldwide'.

[121] See Felice B Friedman, Elizabeth Jacobs, and Stanley C Macel, 'Taking Stock of Information Sharing in Securities Matters' (2003) 10 Journal of Financial Crime 37, 43; David A Chaikin, 'The Impact of Swiss Principles of Mutual Assistance on Financial and Fiscal Crimes' (2006) 16 Revenue Law Journal 192, 214.

venture between a Swiss corporation and a Swedish corporation, announced a tender offer for Elsag Bailey. Suspicious stock transactions took place through Swiss banks immediately prior to purchase, leading the SEC to initiate an investigation.[122] At the end of the year, the Swiss Federal Banking Commission (SFBC) accepted a request from the Swiss authorities to record the accounts involved in the transactions to identify the individuals who made them.

However, the account holder challenged the SFBC's decision in a Swiss court, arguing that the transfer of the information did not meet the requirements of Switzerland's data protection act.[123] In May 2000, the Swiss Federal Court accepted this claim, ruling that the information could not be given unless the SEC provided specific grounds for its confidentiality. The decision was supported by the Supreme Court.[124] The court found that the SEC had not met the requirements of the Swiss Federal Law on Securities Exchanges and Trading, which includes conditions on the transfer of non-public information to foreign securities regulators.[125] The court held that the SEC's request had not provided sufficient guarantees of confidentiality. The Swiss Supreme Court was concerned that if the information was passed on to the SEC, it could be made public in proceedings involving the SEC or disclosed to tax authorities who would not otherwise have access to the information.

The SEC argued that a written promise to keep the information secret was sufficient, but the court found this promise vague and inadequate, as it did not guarantee that the information would not be passed on to other regulators. Despite efforts by the SEC and the SFBC to address these concerns, the court rejected to allow the SFBC to cooperate. Critics argued that the court failed to distinguish between 'disclosures' and 'use' of information in this case, as the 'use' of information in litigation proceedings is distinct from the 'disclosures' of information in violation of confidentiality.[126] Denying the former would make it meaningless to request information.

5. Rights of the Individuals

5.1 Protection of Financial Privacy

Investigation on securities fraud involves law enforcement authorities' obtaining of user's data. Users include individuals and corporations to keep their financial

[122] *SEC v Euro Sec Fund*, No 98-7347 (SDNY 25 September 2000).
[123] *W, X, Y & Z v Swiss Banking Commission*, 2A.355/1999 (1 May 2000).
[124] *A, B, C & D v Swiss Banking Commission*, 2A.349/2001/bmt (20 December 2001).
[125] BEHG (n 87) art 38.
[126] Friedman, Jacobs, and Macel (n 121) 43.

information confidential and secure from unauthorized access or disclosure. The targeted information includes personal financial data, such as bank account balances, investment portfolios, and credit card transactions, as well as business financial records, such as revenue, profits, and expenses. The question arises as to whether the enforcement aligns with the protection of financial privacy.

Financial privacy is protected by laws and regulations governing financial information collection, use, and disclosure by financial institutions and government agencies. These laws may require financial institutions to obtain consent from customers before sharing their financial information with third parties. They may impose penalties for unauthorized disclosure or misuse of financial information.

There are generally two contrasting views on financial privacy. A view claims that financial privacy is a fundamental human right. This standpoint underscores the importance of protecting individuals from intrusive surveillance and data misuse. It also supports personal autonomy concerning financial decisions.[127] The other view emphasizes that transparency is necessary for ensuring accountability and integrity in financial systems and preventing unlawful activities. It characterizes financial privacy as the customer's contractual right against the financial institution. These views often reflect the regulatory and cultural differences between the European Union and the United States.[128] A balanced approach is possible, where financial privacy is protected with statutory exceptions for legitimate governmental interests. This standpoint supports targeted and limited disclosure of financial information with adequate safeguards to protect privacy.

European countries pioneered the establishment of international protection of privacy rights. Two years after the Universal Declaration of Human Rights was adopted, the Convention for the Protection of Human Rights and Fundamental Freedoms (European Convention on Human Rights) provided privacy protection.[129] The concept of privacy was characterized as part of fundamental human rights, and the criteria for its limitations were strict. Information protection laws were enacted in member States of the European Community in the 1970s when banks and other financial institutions began to conduct financial transactions based on electronic information, as Chapter 11 will discuss in detail. It became problematic that the standards for information protection in member countries were not uniform.

[127] While the argument is not confined to financial privacy, Mills argue that the increase in intrusiveness into personal privacy harms individuals and society. He argues that personal autonomy, private property, personal information, and physical space help the privacy interests. Jon L Mills, *Privacy: The Lost Rights* (OUP 2008) 13.

[128] Virginia Boyd, 'Financial Privacy in the United States and the European Union: A Path to Transatlantic Regulatory Harmonization' (2006) 24 Berkeley Journal of International Law 939; David A Tallman, 'Financial Institutions and the Safe Harbor Agreement: Securing Cross-Border Financial Data Flows' (2002) 34 Law and Policy in International Business 747.

[129] European Convention for the Protection of Human Rights and Fundamental Freedoms (adopted on 4 November 1950, entered into force on 3 September 1953), art 8, 213 UNTS 222.

In 1995, the European Community Council adopted the Data Protection Directive 95/46/EC, which allowed for the exchange of personal information in the internal market and uniform privacy protection for data protection.[130] In particular, the Directive stipulated that when an EU company did business with a company outside the European Union, it could transfer information only after it had obtained consent to use it to the extent permitted under EU law. Similarly, in 2004, Canada enacted a law prohibiting companies from transferring personal information they hold to other countries unless those countries provide the same level of privacy protection, a measure considered equivalent to that of the European Union.[131]

On the other hand, the latter view is supported mainly in the United States. The Gramm–Leach–Bliley Act of 1999 abolished the separation of banks and securities firms established under the Glass–Steagall Act of 1933.[132] The act incorporated a chapter that outlined the obligations of financial institutions to safeguard information, establishing comprehensive regulations for the protection of financial data that were previously fragmented across different fields and State laws. However, there is no particular restriction regarding criminal investigations, so financial institutions must disclose information, and customers would have no opportunity to disagree with the procedure. In 1978, the Right to Financial Privacy Act was enacted, which grants customers of financial institutions a measure of privacy from federal government scrutiny by requiring government authorities to follow specific procedures when seeking access to financial records. It also imposes obligations and restrictions on financial institutions before releasing such information.[133] The Act was enacted in response to *United States v. Miller* in 1976 where the Supreme Court held that financial records belong to the institution, not the customer, thereby denying customers the right to challenge government access to those records.[134]

Virginia Boyd argued in 2006 that the differences between information protection standards and law enforcement mechanisms in the financial sector have resulted in a divergence in international privacy standards.[135] Without international standards, the 1995 EU Directive, which prohibited data transfers to countries that do not provide adequate protection, was regarded as the most ambitious attempt to protect individuals' privacy. On the other hand, the United States does not have a

[130] Directive 95/46/EC of the European Parliament and of the Council of 24 October 1995 on the protection of individuals with regard to the processing of personal data and on the free movement of such data (Data Protection Directive) [1995] OJ L281/31, arts 25 and 31(1).

[131] Personal Informational Protection and Electronic Documents Act (PIPEDA), RSC 2004, c 5, sch 1, s 4.1, principle 1.

[132] Financial Services Modernization Act of 1999 (Gramm–Leach–Bliley Act), Pub L No 106-102, 113 Stat 1338; 15 USC ss 6801–6809.

[133] Right to Financial Privacy Act, Pub L 95-630, 92 Stat 3641 (1978).

[134] *United States v Miller*, 425 US 435 (1976).

[135] Boyd (n 128).

law prohibiting the transfer of such information. The right to privacy is not viewed as a fundamental constitutional right, like the right to freedom or equality. Instead, it is considered a relative concept defined and protected differently by various laws.

5.2 Protection of Fundamental Rights through Domestic Civil and Administrative Procedures

The protection of fundamental rights in the investigation of securities fraud is carried out through civil, administrative, and criminal procedures at the domestic level. The suppression of securities fraud, as described in Section 2, largely depends on the broad administrative authorities. However, such authorities are subject to constitutional and statutory regulations. As articulated in Section 4, most of the jurisdictions maintain the distinction between the legal branches and does not allow the law enforcement authorities to bypass the strict criminal procedures by relying on civil or administrative procedures.

While the US SEC has taken flexible approach, its authority remains constrained by certain limits. On 27 June 2024, the US Supreme Court in *SEC v Jarkesy* held that when the SEC seeks civil penalties against a defendant for securities fraud, the Seventh Amendment to the US Constitution entitles the defendant to a jury trial. The Amendment provides that 'the right of trial by jury shall be preserved' in lawsuits.[136] In other words, it held that the SEC did not have the power to take administrative action against securities firms and other regulated businesses. When it does, it will be required to bring a civil case in court against the operators. The impact of the decision may extend to other federal agencies such as the Federal Trade Commission, the Internal Revenue Service, and the Environmental Protection Agency. This case may present the potential shift in the US legal practice.

6. Concluding Remarks

Obtaining information on securities offences can be achieved through existing commissions and MLATs, but practical problems may arise, such as delays and inefficiencies. The jurisdiction of the host country of a stock exchange regarding securities crimes is widely recognized based on either the territorial principle or the personal principle, regardless of the underlying basis of that jurisdiction. However, if unilateral law enforcement activities for evidence collection do not align with the legal systems of other countries, legal friction may arise, as observed in cases of violations of competition laws and economic sanction laws.

[136] *Securities and Exchange Commission v Jarkesy et al* 603 US 109 (2024) <https://www.supremecourt.gov/opinions/23pdf/22-859_1924.pdf>.

To facilitate the exchange of information between financial authorities on securities crimes, domestic laws in many countries have expanded the powers of those authorities. This trend, which has been instrumental in enhancing the regulation of other economic offences, is highly important.

Furthermore, financial authorities from different countries also collaborate through MOUs, even though such agreements are not legally binding. These MOUs are established to overcome the limitations of commissioning. It is important to note that these MOUs do not pertain to criminal matters; thus, they are marked by collaboration without the need for judicial review, which is typically needed for mutual legal assistance.

The cooperation between financial authorities alone is insufficient to establish criminal liability. At the domestic level, in some countries, such as Japan, information exchanged between financial authorities may not be admissible as evidence in criminal proceedings in other countries. Nevertheless, these legislative changes have facilitated the gathering of relevant information through these networks, the identification of crucial evidence that requires mutual legal assistance, and the referral of relevant information for prosecution.

Regarding the protection of the rights of private individuals, several measures have been implemented, particularly concerning the confidentiality obligation imposed on parties within a MOU. These measures are intended to ensure that sensitive information remains protected. However, private individuals do not possess the additional right to file an objection against the cooperation facilitated by these arrangements. They may challenge the legality of such cooperation in the courts of the country where the request is made, but thus far, all such cases have been dismissed.

Furthermore, there is a need for a more comprehensive examination of how financial privacy can be balanced with the requirements of regulatory compliance and international cooperation. As financial markets continue to evolve, it is essential to engage in broader discourse about the protection of financial privacy and the rights of private individuals while maintaining the integrity of financial systems.

8
Tax Offences

1. Introduction

A tax offence is an act of an individual or an entity to wilfully and intentionally falsify information on a tax return to limit tax liability. It entails an act or omission that violates tax laws and regulations, such as failing to under-report income, claiming false deductions, failing to comply with tax filing requirements, or using false identification information. Tax offences can range from minor infractions to severe crimes, depending on the severity of the violation.

Examples of tax offences include non-compliance offences (such as failure to provide the required information, documents, or returns), intentional tax offences (such as deliberate failure to comply with tax law to obtain financial advantage), and specific offences (such as entering an arrangement that would make a person unable to pay tax).[1] The elements of tax offences vary by State, as the requirements of tax bases, tax rates, sanctions for violations of the law, and the distinction between legal tax savings and unlawful tax evasion differ. Multinational corporations and individuals often make use of these gaps among jurisdictions.

There are primarily two grounds for applying tax laws: the source of the revenue and the residence of the taxpayer.[2] Source jurisdiction means that a State can tax income and revenue earned or generated within the State. Residence jurisdiction means that a State can tax worldwide income its residents earn. For tax purposes, a resident is defined by specific criteria, such as domicile in the case of a natural person or permanent establishment in the case of a corporation.[3] Therefore, the scope of the prescriptive jurisdiction could be wide-reaching.

The issue in the present context concerns enforcement jurisdiction. Tax authorities use a mix of procedures to detect and investigate tax crimes. Their primary source is the reports from the taxpayers, financial institutions, and employers. Tax

[1] OECD, 'Fighting Tax Crime—The Ten Global Principles, Second Edition' (17 June 2021) 16 <https://www.oecd.org/en/publications/fighting-tax-crime-the-ten-global-principles-second-edition_006a6512-en.html>. All websites were last accessed on 31 March 2025.

[2] Reuven S Avi-Yonah, *Advanced Introduction to International Tax Law* (3rd edn, Routledge 2021) 7. See also American Law Institute, *Restatement of the Law Fourth, The Foreign Relations Law of the United States* (American Law Institute Publishers 2018) s 411.

[3] There are debates about the criteria for activities carried out within the State and the definition of 'domicile' under each national law, which is beyond the scope of this chapter. See Philip Baker, 'Some Thoughts on Jurisdiction and Nexus' in Guglielmo Maisto (ed), *Current Tax Treaty Issues. 50th Anniversary of the International Tax Group* (IBFD Publications 2020) 446.

International Law and the Investigation of Transnational Crimes. Yurika Ishii, Oxford University Press.
 DOI: 10.1093/9780198957089.003.0008

authorities can identify inconsistencies in tax return information by verifying records obtained from such third-party sources. In addition, banks and other financial institutions must submit information on suspicious activity to the authorities, including unexplained large deposits or transfers, which is the rule developed through anti-money laundering regulations.

Collecting tax information across borders entails many issues. States have created multilayered networks of tax information exchange to overcome this limitation. The exchange of information on tax incomes provided in double-tax treaties is an essential tool for investigating tax crimes. In addition, States started to conclude the tax information exchange agreements (TIEAs) to strengthen co-ordination on a bilateral basis. The Organisation for Economic Co-operation and Development (OECD) Global Forum on Transparency and Exchange of Information for Tax Purposes (Global Forum) and the subsequent enforcement mechanism of the common reporting standard (CRS) constitute new steps forward, as discussed in the following sections. As the following sections will examine, today, States utilize these mechanisms, which consist of domestic tax regimes and multilayered tax treaties, to obtain tax information from foreign authorities.

One of the most significant advances in the investigation of tax crimes has been the formal authorization of the use of tax information in criminal proceedings. Many agreements allow recipient countries to share financial and tax information from these networks with law enforcement authorities. By integrating tax records into criminal investigations, authorities can better track illicit financial activities, including money laundering and other financial crimes.

With these characteristics in mind, this chapter focuses on the authorities' collecting of tax information across borders. Section 2 sets the stage for understanding the proliferation of offshore financial centres and the role of bank secrecy. Section 3 then explores the historical development of multilayered networks to exchange tax information, underscoring key model treaties and the increasing mechanisms for information exchange. Significant instruments discussed include the OECD Convention on Mutual Assistance in Tax Administration and Enforcement (the OECD Tax Administration Convention) and various TIEAs. Further, Section 4 examines the scope and application of information exchange in criminal procedures, addressing issues such as double criminality, grounds for refusal, confidentiality, and the impact of bank secrecy laws. The role of mutual legal assistance treaties (MLATs) in criminal matters is also scrutinized. The discussion then delves into the historical and legal backgrounds that have shaped the use of tax information in criminal investigations. The following focus is on methods of obtaining evidence from financial institutions. The chapter delves into the US measures, from the QIs programme to the Foreign Account Tax Compliance Act (FATCA). Then, Section 5 will examine the efforts of the OECD Global Forum. Lastly, Section 6 argues that protecting individual rights forms a crucial part of the discussion, emphasizing taxpayer rights and the importance of financial privacy amidst growing transparency demands.

2. Characteristics of Collecting Tax Information Across Borders

2.1 Creation and Proliferation of Offshore Markets

Tax law represents the State's fiscal policy. Unlike criminal law, which by its very nature has many common elements, tax law differs substantially from one country to another. In addition, tax regulations of developed States internalize offshore markets or offshore financial centres, which are financial markets outside the investor's home country. Typically, offshore financial centres offer favourable regulatory and tax conditions for non-resident individuals and companies, including benefits such as bank secrecy. Such asymmetries characterize cross-border tax enforcement.

The modern origin of offshore markets can be traced back to the United Kingdom's establishment of the Eurodollar market in the 1960s.[4] Britain created the mechanism to protect its financial institutions from the devaluation of the pound that followed the Suez crisis.[5] In 1963, the Bank of England began differentiating between 'onshore' and 'offshore' transactions, favouring the latter regarding taxation and regulation to attract foreign financial institutions (FFIs).[6]

There was disagreement about whether a legal entity was considered a resident for tax purposes if its significant business activities were not conducted in the country where it was registered. A court set the precedent that even if a company is registered in the United Kingdom, it may not be required to pay taxes under UK law unless it exercises management and control of the company within the UK territory.[7]

[4] For the historical development of the offshore financial centre and its nature, see Rose-Marie Belle Antoine, *Confidentiality in Offshore Financial Law* (2nd edn, OUP 2014) 3; Dora Neo, 'A Conceptual Overview of Bank Secrecy,' in Sandra Booysen and Dora Neo (eds), *Can Banks Still Keep a Secret?* (CUP 2017) 3. For the economic significance of Eurodollar market, see Milton Friedman, 'The Euro-Dollar Market: Some First Principles' [1969] Morgan Guaranty Survey 4; Sol Picciotto, *International Business Taxation: A Study in the Internationalization of Business Regulation* (Quorum Books 1992).

[5] Ronen Palan, *Tax Havens: How Globalization Really Works* (Richard Murphy and Christian Chavagneux eds, Cornell UP 2010) 107. The Suez Crisis of 1956 costed GBP 500 million and the value of the currency decreased.

[6] JML, 'Report for Hamilton' (19 October 1961) EID 10/19; 'Draft Report of BIS Meeting on Eurodollar Market' (13 January 1963) EID 10/22.

[7] The case *Todd v Egyptian Delta Land and Investment Co Ltd* (1928) 14 TC 119, involved the Egyptian Delta Land and Investment Company, which was registered in London in 1904 and had its headquarters in Cairo, Egypt, which was a British colony at the time. The company's business was buying and leasing land in Egypt. The issue in the case was whether the company could be considered a resident of the United Kingdom for tax purposes. The court rejected the notion that the company was a UK resident based on the criterion presented. See Palan (n 5) 126; John O'Brien, *Conflict of Laws* (Taylor & Francis 1999) 84; Subhajit Basu, *Global Perspectives on E-Commerce Taxation Law* (Ashgate 2007) 38.

The United States followed suit to prevent the outflow of dollars. During the 1950s, amidst the tensions of the Cold War, countries became reluctant to exchange their gold for US dollars, concerning potential devaluation and economic instability. This shift was largely due to the significant rise in US military spending and foreign aid.

The US government enacted the Interest Equalization Tax (IET) Act in response.[8] IET was a federal tax imposed on the acquisition cost of foreign stocks and bonds purchased by US citizens. Its purpose was to reduce the capital outflow from the United States and to address the balance of payment deficits by dissuading American investment in foreign securities and encouraging investment in domestic securities. As a result, US corporations began registering themselves in offshore markets. In the 1970s, the rise of neoliberalism pushed for the growth of offshore markets, the deregulation of financial markets in the United Kingdom and the United States, and oil crises. These factors contributed to expanding the Eurodollar market, where governments began procuring US dollars. The United States abolished the IET Act in 1974 due to significant changes in economic and political conditions since the early 1960s, including the adoption of floating exchange rates in 1971 and the increasing integration of global trade and investment markets.

Such offshore markets began to spread in the United Kingdom's former colonies and Caribbean States. In 2000, the International Monetary Fund (IMF) published a list of sixty-nine countries and territories with major offshore markets.[9] The list included Bermuda, the Cayman Islands, the British Virgin Islands, Gibraltar, the Turks and Caicos Islands, Anguilla, and Montserrat, which are British Overseas Territories; Jersey, Gandhi Island, and the Isle of Man, which are Crown Dependencies; Hong Kong, a former colony and later a dependent territory; and Singapore, Malaysia, Bahrain, and Cyprus, former colonies. During the 1920s, the British Empire employed the Financial Act of 1920 to incentivize companies operating in British territory to invest in the domestic market. The government provided preferential tax rates to the colonies by permitting a deduction from the Dominion or colonial tax rate of up to 50 per cent of the UK rate for transactions within the British Empire.[10]

In the meantime, US corporations expanded to the Caribbean islands of the Bahamas, the Netherlands Antilles, the Cayman Islands, and Panama to utilize the IET.[11] Offshore markets in the region emerged due to the British Empire's decline and the United States's ascendance as a dominant power in the nineteenth century. The United States tried to eliminate European influence in the region. After the

[8] Interest Equalization Tax Act, Pub L No 88-563, 78 Stat 827 (1963).

[9] IMF Monetary and Exchange Affairs Department, 'Offshore Financial Centers IMF Background Paper' (23 June 2000) <https://www.imf.org/external/np/mae/oshore/2000/eng/back.htm>.

[10] Picciotto (n 4) 14.

[11] ibid 121.

Spanish–American War of 1898, the United States incorporated Puerto Rico as its federal district, established Cuba as a protectorate, supported Panama's independence from Colombia, and developed the Panama Canal Zone as a US leasehold for canal development. However, the United States did not incorporate the Lesser Antilles into its territory. Since the British colonization of these islands in the mid-seventeenth century, their primary industry has been the cultivation of sugar plantations using enslaved people. After the Civil War in 1865, labour-intensive industries in the United States that relied on enslaved people declined. As a result, the Lesser Antilles remained under British possession. In 1958, the British attempted to establish a separate nation called the West Indian Federation. However, the organization was dissolved four years later in 1962.

Since the 1960s, countries with limited industrial infrastructure have increasingly leveraged the growth of the UK offshore market. The Cayman Islands, the Bahamas, and Bermuda led this movement.[12] The West Indies Associated States Council of Ministers was established in 1966, and the Eastern Caribbean Common Market became the basis of regional cooperation in 1968. The Organisation of Eastern Caribbean States was established in 1981, further strengthening economic ties between these countries. Being English-speaking and having inherited the British legal system, these countries had social and cultural grounding that allured US companies.

Neoliberalism pushed for the development of offshore markets in the 1970s in the United Kingdom and the United States. Their policies aimed to stimulate the private economic sector for increased productivity and preserve market functioning to address the adverse effects of excessive productive activity. In the late 1970s, pro-competitive policies were implemented, State-owned enterprises were privatized in the United Kingdom and the United States, and deregulation occurred in financial and labour markets. The 1973 Oil Crisis further fuelled the expansion of the Euromarket, as governments faced fund shortages in purchasing oil due to soaring oil prices, leading them to raise dollars through the offshore centres. Countries began to regulate capital within their borders and move away from the Bretton Woods monetary system based on the gold and dollar standards.[13]

2.2 Bank Secrecy

A significant impediment to tax crime investigations is the issue of bank secrecy. Banks and other financial institutions are mandated to maintain the confidentiality

[12] See the autobiography of the First Financial Secretary of the Cayman Islands, Vassel Johson, *As I See It: How Cayman Became a Leading Financial Centre* (Book Guild Ltd 2001).

[13] Eric Helleiner, *States and the Reemergence of Global Finance: From Bretton Woods to the 1990s* (Cornell UP 1994) 82.

of their clients' tax information under the contractual relationship between the customer and the bank. In addition, States enact legislation to protect financial information more rigorously than other information obtainable through other business transactions. For instance, the UK Bankers' Books Evidence Act 1879 provide that

> [a] banker or officer of a bank shall not, in any legal proceeding to which the bank is not a party, be compellable to produce any banker's book the contents . . . , or to appear as a witness to prove the matters, transactions, and accounts therein recorded, unless by order of a judge made for special cause.[14]

However, these laws can become excessively stringent, thereby restricting third parties, including the State, from conducting criminal investigations. Such confidentiality measures attract individuals seeking to avoid disclosing their information to public authorities.

The offshore markets created a division between the country where financial capital was located and the country where taxes were imposed. The taxing States needed to obtain financial information abroad through various means. In response, countries with offshore markets enacted banking secrecy laws to prevent such attempts and attract financial institutions to their shores. Several jurisdictions, including Switzerland,[15] the Cayman Islands,[16] Panama,[17] Uruguay,[18] and Singapore,[19] have enacted laws prohibiting financial institutions and their employees from disclosing customer information to foreign authorities, which would invite criminal sanctions.

These statutes impose legal obligations on financial institutions or their employees to maintain strict confidentiality of customer information and criminal penalties for unauthorized disclosures. The following sections will examine the cases of Switzerland and the Caribbean countries, each of which has taken a distinct approach to establishing bank secrecy laws.

2.2.1 Switzerland

Switzerland's financial market developed significantly in the mid-nineteenth century. The introduction of railways from Germany and the progress of the Industrial Revolution played a key role in fostering progress. The financial sector became Switzerland's dominant industry, driving its development and economic

[14] Bankers' Books Evidence Act 1879, c 11, s 6.

[15] Bundesgesetz über die Banken und Sparkassen (Bankengesetz, BankG) vom 8. November 1934, art 47; Schweizerisches Strafgesetzbuch vom 21. Dezember 1937, art 273.

[16] Confidential Relationships (Preservation) Law, Law 16 of 8 September 1976.

[17] Coded Bank Accounts, Law 8 of 28 January 1959; Commercial Code, arts 89, 93, Law 17 of 30 January 1961.

[18] Sistema de Intermediación Financiera, s 15.322 [1982] Diario Oficial 59.

[19] Banking Act, Act 41 of 1970, art 47(4).

growth.[20] During the 1920s, European countries faced a period of economic recession, leading to increased taxes for citizens. As a result, wealthy citizens chose to deposit their money in Swiss banks. In response, the governments sought information about individual deposits from Swiss authorities.[21] Moreover, the Nazi regime required Jews to report foreign deposits, and German State police conducted covert investigations of accounts held in Swiss territory through Swiss bankers.[22] Legal provisions were implemented to prevent financial institution officials from disclosing information to foreign authorities and imposing criminal penalties for any violations to address such concerns.

The initial measure taken to safeguard the interests of bank depositors was implemented in the Banking Act of 1934. This Act established regulations on reserves, mandated annual financial reporting, and required independent auditing by certified accountants.[23] The provision stipulated that financial institution officials have the legal duty to maintain the confidentiality of client information. Infringement or aiding in violating this obligation could result in criminal prosecution, including fines and imprisonment.[24] This provision is in place to safeguard the interests of the customer rather than those of the financial institution. Financial institutions cannot decline to disclose the information if the customer has been authorized to do so.[25] In addition, the Criminal Code of 1937 prohibited the disclosure of trade or business secrets to foreign authorities.[26]

The strictness of Swiss banking legislation may not be due to the stringency of the Banking Act itself but because of the limited powers of government and more robust cantonal authorities.[27] Tax laws fall under the jurisdiction of the cantons, and tax authorities at the federal level are not authorized to order banks to provide information on customer accounts or transactions based on misdemeanours. The

[20] For the history of the Switzerland's bank secrecy laws, see Henri B Meier, John E Marthinsen, and Pascal A Gantenbein, *Swiss Banking Secrecy* (John Wiley & Sons, Inc 2012) 98.

[21] ibid 108.

[22] Peter C Honegger, 'Swiss Banking Secrecy' [1990] Butterworths Journal of International Banking and Financial Law 344; Swiss Bank Corporation, *The Truth about Swiss Banking* (Swiss Bank Corporation 1972) 2. See also Hermine Herta Meyer, 'Banking Secret and Economic Espionage in Switzerland' (1954) 23 George Washington Law Review 284.

[23] The law was amended in 1971, but its policies on the bank secrecy remained the same.

[24] BankG (n 15) art 47. The statute prescribes a penalty of either a fine of Swiss Francs 2,000 or a maximum imprisonment of six months for intentional violations. Negligent violations carry a fine of Swiss Francs 1,000.

[25] Beat Kleiner, Renate Schwob, and Christoph Winzeler, 'Art. 47' in Daniel Bodmer, Beat Kleiner, and Benno Lutz (eds), *Kommentar zum Bundesgesetz über die Banken und Sparkassen vom 8. November 1934 sowie zu der Verordnung vom 17. Mai 1972 und der Vollziehungsverordnung vom 30. August 1961* (Schulthess Polygraphischer Verlag 2014) Rn 1.

[26] Strafgesetzbuch vom 21. Dezember 1937, art 273. The disclosure or unauthorized access of trade or business secrets to foreign entities, their officials, or agents may result in a prison sentence of up to three years or a monetary fine. In severe cases, the prison sentence may not be less than one year and can be accompanied by a monetary penalty.

[27] Meyer (n 22) 30.

elements and penalties of tax offences vary between cantons, making it challenging for foreign authorities to access financial information from Swiss banks.

2.2.2 Caribbean Countries

Caribbean countries with offshore centres enacted bank secrecy laws as well. As common law jurisdictions, they used to rely on the 1924 *Tournier* case from the UK Court of Appeal regarding bank secrecy.[28] The judgment held that the disclosure of the information is justified when disclosure is under compulsion by law, where there is a duty to the public to disclose, where the interests of the bank require disclosure, or where the disclosure is made by the express or implied consent of the customer. However, some countries established statutory laws to enforce bank secrecy.[29]

It was partly a response to the US proactive law enforcement activities. In the mid-1960s, the United States sought access to banking information in the Caribbean to address drug offences. The Internal Revenue Service (IRS) launched 'Operation Trade Wind' in 1965, which involved law enforcement operations collecting information on fund movements in tax havens in the region.[30] The organization investigated the use of offshore accounts by US citizens seeking to evade tax obligations and conceal assets, some suspected to originate from criminal activities.

For instance, the Bahamas adopted the Banks and Trust Companies Regulation Act in 1965.[31] It codified the *Tournier* judgment, which was only applicable as common law. Its policy got rigorous after IRS officials stole a suitcase containing Bahamian bank documents to collect evidence as a part of the operation.[32] In 2000, the US Financial Crimes Enforcement Network (FinCEN) assessed the Bahamas as having one of the strictest bank secrecy regulations.[33]

[28] Court of Appeal, *Tournier v National Provincial and Union Bank of England* [1924] 1 KB 461, 473.

[29] See also Peter D Maynard, 'Offshore Banking Secrecy: Myth or Reality?' (1998) 1 Journal of Money Laundering Control 316.

[30] US Congress, House Committee on Government Operations, *Oversight Hearings into the Operations of the IRS (Operation Tradewinds, Project Haven, and Narcotics Traffickers Tax Program): Hearings before a Subcommittee of the Committee on Government Operations, House of Representatives, Ninety-fourth Congress, First session, October 6, November 4 and 11, 1975* (US Government Printing Office 1976). For the US policy to expand its jurisdictional scope to collect tax information from Carribean countries, see also Antoine (n 4) 307, 318.

[31] Banks and Trust Companies Regulation Act 1965 c 287, reprinted in 107-1 'Hearings: Role of U.S. Correspondent Banking in International Money Laundering' (2001) 3 Senate Hearing 107-84, 2584.

[32] *United States v Payner* 447 US 727 (1980). The US Supreme Court declined to exclude the evidence as tainted, ruling that the respondent lacked standing under the Fourth Amendment to suppress documents unlawfully seized from a third-party bank officer. The Court reasoned that a defendant's constitutional rights are violated only when the challenged conduct infringes upon their legitimate expectation of privacy. Furthermore, it held that the federal courts' supervisory power does not permit the suppression of otherwise admissible evidence solely because it was unlawfully obtained from a third party not before the court.

[33] United States Department of the Treasury Financial Crimes Enforcement Network, 'FinCEN Advisory: Transactions Involving The Bahamas' (July 2000) <https://www.fincen.gov/sites/default/files/advisory/advis13.pdf>.

The Cayman Islands enacted the Confidential Relationships (Preservation) Law in 1976.[34] The trigger was also a case where IRS officials subpoenaed a Cayman banker, Anthony R Field, when he landed at Miami airport. A grand jury looked into possible criminal violations of the US tax laws, focusing on using foreign banks to evade tax enforcement. Field refused to answer grand jury questions as he would have breached Cayman law. The US Fifth Circuit weighed the benefits of upholding US tax laws against the harm caused to the banker by breaching the Cayman Bank Secrecy Act. It ultimately concluded that the benefits of enforcing the tax laws outweighed the negative consequences to the banker, and therefore, the banker was required to testify.[35]

2.3 Summary

The challenge of international tax investigations lies in that specific countries control the tax information, and each nation has the sovereign right to withhold that information. Offshore markets emerged as 'commercialized sovereignty'[36] in which States utilize their sovereign authority to offer favourable regulatory environments, tax incentives, and other commercial benefits to attract multinational corporations, investors, and financial institutions. This circumstance created challenges in exchanging financial information.

3. Expansion of the Scope of Cooperation through Tax Agreements

3.1 Historical Development of the Exchange of Information through Tax Agreements

3.1.1 Bilateral Tax Agreements in the Nineteenth Century

States have developed complex information-sharing networks to meet the challenges. The main concern is that these arrangements were initially designed for administrative cooperation. However, driven by the need to combat tax fraud, money laundering, and other serious crimes, States have begun to agree to use this information for criminal investigation purposes.

Before addressing this issue, which will be examined in Section 4, this section outlines the historical development of tax treaties. Bilateral tax agreements have been in place since the 1840s.[37] However, cooperation between States was typically

[34] Confidential Relationships (Preservation) Law (n 16).

[35] *United States v Anthony R Field* 532 2d 404 (1976).

[36] Ronen Palan, 'Tax Havens and the Commercialization of State Sovereignty' (2002) 56 International Organization 151.

[37] Early practices included France and Belgium, Convention Concluded at Brussels on 12 August 1843, regulating the Relations between the Administrative Services of France and Belgium, translated

based on geographic and cultural connections, similar to the practice of letters rogatory. In its initial form, the exchange of information clauses emerged in the 1920s between the German Reich and its neighbouring countries. For instance, a treaty between the German Empire and Czechoslovakia, signed in 1921, stipulated mutual assistance for all tax information and documents.[38] The treaty provided three grounds for refusal of such assistance: (1) if the taxpayer was a national of the requested State, (2) if the provision of assistance would impact the sovereign rights or security of the requested State, and (3) if the provision of assistance involved information or statements of a third party who was not a taxpayer and could not be obtained under the law of the requested State or any other case where law enforcement could only be carried out in disregard of the principles of trade, commerce, or industrial secrecy. These three grounds for refusal were commonly included in other treaties concluded during the same period.

In 1922, the constituent States of the former Austro-Hungarian Empire, Austria, Hungary, Poland, Italy, Romania, and the Kingdom of Serbian Croatia concluded a tax treaty. However, it briefly provided mutual assistance on a reciprocal basis.[39]

After the First World War, the League of Nations established the Economic and Financial Organization and Fiscal Commission as its suborganization in 1920. The main mandate of the Fiscal Commission was to eliminate double taxation and pent tax avoidance.[40] In 1928, four draft model tax treaties were adopted.[41]

However, experts were aware of the difficulties of administrative cooperation on tax matters. The report submitted in 1925 before the Committee noted that States strongly desired to eliminate double taxation. Nonetheless, there was resistance

in League of Nations, *Double Taxation and Fiscal Evasion, Collection of International Agreements and Internal Legal Provisions for the Prevention of Double Taxation and Fiscal Evasion* (C.345.M.102. 1928. II, Geneva, 1 October 1928) 211; Netherland and Belgium, Convention regulating the Relations between the Administrative Services of Netherlands and Belgium (signed on 24 May 1845), translated in ibid 213; Belgium and Luxemburg, Convention regulating the Relations between the Administrative Services of Belgium and Luxemburg (11 October 1845), translated in ibid 213. For the historical development, Edwin RA Seligman, *Double Taxation and International Fiscal Cooperation* (Macmillan 1928) 52; Christian Freiherr von Roenne, 'The Very Beginning—The First Tax Treaties' in Thomas Ecker and Gernot Ressler (eds), *History of Tax Treaties: The Relevance of the OECD Documents for the Interpretation of Tax Treaties* (Linde 2011) 32.

[38] Germany and Czechoslovakia, Treaty between the German Reich and the Czechoslovak Republic concerning Legal Safeguards and Legal Assistance in Matters of Taxation (signed at Prague, 31 December 1921) 17 LNTS No 447B, translated and reproduced in League of Nations (n 37) 215.

[39] Autriche, Hongrie, Italie, Pologne, Roumanie, Etat Serbe-Croate-Slovene, Convention pour eviter la double imposition, signée a Rome, le 6 avril 1922, arts 12, 28 *Nouveau Recueil General de Traites et Autres Actes aux Rapports de Droit International* 3d ser, 457 (1934).

[40] League of Nations, *Report on Double Taxation* (Doc E.F.S. 73.F.19, 1923); League of Nations, *Report Presented by the Commission of Technical Experts on Double Taxation and Tax Evasion* (Doc C.216.M.85, 1927) 11; Klaus Vogel, 'Double Tax Treaties and Their Interpretation' (1986) 4 International Tax and Business Law 1.

[41] League of Nations, *Double Taxation and Tax Evasion Report, Presented by the General Meeting of Government Experts on Double Taxation and Tax Evasion*, vol II (1928) 49.

from each State to prevent tax avoidance by cooperating with other States.[42] In a book published in 1928, Edward Seligman, an American economist and one of the report's authors, attributed the slow pace of information exchange to economic reasons.[43] While relevant tax information was submitted to the requesting tax authorities, cooperation was hindered if the other State party failed to reciprocate, reducing the incentive to share information. Additionally, disclosing customer information to a foreign authority often conflicted with the interests of banks.

As a result, the 1928 Model Convention on Administrative Cooperation in Tax Matters provided administrative assistance, including information exchange, only to prevent double taxation.[44] In addition, the drafters underscored the preservation of each country's sovereignty. When information is not legally accessible, it is not subject to exchange under domestic fiscal laws and public policy, including the banking secrecy law. As a result, in the 1920s, regulations on information exchange played only a minor role in national implementation.

In the 1930s, the tax agreement included the information exchange clause. Countries started to conclude bilateral tax treaties following the model taxation conventions.[45] The information exchange clause increased in the mid-1930s. For instance, a collection of taxation treaties published by the League of Nations in 1933 featured mutual assistance provisions of treaties between Belgium and Luxembourg,[46] France and Belgium,[47] Italy and Belgium,[48] and Austria and Poland.[49] Furthermore, the Belgium–Netherlands Treaty of 1933 specifically outlined the provision of information necessary for tax collection.

In 1939, the League of Nations Fiscal Committee proposed adopting an amended model of a bilateral convention for administrative assistance for tax matters. Following this proposal, the Mexico Model Convention was adopted in 1943,[50] and the London Model Convention was adopted in 1946.[51] The

[42] League of Nations, *Report and Resolutions submitted by the Technical Experts to the Financial Committee of the League of Nations* (7 February 1925). The resolution on tax evasion states that '[e]ach State shall recover within its territory, in accordance with its own law, taxes due in another State, including taxes due from person not nationals of the latter State. The State to which such an application is made may not, however, be requested to apply any method of execution not provided for under the law of the State making the application.' ibid 35.

[43] Seligman (n 37) 52.

[44] League of Nations (n 41).

[45] Picciotto (n 4) 25.

[46] League of Nations, *Double Taxation and Fiscal Evasion, Collection of International Agreements and Internal Legal Provisions for the Prevention of Double Taxation and Fiscal Evasion*, vol V (1933) 7, art 11.

[47] ibid 58, art 15.

[48] League of Nations (n 46) 64, art 14. The treaty explicitly provided mutual assistance in exchanging documents to assess and collect taxes outlined in the treaty.

[49] ibid 44, art 18.

[50] Model Bilateral Convention for the Establishment of Reciprocal Administrative Assistance for the Assessment and Collection of Direct Taxes, Mexico Draft, reproduced in League of Nations, *Report on the Work of the Tenth Session of the Committee* (1946) 58.

[51] Model Bilateral Convention for the Establishment of Reciprocal Administrative Assistance for the Assessment and Collection of Taxes on Income, Property, Estates and Successions, London Draft, reproduced in League of Nations (n 50) 59.

information exchange provisions included in both model conventions, which presupposed a continuous and repeated exchange of information, represented more stringent obligations than the prevailing standards of State execution at the time.

3.1.2 Model Treaties

Before the Second World War, the exchange of information between States was restricted and limited exclusively to administrative matters. In addition, one of the hurdles to closer cooperation was the 'revenue rule', which meant that one State would not assist in enforcing tax debts owed to another State. It is a common rule that a State does not entertain a suit brought by a foreign sovereignty to enforce the penal or revenue laws of that foreign State. The earliest case appeared in the early eighteenth century in the English courts.[52] The jurisdiction to prescribe and the jurisdiction to enforce taxes were closely linked. Under this rule, taxes can only be collected if the taxpayer was physically present in the jurisdiction or had property on its territory.

In contrast, post-war practices indicate a significant shift towards closer cooperation among States in the suppression of tax fraud within their respective jurisdictions. States recognized the necessity of working together to combat tax evasion and fraud effectively. These efforts led to the development of agreements to facilitate the exchange of information for administrative and criminal investigative purposes. As networks of exchange of information on tax matters expanded, States started to design an international cooperation mechanism to allow them to use the information in criminal procedures. In addition, as a State began to seek the assistance of other States to collect taxes, the revenue rule became subject to wider exceptions.

While there are numerous double taxation prevention treaties, model treaties offer valuable insights into trends in State implementation. There are three significant lines of model treaties after World War II.[53]

The first is the OECD Model Convention. The OECD took over and introduced model tax treaties in 1963 and 1977, which have since been updated.[54] The OECD

[52] The earliest reported case that dealt the revenue rule is *Attorney General v Lutwydge* (1729) Bumb 280, 145 ER 674. The English court held that it would not enforce import duties of Scotland. For the historical development of the revenue rule, see Brenda Mallinak, 'The Revenue Rule: A Common Law Doctrine for the Twenty-First Century' (2006) 16 Duke Journal of Comparative and International Law 79.

[53] Mathias Benedict Knittel, 'Articles 25, 26 and 27 Administrative Cooperation' in Thomas Ecker and Gernot Ressler (eds), *History of Tax Treaties: The Relevance of the OECD Documents for the Interpretation of Tax Treaties* (Linde 2011) 19.

[54] OECD, *1963 and 1977 OECD Model Income Tax Treaties and Commentaries* (C van Raad ed, Kluwer Law and Taxation 1990); OECD, *Model Tax Convention on Income and on Capital 2010* (OECD Publishing 2012). See Klaus Vogel, *Klaus Vogel on Double Taxation Conventions: A Commentary to the OECD-, UN-, and US Model Conventions for the Avoidance of Double Taxation on Income and Capital, with Particular Reference to German Treaty Practice* (Kluwer Law International 1997) 1399. The OECD Model Convention has been revised since 1992, in 1994, 1995, 1997, 2000, 2003, 2005, 2008, 2010, and 2017.

Model Convention is an internal organizational document developed by the OECD Tax Committee and adopted by the Council of Ministers.[55] However, it serves as a reference for treaty negotiators when constructing treaties, not only among OECD member states but also when negotiating with non-member States. Member states also have the opportunity to express their views on the Model Convention within the OECD structures. Therefore, the rules in the Model Convention provide important insights into the implementation of national tax laws.

The OECD Model Convention has been amended more frequently than other conventions, which have been amended every two or three years, with the most recent version established in September 2017.[56] The 2003 version included Article 27, which provided assistance with comprehensive information collection.[57] It provides that States shall assist other States 'in the collection of tax to the extent needed to ensure that any exemption or reduced rate of tax granted under this Convention shall not be enjoyed by persons not entitled to such benefits'.[58] On the other hand, it has a reservation that this clause shall not be construed to impose a State the obligation 'to carry out administrative measures at variance with the laws and administrative practice of that or of the other Contracting State' or 'to carry out measures which would be contrary to public policy (ordre public)'.[59]

The second is model treaties prepared by the US Treasury Department, which were developed in 1996, 2006, and 2016.[60] The US Model Treaty is often the first template US negotiators use when concluding tax treaties with other countries, and significantly influences treaty drafting. Nevertheless, the concluded treaties may deviate from the US Model Treaty in certain instances despite its notable influence on the general trajectory.[61]

[55] The establishment of the Organization for European Economic Cooperation (OEEC) in 1948 was a key step in the implementation of the Marshall Plan. Subsequently, in the early 1950s, the OEEC began advocating for the elimination of double taxation in order to stimulate economic exchange between Europe and the United States. It led to the creation of a Finance Committee in 1956, which aimed to standardize the content of bilateral tax treaties. In 1961, the United States and Canada joined as major members, leading to the reorganization of the OEEC into the Organization for Economic Cooperation and Development (OECD). In 1963, the OECD adopted the first draft model tax convention, titled 'Draft Double Taxation Convention on Income and Capital'. Council, *Third Report of the Fiscal Committee to the Council* (13 July 1960) C(60)157, 12.

[56] Updates of the 1992 Model Convention were published in 1994, 1995, 1997, 1998, 2000, 2003, 2005, 2008, 2010, 2014, and 2017. For the OECD's efforts to suppress tax frauds since the 1990s, see David S Kerzner and David W Chodikoff, *International Tax Evasion in the Global Information Age* (Palgrave Macmillan 2016) 53.

[57] OECD, 'Model Tax Convention on Income and on Capital: Condensed Version 2003' (29 January 2003) 295 <https://www.oecd-ilibrary.org/taxation/model-tax-convention-on-income-and-on-capital-condensed-version-2003_mtc_cond-2003-en>.

[58] OECD Model Convention of 2003, art 27(1).

[59] ibid art 27(8)(a)(b).

[60] United States Model Tax Convention of 20 September 1996; United States Model Tax Convention of 15 November 2006. See Martin B Tittle, *The Integrated 2006 United States Model Income Tax Treaty* (Reuven S Avi-Yonah ed, Vandeplas Publishing 2008).

[61] Reuven S Avi-Yonah, *International Tax as International Law: An Analysis of the International Tax Regime* (CUP 2006) 169.

The third is the UN Model Convention on Taxation, adopted in 1980 and 2001.[62] In 1967, a resolution was passed by the United Nations Economic and Social Council (ECOSOC) advocating for the conclusion of tax treaties between developed and developing countries.[63] Subsequently, an ad hoc committee of experts on tax treaties was established under the ECOSOC in 1968. This committee drafted the Commission's guide to treaty negotiations, published in 1979, and the first model treaty, established in 1980. Another Model Convention was introduced in 2001, along with a guide in 2003, in response to changing economic circumstances in the 1990s. The current Committee of Experts on International Cooperation in Tax Matters was established in 2005. The UN Model Convention differs from the OECD Model Convention in its approach to eliminating double taxation, as it prioritizes source-based taxation, which means taxing investments in the host country rather than relying on the residence principle. However, the UN Model Convention's influence is limited, as OECD member states often refer to the OECD Model Convention in their tax treaty negotiations with non-member States.

3.1.3 OECD Convention on Mutual Assistance in Tax Administration and Enforcement

In the late 1990s, the OECD started to take a proactive approach to combat offshore tax evasion. The OECD adopted the Convention on Mutual Assistance in Tax Administration and Enforcement in 1988 as a response to the growing need to address tax fraud and evasion and to enhance international cooperation in tax matters.[64] The Convention has since been revised several times to reflect changes. The most recent version of the Convention was adopted in 2010 and entered into effect in 2011.[65] All Group of Twenty countries, including non-member States of the OECD, have signed the Convention.

The Convention provides a framework for countries to exchange information and assist each other in tax matters, including collecting taxes, investigating tax crimes, and enforcing tax laws.[66] It provides a wide range of measures, including the exchange of information, the service of documents, and the provision of testimony by witnesses.[67] States are obliged to assist other member states in accordance with their domestic laws and regulations. The Convention also includes safeguards

[62] United Nations Economic and Social Affairs, *United Nations Model Double Taxation Convention between Developed and Developing Countries* (United Nations 2017) vii–viii <https://www.un.org/esa/ffd/wp-content/uploads/2018/05/MDT_2017.pdf>.

[63] For the historical backgrounds, see ibid vii.

[64] Convention on Mutual Administrative Assistance in Tax Matters (adopted on 25 January 1988, entered into force on 1 April 1995) (1988) 1966 UNTS 270.

[65] Protocol amending the Convention on Mutual Administrative Assistance in Tax Matters (adopted on 27 May 2010, entered into force on 1 June 2011) 2763 UNTS 6.

[66] ibid art 18.

[67] ibid.

to protect the confidentiality of information exchanged.[68] The information obtained under the procedure shall be treated as secret and protected in the same manner as information obtained under the domestic law of that requesting State.[69] In other words, the receiving State must protect the data to the extent necessary to ensure the necessary level of personal data protection in the supplying State.[70]

3.1.4 Tax Information Exchange Agreements

Since the early 2000s, States have started to conclude TIEAs, bilateral agreements designed to facilitate the exchange of tax information between tax authorities. The United States started to conclude such agreements with Caribbean countries and British Overseas Territories such as Antigua and Barbuda, the Cayman Islands, the Bahamas, the British Virgin Islands, the Netherlands Antilles, Guernsey, the Isle of Man, Jersey, and Aruba in the early 2000s.[71] European countries followed.[72] The OECD developed a TIEA model that provides a framework for countries to negotiate their agreements in 2002.

The agreements generally mandate the exchange of information upon request and outline the specific types of information that can be shared, such as details about bank accounts, the ownership of companies, and other financial assets relevant to tax enforcement. They also include provisions to safeguard the confidentiality of the exchanged information and ensure that it is used exclusively for tax purposes. Additionally, these agreements establish procedures for resolving any disputes between the parties.

The effectiveness of TIEAs in combating tax evasion and avoidance has been the subject of some debate. Some critics argue that such agreements are insufficient for addressing the root causes of tax evasion and that they may be used to unfairly target certain individuals or groups. Others argue that TIEAs are important for promoting transparency and accountability in the global financial system and can help reduce tax evasion and avoidance opportunities.

3.2 Scope of Exchange

A key issue in adopting the model treaties was whether tax information exchange between State parties should be limited to mutual assistance in a tax treaty (referred to as a 'minor information clause') or should also include other information

[68] ibid art 22(1).
[69] ibid.
[70] ibid.
[71] For the list of treaties, see US Department of Treasury, 'Tax Information Exchange Agreements (TIEAs)' <https://home.treasury.gov/policy-issues/tax-policy/tax-information-exchange-agreements-tieas>.
[72] OECD, 'Tax Information Exchange Agreements (TIEAs)' (16 July 2012) < https://web-archive.oecd.org/2012-07-16/71427-taxinformationexchangeagreementstieas.htm>.

related to the enforcement of tax law (referred to as a 'major information clause').[73] A minor information clause means that assistance will be provided for the information on domestic tax interest, which is necessary for requesting State taxation. A major information clause means that the State party is obliged to provide information that the other country requires even when the information is not directly linked with the treaty's purpose, primarily to avoid double taxation, and that the exchange is not reciprocal.

From the outset, the US Model Convention set the major information clause, as it covered all taxes as subject to information exchange, not just those subject to mutual assistance. To this end, the United States can use the information exchange mechanism of tax treaties to assess its tax assets. The United States took the position that information exchange is essential for mutual tax law enforcement and has taken a diplomatic stance that it will not conclude a treaty unless provisions for information exchange are inserted. It took nearly twenty years for the US–Israel tax treaty to be concluded after negotiations because Israel did not agree to cooperate in exchanging information.[74] A TIEA generally covers the US federal income tax and various other taxes. In addition, there are provisions to allow administrative officials in the requesting country to conduct interviews and inspect records within the requested country.

Courts have dealt with the issue of obtaining information when tax claims do not arise in the country where the information is located. For instance, in 1976, the US Second Circuit held that if Canada needed information to establish the tax claims of Canadian citizens, the IRS could subpoena the relevant company solely to provide the information. However, the United States did not hold this tax liability.[75]

Initially, the OECD Model Convention took a more limited approach than the United States. The 1992 Model Convention provided information on non-residents subject to exchange, but this limited such exchange to the information on taxes listed in the Convention. The United States and Mexico withhold their reservation to this provision. The OECD Committee on Fiscal Affairs' report 1994 highlighted that limiting information exchange based solely on taxable profit may result in very little information sharing. Therefore, the report advises the countries involved to minimize such requirements whenever possible to maintain effective reciprocity.[76]

[73] Vogel (n 54) 1403.

[74] Avi-Yonah (n 61) 174.

[75] *United States v A L Burbank & Co Ltd and Bank of Tokyo Ltd* 525 F 2d 9 (2nd Cir 1976), cert denied 96 S Ct 2647 (1976). See Philip Baker, *Double Taxation Conventions and International Tax Law: A Manual on the OECD Model Tax Convention on Income and on Capital of 1992* (2nd edn, Sweet & Maxwell 1994) 442.

[76] OECD, *Tax Information Exchange between OECD Member Countries: A Survey of Current Practices* (OECD Publications and Information Centre 1994) 26.

However, the 1988 Tax Convention provided for a wide range of exchanges of information relating to the imposition and collection of taxes, the collection and enforcement of tax claims, and the referral or initiation of prosecutions to executive or judicial authorities.[77] Furthermore, the 2010 Protocol requires that any State that receives a request for information per the Convention take the necessary steps to obtain such information, even if this is not necessary for its tax purposes.[78] In its terms, '[t]he Parties shall exchange any information . . . that is foreseeably relevant for the administration or enforcement of their domestic laws concerning the taxes covered by this Convention'.[79] The Convention neither specifies that the protection of individual rights is compromised nor mandates the provision of information that reveals trade secrets, business processes, or information that goes against public order. However, these restrictions should not be construed as allowing a refusal to provide information only because they are not necessary for tax purposes.[80]

The 2011 UN Model Convention, adopted in response to the financial crisis, includes provisions for exchanging all tax-related information among countries. Article 26, the provision on the exchange of information, was substantially modified to expand and clarify the information's scope and limit the exceptions to the obligations. The revised version of Article 26(1) included the exchange of information with respect to taxes not mentioned at the beginning of the instrument.[81] In addition, Article 26(4) removed the requirement for a domestic tax interest. The provision and the Commentary were revised in 2014. Following the update of the OECD Model Convention in 2012, Article 26(2) was amended to allow the competent authorities to use information received for other purposes provided such use is allowed under the laws of both States and the competent authority of the supplying State authorizes such use.[82] The Commentary has also been expanded to, among other things, develop the interpretation of the 'foreseeable relevance' standard and explicitly refer to the term 'fishing expeditions' as an element in determining foreseeable relevance.[83]

In summary, despite differences in detail, all three model treaties are designed to exchange a wide range of information that is expected to be relevant to enforcing the tax laws of the countries involved. In other words, the major information clause has been adopted rather than the minor information clause that is limited to the taxes that the treaty captures or the tax information of residents. It is also observed that the OECD Model Convention has influenced the UN Model

[77] Convention on Mutual Administrative Assistance in Tax Matters (n 64).
[78] Protocol amending the Convention on Mutual Administrative Assistance in Tax Matters (n 65).
[79] Convention on Mutual Administrative Assistance in Tax Matters (n 64) art 4(1).
[80] ibid art 5(3).
[81] United Nations Economic and Social Affairs (n 62) 636, para 4.
[82] ibid.
[83] ibid.

Convention, leading it to align with the latter. A key difference between Article 26 of the UN Model Convention and its OECD counterpart is the inclusion of a sentence in paragraph 1 emphasizing the exchange of information to prevent tax avoidance and evasion. This clarification, which was added in 2011, was particularly supported by developing countries to align the article's text with its existing commentary.[84]

Even if this requirement is abolished, the question persists as to whether requests must be confined to specific information regarding an individual or whether broader requests for information that do not specify an individual are permissible. In this context, both the 2010 OECD Model Convention and the 2011 UN Model Convention encompass information that is expected to 'be associated with' the enforcement of tax laws in the relevant country.

The US Model Convention dictates the latter view. As Section 5 discusses, the United States frequently uses anonymous subpoenas ('John Doe' summons) as a means of unilateral law enforcement, which seeks comprehensive requests for information disclosure without identifying individuals. It allows the exchange of information under the treaty to be conducted on the same basis as in an anonymous subpoena. Moreover, unlike unilateral law enforcement, the committee does not consider such cases, and the scope of information gathering tends to increase.

Another key issue is the confidentiality of taxpayer's information, which, in the words of a report of the OECD in 2014, is a 'fundamental cornerstone' of tax systems.[85] Taxpayers must be assured that their sensitive financial information remains protected from unauthorized disclosure, whether intentional or accidental. Confidence in international tax information exchanges depends on ensuring that exchanged data is used and disclosed strictly in accordance with the governing agreements. Maintaining confidentiality at the international level requires a robust legal framework supported by effective systems and procedures to prevent unauthorized disclosures and uphold compliance in practice.

For this purpose, the agreements on the exchange of information contain provisions that the requesting and requested States maintain the same level of confidentiality with the latter State when handling the exchanged information. Tax treaties commonly include strict confidentiality provisions to protect taxpayer information during exchanges between jurisdictions, albeit with minor differences.[86]

[84] ibid 637, para 4.4.

[85] OECD, *Keeping It Safe: The OECD Guide on the Protection of Confidentiality of Information Exchanged for Tax Purposes* (OECD 2014) 5 <https://web-archive.oecd.org/2014-03-13/206532-keeping-it-safe-report.pdf>.

[86] See the OECD Model Tax Convention, art 26; the Model Agreement on Exchange of Information on Tax Matters, art 8; 1988 Tax Convention, art 22.

These provisions ensure that both the information provided in a request and the information received in response remain secure. The exchanged information may only be used for specific, agreed-upon purposes, such as tax assessment or enforcement. It may only be disclosed to designated persons or authorities responsible for these functions.

3.3 Grounds for Refusal

Tax treaties did not include many grounds for refusal compared to criminal assistance treaties. During the League of Nations era, treaties did not establish specific grounds for declining requests. It was presumed that the enforcement of these treaties relies on the national laws of the involved countries, and the expectation was that requests could be rejected if they contradicted these laws.

Both the Mexican Model Convention of 1943 and the London Model Convention of 1946 established specific grounds for rejecting requests for assistance.[87] The reasons for declining enforcement assistance are similar in both model conventions and include the following: (1) when the information is not obtainable under the legislation of either the requesting or the receiving State; (2) when the assistance necessitates an administrative or judicial act that is incompatible with the legislation of either State; (3) when fulfilling the assistance would breach professional, industrial, or trade secrets; (4) when the information pertains to a taxpayer who is a citizen of the requested State; and (5) when, in the judgment of the requested State, fulfilling the assistance would undermine its security or sovereign rights.[88]

In the 1950s, the US Model Convention included similar provisions in its treaty, where the requested State could refuse assistance if (1) it would have to deviate from its legislation to obtain the relevant information; (2) the assistance would be against its sovereignty, security, or public policy; or (3) equivalent information was not available in the requesting State. However, by the 1970s, using sovereignty and security as grounds for refusal became less frequent. Its 1996 version requires compliance only with the national laws of the partner country without any grounds for refusal.[89] In summary, States agreed to narrow the grounds for refusal to the minimum and eliminate barriers to fostering cooperation.

[87] League of Nations, *London and Mexico Model Tax Conventions: Commentary and Text* (League of Nations 1946) 54. See Mexico Model Convention, art 5; London Model Convention, art 5.

[88] League of Nations (n 87).

[89] United States Model Income Tax Convention (20 September 1996) art 26, available at US IRS, 'United States Model—Tax Treaty Documents' (*Internal Revenue Service*, 19 August 2024) <https://www.irs.gov/businesses/international-businesses/united-states-model-tax-treaty-documents>.

3.4 Information Obtained through the Anti-Money Laundering Regulations

A significant development in the late 2000s was that States began to require financial institutions and other entities to collect and report information as part of the anti-money laundering and countering the financing of terrorism (AML/CFT) regulations.

The scope of information accessible to the tax authorities expanded due to the broadened the AML/CFT regulations. For instance, one of the significant challenges in collecting financial information is identifying beneficial ownership. Beneficial owners are individuals who own or control interests in corporate vehicles, such as companies, trusts, foundations, partnerships, and other types of legal entities and arrangements. These structures are used to conduct a wide variety of commercial and entrepreneurial activities. As a result of the AML/CFT regulations, financial institutions now must collect their information.

After the financial crisis of 2008–2009, States and jurisdictions recognized the unfairness of substantial taxable resources being diverted to offshore markets, necessitating a closer examination of financial transactions and increased transparency and accountability. Efforts to expose the real ownership of these entities began in the 1990s, driven by the systematic abuse of offshore markets. Journalistic investigations such as the LuxLeaks in 2014[90] and the Panama Papers in 2016[91] further accelerated this development. As a result, States reached agreements on various mechanisms for closer cooperation. These developments will be examined in detail in Section 5 of this chapter and Chapter 11.

4. Use of Tax Information in Criminal Procedures

4.1 Overcoming the Limits of Tax Agreements

As described in Section 3, the double taxation treaty was initially intended to eliminate double taxation by excluding overlapping jurisdictions. The exchange of information mechanisms was established for this purpose. However, States have started to agree to use information related to tax fraud in criminal proceedings as they developed the networks of tax agreements. This section examines relevant

[90] LuxLeaks (Luxembourg Leaks) is a name of a scandal exposed in an investigation conducted by International Consortium of Investigative Journalists. It concerns confidential information about Luxembourg's tax rulings set up by PricewaterhouseCoopers International Limited (PwC) from 2002 to 2010.

[91] The Panama Papers are a leak of more than 11.5 million financial and legal records hidden by secretive offshore companies that International Consortium of Investigative Journalists exposed.

issues and how States overcame obstacles in exchanging information, including bank secrecy.

4.1.1 Double Criminality

The first issue is the requirement of double criminality, namely whether the act that is the subject of the request for information constitutes a crime under the domestic law of the country of interest for the country that received the request to provide information to the other country. The double criminality requirement was an obstacle to the exchange of information because the elements of tax crimes vary from country to country.[92]

The approach that was employed was that States require double criminality only in an abstract term. The United States introduced a mechanism for exchanging information on 'tax fraud and the like' in the information exchange provisions of bilateral tax treaties concluded from the 1950s to the 1970s, without regard to the differences in constituent elements. Because the scope of the term 'the like' is broad, some agreements adopt the term 'fraud and fiscal evasion'.[93]

In addition, when the United States started to conclude TIEAs, the governments envisioned using information obtained through information exchange under tax treaties for criminal proceedings from the outset. The detailed procedures of TIEAs are often established to ensure that the documents and statements obtained can be used in civil and criminal proceedings. The 1977 OECD Model Convention and the 2011 United Nations Model Convention endorsed this approach. It is difficult to distinguish between tax avoidance and tax evasion until relevant information is obtained. Thus, it is useful for countries to share information on tax avoidance to deter such behaviour and promote compliance with tax laws.

4.1.2 Confidentiality

The use of administrative cooperation information in criminal proceedings raises a confidentiality question. The issue has been recognized since the time of the League of Nations. Both the Mexico Model Treaty and the London Model Treaty addressed this issue.[94] These treaties mandate that the authorities of the requesting States treat acquired information with the same level of confidentiality as they would treat their own country's information. According to the 1963 OECD Model Treaty, any information exchanged must be kept confidential and cannot be disclosed to anyone other than the relevant individuals or authorities. The commentary states that the 'authorities' included the Courts.[95]

92 Michael Abbell, *Obtaining Evidence Abroad in Criminal Cases 2010* (Brill 2010) 111.
93 United Nations Economic and Social Affairs (n 62) 636.
94 Mexico Draft Convention (n 50) art 6; London Draft Convention (n 51) art 6.
95 OECD, *1963 and 1977 OECD Model Income Tax Treaties and Commentaries* (n 54) art 26, para 9.

The discourse has shifted from the general obligation of maintaining confidentiality of information to the specific requisites concerning its application in criminal trials. Employing such information in criminal cases is imperative for the efficient exchange of information. However, prior authorization from the information provider was deemed indispensable due to the public nature of criminal proceedings.

The United States insisted that confidential information obtained through agreement be admissible in any legal proceedings.[96] This position is reflected in its 1996 and 2006 model treaties, which mandate the exchange of information related to tax assessments, collections, implementation or prosecution, and complaint decisions.[97] However, the 1977 OECD Model Treaty stipulates that consent must first be obtained from the information provider before the information can be used in criminal proceedings.[98]

The general trend shifts towards the US approach. The OECD Tax Administrative Assistance Convention of 1988 requires prior permission or a special agreement from the information provider to use the information obtained as evidence in criminal proceedings.[99] The 2010 protocol eliminated the need for consent and established a duty to exchange any information related to the operation or enforcement of tax laws of a contracting State.[100]

The level of compliance with the obligation of confidentiality varies, and taxpayers may have limited opportunities to raise objections. While the use of information in criminal proceedings is generally considered a question of the State's rights and obligations rather than for the benefit of taxpayers, there may be instances where the importance of the consent requirement may be minimal in practice.

For instance, in a 1992 case, the New Zealand tax authority obtained information from its Australian counterpart based on the tax treaty and utilized it to prosecute a New Zealand taxpayer.[101] Although the Australian tax authority had not explicitly consented, it raised no objections to using the information. As a result, the New Zealand court deemed the use of the information valid. This case underscores the discretion of the information-receiving country in using the information acquired for tax assistance.

4.1.3 Bank Secrecy

The main obstacle in setting up information mechanisms was bank secrecy laws as grounds for refusing judicial cooperation. The use of jurisdictions with rigorous

[96] Vogel (n 54) 1432; Tonny Schenk-Geers, *International Exchange of Information and the Protection of Taxpayers* (Kluwer Law International 2009) 136.

[97] United States Model Convention, art 26(1).

[98] OECD Model Convention 2010, art 26(2).

[99] OECD Mutual Assistance on Tax Convention (n 64), art 4.

[100] Protocol (n 65), art 4(2).

[101] *Commissioner of Inland Revenue v E R Squibb & Sons (NZ) Ltd* (1992) 14 NZTC 9, 146 (CA).

bank secrecy as a repository for illicit tax avoidance has been a persistent problem since the 1970s. However, against the growing necessity for States to obtain information from FFIs and the mounting international pressure against offshore markets, jurisdictions known for their stringent bank secrecy laws were compelled to alter their policies. These changes reflect a global shift towards transparency and cooperation in financial matters. States increasingly recognize the importance of accessing financial data to effectively combat tax evasion and other illicit activities.

(1) OECD's Efforts to Suppress Harmful Tax Practices

The OECD took the lead in eliminating unfair practices of offshore markets. On the other hand, there was the common ground that tax policies should be neutral. Such policies should be designed to avoid influencing the flow of capital across borders, thereby preserving economic efficiency within the global market.[102] Furthermore, these policies must adhere to the principles of equity, ensuring fairness across different country levels.

The 1992 OECD Model Convention articulates that provisions pertaining to information exchange should not be interpreted as granting access to information that is not obtainable under the laws or in the normal course of the administration of either party.[103]

The controversy surrounding the provisions for exchanging information is intertwined with the broader challenge of tax competition between offshore market jurisdictions and OECD nations. Given the significantly lower tax rates in tax havens, numerous companies developed sophisticated strategies to establish subsidiaries in these jurisdictions and channel their income through them. This practice prevents earnings from entering their home country, circumventing domestic taxation.

The OECD released the 1998 Report on Harmful Tax Competition to address this issue.[104] The report aimed to ensure that the home country levied the appropriate taxes. A harmful tax regime is defined as a tax system that meets four criteria: (1) a zero or nominal effective tax rate, (2) a lack of effective means for exchanging information, (3) a lack of transparency, and (4) a lack of substantive activity. In this context, transparency in the third criterion refers to applying the law consistently to taxpayers in similar situations and ensuring that tax authorities have access to the necessary information to make decisions about the taxpayer's status.[105]

[102] Kerzner and Chodikoff (n 56) 55.

[103] OECD, 'Model Tax Convention on Income and on Capital: Condensed Version September 1992' (1992) 39, art 26(2)(b) <https://www.oecd.org/en/publications/1992/10/model-tax-convention-on-income-and-on-capital-condensed-version-september-1992_g1g96efa.html>.

[104] OECD, 'Harmful Tax Competition: An Emerging Global Issue' (1998) 26.

[105] OECD, 'Progress Report on Addressing Harmful Tax Practices' (2001) para 6.

The OECD maintained that low tax rates alone do not constitute harmful tax practices.[106] The mere existence of a low effective tax rate is not necessarily an indication of harmful tax activity. Transparency and effective exchange of information should be the standards for cooperation. The organization recognizes that tax competition can be beneficial because it fosters the liberalization of international trade and investment. However, it argues that significantly lower tax rates, such as those offered by tax havens, change the relationship between trade, investment, and taxation and must be addressed.

In 2000, the OECD released a report designating thirty-five tax havens as non-cooperative.[107] The response from offshore market countries can be broken down into two parts.

First, countries such as Switzerland, Luxembourg, Austria, and Belgium—which had attracted businesses with preferential tax treatment and strict confidentiality rules—initially opposed transparency standards. However, they were eventually forced to broaden their disclosure requirements when the European Union introduced the Savings Directive in 2003.[108] The Directive called for the automatic exchange of information between countries to ensure efficient taxation of interest income on savings paid to beneficiaries across borders. At first, Austria, Belgium, and Luxembourg were exempted from this requirement and instead were required to levy withholding tax on savings. Switzerland signed a similar agreement with the European Community in 2004.[109] In 2009, these four countries withdrew their reservations to Article 26 of the OECD Model Convention.[110]

[106] OECD, 'Harmful Tax Competition' (n 104) para 21.

[107] OECD, 'Towards Global Tax Co-Operation, Report to the 2000 Ministerial Council Meeting and Recommendations by the Committee on Fiscal Affairs: Progress in Identifying and Eliminating Harmful Tax Practices' (2000). The designated countries were Anguilla, Antigua and Barbuda, Dutch Aruba, British Cook Islands, Cyprus, Dominican Republic, Bahamas, Bahrain, Bermuda, Belize, British Virgin Islands, British Cayman Islands, Gibraltar, Grenada, British Guernsey, British Isle of Man, Jersey, British Liberia, Malta, San Marino, Marshall Islands, Mauritius, British Montserrat, Nauru, Netherlands Antilles, Niue, Panama, Samoa, Seychelles, St Lucia, St Kitts and Nevis, St Vincent and the Grenadines, British Turks and Caicos Islands Vanuatu, and the US Virgin Islands. It is the approach followed by the FATF in relation to the regulation of money laundering offences. The FATF has designated the Bahamas, Cayman Islands, Cook Islands, Dominican Republic, Israel, Lebanon, Liechtenstein, Marshall Islands, Nauru, Niue Panama, the Philippines, Russia, St Kitts and Nevis, St Vincent and the Grenadines (designated from the beginning of June 2000; FATF, Annual NCCT Report, June 2000, para 64), Egypt, Guatemala, Hungary, the Indonesia, Myanmar, and Nigeria (added in June 2001; FATF, Annual NCCT Report, June 2001, para 1). The nine overlapping countries and territories are the Bahamas, Cook Islands, Dominican Republic, Marshall Islands, Nauru, Niue, Panama, St Kitts and Nevis, and St Vincent and the Grenadines. For an analysis on the political aspects of this issue, see Jason Campbell Sharman, *Havens in a Storm: The Struggle for Global Tax Regulation* (Cornell UP 2006).

[108] Council Directive 2003/48/EC of 3 June 2003 on Taxation of Savings Income in the Form of Interest Payments [2003] OJ L157/38 (23 June 2003).

[109] Memorandum of Understanding between the European Community and the Swiss Confederation (signed and entered into force on 24 October 2004) [2004] OJ L385/43.

[110] OECD, 'Promoting Transparency and Exchange of Information for Tax Purposes' (2010) para 9.

Second, when information exchange treaties are established between OECD and non-OECD member countries, a clause known as the Isle of Man clause used to be often included. This clause stipulates that reforms within the country will not occur until all OECD member countries commit to the same standards. The OECD established the Global Forum in 2000 to facilitate discussions with offshore jurisdictions. The forum focused on identifying and eliminating 'harmful tax activities', particularly those related to lack of transparency and effective exchange of information.

Non-member States are considered 'cooperative jurisdictions' if they meet certain conditions, including the establishment of a legal framework for the exchange of information on requests with appropriate safeguards and the abolition of the requirement of 'double incrimination' in tax offences. In 2005, Article 26 was amended to include a provision that prohibits refusal to provide information on the grounds of banking secrecy, thereby encouraging countries to develop an effective exchange of information systems.

(2) Switzerland

(a) The US–Swiss Information Exchange

Switzerland has maintained stringent regulations for disclosing financial information, as described in Section 2. However, it eventually changed its policy as the United States imposed pressure.

The initial tax treaty between the United States and Switzerland in 1951 outlined a narrow obligation to exchange information.[111] This approach allowed for the exchange of information to implement the treaty. However, the received information must be treated as confidential and not disclosed to any third parties except those involved in the assessment and collection of taxes. The use of such information in judicial proceedings was prohibited.[112]

With the main aim of changing this and dealing with organized crime, the Mutual Assistance in Criminal Justice Treaty was created between the United States and Switzerland in 1973.[113] For the first time, the treaty promised that banking secrecy legislation alone would not be grounds for denial of judicial assistance. The treaty primarily addresses organized crime, and tax crimes per se are explicitly excluded from the treaty's scope. However, it was stipulated that governments charging people with tax crimes are eligible for assistance if they are committed to preventing organized crime.[114]

[111] Convention between the United States of America and the Swiss Confederation for the Avoidance of Double Taxation with Respect to Taxes on Income (signed on 24 May 1951) 3 UST 3972; TIAS 2533; 165 UNTS 51.

[112] ibid art 7(2).

[113] Mutual Assistance in Criminal Matters (signed on 25 May 1973) 27.2 UST 2019; TIAS 8302; 1052 UNTS 61.

[114] ibid art 2(1)(c)(5).

Individuals requested to provide a statement in the requested State are legally obligated to appear, testify, and produce relevant documents, records, and physical evidence. Generally, they may refuse if a witness has legitimate grounds for refusing to provide a statement or evidence in criminal proceedings in the requested State. These grounds include the following: (1) if the request pertains to the investigation or prosecution of a serious offence, (2) if the disclosure of the evidence is material for establishing or proving a fact that is of significant importance to the investigation or proceedings, (3) if the United States has made reasonable efforts to obtain the evidence through other means but has been unsuccessful, and (d) if the witness is a person who has been subjected to a criminal investigation or proceedings in the requested State.[115]

The treaty allows Swiss authorities to disclose confidential information, such as bank secrets or commercial secrets, if the United States has tried but failed to obtain the evidence through other means and if the disclosed facts pertain to individuals who are presumed not to be involved in the offence mentioned in the request, as per established law.

The exchange of information on tax offences was first introduced in 1996 as a double taxation agreement, which replaced the 1951 treaty.[116] The updated treaty explicitly stated that the exchange of information covered 'tax fraud and the like' and that the application of banking secrecy legislation would not be a barrier. However, it should be noted that in Switzerland, the responsibility for determining personal income tax and corporate income tax liabilities lies with the tax office, and the taxpayer's declaration serves as a reference for exercising the tax office's powers. As a result, this provision applied to acts such as falsifying accounting books and bank account documents. Nevertheless, it did not encompass making a false statement on a tax return itself. Therefore, the failure of a US taxpayer to declare income on a specific form was not considered a criminal offence or subject to judicial assistance. Furthermore, Article 26(3) of the treaty stipulated that the provision for information exchange does not impose an obligation on a State party to take administrative measures that would conflict with its sovereignty, security, or public restrictions or to provide specific information that cannot be obtained under its own or the requesting State party's legislation.

(b) UBS Affair

The UBS affair, which occurred from 2008 to 2010, exemplified a significant development in information exchange between the United States and Switzerland.[117]

[115] ibid art 10(2).

[116] Convention between the United States of America and the Swiss Confederation for the Avoidance of Double Taxation with Respect to Taxes on Income (signed on 2 October 1996) KAV 4915.

[117] For more information on the history of the case, see the website of the Swiss Federal Office of Justice, UBS case <http://www.ejpd.admin.ch/content/ejpd/en/home/themen/wirtschaft/ref_fallubs.html>; US Department of Justice, 'UBS Enters into Deferred Prosecution Agreement' (18 February 2009) <http://www.justice.gov/opa/pr/2009/February/09-tax-136.html>.

While the structure of the *UBS* case was not distinct from previous unilateral law enforcement cases, it garnered significant attention because the United States attempted to collect a large amount of unspecified information *en masse* and because the case was brought forth in Switzerland.

In November 2008, senior executives of UBS, the largest bank in Switzerland, were indicted in the US federal court for conspiring to conceal the assets of US taxpayers. A US taxpayer was also charged in June 2008 in a federal district court for failing to file income tax returns per the required form, and the IRS's anonymous summons was granted in the District Court for accounts held by the US taxpayer with UBS. The US government demanded that the Swiss government provide information under the tax treaty, but no judicial assistance was provided. The UBS was specifically required to produce personal information about US taxpayers without filing income tax returns as needed. Nevertheless, the Swiss government did not provide the requested information under the tax treaty.[118]

In February 2009, the UBS entered a deferred prosecution agreement with the US Department of Justice (DOJ). It admitted, in the text of the agreement, that its employees had assisted US citizens in establishing accounts with offshore corporations between 2000 and 2007 to conceal their assets.[119] The next day, the IRS filed a suit in the Federal District Court to enforce an anonymous summons, which effectively ordered the production of account information for more than 52,000 taxpayers.

In response, in April 2009, the Swiss government filed an *amicus curie* in the Federal District Court, seeking to dismiss the summons, arguing that the Swiss legal system should be respected.[120] First, it claimed that the double taxation treaty between the United States and Switzerland existed, and that any attempt by the United States to obtain information through a subpoena would violate that treaty. Second, it stated that enforcing the subpoena would directly contravene Swiss law. Third, the IRS cannot reasonably be expected to receive information based on blanket requests or fishing expeditions. Fourth, it argues that implementing subpoenas goes against the principles of international comity.

The main responses from the DOJ were as follows. First, Congress has granted the IRS the power to seek broad subpoenas. The Right to Financial Privacy Rights Act of 1978 and the Fourth Amendment to the Constitution, which governed the privacy of personal banking information in the United States, did not prohibit the implementation of subpoenas. Bank account holders have no reasonable expectation of privacy in financial or transactional records held by banks or others

[118] *United States v UBS AG*, 'Declaration of Barry B. Shott' (entered on FLSD Docket 19 February 2009) para 17.

[119] *United States v UBS AG*, Case No 09-60033-CR-COHN, United States District Court Southern District of Florida.

[120] *United States v UBS AG*, Amicus Brief of the Government of Switzerland, Case No 09-20423-Civ-Gold/Mcaliley, US District Court for the Southern District of Florida, Miami Division.

that must be reported to the government. Additionally, the principle of non-enforcement of foreign tax claims, also known as the revenue rule, did not apply in this case, as the subpoena is a request for information and not for enforcing a tax claim.

In addition, the reliance on the principle of international comity supports the conclusion that implementing the subpoena is better. Concessions would not serve the best interests of the United States, as the treaty would not prevent the IRS from obtaining information. Even if the court were to balance interests, the Swiss government's argument that the subpoena should not be implemented based on comity theory is invalid. While the interests of Switzerland and the United States in enforcing their respective laws must be considered equally, the enforcement of a subpoena is civil. In contrast, Swiss law was violated because acting pursuant to a subpoena is criminal.

To resolve the dispute, the two governments signed an agreement in August 2009 (the 2009 Agreement), resulting in a settlement between the IRS and UBS.[121] In addition, the two parties agreed to amend the 1996 double taxation agreement.[122] The key aspect of this revision is the exchange of information. The distinction between tax evasion and tax fraud has been eliminated for both individual and group requests. The Swiss authorities agreed to provide the IRS with the account information of 4,450 US taxpayers who held accounts with UBS.

In the meantime, a US taxpayer with an account with UBS filed a lawsuit in the Swiss Federal Administrative Court, seeking to declare that the measure was unconstitutional. In January 2010, the court ruled that the 2009 Agreement did not comply with the information exchange provisions of the existing US–Swiss tax treaty and that the Swiss authorities had no legal basis to provide information to the United States.[123] The court stated that the agreement lacked the necessary basis for providing information to the United States. It was merely a memorandum of understanding and did not change or amend the content of the US–Swiss tax treaty. The court further emphasized that judicial assistance would be provided if the acts falling within the categories set out in the annexe to the agreement were already provided for in the US–Swiss tax treaty and that the agreement did not modify or amend the content of the US–Swiss tax treaty. Subsequently, in August,

[121] Agreement on the Request for Information from the Internal Revenue Service of the United States of America Regarding UBS AG (Switzerland–US, 19 August 2009) <https://www.justice.gov/archive/opa/documents/us-swiss-agreement.pdf>.

[122] Protocol Amending the Convention for the Avoidance of Double Taxation and the Prevention of Fiscal Evasion with Respect to Taxes on Income, Switzerland–US (signed on 23 September 2009, entered into force on 19 September 2019) <https://www.irs.gov/businesses/international-businesses/switzerland-tax-treaty-documents>. See also Technical Explanation of the Protocol available at US Department of the Treasury (2011) <https://home.treasury.gov/system/files/131/Treaty-Switzerland-Protocol-TE-9-23-2009.pdf>.

[123] BVGE, Auszug aus dem Urteil der Abteilung I. S. A. gegen Eidgenössische Steuerverwaltung, Task Force Amtshilfe USA A-7789/2009 vom 21. Januar 2010.

the Swiss government published information on approximately 4,450 UBS accounts belonging to US citizens.

As a result of the UBS affairs, the IRS pursued and obtained anonymous subpoenas against financial institutions in more than thirty countries. The United States also initiated investigations into other major Swiss financial institutions in addition to the UBS, alleging their involvement in aiding and abetting tax evasion. For instance, in 2009, Credit Suisse entered into a deferred prosecution agreement with the DOJ and agreed to pay fines.[124]

The US government implemented additional measures. First, it clarified its policy of requiring US taxpayers to voluntarily disclose information and reducing sanctions for those who voluntarily disclose undeclared income from foreign accounts.[125] This voluntary disclosure programme was not limited to Switzerland but encompassed bank account information in more than sixty jurisdictions.

Second, the IRS sought the issuance of anonymous subpoenas in ten district courts to obtain identifying information in other jurisdictions. For instance, it required information of Norwegian individuals held by US financial institutions.[126] Seven district courts granted these subpoenas for the first time. The Norwegian government initiated the case under the information exchange provisions of a tax treaty between Norway and the United States.

(c) EU–Switzerland Relations

Switzerland's policy shift towards its relationship with the United States has led to changes in its relationship with the European Union. The European Union, which has a mandate to harmonize tax laws among its Member States, has taken measures to prevent tax evasion by individuals who transfer their assets outside the region.[127] To achieve this, the European Union has entered into tax treaties with neighbouring countries, including Switzerland, to ensure that interest income earned by individuals from outside their country of residence is effectively taxed in their country of residence. As part of this effort, the automatic exchange of taxation information now takes place between the country where the interest is paid and the country where the interest is received, making it easier to effectively tax interest income.

[124] *United States v Credit Suisse AG*, Deferred Prosecution Agreement (16 December 2009) <https://www.justice.gov/archives/opa/press-release/file/978871/dl>.

[125] US Senate, Permanent Subcommittee on Investigations, 'Offshore Tax Evasion: The Effort to Collect Unpaid Taxes on Billions in Hidden Offshore Accounts, Majority and Minority Staff Report' (26 February 2014) 10 <https://www.hsgac.senate.gov/wp-content/uploads/imo/media/doc/REPORT%20-%20OFFSHORE%20TAX%20EVASION%20(Feb%2026%202014,%205-15-14%20FINAL).pdf>.

[126] US DOJ, 'Federal Courts Authorize Service of John Doe Summonses Seeking Identities of Persons Using Payment Cards in Norway' (29 July 2013) <http://www.justice.gov/tax/2013/txdv13856.htm>. See also Bruce Zagaris, 'U.S. Court Authorizes First Use of John Doe Summonses on Behalf of Foreign Government' (2013) 29 International Law Enforcement Reporter 47.

[127] Council Directive 2003/48/EC (n 108).

(3) British Overseas Territories

Compared to Switzerland, dealing with the British Overseas Territories tax havens in the Caribbean proved less challenging. In the 1970s, tax fraud escalated in the United States, and offshore markets in the Caribbean became favoured destinations due to their banking secrecy laws and position outside the enforcement jurisdiction of the United States. Furthermore, the deregulation since the 1980s made it easier for funds to flow out of the country, as OECD countries relaxed restrictions on international investment and foreign exchange regulations.[128] As multinational corporations engaged in rapidly increasing international transactions during the same period, many subsidiaries were established in offshore markets, increasing the risk of illegal tax avoidance.

In response, from the mid-1980s to the early 1990s, the United States initiated TIEAs with Caribbean countries to facilitate information exchange.[129] To encourage the conclusion of these agreements, the United States introduced tax incentives such as deductions for costs related to treaty maintenance.[130] It also provided preferential treatment for certain investments and loans made by US companies to these countries, although such preferential treatment has been phased out since 1996.[131] The US TIEA also includes provisions for the availability of information in a form that can be used in civil and criminal trials in the United States and prohibits the use of banking secrecy laws as a means of support.

Simultaneously, the United States has also urged Latin American countries to legislate, particularly in cases involving proceeds of crime, to require disclosure of banking information to authorities and enable asset seizure upon request.[132] While bank secrecy laws have not been repealed in these countries, they are no longer commonly accepted as grounds for refusing information exchange requests.

4.1.4 Summary

Today, offshore financial markets find it challenging to refuse cooperation with major financial States due to the erosion of bank secrecy. Although the issue has not been entirely eradicated, the trend towards financial transparency and regulatory compliance has significantly diminished the ability of these markets to shield information. In addition, the elimination of bank secrecy has also aligned with AML/CFT regulations, which will be briefly mentioned in Section 6 of this chapter and thoroughly examined in Chapter 11. This shift underscores the importance of international collaboration in upholding financial integrity and suppressing tax fraud and other unlawful activities.

128 OECD (n 76).

129 See Bruce Zagaris and Richard A Gordon, *International Exchange of Tax Information: Recent Developments* (Practising Law Institute 1985).

130 26 USC 274(h)(6).

131 26 USC 936(d)(4). This provision was repealed in 2018.

132 Abbell (n 92).

4.2 Mutual Legal Assistance Treaties on Criminal Matters

In the meantime, cooperation was growing in addressing tax crimes through mutual legal assistance in criminal matters. Historically, tax-related offences were excluded from the scope of the MLATs due to the established principle of fiscal offence exception. States started to abolish this principle. The 1959 European Convention on Mutual Assistance in Criminal Justice initially allowed for the refusal of assistance in cases involving fiscal offences.[133] However, the 1978 Additional Protocol expanded the scope of assistance to cover fiscal offences that a request for assistance cannot be denied based on different constituent elements of a tax crime.[134] It coincides with the rules under extradition treaties. According to the 1978 Second Additional Protocol to the European Convention on Extradition, if a crime is of 'the same nature' as the crime that is the basis for the extradition request exists in the requested country, including tax crimes, it may be included as an extraditable crime.[135]

Additionally, the 1985 Schengen Agreement among the Benelux countries, France, and Germany explicitly includes provisions for judicial assistance in fiscal crimes, including tax offences.[136] Furthermore, bilateral extradition treaties entered the United States and have increasingly included provisions for tax crimes since the 1970s. This trend was pronounced in extradition treaties, such as the European Convention on Extradition adopted by the Council of Europe in 1957, which mandates extradition for tax offences, subject to mutual agreement among member States.

5. Obtaining Evidence from Financial Institutions

5.1 The US Jurisdictional Arms for Collecting Tax Information

5.1.1 Qualified Intermediaries

The United States developed a mechanism to obtain information through FFIs. It started as a voluntary disclosure. In the United States, when foreign persons or corporations not residing in the United States earn interest, dividends, or other income from US securities, a 30 per cent withholding tax is levied on the total

[133] European Convention on Mutual Assistance in Criminal Matters, art 2(a).

[134] Additional Protocol to the European Convention on Mutual Assistance in Criminal Matters (adopted on 17 March 1978, entered into force on 12 April 1982) ETS 99, art 2(2).

[135] Second Additional Protocol to the European Convention on Extradition (adopted on 17 March 1978, entered into force on 5 June 1983) ETS 98, art 2(1).

[136] Agreement between the Governments of the States of the Benelux Economic Union, the Federal Republic of Germany and the French Republic on the gradual abolition of checks at their common borders, art 48(1) [2000] OJ L 239/13.

amount. However, there may be tax agreements between the beneficiary's foreign domicile country and the United States to reduce the withholding rate.

Until the early 1980s, withholding agents were required to apply for a reduced tax rate based on the tax treaty with the beneficiary's country of foreign domicile unless they had specific knowledge that the beneficiary was not a resident of a tax treaty country eligible for the reduced rate. This meant that beneficiaries from tax treaty countries automatically received a reduced tax rate on US-sourced income. However, with the rapid increase in international transactions, there were no mechanisms to verify the identity of non-US residents or foreign corporations, leading to fraudulent activities where US persons falsely claimed to be foreign nationals. In response, the IRS has been working since the early 1980s to prevent fraud and tighten rules for foreign investors, although no specific rules were adopted.

Subsequently, in 1997, the IRS introduced significant changes to the procedures for withholding US-source income from non-resident aliens or foreign corporations investing in the United States. The IRS designated certain FFIs or foreign branches of US financial institutions as QIs, which allowed beneficiaries to enjoy reduced tax rates when investing through these designated intermediaries. The QI verifies the identity of the IRS and the beneficiary, but the process is simpler than that for financial institutions that are not QIs. The QI regime has been in effect since 2001, and other developed countries have adopted similar regimes.

5.1.2 Foreign Account Tax Compliance Act

Due to large-scale tax crimes involving UBS, as described in Section 4.1.3, the United States enacted the FATCA in 2010.[137] The FATCA imposes certain restrictions on obtaining information about US persons directly from FFIs. FFIs can agree with the IRS, known as the Foreign Financial Institution Agreement (FFI Agreement), to identify accounts held by US persons and report them to the IRS. The definition of a 'financial institution' includes not only banks but also companies engaged in the custody of financial assets, investment, and insurance. Failure to enter into such an agreement or register with the IRS will result in US corporations' dividends, interest, and other payments being subject to a 30 per cent withholding tax.[138]

The extraterritorial application of FACTA may conflict with the legal system of the country in which the FFI is located and because it increases administrative and other burdens on entities. In response, regulations have been established to promote international cooperation between the country in which the FFI is located

[137] Foreign Account Tax Compliance Act, Pub L No 111-147, 124 Stat 97-117 (2010). Final rule published in 2013, effective the following year 2014.

[138] FATCA registration country jurisdiction listing is available at IRS's website <https://www.irs.gov/businesses/corporations/fatca-registration-country-jurisdiction-listing>.

and the United States to eliminate legal barriers to compliance with the FATCA by the financial institution in question.

The United Kingdom, France, Germany, Spain, and Italy were the first countries that agreed with the United States to advance the principles of FATCA under the concept of bilateral intergovernmental agreements (IGAs) to address the legal barriers financial institutions face in complying with FATCA. However, the basis on which information is provided varies from country to country and region. In some cases, domestic laws may require financial institutions to provide information on the accounts of US persons based on inter-agency agreements. In such cases, the account holder would be obligated to provide the information under domestic law. For instance, the United Kingdom[139] amended its national laws to implement the FATCA, allowing for such provisions under the authority of tax authorities.

In addition, the United States signed IGAs to improve international tax compliance and implement the FATCA with over 110 jurisdictions.[140] The arrangements are to address legal impediments to compliance, simplify practical implementation, and reduce costs of the FFIs.

There are two models of such agreements.[141] Under the Model 1 IGA, the partner jurisdiction agrees to report to the IRS specified information about the US accounts maintained by FFIs located in the jurisdiction. The competent authority of the partner jurisdiction reports the information submitted by the FFIs. The exchange of information may be on a reciprocal or non-reciprocal basis.

Under the Model 2 IGA, the partner jurisdiction agrees to direct and enable all relevant FFIs located in the jurisdiction to report specified information about their US accounts directly to the IRS. In general, the competent authority of the partner jurisdiction would agree to instruct and enable FIs in the country to register with the IRS and certify their compliance with FATCA, as they are subject to the regulation. The authority accepts and promptly honours group requests by the US competent authority for additional information about US accounts identified as recalcitrant and reported on an aggregate basis by FIs of the counterparty. The authority of the counterparty would obtain the requested information from the identified FIs and promptly exchange the information with the US competent authority under the bilateral tax agreements.

In exchange, the US authorities would eliminate the obligation of each FFI in the counterparty to enter into a separate FFI agreement directly with the IRS. The US authorities also eliminate US withholding under FATCA on payments to FIs

139 The International Tax Compliance (United States of America) Regulations 2013, No 1962, s 2.

140 The texts of the FATCA IGAs are available at US Department of State's website <https://home.treasury.gov/policy-issues/tax-policy/foreign-account-tax-compliance-act>.

141 US IRS, 'FATCA Information for Governments' <https://www.irs.gov/businesses/corporations/fatca-governments>. See also Raymond J Holst, Jiyeon Lee-Lim, and William Lu, 'Intergovernmental Agreements Under FATCA: Comparing the Two Models' [2013] White Paper, Latham & Watkins <https://www.lexology.com/library/detail.aspx?g=4de3f6cb-1825-4a58-97b6-6b18ec2383b9>.

in the counterparty that have registered or entered into an FFI agreement with the IRS and conduct due diligence and reporting in a manner consistent with FATCA requirements or are treated as deemed compliant or exempt pursuant to the IGA's framework, in other words, by identifying all such financial institutions as participating FFIs, deemed-compliant FFIs or exempt as appropriate. It would also provide other measures to reduce burdens and simplify the implementation of FATCA.

In summary, the United States constructed the mechanism to collect information from the FFIs based on either the institution's consent or the agreement with the partner jurisdiction.

5.2 OECD Global Forum and the Common Reporting Standards

FATCA is an indirect form of law enforcement that faces challenges during judicial proceedings and can lead to tension with the country where the financial institution is located. This triggered the establishment of a mechanism for information exchange through a regulatory network. Efforts have been made to prevent multinational corporations and others from avoiding taxation by shifting their income from high-tax jurisdictions to low-tax or no-tax jurisdictions through international transactions among related parties, known as tax base erosion and profit shifting.[142] A growing need emerged to prevent opaque flows of funds to offshore markets and ensure proper tax collection through international cooperation and implementing mechanisms.

The Global Forum has provided the foundation for this effort. It serves as a forum for mutual examination of legislation on the exchange of tax information and involves mainly OECD members and offshore market countries. It was originally established in 2001 and reorganized in 2014. The OECD adopted a model cooperation agreement between tax authorities and the CRS, an international standard for the automatic annual exchange of financial account information related to non-residents between tax authorities in 2014. The CRS mandates that the tax authorities of each country receive reports on financial account information held by non-residents from financial institutions within their country and share this information with the tax authorities of the non-resident's country of residence in accordance with the information exchange provisions of tax treaties and other agreements. The account information includes the holder's personal identification information, account balance, total annual interest receipts, dividends, and other financial transactions.

[142] OECD, 'Action Plan on Base Erosion and Profit Shifting' (19 July 2013) <https://www.oecd.org/en/publications/action-plan-on-base-erosion-and-profit-shifting_9789264202719-en.html>.

The legal basis for the exchange of information by tax authorities is typically the administrative law competence provisions of the tax authorities and the information exchange provisions of individual treaties. Some countries, such as the United Kingdom, have amended their national laws to implement the FATCA as previously stated. In contrast, others, such as Japan, have not made any amendments and rely on their existing powers to exchange information.

The network between tax authorities is developed through a global forum, which determines the basis for exchanging information. Notably, the CRS requires countries to exchange information even if they have no taxable interests and not to refuse requests based on bank secrecy legislation or bilateral taxability requirements. It has been described as going beyond the conventional level of cooperation and expanding and deepening the treaty network through multilateral dialogue and monitoring.

Another remarkable development is the establishment of the Crypto-Asset Reporting Framework (CARF) in 2023.[143] Crypto-assets are digital assets that leverage distributed ledger technology (DLT), such as blockchain, to enable secure transactions, ownership, and transfer. DLT allows financial transactions to occur directly between peers without the control or authorization of a third party, including States and financial institutions. It represents a transformative shift, as conventional financial systems rely on State-backed authorization to ensure the stability and economic value of money.[144] Such a transaction can be done on a peer-to-peer basis and through a service provider.

The CARF consists of three components. First, the rules and related commentary are designed to be transposed into domestic law to collect information from the crypto-asset service providers with a relevant nexus to the jurisdiction.[145] Second, the framework includes a Multilateral Competent Authority Agreement on Automatic Exchange of Information pursuant to the CARF.[146] Third, an electronic format (XML schema) is used by competent authorities for purposes of

[143] The text of the CARF is available at OECD, 'International Standards for Automatic Exchange of Information in Tax Matters: Crypto-Asset Reporting Framework and 2023 update to the Common Reporting Standard (15 July 2014) <https://doi.org/10.1787/896d79d1-en>.

[144] For an extensive description on the features of the DLT from legal perspectives, see Tetsuo Morishita, 'Technical Description of DLT for Conflicts Lawyers' in Andrea Bonomi, Matthias Lehmann, and Shaheeza Lalani (eds), *Blockchain and Private International Law* (Brill 2023) 51.

[145] Service providers will be subject to the rules if they meet any of the following conditions within a jurisdiction that has adopted the framework: (1) they are tax residents, (2) they are both incorporated or organized under the jurisdiction's laws and either possess legal personality or are subject to tax reporting obligations, (3) they are managed from the jurisdiction, (4) they maintain a regular place of business there, or (5) they conduct relevant transactions through a branch based in the jurisdiction. To prevent duplicative reporting when a service provider has nexus with multiple jurisdictions, the framework establishes a hierarchy of nexus rules. Additionally, it includes a provision for cases where a service provider has nexus in two jurisdictions based on the same type of nexus. OECD (n 143) 17.

[146] ibid 69.

exchanging the CARF information, as well as by service providers to report CARF information to tax administrations, as permitted by their domestic law.[147]

Careful assessment is needed to determine whether establishing such a regulatory framework has taken the exchange of tax information out of the realm of not being directly regulated by international law and into a scheme that regulates the parts common to national laws under international law.[148] The degree of obligation of States is an important aspect of international jurisprudence. The CRS are not legally binding under any convention, and authorities comply with them voluntarily because non-compliance will disadvantage their financial institutions. They, therefore, remain part of domestic law enforcement and do not constitute a legal obligation under international law. Nevertheless, they have a significant de facto impact on cross-border investigations of financial crimes.

6. Protection of Individual Rights

6.1 The Concept of Taxpayer's Rights

With the advancement of information exchange mechanisms and the increase in the volume of information exchanged, there have been debates on how to protect the rights of private individuals.

Basic taxpayer rights include the right to information, assistance, appeal, fair taxation, certainty, and privacy. According to the OECD's survey published in 1990, the member States of the organization have had domestic legislation to ensure these rights.[149] Certain constitutional rights, such as the right to access government-held information and the right to property, extend to taxation measures. However, as described in the previous sections, revenue authorities in many countries have started to take stringent measures to counter tax avoidance and evasion. They also led to more complex tax rules and frequent legislative changes. These shifts increased the risk of double taxation and made it difficult for taxpayers to plan their financial affairs. The compliance burden grew as the rules required time and resources to ensure adherence to the latest rules and reporting obligations. Constitutional rules are inadequate to fully safeguard the rights and interests of individuals.

[147] The text of the amended CRS is available at OECD, 'Amended Common Reporting Standard XML Schema' (1 October 2024) <https://www.oecd.org/en/publications/amended-common-reporting-standard-xml-schema_dd7ee57a-en.html>.

[148] For the nature of the CRS, see Yoshihiro Masui, 'Sozeijoyaku Ni Motozuku Joho Kokan' (2011) 30 Kinyu Kenkyu 253.

[149] OECD, Committee on Fiscal Affairs, *Taxpayer's Rights and Obligations: A Survey of the Legal Situations in OECD Countries* (OECD 1990).

Recognizing the importance of protecting taxpayers' rights, the OECD started to establish principles that balance tax enforcement with fairness in the 1990s.[150] It has developed the ideas of a transparent and cooperative approach to tax compliance and an enhanced relationship between tax authorities and taxpayers. OECD member States, including the United States,[151] the United Kingdom,[152] and France,[153] have issued the taxpayer's charter or other guidance that clarifies the rights of the taxpayers. Furthermore, the European Commission has also taken steps to improve taxpayer protections. In 2012, it introduced an action plan that included the concept of a taxpayer's code aimed at setting out clear rights and obligations for taxpayers within the European Union.[154] These rights include the right to privacy and confidentiality of tax information, the right to appeal a tax assessment or decision, and the right to receive reasonable assistance from tax authorities.

6.2 Taxpayer's Right to Privacy in the Exchange of Tax Information

The domestic rules concerning the taxpayers' rights may not fully cover situations where the taxing government seeks to obtain information on assets located in another country. The OECD recommends that domestic laws must be in place to protect the confidentiality of tax information, and there should be treaty obligations to the same effect. Effective penalties must be in place for unauthorized disclosure of exchanged information. Beyond confidentiality, there are several claims that States should respect the privacy rights in a cross-border investigation.

In his work published in 2009, Tonny Schenk-Geers focused on the taxpayer's legal position in exchanging tax-related information between States based on various agreements.[155] He mainly noted that States had a legal duty to protect the interests of their internal taxpayers or suppliers of information, apart from the obligation to protect the interests of the contracting States. In this context, he underscores the government's duty to inform the tax-payer concerning the decision to exchange information, and specific requirements and grounds of appeal must be provided.

In his 2010 paper, Arthur Cockfield emphasized the need for fairness in the rules and policies governing information exchange. He expressed concern about

[150] ibid.

[151] US IRS, 'Taxpayer Bill of Rights' (2024) <https://www.irs.gov/taxpayer-bill-of-rights>.

[152] UK HMRC, 'Corporate Report: The HMRC Charter' (*GOV.UK*, 30 July 2024) <https://www.gov.uk/government/publications/hmrc-charter/the-hmrc-charter>.

[153] Les ministères économiques et financiers, 'La charte des droits et obligations du contribuable vérifié' (2024) <https://www.economie.gouv.fr/dgfip/charte-des-droits-et-obligations-contribuable-verifie>.

[154] European Commission, 'Guidelines for a Model for A European Taxpayers' Code' (2016) Ref No Ares(2016)6598744 <https://taxation-customs.ec.europa.eu/system/files/2016-11/guidelines_for_a_model_for_a_european_taxpayers_code_en.pdf>.

[155] Schenk-Geers (n 96) 297.

the potential undemocratic constraints on individuals' right to information, particularly due to the impact of information technology and post-9/11 developments.[156] Efficient exchange of information can be achieved by promoting the exchange of electronic data while also ensuring that taxpayers' rights are respected. Both aspects are crucial for effective information exchange.

However, the implementation of tax agreements has not been consistent across these countries, and a common standard has not been established. It has not been fully established at the international level that these rights are guaranteed in the country where the assets are located or that private individuals can legally invoke them in tax imposition.

6.3 Financial Privacy

From the viewpoint of ensuring financial privacy, an approach is to prohibit the provision of information to a country that does not provide privacy protection equivalent to that of its own country. The EU Protection Directive and Canadian law are based on this view. Such differences in privacy standards also affect the disclosure of evidence in civil litigation. To overcome this problem, it is noteworthy that in 2008, the Sedona Conference, an academic organization, adopted the principles addressing electronic discovery. Substantial discovery must meet certain requirements, including considerations of data privacy laws in the jurisdiction where the information is located, obligations of parties to retain relevant information in the lawsuit jurisdiction and data location, and the purpose and scope of the discovery process. It also provides for agreements or, if necessary, court orders on measures to protect privileges, privacy, trade secrets, and other confidential information in disclosure procedures.[157]

However, the variance of the concepts of privacy affects the establishment of a network of international cooperation on the exchange of tax information. When standards for protecting individual rights differ from each other, cross-border tax regulations may lead to disputes between the law-enforcing country and the

[156] Arthur J Cockfield, 'Protecting Taxpayer Privacy Rights under Enhanced Cross-Border Tax Information Exchange: Toward a Multilateral Taxpayer Bill of Rights' (2010) 42 University of British Columbia Law Review 420; Arthur J Cockfield, 'The Rise of the OECD as Informal World Tax Organization through National Responses to E-Commerce Tax Challenges' (2005) 8 Yale Journal of Law and Technology 136; Arthur J Cockfield, 'A Comparative Analysis of Canadian and Foreign Private Sector Privacy Laws' in Elia Zureik (ed), *Surveillance, Privacy, and the Globalization of Personal Information* (McGill-Queens UP 2009) 50.

[157] The Sedona Conference, *The Sedona Canada Principles Addressing Electronic Discovery* (January 2008) <https://www.thesedonaconference.org/publication/The_Sedona_Canada_Principles>. The latest version in 2018 is available at The Sedona Principles, 'Third Edition: Best Practices, Recommendations & Principles for Addressing Electronic Document Production,' 19 Sedona Conference Journal 1 (2018).

affected individuals over whether financial institutions should disclose information to foreign authorities.

6.4 Development of the Concept of Taxpayers' Rights through Court Jurisprudence

There is a limited number of case law addressing taxpayers' rights in the context of cross-border investigation. It is notable that the European Court of Human Rights (ECtHR) and the Court of Justice of the European Union (CJEU) played a significant role in articulating the right to privacy in the information exchange.[158] The European Convention on Human Rights (ECHR) Article 8 and the EU Charter on Fundamental Rights Article 7 provide the right to respect for private and family life, home, and correspondence or communication. In addition, the EU Charter on Fundamental Rights Article 8 explicitly provides the protection of personal data. There are several cases where the courts interpreted these provisions in the context of the exchange of tax information. However, the cases are not consistent concerning the protection of privacy rights.

The ECtHR, in the *GSB v Switzerland* case in 2015, approved the law enforcing the country's wide margin concerning the exchange of tax information.[159] The case was about the transmission of the applicant's bank account information to the US tax authorities in connection with an administrative cooperation agreement between Switzerland and the United States. In the USB affair, the Swiss Financial Market Supervisory Authority had ordered UBS to transmit the applicant's file in accordance with the arrangement between the authority and the IRS.

The Switzerland Federal Administrative Court held that the conditions set out in the ECHR for any interference with private or family life were met in the instant case, considering that the important economic interests at stake for the country and Switzerland's interest in being able to honour its international commitments outweighed the individual interest of the persons concerned by the mutual assistance in keeping their financial situation secret.

The applicant alleged that the disclosure of his bank details constituted a violation of his right to respect his private life. The Court acknowledged that Switzerland had a wide margin of appreciation in the case, as the disputed disclosure pertained

[158] These developments are closely observed in the Japanese academic community as well. See, for instance, Yoshihiro Masui, 'Kazei Jōhō No Kōkan to Ōshū Jinken Jōyaku [Exchange of Tax Information and Human Rights Treaties]' (2017) 123 Hogaku Shinpo 333; Takeshi Fujitani, 'Kazei mokuteki no jōhō kōkan seido no gurōbaruka to kokunai saibansho no yakuwari' [Globalisation of Information Exchange Systems for Taxation Purposes and the Role of National Courts] (2018) 69(1) Shakai Kagaku Kenkyu 39.

[159] *GSB v Switzerland* App No 28601/11 (22 December 2015). The case also concerned the non-discrimination principle, provided under ECHR art 14, but this section will only deal with the privacy right under ECHR art 8.

solely to the applicant's bank data, which is 'purely financial information'.[160] It did not involve the transmission of intimate details or data closely linked to his identity, which would have required enhanced protection.[161] It also stated that Switzerland had an important interest in accepting the United States request for administrative mutual assistance so that it could avert major conflicts with the United States.[162] The measure was carried out as part of a mutual assistance procedure, not in connection with any actual criminal proceedings in the United States. It represented only a preliminary stage to potential criminal proceedings.[163] Given the circumstances and the non-personal nature of the disclosed data, the Court found it reasonable for Switzerland to prioritize the public interest in resolving the matter with the United States over the applicant's private interest and found that Switzerland did not exceed its margin of appreciation.[164]

The CJEU took a different approach from the ECtHR. Previously in *Sabou* case, the Court held that relevant instruments concerning information exchange did not grant a taxpayer of a member State the right to be informed of a request for assistance, even when the request aims to verify information submitted in the taxpayer's income tax return. Nor do they entitled the taxpayer to participate in formulating the request or to be involved in the examination of witnesses carried out by the requested member State. Accordingly, the Court adopted a distinctly State-centric approach.[165] However, in the *Berlioz Investment Fund SA* case,[166] the Luxembourg corporation was subject to an information request from the French law enforcement authority, which sought assistance from the Luxembourg authority under the administrative cooperation mechanism established by Directive 2011/16.[167] The company refused to comply, leading the authority to impose a financial penalty. In response, the corporation contested the request, questioning the relevance of the information sought by the Luxembourg authorities.

The CJEU clarified the application of the EU Charter on Fundamental Rights in the context of administrative cooperation in taxation under Council Directive 2011/16/EU. It ruled that a Member State enforces EU law when it imposes financial penalties on individuals refusing to provide information in cross-border tax inquiries, thereby making the Charter applicable. The Court affirmed that individuals penalized for non-compliance with an information request have the right to challenge the legality of the request under Article 47 of the Charter. Furthermore,

[160] ibid para 93.
[161] ibid.
[162] ibid para 94.
[163] ibid.
[164] ibid para 97.
[165] Case C-276/12 *Jiří Sabou v Finanční ředitelství pro hlavní město Prahu* [2013] ECLI:EU:C:2013:678 (Grand Chamber) paras 30–46.
[166] Case C-682/15 *Berlioz Investment Fund SA v Directeur de l'administration des contributions directes* [2017] ECLI:EU:C:2017:373 (Grand Chamber).
[167] Council Directive 2011/16/EU of 15 February 2011 on administrative cooperation in the field of taxation and repealing Directive 77/799/EEC [2011] OJ L64/1.

the principle of 'foreseeable relevance' is a key condition for the validity of such requests, requiring the requested authority to assess whether the information sought is relevant to the tax investigation. While national courts can review penalties and the legality of information requests, their scrutiny of relevance is limited to cases where the information is manifestly irrelevant. Additionally, courts must have access to the full request for information, but the individual concerned does not, as confidentiality under Article 16 of Directive 2011/16 must be maintained. However, the individual must receive sufficient information to exercise their right to a fair hearing.

These developments merit attention as attempts to establish common standards of protection in the field of taxation, extending beyond the safeguarding of rights within individual jurisdictions. Nonetheless, in other States than the European Union, consistent and sufficient State practice in this area appears to remain limited.

7. Concluding Remarks

The main findings of this chapter are summarized below. First, tax crimes have been excluded from criminal justice cooperation as a form of fiscal crime but have been replaced with cooperation through tax treaties. However, provisions for information exchange in tax treaties have evolved, indicating that tax law has undergone its development. For instance, mutual assistance based on the Bank Secrecy Act is no longer feasible, highlighting the changing nature of tax law since the 1970s.

States used to constrain the scope of information exchange to preserve national sovereignty. These limitations are incorporated in treaty provisions on information exchange and may include considerations such as home taxation interests, double criminality requirements, and other measures. Additionally, negotiations have occurred in some countries to prohibit banking secrecy legislation.

Second, tax law has a broad scope of application, allowing for taxation of income generated within the home country as well as the income of its citizens. This has led to the enactment of measures such as the FATCA and establishing a network of regulatory authorities to facilitate information exchange through non-binding agreements, bypassing coordination through treaties. However, these measures are accepted due to the established jurisdictional basis.

Third, an ongoing debate exists about harmonizing disclosure standards to third parties or authorities regarding financial information. Demands for transparency have led to the emergence of standards for the disclosure of information, which tend to undermine the need to keep information secret, particularly in the case of tax obligations. Furthermore, financial institutions must increasingly disclose information extensively concerning tax offences. Bank secrecy legislation, which previously prohibited the disclosure of information to foreign authorities, tends to be amended. Refusing assistance solely based on bank secrecy legislation is no longer permissible. This situation, where taxpayers' rights to information and financial privacy are unduly restricted, resembles the vulnerable position of private individuals in criminal assistance as discussed in Chapter 3. The lack of international coordination in this regard seems to be evident.

9
Foreign Bribery

1. Introduction

Bribery is an act of offering, giving, receiving, or soliciting something of value to influence the actions of an individual holding a public or legal duty. The item of value could be money, gifts, favours, or anything else that might be considered valuable to the recipient. Foreign bribery is an act to offer, promise, or give any undue pecuniary or other advantage to foreign public officials to gain or retain an improper advantage in business or other transactions.

The Convention on Combating Bribery of Foreign Public Officials in International Business Transactions (OECD Anti-Bribery Convention) of 1997 defines the elements of the crimes, which is the minimum criteria for the member States to criminalize.[1] Article 1(1) defines the crime as the act

> to offer, promise or give any undue pecuniary or other advantages, whether directly or through intermediaries, to a foreign public official, for that official or a third party, so that the official act or refrain from acting concerning the performance of official duties, to obtain or retain business or other improper advantage in the conduct of international business.

Article 2 obliges member States to take measures to establish the liability of legal persons for the bribery of a foreign public official. As of August 2024, the Convention enjoys forty-six parties, including thirty-eight OECD (Organisation for Economic Co-operation and Development) and eight non-OECD countries: Argentina, Brazil, Bulgaria, Croatia, Peru, Russia, and South Africa. These countries account for almost 80 per cent of world exports and nearly 90 per cent of global outward flows of foreign direct investments.[2] It is noted that China and India, despite being major economies, are not parties to the agreement.

The need for regulations on foreign bribery emerged out of economic globalization. The US commodity and futures trading firms, which have been facilitating transactions of natural resources from developing countries since the 1960s,

[1] Convention on Combating Bribery of Foreign Public Officials in International Business Transactions (adopted on 21 November 1997, entered into force on 15 February 1999) OECD/LEGAL/0293.

[2] OECD, 'Fighting Foreign Bribery' <https://www.oecd.org/en/topics/sub-issues/fighting-foreign-bribery.html>. All websites were last accessed on 31 March 2025.

International Law and the Investigation of Transnational Crimes. Yurika Ishii, Oxford University Press.
 DOI: 10.1093/9780198957089.003.0009

played a pivotal role in expanding international trade.[3] They acted as intermediaries, linking resource-rich nations with the world's financial centres. The corporations formed specific connections with foreign senior officials during the process, often through providing gifts, financial support, and other benefits. Bribing local officials was particularly prevalent in developing countries, where regulations were frequently weak or non-existent. Another aspect of corruption during the Cold War was the use of bribery by both the West and the Soviet Union, employing corporations as tools to secure and expand their influence. As Michael Reisman articulated in 1979, the interconnection between the American commercial system, modern representational government, and the nation-state system led to the tolerance of foreign bribery.[4]

Since the end of the Cold War, there has been a significant shift in public attitudes against corruption, which led to the adoption of the OECD Anti-Bribery Convention and the United Nations Convention against Corruption (UNCAC) in 2003.

Prohibiting bribery of foreign public officials in only one country puts that country's companies at a competitive disadvantage. Therefore, harmonizing national laws at the international level was essential for establishing regulations on the offence. As detailed in Section 2, the OECD served as the primary forum for this effort. In this context, Kevin Davis illustrates the key elements of transnational bribery law in action, examining the law through the 'OECD paradigm' and the 'anti-imperialist critique'.[5] He rightly argues that the modern regime on foreign bribery is based on the premise that broad prohibitions on bribery, targeting a wide range of actors, imposing stiff sanctions, and involving multiple agencies in the enforcement process are necessary.[6]

On the other hand, investigations into foreign bribery have several unique challenges. The prime difficulty is the detection of the offence. Corporations use their front companies to pay illicit money. The officials who demand and receive kickbacks do not cooperate. States must proactively gather information from diverse sources, including the mass media, reporting persons, public agencies, foreign authorities, and the private sector. Financial, banking, and company information,

[3] Javier Blas and Jack Farchy describe how commodities corporations secured access to natural resources in developing countries by building networks with government officials. These US commodity firms also expanded trade networks among developed countries, including the United States, the European Union, Japan, and the Republic of Korea, thereby contributing to the globalization of the economy. Javier Blas and Jack Farchy, *The World for Sale: Money, Power, and the Traders Who Barter the Earth's Resources* (OUP 2021).

[4] W Michael Reisman, *Folded Lies: Bribery, Crusades, and Reforms* (Free Press 1979).

[5] Kevin Davis, *Between Impunity and Imperialism: The Regulation of Transnational Bribery* (OUP 2019) 1–18.

[6] Davis calls this response the 'OECD paradigm'. On the other hand, the 'anti-imperialist critique', a significant challenge to the OECD paradigm, acknowledges the seriousness of transnational bribery but questions the conventional responses.

including beneficial ownership and asset tracing, are necessary.[7] However, there remains a significant divergence in the enforcement of bribery law.[8] Therefore, States may use investigative measures for tax offences and anti-money laundering regulations to scrutinize foreign bribery. This chapter focuses on the specific characteristics of these investigation methods.

Section 2 first overviews the harmonization process of the substantive laws in the following part. Then, Section 3 explores challenges in cross-border law enforcement to investigate foreign bribery. There are not so much of jurisdictional challenges for the authorities. However, the practice of law enforcement is limited. In this context, the focus is on the US Foreign Corrupt Practices Act (FCPA), the UK Unexplained Wealth Order (UWO), and Australia's anti-bribery laws, the most robust legal frameworks governing foreign bribery. It examines their key provisions, enforcement mechanisms, and their impact on global anti-bribery efforts. It will also highlight gaps in cross-border investigations in other States and regions. Section 4 explores various informal arrangements to combat foreign bribery, emphasizing their roles and effectiveness. The section covers the limitations of the UNCAC and mutual legal assistance treaties (MLATs) in effectively addressing foreign corruption across borders. It deals with informal direct cooperation with governments and corporations in detecting and preventing foreign bribery. It also examines how incentivizing the reporting of foreign bribery can lead to more effective enforcement and prevention. Section 5 briefly addresses the issue of the protection of fundamental rights, with particular reference to the fact that companies may be subject to multiple jurisdictions.

This chapter does not specifically address the demand side of foreign bribery because it necessitates a separate and distinct analysis. It is noted that the OECD's 2021 recommendation urges member states to address the demand side of bribery.[9] In addition, certain countries, including the United Kingdom,[10] Germany,[11] France,[12] and the United States,[13] have enacted laws that criminalize the demand side of foreign bribery, targeting foreign officials who solicit or accept bribes from individuals or businesses within their jurisdiction.

[7] OECD, 'Recommendation of the Council for Further Combating Bribery of Foreign Public Officials in International Business Transactions' (adopted 26 November 2009, amended 26 November 2021) OECD/LEGAL/0378, para X(i) <https://legalinstruments.oecd.org/en/instruments/oecd-legal-0378>.

[8] Davis (n 5) 161.

[9] OECD, 'Recommendation of the Council for Further Combating Bribery of Foreign Public Officials in International Business Transactions, OECD/LEGAL/0378' (26 November 2021) s XII <https://legalinstruments.oecd.org/en/instruments/OECD-LEGAL-0378>.

[10] Bribery Act 2010, c 23, s 2.

[11] Gesetz zur Bekämpfung der Korruption (Korruptionsbekämpfungsgesetz) 2006, BGBl I 1593, s 332.

[12] Loi n° 2016-1691 du 9 décembre 2016 relative à la transparence, à la lutte contre la corruption et à la modernisation de la vie économique, art 7.

[13] Foreign Extortion Prevention Act, Pub L No 115-165, 132 Stat 1245 (2018), s 3.

2. Harmonization of the Substantive Law

2.1 The Necessity for Harmonization

The first challenge to the suppression of foreign bribery is harmonizing the substantive laws among States and establishing international cooperation mechanisms. Before the 1970s, corrupt foreign practices were widespread and broadly accepted as a standard part of business in developing States. Many countries paid no heed to such practices and allowed corporations to deduct foreign bribes as legitimate business expenses on their financial statements. This tacit approval of bribery created an environment where unethical behaviour flourished, undermining fair competition and perpetuating corruption in developed and developing nations. During this period, the lack of stringent regulations and enforcement mechanisms enabled corporations to engage in bribery without significant legal or financial repercussions.

The FCPA was the first domestic law that criminalized foreign bribery.[14] Before this legislation, the US trading firms often resorted to corrupt practices to secure favourable terms and expedite transactions. From the end of the 1960s to the early 1970s, several scandals occurred. For instance, in 1974, it was discovered that the United Brands Company paid a USD 2.5 million bribe to the Honduran President to obtain tax reductions ('Bananagate'). In 1974, Honduras passed a law to raise the tax on banana exports. However, the company tried to beat other competitors, namely Standard Fruit and the Del Monte Corporation, by obtaining favourable treatment.[15] In 1977, it was revealed that Esso Italiana, Exxon's subsidiary, had made improper payments of more than USD 40 million to an Italian political party to suspend nuclear energy development and continue relying on oil in electrical power plants.[16] Then, the Lockheed affair was accused in 1977. The US airline bribed government officials in several countries, including Japan, the Netherlands, Italy, West Germany, and Saudi Arabia, to secure passenger and fighter aircraft orders.[17] Following these cases, the Securities and Exchange Commission (SEC) investigated the accounts of US companies and found that other companies also were engaged in similar practices of bribing foreign officials. Congress adopted the FCPA to suppress such conduct in the same year.

[14] Foreign Corrupt Practices Act, Pub L No 95-213, 91 Stat 1494 (1977), 15 USC 78dd-1, 78dd-2. For its background, see also Mark Pieth, 'Introduction' in Mark Pieth, Lucinda A Low, and Nicola Bonucci (eds), *The OECD Convention on Bribery* (2nd edn, CUP 2013) 11.

[15] Against this background was the cartel among banana exporting countries to North American market (namely Colombia, Costa Rica, Ecuador, Guatemala, Honduras, Nicaragua, and Panama) to fix the fruit's price.

[16] AP, 'Italian Exxon Official Resists S.E.C. Decree' *New York Times* (29 September 1977) 91.

[17] Peter W Schroth, 'The United States and the International Bribery Conventions' (2002) 50 American Journal of Comparative Law 593.

The FCPA underwent revisions in 1988, introducing amendments that relaxed certain requirements.[18] The standard for third-party liability was modified from 'knowing or having reason to know' to simply 'knowing', thereby removing the 'having reason to know' element.[19] The scope of exceptions and affirmative defences, such as those for facilitation payments, lawful payments, and reasonable and bona fide expenditures, was broadened.[20] On the other hand, the revisions also imposed a new requirement on the President to engage in negotiations to establish an international agreement to combat foreign bribery.

2.2 OECD Anti-Bribery Convention

2.2.1 Background

Following the enactment of the FCPA, the United States led the adoption of the Anti-Bribery Convention, which addressed concerns that US corporations may face a competitive disadvantage against other corporations operating in developing countries where bribery is a common and often necessary practice.[21]

Even during congressional deliberations on the FCPA, concerns arose that including in US law provisions that prohibited bribery would allow US companies to decline requests for bribes, thereby curbing unnecessary expenditures.[22] Moreover, the FCPA safeguards US diplomatic relations by discouraging US companies from offering large bribes to foreign officials or dignitaries, which could engender negative diplomatic ramifications.[23]

As US companies became more aware of the inequity caused by the FCPA, they appealed to Congress to repeal it. Congress chose to preserve the law and address the issue of foreign public official bribery by companies from other nations. In 1988, Congress directed the President to negotiate an international agreement with the OECD to ban foreign public official bribery and report to Congress on the progress made within one year.[24]

In 1989, the United States complained to the OECD Committee on International Investment Multinational Enterprises, asserting that corrupt payments made to

[18] Pieth (n 14) 12–13.

[19] 15 USC 78dd-2. The DOJ had testified that its policy is only to prosecute those cases where 'the evidence of awareness—whether direct or circumstantial—was so clear as to constitute actual knowledge of the bribe scheme'. Senate Subcommittee on Securities and on International Finance and Monetary Policy, 99th Cong 2d Sess, 10 June 1986.

[20] 15 USC 78dd-1(b).

[21] Alejandro Posadas, 'Combating Corruption under International Law' (1999) 10 Duke Journal of Comparative and International Law 345, 381.

[22] House Report No 95-640, Senate Report No 95-114, House Conference Report No 95-831, House Conference Report No 100-576.

[23] Donald R Cruver, *Complying with the Foreign Corrupt Practices Act: A Guide for U.S. Firms Doing Business in the International Marketplace* (American Bar Association 1994) 4.

[24] Omnibus Trade and Competitiveness Act, Pub L No 100-418, 102 Stat 1107 (1988), s 5003(d)(1).

foreign officials in international trade created an unfair competitive environment. The United States proposed a convention on anti-corruption, which the OECD adopted in November 1997 after policy recommendations and other measures designed to prohibit bribery were implemented.[25]

2.2.2 Overview of the Convention

The Convention requires member states to criminalize foreign bribery and violations of specified accounting standards within their territory or by nationals. Furthermore, those parties that have made bribery of their public officials a predicate offence in their money laundering legislation are required to apply the same legislation to bribery of foreign public officials, regardless of where the bribery is committed.

To ensure the effectiveness of the criminalization provided by the Convention, the OECD has introduced a peer review system, which thoroughly examines member States' legislation and encourages them to enact or amend legislation to meet the standards of the Convention, as Section 3.6 will discuss. The OECD has thus established a systematic monitoring programme to promote the full implementation of these instruments across member countries.

The OECD has made several recommendations to enhance legal assistance to suppress this crime. The OECD Working Group on Bribery, composed of forty-four member States, oversees implementing and enforcing the Anti-Bribery Convention and Recommendation. In 2009, a recommendation was made that criminal assistance for bribing foreign public officials be bolstered and called for MLATs.[26] Furthermore, the organization issued an elaborate report in 2012 on various types of criminal aid.[27] In 2021, the OECD Council adopted a revised Recommendation to address challenges, good practices, and cross-cutting issues concerning foreign bribery. In addition, the OECD's Committee on Fiscal Affairs also monitors whether member states allow the tax deductibility of foreign bribes.[28] Other significant instruments include the 2009 Recommendation on Tax Measures for Further Combating Bribery of Foreign Public Officials in International Business Transactions and the 2006 Recommendation on Bribery and Officially Supported Export Credits.[29]

In addition, the OECD coordinates civil and collateral sanctions by recommending restrictions on the granting of official export credit as a broad public

[25] 1994 Council Recommendation on International Business Transactions, C(94)75/FINAL, 27 May 1994; 1996 Recommendation on the Tax Deductibility of Bribes, C(96)27/FINAL, 17 April 1996.

[26] 2009 Council Recommendation on Tax Measures for Further Combating Bribery of Foreign Public Officials in International Business Transactions, OECD/LEGAL/0371.

[27] OECD, 'Typology on Mutual Legal Assistance in Foreign Bribery Cases' (20 April 2012) <https://www.oecd.org/en/publications/typology-on-mutual-legal-assistance-in-foreign-bribery-cases_a61063e4-en.html>.

[28] OECD (n 7).

[29] OECD, 'Recommendation of the Council on Bribery and Officially Supported Export Credits' (2006) OECD/LEGAL/0348 <https://legalinstruments.oecd.org/public/doc/201/201.en.pdf>.

sanction for the offence of bribery of foreign public officials. This public export credit is trade insurance granted after an examination by a credit-granting organization in each country. For multinational corporations, the loss of export credit can effectively mean an end to their trading, incentivizing them to refrain from bribery. In 2006, the OECD recommended countries take appropriate measures to deter foreign bribery in transactions benefiting from official export credit support, including establishing penal and administrative sanctions.[30] To improve the implementation of these guidelines, the OECD's Committee on Fiscal Affairs monitors whether member States allow the tax deductibility of foreign bribes.

Harmonization of the regulation of foreign bribery requires coordination in other fields. Some countries previously allowed corporations to deduct hush money payments from their taxes. The OECD recommended that countries abolish such practices in 1996.[31] It undermines the tax system's integrity and sends the message that it is acceptable to engage in unethical behaviour. Implementing regulations with a wide range of sanctions and a peer review system is not uncommon in economic law fields but was a novel approach in criminal law.

In contrast to the detailed regulations regarding substantive law, the obligations for enforcement and mutual assistance obliged under the Convention are relatively simple.

The Convention provides that '[i]nvestigation and prosecution of the bribery of a foreign public official shall be subject to the applicable rules and principles of each Party'.[32] It also provides that such measures 'shall not be influenced by considerations of national economic interest, the potential effect upon relations with another State or the identity of the natural or legal persons involved'.[33]

Member States must provide timely and effective legal help to other State Parties 'to the fullest extent possible'.[34] Furthermore, they must promptly inform the receiving State Party of any additional information or documentation necessary to respond to the request and update them on the status or outcome of their consideration.

To ensure that discrepancies in the substantive law do not hinder proceedings, the Convention considers the requirement of double criminality to have been met concerning the offences outlined in the Convention.[35] Additionally, States parties cannot refuse to provide mutual legal assistance because of bank secrecy.[36]

[30] OECD, '2006 Action Statement on Bribery and Officially Supported Export Credits' (2006) TD/ECG(2006)11 <https://www.oecd.org/en/topics/sub-issues/bribery-and-export-credits.html>.

[31] OECD, 'Recommendation of the Council on the Tax Deductibility of Bribes to Foreign Public Officials' (1996) OECD/LEGAL/0286 <https://legalinstruments.oecd.org/en/instruments/OECD-LEGAL-0276>. The Recommendation was abrogated on 25 May 2009.

[32] OECD Bribery Convention (n 1), art 5.

[33] ibid.

[34] ibid art 9(1).

[35] ibid art 9(2).

[36] ibid art 9(3).

Member States must also establish an authority with jurisdiction over mutual assistance under the Convention.[37]

However, the Convention does not specify the substance of assistance that member states are obligated to provide, and its enforcement is not without obstacles. For instance, in most countries, waiving bank secrecy requires strong evidence of a criminal offence and a link between the offence and the requested information.[38] 'Fishing expeditions' to find foreign bank accounts are generally not accepted.[39] Access to confidential accounts can be further restricted, especially in non-criminal cases against legal entities.[40] Furthermore, long delays may occur when they request search warrants or legal authorizations for the lifting of bank secrecy.[41] By large, these treaty rules are as limited as a conventional MLAT. As Sections 3 and 4 will discuss, States use other informal means to gather information and evidence than the treaty mechanism.

2.3 United Nations Convention against Corruption

The UNCAC also mandates criminalizing foreign bribery and more comprehensive mandatory assistance provisions. The UN General Assembly launched efforts against corruption in the 1990s after the Cold War had ended, and Western countries were no longer hesitant to address corruption in developing nations. Despite earlier General Assembly resolutions condemning corruption, progress was not made towards regulating corruption until the Declaration against Corruption and Bribery in International Commercial Transactions was adopted in 1996.[42] This declaration spurred the development of the World Bank's Anti-Corruption Strategy and the World Trade Organization's mandate for transparency in government procurement agreements.[43]

In 2003, after two years of drafting by an ad hoc committee, the UN General Assembly adopted the UNCAC. The OECD member States and other developed countries had already ratified the OECD Anti-Bribery Convention and actively

[37] ibid art 11.

[38] Maurice Harari and Delphine Jobin, 'International Co-Operation' in Mark Pieth, Lucinda A Low ,and Nicola Bonucci (eds), *The OECD Convention on Bribery* (2nd edn, CUP 2013) 516–17.

[39] ibid.

[40] ibid.

[41] ibid.

[42] UNGA Res 51/191 (1996) *United Nations Declaration against Corruption and Bribery in International Commercial Transactions*; UNGA Res 51/59 (1996), *Action against Corruption*, UN Doc A/RES/51/59.

[43] World Trade Organization, Agreement on Government Procurement (adopted on 15 April 1994, entered into force on 1 January 1996) 1915 UNTS 103, art 17.

participated in the drafting process.[44] The UNCAC contains provisions for mutual assistance, specifically for recovering property transferred through bribery.

On the other hand, the UNCAC only required member States to comply with the obligation of a State party to exchange financial intelligence to be 'within the conditions prescribed by its domestic law'.[45] While the combat against corruption has been an important agenda for the United Nations, there is no effective enforcement mechanism equivalent to the ones established by the OECD. As a result, the instrument has not been widely used to address foreign bribery.

3. Limited Law Enforcement Practice

3.1 Lack of Jurisdictional Conflicts

This section explores some of the most comprehensive legislations addressing foreign bribery, which require individuals and corporations to disclose unexplained financial resources. Such regulation aligns with anti-money laundering regulations, which Chapter 11 will examine.

The jurisdictional reach of these laws is generally broad. However, States have sufficient nexus in practice based on factors such as the corporation being established under their laws, being registered on their securities exchange, or conducting business in their market. Some cases may not neatly fit on a conventional basis such as territoriality or personality. However, if the corporation is listed, States may assert jurisdiction to maintain a stable market. In addition, the official commentary of the OECD Anti-Bribery Convention articulates that '[t]he territorial basis for jurisdiction should be interpreted broadly so that an extensive physical connection to the bribery act is not required'.[46] As a result, there are minimal conflicts among States in their implementation.

3.2 The US Foreign Corrupt Practices Act

As explained in the previous section, the FCPA was the first anti-foreign bribery law and the most robust one to this date. The notable features of the FCPA include

[44] United Nations Convention against Corruption (adopted on 31 October 2003, entered into force on 14 December 2005) 2349 UNTS 41 (UNCAC). It is noted that the United States and Canada declared that they would not amend their domestic laws. United Nations Office on Drugs and Crime, 'Declarations and Reservation' (14 August 2008) <http://www.unodc.org/documents/treaties/UNCAC/ReservationsDeclarations/DeclarationsAndReservations14Aug2008.pdf>.

[45] UNCAC (n 44), art 14(1)(b).

[46] OECD, 'Commentaries on the Convention on Combating Bribery of Foreign Public Officials in International Business Transactions, Adopted by the Negotiating Conference on 21 November 1997' (1997) para 25 <https://www.oecd-ilibrary.org/docserver/2bfa620e-en.pdf>.

its expansive jurisdictional reach that covers domestic and foreign actors. It prohibits bribery of foreign officials by securities issuers registered with the US securities exchange, US citizens, or US-domiciled corporations, regardless of nationality. Corporations are subject to the parent company's liability to its subsidiaries, and in a merger, the surviving or newly formed entity assumes the liabilities of the merged or acquired company. The FCPA also covers conspiracies and holds corporations liable, including their subsidiaries, in the case of mergers. It covers cases where a phone conversation takes place between a US person and someone overseas or when an email is sent to a party in the United States. Additionally, using a US correspondent account can trigger the FCPA, as payments made in US dollars through such accounts involve US financial institutions, creating a sufficient connection between the conduct and the United States.

Violations of the FCPA may result in criminal sanctions and substantial collateral repercussions, including being barred from contracting with the federal government, cross-debarred by multilateral development banks, and suspending or losing certain export privileges.[47]

The FCPA offence is subject to regulation by other laws. The Public Company Accounting Reform and Investor Protection Act of 2002 (SOX Act), enacted in response to the Enron scandal,[48] imposed accountability on directors for the accuracy and sufficiency of corporate financial reports.[49] The SOX Act also reinforces internal controls on financial reporting and forbids document tampering.

Both the US Department of Justice (DOJ) and the SEC are in charge of enforcing the law. The DOJ may pursue criminal charges, and the SEC may pursue civil charges. The two agencies may work together, and the Federal Bureau of Investigation's International Corruption Division may investigate cases in foreign countries. The SEC has been rigorously enforcing the law since the late 2000s.[50] In 2010, the SEC's Enforcement Division created a specialized unit to further strengthen its enforcement of the FCPA.

Although the FCPA was passed in the United States in 1977, it was rarely applied to foreign companies until the 2000s, when there was a significant increase in enforcement by the DOJ and SEC, as demonstrated by Brandon Garrett.[51]

[47] Criminal Division of the US DOJ and Enforcement Division of the US SEC, *A Resource Guide to the US Foreign Corrupt Practices Act* (2012) 72. For the concrete scenarios that trigger FCPA, see US DOJ, 'A Resource Guide to the U.S. Foreign Corrupt Practices Act' (2020 2nd edn) 9-18 <https://www.justice.gov/criminal/criminal-fraud/file/1292051/dl?inline>.

[48] Enron, a major US energy company at the time, committed accounting fraud to conceal debt and exaggerate profits. It declared bankruptcy in 2001 after its actions were exposed. The impact was significant, as the company's collapse led to the loss of approximately 4,000 jobs and USD 74 billion in shareholder value.

[49] Public Company Accounting Reform and Investor Protection Act, Pub L No 107-204, 116 Stat 745 (2002).

[50] SEC, 'SEC Enforcement Actions: FCPA Cases' (2024) <https://www.sec.gov/enforce/sec-enforcement-actions-fcpa-cases>.

[51] Brandon L Garrett, 'Globalized Corporate Prosecutions' (2011) 97 Virginia Law Review 1775.

Authorities and companies often reach plea deals or deferred prosecution agreements (DPAs) when pursuing corporate criminal liability, particularly for this crime, as Chapter 5 described. Companies agreeing to these settlements, rather than undergoing a criminal trial and risking being delisted from the stock exchange, is more advantageous. These agreements allow for the collection of information and evidence on the case and installing an independent monitor within the company to report on its activities. This approach enables the United States to enforce its laws without relying on mutual assistance treaties to collect information and evidence from foreign companies.

3.3 The UK Bribery Act and Unknown Wealth Order

Another example of robust legislation is that of the United Kingdom. The regulation of bribery in the United Kingdom has changed over time.[52] Although individual statutes and case law previously governed bribery, in 2010, these were consolidated into the new Bribery Act.[53] The Bribery Act applies to any UK-based legal entity conducting part or all of its business in the UK territory. However, it should be noted that the legislation permits law enforcement against legal entities outside the United Kingdom. The UK Ministry of Justice guidelines permit subsidiaries to operate independently of their parent company.[54] The mere existence of a parent–subsidiary relationship does not qualify a subsidiary as conducting business in the United Kingdom. Nonetheless, suppose that the foreign parent company uses the subsidiary to conduct business in the United Kingdom or exercises some degree of control over the subsidiary's business. In that case, the Act applies to the parent company.

In 2013, the United Kingdom introduced DPAs, similar to the US approach, and changed its sentencing criteria to include fines and the potential disqualification of directors.[55] Breaches of the Bribery Act can result in penalties, confiscation of proceeds under the Proceeds of Crime Act 2002,[56] and disqualification of directors under the Company Directors Disqualification Act 1986.[57]

Despite the broad scope of the Bribery Act, the United Kingdom tends to use DPAs selectively. In 2014, the Serious Fraud Office (SFO) investigated the UK

[52] Public Bodies Corrupt Practices Act 1889, 52 & 53 Vict c 69; Prevention of Corruption Act 1906, 6 Edw 7 c 34; Prevention of Corruption Act 1916, 6 & 7 Geo 5 c 64.

[53] Bribery Act 2010, c 23.

[54] United Kingdom Ministry of Justice, *Bribery Act 2010 Guidance* (2010) 15.

[55] Crime and Courts Act 2013, c 22, sch 17. See also Sentencing Council, 'Fraud, Bribery and Money Laundering Offences: Definitive Guideline' (effective from 1 October 2014) <http://www.sentencingcouncil.org.uk/wp-content/uploads/Fraud_bribery_and_money_laundering_offences_-_Definitive_guideline.pdf>.

[56] Proceeds of Crime Act 2002, c 29.

[57] Company Directors Disqualification Act 1986, c 46.

subsidiary of Alstrom, a French-based electrical company, for alleged bribery of senior officials in India, Poland, Tunisia, and other countries between 2000 and 2006. The SFO concluded a DPA with the company rather than imposing a fine.

A significant development is the establishment of an UWO, a legal tool introduced by the Criminal Finances Act of 2017. It is a court order that a British court can issue, compelling the individuals to disclose the sources of their unexplained wealth. The authorities can target assets owned by individuals suspected of involvement in serious crime, including politically exposed persons. An enforcement authority may apply for an order to the High Court. The court must be satisfied that (1) there is reasonable cause to believe the individual holds the asset, (2) the value of the asset exceeds GBP 50,000, and (3) the respondent is a politically exposed person, or there are reasonable grounds to suspect involvement in serious crime. Suppose individuals fail to provide a satisfactory account. In that case, their assets may be seized following a successful appeal to the High Court by an enforcement authority, such as the National Crime Agency, Financial Conduct Authority, and Her Majesty's Revenue and Customs; the Director of the SFO; and the Directors of Public Prosecutions.

The effectiveness of this mechanism is in question. The first case where this order was used was against Zamira Hajiyeva, the wife of a jailed Azerbaijani banker. She was ordered to explain the source of her wealth, including a GBP 15 million property in London.

The UWOs reverse the traditional burden of proof, requiring individuals to prove the legitimacy of their wealth. This shift raises concerns about due process and the presumption of innocence.

Besides these legal issues, there are questions concerning the effectiveness. First, the criteria for obtaining a UWO, such as proving a connection to serious crime or political exposure and demonstrating that the property's value exceeds GBP 50,000, can be difficult to meet. Second, wealthy individuals often use sophisticated methods to conceal their assets, such as complex corporate structures and offshore accounts. As a result, since their introduction, the number of UWOs issued has been relatively low.[58]

Despite these challenges, the UWO represents a significant step forward in the suppression of foreign bribery. The legislation, though not without its limitations, has introduced a novel mechanism to target and disrupt the accumulation of unexplained wealth by individuals or corporations who might otherwise evade scrutiny. Even if the current number of UWOs issued is low, the legislation makes it clear that unexplained wealth will not be tolerated. The UWO should be viewed

[58] Ali Shalchi, 'Unexplained Wealth Orders' (14 April 2022) <https://commonslibrary.parliament.uk/research-briefings/cbp-9098/>. By February 2022, only nine orders had been issued, relating to four cases. None have been obtained since the end of 2019.

as a progressive piece of legislation that holds significant promise in the ongoing effort to combat financial crime.

The United Kingdom enacted the Economic Crime (Transparency and Enforcement) Act in March 2022. This legislation introduced substantial reforms to the UWO regime, aiming to simplify their acquisition, enforcement, and monitoring.[59] Its effectiveness is yet to be proven.

3.4 Australia's Crimes Legislation Amendment (Combatting Foreign Bribery) Bill 2023

Australia is another notable country that has vigorously enforced its anti-bribery law. After it ratified the OECD Convention in 1999, it enacted the Criminal Code Amendment (Bribery of Foreign Officials) Act in the same year, which inserted relevant provisions into the Criminal Code Act 1995 (Criminal Code) to criminalize foreign public officials. Since challenges existed in the implementation of the law, the Crimes Legislation Amendment (Combatting Foreign Bribery) Bill 2023 was passed in 2024.

Under the present law, bribing a foreign public official is a crime under the Criminal Code.[60] A corporation can be liable for foreign bribery because of the actions of its top-level management or board of directors, employees, and agents.[61]

In addition, a corporation can be held liable for failing to prevent an offence committed by its 'associate',[62] a term that is broadly defined.[63] A defence available to companies is to establish that they have 'adequate procedures' in place to prevent such conduct. The Bill provides that the Attorney General must publish guidance on what qualifies as adequate procedures.

Australia's foreign bribery laws apply to conduct occurring outside Australia where the offence is committed by an Australian citizen or resident or by an Australian corporation.[64] Conducting lawful acts in foreign public officials' countries[65] and the facilitation payments[66] constitute defences for the offence.

[59] Economic Crime (Transparency and Enforcement) Act 2022, c 10, ss 45–53. The law was enacted in response to Russia's invasion against Ukraine in February 2022. The United Kingdom has been a key destination for Russian wealth investment, and the law aims to monitor these transactions.

[60] Criminal Code Act 1995, No 12, s 70.2.

[61] ibid division 12.

[62] ibid s 70.5A. It is an absolute liability. Before this legislation, a corporation was not criminally responsible for bribery by its employees, agents, or officers, if it can prove it has exercised due diligence to prevent the crime. The current law abolished such a defence.

[63] ibid s 70.1 defines 'associate'. A person is an 'associate' if person is an officer, employee, agent, or contractor of the other person is a subsidiary of the other person; is controlled by the other person, or otherwise performs services for or on behalf of the other person.

[64] Australian corporation means the ones incorporated by or under a law of the Commonwealth or of a State or territory.

[65] Criminal Code, s 70.3. This defence does not apply in relation to local customs that are not evidenced by a written law.

[66] ibid s 70.4.

One of the main reasons for the amendments was the challenges in securing prosecutions for foreign bribery offences. For several years, it lagged behind other countries in enforcement.[67] The first Australian prosecutions for foreign bribery commenced in 2011, and since then, seven convictions have been obtained across two prosecutions.

The government has tried to improve the efficiency in collecting the necessary information to prove the case. One such attempt was the introduction of DPAs. The Crimes Legislation Amendment (Combatting Corporate Crime) Bill 2017 and the following Crimes Legislation Amendment (Combatting Corporate Crime) Bill 2019 proposed introducing the mechanism. The proposed bills provided that DPAs would apply only to legal entities, not individuals, and would require approval from a former judicial officer. However, they did not pass. The government's proposal to include a DPA mechanism in the 2023 legislation was rejected in the end.[68]

3.5 Challenges in the Enforcement of Anti-Foreign Bribery Acts

As a result of the harmonization efforts as described in Section 2, most OECD member States now have anti-foreign bribery acts. Nevertheless, their enforcement has proven challenging. Most countries are hesitant to investigate foreign companies for offences. Restrictive prosecution discretion and court interpretation limit enforcement laws prohibiting foreign bribery.

For instance, France amended its Criminal Code in 2000 to criminalize foreign bribery.[69] Corporate liability includes fines[70] and various penalties, such as a prohibition on doing business in the place where the offence was committed for up to five years, placement under judicial supervision, closure of the department in which the offence was committed, disqualification from public procurement, and a prohibition on cheque writing.[71] However, their enforcement policy is limited. Only one prosecution against a foreign public official for bribery has been carried out in the fourteen years since the law was amended, raising concerns expressed by the OECD in 2012.[72]

[67] Cat Baker, 'Australia's Implementation of the OECD Anti-Bribery Convention' (28 August 2019) <https://www.aph.gov.au/About_Parliament/Parliamentary_Departments/Parliamentary_Library/pubs/rp/rp1920/Anti-BriberyConvention>.

[68] See Crimes Legislation Amendment (Combatting Foreign Bribery) Bill 2023, Act No 47. The statutory review of the operation of the amendments after eighteen months will be tabled in the Parliament and will provide another opportunity to consider the introduction of a DPA regime.

[69] Code penal, arts 435-3, 435-4; Loi n° 2000-595 du 30 juin 2000 modifiant le code pénal et le code de procédure pénale relative à la lutte contre la corruption.

[70] ibid art 435-6, 1°.

[71] ibid art 435-6, 2°.

[72] OECD, 'OECD Seriously Concerned at Lack of Foreign Bribery Convictions in France, But Recognises Recent Efforts to Ensure Independence of Prosecutors' (23 October 2012) <http://www.oecd.org/corruption/oecdseriouslyconcernedatlackofforeignbriberyconvictionsinfrancebutrecognis

However, France subsequently implemented a series of structural reforms aimed at addressing foreign bribery offences. The Law on Transparency, the Fight against Corruption and the Modernization of Economic Life (known as 'Loi Sapin II') of 2016 made the institutional reforms by introducing *Convention judiciaire d'intérêt public* and establishing Anti-Corruption Agency (*Agence française anticorruption*) , a specialised investigative unit for economic and financial crimes.[73] Between 2012 and 2021, sanctions were imposed in 14 cases, including two multi-national corporations. In its 2021 evaluation, the OECD observed that the strategic emphasis on resolving foreign bribery cases through this non-trial mechanism represented a major shift in the approach to corporate liability.[74]

In Germany, the ratification of the OECD Anti-Bribery Convention resulted in amendments to the Criminal Code in 1998.[75] Additionally, it enacted the International Bribery Act, which criminalizes the bribery of foreign public officials and officials of international organizations,[76] and the EU Bribery Act to suppress bribery of EU public officials.[77] Moreover, the government released guidelines on the corruption of foreign public officials.[78] Germany has indeed enforced these laws and has taken stringent action against its corrupt companies in procurement contracts for aid, especially in Africa. However, the OECD 2021 evaluation report comments that 'Germany's enforcement of its corporate liability regime remains critically low.'[79] It was primarily because the country did not sufficiently implement the OECD's recommendations on detecting foreign bribery.

Japan criminalized foreign bribery per its Unfair Competition Prevention Act of 2000. At that time, the Japanese Penal Code did not include a mechanism to hold

esrecenteffortstoensureindependenceofprosecutors.htm>. It is noted that, in 2013, Total SA, a multinational oil corporation, was accused of bribing senior Iraqi officials to secure contracts under the UN Oil-for-Food Programme. The Paris Tribunal applied a restrictive interpretation of the elements of foreign bribery, underscoring the absence of unjust enrichment, and acquitted the charges (Tribunal de grande instance de Paris, du 10 janvier 2013, n 2011-10303). Its ruling was later overturned by the Court of Appeal (Cour d'appel, Paris, du 26 fevrier 2016, n 2015-13243). See also *Total SA and Vitol SA v France* App Nos 34634/18 and 43546/18 (12 October 2023).

[73] Loi no 2016-1691 du 9 décembre 2016 relative à la transparence, à la lutte contre la corruption et à la modernisation de la vie économique ('Loi Sapin II'). For the introduction of non-trial mechanisms in France, see also Chapter 5, Section 3.3.

[74] OECD, 'Implementing the OECD Anti-Bribery Convention Phase 4 Report: France' (2021) 9 <https://doi.org/10.1787/2c7d8500-en>.

[75] StGB, arts 299(3), 299–302, 331–338, 108b–198e.

[76] Gesetz zur Bekämpfung internationaler Bestechung vom 10. September 1998, BGBl 1998 II S 2327.

[77] EU-Bestechungsgesetz vom 10. September 1998, BGBl 1998 II S 2340. Partially amended in 2004, Gesetzes vom 21. Juli 2004, BGBl I S 1763.

[78] Richtlinie der Bundesregierung zur Korruptionsprävention in der Bundesverwaltung (30 July 2004) <https://www.umweltbundesamt.de/sites/default/files/medien/377/dokumente/richtlinie_der_bundesregierung_zur_korruptionspraevention.pdf>.

[79] OECD, 'Implementing the OECD Anti-Bribery Convention Phase 4 Follow-Up Report: Germany' (2021) 3 <https://doi.org/10.1787/4293ecc0-en>. According to the report, corporate liability was only established against nine percent of the cases.

legal persons criminally liable. Additionally, it lacked personal jurisdiction over foreign bribery. The Japanese Diet established the offence as a part of the specialized criminal law to address these limits.[80] In addition, the Ministry of Economy, Trade and Industry issued the 'Guidelines for Preventing Bribery of Foreign Public Officials' to support companies' voluntary and preventative approaches to preventing bribery of foreign public officials.[81]

However, there were several issues concerning the effectiveness of the Japanese law. The jurisdictional scope was too narrow because it did not cover foreign bribery committed by non-Japanese employees or agents outside Japan. In addition, the fines imposed are relatively low compared to other OECD member States. As a result, the number of cases of bribery is significantly low, given the size of the Japanese economy and the fact that Japanese companies operate in high-risk areas and sectors.[82] In 2023, Japan amended the law in response to these shortcomings.[83] Statutory penalties have been increased for both natural and legal persons, and bribery by foreign employees of Japanese companies abroad has been made punishable.

3.6 OECD's Peer Review on the Implementation of the Convention

The OECD recommends that member States periodically review their laws and approaches to enforcing the OECD Anti-Bribery Convention.[84] The OECD Working Group on Bribery in International Business Transactions, which was established in 1994, is in charge of monitoring the implementation and enforcement of the OECD Anti-Bribery Convention and relevant OECD recommendations.[85] The Working Group publishes monitoring reports on each country's progress in implementing and enforcing the Convention. These reports reflect the findings of a field visit to the country under review and the views of stakeholders such as civil society, the private sector, and academia.[86]

This mechanism came after the peer-review mechanism under the Financial Action Task Force on money laundering and terrorism financing, as Chapter 11 will explain. However, the reports on foreign bribery carry less immediate impact

[80] Law to Amend the Unfair Competition Prevention Law, Act No 51 of 2004, amending Unfair Competition Prevention Act, Act No 47 of 1993, art 18.

[81] METI, 'Gaikoku Kōmuin Zōwai Bōshi Shishin' (2004) <https://www.meti.go.jp/policy/external_economy/zouwai/pdf/GaikokukoumuinzouwaiBoushiShishin.pdf>.

[82] OECD, 'Japan and the OECD Anti-Bribery Convention' (2024) <https://www.oecd.org/en/topics/sub-issues/fighting-foreign-bribery/japan-country-monitoring.html>.

[83] Amendment of Unfair Competition Prevention Act, Act No 51 of 2023, art 21(11).

[84] The 2021 OECD Recommendation (n 28) para VI (i)–(iii).

[85] The instruments include recommendations such as OECD (n 9).

[86] OECD, 'OECD Anti-Bribery Convention and the Country Monitoring Process' (2024) <https://www.oecd.org/content/dam/oecd/en/topics/policy-sub-issues/fighting-foreign-bribery/oecd-anti-bribery-convention-country-monitoring-process.pdf>.

because they do not directly affect the practices of financial institutions. Instead, it serves as a guideline, urging States to strengthen their anti-bribery measures and legal frameworks. As outlined in the previous section, countries have adjusted their domestic laws to align with established international standards. With this regard, the OECD's peer-review process has played a meaningful role in fostering consistency among national laws.

4. Informal and Enhanced International Cooperation

4.1 Limits of the Mutual Legal Assistance Mechanisms

The OECD Anti-Bribery Convention aim to facilitate bilateral cooperation by harmonizing collaboration methods. Since the instrument was adopted, the number of countries criminalizing the offence of bribery of foreign public officials in their national laws has increased. All member States of the OECD enacted domestic laws but with varying penalties and criminal liability provisions.[87]

However, the constraints of mutual legal assistance mechanisms persisted. The OECD report in 2012 titled 'A Typology of Legal Mutual Assistance in Foreign Bribery Cases' highlights that mutual legal assistance in cases involving the bribery of foreign public officials remains a challenge.[88] The report highlights various problems, such as non-cooperation from the recipient State, insufficient resources to carry out the request, and non-compliance with the condition of double criminality. These issues are similar to those encountered in the UNTOC.

Foreign bribery poses an additional risk. When evidence is obtained through a mutual assistance treaty, the implicated officials may become aware of the investigation, potentially leading to the destruction of evidence or concealment of illicit gains. As a result, efforts to curb foreign bribery have been limited.[89] Data protection laws further complicate cross-border cooperation. To facilitate effective international collaboration in investigating foreign bribery and related offences, the OECD advises member countries to ensure that data protection regulations do not unnecessarily obstruct the exchange of economic or commercial information.[90]

[87] The status of the national implementation of the Convention can be found on the website that publishes the results of OECD peer reviews, 'Country Reports on the Implementation of the OECD Anti-Bribery Convention' <https://www.oecd.org/en/topics/fighting-foreign-bribery.html>.

[88] OECD (n 27)25.

[89] ibid 44.

[90] ibid 62.

4.2 Informal Cooperation Between Law Enforcement Authorities

Some States engage in informal cooperation to overcome these limitations, including ad hoc joint investigations.

The United States, the EU member States, the United Kingdom, and Australia started to employ informal cooperation alongside formal processes stipulated under mutual assistance treaties. The use of a mutual assistance treaty is an arduous and time-consuming undertaking. To overcome these challenges, they utilize summary information exchanges to establish the investigation's trajectory and procure evidence at the final stage that would otherwise be attainable only through applying a mutual assistance treaty.[91]

The 2012 OECD report above explored how law enforcement officials from different countries can work together when investigating foreign bribery cases.[92] The two main approaches discussed involve maintaining separate but parallel investigations or forming a joint investigation team (JIT) in which two authorities share the evidence and coordinate actions. The latter can facilitate communication about investigative and prosecution strategies, foster best practices, prevent the duplication of efforts, reduce the risk of premature disclosure of information, and provide a rapid response mechanism. In addition, direct communication between authorities in the early stages of an investigation has advantages over cooperation, according to formal assistance treaties. Doing so is more straightforward and carries a lower risk of information leakage, especially in bribery, where passing investigative information to the other country's government officials must be avoided. The two approaches are not mutually exclusive, and elements of a JIT can be incorporated into parallel investigations. Informal mechanisms for parallel investigations can also help determine whether a JIT is likely to be effective in establishing parameters for a JIT.

However, since these forms of cooperation operate within the scope of each country's national laws, concerns arise about the confidentiality of the information, individual rights to privacy, and the privilege of secrecy. In some cases, sharing evidence via electronic media could lead to the exchange of bulk information that should be protected under national law.

In several cases, multiple States have cooperated in investigations, a practice that became more prominent in the late 2000s. For example, the DOJ and SEC worked closely with German authorities while investigating Siemens AG, a German multinational corporation. Siemens AG and its subsidiaries in Argentina, Bangladesh, and Venezuela agreed to pay over USD 450 million in fines.[93] It has been disclosed that Siemens AG has engaged in a systematic effort to falsify its corporate books and records and knowingly failed to implement and circumvent existing internal controls since the mid-1990s. Siemens AG was listed on the New York Stock Exchange

[91] ibid 47.
[92] ibid.
[93] Alexandra Wrage and Anne Richardson, 'Siemens AG: Violations of the Foreign Corrupt Practices Act' (2009) 48 International Legal Materials 232.

in 2001, and from that time until approximately 2007, Siemens AG made payments totalling approximately USD 1.36 billion through various mechanisms.[94]

Intergovernmental cooperation has expanded since then. For example, the US DOJ worked with the United Kingdom, Switzerland, and France to investigate Alstom SA, a French power and transportation company that allegedly bribed officials in Indonesia, Saudi Arabia, Egypt, and the Bahamas.[95] The corporation agreed to pay USD 772 million in 2014.

In another case, authorities in Brazil, the United States, and Switzerland closely worked on the investigation concerning Odebrecht SA, a Brazilian construction conglomerate, and Braskem, a Brazilian petrochemical company.[96] In 2016, the two corporations pleaded guilty and agreed to pay USD 3.5 billion as they violated the FCPA. According to the US Office of Foreign Affairs, the guilty plea resulted from 'an extraordinary multinational effort' to 'identify, investigate and prosecute a complex and long-lasting corruption scheme'.[97]

In 2014, GlaxoSmithKline plc, a British pharmaceutical and biotechnology company, became subject to investigation by China, the United States, and the United Kingdom under the Chinese Anti-Unfair Competition Law, the US FCPA, and the UK Bribery Act, respectively. The company set a record USD 489 million (3 billion Chinese Yuan) in China for engaging in bribery to promote their products and issued a public apology to the Chinese populace. Company executives were convicted. The United States also fined the corporation under the FCPA. On the other hand, the UK SFO concluded its investigation in 2019, citing a lack of sufficient evidence to proceed with legal action.[98]

4.3 Informal Cooperation with Corporations

4.3.1 Deferred Prosecution Agreements

Because the detection and the collection of evidence are the significant challenges in investigating foreign bribery, States often use DPAs, as described in Chapter 5. The importance of negotiated settlements to investigate foreign bribery cases is well recognized.[99]

94 US DOJ, '08-1105: Siemens AG and Three Subsidiaries Plead Guilty to Foreign Corrupt Practices Act Violations and Agree to Pay $450 Million in Combined Criminal Fines (2008-12-15)' (15 December 2008) <https://www.justice.gov/archive/opa/pr/2008/December/08-crm-1105.html>.

95 ibid.

96 US Office of Public Affairs, 'Odebrecht and Braskem Plead Guilty and Agree to Pay at Least $3.5 Billion in Global Penalties to Resolve Largest Foreign Bribery Case in History | United States Department of Justice' (21 December 2016) <https://www.justice.gov/opa/pr/odebrecht-and-braskem-plead-guilty-and-agree-pay-least-35-billion-global-penalties-resolve>.

97 ibid.

98 See Department of Justice, GlaxoSmithKline to Plead Guilty and Pay $3 Billion to Resolve Fraud Allegations and Failure to Report Safety Data (2 July 2012) <https://www.justice.gov/archives/opa/pr/glaxosmithkline-plead-guilty-and-pay-3-billion-resolve-fraud-allegations-and-failure-report>.

99 Brandon L Garrett, *Too Big to Jail: How Prosecutors Compromise with Corporations* (Harvard UP 2014).

As explained in Section 3.2, the United States often employs parallel investigations in its law enforcement actions against foreign companies. The 2006 *Siemens* case is a notable example of this approach in the context of foreign bribery.[100] The conglomerate Siemens AG, headquartered in Munich, was found to have violated the law through bribery, obtaining commercial benefits in several countries, and accounting for misrepresentations of its expenditures. The DOJ negotiated a plea agreement with Siemens in 2008 and shared information about the case with German authorities to aid their prosecution. Siemens paid USD 814 million to Germany and USD 800 million to the United States. However, neither the parent company nor its affiliates lost their entitlements to participate in government tenders. In other words, the corporation avoided the worst punishment.[101]

Another earlier instance is the *BAE Systems* Case.[102] The defence contractor with its headquarters in the United Kingdom was accused of obtaining the deals of fighter jets and ground attack aircraft with the Kingdom of Saudi Arabia (KSA) since the 1980s in exchange for massive bribes to the Saudi royal families and false accounting. Foreign bribery became a crime in the United Kingdom in 2002.[103] Although the SFO started an investigation in 2004, it dropped the case in 2006 as KSA suggested withdrawal from diplomatic cooperation with the United Kingdom on security and intelligence.[104] Non-governmental organizations in the United Kingdom brought a claim before the court that SFO acted in contradiction with the OECD Bribery Convention and the principle of the rule of law. The High Court decided it was unlawful for the Director of the SFO to stop the investigation.[105] However, the judgment was overturned by the House of Lords.[106]

In 2007, the United States began to investigate the case without the assistance of the UK government. DOJ alleged that certain payments served as the factual predicate for the conspiracy charge, such as defrauding the United States, making false statements to the United States, and violating Arms Export Control Act and International Traffic Arms Regulations.[107] It obtained information from its CEO

[100] For an overview of the case, see US DOJ, 'Re: United States v Siemens Aktiengesellschaft' (15 December 2008) <https://www.justice.gov/sites/default/files/criminal-fraud/legacy/2013/05/02/12-15-08siemens-statement.pdf>. The plea agreement listed specific benefits gained for procurement contracts in Iraq under the UN Oil-for-Food programme, laying a railway line in Venezuela and developing a mobile phone network in Bangladesh, a power plant in Israel, and a traffic control system in Russia. Wrage and Richardson (n 93).

[101] For the details of this case, see Hartmut Berghoff, '"Organised Irresponsibility"? The Siemens Corruption Scandal of the 1990s and 2000s' (2018) 60 Business History 423; Wrage and Richardson (n 93).

[102] Charles F Smith and Brittany D Parling, '"American Imperialism" : A Practitioner's Experience with Extraterritorial Enforcement of the FCPA' (2012) 2012 The University of Chicago Legal Forum 237, 245; Garrett (n 51) 1840.

[103] Anti-Terrorism, Crime and Security Act 2001, c 24, s 107.

[104] Smith and Parling (n 102) 245; Garrett (n 51) 1840.

[105] High Court of Justice [2008] EWHC 714 (Admin), Case No CO/1567/2007, 10 April 2008.

[106] House of Lords [2008] UKHL 60.

[107] *US v BAE Systems plc*, 'United States' Sentencing Memorandum', Case 1:10-cr-00035-JDB (DDC, 22 February 2010) 2.

directors and through many additional subpoenas in the United States to employees of BAE systems. In 2010, BAE entered into a plea agreement, admitting it conspired to defraud the United States by making false statements about its FCPA compliance programme and paying a vast fine.[108] It was agreed that a UK citizen, acceptable to BAE and the DOJ and approved by the UK government, serve as an independent monitor.[109] However, it was not debarred from future international deals because it was not convicted of bribery.

In April 2010, the United Kingdom enacted the Bribery Act, and the SFO adopted a guideline for corporate prosecution similar to that of the DOJ. Brandon Garrett comments that 'it is less likely that the same tensions would exist today now that the United States and United Kingdom share a similar approach'.[110] However, the real issue in the *BAE* case was not the lack of substantive law in the United Kingdom. It was the discretion left to the UK government to let its major firm continue its business and handle the diplomatic relationship with KSA. The United States' action showed that the scope of such allowance has been narrowed down. The enforcement tool played an important role because the corporation could have failed in the plea agreement, and the unilateral law enforcement against the corporation might have invited political controversy between the relevant States.

The fairness and transparency of the DPA were questioned in the SNC-Lavalin affair.[111] SNC-Lavalin, which subsequently altered its name to AtkinsRéalis, is a company based in Canada that offers engineering, procurement, and construction services. In 2015, Canadian authorities charged the company, a public contractor, with bribery and fraud. Evidence showed that the company bribed Libyan senior officials, including USD 1.9 million incurred during a trip to Canada by Al-Saadi Gaddafi, then-Libyan leader, in 2008. The conviction of the company would have excluded the company from public contracts. Later, a Parliamentary ethics report affirmed that the Canadian Prime Minister influenced the Attorney General to conclude a DPA in light of the company's size and significance. The corporate case ended with an SNC-Lavalin subsidiary pleading guilty to fraud, resulting in one individual's conviction. No other fraud or corruption charges were pursued against the SNC-Lavalin companies.

4.3.2 Incentivization of the Reporting

The 2021 OECD Recommendation lists several specific measures for encouraging such reporting.[112] For instance, States can establish policies and procedures for natural persons, including public officials, to report such suspicions to competent

[108] US DOJ, BAE Systems PLC Pleads Guilty and Ordered to Pay $400 Million Criminal Fine' (1 March 2010) <http://www.justice.gov/opa/pr/2010/March/10-crm-209.html>.

[109] ibid para 12.

[110] Garrett (n 51) 1842.

[111] ibid.

[112] OECD (n 9).

authorities, allowing for confidential and, where appropriate, anonymous reporting. It is also recommended that member states provide accessible and diversified channels for reporting such suspicions.

Appropriate measures should be taken to allow public officials to report suspected acts of foreign bribery detected during their work. Officials are in a position to detect the offence when they are in public agencies and interact with or have information regarding companies operating abroad.

Incentivizing corporations to cooperate is crucial for promoting compliance with foreign bribery laws. On the one hand, governments can use a range of administrative measures, such as withholding public subsidies, licences, public procurement contracts, contracts funded by official development assistance, officially supported export credits, and other public benefits.[113]

On the other hand, governments can rely on non-trial resolutions to ensure that corporations cooperate. Non-trial resolutions refer to mechanisms developed and used to resolve matters without a full court or administrative proceeding based on a negotiated agreement with a natural or legal person and a prosecuting or other authority.[114] The DPAs and other informal arrangements are useful for encouraging persons related to foreign bribery to inform the authorities to investigate and prosecute the offenders.[115]

The OECD recommends that member states use such resolutions to resolve criminal, administrative, and civil cases. At the same time, the OECD also suggests that these resolutions follow due process, transparency, and accountability principles and provide clear and publicly accessible information on their advantages. Member countries should develop clear criteria for using non-trial resolutions and ensure that foreign bribery resolved by non-trial resolutions is punished with transparent, effective, proportionate, and dissuasive sanctions.[116]

To prevent and detect foreign bribery effectively, companies should develop internal controls, ethics, and compliance programmes based on a risk assessment that considers their unique circumstances, including the risks of foreign bribery that they face. These risks may arise from a company's geographic location, industry sector, regulatory environment, potential clients and business partners, transactions with foreign governments, or third parties' use. It states that a company should regularly monitor and reassess these risks and circumstances to determine how to allocate compliance resources and ensure the ongoing effectiveness of its internal controls, ethics, and compliance programmes.

The 2021 OECD Recommendation calls for member countries to establish legal and institutional frameworks to protect reporting persons who report on

[113] ibid para IV(ix).
[114] ibid.
[115] ibid para XVIII.
[116] ibid.

suspected foreign bribery cases in a work-related context.[117] It states that the framework should provide sufficient protection against any retaliatory action to persons in the private or public sector who report such cases, including providing confidentiality of the reporting person's identity and the content of the report. The Recommendation also includes providing broad definitions of retaliation and offering appropriate remedies and sanctions against retaliating individuals or entities. Additionally, the framework should be periodically reviewed for effectiveness, and incentives should be considered for making reports that qualify for protection. As this description shows, the investigation of foreign bribery is characterized by the need for extensive arrangements to gather information.

5. Protection of Fundamental Rights

As investigations into foreign bribery become more intrusive, potential issues related to privacy, due process, fairness, and accountability may arise. However, such concerns about fundamental rights are not unique to foreign bribery cases. They are also prevalent in securities fraud regulations, where administrative authorities often conduct criminal investigations or money laundering regulations, which may lead to possible intrusions on privacy. In practice, though, it is rare for these issues to surface, as legal frameworks and oversight mechanisms are typically in place to safeguard against such infringements.

A key issue to foreign bribery investigation arises when multiple authorities conduct independent investigations without jurisdictional coordination, potentially leading to legal entities and individuals being subject to double sanctions. Currently, no universally applicable legal principle exists regarding the doctrine of *res judicata* when it comes to cross-border law enforcement. It is handled only per the laws of the jurisdiction in which the case is heard.

For example, US law applies to foreign companies involved in official bribery offences, regardless of court judgments or rulings in other countries, due to its broad jurisdictional scope. As a result, multiple law enforcement authorities may impose overlapping sanctions, with the United States actively enforcing its laws. The issue is whether such sanctions that may lead to double punishment are permissible. Although the US Constitution prohibits multiple criminal prosecutions by the US government for the same offence that puts individuals in danger of life or limb more than once, this prohibition does not extend to international cases. Therefore, under domestic US law, multiple prosecutions for foreign companies are allowed and not disputed.

[117] ibid para XXII.

The US authorities may, at their discretion, consider the amount paid in other jurisdictions. In 2017, UK manufacturer Rolls-Royce plc entered into a DPA and admitted that it conspired to violate the FCPA in Thailand, Brazil, Kazakhstan, Azerbaijan, Angola, and Iraq.[118] At the same time, the company also reached settlements with the United Kingdom's SFO and Brazil's Ministério Público Federal (MPF). As part of its leniency agreement with the MPF, Rolls-Royce also agreed to pay a penalty of approximately USD 25.5 million for its role in a conspiracy to bribe foreign officials in Brazil between 2005 and 2008. As the conduct underlying the MPF resolution overlaps with that addressed in part of the Department's resolution, the Department credited the amount Rolls-Royce agreed to pay in Brazil towards the total fine imposed in the United States.

To take another example, French courts count that another country already penalized the defendant. Two cases of Vitol and Clearstream concerning foreign bribery are particularly noteworthy. In the former case, the French authorities investigated allegations that Vitol, an oil company based in the Netherlands, had bribed senior Iraqi officials in the UN Oil-for-Food programme. The Paris Court of First Instance ruled that the prosecution in France was blocked due to a plea bargain between Vitol and US authorities.[119] In the situation involving Jeffrey Tesler, the managing director of Clearstream, a Luxembourg-based company that faced accusations of bribery related to the creation of natural gas facilities in Nigeria, the Paris Court of First Instance determined that legal action could not proceed. This decision was based on Tesler's prior plea agreement with the United States in 2011, which resulted in his serving a twenty-one-month prison sentence.[120]

The 2021 OECD Recommendation outlines several key measures that member states are encouraged to adopt to enhance international cooperation in the investigation and prosecution of foreign bribery cases. Among the most significant of these measures is the emphasis on direct coordination during concurrent or parallel investigations and prosecutions. It includes the sharing of information and evidence between jurisdictions to ensure that investigations are as comprehensive and efficient as possible.

The Recommendation also advises that when multiple member States have jurisdiction over a single case, there should be consultations throughout the investigation, prosecution, and resolution of the case. As explored in this chapter, such cooperation is vital for avoiding conflicts and ensuring that the legal actions taken are harmonized across jurisdictions. The Recommendation, however,

[118] US DOJ, Office of Public Affairs, 'Rolls-Royce Plc Agrees to Pay $170 Million Criminal Penalty to Resolve Foreign Corrupt Practices Act Case' (17 January 2017) <https://www.justice.gov/opa/pr/rolls-royce-plc-agrees-pay-170-million-criminal-penalty-resolve-foreign-corrupt-practices-act>.

[119] Tribunal de grande instance de Paris, 11ème chambre correctionnelle, du 20 janvier 2013.

[120] Tribunal de grande instance de Paris, 11ème chambre correctionnelle, du 24 Juin 2014. See Radha Ivory and Tina Søreide, 'The International Endorsement of Corporate Settlements in Foreign Bribery Cases' (2020) 69 International and Comparative Law Quarterly 945.

acknowledges the inherent risks associated with prosecuting the same individual in different jurisdictions for the same criminal conduct, a situation that could potentially lead to issues of double jeopardy or conflicting legal outcomes.

It is noted that the establishment of joint or parallel investigative teams mostly takes place between European countries and the United States. This indicates that while the framework for cooperation is in place, its practical application remains limited. The uneven enforcement across member parties remains one of the concerns. Moreover, while the OECD's peer review mechanism is widely regarded as a strength, achieving full compliance with its follow-up recommendations continues to be a remaining issue.

6. Concluding Remarks

The OECD Anti-Bribery Convention and the UNCAC require assistance to be provided per national law. This assistance is similar to those designed for drug offences and organized crime. However, cooperation is to be carried out on a reciprocal basis, and the MLATs could be viewed as a last resort due to the difficulty of collecting evidence in cases involving the bribery of foreign public officials. Therefore, governments increasingly rely on ad hoc or informal intergovernment cooperation, such as parallel or joint investigations, as well as direct cooperation with corporations through guilty plea and DPAs, to effectively gather information.

10

Terrorism

1. Introduction

1.1 Obligation to Suppress Terrorism under International Law

The international community has developed various frameworks to suppress terrorism, encompassing multilateral treaties, conventions, regional agreements, and national legislation. The 9/11 terrorist attacks on 2001 marked a pivotal shift in global counterterrorism policies. A series of significant changes unfolded, coinciding with other acts of mass terrorism perpetrated by radical extremists in the early 2000s. Notable among these incidents were the Bali bombing on 12 October 2002, carried out by Jemaah Islamiyah; the Madrid train bombings on 11 March 2004, attributed to extremists with ties to al-Qaida (also known as al-Qaeda); and the London bombings on 7 July 2005, executed by British nationals influenced by radical ideologies. These events prompted widespread shifts in global security policies, international relations, and the perception of terrorism as a critical threat to global stability. It became evident that it necessitates cooperation at every level, from international collaborations to inter-agency partnerships and direct cooperation between governments and the private sector.[1]

One of the challenges in the international suppression of terrorism has been the absence of a universally accepted, comprehensive definition of the crime.[2] However, it has been addressed through the following practice at the international level.

First, efforts have been made through multilateral and regional treaties to cover a vast extent of crimes. Historically, suppression of terrorism began during the inter-war period with the drafting of the Convention on the Prevention and Punishment of Terrorism. Although it was adopted by the General Assembly of

[1] Cherif M Bassiouni, 'Mixed Model of The International Criminal Justice' in Cherif M Bassiouni (ed), *International Criminal Law, Volume 3: International Enforcement* (Martinus Nijhoff 2008) 155.

[2] Ben Saul, *Defining Terrorism in International Law* (OUP 2006) 1.

International Law and the Investigation of Transnational Crimes. Yurika Ishii, Oxford University Press.
 DOI: 10.1093/9780198957089.003.0010

the League of Nations in 1937, it never came into effect.[3] Subsequently, substantial international regulation in specific crimes took shape with the adoption of the Tokyo Convention on the Prevention of Hijacking in 1963.[4] Since the 1970s, conventions aimed at preventing specific types of terrorism have been adopted by the United Nations and other organizations. These instruments are open for signature by all States, obligating member states to criminalize these acts in their national laws.

The International Convention for the Suppression of the Financing of Terrorism (ICSFT) of 1999 requires member States to criminalize an offence to provide or collect funds for acts of terrorism. The instrument encompasses crimes defined under existing anti-terrorism conventions, as well as any act

> intended to cause death or serious bodily injury to a civilian or to any other person not taking an active part in the hostilities in a situation of armed conflict, when the purpose of such an act, by its nature or context, is to intimidate a population or to compel a government or an international organization to do or to abstain from doing any act.[5]

Second is the harmonization of substantive laws led by the United Nations, which has facilitated a more unified approach to defining and combating terrorism at the international level. The UN Security Council addressed in 2004 that

> criminal acts, including against civilians, committed with the intent to cause death or serious bodily injury, or taking of hostages, with the purpose to provoke a state of terror in the general public or a group of persons or particular persons, intimidate a population or compel a government or an international organization to do or to abstain from doing any act', which 'constitute offences within the scope of and as defined in the international conventions and protocols relating to terrorism [are under no circumstances justifiable].[6]

The Security Council then called upon States 'to prevent such acts and, if not prevented, to ensure that they are punished by penalties consistent with their grave

[3] League of Nations, *Proceedings of the International Conference on the Repression of Terrorism* (Doc C.94.M.47, 1938.V.3) 49. For the background, see Thomas M Franck and Bert B Lockwood Jr, 'Preliminary Thoughts towards an International Convention on Terrorism' (1974) 68 American Journal of International Law 69.

[4] Convention on Offences and Certain Other Acts Committed on Board Aircraft (concluded on 14 September 1963, entered into force on 4 December 1969) 704 UNTS 219. The 1963 Tokyo Convention does not provide for the *aut dedere aut judcaire* principle and differs from other conventions in its allocation of jurisdiction structure.

[5] International Convention for the Suppression of the Financing of Terrorism (ICSFT) (adopted on 9 December 1999, entered into force on 10 April 2002) 2178 UNTS 197, art 2(1)(b).

[6] S/RES/1566 (2004) para 3.

nature'.[7] The UN General Assembly established the Global Counterterrorism Strategy in 2006 to promote national, regional, and international efforts to counterterrorism. The UN Office of Counterterrorism was established in 2017,[8] and it aims to coordinate and build capacity to support Member States in implementing practical measures to prevent and counter terrorism through various activities, projects, and programmes.

There are distinct characteristics of terrorism defined under multilateral treaties compared to other organized crime. Terrorism is of such a nature that preventing it is not merely a matter of national interest but also of international concern.[9] Therefore, the preventive measures or legal frameworks outlined in the convention are designed to protect broader international security and stability rather than being confined to the jurisdiction or interests of any single nation.

Treaties require domestic criminalization to the extent that the targeted crimes can be identified by extracting common legal interests of the international community that are distinct from domestic legal interests. These include acts such as the unlawful seizure of aircraft or ships;[10] the taking of hostages with prescribed demands on a State;[11] acts that impede trade and diplomacy between States, such as violence against internationally protected heads of State, diplomats, and others,[12]

[7] ibid.

[8] A/71/291 (2017).

[9] Japanese scholars have paid close attention to the structure of the conventions designed to combat terrorism. Sōji Yamamoto provided a detailed analysis of the structure of the terrorism conventions, noting that they serve both the 'traditional function of international cooperation to concentrate criminal jurisdiction on certain States' and a 'new function of international cooperation' to oblige multiple States to exercise their jurisdictionFor a comprehensive analysis of major counterterrorism conventions, see also Naoya Okuwaki, 'Kokusaihō Kara Mita Kokusai Keiji Kyōryoku No Gendaiteki Tenkai' (2003) 278 Hogaku Kyoushitsu 4; Kazuhiro Nakatani, 'Terorizumu Ni Taisuru Sho Taiō to Kokusaihō' in Atsushi Yamaguchi and Kazuhiro Nakatani (eds), *Anzen Hoshō to Kokusai Hanzai* (Tokyo UP 2005); Takayo Andō, *Kokusai Terorizumu Ni Taisuru Hōteki Kisei No Kōzō: Terorizumu Bōshi Kanren Shojōyaku Ni Okeru Saiban Kankatsuken No Kentō* [*The Structure of Legal Control of International Terrorism*] (Shohan, Kokusai Shoin 2020).

[10] Convention for the Suppression of Unlawful Seizure of Aircraft (signed on 16 December 1970, entered into force on 14 October 1971) 860 UNTS 105; Convention for the Suppression of Unlawful Acts against the Safety of Civil Aviation (signed on 23 September 1971, entered into force on 26 January 1973) 974 UNTS 178; Convention for the Suppression of Unlawful Acts against the Safety of Maritime Navigation (adopted on 10 March, 1988, entered into force on 1 March, 1992) 1678 UNTS 201; Protocol for the Suppression of Unlawful Acts against the Safety of Fixed Platforms Located on the Continental Shelf (adopted on 10 March 1988, entered into force on 1 March 1992) 1678 UNTS 304. See also Protocol for the Suppression of Unlawful Acts of Violence at Airports Serving International Civil Aviation, supplement to the Convention for the Suppression of Unlawful Acts of Violence against the Safety of Civil Aviation (signed on 24 February 1988, entered into force on 6 August 1989) 1589 UNTS 473.

[11] International Convention against the Taking of Hostages (adopted on 17 December 1979, entered into force on 3 June 1983) 1316 UNTS 205.

[12] Convention on the Prevention and Punishment of Crimes against Internationally Protected Persons, including Diplomatic Agents (adopted on 14 December 1973, entered into force on 20 February 1977) 1035 UNTS 167.

or acts that pose a significant risk of proliferation of weapons of mass destruction;[13] and other forms of mass violence[14] and terrorist financing.[15]

The instruments oblige the member States to exercise prescriptive jurisdiction by incorporating *aut dedere aut judicaire* provisions. Before the 1970 Convention for the Prevention of the Unlawful Taking of Aircraft, international law had minimal involvement in determining what constitutes a punishable or extraditable offence. In contrast, counterterrorism treaties impose an obligation on States to decide whether to prosecute suspects when they are within their jurisdiction or hand them over to the relevant State. This marked a significant shift in jurisdictional rules, as it establishes a principle at the international level aimed at preventing offenders from taking refuge in safe havens.

1.2 Challenges in Investigating Terrorism: A New Form of Jurisdictional Conflicts?

Notwithstanding these mechanisms to oblige States to suppress terrorism, few robust investigative frameworks have been established at the multilateral level. The obligations under anti-terrorism conventions to provide legal assistance are generally limited to counter the global security threat. Instruments typically include the caveat that the States shall carry out their obligations 'in a manner consistent with the principles of sovereign equality and territorial integrity of States and that of non-intervention in the domestic affairs of other States'.[16] The criminal assistance mechanisms provided under these treaties do not fundamentally differ from that under conventional mutual legal assistance agreements.

The investigation of terrorism necessitates a comprehensive and multifaceted approach. Terrorism arises from a complex of economic, societal, historical, and religious factors. Addressing such crimes requires a thorough examination of various aspects of human activity. States have developed extensive mechanisms for collecting information on ordinary citizens in their domestic spheres. As a result,

[13] Convention on the Physical Protection of Nuclear Material (signed on 3 March 1980, entered into force on 8 February 1987) 1456 UNTS 101.

[14] International Convention for the Suppression of Terrorist Bombings (adopted on 15 December 1997, entered into force on 23 May 2001) 2149 UNTS 256; International Convention for the Suppression of Acts of Nuclear Terrorism (adopted on 14 September 2005, entered into force on 7 July 2007) UNGA Res 59/290 (13 April 2005) UN Doc A/RES/59/290; Convention on the Safety of United Nations and Associated Personnel (adopted on 15 December 1994, entered into force on 15 January 1999) 2051 UNTS 363. See also the Convention on the Marking of Plastic Explosives for Detection (signed on 1 March 1991, entered into force on 21 June 1998) 2122 UNTS 359. The instrument obliges the addition of detection materials to plastic explosives, prohibits the manufacture and transfer of plastic explosives without identification measures, and obliges the disposal of such explosives but does not mandate criminal assistance.

[15] ICSFT, art 2(1).

[16] See, for instance, ICSFT art 20.

some countries have developed more effective mechanisms than the conventions require to investigate terrorism using a variety of approaches.

The digital transformation has coincidentally occurred across numerous countries, including many developing nations. This shift towards electronically collecting personal information is primarily driven by increased efficiency, enhanced convenience, and the expansion of the digital marketplace. Nevertheless, adopting centralized databases, single identity systems for all citizens, and biometric registration, such as fingerprint-based identification, may lead to potentially intrusive investigative practices.

This motif has been explored in many other works, particularly in the field of data protection law. Most recently, in her 2023 work, Mistale Taylor examined transatlantic jurisdictional conflicts in data protection law and the role of the fundamental right to data protection in shaping the European Union's exercise of extraterritorial jurisdiction.[17] However, such disputes in the context of criminal investigations have received limited scholarly attention.

In this regard, the key argument of this chapter is that the form of jurisdictional conflicts has shifted from the conflict of national interests to the tension between the demand to maintain global security and the privacy and security of individuals. The current tensions are predominantly between the United States and the European Union, primarily driven by the European Union's market size and stringent regulatory frameworks, which significantly affect the US companies operating within its jurisdiction. The disparity in regulatory approaches regarding data privacy and market competition has led to friction between these two major economic powers. This chapter will explore the potential challenges that may arise or have already emerged as a result of these developments.

With this regard, the focus of this chapter is on the collection of intelligence information by governments, as well as information on natural persons, including transport details, biometric data, and biogenetic information. Its purpose is not to delve into the specifics of national legislation. Instead, it seeks to identify common challenges faced by countries that have established robust counterterrorism legislative mechanisms.

Issues related to the collection of financial data from the private sector will be addressed in Chapter 11, and communication data will be covered in Chapter 12. This book does not cover issues related to the 'War on Terror', including the use of 'enhanced investigation' methods, as they require a separate analysis. For the same reason, it does not specifically address the terrorist interrogation by the Central Intelligence Agency (CIA) of the United States in a third country after the 9/11 attacks.

[17] Mistale Taylor, *Transatlantic Jurisdictional Conflicts in Data Protection Law: Fundamental Rights, Privacy and Extraterritoriality* (CUP 2023). Taylor's work deals with the reach of EU data protection law in data transfers to the United States for counterterrorism purposes, albeit in specific contexts.

1.3 Structure of This Chapter

Section 2 will commence by examining the issues arising from the expansion of national security authorities to combat terrorism in areas such as surveillance, with particular attention given to the growing tensions between the United States and the European Union over data privacy. Section 3 will deal with the issues concerning the terrorist screening. Section 4 will address the conflicts surrounding the increased exchange of airline passenger name records (PNRs). It will explore the legal frameworks and security imperatives driving PNR data sharing agreements, as well as the privacy concerns and regulatory challenges these exchanges pose, particularly in the transatlantic context. Finally, Section 5 will delve into the complexities surrounding the exchange of biometric and biogenetic information. Sections 3 and 4 will explore the implications of these exchanges for both national security and individual privacy, considering the ethical, legal, and operational challenges they present. Special emphasis will be placed on the implications of these practices for civil liberties, data protection standards, and the role of emerging technologies in shaping future security policies.

2. Counterterrorism Intelligence Operations

2.1 Key Issues

In response to the evolving nature of terrorism, following a series of high-profile mass terrorist attacks, States have significantly expanded their surveillance and intelligence gathering capabilities. These enhanced national security measures have been implemented with the aim of preventing future offences and responding effectively to terrorism-related threats. However, this shift has introduced complex issues when the information gathered through intelligence operations is later used in criminal prosecutions, considering due process rights and fair trial.

Investigations focus on individuals involved in criminal activities, operating within the boundaries of a State's legal system, while intelligence operations primarily aim at foreign enemies and national security threats. However, the counterterrorism practice shows that domestic law enforcement agencies increasingly engage in intelligence gathering and pre-emptive measures, activities once reserved for national security agencies. This convergence complicates legal distinctions and raises important questions about the appropriate balance between law enforcement powers and the protection of individual rights.

The narrative that the terrorists are 'enemies' blurred the distinction between the criminal procedure, which is supposed to be applicable to their own people, and the intelligence operation, of which the original primary purpose was to look after foreigners.

Separation of law enforcement and intelligence agencies is commonly established in national legislation to ensure the integrity of the criminal procedure. When the police authorities require the compelled acquisition of information or evidence, they are generally obliged to obtain a court warrant and employ measures that are strictly necessary. The procedure is to protect individuals' fundamental rights, including the right to privacy, and to restrict the authorities from abusing their power. It is not only the duty of States under their domestic laws but also the obligation under international human rights law. The International Covenant on Civil and Political Rights (ICCPR) Article 9(1) provides that '[n]o one shall be deprived of his liberty except on such grounds and in accordance with such procedure as are established by law'.

On the other hand, intelligence gathering activities are conducted covertly, thereby operating outside the purview of judicial oversight. The information acquired by intelligence agencies conventionally consists of publicly available data, encompassing press articles and information sourced from foreign embassies, which normally poses minimal legal concerns vis-à-vis citizens in general.

However, suppressing terrorist organizations requires both intelligence gathering and investigative efforts. The risk emerges that the authorities can bypass the hefty criminal procedure when intelligence agencies gather and analyse information, subsequently utilized by judicial investigative authorities as a part of the evidence.[18]

This tension between the need for robust security measures and fundamental human rights forms a central debate in contemporary law and policy on counterterrorism. At the heart of this debate is the question of whether expanded national authority in the realm of counterterrorism undermines fundamental legal protections, such as the right to a fair trial, the right to privacy, and the presumption of innocence. Framing the issue solely as a choice between prioritizing the protection of due process rights, which shield individuals from governmental overreach, and giving precedence to national security concerns in the interest of public safety may be an oversimplification. The necessity of pre-emptive intelligence gathering could be justified to enhance the safety of individuals and prevent potential threats. However, this approach carries significant risks of undermining the legal safeguards that form the foundation of democratic governance.

A key factor complicating this issue is the significant variation among States in both the perceived necessity for counterterrorism measures and their capacity to implement them, as well as the differing levels of data privacy protection. These

[18] Marianne FH Hirsch Ballin, *Anticipative Criminal Investigation: Theory and Counterterrorism Practice in the Netherlands and the United States* (TMC Asser Press 2012); Norman C Bay, 'Executive Power and the War on Terror' (2005) 83 Denver University Law Review 335; Stephen J Schulhofer, *The Enemy Within: Intelligence Gathering, Law Enforcement, and Civil Liberties in the Wake of September 11* (Century Foundation Press 2002); Paul Rosenzweig, 'Civil Liberty and the Response to Terrorism' (2003) 42 Duquesne Law Review 663.

discrepancies make it challenging to harmonize approaches across jurisdictions, leading to potential conflicts, particularly among major markets that adopt divergent policies. The lack of uniformity in how counterterrorism strategies are implemented further exacerbates tensions as States pursue varying priorities based on their unique security needs and regulatory frameworks.

The following section will explore how different legal systems have navigated these competing interests and the extent to which enhanced national authority to counter terrorism may impact the rights of individuals. Additionally, it will consider whether striking a balance between these two objectives is feasible in practice or whether one must inevitably give way to the other in the face of modern security challenges.

2.2 The US Law and Policy

2.2.1 Basic Legislations

The United States has implemented one of the most comprehensive policies in investigating terrorist activities and addressing these threats. It possessed the military capabilities necessary to enforce its policy, a capacity that is not available to most States. Moreover, its robust financial and communication networks, coupled with its expansive market, enable the country to extend its jurisdictional reach to foreign individuals and entities, raising international concerns.

Domestic laws in the United States introduced substantial modifications to the long-standing principle of separating law enforcement authorities and intelligence agencies in matters related to foreign terrorists. In general, the Department of Justice (DOJ) and the Federal Bureau of Investigation (FBI) are entrusted with handling criminal proceedings, while the CIA and the National Security Agency (NSA) primarily focus on intelligence operations. Historically, the CIA and NSA have employed diverse methods to collect information within foreign jurisdictions. The Fourth Amendment of the Constitution ensures the protection of an individual's right to privacy. In 1972, the Supreme Court affirmed that the President possesses constitutional authority to enact measures essential for national security, but such measures must align with the principles outlined in the Fourth Amendment.[19] The Constitution does not relieve the President from the responsibility of upholding the right to privacy.

On the other hand, it has been the United States's approach that the Constitutional protection would not extend beyond its territory. During the Cold War in 1978, the United States introduced the Foreign Intelligence Surveillance Act (FISA) to facilitate the interception of communications conducted by foreign

[19] *United States v United States District Court* 407 US 297, 320 (1972).

government intelligence agencies within the country. The primary objective of this law was to safeguard national security interests while implementing judicial oversight over intelligence operations conducted on US soil. The legislation granted the CIA the authority to intercept communications classified as 'foreign intelligence' involving 'foreign powers' and 'agents for foreign powers' without the need for a court warrant. The FISA warrants, which have lower evidence requirements than criminal search or communication interception warrants, have raised concerns about potentially bypassing the stricter warrant standards set by the Fourth Amendment when used to investigate criminal offences.

In 1981, the US government issued Executive Order 12333 regarding its intelligence activities.[20] The order was subsequently amended in 2003, 2004, and 2008. The latest order provides that intelligence efforts should be on detecting and countering several key threats. These include espionage and other activities directed by foreign powers or their intelligence services against the United States and its interests. Additionally, there must be a strong emphasis on identifying and neutralizing threats posed by terrorism. Finally, addressing the risks associated with the development, possession, proliferation, or use of weapons of mass destruction is essential for safeguarding national security.[21]

In addition, Communications Assistance for Law Enforcement Act of 1994 was enacted to require telecommunications carriers and manufacturers to assist law enforcement in executing electronic surveillance pursuant to court orders or other lawful authorization.[22]

The foreign intelligence exception to the Fourth Amendment's warrant requirement is well-established in the case law. When US authorities, with the consent of a foreign country, search the residence or premises of a foreign terrorist suspect outside the United States, the search is not subject to Fourth Amendment restrictions even against a US citizen. In the case of *Al-Hajj* before the Second Circuit decided in 2008, Wadih El-Hage, also known as Al-Hajj, a US citizen, faced accusations of conspiring with al-Qaida leader Bin Laden in a plot to bomb the US embassy in Kenya on 7 August 1998.[23] During the spring of 1996, the US intelligence community discovered the existence of an al-Qaida cell in Kenya and intercepted five telephone communications between August 1996 and August 1997. Although they obtained authorization from Kenyan authorities, they did not acquire a warrant from the US judicial branch. One of the intercepted phones was located in the residence where Al-Hajj lived. In 1997, the Attorney General authorized the collection of information specifically targeting the defendant, and this

[20] Executive Order 12333, 'United States Intelligence Activities' (4 December 1981) 46 FR 59941, 3 CFR, 1981, as amended by Executive Orders 13284 (2003), 13355 (2004), and 13470 (2008).

[21] ibid para 1.1(b).

[22] Communications Assistance for Law Enforcement Act (CALEA), Pub L No 103-414, 108 Stat 4279 (1994).

[23] *In re Terrorist Bombings of US Embassies in East Africa* 552 F 3d 157 (2d Cir 2008).

authorization was renewed in July 1997. In August 1997, US and Kenyan authorities collaborated to search Al-Hajj's residence. Although they were presented with a warrant issued by the Kenyan authorities, stating that the search was for stolen property, the US agents searched the entire residence rather than focusing solely on the stolen property. As a result, the accused contested the admissibility of the evidence obtained during the search, questioning its legality. The Second Circuit Court of Appeals rejected the claims, noting, among other reasons, that the Fourth Amendment's reasonableness requirement, rather than the warrant requirement, applies to extraterritorial searches of US citizens, and that the search in question was reasonable.

In the case of *Verdugo Urquidez*, it was already established by the Supreme Court that when US authorities, with the consent of a foreign country, search the residence or premises of a foreign terrorist suspect outside the United States, the search is not subject to Fourth Amendment restrictions. The Court relied on Executive Order 12333, which grants the Attorney General the authority to authorize searches for intelligence purposes using techniques that would require a warrant if conducted for law enforcement purposes against US citizens abroad. However, the Court recognized a foreign intelligence collection exception for searches targeting foreign powers or their agents. This exception was justified by the executive branch's constitutional authority in foreign affairs matters. As a result, the Second Circuit Court of Appeals accepted the exclusion of the warrant requirement.[24]

2.2.2 Post-9/11 Attacks Legislations

The 9/11 attacks prompted the acceleration of US counterterrorism policies. The Uniting and Strengthening America by Providing Appropriate Tools Required to Intercept and Obstruct Terrorism Act of 2001 (PATRIOT Act) was enacted along with subsequent legislative amendments, effectively facilitating information acquisition by various agencies within the United States.[25] These amendments to US domestic law significantly expanded the government's capacity to gather information and use it in subsequent criminal proceedings.

First, the PATRIOT Act amended the Communications Interception Act and granted the Director of the FBI and others the authority to obtain meta-information from telecommunications companies.[26] This meta-information includes details like the location, number of calls, duration, and telephone numbers involved while

[24] *United States v Verdugo-Urquidez*, 494 US 259, 260 (1990). The Court did not hold that the Constitutional protection is limited to the US citizens, but held that the defendant's 'legal but involuntary presence' on US soil, resulting from his arrest, did not establish a sufficient connection with the country to invoke the Fourth Amendment.

[25] Uniting and Strengthening America by Providing Appropriate Tools Required to Intercept and Obstruct Terrorism Act (PATRIOT Act), Pub L No 107-56, 115 Stat 272 (2001).

[26] ibid, s 215.

excluding the actual content of the calls. The purpose of these amendments was to enhance efforts in countering international terrorism. In simpler terms, the amended act allowed the use of telephone number recorders, known as pen registers, if they were employed in investigations related to international terrorism or covert intelligence activities.[27] Additionally, the Act determined that the comprehensive acquisition of business records is permissible when it is conducted for the purpose of investigating international terrorism.[28]

Second, the Electronic Communications Privacy Act underwent amendments that broadened the range of records accessible from electronic communications service providers. These amendments eliminated the need for court review in certain cases and mandated the disclosure of payment-related information, such as bank account or credit card numbers, when authorities are investigating a terrorism offence. Consequently, the revised law permits the disclosure of payment methods and details, including bank account or credit card numbers.[29]

Third, amendments have been made to the FISA under the PATRIOT Act, expanding its scope to encompass international terrorist organizations as well as foreign political organizations that have no affiliation with foreign powers. These amendments establish that the procedures and limitations associated with wire communications interception, oral conversations interception, and electronic communications interception for criminal investigations do not apply to agencies engaged in collecting foreign intelligence information.[30] In addition, the FISA Amendments Act, enacted in 2008, enables intelligence agencies to identify with whom terrorists are communicating, what is being discussed, and what plans may be underway. The distinction between foreigners and the US citizens is maintained. The Act authorises surveillance targeting foreign persons reasonably believed to be located outside the United States. It mandates court orders for targeting US persons for foreign intelligence purposes, regardless of their location, and requires judicial review of procedures designed to protect information concerning US citizens.[31]

The PATRIOT Act grants authorization for electronic searches and physical searches of international terrorist organizations without the requirement of a court warrant. It includes the use of a national security letter (NSL), which is an administrative order issued by the FBI to gather information for national security purposes. The authority can use NSLs to obtain data about a person's communications,

[27] ibid s 214.
[28] ibid s 215.
[29] ibid s 210.
[30] ibid ss 206 and 215.
[31] An Act to amend the Foreign Intelligence Surveillance Act of 1978 to Establish a Procedure for Authorizing Certain Acquisitions of Foreign Intelligence, and for Other Purposes, Pub L No 110-261, 122 Stat 2436 (2008).

transactions, or financial activities from third parties, such as telecommunications companies, financial institutions, and internet service providers.[32] The recipients of the order are prohibited from disclosing that they received the letter. In 2005, the PATRIOT Improvement and Reauthorization Act allowed for judicial review of NSLs. A federal judge could repeal or modify an NSL if the court found the request for information was unreasonable, oppressive, or otherwise unlawful.[33]

The debate over whether the NSA's surveillance activities under section 215 of the PATRIOT Act undermine individuals' legitimate expectations of privacy has been ongoing at various levels. In response to the FBI's failure to prevent the 9/11 attacks, despite prior knowledge of the plans, Congress enacted the Intelligence Reform and Terrorism Prevention Act in 2004.[34] This Act aimed to enhance intelligence sharing between the Intelligence and Criminal Investigation Divisions, reinforcing investigations to detect and prevent future incidents. While it is necessary to involve a wide range of authorities to effectively combat terrorism, it raised concerns about potential abuses of law enforcement authority, infringement on individual privacy and civil rights, and the possible compromise of the criminal justice system's integrity.

The PRISM programme, operating under section 702 of the FISA, emerged as part of these efforts. This surveillance initiative required major US communication service providers, such as Google, Yahoo, Facebook, and others, to supply records of their users' activities. Although the programme was intended to collect information on foreign nationals' behaviours, which was deemed consistent with the Fourth Amendment, it faced criticism for the potential misuse of intelligence operations in domestic criminal inquiries.[35]

The debate intensified when judicial decisions regarding NSA surveillance were divided in the early 2010s. The District Court for the District of Columbia ruled that the NSA's surveillance programme violated the Fourth Amendment, distinguishing it from the established jurisprudence, which relied on third-party jurisprudence.[36] The court highlighted the significant increase in the amount of information collected by the government and its enhanced analytical capabilities as the key distinction. Conversely, the US District Court for the Southern District of

[32] For the jurisdictional issues, see Darryl Brown, 'Extraterritorial Ambit through Offence Definitions, Technology and Economic Power' in Micheál Ó Floinn and others (eds), *Transformations in Criminal Jurisdiction* (Hart 2023) 78.

[33] The PATRIOT Improvement and Reauthorization Act, Pub L No 109-177, 120 Stat 192 (2006).

[34] Intelligence Reform and Terrorism Prevention Act, Pub L No 108-458, 118 Stat 3638 (2004).

[35] Director of National Intelligence, 'Facts on the Collection of Intelligence Pursuant to Section 702 of the Foreign Intelligence Surveillance Act' (8 June 2013) <https://nsarchive2.gwu.edu/NSAEBB/NSAEBB436/docs/EBB-070.pdf>. All websites were last accessed on 31 March 2025.

[36] *Klayman v Obama* 957 F 2d 1 (DDC 2013). The Supreme Court's holding in *Smith v Maryland* 442 US 735 (1979) was that the installation and use of a pen register by the police to obtain information on a suspect's telephone calls was not a 'search' within the meaning of the Fourth Amendment to the Constitution and therefore no search warrant was required.

New York held that these changes were merely quantitative, and the legal principles established in the Smith decision still applied, deeming the NSA's programme constitutional.[37] However, this decision was later overturned by the Circuit Court, which concluded that section 215 of the Patriot Act exceeded the powers granted to Congress by the Constitution.[38]

In response to the growing controversy, independent expert panels within the executive branch recommended improvements to surveillance programmes. For example, the Presidential Review Panel on Intelligence and Communications Technology[39] and the Civil Liberties and Privacy Oversight Board[40] proposed reforms. In 2014, the Obama Administration released a proposal to reform NSA surveillance activities, which included ending the metadata programme under section 215 of the Patriot Act. Additionally, following media reports exposing details of the US surveillance programme, a special working group established by the Commission published a report advocating for enhancements to the operation of section 702 of the FISA.

2.3 Other Countries' Legislations on Surveillance Programme

It is noted that, from the 1990s to the 2010s, other governments have increasingly expanded their surveillance capabilities, often justifying these measures as necessary for national security and counterterrorism. It has been facilitated by advancements in digital technology, allowing States to monitor communications and internet activity on an unprecedented scale.[41]

First, countries with solid democratic institutions and legal protections have expanded their surveillance laws. These measures often involve metadata retention, bulk interception of communications, and government access to encrypted data. While these measures are subject to judicial oversight and public scrutiny, concerns persist regarding their implications for privacy and fundamental freedoms.

[37] *ACLU v Clapper*, No 13 Civ 3994 (SDNY 2013).

[38] *ACLU v Clapper* (2nd Cir, 7 May 2015) Docket No 14-42-cv.

[39] President's Review Group on Intelligence and Communications Technologies, Liberty and Security in a Changing World: Report and Recommendations of The President's Review Group on Intelligence and Communications Technologies (12 December 2013) <https://obamawhitehouse.archives.gov/sites/default/files/docs/2013-12-12_rg_final_report.pdf>.

[40] Privacy and Civil Liberties Oversight Board, Report on the Telephone Records Program Conducted under Section 215 of the USA PATRIOT Act and on the Operations of the Foreign Intelligence Surveillance Court (23 January 2014) <https://s3.amazonaws.com/s3.documentcloud.org/documents/1008957/final-report.pdf>.

[41] For a comprehensive analysis of State practice, see Fred H Cate and James X Dempsey, *Bulk Collection: Systematic Government Access to Private-Sector Data* (OUP 2017). This section does not get into the criminal procedural laws that relates to bulk collection. It is also noted that many developed countries do not have surveillance programmes. In Japan, for example, there is no similar legislation for such a programme.

In Germany, the Act on Restrictions on the Secrecy of the Mail, Post, and Telecommunications (commonly known as the G10 Act) serves as the primary legal framework.[42] It grants intelligence agencies the power to monitor communications for national security purposes. In addition the Data Retention Act of 2015 mandates the retention of communication metadata by service providers for a specified period, enabling access by law enforcement and intelligence agencies for national security investigations.[43]

France grants its data protection authority, the National Commission on Informatics and Liberty (Commission Nationale de l'Informatique et des Libertés), the power to collect and analyse mass metadata.[44] The organization, established under the Information Technology, Data Files, and Civil Liberty Act of 1978,[45] operates under the Internal Security Code amended in 2012 to identify suspicious behaviour patterns.[46] In 2015, the country enacted the Intelligence Act to establish an independent oversight body, the Commission for Oversight of Intelligence Gathering Techniques (Commission Nationale de Contrôle des Techniques de Renseignement).[47]

In the United Kingdom, the Interception of Communications Act 1985 was among the first legal frameworks governing State surveillance.[48] It has since been succeeded by more comprehensive legislation, most notably the Investigatory Powers Act 2016.[49] This instrument significantly expanded the government's surveillance powers, including bulk data collection, internet connection records, and mandatory cooperation from communication service providers.

[42] Gesetz zur Beschränkung des Brief-, Post- und Fernmeldegeheimnisses (Artikel 10-Gesetz) BGBl 2001 I, 1254, 2298; BGBl 2023 I Nr 413. This 'Article 10 Act' permits restrictions on the privacy of correspondence, posts, and telecommunications to protect the free democratic basic order or the existence or security of the Federation or a State. See Paul M Schwartz, 'Systematic Government Access to Private-Sector Data in Germany' in Fred H Cate and James X Dempsey (eds), *Bulk Collection: Systematic Government Access to Private-Sector Data* (1st edn, OUP 2017) 64. The law was last amended in 2023. The current Section 3 stipulates that the data may be used for the investigation of certain serious crimes, while Section 6 sets out detailed conditions to ensure due process. In addition, Section 7a permits the Federal Intelligence Service (*Bundesnachrichtendienst*) to transfer personal data obtained through intelligence activities, subject to the approval of the Federal Chancellery (*Bundeskanzleramt*) and compliance with specified conditions.

[43] Gesetz zur Einführung einer Speicherpflicht und einer Höchstspeicherfrist für Verkehrsdaten (DE) BGBl I 2015, 2218.

[44] See Winston J Maxwell, 'Systematic Government Access to Private-Sector Data in France' in Fred H Cate and James X Dempsey (eds), *Bulk Collection: Systematic Government Access to Private-Sector Data* (1st edn, OUP 2017) 49.

[45] Loi n° 78-17 du 6 janvier 1978 relative à l'informatique, aux fichiers et aux libertés.

[46] Ordonnance n°2012-351 du 12 mars 2012.

[47] Loi n° 2015-912 du 24 juillet 2015 relative au renseignement.

[48] Interception of Communications Act 1985, c 56.

[49] Investigatory Powers Act 2016, c 25. It authorises designated authorities to access internet connection records, subject to oversight by the Investigatory Powers Commission, an institution established under the legislation. See also Regulation of Investigatory Powers Act 2000, c 23, which regulates the powers of public bodies to carry out surveillance and interception of communications, including the acquisition of communication data for national security purposes.

Australia has also enacted a series of laws that enhance government surveillance capabilities. The Telecommunications (Interception and Access) Act of 1979 provides intelligence agencies with access to communications.[50] The Data Retention Law of 2015, which amended the 1979 law, mandates internet service providers to store metadata for two years, allowing law enforcement to access this data without requiring a warrant in many cases.[51] Furthermore, the Telecommunications and Other Legislation Amendment (Assistance and Access) Act of 2018 compels technology companies to provide authorities access to encrypted communications, raising concerns about potential vulnerabilities in cybersecurity.[52]

Canada has implemented surveillance measures primarily through the Anti-Terrorism Act of 2015, which expanded the powers of the Canadian Security Intelligence Service to collect and share intelligence with domestic and international partners.[53] The Communications Security Establishment Act of 2019 further strengthened Canada's intelligence gathering abilities, including provisions for mass surveillance.[54]

Second, some countries employ surveillance systems primarily as tools for political control, censorship, and repression. Russia has developed an extensive surveillance infrastructure over the years. The System of Operational-Investigative Measures, initially introduced in 1995, enables the Federal Security Service to intercept and store all electronic communications in the country. The Yarovaya Law of 2016 further expanded these capabilities by requiring telecom providers to store metadata and content for up to six months and granting security agencies access to this information.[55] Additionally, the Sovereign Internet Law 2019 allows the Russian government to isolate the country's internet infrastructure, which enables the authorities to conduct deep surveillance.[56]

China has also promoted State control over the cyber domain. The Cybersecurity Law of 2017 mandates data localization, requiring companies to

[50] Telecommunications (Interception and Access) Act, Act No 114 of 1979.

[51] Telecommunications (Interception and Access) Amendment (Data Retention) Act, Act No 39 of 2015.

[52] Telecommunications and Other Legislation Amendment (Assistance and Access) Act, No 148 of 2018. See also Surveillance Legislation Amendment (Identify and Disrupt) Act 2021. It allows police officers to disrupt data through modification and deletion of data to frustrate the commission of serious offences, to collect intelligence on serious criminal activity carried out by criminal networks operating online, and to take over the control of a person's online account to gather evidence about criminal activity to further a criminal investigation. For an overview of this act, see Australian Government, Department of Home Affairs, 'Surveillance Legislation Amendment (Identify and Disrupt) Act 2021' (2021) <https://www.homeaffairs.gov.au/about-us/our-portfolios/national-security/lawful-access-telecommunications/surveillance-legislation-amendment-identify-and-disrupt-act-2021>.

[53] Anti-Terrorism Act (SC 2015), c 20.

[54] Communications Security Establishment Act (SC 2019), c 13, s 76.

[55] Federal Law of 06.07.2016 No 374-FZ; Federal Law of 06.07.2016 No 375-FZ.

[56] Federal Law of 01.05.2019 No 90-FZ. See Carolina Vendil Pallin, 'Russian Information Security and Warfare' in Roger Kanet (ed) *The Routledge Handbook of Russian Security* (Routledge 2019) 203, 205.

store data within China and provide authorities with access when requested.[57] The National Intelligence Law of 2017 obligates organizations and individuals to assist in intelligence gathering efforts, effectively compelling businesses and citizens to participate in State surveillance.[58] In addition, the Golden Shield Project (commonly known as the Great Firewall) enables widespread internet censorship and monitoring, restricting access to foreign information sources and regulating online discourse. China employs a vast network of surveillance technologies, including facial recognition, artificial intelligence (AI)-driven monitoring, and extensive CCTV camera networks. China's Social Credit System integrates surveillance into daily life, assessing citizens' behaviour and imposing consequences for actions deemed undesirable by the State.

Countries in the Middle East have also expanded their surveillance capabilities, often in ways that restrict civil liberties and suppress political dissent. For instance, Saudi Arabia has implemented a sophisticated surveillance regime to monitor online activities and track individuals perceived as threats to national security. Additionally, strict censorship laws limit freedom of expression, with authorities closely monitoring social media platforms.[59]

These practices demonstrate that the US data collection and surveillance policies are not an exceptional case. However, what set the United States apart was its role as the headquarters for major global information technology corporations, which amassed vast amounts of user data from individuals and institutions in other countries. This global reach of the US-based companies allowed the US government to access their data.

2.4 Conflicts Concerning the Data Transfer and the Protection of Human Rights and Privacy

Prior to the 9/11 attacks and the subsequent legislations, as described in Section 2.2, the US law and policy shook the EU–US relationship because there has been an extensive divergence between the two entities.[60] The debate revolves around

[57] Cybersecurity Law (enacted on 7 November 2016) <https://www.gov.cn/xinwen/2016-11/07/content_5129723.htm>.

[58] National Intelligence Law (enacted on 27 June 2017) <http://www.npc.gov.cn/zgrdw/npc/xinwen/2018-06/12/content_2055873.htm>. For an overview of China's surveillance mechanisms, see Zhizheng Wang, 'Systematic Government Access to Private Sector Data in China,' in Fred H Cate and James X Dempsey (eds), *Bulk Collection: Systematic Government Access to Private-Sector Data* (OUP 2017) 241.

[59] The government possesses extensive powers to control digital information, primarily under the following legislative instruments: the Anti-Cyber Crime Law of 2007, Royal Decree No M/17; the Law of Combating Crimes of Terrorism and its Financing of 2017, Royal Decree No M21/1439; the Law of Printed Materials and Publication of 2003, Royal Decree No M/32, amended in 2011.

[60] For the backgrounds of the tensions between the United States and the European Union in the 2000s, see David A Tallman, 'Financial Institutions and the Safe Harbor Agreement: Securing Cross-Border Financial Data Flows' (2002) 34 Law and Policy in International Business 747, 754; Gregory Shaffer, 'Globalization and Social Protection: The Impact of EU and International Rules in the

whether data transfers from the European Union to the United States are permissible if the former deems the latter's data protection inadequate.

Since 1973, several European countries have enacted national laws to restrict the cross-border transfer of data collected within their territories due to privacy concerns.[61] This process was later harmonized by the EU Directive 95/46, which prohibited data transfers to countries that did not provide adequate levels of data protection.[62] Directive 95/46 created a situation where subsidiaries of US companies operating in Europe are prohibited from transferring data related to commercial transactions while adhering to US law.[63]

To address the disparities, the US Department of Commerce (DOC) and the European Commission agreed to establish the Safe Harbor Frameworks in 2000. This agreement was non-binding and enabled organizations participating in the framework to transfer data from the European Economic Area to regions outside the area. The European Commission endorsed this agreement in Decision 2000/520.[64] Under this framework, participating companies must adhere to principles of transparency, users' consent and choice, third-party compliance, access, security, relevance, and dispute resolution. These principles serve as guidelines for companies participating in the framework to safeguard privacy and provide individuals with certain rights and protections regarding their personal data.

Participating organizations in the framework are allowed to transfer information under EU law if they have been vetted by the DOC and certified as meeting the adequate protection standard required under the EU law. Additionally, these organizations are exempt from the prior authorization procedure for data transfers that EU Member States must typically undertake under Directive 95/46, or they may receive automatic authorization. Compliance with the Safe Harbor Privacy Principles outlined by the framework was mandatory for participating organizations, and they are expected to self-regulate privacy protection.

If a participating organization fails to comply with these standards, there are two avenues for enforcement. One was the private sector enforcement, and the other was the law enforcement by the US government. In the case of private sector

Ratcheting Up of US Data Privacy Standards' (2000) 25 Yale Journal of International Law 1. For the latest practice, see Taylor (n 17) 95.

[61] Sweden adopted Dataskyddslag (Swedish Data Act) (1973:289), and West Germany enacted Bundesdatenschutzgesetz (BDSG) (adopted on 27 January 1977, entered into force on 1 January 1978) BGBl I 201.

[62] Directive 95/46/EC of the European Parliament and of the Council of 24 October 1995 on the protection of individuals with regard to the processing of personal data and on the free movement of such data [1995] OJ L281/31.

[63] ibid.

[64] Commission Decision of 26 July 2000 pursuant to Directive 95/46/EC of the European Parliament and of the Council on the adequacy of the protection provided by the safe harbour privacy principles and related frequently asked questions issued by the US Department of Commerce (notified under document number C(2000) 2441) [2000] OJ L215/7.

enforcement, companies must establish an independent dispute resolution body to investigate and resolve individual claims, with appropriate dispute resolution mechanisms and remedies in place. If a breach occurs, it must be publicly disclosed, and the data involved must be deleted. As for enforcement by the US government, the primary responsibility lies with the Federal Trade Commission (FTC) to ensure compliance with the standards. Administrative penalties can be imposed for non-compliance. If a private sector dispute resolution body or another entity determines that the standards have not been met, it must notify the DOC. Since the establishment of the framework in 2000, over 4,400 US organizations have participated and conducted activities within the European region.

Switzerland also implemented a data protection law in 1992, which came into effect in 1993 and was subsequently amended in 2008.[65] The amendment specified that data transfers will not take place if Switzerland is not deemed compliant with privacy protection. Consequently, the US DOC has established a similar safe harbour framework with Swiss competent authorities.[66]

The Safe Harbor Framework had little relevance to counterterrorism regulations. However, afterwards, the United States expanded its access to individuals' information through the implementation of the PATRIOT Act and subsequent legislative changes. It raised concerns that US authorities were monitoring the personal data of individuals within the European Union.

In October 2015, the European Court of Justice (ECJ) declared the Commission's decision approving the Safe Harbor Framework invalid in the *Schrems* case.[67] In 2013, the existence of the PRISM programme, which involved surveillance by the NSA and other agencies, including Facebook, came to light. This revelation prompted an Austrian citizen, Max Schrems, to file a petition with the Irish Data Protection Authority, requesting an investigation into the legality of Facebook's data transfers, particularly those conducted under the Safe Harbor Framework.

The ECJ clarified that EU member States have the authority to assess whether the destination country ensures adequate data protection when transferring data outside the European Union. The court further emphasized that the 1995 Directive does not limit the powers of national supervisory bodies, even if the Commission finds that the framework's requirements are met. Consequently, the ECJ ruled the Safe Harbor Framework invalid, stating that the Irish Data Protection Authority

[65] Bundesgesetz über den Datenschutz (DSG) vom 19. Juni 1992.

[66] US–Swiss Safe Harbour Privacy Principles, issued by the US Department of Commerce on 16 February 1999.

[67] Case C-362/14 *Maximillian Schrems v Data Protection Commissioner* ECLI:EU:C:2015:650 (Judgment) (ECJ, 6 October 2015). Initially, the Irish data protection agency declined to investigate the case, citing the belief that the data transfers under the Safe Harbor Framework were adequately protected. In response, the High Court sought a preliminary ruling from the ECJ to determine whether the Irish data protection agency could examine the Commission's decision on the validity of the Safe Harbor Framework.

was obligated to investigate the individual's complaint and assess whether Facebook's transfer of personal data of EU citizens to the United States complied with the 1995 Directive.[68]

In February 2016, the Commission and the United States reached an agreement to introduce a new cooperative framework known as the Privacy Shield. This framework fulfilled the requirements outlined by the ECJ. The Privacy Shield imposed stronger data protection obligations on US companies and established administrative penalties for non-compliance. It also stipulated that the US DOC, in collaboration with the FTC and data protection authorities of the member States, would oversee monitoring and enforcement of privacy breaches. Additionally, EU citizens gained the ability to raise data protection inquiries and complaints through a newly established ombudsperson, with companies obliged to respond within forty-five days. This bilateral arrangement between the European Union and the United States provided individuals with the means to seek legal recourse for privacy violations.

In the Court of Justice of the European Union ruling in July 2020, *Schrems II*, the Court held that the Privacy Shield was invalid because it did not adequately protect EU citizens' data from US government surveillance practices, such as those conducted by the NSA. Max Schrems again brought the case to challenge the transfer of personal data from the European Union to the United States under the arrangement. The ruling stressed that US surveillance laws, particularly those related to national security, did not meet the standards of the General Data Protection Regulation (GDPR), as they lacked sufficient safeguards for EU citizens' data.

In the aftermath of *Schrems II*, the United States and the European Union sought to develop a new framework to facilitate transatlantic data flows while addressing the court's concerns. This led to the announcement of the EU–US Data Privacy Framework of 2023.[69] The Framework aims to restore the legal basis for data transfers by introducing enhanced protections for EU citizens' data, including commitments from the US government to limit its surveillance activities and ensure stronger oversight. Key features of the new framework include establishing an independent redress mechanism for EU citizens whose data privacy is violated and stronger safeguards for data handling by US companies. While the arrangement represents progress in aligning US and EU privacy standards, concerns remain regarding its viability in the long term and whether it can withstand legal scrutiny, particularly in light of the rigorous privacy standards set by the GDPR. In addition, in 2022, the President of the United States introduced changes to how intelligence activities are overseen. The Executive Order 14086 established an independent

[68] ibid para 106.

[69] Commission Implementing Decision (EU) 2023/1795 of 10 July 2023 pursuant to Regulation (EU) 2016/679 of the European Parliament and of the Council on the adequate level of protection of personal data under the EU–US Data Privacy Framework [2023] OJ L231/118, Annex I.

and enforceable process that allows individuals, under certain conditions, to file a complaint if they believe their personal information was collected by US intelligence agencies in a way that broke US law.[70]

The tension between national security and human rights is often seen as a cliché. However, when data transfer is involved, the division represents a new variation of jurisdictional conflict. As a solution, the United States and the European Union agreed to cooperate to mitigate disputes over data protection, security, and the free flow of information. Although the cooperation mechanism remains State-centric in nature, the inclusion of procedural safeguards, oversight structures, and channels for individual redress allows it to strike a balance between the need of national security and international cooperation, on the one hand, and the protection of individual rights and freedoms, on the other.

3. Terrorist Screening Information

3.1 Key Issues

Countries have started to collect and store terrorism screening information, which is used by government agencies to identify individuals who may pose a security or terrorism threat. The information includes personal identifiers, such as names, dates of birth, and biometric data; behavioural indicators, such as information about suspicious activities or patterns; connections to known or suspected terrorists, organizations, or extremist groups; and travel patterns or destinations that may indicate potential threats.[71] The data is often used by various agencies, including intelligence, law enforcement, customs, and border protection, to support national security efforts and protect public safety.

Major countries have commonly established integrated government agencies or bureaus to coordinate and enhance their efforts in countering terrorism. A notable development took place in the United States. One of the causes of the 9/11 attacks was the compartmentalization of the departments in the US government, as stated in the previous section. Agencies did not convey necessary information to other relevant bureaus to prevent the terrorists from entering the United States. The Department of Homeland Security (DHS) was established to fill the gap in 2003. Its function is to oversee counterterrorism, law enforcement, border security, and inspection activities.

[70] Executive Order 14086 (7 October 2022).

[71] US DOS, 'Programs and Initiatives' <https://www.state.gov/bureau-of-counterterrorism-programs-and-initiatives/>. All websites were last accessed on 31 March 2025.

In the European Union, the Europol has enhanced collaboration between member states by sharing critical intelligence on transnational threats, addressing issues of fragmentation, and improving coordinated responses to terrorism and organized crime. Japan strengthened its counterterrorism measures through the establishment of the Counterterrorism Unit to enhance information sharing and coordination among various ministries and security agencies. From an international law perspective, the challenge lies in how governments can effectively share such information.

Even when States did not create a new agency, they often strengthened the mandates of existing authorities. For example, in the United Kingdom, the powers of MI5, which is the security service, were expanded to enhance its ability to counterterrorism.[72] Similarly, in Germany, the Federal Office for the Protection of the Constitution (*Bundesamt für Verfassungsschutz*, BfV) allowed an increase in its authority to monitor and prevent terrorist activities.[73] In France, the *Direction générale de la Sécurité intérieure* (General Directorate for Internal Security), established in 2008, was bolstered to improve its counterterrorism capabilities.[74] Mandates of the Japanese National Police Agency and Public Security Intelligence Agency expanded following the ratification of the ICSFT and other anti-terrorism conventions after the 9/11 attacks.[75]

As States move towards more robust information collection on suspicious activities, they began to take balance on two demands. On the one hand, the integration of information systems is essential for effectively countering terrorism. A compartmentalized system, where data and intelligence are siloed, can hinder timely responses to emerging threats and the ability to address the complexities of modern terrorism is significantly diminished. On the other hand, serious human rights violations may emerge that could undermine the integrity of the criminal justice process without appropriate governance. The central challenge is to develop a robust regulatory framework that clearly delineates how and under what

[72] The role and responsibilities of M15 is provided under Security Service Act 1989, c 5. The Security Service Act 1989, the Intelligence Services Act 1994, the Regulation of Investigatory Powers Act 2000, and the Investigatory Powers Act 2016 provide the legal framework for its intelligence gathering activities.

[73] The mandate of BfV is provided under Act on Cooperation between the Federation and the Länder in Matters relating to the Protection of the Constitution and on the Federal Office for the Protection of the Constitution (Gesetz über die Zusammenarbeit des Bundes und der Länder in Angelegenheiten des Verfassungsschutzes und über das Bundesamt für Verfassungsschutz (BVerfSchG)), enacted in 1950 (BGBl 682) and amended in 1990 (BGBl I 2954, 2970).

[74] The agency was created in 2008 as *Direction centrale du renseignement intérieur* (Central Directorate of Interior Intelligence), merging *Direction centrale des renseignements généraux* and *Direction de la surveillance du territoire* of the French National Police. The name was changed to *Direction générale de la Sécurité intérieure* and its organizational authority changed, under Décret n° 2014-445. The legal basis for the surveillance is provided under the Intelligence Act (n° 2015-912 du 24 juillet 2015 relative au renseignement).

[75] The expansion took place under a series of legislations, subsequent to Japan's ratification of the ICSFT, including the Act on the Punishment of Financing to Offences of Public Intimidation, Act No 67 of 2002.

conditions shared intelligence can be used. This framework must balance the need for swift and effective counterterrorism measures with the need to protect individuals' rights and ensure that legal procedures remain fair and transparent. The following part section examine mechanisms for exchanging information to fufil these demands.

3.2 HSPD-6 Agreement

In the United States, the Homeland Security Presidential Directive 6 (HSPD-6), which the President issued in September 2003, called for the establishment and use of a single consolidated terrorist watchlist to improve the identification, screening, and tracking of individuals known or suspected to be or have been engaged in conduct constituting, in preparation for, in aid of, or related to terrorism ('known or suspected terrorists') and their supporters.[76]

Consequently, the government established the Terrorist Screening Database (TSDB), which is a comprehensive repository maintained by the FBI Terrorist Screening Center. The government also established the Terrorism Threat Integration Centre, which was established in May 2003, to facilitate the effective integration and analysis of such information. It was subsequently reorganized into the National Counterterrorism Centre in 2004. In July 2010, the DHS introduced the Watchlist Service, which was designed to facilitate the transfer of TSDB data from the Terrorist Screening Center to the DHS. The Watchlist Service maintains an up-to-date copy of the TSDB, which contains personally identifiable information. The information pertaining to individuals engaged in terrorist activities is employed, in accordance with the relevant legislation, for the purpose of screening processes conducted by a range of entities, including the US federal, State, and local governments, foreign governments, and the private sector, as well as for diplomatic, military, intelligence, law enforcement, immigration, and visa-related purposes.

The HSPD-6 requires the government to conclude agreements (HSPD-6 Agreement) with foreign governments for the exchange of terrorism screening information. The primary objective of the HSPD-6 Agreements is to share terrorist watchlist information between the United States and partner countries. This includes data on known or suspected terrorists, which can be used for border security, immigration screening, and law enforcement purposes. The Agreement facilitates the mutual exchange of information on suspected terrorist activities,

[76] US Department of Homeland Security, DHS/ALL/PIA-027(e) DHS Watchlist Service (10 July 2020) <https://www.dhs.gov/sites/default/files/publications/privacy-pia-dhsall027d-watchlistservice-july2020.pdf>.

ensuring reciprocity. As of December 2024, the United States has successfully concluded agreements with approximately forty countries.[77]

Moreover, the Terrorist Interdiction Program's Personal Identification Secure Comparison and Evaluation System offers partner countries assistance with border security, with the objective of identifying instances of cross-border travel by terrorists.[78]

3.3 Preventing and Combating Serious Crime Agreements

A Preventing and Combating Serious Crime Agreement (PCSC Agreement) is a bilateral treaty that establishes a framework for the exchange of personal information, including fingerprints. Its primary objective is to prevent and investigate serious crimes by facilitating the rapid exchange of information between countries and territories that have visa waiver agreements with the United States.

After the 9/11 attacks, the National Commission on Terrorist Attacks upon the United States recommended the US Congress reinforce the immigration control system.[79] In response, the Recommendations Implementation Act of 2007 was enacted, mandating the implementation of these recommendations.[80] The US government was required to include provisions in visa waiver agreements that facilitate the sharing of information with relevant countries regarding potential threats to US security posed by individuals entering the country.

These agreements generally outline the following procedures, although specific details vary between partner countries.[81] First, the core mechanism of the PCSC Agreement is 'automated querying'. A party may request the counterpart's authorities to check if the individual's fingerprint information is registered in the database held by the police authorities of their respective country. When an automated query is initiated, the system responds with either a match, providing a reference number, or no match. If a match is found, fingerprint data accompanies the response for verification. The queried party may request an explanation for the query if no further information is sought after the match, and technical details for automated querying are to be specified through implementing arrangements between the national contact points.

[77] For an overview, see United States Government Accountability Office, 'Visa Waiver Program: Additional Actions Needed to Address Risks and Strengthen Overstay Enforcement' (2011) <https://www.gao.gov/products/gao-12-287t>.

[78] US DOS (n 71).

[79] The National Commission on Terrorist Attacks upon the United States, *The 9/11 Commission Report* (22 July 2004) 383–89 <http://www.9-11commission.gov/report/911Report.pdf>.

[80] Implementing Recommendations of the 9/11 Commission Act, Pub L No 110-53, 121 Stat 266 (2007) s 711.

[81] The following explanation is based on the US–Japan Agreement (signed on 7 February 2014, entered into force on 5 January 2019) <https://www.state.gov/wp-content/uploads/2019/02/19-105-Japan-Law-Enforcemt-Coop.pdf>.

The databases of the counterpart country's police authorities must include the fingerprints of individuals who have been indicted for insufficient charges or acquitted, in addition to convicted individuals. If fingerprints are registered, the images are automatically transmitted to the counterparty, and the counterpart country's police authorities are obligated to respond to the inquiry. Second, if a relevant person is identified, the US side will share the suspect's name, gender, date of birth, previous arrests, sentencing results, and other relevant information with the counterpart country, specifying the purpose of the investigation. The counterpart country's police authorities are generally required to provide this information, although they may refuse in exceptional circumstances.

Agreements ensure the careful handling and deletion of fingerprint data. Once the query response is provided, both the querying and queried contact points are required to delete the data unless needed for follow-up. The data may only be used for specific purposes, such as investigating serious crimes, preventing threats to public security, or immigration-related purposes. If the data is needed for other purposes, prior consent must be obtained. Parties are restricted from sharing the information with third parties without written consent, and conditions on data usage may be imposed and must be respected.

The agreement emphasizes the need for organizational, technical, and security measures to protect the information shared, including encryption where necessary. In cases where incorrect or unreliable information is shared, the party responsible must notify the other party, and appropriate steps must be taken to correct, delete, or withhold the erroneous data.

The cooperation framework established by the PCSC Agreement differs from a traditional mutual legal assistance treaty (MLAT) in that the requested administrative authorities do not have the discretion to refuse the provision of information, at least during the initial stage.

The protection standards under the PCSC Agreements differ from those in domestic procedures, which normally require court authorization. A notable divergence arises in that the protection of human rights under the PCSC Agreements is less stringent compared to domestic procedures. This disparity raises concerns about the adequacy of safeguards in international cooperation agreements. The more relaxed standards under the PCSC Agreements could potentially offer less protection for individual rights compared to domestic legal frameworks. As part of its negotiation strategy, the United States has adopted a policy of not renewing visa waiver agreements unless the counterpart country concludes a PCSC Agreement.[82] However, no legal disputes have materialized to date.

[82] Paul Luif and Florian Trauner, 'The Prüm Process: The Effects of Enhanced Cooperation within Europe and with the United States in Combating Serious Crime' in Ronald L Holzhacker and Paul Luif (eds), *Freedom, Security and Justice in the European Union* (Springer New York 2014).

4. Airline Passenger Name Record

4.1 Key Issues

Regulation of immigration and transportation is the core of terrorism regulation. The States of departure have a certain degree of control over the air travel flow prior to the arrival of the passenger in the country of destination. With this regard, the identification of the travellers is essential. The passenger-related information from carriers or airlines to border control authorities falls into two main streams: Advance Passenger Information (API), which is generated during the check-in, and PNR, which is generated during the booking or buying of an air ticket. Both are subject to the guidelines of the International Civil Aviation Organization (ICAO).[83]

4.2 Disputes between the United States and the European Union

In November 2001, two months after the 9/11 attacks, the United States enacted the Aviation and Transportation Security Act.[84] The law required airlines operating flights to or from US airports connecting with foreign countries to provide personal passenger information to border control authorities, including DHS. This measure aimed to enhance immigration control and did not face jurisdictional challenges.

Previously, the US Customs Service used to receive passenger information from air carriers on a voluntary basis. Then, the DHS established the Advanced Passenger Information System, which is an electronic data interchange system for the carriers to transmit such data to the Customs and Border Protection, a successor of the Customs Service.[85]

However, it created a legal predicament for EU-registered airline companies. On the one hand, these airlines were obligated to share passenger personal data

[83] The API Guidelines were developed in 1993 by the World Customs Organization (WCO) in co-operation with the International Air Transport Association (IATA). Subsequently, the two and ICAO jointly published WCO/IATA/ICAO Guidelines on Advance Passenger Information in 2003, 2010, and 2013. Since 2010, the WCO/IATA/ICAO API Contact Committee worked on updating the electronic reporting standards for PNR. The API Contact Committee also developed guidelines for PNR and PNRGOV standards, which are complementary to Doc 9944, ICAO's guidelines on PNR. These guidelines reflect the consensus achieved between the WCO, IATA, and ICAO on matters concerning the reporting of passenger information to governments. ICAO Security and Facilitation, 'Facilitation Programme—API Guidelines and PNR Reporting Standards' <https://www.icao.int/Security/FAL/SitePages/API%20Guidelines%20and%20PNR%20Reporting%20Standards.aspx>.

[84] Aviation and Transportation Security Act, Pub L No107-71, 115 Stat 597 (2001), 49 USC 44909(c)(3).

[85] US CBP, 'Fact Sheet: APIS—Preventing Terrorists from Boarding International Flights and Vessels Destined for or Departing from the U.S.' (11 December 2013) <https://www.cbp.gov/sites/default/files/documents/apis_factsheet_3.pdf>.

with the DHS in compliance with US law. Failure to comply could result in fines and revocation of landing rights for the airline. On the other hand, the European Union had previously adopted the Data Protection Directive 95/46/EC in 1995, which prohibited companies subject to the jurisdiction of member States from sharing personal data collected for air transport services with third parties for other purposes. Such use of information would not satisfy the requirement. Additionally, the Directive stipulated that personal data could only be transferred to countries outside the European Union if those countries ensured an adequate level of protection. The determination of adequacy was the responsibility of the European Commission. However, the Commission's jurisdiction was limited to matters relating to the Internal Market (Pillar I) of the EU Treaty, while matters related to justice and security (Pillar III) fell under the exclusive jurisdiction of individual member states. Therefore, the Commission lacked the authority to decide the matter. Consequently, each airline company faced the risk of violating data protection laws in their respective countries of registration.

To address this situation and facilitate the smooth exchange of information, the US government and the European Commission initiated discussions in December 2001.[86] Their aim was to establish a framework for collecting passengers' personal data that would satisfy the requirements of both parties. Subsequently, an agreement was signed in May 2004 to resolve these issues.[87] The European Council also issued Directive 2004/82/EC on the obligation of carriers to communicate passenger data without the opinion of the European Parliament as it was emergent.[88]

The aim of the agreement was to set the basis for the transfer of PNR data by carriers operating passenger flights between the European Union and the United States and the subsequent use of that data by the DHS. Its main aim was to prevent, detect, investigate, and prosecute terrorist offences and related crimes, as well as other serious cross-border crimes punishable by a sentence of imprisonment of at least three years. PNR data is the information voluntarily provided by passengers and collected by air carriers during the reservation and check-in procedures. It includes information such as name, dates of travel and travel itinerary, ticket information, contact information, payment and billing information, travel agent, seat number, and baggage information.

At the time of negotiation, the parties disagreed regarding the permissible use of transferred information for US domestic crimes. The United States proposed that personal data could be utilized for immigration control and dealing with domestic

[86] For the background, see Evelien Brouwer, 'The EU Passenger Name Record (PNR) System and Human Rights: Transferring Passenger Data or Passenger Freedom?', vol 320 (*Centre for European Policy Studies*, 3 September 2009).

[87] US DOS, 'Executive Agreement with the EC re the processing and transfer of passenger name record data by air carriers to the U.S. Department of Homeland Security (signed on 28 May 2004)' <https://2009-2017.state.gov/s/l/2004/78081.htm>.

[88] Council Directive 2004/82/EC of 29 April 2004 on the obligation of carriers to communicate passenger data [2004] OJ L261/24.

crime. However, the Commission contended that this broad use went beyond the intended purpose. Eventually, it was agreed that the use of transferred information would exclude dealing with domestic crime. The information would only be shared for terrorism-related offences and other serious cross-border offences, including organized crime. Furthermore, the United States would be prohibited from employing the information for any other purpose, such as controlling individuals who entered the country illegally.

The scope of the data to be provided and the treatment of sensitive information, such as ethnic origin, religion, or belief, were subjects of debate. Ultimately, it was stipulated that such sensitive information would not be included in the provision of data.

Regarding the retention period of the data, initial discussions saw the United States advocating for a storage duration of fifty years, while the Commission insisted on three years. Ultimately, it was agreed that the DHS would retain the information for a period of three and a half years.

The Commission conducted an assessment and determined that the US domestic law satisfied the adequacy requirement. The treaty was then concluded based on a decision by the Council of Europe, which holds the authority to finalize such treaties.

Both civil society organizations and EU institutions, particularly the European Parliament, voiced criticism of the agreement because it may conflict with the European Data Protection Directive. The Article 29 Working Group, an independent advisory body established under Article 29 of the Data Protection Directive, had expressed the need to ensure respect for fundamental human rights and freedoms, including the right to privacy and data protection, without being constrained by the imperatives of US domestic security.[89] Furthermore, concerns were raised regarding the sharing of information by the DHS with other law enforcement agencies, including the DOJ, as there were no specific measures in US domestic law to prevent such sharing.

In July 2004, civil society organizations prompted the European Parliament to appeal to the ECJ to annul the Commission's decision regarding the adequacy of the agreement and the European Council's decision to approve the conclusion of the PNR Agreement.[90] The core of the case revolved around the fact that the transfer of information under the PNR Agreement fell under Pillar III, focused on countering terrorist crime rather than Pillar I, and the Commission lacked the authority to make that determination. Additionally, the Council's decision, which relied on a provision in the EC Treaty on the Establishment of the Internal Market

[89] Article 29 Working Party, 'Opinion 6/2002 on Transmission of Passenger Manifest Information and Other Data from Airlines to the United States' (adopted on 24 October 2002) 11647/02/EN WP 66.

[90] Joined Cases C-317/04 and C-318/04, *European Parliament v Council of the European Union and Commission of the European Communities* ECLI:EU:C:2006:346 (Judgment) (30 May 2006).

and Other Matters,[91] was deemed irrelevant as the conclusion of the Agreement pertained solely to the transfer of information to the United States. Consequently, the Council was deemed to lack the necessary authority.

The ECJ acknowledged the European Parliament's complaint and declared the Commission and Council decisions on the 2004 Agreement invalid. However, the ECJ's ruling was confined to the issue of competence overreach and did not address the question of whether the transfer of personal data violated the right to privacy under the European Convention on Human Rights or if the Agreement contradicted the principle of proportionality based on substantive law.[92]

Under the direct oversight of the European Council, supported by the European Commission, renegotiations between the United States and the European Union were initiated. Throughout the negotiations, the interim agreement remained in effect. The renewed instrument stipulated that the Council would take the necessary steps to ensure that the US information protection measures aligned with EU standards. It was also mandated that airline operators conducting international air traffic to or from the United States would provide passenger information to the DHS.[93]

The present agreement provides that the use of PNR data will be limited to the prevention, detection, investigation, and prosecution of terrorist offences or other transnational crimes. The parties are obliged to implement stringent measures for data security and integrity. Individuals will possess the right to access their PNR data stored in the United States. If any inaccuracies are found, the information must be promptly corrected or deleted. The utilization of PNR data will be restricted for a specified duration. For transnational crime, the data will be retained for ten years, while for terrorism-related purposes, it will be retained for fifteen years. After a period of six months, personally identifiable information within the PNR data will be anonymized. Furthermore, after five years, the PNR data will be transferred to a dormant database with additional safeguards in place.[94]

The agreement further outlined that the United States would collect passenger information and utilize it for the prevention, detection, investigation, and prosecution of terrorist attacks and related crimes. It would also be used for international crimes that carry a minimum imprisonment term of three years under the US law.[95]

Compared to the 2004 Agreement, the 2007 Agreement reduced the types of information to be transferred. The DHS stated that certain exceptional cases would allow for specific uses of sensitive information, particularly when the life of the

[91] Treaty establishing the European Community [2002] OJ C325/33, art 95.

[92] Mario Mendez, 'Passenger Name Record Agreement and European Court of Justice' (2007) 3 European Constitutional Law Review 127.

[93] Agreement between the European Union and the United States of America on the processing and transfer of Passenger Name Record (PNR) data by air carriers to the United States Department of Homeland Security (DHS) (the 2007 PNR Agreement), OJ L 204, 4 August 2007, 16–25.

[94] ibid art 7.

[95] The 2007 PNR Agreement, art 4.

individual in question or another person would be endangered or severely compromised. Information that requires careful handling, such as a passenger's race, religion, political beliefs, health, or sex life, would be mechanically screened and protected. However, in exceptional circumstances where human life is at risk, this information may be utilized. The determination of what information qualifies for cautious handling and protection would be established by US authorities separately.[96]

Regarding data retention, under the 2007 Agreement, passenger information is initially loaded into an operational analytical database. After six months, personal identifying details such as names, contact information, and special services associated with individual passengers are depersonalized and shielded. Within five years of loading, the depersonalized data is transferred to an inactive database, where it can be stored for up to ten years. Access to this dormant database requires approval from a senior official within the Department designated by the Secretary of Homeland Security. Additionally, if the information pertains to an international crime carrying a minimum imprisonment term of three years or more, the depersonalization period can be extended to five years, subject to review.[97]

The Agreement also grants EU citizens the right to seek administrative and judicial remedies under the US law if their information is used in contravention of the Agreement. They also possess the right to challenge decisions made by US authorities regarding the use and processing of their information and can request a review by the Federal Court.[98]

The PNR Agreement has not only been implemented between the United States and the European Union but has also been extended to other regions. Consequently, the information management systems established under the Agreement's framework are expected to be adopted by airlines across the countries.

4.3 Standard Setting in the International Civil Aviation Organization

The ICAO is responsible for developing standards and guidelines for the collection, use, processing, and protection of PNR data. The initial standard was published in 2013 and has since been updated. In 2017, the UN Security Council adopted Resolution 2396 (2017), which mandates all UN member states to develop

[96] ibid art 6.

[97] ibid art 8.

[98] ibid art 3. The European Union concluded the PNR Agreement with other countries including Australia and Canada. Agreement between the European Union and Australia on the processing and transfer of Passenger Name Record (PNR) data by air carriers to the Australian Customs and Border Protection Service [2012] OJ L186/4; Agreement between the European Community and the Government of Canada on the processing of Advance Passenger Information and Passenger Name Record (PNR) data [2006] OJ L82/15.

capabilities for collecting, processing, and analysing PNR data in furtherance of ICAO standards and recommended practices.[99] The Security Council also stated that the States should 'ensure PNR data is used by and shared with all their competent national authorities, with full respect for human rights and fundamental freedoms' for a limited purpose of preventing, detecting, and investigating terrorist offences and related travel.[100]

5. Biometrics and Biogenetic Information

5.1 Key Issues

Biometrics are body measurements and calculations that represent human characteristics, such as facial images and fingerprints. Biogenetic information includes deoxyribonucleic acid (DNA). The use of biometric and biogenetic technologies for the suppression of terrorism—or, more broadly, for border management and surveillance—has become increasingly prevalent. Current trends demonstrate the deployment of advanced technologies to capture and analyse biometric data, including fingerprints, iris scans, facial recognition, vein patterns, DNA, and behavioural biometrics. Additionally, there is a growing collection of biometric data from both physical spaces, such as public areas, including border control areas, and digital environments, including social media platforms. Governments have developed centralized databases of biometric data with enhanced interoperability between different systems.

There has been a growing promotion for the dissemination of biometric data across national borders for the suppression of terrorism at the international level. The United Nations has made efforts to encourage all States to use such data by establishing the necessary systems. For instance, in 2017, the UN Security Council obliged member States to 'develop and implement systems to collect biometric data, which could include fingerprints, photographs, facial recognition, and other relevant identifying biometric data' to 'responsibly and properly identify terrorists'.[101] In 2018, the UN Security Council's Counter-Terrorism Committee endorsed the need to utilize biometrics data by adopting an Addendum to the Guiding Principles on Foreign Terrorist Fighters or the Madrid Guiding Principles[102] and assorting good practices.[103]

[99] UNSC Res 2396 (21 December 2017) UN Doc S/RES/2396, para 12.
[100] ibid.
[101] ibid para 15.
[102] UN Doc S/2018/1177, Annex, Addendum to the Guiding Principles on Foreign Terrorist Fighters (2018), paras 17–18.
[103] UNOTC and UNSC CTED, 'United Nations Compendium of Recommended Practices for the Responsible Use and Sharing of Biometrics in Counter-Terrorism' (18 June 2018) <https://www.unodc.org/pdf/terrorism/Compendium-Biometrics/Compendium-biometrics-final-version-LATEST_18_JUNE_2018_optimized.pdf>.

Furthermore, it is observed that technology corporations providing systems for data utilization often maintain close ties with governments that rely on their products. For example, companies developing surveillance technologies or smart city infrastructure often collaborate with governments for public security purposes.[104] This sort of close relationship may drive the expansion of more intrusive surveillance practices.

On the other hand, the use of biometrics and biogenetic information for terrorism investigations raises several legal issues in relation to privacy, due process, and discrimination. There are several cases from domestic courts and the European Court of Human Rights (ECtHR) but relatively few from public international dispute settlement forums. The key legal challenges are as follows.

First, the primary legal concern regarding the use of biometrics and biogenetic information is the governance of data collection and retention in government databases. If there are no explicit restrictions on how this information is managed, the government could retain personal data for disproportionately long periods without appropriate safeguards. The storage of biometric data, such as facial images, fingerprints, or DNA, can lead to extensive government surveillance capabilities that may infringe on individual privacy. There are concerns about its use for purposes beyond the initial investigation, such as in other criminal cases and civil matters.

In the 2008 case of *S and Marper v the United Kingdom*, the ECtHR held that the indefinite retention of DNA samples from individuals not convicted of crimes violated their right to privacy under Article 8 of the European Convention on Human Rights.[105] Under section 64 of the UK Police and Criminal Evidence Act 1984, authorities are allowed to collect biometric information. The applicants, whose fingerprints and DNA were taken when they were arrested, one of whom was acquitted, and the other's case discontinued, requested the destruction of their biometric data. However, the police refused. The applicants sought judicial review, but the Administrative Court rejected their claim in 2001, a decision upheld by the Court of Appeal and subsequently the House of Lords.

The ECtHR unanimously found that retaining the applicants' biometric data breached Article 8, which protects the right to respect for private and family life. The core issue was whether the interference with this right was lawful, pursued a legitimate aim, and was necessary in a democratic society. While the Court acknowledged that the retention of such data could serve the legitimate purpose of crime detection and prevention, it emphasized that the relevant question was

[104] Privacy International, 'Briefing on the Responsible Use and Sharing of Biometric Data in Counter-Terrorism' (17 July 2020) <https://privacyinternational.org/advocacy/4064/briefing-responsible-use-and-sharing-biometric-data-counter-terrorism>.

[105] *S and Marper v United Kingdom* App Nos 30562/04 and 30566/04 (Judgment) (ECtHR, 4 December 2008).

whether retaining the data of individuals suspected but not convicted of crimes was justified. The retention policy applied without regard to the nature or severity of the offence or the suspect's age, and there were limited opportunities for acquitted individuals to have their data removed or destroyed. The Court found that this blanket and indiscriminate retention failed to strike a fair balance between public and private interests and that the United Kingdom had exceeded the acceptable margin of appreciation.[106]

Second, the advancement of biometric technologies, particularly facial recognition, has enabled the government to engage in mass surveillance. This could have an impact on the private realm, as individuals may be monitored in public spaces. The deployment of such technology may risk creating a situation where individuals' movements are tracked, potentially chilling free expression and freedom of association. The US FBI Criminal Justice Information Services Division developed and integrated a system, the Next Generation Identification, which is an electronic repository of biometric information.[107]

Third, the use of biometric systems, such as facial recognition technology, has been shown to produce less accurate results for certain racial and ethnic groups, leading to biased enforcement actions. It can result in discriminatory practices in law enforcement, where innocent individuals from racial minorities are disproportionately targeted or wrongly accused based on faulty biometric identification.

These potential intrusions against privacy may be accelerated because of the use of AI. The potential for intrusions against privacy may be exacerbated by the increased utilization of AI. The capacity of AI systems to process vast amounts of personal data facilitates the gathering, analysis, and potential misuse of this sensitive information.

While legislative frameworks and case law address certain issues related to the use of biometrics and biogenetic information, governments often store this data indefinitely or without adhering to robust procedural safeguards. The nature of the technology itself necessitates that this information be stored to be practically utilized for the purposes of identifying a person.

A critical aspect of this debate is the need for clear rules regarding due process, transparency, and accountability, as well as established procedures for redress in cases of misuse or abuse of such information. States have started to protect privacy interests concerning biometric and biogenetic information in the context of the protection of personal information. There are a number of approaches that could be considered in terms of harmonization. Domestic laws on personal information

[106] ibid para 119.

[107] Law Enforcement Resources, 'Next Generation Identification (NGI)' <https://le.fbi.gov/science-and-lab/biometrics-and-fingerprints/biometrics/next-generation-identification-ngi>. The FBI has utilized this system at full operational capacity since 2014.

protection and the EU GDPR set certain standards for the protection of personal data, including biometric and biogenetic information. The Council of Europe's Convention 108+, which is the modernized Convention for the Protection of Individuals with Regard to the Processing of Personal Data, also obliges member States to protect this information as personal information.

These frameworks are region-specific, and no universal standard exists to regulate the indefinite storage of such sensitive information. Outside Europe, many countries have varied approaches to biometrics, with some adopting stringent safeguards and others offering little to no regulation.

For example, in the United States, while there are privacy protections at the State level, such as Illinois' Biometric Information Privacy Act,[108] there is no federal standard governing the collection and retention of biometric data across the country.

In 2016, India revised and replaced the National Identification Authority of India Bill of 2010 with the Aadhaar (Targeted Delivery of Financial and Other Subsidies, Benefits, and Services) Act. While the 2016 Act retained many of the provisions from the 2010 Bill, it introduced significant changes. Notably, the new legislation expanded the scope of information accessible to investigative agencies. Under the Aadhaar Act, authorities can now request not only authentication limited to biometric verification but also additional information related to an individual's identity.[109]

Another significant aspect of biometric data retention is the distinction made between nationals and immigrants, with the latter often subject to different and sometimes less protective rules. For instance, many countries retain the biometric information of immigrants and asylum seekers for much longer periods than that of their own citizens. This differential treatment raises questions under human rights law, particularly considering principles such as equality before the law and non-discrimination. The ICCPR and the Universal Declaration of Human Rights underscore the right to privacy and protection from arbitrary interference, irrespective of nationality. The lack of a uniform global standard governing the retention of immigrants' biometric data continues to leave these individuals vulnerable to potential abuse or misuse of their personal information.

[108] The Biometric Information Privacy Act, PA 95-994, 740 ILCS 14/1 (Illinois).

[109] National Identification Authority of India Bill of 2010 <https://prsindia.org/files/bills_acts/bills_parliament/2010/The_National_Identification_Authority_of_India_Bill,_2010.pdf>; The Aadhaar (Targeted Delivery of Financial and Other Subsidies, Benefits and Services) Act, No 18 of 2016 <https://uidai.gov.in/images/targeted_delivery_of_financial_and_other_subsidies_benefits_and_services_13072016.pdf>.

5.2 Intergovernmental Cooperation

5.2.1 Challenges in Intergovernmental Cooperation

Intergovernmental cooperation on the sharing of biometric and biogenetic data is necessary to enhance the suppression of terrorism. However, it also poses several legal challenges.

First is the lack of uniform standards governing the use and sharing of biometric and biogenetic data across borders. Different countries follow distinctive legal frameworks, data protection standards, and technical protocols, making it difficult to establish seamless data sharing mechanisms. The information derived from biometrics and biogenetics is of a highly sensitive nature. Some countries have stringent protection legislation pertaining to such data, while others lack equivalent rules. It may lead to inconsistencies in how data is handled and affect the reliability of intergovernmental cooperation.

The second is the disparities in technological standards. Some nations may have advanced systems in place for handling such data, while others may lack the infrastructure or expertise to manage and exchange information effectively. This disparity in technological capacities can lead to the lack of uniform standards, which makes the data useless in a certain context.

Overall, these challenges affect the integrity of the data, which is necessary for the information to be used in criminal procedures.[110] The following section will examine the efforts made by States to address and overcome them, mainly through the harmonization of national laws.

5.2.2 Biometric Data Sharing Arrangements

Countries may establish bilateral or multilateral agreements for the exchange of biometric data. These agreements typically define the categories of data to be shared, the purposes of the exchange, the data protection measures, and the legal frameworks governing such cooperation.

A notable regional development in this area is the adoption of the Prüm Treaty of 2005 by several EU member states.[111] The treaty provides a legal framework for the exchange of DNA profiles, fingerprints, and vehicle registration data between the signatories. Member States can compare and match biometric information to identify potential matches across different databases. This cooperation

[110] Carole McCartney, 'Forensic Data Exchange: Ensuring Integrity' (2015) 47 Australian Journal of Forensic Sciences 36.

[111] Convention on the Stepping Up of Cross-border Cooperation, Particularly in Combating Terrorism, Cross-border Crime and Illegal Migration (Prüm Convention) (adopted on 27 May 2005, entered into force on 1 November 2006) 2617 UNTS 3. The Prüm Convention was signed on 2005 and open to all members of the European Union. The current member countries are Austria, Belgium, France, Germany, Luxembourg, the Netherlands, and Spain. It also contains provisions for close law enforcement cooperation.

significantly enhances the sharing of biometric data for law enforcement and national security purposes.

The EU Council Decision 2008/615/JHA includes key elements of the Convention on the stepping up of intergovernmental cooperation in combating terrorism and other cross-border cooperation. The Eurodac system further exemplifies a regional approach to biometric data exchange, enabling the collection and comparison of fingerprints for asylum and immigration purposes. Nevertheless, these systems remain a regional initiative, limited to EU member states.

Another significant effort in biometric data exchange is the establishment of interoperability between government databases. For example, the US DHS has developed interoperability between its systems, Automated Biometric Identification System, which was later replaced by Homeland Advanced Recognition Technology System, and partner country databases. This is achieved through the use of advanced encryption protocols, public internet networks, DHS OneNet, and the Customs and Border Protection Gateway, facilitating the secure sharing of biometric and biographic data.

5.2.3 Technological Standards

To enhance the interoperability of the databases, harmonization of technological standards is necessary. In 2014, International Organization for Standardization (ISO) and International Electrotechnical Commission (IEC) adopted ISO/IEC 17025, which is 'the international standard for testing and calibration laboratories. It sets out requirements for the competence, impartiality, and consistent operation of laboratories, ensuring the accuracy and reliability of their testing and calibration results.'[112] The EU has proactively utilized this standard. The Council Framework Decision requires that forensic laboratories and police agencies to have ISO/IEC 17025 accreditation.[113]

5.3 Administration Cooperation through International Organizations

International organizations made efforts to establish interoperability between different biometric systems, enabling seamless sharing and matching of biometric data across borders.

International standards developed by the ICAO help ensure compatibility and consistency in biometric data formats and technologies. ICAO is in charge

[112] ISO, 'ISO/IEC 17025—Testing and Calibration Laboratories' (26 January 2021) <https://www.iso.org/ISO-IEC-17025-testing-and-calibration-laboratories.html>. For a critical assessment of this decision, see McCartney (n 110).

[113] Carole McCartney, Rafaela Granja, and Eric Töpfer, 'Biometric Forensic Identity Databases in Europe: Precariously Balanced or Faulty Scales?' in Andrew Roberts, Joe Purshouse, and Jason Bosland (eds), *Privacy, Technology, and the Criminal Process* (Routledge 2024) 110.

of standardization of the travel documents, such as passports. Its standards require member States to store 'mandatory globally interoperable biometric data' in Machine Readable Travel Documents.[114] The latest version in 2021 requires facial recognition to be stored, while fingerprint and iris recognition is optional. ICAO requires the capacity for data retrieval for a period of ten years, which is the recommended maximum validity period for a travel document. Absence of proprietary elements, ensuring that any investments made by States or organizations in biometrics are safeguarded against changes in infrastructure or suppliers.

Furthermore, the International Criminal Police Organization operates forensic databases that store biometric data, including fingerprints, facial images, and DNA profiles. Member countries can submit and access this data to aid investigations and identify individuals involved in criminal activities across borders. More than 190 jurisdictions are connected through a network.[115]

Although these standards do not directly relate to the MLAT and member States cannot compel other States to share information automatically, they still play a vital role in enhancing police cooperation. By adhering to these standards, States actively strengthen their capacities to collect and store biometric data. The implementation of common practices promotes a more efficient and effective framework for cooperation, even without mandatory information exchange. This proactive approach fosters smoother collaboration and coordination between agencies across borders.

6. Concluding Remarks

As terrorist investigations increasingly depend on the broad collection of communications and financial transaction records, tensions surrounding privacy protection have intensified. Moreover, the distinction between judicial and intelligence agencies has blurred in the context of terrorism-related offences. Enhanced cooperation between these sectors raises concerns about potentially undermining due process.

Creating mechanisms for the cross-border exchange of information related to terrorism offences poses a significant challenge due to the varying privacy protection standards across countries and regions. As this chapter discussed, the United States and its allies addressed this challenge by establishing a network of non-reciprocal or informal agreements, diverging from conventional MLATs.

114 ICAO Doc 9303, *Machine Readable Travel Documents* (8th edn, ICAO 2021) Part 9: Deployment of Biometric Identification and Electronic Storage of Data in MRTDs <https://www.icao.int/publications/documents/9303_p9_cons_en.pdf>.

115 It is reported that there are 18 databases, 100 million police records, 20 million searches per day regarding variety of information such as nominal data, forensic data, documents, and motor vehicles. UNOTC and UNSC CTED (n 103).

In the context of terrorism offences, private individuals lack the ability to seek redress for procedural violations committed extraterritorially in the jurisdictional country, and there have been no efforts to establish new legal remedies for such cases. While joint investigations have been carried out for terrorism offences, no initiatives have aimed to streamline subsequent criminal proceedings by adjusting relevant laws, as has been done for drug offences and organized crime. However, the United States's efforts to strengthen cooperation through bilateral treaties may lead to more unified procedures, potentially reducing the scope for procedural violations.

PART III

DIRECT COOPERATION BETWEEN GOVERNMENTS AND PRIVATE SECTORS

11
Financial Institutions

1. Introduction

This chapter examines the collaboration between governments and financial institutions in tackling financial crimes, with particular emphasis on the implementation and enforcement of anti-money laundering and combating the financing of terrorism (AML/CFT) regulations.[1] It explores how this partnership enhances the resilience of financial systems, ensures adherence to international standards, and mitigates the risks posed by money laundering and terrorist financing.

The criminal act of money laundering is the concealment of the origin of money obtained through illegal activities. The conduct involves knowingly using, transferring, or hiding money or property obtained through predicate offences, intending to disguise its origin or aiding others in avoiding legal responsibility for crimes.[2] The offence of financing terrorism is to provide funds with the knowledge that they will be used to commit a terrorist act.[3] A person may be held criminally liable for financing terrorism even if the provided funds did not directly contribute to the commission of a terrorist act. Both offences involve the act of concealing the trail of financial transactions.

Money laundering is a complex process. The ability of law enforcement to obtain information on suspicious transactions is key to the regulation. Financial institutions and other business entities are required to verify the identity of account holders, report suspicious transactions, and maintain transaction records to regulate both money laundering and financing of terrorism. In the early stages, the AML/CFT regulations primarily focused on suppressing predicate offences, which are the underlying criminal acts that generate illicit proceeds, subsequently concealed or disguised through money laundering activities. However, there has been a shift towards a more comprehensive approach that stresses identifying and curbing unknown and opaque money flows. The current approach aims to disrupt both the sources of illicit funds and the mechanisms used to obscure them.

[1] The author previously discussed the issues arising out of the private-to-private information sharing in Yurika Ishii, 'Information Sharing with the Private Sector under Anti-Money Laundering and Countering the Financing of Terrorism Regulations' (*Research Institute of Economy, Trade and Industry*, January 2024) 24-E-010 <https://www.rieti.go.jp/en/publications/summary/24010014.html>. All websites were last accessed on 31 March 2025.

[2] UNTOC, art 6(2). For the concept of the money laundering, see Dennis Cox, *Handbook of Anti-Money Laundering* (Wiley 2014) 15.

[3] International Convention for the Suppression of the Financing of Terrorism (ICSFT) (adopted on 9 December 1999, entered into force on 10 April 2002) 2178 UNTS 197, art 2.

International Law and the Investigation of Transnational Crimes. Yurika Ishii, Oxford University Press.
 DOI: 10.1093/9780198957089.003.0011

As Section 2 describes, at the international level, States are obliged to renounce both money laundering and financing of terrorism as mandated by international treaties. In addition, the UN Security Council Resolution 1373 (2001), which was adopted immediately after the 9/11 attacks, decided that member States must prevent 'those who finance . . . terrorist acts from using their respective territories for those purposes against other States or their citizens'.[4] It also required member States to afford one another 'the greatest measure of assistance in connection with criminal investigations or criminal proceedings relating to the financing or support of terrorist acts, including assistance in obtaining evidence in their possession necessary for the proceedings'.[5]

The nature, history, and legal implications of government-to-government information sharing for the AML/CFT regulations have been extensively studied since the early 2000s.[6] Challenges associated with information exchange through conventional government-to-government channels are largely dealt with in Part I of this volume. In addition, chapters in Part II explained how the AML/CFT regulations are used to investigate other economic crimes.

This chapter focuses on the direct cooperation between governments and the private sector, particularly financial institutions, and information-sharing mechanisms among these entities. The key issue is how such cooperation can be reconciled with data protection and privacy (DPP) regulations.

Section 2 will briefly describe the basis for information sharing under the AML/CFT regulations at the international level. Then, Section 3 will discuss the potential conflicts between the AML/CFT regulations and the DPP legislation. Section 4 deals with the issues concerning direct cooperation between the government and private sectors, and Section 5 deals with information sharing among private sectors.

2. Obligations under International Law for Government Information Sharing

2.1 Basic Obligations of Financial Institutions under the AML/CFT Regulations

The AML/CFT regulation aims to prevent and suppress the concealment of the origin of the fund. For this purpose, financial institutions and other designated

[4] UNSC Res 1373 (28 September 2001) UN Doc S/RES/1373, para 2(d).

[5] ibid para 2(f).

[6] William C Gilmore, *Dirty Money: The Evolution of International Measures to Counter Money Laundering and the Financing of Terrorism* (Council of Europe Publication 2004); Guy Stessens, *Money Laundering: A New International Law Enforcement Model* (CUP 2000); Mark Pieth and Gemma Aiolfi, *A Comparative Guide to Anti-Money Laundering: A Critical Analysis of Systems in Singapore, Switzerland, the UK and the USA* (Edward Elgar Publishing 2004); Margaret E Beare, *Critical Reflections on Transnational Organized Crime, Money Laundering and Corruption* (University of Toronto Press 2003).

service operators must comply with certain rules and principles. The source of such obligation is primarily the domestic laws of States that have jurisdiction over those institutions. Still, such domestic laws reflect multilayered norms, including multilateral treaties, the UN Security Council resolutions, and the Financial Action Task Force (FATF) recommendations.

The FATF, an intergovernmental body, has established detailed standards for implementing the AML/CFT regulations.[7] A detailed analysis of the substantive obligations is beyond the scope of this volume. However, an overview of the key pillars of the regulations is essential.

First is the customer due diligence (CDD). It requires financial institutions and other regulated entities to verify the identity of their clients and the nature of their transactions (the 'Know Your Customer' principle). Financial institutions must continually monitor transactions for suspicious activity and ensure that the customer's profile remains accurate. When the customer is legal, institutions must identify and verify beneficial owners and understand the organizational control structure.[8] Institutions must ensure the customers are not individuals, entities, or countries subject to sanctions.[9]

Since its Forty Recommendations published in 2012, the FATF has clarified that entities must adopt a risk-based approach. In other words, financial institutions must assess the risk associated with customers, transactions, and geographical locations and apply the appropriate scrutiny level. High-risk clients, such as those with complex ownership structures or connections to politically exposed persons, require heightened scrutiny. Necessary measures include verifying the source of funds, evaluating business relationships, and conducting frequent monitoring.

Second is the obligation of suspicious activity reports (SARs). Financial institutions and other designated entities must notify the government authorities if they detect transactions that may indicate money laundering or other illegal activities. The FATF Recommendation mandates reporting obligations to the authorities for 'gatekeeper' professionals, including real estate brokers, precious metals traders, lawyers, notaries, and accountants. However, the scope is defined in national laws.[10] The records of customer identification and transactions must be kept for a specified period and made available to authorities upon request.

Lastly, the institutions must implement internal controls and compliance to ensure adherence to legal and regulatory requirements. Responsibilities that

[7] FATF, *International Standards on Combating Money Laundering and the Financing of Terrorism & Proliferation* (FATF 2012; last updated in 2025) <https://www.fatf-gafi.org/en/publications/Fatfrecommendations/Fatf-recommendations.html>.

[8] In 2022, the FATF has adopted a detailed guideline concerning beneficial ownership for legal persons. FATF, 'Guidance on Beneficial Ownership for Legal Persons' (10 March 2023) <http://www.fatf-gafi.org/publications/FATFrecommendations/guidance-beneficial-ownership-legal-persons.html>.

[9] FATF, 'International Best Practices: Targeted Financial Sanctions Related to Terrorism and Terrorist Financing Recommendation 6' (June 2013) <https://www.fatf-gafi.org/en/publications/Fatfrecommendations/Bpp-finsanctions-tf-r6.html>.

[10] FATF (n 7) recommendation 7.

could lead to conflicts of interest must be assigned to different individuals or departments. Institutions must regularly train their employees on the anti-money laundering (AML) policies, procedures, and red flags associated with suspicious activities. Institutions should update training programmes to reflect changes in regulations and emerging risks.

Furthermore, institutions must designate a compliance officer responsible for overseeing the AML/CFT programmes.[11] Regular and independent reviews of the AML programme are required to assess its effectiveness. Internal auditors or external third parties may conduct these audits.

2.2 Sources of AML/CFT Regulations

2.2.1 Obligations under Multinational Conventions

The AML/CFT regulations are based on both international law and domestic laws of each State. This section overviews the basic instruments for financial institutions to comply with the regulations.

Money laundering was not prohibited until the United States, for the first time, enacted a domestic law to that effect in 1986. Individuals could be punished for tax evasion, fraud, or violations of banking regulations. However, concealing the origins of illicitly obtained money was not addressed as a crime. In 1970, Congress enacted the Bank Records Act as part of the nation's efforts to combat drug-related offences, requiring banks to report suspicious transactions.[12] In 1986, the Bank Records Act was amended along with the introduction of the Money Laundering Control Act, which defined money laundering as an offence.[13] Restrictions on money laundering offences in countries other than the United States were initially limited, prompting the United States to urge other nations to criminalize money laundering during the late 1980s. In addition, the G7 Summit 1989 decided to establish the FATF, which adopted the first Forty Recommendations in 1990. During

[11] For instance, the United Kingdom designates a Money Laundering Reporting Officer (MLRO), a role first established under the UK Money Laundering Regulations 2007 (SI 2007/2157). The regulation was later replaced by the Money Laundering, Terrorist Financing, and Transfer of Funds (Information on the Payer) Regulations 2017 (SI 2017/692), the core responsibilities of the Money Laundering Reporting Officer have remained unchanged.

[12] The Bank Records and Foreign Transactions Act, Pub L No 91-508, 84 Stat 1114 (1970), Title II, The Currency and Foreign Transactions Reporting Act, 18 USC 5311.

[13] The Money Laundering Control Act, Pub L No 99-570, 100 Stat 3207–3239 (1986), s 1351–67. In addition, the Money Laundering Prosecution Improvement Act, Pub L 100-690, 102 Stat 4354 (1988) and Money Laundering Suppression Act, Pub L No 103-325, 108 Stat 2243 (1994), developed the enforcement mechanism of the AML regulations. For the historical development in the 1980s, see Ronald K Noble, 'A New Anti-Crime Framework for the World: Merging the Objective and Subjective Models for Fighting Money Laundering' (1997) 30 NYU Journal of International Law and Policy 79; Frank C Razzano, 'American Money Laundering Statutes: The Case for a Worldwide System of Banking Compliance Programs' (1994) 3 Journal of International Law and Practice 277.

the late 1980s and early 1990s, the United Kingdom,[14] France,[15] Switzerland,[16] Japan,[17] and others each criminalized money laundering, albeit with varying underlying laws, objectives, and requirements.[18]

To achieve harmonization and establish mechanisms for international cooperation in dealing with crime, the Drug Convention,[19] the United Nations Convention against Transnational Organized Crime (UNTOC),[20] the United Nations Convention against Corruption (UNCAC),[21] and the recommendations of the FATF served as the significant basis. The inclusion of provisions criminalizing money laundering in the UNCAC was motivated by recognizing the linkages between the UNCAC and the UNTOC and the perceived interrelationship between money laundering and corruption.[22] Moreover, the Council of Europe (CoE) Convention on Laundering, Search, Seizure, and Confiscation of the Proceeds of Crime aims to harmonize laws governing money laundering offences among the Member States of the CoE.[23]

The Office for Drug Control and Crime Prevention, which is in charge of suppressing transnational crimes, started to manage the Global Programme Against Money Laundering, which provides technical support for criminal investigations. The UNODC established the International Money Laundering Information Network in 1998, which is a network to facilitate exchanges of information and intelligence on money laundering and related crimes among law enforcement agencies and financial institutions.

[14] In the United Kingdom, money laundering of proceeds from drug offences was criminalized under Drug Trafficking Offences Act 1986, c 32, art 24(1). Such an act became criminalized in 1990 under Criminal Justice International Cooperation Act 1990, c 5, art 14(1)–(3) and the detailed procedure was established under Proceeds of Crime Act 2002, c 29, which was amended in 2005.

[15] In France, money laundering of proceeds from drug-related crimes was criminalized in 1987. See Code de la santé publique, art 627(1)–(3). The money laundering was comprehensively prohibited in 1996. See Loi no 96-392 du 13 mai 1996 relative à la lutte contre le blanchiment et le trafic des stupéfiants et à la coopération internationale en matière de saisie et de confiscation des produits du crime, JORF n°112 du 14 mai 1996, 7208.

[16] Code Pénal, art 305bis, 305ter.

[17] Special Narcotics Law, Act No 94 of 1991. Japan enacted the Act on Prevention of Transfer of Criminal Proceeds, Act No 22 of 2007, to comprehensively regulate money laundering. For the Japanese approach on money laundering after the 2010s, see Ryu Nakasaki, *Hanzai Shūeki Iten Bōshi Hō* (Independently published, 8th edn, 2025).

[18] Pieth and Aiolfi (n 6) 12.

[19] Drug Convention, art 3(b). The UN commentary states that '[t]heir content and drafting style owe much to the then current legislation of the United States in this area'. United Nations, 'Commentary on the United Nations Convention against Illicit Traffic in Narcotic Drugs and Psychotropic Substances 1988' (1998) UN Doc E/CN.7/590, 62 <https://digitallibrary.un.org/record/266894>.

[20] UNTOC, art 6.

[21] UNCAC, art 26.

[22] For case studies on the relationship between money laundering and corruption, see David A Chaikin, *Corruption and Money Laundering: A Symbiotic Relationship* (Palgrave Macmillan 2009); Beare (n 6).

[23] Council of Europe, Criminal Law Convention on Corruption (opened for signature on 27 January 1999, entered into force on 1 July 2002) ETS No 173. See also Council of Europe, Civil Law Convention on Corruption (opened for signature on 4 November 1999, entered into force on 1 November 2003) ETS No 174.

In the meantime, the International Convention for the Suppression of the Financing of Terrorism (ICSFT) was adopted by the United Nations in 1999. It requires member states to criminalize terrorist financing, establish jurisdictions to prosecute offenders, and impose extradition or prosecution obligations on the State where the suspect is located to prevent evasion of prosecution.[24] Additionally, the convention requires implementing legal measures to identify, detect, freeze, and seize funds intended for terrorism and the proceeds derived from terrorist activities.[25] While the instrument does not provide for the money laundering regulation, there is a significant procedural overlap between the regulation of the crime of financing terrorism and that of money laundering.[26]

Other international conventions have also been established to address the offence. The Organization of American States adopted the Anti-Terrorism Convention in 2002,[27] while the CoE agreed on the Convention on the Freezing of the Proceeds of Crime and the Prevention of the Financing of Terrorism in 2005.[28] These conventions share similar procedural obligations and address the crime of terrorist financing in conjunction with money laundering.

2.2.2 Financial Action Task Force Recommendations

(1) Organizational Structure and the Mandates

The key to the AML/CFT regulations is the FATF Recommendations. The FATF is an intergovernmental body, and as of October 2024, there are forty member States. Its plenary, where its members participate, adopts recommendations, standards, and guidance. The FATF membership is restricted to countries capable of complying with the Recommendations.[29] There are Associate Members, which are FATF-style regional bodies, as designated by the FATF, that participate in the work of the FATF.

The FATF's main objectives are to facilitate the implementation of AML regulations under the Drug Convention and other treaties by (1) establishing and reviewing international standards on AML, (2) evaluating the extent of implementation of those standards, (3) recommending compliance with the FATF

[24] ICSFT, art 2.

[25] ibid art 8.

[26] The International Court of Justice held its interpretation regarding the scope and obligations of the ICSFT in detail. See Chapter 2, Section 5.3, of this volume. Application of the International Convention for the Suppression of the Financing of Terrorism and of the International Convention on the Elimination of All Forms of Racial Discrimination (*Ukraine v Russian Federation*) (Judgment) (ICJ, 31 January 2024) <https://www.icj-cij.org/case/166/judgments>.

[27] Inter-American Convention against Terrorism (adopted on 3 June 2002, entered into force on 10 July 2003) OAS Treaty A-66.

[28] Council of Europe Convention on Laundering, Search, Seizure and Confiscation of the Proceeds from Crime and on the Financing of Terrorism (adopted on 16 May 2005, entered into force on 1 May 2008) CETS No 198.

[29] FATF, 'Mandate of the Financial Action Task Force' (2019) <https://www.fatf-gafi.org/en/the-fatf/mandate-of-the-fatf.html#accordion-ffd0cfcabc-item-145fe38728>.

Recommendations in countries and territories that are not FATF participants, and (4) researching money laundering and terrorist financing *modus operandi* and trends.

In 1990, the FATF issued its first Forty Recommendations, which set out guidelines for regulating money laundering offences. Following the 9/11 attacks in 2001, the organization expanded its mandate to deal with the issue of the financing of terrorism. They set specific standards for the domestic regulation of money laundering and terrorist financing crimes, with particular criteria for regulating these crimes. The most recent version of the document was adopted in 2012 and has since been updated.

The FATF Recommendations are not legally binding. They were deliberately designed as such to speed up decision-making on technical matters.[30] However, if a financial institution does not comply with the standards, other States may restrict its transactions. The system's power comes from the cost of non-compliance, namely exclusion from the US- or EU-based private financial infrastructure.[31] The member States are to domestically implement the recommendations as binding law. In addition, the FATF has implemented a peer review system to provide feedback to member States that do not comply with the regulations.

The FATF's mandate has expanded over time. After the 9/11 attacks in 2001, the organization broadened its scope to include combating the financing of terrorism.[32] The Forty Recommendations incorporated measures to prevent proliferation financing, specifically targeting the funding of weapons of mass destruction programmes. Against the background is the Security Council Resolutions that require member States to implement these measures.[33]

The FATF created regional counterparts, or FATF-style regional bodies, to promote AML efforts tailored to regional cooperation practices. There are now nine such regional bodies beginning with the Caribbean FATF. In parallel, the FATF expanded its AML framework through the Egmont Group, formed in 1995. This

[30] For an overview of the FATF's institutional characteristics that enable flexibility in harmonizing domestic standards, see Junji Nakagawa, *International Harmonization of Economic Regulation* (OUP 2011) 279.

[31] For the impact of such a mechanism, James Cockayne, 'Counterterrorism and Transnational Crime' in Jacob Katz Cogan, Ian Hurd, and Ian Johnstone (eds), *The Oxford Handbook of International Organizations* (1st edn, OUP 2017) 216. See also Joost Pauwelyn, Ramses Wessel, and Jan Wouters, 'When Structures Become Shackles: Stagnation and Dynamics in International Lawmaking' (2014) 25 European Journal of International Law 733, 746.

[32] In October 2001, it adopted Special Nine Recommendations to set out the basic framework to detect, prevent, and suppress the financing of terrorism and terrorist acts. FATF, 'IX Special Recommendations' (October 2001) <https://www.fatf-gafi.org/en/publications/Fatfrecommendations/Ixspecialrecommendations.html>. These recommendations were integrated and published in the Forty Recommendations in 2012.

[33] FATF, 'FATF Guidance, The Implementation of Financial Provisions of United Nations Security Council Resolutions to Counter the Proliferation of Weapons of Mass Destruction' (June 2013) <https://www.fatf-gafi.org/content/dam/fatf-gafi/guidance/Guidance-UNSCRS-Prolif-WMD.pdf.coredownload.pdf>.

group, composed of financial intelligence units (FIUs) from various countries, focused on sharing information and expertise to strengthen AML systems globally, thereby becoming a key mechanism for international AML cooperation.

(2) Harmonization of National Legislations of Non-Member States of the FATF

The FATF member countries have developed national legislation on money laundering since the 1990s. However, non-member countries did not, partly due to the cost of implementing AML measures and conflicting policies that prioritize investor confidentiality. Nonetheless, if AML measures are not implemented in non-member countries, the regulations imposed by FATF member states will be ineffective. Therefore, the FATF has pushed non-member states to adopt its standards in three ways.

First, the FATF's standards have been adopted by incorporating the Forty Recommendations by G8 summit participating countries into the international cooperation framework for building and maintaining a stable global financial system. These standards are to be followed by the countries involved. The G8 member States developed the international financial architecture in response to the global economic turmoil of the late 1990s, including the Russian economic crisis of 1997 and the Asian currency crisis of 1998. Its primary objective is strengthening international cooperation in regulating and monitoring the financial system.

The International Monetary Fund (IMF) is the primary mechanism for international cooperation to maintain a stable global financial system. Its purpose is to stabilize exchange rates, balance the balance of payments, and provide loans to member countries when necessary. The constituent instrument requires the IMF to 'oversee the compliance of each member with its obligations'.[34] Under this provision, the IMF can survey and monitor member countries' economic and financial sector policies. It enables the IMF to analyse risks to the currency system and other aspects of a member country's domestic policies, such as fiscal, monetary, and exchange rate matters, and provide policy advice accordingly. Since the economic crisis of 1998, the scope of IMF monitoring has expanded to address the globalization of the economy and large-scale private capital flows. One of the items assessed in the monitoring is whether countries comply with international standards and rules on financial regimes, including the FATF Forty Recommendations.

The IMF and the World Bank jointly initiated the Financial Sector Assessment Programme in 1999 to evaluate member countries' adherence to consistent standards.

Additionally, the G7 established the Financial Stability Forum (FSF) in 1999, which was reorganized into the Financial Stability Board in 2014. The objective

[34] Agreement of the International Monetary Fund (signed on 22 July 1944, entered into force 27 December 1945) 2 UNTS 39, art 4.

of the FSF was to monitor markets in member countries and promote a sound financial system. As part of its monitoring criteria, the FSF refers to the Forty Recommendations set by the FATF.

The Basel Committee on Banking Supervision, the International Association of Insurance Supervisors, and the International Organization of Securities Commissions have recommended adherence to the Forty Recommendations when it comes to cross-border fund transfers. Integrating the FATF standards into international financial architectures imposes the obligations on States to comply with these guidelines.

Second, the FATF mandates its member countries to ensure that financial institutions operating within their jurisdiction exercise due diligence when conducting transactions with individuals, legal entities, or financial institutions from countries or territories that fail to comply with the FATF's recommendations. Financial institutions must 'apply enhanced due diligence measures to business relationships and transactions with natural and legal persons, and financial institutions, from countries for which the FATF calls for this'.[35] Additionally, if branches or subsidiaries of financial institutions located within a member country operate in a non-cooperative jurisdiction, they are required to verify the identity of their customers.

Third, the FATF has published a list of countries and territories that are non-compliant with AML regulations, imposing a special obligation on financial institutions in member countries when carrying out transactions with these listed entities.

Initially, the FATF was not willing to identify any countries that had or had not adequate AML measures in place. Its 1990 report stressed that non-cooperative jurisdictions sought to gain an advantage by avoiding national regulations and not implementing FATF Recommendations due to administrative costs. However, the report concluded that creating a list of these countries and territories was unnecessary. Instead, the FATF recommended using public and peer pressure to encourage non-cooperative countries to cooperate with its recommendations. Consequently, the 1990 Recommendations, Recommendations 21 and 22, only imposed a special duty of care on FATF member country financial institutions when dealing with individuals, legal entities, and financial institutions from countries and territories that did not comply with the Recommendations or were only partially compliant.[36]

An example of the exploitation of regulatory loopholes despite increased regulation was the Seychelles Economic Development Act of 1995.[37] The act allowed foreign investors investing more than USD 10 million in licensed financial

35 FATF (n 7) recommendation 19.

36 FATF, *Report 1990-1991* (1991) 16 <https://www.fatf-gafi.org/content/dam/fatf-gafi/annual-reports/1990%201991%20ENG.pdf>.

37 Economic Development Act, Act No 20 of 1995, Official Gazette, Supplement (4 December 1995) 275–82.

instruments in Seychelles to be exempt from criminal prosecution for all offences and asset confiscation, except in cases of violent crimes and illegal drug trafficking within Seychelles.[38] It also provided immunity from compulsory acquisition or sequestration of the assets belonging to an investor other than a confiscation or forfeiture made by the court concerning such a criminal proceeding.[39] In response, the FATF General Assembly issued a press release in 1996 urging member and non-member states to enforce Recommendation 21 concerning Seychelles and to exert pressure on Seychelles to repeal the legislation.[40] Subsequently, the country and the FATF held discussions on the issue, and in March 1996, Seychelles enacted the Money Laundering Control Act.[41] However, the Act did not amend the exemptions in the Economic Development Act, and was repealed only in July 2000.[42]

In May 1998, the G7 Finance Ministers Summit recognized the issue of non-member countries of the FATF passing legislation that undermines the effectiveness of international AML measures. They requested the FATF to consider measures to address this problem. As a result, the FATF established a working group on non-cooperative countries and regions to evaluate the issue. The working group's report, released in February 2000, presented four criteria for determining whether a country or region is non-cooperative: (1) inadequate financial regulation, (2) lack of regulations concerning money laundering, (3) insufficient international cooperation, and (4) inadequate resources to prevent or detect money laundering activities.

The FATF identified twenty-three jurisdictions as non-cooperative based on the criteria outlined in the working group's report.[43] The areas identified as non-cooperative overlap with those identified in the Organisation for Economic Co-operation and Development (OECD)'s Harmful Tax Competition Practices report. The report emphasized the importance of transparency criteria and co-operation with information exchange.

The FATF continued to monitor non-cooperative jurisdictions and urged them to improve their implementation of AML measures. As countries and jurisdictions progressed, they were removed from the non-cooperative list. In many cases, improvements were based on enacting new money laundering control laws rather than the extent of their implementation. For instance, the Cayman Islands

38 ibid s 5(7)(a).

39 ibid s 5(7)(b).

40 FATF, 'Financial Action Task Force on Money Laundering: Annual Report 1995–1996' (28 June 1996) 17 <https://www.fatf-gafi.org/content/dam/fatf-gafi/annual-reports/1995%201996%20ENG.pdf>.

41 ibid. See also Stessens (n 6) 199–208; Gilmore (n 6) 142.

42 Economic Development (Repeal) Act, Act No 9 of 2000, Official Gazette, Acts (2 August 2000) 57–58.

43 The FATF made these designations three times, in June 2000, 2001, and 2002. See FATF, 'About the Non-Cooperative Countries and Territories NCCT Initiative' <https://www.fatf-gafi.org/en/publications/Fatfgeneral/Aboutthenon-cooperativecountriesandterritoriesncctinitiative.html>.

introduced money laundering regulations in 2000 under its Proceeds of Crime Act, which imposed reporting requirements on financial institutions.[44] Similarly, the Virgin Islands enacted money laundering regulations in 2008 under its Proceeds of Crime Act of 1997, prohibiting financial institutions from doing business with shell banks.[45] Compliance with this requirement resulted in their removal from the list.

The FATF continually identifies and reviews jurisdictions with strategic AML/CFT deficiencies that pose risks to the international financial system and closely monitors their progress. The FATF's International Co-operation Review Group oversees this process, which four regional Joint Groups carry out. Jurisdictions under review may meet face-to-face with the Joint Group to discuss its analysis before FATF plenary meetings. The FATF established this process in 2007 and updated it in 2009 and 2015 to reflect revised FATF standards and the mutual evaluation process.[46]

Initially, the list of non-cooperative jurisdictions was unbalanced, with stricter criteria for designation than the 'Forty Recommendations', which were used to assess the implementation of the Recommendations by member States or the criteria for assessment when joining the FATF. Additionally, no FATF member State had ever been designated as a non-cooperative country or territory. Certain countries, such as Austria, Switzerland, and Luxembourg, were not considered for designation despite concerns about their regulatory transparency. Moreover, the list has been accused of bias towards tax havens with offshore markets. In contrast, Southeast Asian and Middle Eastern countries with strict regulations on foreign capital but lack transparency in regulation have not been included. The FATF revised its approach to address these concerns and to improve fairness and transparency.

It is noted that the FATF's call for non-member countries to adopt and implement its standards is tied to capacity-building efforts. Enforcing AML regulations involves substantial administrative costs, such as setting up a FIU, fostering co-operation with financial institutions, and bolstering law enforcement capabilities.[47] To support this, the FATF has established capacity-building programmes.[48]

44 The Proceeds of Criminal Conduct Law (1999 Revision), The Money Laundering Regulations 2000, Supplement No 1, Extraordinary Gazette No 9 (7 August 2000).

45 Proceeds of Criminal Conduct Act 1997, No 5; Anti-Money Laundering and Terrorist Financing Code of Practice 2008, No 22 <https://www.fiabvi.vg/Portals/0/Anti-Money-Laundering-and-Terrorist-Financing-Code-of-Practice-2008.pdf>. Section 34 of the 2008 Act prohibits an entity from entering into or maintain a correspondent relationship with a shell bank and from keeping or maintaining an anonymous account or an account in a fictitious name. For the implementation of the AML/CFT regulations in Caribbean States, see also Rose Marie Belle Antoine, *Confidentiality in Offshore Financial Law* (OUP, 2nd edn, 2014) 87.

46 FATF, 'High-Risk and Other Monitored Jurisdictions' <https://www.fatf-gafi.org/en/publications/High-risk-and-other-monitored-jurisdictions/More-on-high-risk-and-non-cooperative-jurisdictions.html>.

47 Stessens (n 6) 199.

48 FATF, 'Guidance on Capacity Building for Mutual Evaluations and Implementation of the FATF Standards' (29 February 2008) <https://www.fatf-gafi.org/content/dam/fatf-gafi/guidance/Capacity%20building%20LCC.pdf.coredownload.pdf>.

Additionally, the UNTOC contains provisions to support developing countries in addressing these challenges.[49]

2.2.3 Self-Regulations of Financial Institutions

Financial institutions moved towards forming networks to ensure compliance with the AML/CFT regulations. The Wolfsberg Group, comprising twelve central banks from the United States, the United Kingdom, Switzerland, Germany, France, and Japan, took the lead.[50] Starting with adopting the Anti-Money Laundering Principles in 2000, the group has developed several guidelines to control terrorist financing, establish and maintain correspondent relationships between banks, and other guidelines on laundering. The Principles are a non-binding set of best practice guidelines on relationships between private bankers and clients. Banks that engage in business with financial institutions, which are members of these regulatory groups, must adhere to the established guidelines. These regulations became effective, and as such, a business relationship ensures broader compliance.

3. Data Protection and Privacy Legislations and the AML/CFT Regulations

3.1 Obligations under DPP Regulations

The obligations placed on financial institutions to collect data under AML/CFT regulations may conflict with the underlying principles of DPP laws. The DPP legislation establishes, among other things, the security management obligations of businesses concerning data handling, including non-personal information.[51] The primary purpose is to require companies to manage data for industrial promotion and security purposes. The data related to a transaction might not inherently qualify as personal information. Nevertheless, if the transaction record contains

[49] UNTOC, arts 28, 30–31.

[50] The following banks form the constituent group: ABN AMRO from the Netherlands, Banco Santander from Spain, Bank of Tokyo-Mitsubishi UFJ from Japan, Barclays from the United Kingdom, Citigroup from the United States, Credit Suisse from Switzerland, Deutsche Bank from Germany, Goldman Sachs from the United States, HSBC from the United Kingdom, JP Morgan Chase from the United States, Société Générale from France, and UBS from Switzerland. See Gemma Aiolfi and Hans-Peter Bauer, 'The Wolfsberg Group' in Mark Pieth (ed), *Collective Action: Innovative Strategies to Prevent Corruption* (Dike Verlag 2012); Kris Hinterseer, 'The Wolfsberg Anti-Money Laundering Principles' (2001) 5 Journal of Money Laundering Control 25 <https://www.emerald.com/insight/content/doi/10.1108/eb027291/full/html>.

[51] China, Data Security Law (adopted on 10 June 2021) <http://www.npc.gov.cn/npc/c30834/202106/7c9af12f51334a73b56d7938f99a788a.shtml>; India, Information Technology Act 2000, The Information Technology (Reasonable Security Practices and Procedures and Sensitive Personal Data or Information) Rules 2011 (Notification of the Department of Information Technology, 11 April 2011).

the individuals' identities, then the DPP legislation applies. The OECD has worked on harmonizing data protection principles. It renewed the 1980 Guideline in 2013 and set out eight basic principles: collection limitation, data quality, purpose specification, use limitation, security safeguards, openness, individual participation, and accountability.[52]

Collecting financial information can be particularly invasive, as it may expose details about a person's activities. However, this issue has received less attention, partly because not all financial information qualifies as personal information. In addition, gaps may exist between AML/CFT regulations and DPP regulations, as different regulatory bodies typically oversee them.

States have increasingly promoted collaboration among private sector entities after the FATF adopted the Forty Recommendations in 2012. The practice involves encouraging these entities to combine their data resources and employ artificial intelligence (AI) technology to identify and filter suspicious customers and transactions. Information sharing can yield several benefits when executed effectively, including enhancing cybersecurity, driving innovation, and improving operational efficiency. However, it also raises concerns about privacy, security, and competition that must be carefully addressed and managed. Issues would be compounded if such information sharing becomes mandatory as part of the regulations. Additionally, information sharing may transcend national borders. In such a scenario, requiring entities to share such information could conflict with national privacy laws, other human rights norms, and DPP legislation.

In general, the digitalization of transactions can enhance the effectiveness of regulatory efforts. Banks can amass extensive data, including usage patterns of automated teller machines and mobile net banking systems, along with audio and visual data from these interactions. Users also have the option to voluntarily provide supplementary transaction-related information, such as shopping histories and travel records. AI can detect suspicious transactions and patterns that might indicate money laundering activities. The technology can also provide constant real-time monitoring of transactions, reducing manual reviews and operational expenses.

On the other hand, the risks of data-driven technologies have been well recognized. The consequences of profiling with data may harm personal privacy and safety by making it difficult for individuals to make autonomous choices. It may also foster social discrimination. For example, financial institutions may unfairly target specific demographics or regions. Legitimate transactions from

[52] OECD, '*Recommendation of the Council concerning Guidelines Governing the Protection of Privacy and Transborder Flows of Personal Data*' (adopted on 23 September 1980, amended on 11 July 2013) OECD/LEGAL/0188 <https://www.oecd.org/en/topics/privacy-principles.html>.

marginalized groups might be flagged more frequently. Legislation and policies are being developed based on data ethics in the design of the technology.[53]

To this end, the OECD adopted a Council Recommendation on AI in May 2019,[54] which led to the launch of the Global Partnership on AI initiative by volunteer countries, including Japan and the European Union, in June 2020.[55] The European Commission also proposed a new regulation on AI in April 2021.[56] Furthermore, the European Commission submitted its proposal for a regulation in 2021. Using AI to assess the trustworthiness of individuals based on their social behaviour or personal characteristics, leading to adverse treatment in unrelated social contexts, is prohibited when done by public authorities or on their behalf for market purposes, service deployment, or general use.[57] Other moves include establishing the OECD Expert Network,[58] creating a special committee in the CoE,[59] and formulating guidelines at the national level.[60]

On the other hand, the DPP legislation's contents vary from jurisdiction to jurisdiction. In addition, government agencies responsible for financial regulations and those overseeing personal information protection operate independently and typically do not engage in collaborative efforts. This results in a distinct gap between these two regulatory frameworks.

3.2 Potential Conflicts

The AML/CFT regulations may cause several concerns when they require financial institutions to collect extensive user data. One of the concerns pertains to the possibility of excessive data collection. In the context of AML/CFT regulations, while collecting information is essential for identifying and preventing illicit

[53] Jessica Fjeld and others, 'Principled Artificial Intelligence: Mapping Consensus in Ethical and Rights-Based Approaches to Principles for AI' (15 January 2020) Berkman Klein Center Research Publication No 2020-1 <http://dx.doi.org/10.2139/ssrn.3518482>. Data ethics is the ethics of evaluating the issues posed by algorithms and formulating morally desirable directions, including the generation, recording, curation, processing, distribution, sharing, and use of data and information.

[54] OECD, *Recommendation of the Council on Artificial Intelligence* (22 May 2019) OECD/LEGAL/0449 <https://legalinstruments.oecd.org/en/instruments/OECD-LEGAL-0449>.

[55] The Global Partnership on Artificial Intelligence <https://gpai.ai>.

[56] EU, 'Proposal for a Regulation of the European Parliament and of the Council Laying Down Harmonised Rules on Artificial Intelligence (Artificial Intelligence Act) and Amending Certain Union Legislative Acts' COM (2021) 206 final; European Commission, 'White Paper on Artificial Intelligence: A European Approach to Excellence and Trust' (19 February 2020) <https://ec.europa.eu/info/publications/white-paper-artificial-intelligence-european-approach-excellence-and-trust_en>.

[57] The Proposal Article 6 provides classification rules for high-risk AI systems.

[58] OECD Network of Experts on Artificial Intelligence (ONE AI) <https://oecd.ai/en/network-of-experts>.

[59] Council of Europe, CAHAI (Ad hoc Committee on Artificial Intelligence) <https://www.coe.int/en/web/artificial-intelligence/cahai>.

[60] See OECD, 'AI Policy Observatory' <https://oecd.ai> for country developments.

financial activities, institutions may gather all data related to users' financial activities, which may be irrelevant to detecting such unlawful conduct. One of the core principles of the DPP legislation is the minimum data principle. It requires the personal data necessary to be collected, stored, or processed for a specific, legitimate purpose and should be used only for that purpose. It could be against this principle if institutions utilize the data for purposes beyond what suppression of the money laundering activities requires. This scenario could involve financial institutions using the data to profile customers' financial credibility.

In addition, financial institutions must keep records of financial transactions for certain years after the business relationship ends or after the transaction date. The FATF Recommendation requires that institutions keep records for at least five years.[61] States must set the same standard for the AML/CFT regulations and the DPP legislation to avoid the potential conflict.

The standards in AML/CFT regulations are not as well established compared to this general trend. It is essential to mitigate the risks of conflicts between different sets of laws. Additionally, regulatory bodies should provide clear guidelines and oversight to ensure responsible digital technologies in AML efforts.

After the FATF adopted its Forty Recommendations in 2012,[62] it advocated for financial institutions to share information concerning financial activity with potential connections to criminal activities. The proposals are reflected in the FATF Recommendations and Immediate Outcomes. The FATF acknowledges numerous legal limitations and operational hurdles that hinder the efficient sharing of information among various financial institutions within the same corporate group and the exchange of information between financial institutions that are not affiliated with each other.

Considering the potential obstacles, the FATF issued a report in 2017 to articulate how to align the demands for information sharing, the FATF Recommendations, and DPP legislation.[63] The report includes case studies, including examples of collaboration with authorities responsible for DPP. In addition to this report, it has published several guidance and documents concerning information sharing among private sector members.[64]

The FATF proposes overarching recommendations for information sharing and collaborative analytics to improve AML/CFT effectiveness.[65] The first is to

[61] FATF (n 7) recommendation 11.

[62] ibid.

[63] FATF, 'FATF Guidance: Private Sector Information Sharing' (2017) <https://www.fatf-gafi.org/en/publications/Fatfgeneral/Guidance-information-sharing.html>.

[64] FATF, 'FATF Recommendations 18 and 23: The Application of Group-Wide Programmes by Non-Financial Businesses and Professions, Explanatory Materials' (2021) <https://www.fatf-gafi.org/content/dam/fatf-gafi/recommendations/Explanatory-Materials-R18-R23.pdf>.

[65] FATF, 'Partnering in the Fight against Financial Crime: Data Protection, Technology and Private Sector Information Sharing' (July 2022) <https://www.fatf-gafi.org/content/dam/fatf-gafi/guidance/Partnering-int-the-fight-against-financial-crime.pdf.coredownload.pdf>.

prepare a data protection impact assessment to define the purpose and objectives of information sharing; the data to be processed; why such data are necessary, reasonable, and proportional to achieve the purpose; and the legal basis and safeguards. The second is to engage with DPP authorities from the beginning of the sharing project at the design stage. The third is to examine safeguards to protect customer data adequately. The FATF is aware that there is no one-size-fits-all solution that addresses AML/CFT/, countering the financing of proliferation of weapons of mass destruction, and DPP objectives for all financial institutions at the global level.

Furthermore, the FATF has adopted the San Jose Principles, which are a set of guidelines to promote cooperation between the public and private sectors concerning the use of innovative financial technologies, including AI and blockchain, and to seek a balance to encourage technological innovation and the management of AML/CFT risks.[66] Most notably, it aims for a regulatory environment that is commercially neutral, respects the level playing field, and minimizes regulatory inconsistency both domestically and internationally. In 2021, the FATF issued further recommendations to enhance these principles.[67]

Nevertheless, privacy issues are not the primary concern of the FATF standards and regulations. It is not mandated to designate how to reconcile these potentially conflicting demands. The resolution of potential conflicts between AML/CFT regulations and DPP legislation is addressed nationally.

Given this context, this section raises potential queries about situations arising within international law due to possible clashes with foreign data protection laws and privacy regulations.

4. Direct Cooperation between the Government and Financial Institutions

From an international law perspective, there seems to be little problem for a government to collect information from entities under its jurisdiction as long as it complies with human rights law. However, this section identifies two issues specific to extensive information-gathering requirements imposed on financial institutions through counterterrorism programmes.

[66] FATF 'FinTech and RegTech Forum 2017' (26 May 2017) <https://www.fatf-gafi.org/en/publications/Fatfgeneral/Fatf-fintech-regtech-forum-may-2017.html>; FATF, 'Opportunities and Challenges of New Technologies for AML/CFT' (July 2021) 52, para 155 <https://www.fatf-gafi.org/content/dam/fatf-gafi/guidance/Opportunities-Challenges-of-New-Technologies-for-AML-CFT.pdf>.

[67] FATF (n 63).

4.1 Enhanced Cooperation between Governments and Financial Institutions

Governments have developed various mechanisms for close cooperation with financial institutions to enhance the ability of financial institutions to identify, assess, and manage risks associated with high-risk customers or transactions.

First, governments and financial institutions exchange sensitive information on high-risk individuals or entities. Governments may provide detailed risk profiles or intelligence on customers suspected of money laundering, terrorist financing, or other financial crimes. An example is the UK Joint Money Laundering Intelligence Taskforce, a partnership between law enforcement and the financial sector to exchange and analyse information relating to money laundering and wider economic threats. The Taskforce comprises over forty financial institutions, the Financial Conduct Authority, Cifas, and law enforcement agencies, namely the National Crime Agency, the His Majesty's Revenue and Customs, the Serious Fraud Office, the City of London Police, and the Metropolitan Police Service.

When financial institutions submit SARs to governmental authorities, the government may provide feedback on trends or specific cases, disclosing information highlighting risky customers. It enables institutions to better refine their monitoring processes for similar risks.

Second, governments often maintain lists of individuals and entities subject to sanctions or considered high-risk for financial crimes. Such lists are published and shared with financial institutions through official databases, including the UN Consolidated Sanctions List and the US Treasury's Office of Foreign Assets Control sanctions list. Financial institutions must screen customers against these lists and report suspicious activities. In cases where governments uncover specific threats or financial crimes, they may engage in targeted intelligence sharing with select financial institutions. Examples may include providing information on individuals or networks involved in illicit activities and allowing institutions to enhance their monitoring of associated accounts or transactions.

Conflicts may occur when the requirements under the FATF standards and the DPP legislation of a State are at odds. Although the FATF instruments are not legally binding, they hold de facto authority, compelling States to comply. The FATF is aware of such risks, as described in Section 3.3, although it does not have a mandate or capacity to look into the DPP legislation. States must ensure that any data collection, retention, or sharing under AML laws aligns with privacy standards, limiting data use to its intended purpose and safeguarding against misuse or unnecessary access.

4.2 The Society for Worldwide Interbank Telecommunications

International conflicts can arise when actions taken by one State impact another. A notable example is the case involving the Society for Worldwide Interbank

Financial Telecommunications (SWIFT). The SWIFT is an institution that facilitates the exchange of financial information, such as fund settlement messages relating to customer transfers, interbank transfers, and securities-related transactions. It operates with over 8,000 registered institutions in more than 200 countries.

The events of the 9/11 attacks had a profound impact on the regulatory landscape governing financial transactions. Following the attacks, the United States implemented the Terrorist Financing Tracking Program (TFTP) and established regulations that exceeded the FATF standards. In response to the attacks, the President issued Executive Order 13224, granting the Treasury Department the authority to identify and freeze the assets of foreign individuals or entities involved in terrorist activities or present a significant risk of such activities.[68] This regulation aims to prevent the provision of financial support to terrorist groups. Consequently, the Treasury Department is empowered to mandate financial institutions to divulge their clients' transaction histories.

As an element of the programme, as mentioned above, the United States has enforced a subpoena with associated penalties upon the SWIFT, mandating data submission. While the organization is headquartered in Belgium, some of its servers were in Washington DC at the time.

Monitoring financial transactions serves not only to investigate terrorist financing and related activities but also to investigate actual terrorist incidents. While the Treasury Department is responsible for tracking terrorist financing, the information gathered is shared with the FBI and other law enforcement agencies to support their investigations. There have been instances in which servers have been confiscated to probe money laundering offences. With the aid of this programme, the United States can track the trading patterns of individuals and entities in foreign countries and reproduce their terrorist networks, thereby precluding the occurrence of terrorist crimes.

There is a contention that the method mentioned above of investigation runs counter to the principle of proportionality. The primary server utilized by SWIFT is situated in Belgium, the organization's headquarters. Consequently, the European Parliament passed a resolution in 2006 proclaiming that data transfers violate the 1995 Data Protection Directive.[69] Moreover, a report issued by a Commission working group revealed that the data protection framework in the United States lacks transparency, and transferring data to the United States would breach the 1995 Directive and contradict key European principles on data protection.[70] The report further asserts that the battle against terrorism can be tackled

[68] Executive Order 13224 (23 September 2001).

[69] European Parliament, Resolution of 6 July 2006 on the Interception of Bank Transfer Date from the SWIFT System by the US Secret Services [2006] OJ C303E/843.

[70] Article 29 Data Protection Working Party, 'Opinion 10/2006 on the Processing of Personal Data by the Society for Worldwide Interbank Financial Telecommunication (SWIFT)' (22 November 2006).

within the existing international framework and that the protection of fundamental rights, which are the foundation of democratic societies, must not be diminished for crime control measures.[71]

There was back and forth between the US Treasury and the European Union concerning using SWIFT data in the TFTP. The Treasury Department asserted that the TFTP has multiple layers of governmental and independent controls to ensure data is used solely for counterterrorism, retained only as necessary, and securely managed.[72] The issue was resolved by establishing an independent authority on the EU side to ensure data protection. The European Commission consulted with the President of the Committee of Permanent Representatives and the President of the Committee on Civil Liberties, Justice and Home Affairs of the European Parliament and decided to appoint an independent authority to monitor compliance to verify the protection of personal data originating in the European Union.[73] In December 2008, the Belgian Data Protection Commission (Commission belge de la Protection de la Vie Privée) concluded that SWIFT complied with all applicable Belgian data protection legislation.[74] In February 2009, the European Commission confirmed that the US Treasury has, from the outset, respected the safeguards in handling personal data obtained from SWIFT under subpoena.[75]

The United States and the European Union agreed in January 2010 to transfer this information to the US Treasury (the TFTP Agreement).[76] This agreement outlines the terms and conditions under which the EU authorities can provide funds settlement message data to US authorities for counterterrorism purposes.[77] It applies to acquiring and utilizing financial payment messages and associated data to prevent, investigate, detect, or prosecute terrorist acts or individuals associated with them.[78] The parties will jointly or individually ensure that providers of international financial settlement message services furnish the US Treasury Department with the requested settlement messages and associated data, with SWIFT currently being the only provider.

[71] ibid.

[72] Letter from United States Department of the Treasury regarding SWIFT/Terrorist Finance Tracking Programme [2007] OJ C166/17.

[73] Reply from European Union to United States Treasury Department—SWIFT/Terrorist Finance Tracking Programme [2007] OJ C166/19.

[74] See SWIFT, 'SWIFT Respects Data Protection Legislation' (10 December 2008) <https://www.swift.com/insights/press-releases/swift-respects-data-protection-legislation>..

[75] SWIFT, 'Subpoenaed Swift Message Data Is Adequately Protected' (18 February 2009) <https://www.swift.com/insights/press-releases/subpoenaed-swift-message-data-is-adequately-protected>.

[76] Agreement between the European Union and the United States of America on the processing and transfer of Financial Messaging Data from the European Union to the United States for the purposes of the Terrorist Finance Tracking Program [2010] OJ L195/5 (27 July 2010). The agreement provided that the US Department of the Treasury shall be regarded as ensuring an adequate level of data protection with respect to the data transferred from the EU to the United States, provided that it continues to comply with the privacy and personal data protection commitments set out therein. Ibid art 8.

[77] ibid art 2.

[78] ibid Annex.

The TFTP Agreement provides Europol's role to ensure that the data on financial transfers requested by the United States and stored in EU territory is necessary and tailored for counterterrorism purposes.[79] In addition, the European Data Protection Supervisor (EDPS) has the authority to inspect Europol's compliance with these requirements.[80]

In addition, an individual has the right to request confirmation that his or her personal data has been processed per the data protection rights under the EU Law Enforcement Directive, Directive 2016/680, on the protection of personal data when used by police and criminal justice authorities.[81]

Furthermore, the SWIFT and the TFTP are subject to oversight by major central banks, including the Federal Reserve Board, Bank of England, European Central Bank, and Bank of Japan, under the leadership of the National Bank of Belgium.[82] The issue was thus resolved by establishing these international cooperative frameworks.

5. Private-to-Private Information Sharing

5.1 Policies to Promote Information Sharing among Private Sectors

Criminals typically exploit the information gaps among institutions by using multiple institutions located in different countries to conceal the origin of the funds so that the institutions would have a limited and fragmented view of the transactions. Accordingly, many countries permit or even require in-group information sharing domestically or as a cross-border practice. Institutions have already shared such information with entities within the same corporation group. For instance, global brands of credit and debit cards require the issuers to convey customer information to their subsidiaries under their internal rules. They share information about their customers when they engage with cross-border payments.[83]

[79] ibid art 4.

[80] Regulation (EU) 2016/794 of the European Parliament and of the Council of 11 May 2016 on the European Union Agency for Law Enforcement Cooperation (Europol) and replacing and repealing Council Decisions 2009/371/JHA, 2009/934/JHA, 2009/935/JHA, 2009/936/JHA and 2009/968/JHA [2016] OJ L135/53.

[81] Directive (EU) 2016/680 of the European Parliament and of the Council of 27 April 2016 on the protection of natural persons with regard to the processing of personal data by competent authorities for the purposes of the prevention, investigation, detection or prosecution of criminal offences or the execution of criminal penalties, and on the free movement of such data, and repealing Council Framework Decision 2008/977/JHA (Law Enforcement Directive) [2016] OJ L119/89.

[82] SWIFT, 'Swift Oversight' <https://www.swift.com/about-us/organisation-governance/swift-oversight>.

[83] FATF, 'Cross-Border Payments: Survey Results on Implementation of FATF Standards' (October 2021) paras 87–88 <https://www.fatf-gafi.org/media/fatf/documents/recommendations/pdfs/Cross-Border-Payments-Survey-Results.pdf>.

FATF's Forty Recommendations of 2012 provided a detailed guideline for countries to permit financial institutions to rely on third parties to take CDD measures.[84] Recommendation 17 stipulates that institutions must promptly gather necessary information about CDD measures, ensure that the third party can provide the needed documentation on request, confirm the third party's compliance with CDD and record-keeping requirements, and consider country risk when choosing the third party's location. Supposing the third party is within the same financial group; adheres to specific CDD, record-keeping, and AML/CFT requirements; and is supervised by a competent authority. The financial institutions may apply specific measures through its group programme, potentially waiving the need for certain preconditions based on its ability to manage the higher country risk.[85]

In addition, Recommendation 18 provides detailed guidelines for internal controls and foreign branches and subsidiaries. Financial groups must implement group-wide programmes against money laundering and terrorism financing, including policies and procedures for sharing information within the group for AML/CFT purposes. They must ensure that their foreign branches and majority-owned subsidiaries apply AML/CFT measures consistent with the home country's requirements. Recommendation 21 further provides that financial institutions and their directors, officers, and employees can disclose that a suspicious transaction report or related information has been submitted so long as it is according to group-wide AML/CTF risk management requirements as set out in Recommendation 18.

The recent development of information-sharing mechanisms is to develop data pooling among multiple institutions and entities and collaborative analytics using privacy-enhancing technologies, such as cryptographical capabilities, and trusted enforcement environments, such as distributed ledger technology. Many countries and private entities have started pilot programmes, often involving entities from different countries.[86]

5.2 Restrictions to the Cross-Border Transfer of the Data

An issue that arises in this context is the cross-border sharing of data. These practices often encompass sharing financial data within and beyond a group of countries. However, different countries have varying levels of data protection

[84] FATF (n 7).

[85] ibid recommendation 17.

[86] For instance, Deloitte and UOB, 'The Case for Artificial Intelligence in Combating Money Laundering and Terrorist Financing', paras 17–18 <https://www2.deloitte.com/mm/en/pages/financial-advisory/articles/the-case-for-artificial-intelligence-in-combating-money-laundering-and-terrorist-financing.html>.

regulations, and sharing information across borders can expose individuals to different privacy standards, potentially leading to inconsistencies in safeguarding their personal information. While not all AML-related data are covered by these DPP legislations, it is necessary at this stage to examine possible conflicts. This issue is directly linked to the transfer of communication data, which will be addressed in Chapter 12.

Such data flows remain permissible when the other country substantially complies with the guidelines or implements sufficient safeguards. It is important to sustain consistent protection in line with the guidelines for the cross-border transfer of personal data between one nation and others. These safeguards should include robust enforcement mechanisms and measures established by the data controller. The imposition of restrictions should be avoided. Governments should balance the limitations of the cross-border sharing of personal data with the existing risks and consider the data's sensitivity and the specific purposes and context of the data processing.[87] In 2007, the Council of the OECD issued a Recommendation on Cross-Border Cooperation in the Enforcement of Laws Protecting Privacy[88] to encourage the member States to 'cooperate across borders in the enforcement of laws protecting privacy'.[89] To this end, there are bilateral and multilateral enforcement arrangements or memoranda of understanding to improve cooperation among privacy enforcement authorities. The regional efforts include the Asia-Pacific Economic Cooperation (APEC) Arrangement for Cross-border Privacy Enforcement.

More than seventy countries have some form of restriction on cross-border transfers in their personal data protection legislation.[90] It is because data can be

[87] Council of Europe Convention for the Protection of Individuals with regard to Automatic Processing of Personal Data (adopted on 28 January 1981, entered into force on 1 October 1985) CETS No 108. The amended Convention is the Protocol amending the Convention for the Protection of Individuals with regard to Automatic Processing of Personal Data (adopted on 10 October 2018) CETS No 223. The APEC has adopted the CBPR, in which Japan, the United States, South Korea, Taiwan, and other countries participate. For practice in Asia, see generally Graham Greenleaf, *Asian Data Privacy Laws* (OUP 2014); Graham Greenleaf, 'Asia's Data Privacy Dilemmas: 2014–2019' (2019) 4 Revista Uruguaya de Protección de Datos Personales 49.

[88] Recommendation of the Council on Cross-border Co-operation in the Enforcement of Laws Protecting Privacy (adopted on 12 June 2007) <https://legalinstruments.oecd.org/en/instruments/OECD-LEGAL-0352>.

[89] More specifically, it recommends that states take appropriate steps to (1) improve their domestic frameworks for privacy law enforcement to better enable their authorities to cooperate with foreign authorities; (2) develop effective international mechanisms to facilitate cross-border privacy law enforcement cooperation; (3) provide mutual assistance to one another in the enforcement of laws protecting privacy, including through notification, complaint referral, investigative assistance, and information sharing, subject to appropriate safeguards; (4) engage relevant stakeholders in discussion and activities aimed at furthering cooperation in the enforcement of laws protecting privacy.

[90] Christopher Kuner, *Transborder Data Flows and Data Privacy Law* (OUP 2013) 1. For domestic legislation information in major countries, see Personal Data Protection Commission, 'Survey of Systems for the Protection of Personal Data in Foreign Countries' <https://www.ppc.go.jp/personalinfo/legal/kaiseihogohou/>. For practice in Asia, see generally Greenleaf, *Asian Data Privacy Laws* (n 87).

easily transferred to another country's territory, and businesses can easily lose adherence to the personal data protection legislation of the source country if the data are not adequately protected in the destination country. It also provides equal footing or a level playing field for domestic operators instead of foreign operators.

The EU General Data Protection Regulation (GDPR) established rigorous requirements for cross-border data transfer. Under this instrument, data transfers must have a legitimate legal basis as provided under the regulation. First, personal data can only be transferred to countries or organizations with adequate data protection. Adequacy is determined by the European Commission, which assesses whether the recipient country or organization's data protection laws and practices meet GDPR standards. Second, if the data transfer is to a country without an adequacy decision, organizations may use standard contractual clauses approved by the European Commission. Standard contractual clauses are predefined legal agreements that ensure that data protection standards are met. Third, multinational organizations can implement binding corporate rules and internal data protection policies approved by EU data protection authorities. Binding corporate rules allow intragroup data transfers while maintaining GDPR compliance. Sometimes, a data protection impact assessment is needed before a data transfer. This assessment evaluates the potential risks to individuals' rights and freedoms when transferring data.

Data subjects retain their rights even when their data are transferred. They can exercise their rights to access, rectify, erase, or restrict the processing of their data and object to the transfer. Data controllers must inform data subjects about the transfer, including its purpose, the categories of data transferred, the recipients, and how they can exercise their rights. Adequate security measures must be in place to protect data during transfer. It includes encryption, access controls, and other technical and organizational measures. First, personal data can only be transferred to countries or organizations with adequate data protection. Adequacy is determined by the European Commission, which assesses whether the recipient country or organization's data protection laws and practices meet GDPR standards. The GDPR influenced many countries to adopt higher standards of DPP legislation because of its broad jurisdictional scope.[91]

Most countries do not prohibit cross-border data transfers per se but rather impose conditions on the transfer. Such situations usually require the consent of the person concerned. However, considering the asymmetry of the information held by operators and users and the formalization of approval, there are problems with allowing transfers if consent is obtained, regardless of the operator's system or country to which the data are being transferred. Therefore, it is often required that the government in the relocation destination ensure that its legal system is

[91] See Anu Bradford, *The Brussels Effect: How the European Union Rules the World* (OUP 2020) 131.

secure or that the operator of the relocation destination has taken appropriate security control measures. In determining their adequacy, they may refer to international standards. An important development with this regard is the Council of Europe's adoption of the Protocol amending the Convention for the Protection of Individuals with regard to Automatic Processing of Personal Data in 2018.[92] Another regional efforts include the Asia-Pacific Economic Cooperation (APEC) Arrangement for Cross-border Privacy Enforcement. APEC adopted the APEC Framework in 2004 and updated it in 2015. There is also the APEC Cross-Border Privacy Rules (CBPR).[93] While these rules are an essential mechanism to enable operators to transfer data across borders within APEC economies, their protection level is not deemed sufficient by the standards of the GDPR.

In addition to privacy protection regulations, some laws require businesses to have the necessary equipment to conduct business in their home country and for data collected in their home country to remain there. Such data are not limited to personal data but may include business and industrial data. Reasons vary from country to country, but some examples include raising barriers to entry for companies from other countries, protecting their industries by imposing such regulations, and preventing sensitive data from being taken to other countries for security reasons.

Such legislation encompasses various types of regulations that (1) require data copies to be retained within the home country; (2) mandate data processing and storage exclusively within the home country, along with the installation of necessary facilities; and (3) extend beyond (2) by prohibiting the export of data or certain items outside the country.[94]

Whether it is the regulation of cross-border transfers in personal data protection legislation or the obligation to store data in-country in data protection legislation, it is impossible to categorically determine whether an AML/CFT regulation or

[92] Council of Europe Convention for the Protection of Individuals with regard to Automatic Processing of Personal Data (adopted on 28 January 1981, entered into force on 1 October 1985) CETS No 108; Protocol amending the Convention for the Protection of Individuals with regard to Automatic Processing of Personal Data (adopted on 10 October 2018) CETS No 223.

[93] Japan allows the cross-border transfer of data when the third party in the foreign State acquires the certificate of the APEC CBPR System. Japan Personal Information Protection Act (Act No 57, 2003), art 28; the Guidelines for the Protection of Personal Information, s 4-1 (November 2016, partially amended in April 2025) <https://www.ppc.go.jp/personalinfo/legal/guidelines_offshore/>. Thailand also uses the CBPR as a benchmark as well. Personal Data Protection Act 2019 (Thailand) s 28. See the following as an unofficial English translation: Personal Data Protection Act, B.E. 2562 (2019) (Unofficial Translation) (27 May 2019) <https://thainetizen.org/wp-content/uploads/2019/11/thailand-personal-data-protection-act-2019-en.pdf>. For a study analysing the practices of Asian countries, see Greenleaf, *Asian Data Privacy Laws* (n 87); Greenleaf, 'Asia's Data Privacy Dilemmas: 2014–2019' (n 87).

[94] Christopher Kuner and OECD, 'Regulation of Transborder Data Flows under Data Protection and Privacy Law: Past, Present and Future' (2011) <https://www.oecd.org/content/dam/oecd/en/publications/reports/2011/12/regulation-of-transborder-data-flows-under-data-protection-and-privacy-law_g17a2074/5kg0s2fk315f-en.pdf>.

measure conflicts with such DPP legislation. It is necessary to examine it substantively in terms of its content, purpose, and effect.

5.3 National Approaches

There may be potential conflicts between policies that encourage the private sector to collect and share information for AML/CFT regulations as explained in Section 5.2. There is no binding international agreement to govern information sharing in the private sector. It is therefore important to observe the developments in the major countries.

5.3.1 The United States

The Uniting and Strengthening America by Providing Appropriate Tools Required to Intercept and Obstruct Terrorism (PATRIOT) Act of 2001 established the private-to-private information-sharing mechanism. The law exempts the liability of the institutions under the US law and any contract or other legally enforceable agreement, including arbitration agreement, for such disclosure or for any failure to provide notice of such disclosure to the person who is the subject of such disclosure. Section 314(b) of the PATRIOT Act allows financial institutions to share information under a safe harbour that offers protection from liability to identify better and report activities that may involve money laundering or terrorist activities. The financial institutions may notify the Treasury Department for registration. Under Section 314(b), participation in information sharing is voluntary. However, the Financial Crimes Enforcement Network (FinCEN), the US FIU, encourages financial institutions to take part.

In 2020, the United States significantly updated its AML/CFT under the Anti-Money Laundering Act.[95] It allows financial institutions to share details regarding suspicious transactions with their overseas branches, subsidiaries, and affiliated entities. The law also requires FinCEN and the Treasury Department to conduct a three-year study on the impact of information sharing.

In January 2022, FinCEN issued a notice seeking public comments on the proposed establishment of a limited-duration pilot programme, which permitted a financial institution with a SAR reporting obligation to share SAR-related information with the institution's foreign branches, subsidiaries, and affiliates to combat illicit finance risk, per the law.[96]

[95] Anti-Money Laundering Act, Pub L No 116-283, 134 Stat 4547 (2020), 31 USC 5301 note, and 31 USC 5311.

[96] FinCEN, 'Pilot Program on Sharing of Suspicious Activity Reports and Related Information With Foreign Branches, Subsidiaries, and Affiliates' (25 January 2022) <https://www.federalregister.gov/documents/2022/01/25/2022-01331/pilot-program-on-sharing-of-suspicious-activity-reports-and-related-information-with-foreign>.

On the other hand, the United States does not have a comprehensive data protection law at the federal level. The country lacks a single data protection authority. Instead, it relies on a patchwork of laws and regulations that cover various aspects of data privacy and security. Its governance is based on a decentralized approach.

The Gramm–Leach–Bliley Act (GLBA), a federal law, requires financial institutions to protect the privacy of consumers' financial information and inform them about their privacy practices. Most financial institutions, including banks, credit unions, and brokerage firms, are subject to GLBA and AML/CFT regulations. These institutions must comply with the provisions of the GLBA to safeguard customer financial information and the AML regulations to detect and prevent money laundering activities.

The GLBA requires financial institutions to maintain the privacy of customer information. The law generally restricts sharing non-public personal information, requiring institutions to obtain customer consent before sharing such data with third parties. However, there are exceptions related to sharing information for AML purposes. Therefore, financial institutions can share customer information with other entities to fulfil their AML obligations without customer consent. Financial institutions must have robust security measures under the GLBA and need effective monitoring and reporting systems to fulfil their AML obligations. Therefore, there is no conflict, at least at the formal level, between the AML/CFT requirements and the DPP legislation.

5.3.2 European Union

In the European Union, including the Schengen Agreement into EU law catalysed a significant boost in judicial cooperation. It was driven by the pressing need to combat organized crime and the desire to enhance money laundering controls within the European Union. Notably, establishing specific economic crime regulations within the European Union aimed at curbing fraud against the European Union also played a role in this development.

In 1990, the CoE adopted the Convention on the Laundering, Search, Seizure, and Confiscation of the Proceeds of Crime.[97] The convention contains more detailed provisions regarding mutual assistance obligations. All EU member states have ratified it and consider it a part of the law that applies between them. The mutual assistance provisions entail exchanging information on the existence, location, nature, legal status, and price of proceeds of crime and converted objects. The specifics of mutual assistance include identifying and tracing such proceeds.[98]

[97] Convention on the Laundering, Search, Seizure, and Confiscation of the Proceeds of Crime (signed on 8 November 1990, entered into force 1 September 1993) CETS 141. See also Council of Europe, *Explanatory Report on the Convention on Laundering, Search, Seizure and Confiscation of the Proceeds from Crime* (Council of Europe Publishing 1991) 22, para 35.

[98] UNODC and IMF, 'Model Legislation on Money Laundering and Financing of Terrorism' (2005) <https://www.imf.org/external/np/leg/amlcft/eng/pdf/amlml05.pdf>.

Starting in 1990, the European Community implemented extensive measures to combat money laundering within its borders. The first action taken was a Council Directive that obligated member states to act against laundering proceeds from drug trafficking under the Drug Convention of 1988.[99] This directive also imposed various requirements on financial institutions based on the FATF Recommendations issued in 1990. These obligations included verifying customers' identities, keeping records, prohibiting suspicious transactions, and reporting on such transactions.

Efforts to combat money laundering were further strengthened in the late 1990s through Pillar III of the EU Treaty, built upon the 1990 Directive. It was accomplished by adopting the 1998 Joint Action by the European Council[100] and the 2001 EU Framework Decision.[101] The latter extended the scope of predicate offences to include serious crimes. The Council passed a directive in 2001 that criminalized actions constituting the predicate offences identified in the 2001 Framework Decision.[102] In response to the FATF's 2003 Recommendation, a new directive was adopted in 2005 to harmonize legislation in EU member states relating to the financing of terrorism.[103] The European Union modernized its regulatory framework in 2015 in response to the 2012 FATF Forty Recommendations.[104] It includes the Fourth Anti-Money Laundering Directive[105] and Regulation 2015/847, which includes the obligation to share information within a group of financial institutions.[106]

The Fifth Anti-Money Laundering Directive of 2018 further expands the obligation of information sharing among the group.[107] One of the purposes includes

[99] Council Directive 91/308/EEC of 10 June 1991 on prevention of the use of the financial system for the purpose of money laundering [1991] OJ L166/77.

[100] Joint Action 98/699/JHA of 3 December 1998 adopted by the Council on the basis of Article K.3 of the Treaty on European Union, on money laundering, the identification, tracing, freezing, seizing and confiscation of instrumentalities and the proceeds from crime [1998] OJ L333/1 (29 December 1998).

[101] Council Framework Decision 2001/500/JHA of 26 June 2001 on money laundering, the identification, tracing, freezing, seizing and confiscation of instrumentalities and the proceeds of crime [2001] OJ L182/1 (5 July 2001).

[102] Council Directive 2001/97/EC [2001] OJ L344/76.

[103] Council Directive 2005/60/EC [2005] OJ L309/15. See also Gilmore (n 6) 189.

[104] European Commission, 'Anti-Money Laundering and Countering the Financing of Terrorism at EU Level' <https://finance.ec.europa.eu/financial-crime/anti-money-laundering-and-countering-financing-terrorism-eu-level_en>.

[105] Directive (EU) 2015/849 of the European Parliament and of the Council of 20 May 2015 on the prevention of the use of the financial system for the purposes of money laundering or terrorist financing, amending Regulation (EU) No 648/2012 of the European Parliament and of the Council, and repealing Directive 2005/60/EC of the European Parliament and of the Council and Commission Directive 2006/70/EC [2015] OJ L141/73. This Directive amended Regulation 648/2012 and repealed Directives 2005/60/EC and 2006/70/EC.

[106] Regulation 648/2012, art 45(8) ('[m]ember States shall ensure that information sharing within the group is allowed. Information on suspicions that funds are the proceeds of criminal activity or are related to terrorist financing reported to the FIU shall be shared within the group unless otherwise instructed by the FIU').

[107] Directive (EU) 2018/843 of the European Parliament and of the Council of 30 May 2018 amending Directive (EU) 2015/849 on the prevention of the use of the financial system for the purposes

improving cooperation and enhancing communication among entities.[108] Article 39(3) provides exceptions for prohibiting information sharing with third parties. It consists of the disclosure between the credit and financial institutions from the member states as long as they belong to the same group or between those entities and their branches and majority-owned subsidiaries established in third countries. It is also conditioned that those branches and majority-owned subsidiaries fully comply with the group-wide policies and procedures and that the group-wide policies and procedures comply with the requirements set out in this directive.

In 2024, the EU adopted the AML Regulation, which became directly applicable in all member States without the need for national implementing measures.[109] Chapter II on the internal policies, controls, and procedures of obliged entities provides the regulation of group information sharing. It requires that the group-wide policies, controls and procedures shall also include data protection policies and policies, controls and procedures for sharing information within the group for AML/CFT purposes.[110] The sharing of information within the group shall cover the identity and characteristics of the customer, its beneficial owners or the person on behalf of whom the customer acts, the nature and purpose of the business relationship, and the suspicions that funds are the proceeds of criminal activity or are related to terrorist financing reported to the FIU. Groups must establish comprehensive group-level policies, controls, and procedures to ensure that the information exchanged per the initial clause receives adequate safeguards for confidentiality, data protection, and its proper use.

Where branches or subsidiaries of obliged entities are in third countries where the minimum AML/CFT requirements are less strict than those set out in this regulation, the obliged entity concerned shall ensure that those branches or subsidiaries comply with the regulation requirements, including provisions concerning data protection or the equivalent.[111]

Where the law of a third country does not permit compliance with the requirements laid down in this Regulation, obliged entities shall take additional measures to ensure that branches and subsidiaries in that third country effectively handle

of money laundering or terrorist financing, and amending Directives 2009/138/EC and 2013/36/EU [2018] OJ L156/43.

[108] Preamble para 46 ('it is important to allow credit and financial institutions to exchange information not only between group members but also with other credit and financial institutions, with due regard to data protection rules as set out in national law').

[109] Regulation (EU) 2024/1624 of the European Parliament and of the Council of 31 May 2024 on the prevention of the use of the financial system for the purposes of money laundering or terrorist financing [2024] OJ L 2024/1624, 19.6.2024. Besides this Regulation, Directive 2024/1640, Regulations 2023/1113 and 2024/1620 form the EU's AML/CFT institutional framework. The Regulation 2024/1620 established the Authority for Anti-Money Laundering and Countering the Financing of Terrorism as a new body responsible for implementing AML regulations.

[110] Regulation 2024/1624 art 16(1).

[111] ibid art 17(1).

the risk of money laundering or terrorist financing and the head office shall inform the supervisors of their home member state. Where the supervisors of the home member state consider that the additional measures are not sufficient, they shall exercise other supervisory actions, including requiring the group not to establish any business relationship, to terminate existing ones or not to undertake transactions, or to close down its operations in the third country.

Furthermore, the Regulation specifies that Anti-Money Laundering Act of 2020 shall develop draft regulatory technical standards and submit them to the Commission for adoption. Those draft regulatory technical standards shall specify the type of additional measures, including the minimum action to be taken by obliged entities where the law of a third country does not permit the implementation of group-wide information sharing and the additional supervisory actions needed in such cases.

There is a potential conflict between the AML/CFT regulation and human rights law. Respect for private life and personal data protection are the rights provided in the EU Charter of Fundamental Rights.[112] It is stated that '[s]uch data must be processed fairly for specified purposes'[113] and '[c]ompliance with these rules shall be subject to control by an independent authority'.[114] The AML measures must be compatible with the Charter and case law of the Court of Justice of the European Union (CJEU). It is noted that GDPR Article 6(1) provides the principles where processing shall be lawful. The data subjects must consent to processing their data for one or more specific purposes, among other requirements. In addition, processing is necessary to execute a contract to which the data subject is a party or to take steps at the data subject's request before entering a contract. The implementation of the AML/CFT regulations will meet these requirements.

The European Data Protection Board (EDPB) adopted a statement[115] that 'the applicable anti-money laundering measures include comprehensive and far-reaching obligations on financial services providers and other obliged entities to identify and know their customers, to monitor transactions undertaken using their services, and to report any suspicious transactions'.[116] Furthermore, the legislation stipulates long retention periods.[117] These measures cover the entire European financial services industry and, therefore, affect, in a comprehensive manner, all persons using financial services each time they use them.[118]

112 Charter of Fundamental Rights of the European Union [2012] OJ C326/391, arts 7 and 8(1).

113 ibid art 8(2).

114 ibid art 8(3).

115 The European Data Protection Board, 'Statement on the Protection of Personal Data Processed in Relation with the Prevention of Money Laundering and Terrorist Financing' (15 December 2020) <https://www.edpb.europa.eu/sites/default/files/files/file1/edpb_statement_20201215_aml_actionplan_en.pdf>.

116 ibid.

117 ibid.

118 ibid.

In this context, the EDPB stresses that the intended update to the AML framework shall not be undertaken without a review of the relationship between the AML measures and the rights to privacy and data protection. In this discussion, the relevance and accuracy of the data collected play a paramount role. The EDPB is convinced that a closer articulation between the two sets of rules would benefit the protection of personal data and the efficiency of the AML framework. In this respect, the EDPB stressed the need for a clear legal basis for processing personal data that states the purposes and limits of such processing in line with Article 5(1) GDPR. In particular, clarity is needed on information sharing and international data transfers, as noted by the EDPS in its opinion on the European Commission's action plan for a comprehensive union policy on preventing money laundering and terrorism financing.[119]

The CJEU judgments concerning the AML measures show the court's stance that disclosing an individual's data to a third party is a serious intrusion and that the Court will carefully scrutinize any such disclosure. In its judgment in 2022, the CJEU Grand Chamber held that provisions of Directive 2018/843 concerning the publication of beneficial ownership registers[120] were incompatible with the Charter of Fundamental Rights.[121] The Court found that while deterring money laundering was a valid objective, making the data available to the general public was neither necessary nor a proportionate way of achieving that objective and was contrary to the Charter. According to this judgment, the financial institutions and other operators must limit the scope of the disclosure in light of the necessity principle.

In a broader context, information sharing relates to the EU Digital Single Market, an effort started in 2015 to integrate national digital markets. The three policy pillars are to improve access to digital goods and services; to create the environment for digital networks and services by providing high-speed, secure, and trustworthy infrastructures and services; and to maximize the growth potential of the digital economy.

5.3.3 United Kingdom

The United Kingdom, one of the financial centres, has rigorous AML/CFT regulations. The United Kingdom criminalized the laundering of proceeds from drug offences through the Drug Trafficking Offences Act 1986[122] and the Criminal Justice

[119] ibid.

[120] Council Directive 2015/849 requires the EU member states to establish a register of beneficial ownership (RBO) containing personal data about the owner of each legal entity, including their name, nationality, and ownership interest, and to make the RBO available to a range of financial entities such as banks. Furthermore, Directive 2018/843 allowed the member states to access the RBO, regardless of whether they could demonstrate a legitimate interest.

[121] Joined Cases C-37/20 & C-601/20, *WM and Sovim SA v Luxembourg Business Registers*, Judgment of the Court (Grand Chamber), 22 November 2022, ECLI:EU:C:2022:912.

[122] Drug Trafficking Offences Act 1986, c 32.

Act 1990.[123] The Proceeds of Crime Act 2002, amended in 2005, further criminalized concealing the source of an offence above a specified amount. Today, its basis is the Terrorism Act 2000, the Proceeds of Crime Act 2002, the Money Laundering, Terrorist Financing and Transfer of Funds (Information on the Payer) Regulations 2017 (MLR 2017),[124] and the Money Laundering and Terrorist Financing (Amendment) Regulations 2019 (MLR 2019). MLR 2017 and MLR 2019 are enacted to implement the rules established under the Fourth and the Fifth EU AML Directives, respectively.

The latest MLR 2019 significantly expanded the scope of application and the CDD obligations provided under MLR 2017. It provided that firms must have 'policies, controls and procedures to identify and scrutinize transactions which are complex or unusually large or have unusual patterns of transactions or which have no apparent economic or legal purpose'.[125] Firms must have group-wide policies, controls, and procedures for sharing information about clients with other group companies for AML/CTF purposes.

In addition, the United Kingdom has strong legislation to prevent and suppress fraud offences. The UK Cifas is essential in information sharing on fraudulent crimes directly connected to money laundering. Cifas is a not-for-profit organization with over 400 members who share fraud and financial crime data to prevent, deter, and detect fraud and broader financial crime.[126] The organization manages the National Fraud Database, the most significant fraud risk database.[127] The member organizations post cases of fraudulent conduct against their organization to the relevant database, enabling other members to compare against their data. The data and intelligence are shared in real time and are available online 24/7. The database holds first- and third-party fraud risks, such as account takeover, identity fraud, false insurance claims, and false applications. The issue remains concerning cross-border data sharing. Cifas' ability to conduct business within the United Kingdom is limited. The financial institutions can earmark funds exiting the United Kingdom but cannot follow the proceeds of crime.

When it left the European Union, the United Kingdom had the Data Protection Act, equivalent to the GDPR.[128] It has similarly strict rules, namely data protection principles, which require the information to be fair, lawful, and transparent. In June 2025, the Data (Use and Access) Act was enacted, introducing a range

[123] Criminal Justice (International Co-operation) Act 1990.

[124] The Money Laundering, Terrorist Financing and Transfer of Funds (Information on the Payer) Regulations, SI 2017/692.

[125] Money Laundering and Terrorist Financing (Amendment) Regulations 2019, SI 2019/1511, reg 14A(10).

[126] 'ECR0037—Evidence on Economic Crime' (8 May 2018) <https://committees.parliament.uk/writtenevidence/89879/html/>.

[127] CIFAS, 'National Fraud Database' <https://www.cifas.org.uk/fraud-prevention-community/combined-threat-protect/national-fraud-database>

[128] Data Protection Act 2018 c 12.

of provisions aimed at supporting the expansion of digital verification services, among other objectives. While it does not replace the Data Protection Act, it introduces notable amendments, including changes to the rules governing cross-border data transfers.[129] These laws may pose challenges, including identifying a lawful ground for processing personal data, compliance with information requirements, protecting customers' data collected through the CDD process, and sharing the data with law enforcement agencies and other institutions. However, Article 5(1) of the Data Protection Act along with the Information Commissioner's Office (ICO)'s guidance on data protection principles, indicates that AML compliance, particularly in relation to data minimisation, retention, and the lawful basis for processing, may be justified where it is carried out under a legal obligation or in the public interest.[130]

5.3.4 China

China enacted the Anti-Money Laundering Act of 2006. The provision of customer identification data, transaction information, and investigative information obtained per AML obligations to other 'units' is required by law.[131] The State Council's anti-money laundering administrative department is responsible for managing a centralized and unified national AML information database and taking the necessary measures to maintain the security of AML information.[132] The administrative department in the State Council in charge of AML may obtain necessary information from relevant State agencies, departments, and institutions, and applicable State agencies, departments, and institutions shall provide such data per the law.[133] Firms, enterprises, and other market entities shall report beneficial ownership information through the relevant information systems of

[129] Data (Use and Access) Act 2025 c 18. See also 'Guidance: Data (Use and Access) Act 2025: data protection and privacy changes' <https://www.gov.uk/guidance/data-use-and-access-act-2025-data-protection-and-privacy-changes>.

[130] Information Commissioner's Office, A guide to the data protection principles <https://ico.org.uk/for-organisations/uk-gdpr-guidance-and-resources/data-protection-principles/a-guide-to-the-data-protection-principles/>. The guide is currently under review.

[131] Anti-Money Laundering Act (adopted on 31 October 2006, entered into force on 1 January 2007), art 6. Most recently, the legislation was updated in 2024 following the FATF's 2019 evaluation report. Anti-Money Laundering Law (adopted on 8 November 2024, entered into effect on 1 January 2025) art 37.

[132] ibid art 14. The centre's main duties include (1) collecting, collating, and preserving information on large-value and suspicious fund transactions and related investigations and case information; (2) analysing and studying information on large-value and suspicious transactions, examining and consulting with relevant departments on clues about suspicious fund transactions, and cooperating with relevant departments in conducting joint investigations on clues of suspicious fund transactions; (3) studying and analysing the ways, means, and development trends of AML crimes, and providing the basis for the formulation of AML policies; (4) researching and formulating technical standards for reporting information on large-value and suspicious transactions in conjunction with relevant departments. See The People's Bank of China, 'Anti-Money Laundering Center' <http://www.pbc.gov.cn/fxqzhongxin/3558093/3558095/index.html>.

[133] ibid art 15.

the market supervision and management department.[134] When financial institutions identify customers through third parties, they shall do so by investigating the CDD management capabilities of such third parties.[135] The State Council may supervise and control financial institutions established in China and their foreign branches.[136]

In the meantime, the People's Bank of China enacted the Measures for the Supervision and Administration of Anti-Money Laundering and Counter-Terrorist Financing of Financial Institutions in August 2021.[137] It enlarged the scope of the organizations subject to the regulation, including loan companies, asset management subsidiaries of commercial banks, non-banking payment institutions, insurance agents, and insurance brokers.

It also provides for the sharing and using information by organizations per laws and regulations.[138] If the local law is stricter for foreign subsidiaries and branches, the local law shall be followed. If this restricts or prohibits the implementation of said laws, the head office must take appropriate supplementary measures to combat AML and report to the People's Bank of China.[139]

On the other hand, since the late 2010s, China has updated its DPP legislation against the growing importance of digital technology. The key DPP legislation includes the Cybersecurity Law of 2017, the Personal Information Protection Law (PIPL) of 2021, and the Data Security Law of 2021. The Personal Information Protection Law sets out comprehensive rules for processing personal information, including consent requirements, data subject rights, cross-border data transfers, and the appointment of data protection officers. It resembles the GDPR but aims to protect national sovereignty and data security, reflecting China's approach. The Data Security Law includes provisions concerning the export of controlled data and security reviews for data processing. In particular, it prohibits operators of important infrastructure from transferring critical data relevant to national security without the authorization of the government authorities.

5.4 Summary

The FATF's efforts align with the digital transformation trends in developed countries. It is necessary that financial institutions, as gatekeepers, have the

[134] ibid art 17.
[135] ibid art 29.
[136] ibid art 24.
[137] Administrative Measures for Anti-Money Laundering and Counter-Terrorist Financing Supervision of Financial Institutions, adopted on April 12, 2021, promulgated on 1 August 2021.
[138] ibid art 12.
[139] ibid art 13. The extraterritorial effect of the China's AML/CFT regulation requires close examination.

responsibility for collecting the relevant information appropriately and allowing the government to access such data.

There are no established international law rules concerning the human rights norm in the context of the AML/CFT regulations beyond the rules already established concerning due process. Democratic values are the foundation of developed countries such as the member states of the G7. However, specific States do not share the same view and instead impose authoritarian regulations.

The analysis shows the importance of data protection and the constitutional values of privacy. However, these elements are often considered secondary in the context of AML/CFT regulations, where law enforcement authorities find it challenging to collect the information. While reconciling two areas is not easy, there are similar situations in other contexts of data governance. At least for the democratic States, the governments must commit themselves to democratic values because otherwise, the digitalization of financial information and sharing of such information would degrade such values. To this end, the law enforcement authority should maintain trust in its government access. In this context, the OECD Declaration on Government Access to Personal Data Held by Private Entities adopted in December 2022 is relevant.[140] It listed the principles of legal basis, legitimate aims, approvals, data handling, transparency, oversight, and redress. In particular, it recommends that '[m]echanisms exist for providing transparency about government access to personal data that balance the interest of individuals and the public to be informed with the need to prevent the disclosure of information that would harm national security or law enforcement activities'.[141]

It is also important to note that government access to business data (G2B relations) is not the same thing as the sharing of information among the private sector (B2B relations) and the provision of information from the government to the business sector (B2G relations). However, in the context of the AML/CFT regulations, financial institutions have the power to manage customers' financial transactions. Customers are in a more vulnerable position, and it is vital to protect their interests to realize democratic mechanisms.

6. Concluding Remarks

Money laundering offences and terrorist financing offences are both specifically identified as offences in various international conventions. The Drug Convention and the UNTOC oblige member States to criminalize money laundering as an

[140] OECD, 'Declaration on Government Access to Personal Data Held by Private Sector Entities' (adopted on 14 December 2022) <https://legalinstruments.oecd.org/en/instruments/OECD-LEGAL-0487>.

[141] ibid principle V.

offence, while the Convention against the Financing of Terrorism identifies terrorist financing as an offence. These conventions also mandate cooperation and information sharing among authorities. Compared to other terrorism offences, the obligations arising from money laundering and terrorist financing offences are more specific in terms of requirements, as they necessitate the appointment of designated authorities to consolidate information and provide detailed legal assistance.

Another significant feature of money laundering regulation is incorporating recommendations issued by the FATF into national legislation in many countries. The legal support provided by the international conventions is often deemed insufficient, and the FATF Recommendations are mandatory for States and financial institutions. These recommendations seek to regulate money laundering and terrorist financing offences by regulating transactions between financial institutions.

For money laundering and terrorist financing offences, obtaining information from financial institutions is of utmost importance. Regulations are, therefore, established to acquire information from home-country entities or foreign entities linked to home-country entities. Compliance with FATF Recommendations is also encouraged in non-FATF member states through tightening regulations on home-country financial institutions.

Mutual aid structures consider restrictions on the rights of private individuals, mainly through regulations on financial institutions. These regulations are explained to customers, and their prior consent is obtained, thereby reducing the potential for objections from private individuals.

12
Communication Service Providers

1. Introduction

This chapter delves into the unique aspects of engaging in direct cooperation with communication service providers within the framework of international law.[1] The contemporary digital era presents new challenges to the international law that governs cross-border criminal investigations. The prevalence of transnational organized crime has fuelled a concomitant increase in the demand for information and evidence located abroad. This chapter explores the challenges in collecting electronic evidence (e-evidence) directly from the private sector. E-evidence is generally data communicated primarily through the internet, including emails, messages exchanged through social network services, documents, and photographs. The data in question comprise two distinct categories: content data and metadata. The former pertains to the substantive content of the communication. The latter is information that confirms the occurrence of the communication, such as the identity of the customer and access log records, including the data associated with the communication's location, date, and time.[2]

States may rely on mutual legal assistance treaties (MLATs) or other forms of intergovernmental cooperation to obtain e-evidence, as explored in Chapter 2. However, they are expensive and lengthy, so offenders may conceal and destroy the materials. Moreover, e-evidence investigations involve various technical components, including digital forensics, that differentiate them from other forms of evidence. Conventional MLATs may not be suitable for facilitating such collaboration. Therefore, States may seek direct assistance from private service providers ('direct cooperation').[3] Where the company may be subject to the jurisdiction

[1] This chapter includes materials published in Japanese in Yurika Ishii, 'Keiji Sosa Ni Okeru Gaikoku Jigyosha Karano Tsushin Joho Shutoku' (2023) 12 Tokyo Journal of International Law 137. It has not been published in English in any form.

[2] The terms 'information' and 'data' have different definitions. However, this chapter will use these terms interchangeably.

[3] Service providers can be categorized into several groups. First, there are carriers, which own or operate telecommunications networks to provide transport services. They provide facilities such as transmission infrastructure, cables, and wireless networks. Second, there are carriage service providers, which provide carriage services, including the transmission of communications such as internet services. Third, there are providers of messaging and call applications. Fourth, there are providers of storage and backup services. Finally, there are general electronic content service providers.

International Law and the Investigation of Transnational Crimes. Yurika Ishii, Oxford University Press.
 DOI: 10.1093/9780198957089.003.0012

of a foreign State, the enforcing State will not normally seek the consent of the home State.

Direct cooperation with communication service providers is not a novel phenomenon. Countries can exert their control over foreign corporations through territorial and personal jurisdictions. However, e-evidence has distinctive features compared to other forms of evidence. It is susceptible to rapid modification and replication, and poses challenges in terms of preservation, integrity, and authenticity.

The question that needs to be addressed is whether there are established distinct rules concerning digital evidence under international law. The rules and guidelines governing digital investigations impact the broader regulation of cyberspace. The core value of the internet, created and operated by private entities, has been accessibility. Ensuring the unobstructed flow of information is essential in safeguarding the freedom of expression as a fundamental human right and promoting economic development by providing a favourable environment for corporations to offer communication services.

The characteristics of information technology (IT) platforms must also be taken into account, as they are deeply rooted in the network economy. Large companies use their extensive user bases, vast data ecosystems, and advanced artificial intelligence capabilities to create self-reinforcing network effects that further consolidate their market dominance. The immense influence of major tech giants such as GAFAM (Google, Apple, Facebook, Amazon, and Microsoft) in the United States and BAT (Baidu, Alibaba, and Tencent) in China is evident, as these companies dominate the market through their extensive integration across multiple sectors and services.[4]

Recent years have seen the rise of 'digital human rights', which encompass rights and freedoms in the digital realm (see Section 4.3). They include the right to privacy, freedom of expression, access to information, and participation in digital spaces without discrimination.

Given these developments and the associated challenges, Section 2 discusses international law rules concerning the jurisdiction of foreign operators. It points out that while the increase of digital communication services has pushed States to employ a flexible jurisdictional basis, a distinct category of 'internet jurisdiction' is not supported by State practice. Section 3 argues that potential conflicts between States concerning law enforcement against communication providers will invite judicial conflicts among relevant States. Section 4 argues that international law cannot reconcile such disputes. Section 5 describes the structures of bilateral agreements and the Second Additional Protocol to the Cybercrime Convention, which is to overcome such conflicts, albeit within like-minded countries.

[4] See Amy Webb, *The Big Nine: How the Tech Titans and Their Thinking Machines Could Warp Humanity* (Public Affairs 2020).

2. Collecting Data From Foreign Communication Service Providers

2.1 Jurisdictional Basis

This section delves into the challenges related to law enforcement States extending their jurisdictional reach to foreign service providers without the consent of another State that holds jurisdiction over the provider.

There is no multilateral treaty governing direct cooperation. Article 18(1) of the Council of Europe Cybercrime Convention of 2001 provides that parties must adopt measures to empower their competent authorities to order 'a person in its territory to submit specified computer data in that person's possession or control, which is stored in a computer system or a computer-data storage medium' and 'a service provider offering its services in the territory of the Party to submit subscriber information relating to such services in that service provider's possession or control'. The former involves content data, and the latter involves metadata. However, member states agreed these measures were limited to their territories during the preparatory work. They do not govern the situation where they extend their jurisdiction to a foreign entity.[5]

The League of Arab States Convention on Combatting Information Technology Offences of 2000 provides that the 'State Party shall commit itself to adopting the procedures necessary to enable the competent authorities to order any person who is acquainted with the functioning of the information technology or the procedures applied to protect the information technology to give the information necessary to complete the procedures'.[6] As such, it is necessary to establish direct cooperation with service providers. It explicitly prohibits the exercise of jurisdiction '*in the territory of another State* the jurisdiction or functions the exercising of which is the exclusively right of the authorities of that other State by virtue of its domestic law' (emphasis added).[7] However, it does not specify a situation where a State extends its jurisdiction to a foreign provider that offers business in the law-enforcing State.

The United Nations Convention against Cybercrime, adopted in 2024, does not contain any provisions authorizing direct cooperation.[8] Driven by Russia and China, the convention strongly emphasizes the protection of territorial sovereignty.[9]

[5] Council of Europe, 'Explanatory Report to the Convention on Cybercrime' (ETS No 185, 2001).
[6] The League of Arab States Convention on Combatting Information Technology Offences, art 27(1).
[7] ibid art 4(2).
[8] United Nations Convention against Cybercrime (adopted on 24 December 2024) UNGA Res 79/243.
[9] See, for instance, ibid art 5(1).

Despite the insufficiency of international regulations in this regard, there is a growing trend wherein an increasing number of laws and regulations explicitly permit access to data stored in extraterritorial repositories. Countries have multiple jurisdictional bases to apply their laws to such entities. The first is the territoriality principle, which states that the provider's services within a particular territory can be a basis for applying relevant laws. While the operators are not physically present in the territory, there seems to be a consensus that foreign operators offering telecommunications services within their territories have the right to exercise jurisdiction based on the principle of territoriality.[10] The second is the personality principle. If a corporation or its subsidiary is registered in a State, the State would possess legal authority over the company based on the nationality.

A relatively novel approach is the targeting theory. Communication service providers and internet operators have become increasingly common in providing services without owning their telecommunications infrastructure or physical presence in a foreign territory. Yet, if a foreign service provider targets activities or customers of a State, then the State can exercise its jurisdiction because the provider is deemed to have minimum contacts with the State. On the other hand, the mere accessibility of a website would not by itself justify legal authority in the location where users can reach the site.[11] The courts look at the nature, effects, and scale of the activities and the intentions of the operators to provide the service either within the territory of or the persons within the law-enforcing State.[12]

The concept is not inherent to cyberspace. However, it emerged in response to internet services, first in the US Courts. In 1997, the US District Court adopted a 'slide scaling test' in a trademark dispute.[13] When it examined whether it has jurisdiction over a defendant in another State, it held that 'the likelihood that personal jurisdiction can be constitutionally exercised is directly proportionate to the nature and quality of commercial activity that an entity conducts over the Internet'.[14] It later developed into the targeting theory to limit territorial and personal jurisdiction.

The theory has been endorsed in other countries and regions. In 2012, the Court of Justice of the European Union (CJEU) supported this theory when it ruled on the scope of the EU Member States' jurisdictional basis over internet services. It held that the

[10] American Law Institute, *Restatement of the Law Fourth, The Foreign Relations Law of the United States* (American Law Institute Publishers 2018) s 407. See also Paul Schwartz, 'Legal Access to the Global Cloud' (2018) 118 Columbia Law Review 1681; Jennifer Daskal, 'Borders and Bits' (2017) 71 Vanderbilt Law Review 179.

[11] See Cedric Ryngaert, 'International Jurisdiction Law' in Austen Parrish and Cedric Ryngaert (eds), *Research Handbook on Extraterritoriality in International Law* (Edward Elgar Publishing 2023) 16.

[12] Julia Hörnle, *Internet Jurisdiction Law and Practice* (OUP 2021) 143.

[13] *Zippo Mfg Co v Zippo Dot Com Inc* 952 F Supp 1119 (WD Pa 1997).

[14] ibid 1124.

> act takes place, at least, in [the law enforcing State] where there is evidence from which it may be concluded that the act discloses an intention on the part of the person performing the act to target members of the public in [the law enforcing State], which is for the national court to assess.[15]

The judgment later came to have broader implications. Today, the EU laws concerning digital activities, including the General Data Protection Regulation (GDPR), incorporate this theory. The jurisdictional nexus in this scenario was the action occurring within the State, such as advertisement and collection of personal data.[16]

From an international legal standpoint, whether other nations raise objections to broadening jurisdiction matters. The extent of international opposition to a State's jurisdiction will hinge on factors such as general agreement on the purpose and aim of regulation and mechanisms that consider comparable foreign regulations as safeguards.[17]

It is noted that there are cautious views among international lawyers. Robert Currie and Stephen Allen, in their writings in the mid-2010s, argued that the consent of the host State of the service provider is required in principle. However, they reserved their position on collecting e-evidence due to the lack of consensus in State practice.[18] Since then, an increasing number of countries have expanded their legal authority over foreign service providers. Furthermore, some argued that it is unlawful to engage in direct cooperation without the host State's consent.[19] The view does not enjoy scholarly support or State practice.

[15] Case C-173/11 *Football Dataco Ltd v Sportradar GmbH* [2012] ECLI:EU:C:2012:642, para 47.

[16] Article 3 of the GDPR provides a wide basis for its application regardless of the fact whether the processing of the data takes place within the European Union. Regulation (EU) 2016/679 of the European Parliament and of the Council of 27 April 2016 on the protection of natural persons regarding the processing of personal data and on the free movement of such data, and repealing Directive 95/46/EC. See also EU Policy Department for Citizens' Rights and Constitutional Affairs Directorate-General for Internal Policies, 'Regulating Targeted and Behavioural Advertising in Digital Services: How to Ensure Users' Informed Consent' (2021).

[17] Cedric Ryngaert, 'Jurisdiction' in Jean D'Aspremont and Sahib Singh (eds), *Concepts for International Law* (Edward Elgar Publishing 2019) 580. According to Nico Krisch, the regulation of global business activities has led to a transformation of international law, resulting in the creation of 'unbound' jurisdictions. This situation allows a few influential States to establish and enforce rules. Nico Krisch, 'Jurisdiction Unbound: (Extra)Territorial Regulation as Global Governance' (2022) 33 European Journal of International Law 481. There is a counter-argument that jurisdiction should be understood as governing the relationships between equal sovereign entities rather than merely regulating cross-border markets. For further insights on this topic, see also Roger O'Keefe, 'Cooperative National Regulation to Secure Transnational Public Goods: A Reply to Nico Krisch' (2022) 33 European Journal of International Law 515.

[18] Robert J Currie, 'Cross-Border Evidence Gathering in Transnational Criminal Investigation: Is the Microsoft Ireland Case the "Next Frontier"?' (2016) 54 Canadian Yearbook of International Law 63; Stephen Allen, 'Enforcing Criminal Jurisdiction in The Clouds and International Law's Enduring Commitment to Territoriality' in Stephen Allen and others (eds), *Oxford Handbook of Jurisdiction in International Law* (OUP 2019).

[19] Bert-Jaap Koops and Morag Goodwin, 'Cyberspace, the Cloud, and Cross-Border Criminal Investigation: The Limits and Possibilities of International Law' (2016) 5 Tilburg Law School Research Paper 1 <http://dx.doi.org/10.2139/ssrn.2698263>. All websites were last accessed on 31 March

The fact that it is data in cyberspace does not affect the assessment on a jurisdictional basis. States assert control over the entity responsible for data administration, not the data itself. The data's physical location is inconsequential in this context. Therefore, the 'loss of location' is not an issue regarding direct cooperation. This scenario draws parallels with instances involving companies possessing physical documents overseas. A company cannot object against the request of the State to which it belongs on the ground that the required documents are held outside the country. The location of the materials is not relevant.[20]

2.2 National and Regional Legislation

2.2.1 Extension of Jurisdictional Arms

This section explores relevant national and regional legislations that allow law enforcement agencies to require communication service providers to disclose the users and communication data they hold.

(1) The United States

The foremost example in this context is the US Clarifying Lawful Overseas Use of Data Act (CLOUD Act) of 2018.[21] This legislation amends the Stored Communications Act (SCA), which outlines the responsibilities of telecommunications providers. Under the CLOUD Act, these providers must store, disclose, and provide customer or subscriber communications and related records to investigative authorities, regardless of whether the data is stored domestically or abroad.[22]

The jurisdictional scope of the CLOUD Act is the same as that of the SCA. The US Department of Justice (DOJ) clarifies that the Act applies to US-based companies, US-owned companies, and companies headquartered in the United States and extends to entities subject to its jurisdiction by providing services to the United

2025. Ulrich Sieber and Carl-Wendelin Neubert argues that the investigation is permissible when it satisfies the necessity doctrine. Ulrich Sieber and Carl-Wendelin Neubert, 'Transnational Criminal Investigations in Cyberspace: Challenges to National Sovereignty' (2017) 20 Max Planck Yearbook of United Nations Law 241. Although instances might arise where a cyber operation by a State could breach international law yet find justification under this doctrine, virtually no State seeks to rationalize direct cooperation using this principle.

[20] Frederick Alexander Mann, 'The Doctrine of International Jurisdiction Revisited after Twenty Years' (1984) 186 Recueil des Cours 9, 49.

[21] Clarifying Lawful Overseas Use of Data Act (CLOUD Act), Pub L No 115-141, 132 Stat 1210 (2018).

[22] ibid s 103(c). CLOUD Act was enacted against the background of *Microsoft Ireland* case before the Second Circuit Court in 2016. *Microsoft Corp v United States (In re a Warrant to Search a Certain E-Mail Account Controlled & Maintained by Microsoft Corp)* 829 F3d 197 (2d Cir 2016). See Jennifer Daskal, 'Microsoft Ireland, the CLOUD Act, and International Law Making 2.0' (2018) 71 Stanford Law Review 9.

States. The determination of sufficient consolidation, warranting the exercise of US jurisdiction, is highly contingent upon the specific circumstances of each case.[23]

However, the CLOUD Act enables service providers to request the modification or revocation of a disclosure order issued by a US court if they have a valid belief that (1) the individual whose data are being requested is neither a US citizen nor a US resident and (2) complying with the disclosure order could substantially breach the laws of a foreign government partnered with the United States through an executive agreement. The service provider can approach a US court to alter or withdraw the specified disclosure order in such cases. The court will consider the factors in the CLOUD Act to determine, based on comity, by applying a multifactor balancing test that considers the interests of both the United States and the foreign country.[24] If the conditions are not met, the operator can still request that the court change or cancel the order based on comity under general law.

The CLOUD Act establishes that the disclosure of data by a US-based provider in response to a direct order from a foreign government will not be deemed unlawful under US law if an executive agreement is in place between the US government and the respective foreign government. To enter into such an agreement, the foreign government must meet several requirements, including approval by the US Attorney General and substantial and procedural protection for human rights, encompassing privacy and freedom of expression. Additionally, the foreign government must have implemented appropriate measures to minimize the acquisition, retention, and dissemination of information on individuals who are US citizens. The agreement will not become effective if a joint resolution, passed by both the House of Representatives and the Senate, raises objections within 180 days after the signing of the agreement.[25]

Most IT companies welcomed the enactment of the CLOUD Act, as the legislation clarified the rules concerning the disclosure of data located abroad.[26] On the other hand, human rights organizations raised concerns.[27] In the words of a coalition of non-governmental organizations, the bill 'would place too much authority in the hands of the executive branch with few mechanisms to prevent abuse'.[28] It

[23] US DOJ, *Promoting Public Safety, Privacy, and the Rule of Law Around the World: the Purpose and Impact of the CLOUD Act, White Paper* (April 2019) 17 <https://www.justice.gov/opa/press-release/file/1153446/download>.

[24] ibid 16.

[25] CLOUD Act (n 21) s 105(a); 18 USC s 2523(b).

[26] See Nishimura Institute of Advanced Legal Studies, 'Report by the CLOUD Act Study Group Ver. 2.0: Legal Analysis and Proposals On Criminal Investigations Obtaining Data Held by Companies' (2023) 10 <https://www.nishimura.com/en/knowledge/publications/92692>.

[27] See ACLU, 'The Cloud Act Is a Dangerous Piece of Legislation' (13 March 2018) <https://www.aclu.org/blog/privacy-technology/internet-privacy/cloud-act-dangerous-piece-legislation>; EFF, 'The CLOUD Act: A Dangerous Expansion of Police Snooping on Cross-Border Data' (8 February 2018) <https://www.eff.org/deeplinks/2018/02/cloud-act-dangerous-expansion-police-snooping-cross-border-data>.

[28] ACLU, 'Coalition Letter on CLOUD Act' (13 March 2018) <https://www.aclu.org/documents/coalition-letter-cloud-act>.

criticized that it would 'allow foreign governments to wiretap on US soil under standards that do not comply with US law' and 'possibly facilitate foreign government access to information that is used to commit human rights abuses, like torture'.[29] Many of their concerns are overstated, as the bill explicitly mandates that the Attorney General cannot establish an executive agreement with a country failing to meet the human rights criteria set by the CLOUD Act. Nonetheless, their assertions highlight the delicate nature of gathering communication data. Section 3 will discuss the potential conflict between the CLOUD Act and other States' privacy laws.

(2) European Union

The EU e-Evidence Regulation, adopted in June 2023, sets up new mechanisms for cross-border investigations.[30] The Regulation will have law enforcement authorities of the member states request evidence directly from service providers in other member states by 'production orders' and ask the data be preserved for up to sixty days by 'preservation orders'. In addition, the European Parliament adopted a directive that mandates service providers that offer services in the European Union to name designated establishments or legal representatives where member state authorities can address electronic evidence requests.[31]

The e-Evidence Regulations contain provisions by which authorities can refuse evidence requests concerning media freedom or fundamental rights violations in the requesting member state. They also guaranteed that when ordering authorities seek sensitive data, including traffic data, except when solely for identification and content data, they will generally need to inform the authorities in the target country to ensure transparency.

It took almost five years for the European Parliament to start working on harmonizing the rules concerning e-evidence.[32] The Regulation expressly provides that it shall not modify the obligation to respect fundamental rights and legal principles, and that any existing obligations applicable to law enforcement or judicial authorities in this regard remain unaffected.[33] It sets out a detailed procedure for issuing production orders, which may only be issued by judicial authorities or

[29] ibid.

[30] Regulation (EU) 2023/1543 of the European Parliament and of the Council of 12 July 2023 on European Production Orders and European Preservation Orders for electronic evidence in criminal proceedings and for the execution of custodial sentences following criminal proceedings [2023] OJ L 191/118.

[31] Directive (EU) 2023/1544 of the European Parliament and of the Council of 12 July 2023 laying down harmonised rules on the designation of designated establishments and the appointment of legal representatives for the purpose of gathering electronic evidence in criminal proceedings [2023] OJ L 191/181.

[32] European Parliament, Resolution of 3 October 2017 on the fight against cybercrime' (2017/2068(INI)) [2018] OJ C346/121 <https://www.europarl.europa.eu/doceo/document/TA-8-2017-0366_EN.html>.

[33] Regulation (n 30) art 1(3). See also ibid art 12(1).

other designated competent authorities acting in their capacity as investigating authorities.[34] The issuance and the execution of such orders are subject to specific conditions designed to safeguard due process.[35] The Regulation expressly provides that it shall not modify the obligation to respect fundamental rights and legal principles, and that any existing obligations applicable to law enforcement or judicial authorities in this regard remain unaffected.[36] It sets out a detailed procedure for issuing production orders, which may only be issued by judicial authorities or other designated competent authorities acting in their capacity as investigating authorities.[37] The issuance and the execution of such orders are subject to specific conditions designed to safeguard due process.[38]

(3) Other State Practice

Other States impose their laws on foreign operators within their jurisdiction. For instance, China's Internet Security Law of 2016 and its corresponding implementing regulations classify operators into two categories: internet operators and critical infrastructure operators.[39] Operators are required to verify the real identities of their users and are obligated to offer technical assistance and cooperation to public security organs and State security agencies.[40] This cooperation aims to facilitate legal national security protection and criminal investigation activities. The law encompasses the extraterritorial data held by operators.[41]

In 2020, Japan expanded the scope of the Telecommunications Act to encompass foreign legal entities, organizations, and individuals with a foreign domicile who plan to engage in telecommunications activities within Japan.[42] In 2018, South Korea revised the Telecommunications Business Act, which included a provision stating that operators offering core telecommunications services abroad must establish a domestic agent. Additionally, such operators are now subject

[34] ibid arts 5–6.
[35] ibid arts 10–11.
[36] Regulation (n 30) art 1(3). See also ibid art 12(1).
[37] ibid arts 5–6.
[38] ibid arts 10–11.
[39] Internet Security Law (Cybersecurity Law), passed by the Standing Committee of the National People's Congress, Cybersecurity Law of the People's Republic of China (adopted 7 November 2016, entered into force 1 June 2017). Internet operators are those who establish, operate, maintain, protect and use the internet in China, while key information infrastructure operators are those internet operators who operate key infrastructure and are designated by the State Council. Internet Security Law of 2016, art 31.
[40] ibid art 24(1).
[41] ibid art 28
[42] Telecommunications Business Law, Law No 86 of 1984 (amended by Law No 30 of 2020) art 10(1)(i); Law on the Protection of Personal Data, Law No 57 of 2003 (amended by Law No 44 of 2020) art 24(2).

to regulatory oversight by the authorities.[43] Other examples include Belgium,[44] Norway, Portugal, Serbia, and Romania.[45]

2.2.2 Basis for Bilateral Agreements

The United Kingdom and Australia have enacted domestic laws granting their law enforcement agencies access to evidence from foreign operators located abroad. The CLOUD Act prompted these legislative actions. Subsequently, both States have concluded data exchange agreements with the United States.

(1) The United Kingdom

In the United Kingdom, the Investigatory Powers Act of 2016 stipulates that it applies to foreign operators, regardless of whether they offer electronic communications services within the United Kingdom or have control over telecommunications systems in the United Kingdom.[46]

In 2019, the United Kingdom enacted the Crime (Overseas Production Orders) Act. It authorizes the government to establish a designated international cooperation arrangement with the country where the addressee operates or is based. The law enables UK authorities to request a UK court order that compels individuals and companies located outside of the United Kingdom, including communication service providers, to furnish electronic data stored outside the United Kingdom when there exists a Designated International Cooperation Agreement between the United Kingdom and the country where the provider is situated.[47] As Section 5.1 describes, the country concluded the data exchange agreement with the United States.

(2) Australia

Australia's Telecommunications Legislation Amendment (International Production Orders) Act (IPO Act), amended in 2021, is another prime example of a broad jurisdictional basis.[48] This bill was adopted to address the

[43] Telecommunications Business Law, Law No 16019 (amended 24 December 2018) art 87.

[44] The Belgian Court of Cassation held in the *Yahoo!* case that there is a difference between a police authority exercising its powers directly extraterritorially and ordering a business operator in the territory to submit the data. In the latter case, the court held that there was no exercise of extraterritorial jurisdiction in relation to the latter submission order, even though the data were outside the country. However, only the traffic data was the subject of the order in this case, and it is expressly stated that the same decision cannot be made for all data. Hof van Cassatie van België, Nr P.13.2082.N, 1 December 2015.

[45] T-CY, 'Transborder Access and Jurisdiction' (6 December 2012) <https://rm.coe.int/16802e79e8>.

[46] Investigatory Powers Act 2016, c 25. The provisions of the Act, such as section 60A(4), apply to operators providing communications services in the United Kingdom or using UK communications systems. There are no qualifications based on the nationality or location of operators.

[47] Crime (Overseas Production Order) Act 2019, c 5.

[48] Telecommunications Legislation Amendment (International Production Orders) Act, Act No 78 of 2021 (IPO Act).

timeliness and effectiveness of collecting communication data.[49] The previous 1997 Telecommunications Act of Australia set up the regulation of service providers and carriers. Nevertheless, it limited its application to entities that are Australian corporations or provide services through Australian network units.[50] In addition, the Telecommunications (Interception and Access) Act 1979 was the basis for the law enforcement authorities to access the communication data. However, it did not have the mechanisms to require foreign providers to submit information to the government.

The IPO Act allows Australian authorities, including the Australian Security Intelligence Organisation, to obtain International Production Orders (IPOs) to collect data directly from foreign communication service providers if a designated international agreement is in place. The only instance is the Australia–US Agreement, which was concluded in 2021. The Agreement is to be reciprocal. The Act allows for exemptions from Australian laws, which would otherwise prohibit Australian providers from disclosing data to a foreign authority.

Eligible judges and an independent nominated Australian Administrative Tribunal (AAT) Member may issue the IPOs. They must consider matters such as privacy implications for the individuals subject to the IPO, the gravity of the conduct constituting the offence being investigated, the gravity of the conduct constituting the offence being investigated, and the extent to which other methods of investigation have been used or are available.

The IPO Act sets the enforcement threshold, which is quite low. A provider must comply with the order if

> a prescribed communications provider provides a service to one or more Australians, or owns or operates a telecommunications network that is used to provide transmission service to one or more Australians, or one or more Australians have posted material on a general electronic content service provided by a prescribed communications provider.[51]

The IPO covers a vast area of investigation, including investigating an offence, monitoring a person subject to a control order relevant to counterterrorism, and

[49] House of Representatives, Telecommunications Legislation Amendment (International Production Orders) Bill 2020, Explanatory Memorandum, paras 4–8, 64–88 <https://parlinfo.aph.gov.au/parlInfo/download/legislation/ems/r6511_ems_0ac5ae09-3e3e-400b-ae5e-680a68af4e45/upload_pdf/733176.pdf;fileType=application%2Fpdf>. See Genna Churches and others, 'Review of the Effectiveness of the Telecommunications Legislation Amendment (International Production Orders) Bill 2020 ("IPO Bill")' (2020) UNSW Law Research Paper No 20-17 <http://dx.doi.org/10.2139/ssrn.3597800 >.

[50] Telecommunication Act, Act No 47 of 1997, ss 87 and 97.

[51] IPO Act, s 125.

carrying out by the Australian Security Intelligence Organisation its functions.[52] There were concerns about human rights issues. However, the explanatory memorandum of the Senate explains that it complies with international human rights treaties, including the International Covenant on Civil and Political Rights (ICCPR), to which Australia is a party.[53] Additional measures are in place at the State level to ensure the proper consideration procedure. Public Interest Monitors operate under the Public Interest Monitor Act 2011 of Victoria, the Police Powers and Responsibilities Act 2000, and the Crime and Corruption Act 2001 in Queensland. These monitors evaluate applications for interception activities from agencies within their respective jurisdictions. Additionally, the Commonwealth Ombudsman and the Attorney-General's Department provide independent oversight over government agencies. This mechanism pertains to adherence to the Act and specific international agreements assigned for such purposes.

The foreign communications provider subject to an IPO must comply with the order. The failure to meet this requirement may result in the imposition of substantial penalties, potentially amounting to a maximum of AUD 10 million for the corporation. The provider may object to an IPO premised upon the contention that said IPO fails to align with the pertinent designated international agreement. The provider must furnish the Commonwealth Attorney-General's Department with a written notice outlining the specific reasons substantiating the incongruity between the IPO and the designated international agreement. In response to the submitted notice, the Department undertakes a comprehensive review and retains the authority to annul the IPO if such action is warranted.

Furthermore, the Criminal Assistance Act in Australia includes provisions for obtaining assistance concerning electronic information and communications data.[54] The act enables the issuance of direct orders against providers in countries with which Australia has agreements. However, it has faced criticism from certain quarters for being excessively intrusive on privacy grounds. This criticism stems from concerns that the act permits investigative actions and surveillance activities to prevent terrorism.[55]

[52] There are three types of IPOs: (1) Interception IPOs, which enable communications to be intercepted and made available to the requesting agency, and which will also enable the agency to acquire telecommunications data (metadata) relating to the intercepted communications or the individual services; (2) Stored Communications IPOs, which require the provider to disclose specified stored data; and (3) Telecommunications Data IPOs, which require the disclosure of specified telecommunications data. For Interception IPOs, the judge or AAT Member must be satisfied that the information would likely assist in connection with the investigation of serious offences. For Stored Communications IPOs and Telecommunications Data IPOs, the judge or AAT Member must be satisfied that there are reasonable grounds for suspecting that the prescribed communications provider holds, or is likely to commence to hold, the relevant stored communications and telecommunications data.

[53] IPO Act, s 19; House of Representatives (n 42).

[54] Mutual Assistance in Criminal Matters Act, Act No 85 of 1987.

[55] Churches and others (n 49).

3. Prohibition of Data Disclosure to Foreign Authorities

Although the investigating State may apply its laws regarding service provision and communication systems, such direct cooperation with foreign providers may be prohibited under another State's laws due to (1) personal data protection legislation and (2) legislation that limits the transfer of data, including non-personal data, outside the country.

3.1 Personal Information Protection Legislation

3.1.1 Overview

Personal data is any information that relates to an identified or identifiable living individual. Examples include a name, an email address, an Internet Protocol address, and a cookie identification. Over seventy countries implement regulations in their data protection legislation to restrict cross-border personal data transfers. The purpose is to prevent operators from transferring data to countries with inadequate data protection measures, which could bypass the originating country's data protection laws. Additionally, these regulations aim to avoid disproportionate burdens on domestic operators competing with foreign providers. Therefore, it generally adopts a broad jurisdictional basis, including the targeting theory. The Brussels effect pushed other States to employ vigorous personal information protection laws.[56] Therefore, the present section explores the EU regulations in detail.

The primary issue in the current context arises when a law-enforcing State seeking communication data fails to offer adequate personal data protection in the context of government access. This situation can deter service providers from transferring data to that law-enforcing State. It does not inherently create a conflict of rules as long as the transfer impact assessment pertains solely to private-to-private data transfers. Nevertheless, providers may face a difficult situation in which they must disclose data to a State's law enforcement authority, potentially putting the data at risk.

[56] For the expansion of the privacy information protection legislation, see Chapter 12, Sections 3.1 and 5.2. See also Christopher Kuner and OECD, 'Regulation of Transborder Data Flows under Data Protection and Privacy Law: Past, Present and Future' (2011) OECD Digital Economy Papers No 187 <https://www.oecd.org/content/dam/oecd/en/publications/reports/2011/12/regulation-of-transborder-data-flows-under-data-protection-and-privacy-law_g17a2074/5kg0s2fk315f-en.pdf>; Christopher Kuner, *Transborder Data Flows and Data Privacy Law* (OUP 2013). For the development in the Asian region, see Graham Greenleaf, *Asian Data Privacy Laws* (OUP 2014); Graham Greenleaf, 'Asia's Data Privacy Dilemmas: 2014–2019' (2019) 4 Revista Uruguaya de Protección de Datos Personales 49.

3.1.2 The European Union

The EU GDPR is one of the most rigorous regulations among the various data protection frameworks.[57] It influenced the privacy and personal information legislations of other States.[58] Anchored in the Charter of Fundamental Rights of the European Union and the Treaty on the Functioning of the European Union, personal data protection is recognized as a fundamental right.[59] Before the GDPR, the 1995 Data Protection Directive prohibited transfers of personal data to third countries lacking sufficient data protection measures.[60] Subsequently, the GDPR, which superseded the Directive, was adopted in 2016 and became enforceable in 2018 within the European Union.

The GDPR primarily governs the safeguarding of personal data held by business operators. It regulates the processing of personal data by controllers or processors operating within the European Economic Area (EEA). The GDPR applies in two scenarios: (1) when the controller or processor has a physical establishment within the EEA and (2) when the controller or processor, without an establishment, offers goods or services to individuals within the EEA or monitors their behaviours. In the latter case, data transfers to destinations outside the EEA are prohibited unless the destination country provides adequate data protection measures.

Under the GDPR, no transfer or disclosure of personal data is allowed solely based on a judgment from a third-country court or at the order of a third-country authority. Exceptions to this prohibition can be made when other grounds stipulated in the Regulation exist, or there is an agreement between the European Union or a member state.

The European Data Protection Supervisory Service (EDPS) and the European Data Protection Board (EDPB) assessed the CLOUD Act immediately after its enactment. According to their joint evaluation, disclosing or otherwise sharing data with US authorities under the CLOUD Act may infringe upon the GDPR.[61] The CLOUD Act empowers US authorities to directly request data from providers

[57] Regulation (EU) 2016/679 on the protection of natural persons regarding the processing of personal data and on the free movement of such data, and repealing Directive 95/46/EC (General Data Protection Regulation) [2016] OJ L119/1.

[58] For the European Union's regulatory impact, see Anu Bradford, *The Brussels Effect: How the European Union Rules the World* (OUP 2020). In addition, Joanne Scott argued that the European Union makes frequent recourse to a legislative technique of 'territorial extension' in order to gain regulatory traction over activities that take place abroad. Joanne Scott, 'Extraterritoriality and Territorial Extension in EU Law' (2014) 62 American Journal of Comparative Law 87.

[59] Charter of Fundamental Rights of the European Union [2012] OJ C326/391, art 8.

[60] Directive 95/46/EC of the European Parliament and of the Council of 24 October 1995 on the protection of individuals regarding the processing of personal data and on the free movement of such data [1995] OJ L281/31.

[61] EDPS–EDPB, 'Annex. Initial legal assessment of the impact of the US CLOUD Act on the EU legal framework for the protection of personal data and the negotiations of an EU-US Agreement on cross-border access to electronic evidence' <https://edpb.europa.eu/sites/edpb/files/files/file2/edpb_edps_joint_response_us_cloudact_annex.pdf>.

without relying on any of the grounds mentioned above, which may conflict with the guidelines issued by the EDPS.[62]

The United States and the European Union have adopted bilateral arrangements to allow their corporations to transfer data to other regions. The International Safe Harbor Privacy Principles was employed since 1998 to govern cross data transfer, as described in Chapter 10, Section 2.4.[63] In 2015, the European Court of Justice held the mechanism was invalid.[64] It led the adoption of the Privacy Shield, which began to operate in 2016. In 2016, a Privacy Shield framework was established among the United States, European Union, and Switzerland to facilitate the transfer of business-to-business data. However, the adequacy of the protection provided in the arrangements had been disputed before the CJEU. Most recently, in the *Schrems II* case in 2020, the Court found that the Privacy Shield 2016 was invalid.[65] One of the issues was whether the US government's access to personal data for national security purposes under the Foreign Intelligence Surveillance Act meets the GDPR requirements. The CJEU found that the US legislation fell short because it did not provide data protection and rights of judicial review and redress available in the European Union. The case illustrates that government access for national security purposes can impede data transfer among private sector entities.

In 2022, the US Department of Commerce and its counterparts, the European Commission, the UK government, and the Swiss Federal Administration, each established new privacy frameworks to address existing concerns.[66] These frameworks require US organizations receiving personal data from their EU, UK, and Swiss counterparts to implement reliable transfer safeguards and to provide privacy protections consistent with their respective laws. Effective privacy protection under these frameworks includes methods to ensure compliance with the core principles; recourse for individuals affected by non-compliance, including the establishment of independent recourse mechanisms; and sanctions for organizations that fail to comply with the principles.

In 2016, alongside the GDPR and the Passenger Name Record Directive, the Law Enforcement Directive (LED) was adopted.[67] The LED introduces a

[62] Besides the data-transfer mechanisms, it is noted that an MLAT was signed between the European Union and the United States in 2003, along with separate MLATs between the United States and EU Member States. Agreement on Mutual Legal Assistance between the European Union and the United States [2003] OJ L181/34.

[63] International Safe Harbor Privacy Principles, 65 Fed Reg 45666 (24 July 2000).

[64] C-362/14 *Maximillian Schrems v Data Protection Commissioner* ECLI:EU:C:2015:650.

[65] C-311/18 *Data Protection Commissioner v Facebook Ireland and Schrems* ECLI:EU:C:2020:559. The decision was based on the existence of a US government programme for the surveillance of personal data under section 702 of FISA and Executive Order 12333, and the lack of a right for data subjects to challenge the processing of their data in a judicial forum.

[66] Data Privacy Framework Program, 'Enforcement of the Data Privacy Framework (DPF) Program' <https://www.dataprivacyframework.gov/program-articles/Enforcement-of-the-Data-Privacy-Framework-(DPF)-Program>.

[67] Directive (EU) 2016/680 of the European Parliament and of the Council of 27 April 2016 on the protection of natural persons with regard to the processing of personal data by competent authorities for the purposes of the prevention, investigation, detection or prosecution of criminal offences

framework different from the GDPR's in balancing public safety and personal data protection. Its purpose is to establish rules for protecting individuals concerning the processing of personal data by authorities, specifically to prevent, investigate, detect, prosecute, or enforce criminal offences, including measures against threats to public safety. Member states differentiate their treatment of personal data based on the data subject's role, such as suspects, convicted individuals, victims, witnesses, and so forth. Furthermore, distinctions are made between personal data and verifying personal data, as well as whether the data requires special attention. It will be maintained if an MLAT exists between the European Union and a third country.

The LED establishes data transfer rules from EU member state authorities to third countries and international organizations. These regulations cover various transfers, including those based on adequacy decisions, transfers with appropriate safeguards in the absence of adequate choices, and transfers considered necessary under specific circumstances. Such circumstances may arise when it is necessary to safeguard the data subject's vital interests or the vital interests of others, protect the data subject's legitimate interests as defined by national laws, prevent immediate and significant threats to public security in an EU member State or a third country, or prevent or investigate crimes in response to specific and individual cases.

3.2 Data Protection Legislation

Data protection legislations define operators' security management responsibilities concerning data handling, including non-personal data. These regulations require businesses to have a suitable infrastructure in their home countries and ensure that data collected within their jurisdictions remain within their countries. The motivations behind implementing such regulations vary across countries but commonly include the desire to create barriers for foreign companies entering the market, safeguard domestic industries, and prevent sensitive data from being moved abroad for security reasons.[68]

The specific provisions within these regulations can vary significantly. They may include obligations such as maintaining a copy of the data within the home country, processing and storing data exclusively within the home country (prohibiting data storage in other countries), establishing local facilities, and, in some

or the execution of criminal penalties, and on the free movement of such data, and repealing Council Framework Decision 2008/977/JHA [2016] OJ L119/89.

[68] Lee Andrew Bygrave, *Data Privacy Law* (OUP 2014); Kuner and OECD (n 56). There are situations where restrictions may be imposed, accounting for the nature of the information itself, such as biometric, mapping, or financial data. For state practice, Anupam Chander and Uyên P Lê, 'Data Nationalism' (2014) 64 Emory Law Journal 677.

cases, prohibiting the removal of data outside the home country. Differentiating these regulations from cross-border transfer restrictions outlined in the Personal Data Protection Act requires a thorough examination based on the measure's content, purpose, and impact.

For instance, China's Internet Safety Law mandates that 'critical information infrastructure operators' store personal data collected within China's borders.[69] This does not outright ban extraterritorial data transfers but necessitates a safety assessment and prohibits transfers in specific prescribed cases. Furthermore, the Data Security Law in China applies only to data processing activities conducted within the country. It imposes data security protection obligations on organizations and individuals involved in data processing. Similarly, India's Information Technology Act compels businesses to retain data within India.[70] Russia[71] and Vietnam[72] also have regulations that mandate data storage within their regions.

3.3 Service Provider's Obligation for Decryption

Individuals exhibit a significant need for encrypted communication to facilitate their transactions. They tend to prefer end-to-end encryption to secure their message. No one, including the service providers and third parties, can access the cryptographic keys except the senders and recipients. The technology is important to protect users from risks of cybercrime, data theft, and violation of privacy. Platformers such as Microsoft, Google, and Apple have expressed their policy on employing this system. On the other hand, there is a demand for law enforcement authorities to access the communication data because criminal networks use encrypted communication platforms to facilitate their illicit activities.

Therefore, a State may issue orders to operators, compelling them to decrypt encrypted data or require the installation of backdoors. A backdoor refers to a deliberate entry point in a software, system, or technology that allows individuals to gain access, bypassing the usual security measures. It can serve legitimate purposes such as maintenance or debugging. However, it can potentially provide a way to manipulate or control the system and collect information without authorization.

Various perspectives and practices exist in response to the increasing severity of terrorism and other threats. Governments of the United States, the United Kingdom, Canada, Australia, and New Zealand (the 'Five Eyes' intelligence

[69] Law of the People's Republic of China on Internet Security (adopted on 10 June 2021) <http://www.npc.gov.cn/npc/c30834/202106/7c9af12f51334a73b56d7938f99a788a.shtml>.

[70] Information Technology Act 2000 (amended in 2011) <https://www.wipo.int/edocs/lexdocs/laws/en/in/in098en.pdf>.

[71] Federal Law No 152-FZ of 27 July 2006 on Personal Data (as amended on 30 December 2020); Regulations on securing personal data being processed in personal data systems, No 781, 2007.

[72] Law on Cybersecurity 2018, No 24/2018/QH14, art 26.

alliance) have repeatedly expressed concern about the risks caused by encryption technology.[73] In 2020, India and Japan, members of the Quadrilateral Security Dialogue, joined in issuing a statement calling on IT companies to develop the backdoors.[74]

Some countries provide legal mechanisms for such measures. For instance, the UK Investigatory Powers Act 2016 authorizes authorities to request the removal of electronic protection within the operator's capabilities.[75] Similarly, Australia's Telecommunications and Other Legislation Amendment (Assistance and Access) Act mandates that operators develop new capabilities and obliges them to co-operate within their capacities.[76]

Conversely, opposing viewpoints highlight concerns about communication security; the burden imposed on operators, including the costs associated with implementing backdoors; and potential disadvantages in international competitiveness compared to companies not subject to decryption requirements.

4. Irreconcilable Jurisdictional Conflicts

4.1 Overview

National legislation on data investigations has been developed with limited effectiveness in international coordination. Consequently, conflicts can arise between the investigating State and the host State of data providers. In the past, the United States applied its own antitrust and export control laws to foreign companies operating outside its borders based on the effects principle, leading to disagreements with European countries. In response, European countries enacted laws prohibiting information disclosure to foreign governments, resulting in conflicts for companies. Since the 1990s, economic policy alignment and improved law enforcement by the United States have led to convergence and resolution of these issues.

However, it is inherently difficult to coordinate conflicting values and interests concerning data investigations among States. There are several issues in question.

[73] Five Country Ministerial, 'Statement of Principles on Access to Evidence and Encryption' (2018) <https://www.homeaffairs.gov.au/nat-security/Pages/statement-of-principles-on-access-to-evidence-and-encryption.aspx>.

[74] US DOJ, Press Release, 'International Statement: End-To-End Encryption and Public Safety' (11 October 2020) <https://www.justice.gov/opa/pr/international-statement-end-end-encryption-and-public-safety>.

[75] Investigatory Powers Act, c 25.

[76] Telecommunications and Other Legislation Amendment (Assistance and Access) Bill 2018. The Act provides for (1) a Technical Assistance Request (a voluntary request for cooperation), (2) a Technical Assistance Notice (a notice requiring operators to cooperate within their capabilities), and (3) Technical Capability Notice (a notice requiring operators to build new capabilities. The Technical Assistance Notice will then be addressed to be granted to the authorities.

First, the guarantee of individual rights to information is the primary factor influencing disputes. The right to privacy varies in its content due to social and cultural values. For instance, the constitutional prominence of the right to privacy and the existence of comprehensive personal data protection laws differs across countries and regions. In the European Union, the right to data protection is safeguarded by the EU Charter of Fundamental Rights.[77] Some countries, such as China, view protecting personal data as protecting individual rights and preserving national sovereignty. Conversely, the United States prioritizes fostering new technologies and industries by enabling data utilization by IT companies. While no federal-level comprehensive data protection law exists, relevant laws exist at the disciplinary and State levels.

It is noted that some countries stick to the strict data protection policy. The practice of Switzerland is noteworthy. It upholds privacy as the constitutional rights.[78] As explained in the context of bank secrecy in Chapter 8, Article 271 of the Swiss Criminal Code prohibits Swiss companies from assisting foreign law enforcement. All foreign authority requests under MLATs and other legal assistance agreements must be reviewed by the Swiss government, as direct cooperation is not permitted. Furthermore, Switzerland has a close access to the EU market and benefits from a strong scientific community and stable IT infrastructure. Therefore, it attracts pro-privacy companies such as Proton, which offers end-to-end encryption services.

Privacy rights and regulations on cross-border data transfers exhibit significant diversity. Efforts have been undertaken to facilitate efficient cross-border data transfers.[79] They include amended Convention 108, which aims to protect data rights while considering the necessity of cross-border transfers.[80] However, the convention is limited by the absence of major States such as the United States and China as participants.

Another major achievement is the Organisation for Economic Co-operation and Development (OECD)'s Declaration on Government Access to Personal Data Held by Private Sector Entities, adopted in 2022. It aims to enhance trust in cross-border data transfers by clarifying the principles through which national security and law enforcement agencies can access personal data within the bounds of existing legal frameworks. The instrument is not universally supported. Even if co-ordination was possible among States regarding information handling, it is limited to countries that adhere to similar human rights norms.

[77] Charter of Fundamental Rights of the European Union [2012] OJ C326/391, art 8.

[78] Switzerland, Federal Constitution (AS 1999 2556) art 13. It amended the Federal Act on Data Protection in 2020 and issued Ordinance on Data Protection and the Ordinance on Data Protection Certification, which came into effect in 2023.

[79] OECD, Recommendation of the Council concerning Guidelines governing the Protection of Privacy and Transborder Flows of Personal Data (2013), C(80)58/FINAL, 11 July 2013, see also C(2013)79.

[80] Protocol Amending the Convention for the Protection of Individuals regarding Automatic Processing of Personal Data (adopted on 10 October 2018) CETS No 223.

The second factor is the potential for conflict diversification. Historical judicial friction, starting from the 1960s, arose partly due to the concentration of multinational corporations in the United States, where the dollar served as the reserve currency. This issue was predominantly caused by the United States until the European Union emerged as a significant player. Presently, there is a similar concentration of major IT companies' headquarters in the United States, although the trend of platforming is also expanding outside the United States. Moreover, over seventy countries have implemented restrictive regulations on cross-border personal data transfers. Consequently, disputes in this area can become increasingly intricate.

In the absence of a higher coordinating mechanism, conflicting jurisdictions lack a means of resolution. Consequently, operators aiming to avoid being entangled in such conflicts may take actions to evade being subjected to the jurisdiction of a specific country. An instance of this is observed in the EEA, where certain US newspapers and the Japanese company Yahoo! Japan decided to withdraw their services following the enforcement of the GDPR. However, if this trend intensifies globally, there is a potential for service providers to cease operations in certain countries to evade being caught in the middle. Consequently, a situation may arise where internet services become unavailable depending on the user's location. This scenario could lead to a fragmented internet (referred to as 'splInternet'), undermining the fundamental nature of transnational information networks.[81]

4.2 Privacy under International Human Rights Law

4.2.1 Historical Development

An additional challenge lies in the restricted coverage of international human rights law. It inadequately tackles issues concerning the investigation of transnational crimes, particularly concerning the right to privacy.

The 1960s saw the transformation of a criminal procedure because computers enabled the authorities to digitize information and to facilitate its collection, storage, reproduction, distribution, and circulation. Furthermore, the proliferation of the internet, which was put to practical use in the private sector in the 1990s, has led to a dramatic increase in the transfer of information across national borders compared to an earlier time.[82] These transformations in information and

[81] It is noted that the key issue is the geopolitical competition among major digital markets. In this context, Anu Bradford argues that the United States, China, and the European Union seek to advance their respective models of digital governance. Anu Bradford, *Digital Empires: The Global Battle to Regulate Technology* (OUP 2023).

[82] Daniel J Solove, 'Privacy and Power: Computer Databases and the Metaphors for Information Privacy' (2000) 53 Stanford Law Review 1393, 1402.

communications technology necessitated new national legislation specifically for information protection from the late 1960s. The Federal Republic of Germany's State of Hess enacted the first general data protection law in 1970.[83] Other countries followed, including Sweden,[84] the United States,[85] West Germany,[86] France,[87] Denmark,[88] Norway,[89] Canada,[90] and the United Kingdom.[91] At their core, these laws reconciled privacy protection with the need for cross-border communication.

There have been attempts to identify common principles for data protection laws. The OECD established an expert group on cross-border data transfer and privacy protection in 1978 and adopted the first Privacy Guidelines in 1980.[92] The basic principles are the free flow of data and legitimate restrictions. In other words, Member States are recommended to take 'all reasonable and appropriate steps to ensure that transborder flows of personal data ... are uninterrupted and secure'.[93] Unless the receiving State does not substantially observe the OECD Guidelines or the re-export of such data would circumvent its domestic privacy legislation, a State should refrain from restricting transborder flows of personal data.[94] A State may restrict the transfer of specific categories of personal data if its domestic privacy laws contain specific regulations tailored to the nature of such data and if the receiving member country lacks equivalent protections.[95] However, the guidelines are more inclined towards fostering cross-border transactions. It specifically provides that 'States should avoid developing laws, policies and practices in the name of the protection of privacy and individual liberties, which would create obstacles to transborder flows of personal data that would exceed requirements for such protection'.[96]

However, there was no harmonization of standards for protecting privacy at the time. The differences in standards between the European Union and the United States illustrate it. In the European Union, the adoption of Directive 95/46 by the EC Council in 1995 harmonized the standards required in the national laws of the EU Member States. The Directive specifies that transfers of personal data outside the territory of the European Union must be subject to the same 'adequate

83 Datenschutzgesetz, 07 October 1970, Hessisches Gesetz-und Verordnungsblatt I, 625.
84 Datalagen, Svensk författningssamling [SFS] 1973:289.
85 Privacy Act, Pub L No 93-579, 88 Stat 1896 (1974), 5 USC 552a.
86 Bundesdatenschutzgesetz (BDSG) (1 January 1979) BGBl I, No 7, 201.
87 Loi 78-17 du 6 janvier 1978 relative à l'informatique, aux fichiers et aux libertés.
88 Lov nr 293 af 8 juni 1978 om private registre mv; lov nr 294 af 8 juni 1978 om offentlige myndigheders registre.
89 Lov om personregistre mm av 9 juni 1978 nr 48.
90 Human Rights Act 1977, SC 1976–77, c 33, s 1.
91 Data Protection Act 1984, c 35.
92 OECD, Guidelines Governing the Protection of Privacy and Transborder Flows of Personal Data, annex to the Recommendation of the Council of 23 September 1980.
93 ibid para 15.
94 ibid para 17.
95 ibid.
96 ibid para 18.

protection' in the destination country as within the European Union.[97] In the European Union, the right to privacy is a fundamental right of the individual and directly implies due process guarantees and the principle of proportionality. The 1995 Directive is based on this assumption.[98]

In contrast, the United States does not comprehensively regulate the rights of individuals to information but has separate legislation for each area of information collection. It aims to promote the free flow of ideas and competition instead of tightening government regulation. There has not been a privacy protection law at the federal level.[99]

Many countries do not have data protection laws. In this regard, as mentioned earlier, the OECD guidelines and the Asia-Pacific Economic Cooperation (APEC)'s Cross-border Privacy Rules Regime[100] are attempting to bring about cooperation between authorities. However, they are not legally binding, and the extent of their implementation is not sufficient.

Data that a service provider has can be metadata (communications data and traffic data) or content data. The former refers to the information on the data, including the communication's origin and destination, route, time, size, duration, and the types of underlying service. The latter is the contents of the communication. National legislation often requires service providers to store such data and to disclose and submit it when the authority requires it.

It is also commonly recognized in national laws in many countries that the right to privacy may be constrained to the extent necessary for the public interest, including criminal regulation. However, criminal investigations through mass data are fraught with the possibility of deviating from the principle of proportionality. There remains a dispute as to the extent of the scope of permissibility.[101] The conditions under which investigative authorities access it differ from country to country. There is no universal standard in this regard, which the subsequent chapters will explore in detail.

[97] Directive 95/46/EC of the European Parliament and of the Council of 24 October 1995 on the protection of individuals with regard to the processing of personal data and on the free movement of such data [1995] OJ L281/31, art 25.

[98] ECJ cases expressly stating this include Joined Cases C-465/00, C-138/01, C-139-01, *Rechnungshof (C-465/00) v Österreichischer Rundfunk and Others and Christa Neukomm (C-138/01) and Joseph Lauermann (C-139/01) v Österreichischer Rundfunk* [2003] OJ C171/3 (19 July 2003). ECtHR cases to this effect include Grand Chamber, *Fressoz and Roire v France* App No 29183/95 (Judgment) (ECtHR 21 January 1999), Reports 1999-I, 1.

[99] In 2022, American Data Privacy and Protection Act was submitted to the Congress but did not pass. See US Congress, House of Representatives, 'American Data Privacy Protection Act, HR 8152, 117th Congress (2022)' <https://www.congress.gov/bill/117th-congress/house-bill/8152/text>.

[100] APEC Cooperation Arrangement for Cross-Border Privacy Enforcement (endorsed on November 2009, commenced on 16 July 2010).

[101] Fred H Cate, *Privacy in the Information Age* (Jessica Kingsley Publishers 1997) 129; Arthur J Cockfield, 'Protecting Taxpayer Privacy Rights under Enhanced Cross-Border Tax Information Exchange: Toward a Multilateral Taxpayer Bill of Rights' (2010) 42 University of British Columbia Law Review 420, fn 84.

4.2.2 Development of Privacy Rights under International Law through the European Court of Human Rights

As global efforts to combat crimes such as organized crime and terrorism become more collaborative, there is a growing trend towards safeguarding the rights of the accused through the clarification and implementation of international human rights standards.[102]

The European Convention on Human Rights (ECHR) leads this practice. Notably, the European Court of Human Rights (ECtHR) enjoys broad jurisdiction in terms of individual petitioning compared to other human rights bodies. Individuals have the right to submit petitions for violations of the Convention per the amendment introduced by Protocol 11 to the ECHR, which became effective in 1998.

The Article 8 of the ECHR provides that '[e]veryone has the right to respect for his private and family life, his home and his correspondence'.[103] Then, it stipulates that '[t]here shall be no interference by a public authority with the exercise of this right' subject to certain exceptions.[104]

The first case where the ECtHR decided on the legality of the interception was *Klass and Others v Germany* of 1978.[105] The court affirmed that 'where a State institutes secret surveillance the existence of which remains unknown to the persons being controlled, with the effect that the surveillance remains unchallengeable, Article 8 could largely be reduced to a nullity'.[106] It also held that the exception to privacy rights has to be narrowly interpreted. In the court's words, '[p]owers of secret surveillance of citizens, characterizing as they do the police State, are tolerable under the Convention only in so far as strictly necessary for safeguarding the democratic institutions'.[107] However, in light of the procedural mechanisms of Germany and of the detailed examination of the contested legislation, the Court concluded that the German legislature was legal 'as being necessary for a democratic society in the interests of national security and for the prevention of disorder or crime', which is one of the exceptions to Article 8(1).[108]

[102] Sabine Gless and John AE Vervaele, 'Law Should Govern: Aspiring General Principles for Transnational Criminal Justice' (2013) 9 Utrecht Law Review 1.

[103] ECHR art 8(1).

[104] ibid art 8(2) ('There shall be no interference by a public authority with the exercise of this right except such as is in accordance with the law and is necessary in a democratic society in the interests of national security, public safety or the economic wellbeing of the country, for the prevention of disorder or crime, for the protection of health or morals, or for the protection of the rights and freedoms of others'). See ECtHR, 'Guide on Article 8 of the Convention—Right to Respect for Private and Family Life' (2022) <https://ks.echr.coe.int/documents/d/echr-ks/guide_art_8_eng>.

[105] *Case of Klass and Others v Germany* App No 5029/71 (Judgment (Merits)) (ECtHR, 6 September 1978).

[106] ibid para 36.

[107] ibid para 42.

[108] ibid para 60.

The ECtHR has emphasized that communications by the authorities should not be arbitrarily monitored. According to the Court, interception of communications must have a legal basis that is publicly available, as established in the leading case of *Weber v Germany* in 2006.[109] In Germany, the 1996 Act, which amended the Interception of Communications and Other Communications Act, granted the Federal Intelligence Agency (Bundesnachrichtendienst) the power to strategically intercept communications and use or transfer the obtained information to other agencies. The Court held that the warrant for interception must specify the nature of the offence; the categories of individuals to be intercepted; the duration of the interception; the procedures for analysing, using, and storing the information obtained; and the timeline for deleting the recorded information.

Furthermore, the Court has also ruled that the acquisition of metadata, which includes information about the telephone number and duration of the call but not the content of the communication, constitutes an interference with the rights protected under Article 8(1). Additionally, the recording of calls by the police, even with the consent of one of the parties to the call, is considered interference by a public authority.

The jurisprudence of the ECtHR has played a significant role in promoting international standards for respecting human rights during investigations.

4.3 Digital Authoritarianism

An obstacle arises from the involvement of national sovereignty and ideology. Certain nations employ digital technologies to oversee, regulate, and influence the information and communication activities of their citizens, frequently compromising individual liberties and privacy. This phenomenon is labelled digital authoritarianism or digital repression in cases where freedom of expression is unduly curtailed. This phenomenon has gained prominence in non-democratic countries, including China, Saudi Arabia, and other Middle Eastern countries, such as Russia. Milder countries, such as Vietnam and India, also shift towards such a trend. While this section does not intend to extensively examine State practice, there are shared elements that render these States incompatible with other democratic nations.

A pivotal aspect of this trend revolves around internet censorship, as described in Chapter 10, Section 2. Governments might utilize advanced surveillance technologies to monitor online activities, allowing them to identify and target individuals expressing dissenting opinions. Authoritarian States frequently quell online activism by subjecting activists to harassment and cyberattacks, thereby silencing

[109] *Weber and Saravia v Germany* App No 54934/00 (Decision) (ECtHR 29 June 2006).

opposition and discouraging civic participation. These governments often resort to blocking access to websites and platforms deemed threatening to their control.

In their pursuit, governments may also resort to propaganda and disinformation tactics. By deploying social media bots, trolls, and State-controlled media outlets, they manipulate public sentiment, propagate falsehoods, and sow confusion. These measures effectively restrict citizens from accessing information and viewpoints that deviate from the official narrative. Simultaneously, they undermine the integrity of independent journalism, which holds the role of the 'fourth estate' in a flourishing democratic landscape.

The motives and origins of this approach differ across States. Nonetheless, the challenge lies in the frequent entanglement of economic interests and the government's desire for control, two aspects that are often intertwined and inseparable.

Tom Ginsburg persuasively argued that democratic and authoritarian governments exhibit distinct perspectives on international law stemming from their unique governance systems.[110] As the dynamics of power among these types of governments change, there will be implications for the global framework of legal principles. While human rights might encounter substantial hurdles in the future, citizens of democratic nations could still experience advantages through collaborative international legal efforts in various domains. It effectively elucidates the scenario of digital authoritarianism.

4.4 Human Rights Protection

4.4.1 The Limits of the International Human Rights Law

Another issue concerns the human rights protection of communication service users. There are established international human rights that may be affected by the extension of the jurisdictional scope. They include protection against arbitrary or unlawful interference with privacy,[111] the right to freedom of expression[112] and association,[113] the right to life, and an effective remedy[114] and fair trial.[115]

The challenge arises when the investigating State's due process standard falls below that of the host State or international human rights law. The handling of data by investigating authorities will adhere to the regulations of the respective country. In digital investigations, it is crucial to establish guidelines concerning

[110] Tom Ginsburg, *Democracies and International Law* (CUP, 2021) 288.
[111] International Covenant on Civil and Political Rights (ICCPR) (adopted on 16 December 1966, entered into force on 23 March 1976) 999 UNTS 171, art 17.
[112] ibid art 19.
[113] ibid art 21.
[114] ibid art 2(3).
[115] ibid art 14.

data retention periods and disposal procedures to safeguard data subjects' rights. Furthermore, there is a growing need to set industry standards for digital forensic techniques to ensure the integrity and precision of data. Despite several efforts to address this issue, as will be elucidated further in the subsequent analysis, establishing international standards remains unresolved.

Moreover, in response to the digital age, the right to privacy strives to empower individuals to assume a proactive role in managing their information, acknowledging the inherent characteristics of data, which can be swiftly transferred, distributed, stored, and utilized in vast quantities. As a result, certain countries and the European Union have enforced stringent requirements to ensure robust safeguarding of privacy for States and operators.

Conversely, privacy rights present challenges in coordination due to their intrinsic nature, as they reflect each country's historical, societal, and cultural contexts. The legal frameworks of various nations often impose varying restrictions on access by investigative authorities, contingent upon the specific content, and characteristics of the information in question, such as subscriber data held by telecommunications providers, communication metadata, and content data. However, the classifications and prerequisites for obtaining warrants diverge across countries. For instance, the US SCA of 1986 stipulates that a subpoena is adequate for acquiring communication metadata, whereas content data necessitates a warrant.[116] In contrast, Japan adopts an alternative approach, asserting that metadata should enjoy the same level of protection as content data, considering it a confidential communication component.

Furthermore, current international human rights law, which upholds the principles of freedom of expression and condemns censorship, fails to provide adequate guidance for managing substantial volumes of data by investigating bodies. While the right to privacy is enshrined in prominent international human rights treaties, such as the ICCPR, it primarily safeguards individuals from government censorship and the dissemination of their private affairs to external parties.

International human rights law is based on a decentralized framework. Consequently, if evidence gathered by an investigating State contravenes the laws of the host State, there is no explicit requirement under international law to exclude such evidence from the criminal trial of the former State.[117] Nonetheless, the host State has the prerogative to implement measures prohibiting operators from cooperating in such cases, potentially leading to an international dispute.

[116] United States Stored Communications Act 1986, Pub L No 99-508, 100 Stat 1848, 1860.

[117] Article 2(1) of the ICCPR requires member States to respect human rights for individuals in the territory or under the jurisdiction, rendering limited provisions for human rights guarantees when criminal investigations involve multiple States. Consequently, in such instances, the decision regarding the exclusion of evidence rests with the court of the respective State.

4.4.2 Digital Human Rights

To overcome the limits of international human rights law, some scholars advocate for digital human rights, which are the rights and principles that pertain to individuals in the digital domain. With the proliferation of digital technologies and their pervasive influence on various aspects of human life, this concept has emerged as a crucial area of study and discourse. It encompasses protecting, promoting, and realizing fundamental human rights in the digital era. It covers conventional rights, such as freedom of expression, privacy, and non-discrimination, as well as novel rights that have emerged due to the unique challenges and opportunities of digital technologies.[118]

There had been a series of efforts to clarify internationally accepted human rights standards to cross-border data flows. For instance, the International Law Commission published a report in 2006 on core principles of data protection law, which it identified as (1) legality and fairness of information collection and processing, (2) data accuracy, (3) specificity and limitation of data collection, (4) proportionality of constraints, (5) transparency, (6) individual participation and specific access rights, (7) non-discrimination, (8) responsibility for loss of data protection, (9) guarantee of independent monitoring bodies and legal sanctions, (10) elimination of unjustified barriers to cross-border information circulation, and (11) durability.[119] However, it did not have much practical impact afterwards.

The digital age has engendered profound transformations in how information is accessed, disseminated, and controlled. It has opened new avenues for communication, participation, and social interaction while raising concerns regarding surveillance, data privacy, and algorithmic biases.

The UN Human Rights Council and the Office of the UN High Commissioner for Human Rights have investigated 'privacy in the digital age'. Additionally, businesses may have a social responsibility to fulfil regarding data handling, as outlined in the Guiding Principles on Business and Human Rights. However, it should be noted that the right to refuse disclosure when requested by a State with jurisdiction in a criminal investigation cannot be considered firmly established in substantive international law.

Digital investigation can potentially infringe upon users' rights, including their right to personal data protection, privacy, and freedom of expression. The nature of communication datasets sets them apart from paper-based information and other

[118] See Yuval Shany, 'Digital Rights and the Outer Limits of International Human Rights Law' (2023) 24 German Law Journal 461.

[119] International Law Commission, *Report on the Work of its Fifty-Eighth Session (1 May to 9 June and 3 July to 11 August 2006)* UN Doc A/61/10, Annex IV, 'Protection of Personal Data in the Transborder Flow of Information', 217.

forms of evidence due to the extensive volume of information in these datasets and their notable impact on privacy boundaries.

In situations where the rights in question are protected by the laws of the jurisdiction and the authorities within the same country gather evidence in a manner that violates those rights, it becomes mandatory to exclude such evidence according to Article 14(1) of the ICCPR, which upholds the right to a fair trial. However, suppose the acquisition of evidence is deemed illegal due to rights violations under the laws of another State yet remains lawful under the jurisdiction where the trial takes place. In that case, the court may need to assess whether excluding the evidence is necessary to safeguard the rights to a fair trial, a robust defence, and an effective remedy. International human rights law has an inherently decentralized nature. It does not require the consideration of the illegality of authorities from other States in cases involving multiple States engaged in a criminal investigation.

Various theoretical endeavours have aimed to address the decentralized nature of international human rights law. However, in practice, the movement to establish a legal framework for it has primarily emerged within the case law of the ECtHR, with little indication of a similar trend beyond Europe.

It is also possible for individuals to attempt to exclude evidence by asserting the violation of their human rights under international law rather than the law of another State. When challenging evidence is obtained from outside the jurisdiction, the extraterritorial application of human rights treaties may arise as a concern, as examined in Chapter 3, Section 4. On one hand, as foreign operators are increasingly mandated to have a representative or agent in their home country for telecommunications purposes if the evidence is obtained through such a representative or agent, this issue is effectively mitigated.

Nevertheless, the difficulty arises because the existing standards within international human rights treaties do not sufficiently address the specific rules concerning electronic evidence acquisition. There are no universally established guidelines on how the forum State's authorities should handle and dispose of data after acquiring it from an operator. There is also a lack of clarity regarding how the rights of the user and third parties can be safeguarded when such evidence is disclosed in court and whether the monitoring of data handling by third parties within the jurisdiction is adequately covered.

Furthermore, the monitoring of data handling by third-party entities in the jurisdiction lacks universally established rules. Although certain countries have differentiated the treatment of data based on their nature, such distinctions are not universally recognized. Moreover, determining the significance of digital privacy is contingent upon each country's political, social, and cultural choices, which inherently pose challenges in achieving harmonization across nations.

5. Direct Cooperation as Prescribed under Treaties

5.1 Data Access Agreements

There has been a growing trend in recent years towards mutual recognition of requests for direct cooperation with operators located in foreign territories to overcome such potential conflicts.

An instance is the bilateral data exchange agreements. They are in response to the CLOUD Act, which provides for executive agreements. As described above, Australia and the United Kingdom have also enacted laws that allow their governments to conclude bilateral exchange agreements. Following national legislation, these executive agreements are expected to be signed between the two countries. Notably, data access agreements have already been established between the United Kingdom and the United States,[120] as well as between the United States and Australia.[121]

For instance, the UK–US Agreement specifies that in cases involving serious crimes with a statutory term of three years or more, direct requests for data disclosure and submission can be made to providers under the jurisdiction of the requesting State. The types of data covered include communication content, communication data, metadata, stored process data, and the account holder's identity. Notably, a unique requirement imposed solely by the United Kingdom involves segregating or deleting information that is deemed unnecessary for criminal investigations and other purposes.

There are instances where the consent of the other State is required for the use of acquired data in prosecution. As an illustration, one can consider situations wherein the United States is investigating a crime that potentially carries the death penalty or when the United Kingdom is involved in a case that encompasses limitations on freedom of expression. Furthermore, as an objection procedure, if a provider from the investigating State believes that an order violates the national law of the other State, they can initially challenge it through the procedure established by the ordering State. If the decision of the ordering State is not adhered to, an objection can be raised with the designated authority of the other State. Both countries engage in consultations, and ultimately, the other country can refuse to enforce the

[120] Agreement on Access to Electronic Data for the Purpose of Countering Serious Crime (3 October 2019) <https://assets.publishing.service.gov.uk/government/uploads/system/uploads/attachment_data/file/836969/CS_USA_6.2019_Agreement_between_the_United_Kingdom_and_the_USA_on_Access_to_Electronic_Data_for_the_Purpose_of_Countering_Serious_Crime.pdf>.

[121] Agreement between the Government of the United States of America and the Government of Australia on Access to Electronic Data for the Purpose of Countering Serious Crime (signed on 15 December 2021) <https://www.justice.gov/dag/cloud-act-agreement-between-governments-us-and-australia>. See also Parliament of Australia, 'CLOUD Act Agreement' <https://www.aph.gov.au/Parliamentary_Business/Committees/Joint/Treaties/CloudActAgreement/Report/section?id=committees%2Freportjnt%2F024997%2F80300>.

order. The application of the EU–US Umbrella Agreement is also provided for in this context.[122]

5.2 Second Additional Protocol of the Cybercrime Convention

The introduction of Second Additional Protocol to the Cybercrime Convention addressed the growing demand for an efficient and simplified means of obtaining subscriber and traffic data from service providers in different contracting States. This Protocol facilitates direct multilateral cooperation, ensuring a smoother process for ordering or requesting the submission of such data.

The acquisition of information is limited to domain name registration and subscriber information. Domain names play a significant role in disseminating malware, botnets, phishing, and other illicit activities. Therefore, direct cooperation focuses on obtaining information about the registrant of a domain, as it plays a critical role in identifying potential suspects involved in such activities.

Each party shall adopt such legislative and other measures as may be necessary to empower its competent authorities, for specific criminal investigations or proceedings, to issue a request to an entity providing domain name registration services in the territory of another party for information in the entity's possession or control for identifying or contacting the registrant of a domain name.[123] This request aims to obtain information held or controlled by the entity, aiming to identify the registrant of a specific domain name or establish communication with the relevant individual. The State party should undertake any necessary legislative or other measures to authorize the entity to issue such a request for information. If the entity refuses to cooperate, the requesting State may ask for an explanation regarding the reasons behind the refusal. Moreover, the requesting State can also seek consultation with the State party where the entity is located to explore alternative means of acquiring the required information.

The State party must also take the legislative and other measures necessary to authorize the issuance of an order directly submitted to the operator concerning the disclosure of subscriber information in the possession or control of an entity in the territory of another State party.

Suppose an order is issued to an organization within a party's territory. In that case, the party may require simultaneous notification of the order, along with supplementary information and a summary of the relevant facts pertaining to the

[122] The Umbrella Agreement does not establish an independent basis for data transfers but sets out appropriate safeguards for data transfers for law enforcement purposes. Agreement between the United States of America and the European Union on the protection of personal information relating to the prevention, investigation, detection, and prosecution of criminal offences [2016] OJ L336/3.

[123] Second Additional Protocol to the Convention on Cybercrime (adopted on 17 November 2021) ETS 185, art 5(1).

investigation or proceedings. Upon receiving such notification or engaging in consultation, the State party holds the authority to instruct the operator not to disclose subscriber information in the following circumstances. The first is when the disclosure could undermine ongoing criminal investigations or proceedings within the State party. The second is when the requested subscriber information falls within the grounds for refusal outlined in the Cybercrime Convention for Judicial Assistance Requests.

Furthermore, States parties have the option to include reservations to Article 7 of the Second Additional Protocol at the time of signing, ratifying, or approving the Convention. They may also choose to exclude the application of this article if the disclosure of certain types of access numbers is deemed incompatible with the fundamental principles of their national legal system.

Additionally, there exists a mechanism to ensure the enforcement of orders issued by other contracting parties for the expeditious submission of subscriber information and communication records. This mechanism entails the involvement of authorities from another State to execute such orders.

Every State party is responsible for ensuring that establishing, implementing, and applying the powers and procedures outlined in this Protocol adhere to the conditions and safeguards established within their respective national laws. Given the diversity of legal systems and cultural backgrounds among States parties, providing precise specifications for the conditions and safeguards applicable to each procedure is not feasible. Instead, the Protocol emphasizes that States parties must offer adequate guarantees of human rights and freedoms and uphold common standards and minimum safeguards that comply with their obligations under relevant international human rights instruments. By doing so, they ensure the protection of individuals' rights and maintain the application of consistent safeguards.

Suppose both the transferring party and the receiving party are bound by an international agreement that establishes a comprehensive framework for protecting personal data and applies to the transfer of data to prevent, detect, investigate, and prosecute criminal offences. In that case, the terms of that agreement shall apply to the personal data received under this Protocol.

5.3 Assessment

The resolution of jurisdictional and human rights concerns arising from direct cooperation, as mentioned in Section 1, can be achieved by implementing the Data Access Agreements and the Second Additional Protocol. Adopting these mechanisms will encourage States to establish a uniform mechanism that will be incorporated into domestic laws. However, direct cooperation can occur only between countries that have adopted similar principles regarding data protection and the transborder transfer of data, as the requesting country determines the applicable law. Moreover, treaties enabling direct cooperation are typically established between countries that share policies beyond judicial cooperation, such as those concerning personal data protection and digital trade. Consequently, internet communication restrictions have already emerged when operators opt out of one country due to conflicts between legal frameworks.

6. Concluding Remarks

An excessively broad jurisdictional scope in direct cooperation can potentially conflict with pertinent privacy and data protection legislation. Historically, such jurisdictional conflicts have manifested, yet their incidence has waned, partly due to economic globalization. Concerning the direct acquisition of communication data, the likelihood of convergence remains uncertain unless a consensus materializes on fundamental values, notably those concerning privacy and human rights. There is no tangible indication of a global consensus on this matter.

Moreover, certain facets of data acquisition fail to neatly align with established norms within the domain of traditional criminal procedure laws. The mere presence of due process guarantees at the point of data acquisition proves insufficient; specific regulations governing data storage and post-acquisition disposal become requisite. Consequently, certain dimensions of data acquisition necessitate the redressal of inherent structural constraints inherent to the criminal procedures. No universally applicable norms have been established to address this challenge.

In prospective developments, it is anticipated the formulation of normative frameworks alongside enhanced cooperation, primarily with OECD nations, which share common democratic principles. Conversely, collaborative efforts on data acquisition involving authoritarian States will likely be based on MLATs. It is imperative to exercise caution in this regard to prevent the potential fragmentation of the global internet infrastructure.

13
Conclusion

1. Consent-Based Investigation of Transnational Crimes

Criminal investigations lie at the core of State sovereignty, embodying a fundamental expression of a State's coercive powers. It is the primary reason why international cooperation in this area remains challenging and, as a result, has slowly progressed. Collaboration in the suppression of cross-border crimes continues to be primarily State-centric. Mutual legal assistance treaties (MLATs), the instruments for facilitating cooperation, operate on a reciprocal basis. States are not obligated to respond to foreign requests for investigative assistance without such legally binding frameworks. Consequently, international cooperation in criminal investigations remains limited, contingent on treaty obligations.

This conventional understanding is still valid. However, it does not give the full picture of the investigation of transnational crime. This book argued that the procedure to obtain the evidence relies on the consent of counterpart States and private enterprises. States obtain an agreement from States where information is located, explicitly and tacitly, formally and informally, through instruments covering criminal and non-criminal matters. States also rely on the consent of corporations, financial institutions, and communication service providers operating in foreign jurisdictions to obtain data and information relevant to investigations. The impetus for States and entities to offer such consent stems from their need to remain integrated within globally interconnected financial, economic, and information networks.

It is a historical fact that the United States led the development of this investigative approach. Its main motivation was to mitigate the national security threats and economic harm posed by transnational crimes, including violations of antitrust laws, securities fraud, and tax fraud, as well as organized crimes and terrorism. Several elements enabled the United States to do so. It has been the home to multinational corporations, mega-financial institutions, and service providers of information technology. Therefore, it was easier for the United States to extend its jurisdiction when the foreign company does business in its territory or belongs to a US corporation group. It also began using mechanisms such as deferred prosecution agreements (DPAs) to reduce the likelihood of corporations disputing jurisdictional issues.

International Law and the Investigation of Transnational Crimes. Yurika Ishii, Oxford University Press.
 DOI: 10.1093/9780198957089.003.0013

It is also noted that the United Kingdom set the foundation by creating the Euro Market and, eventually, offshore financial centres. While the United Kingdom was generally not proactive in addressing transnational crimes beyond its borders, it established the financial architecture in which countries and business sectors are integrated. Then, the United States could use the dollar clearance system as leverage to ensure compliance with its policies as long as the counterparty relies on the currency.

Another key aspect of modern criminal investigations is the shift towards digital information, which has reshaped cross-border investigations. It allows States to access essential data directly through cyberspace or from private entities such as financial institutions and communication service providers without physically entering another State's territory.

The flow of information has grown not only in volume but also in complexity. People now exchange vast amounts of information through mobile devices, tablets, and other digital tools, which have become integral to their daily lives. Each location visited, each search query entered, and each interaction left a digital footprint stored on the operators' personal devices and servers. It enables law enforcement officers to trace an individual's behaviours.

The deepening and expansion of digital technologies, including artificial intelligence (AI), distributed ledger technology, and quantum information communication, have the effect of lowering the boundaries between countries and societies and promoting the global distribution of information. Additionally, societies are steadily transitioning to cashless systems by adopting electronic payments, mobile wallets, and digital currencies. The digitalization of money allows for easier tracking of an individual's behaviours and the movement of funds that may be linked to criminal activities.

This book explored the current practice and standards concerning cross-border investigation in light of these significant societal changes. While it examined how such mechanisms are established, it also paid a close attention to the rights and interests of suspects and defendants. States have a constitutional obligation to safeguard the rights and well-being of individuals within their jurisdiction. It is the duty arising from the delegation of authority by the people to the sovereign. In the contemporary settings, however, States increasingly possess the capacity to intrude upon and scrutinize the private spheres of individuals. Natural persons have a limited capacity under international law. When a State transfers their information to a foreign government, it usually lacks formal standing to object. Additionally, individuals may consent to financial institutions and communication service providers sharing their information with governments as a condition of service use. Nevertheless, such consent is nominal when individuals have little practical alternative because the technology is deeply embedded in their daily life. The primary question of this book has been to what extent international law address this gap.

2. Summary of the Key Findings

2.1 Expanding the Realm of State Jurisdiction

Part I of the book started by exploring the significance and limits of conventional cross-border criminal investigation. Transnational criminal law embedded the State-centric structure as they developed international cooperation mechanisms on criminal matters, including MLATs.[1] While the fundamental principles remain unchanged, the mechanisms of enforcement have evolved. A key development has been the process of globalization, which facilitates the extension of State jurisdiction over foreign entities. Additionally, the digitization of information has significantly enhanced States' capacity to collect and manage data efficiently.

Since the 1970s, States have started to develop multilateral conventions on certain crimes that harm the common interests of the international community. While these instruments required member States to establish prescriptive jurisdiction, the obligations in providing evidence and information were limited as they left a wide range of grounds for refusal and the principle of reciprocity. In addition, the process is time-consuming and costly, making it an inadequate mechanism for effectively combating modern crime.[2]

On the other hand, unique challenges in investigating transnational crimes include complexities in gathering evidence across borders. Law enforcement officers use enhanced forms of investigation, including bulk data collection, to address this difficulty. It raises questions concerning distinctions between criminal investigations and intelligence surveillance.

The State-centric nature of mutual legal assistance limits individual rights under criminal procedural law, such as the right to a fair trial and exclusionary rules in cross-border investigations. The role of international human rights law is limited as it is often decentralized within transnational crime cooperation. There is a gradual shift towards a human-centric approach within scholarly arguments, yet it is not widely supported in practice.[3]

The United States started to exercise its jurisdiction over foreign entities operating in foreign jurisdictions. The issue of unilateral law enforcement sparked intense conflicts between States in the 1980s when affected States objected to the extraterritorial application of US domestic laws to events outside their jurisdiction.[4] However, subsequent adjustments to jurisdictional frameworks have reduced much of the friction between States. There are several backgrounds. First, objections based on jurisdictional principles, such as the effects principle in

[1] Chapter 2, Section 2.
[2] ibid.
[3] Chapter 3, Sections 3–5.
[4] Chapter 4, Section 2.

competition law, the source principle in tax law, which considers economic activity as the point of connection, or arguments that include aspects such as transactions taking place in the home country or being denominated in the home currency and the existence of a connection with the home enterprise, have diminished considerably.[5] Second, States recognized the need to suppress certain transnational crimes and established key instruments such as the Drug Convention, United Nations Convention against Transnational Organized Crime, International Convention for the Suppression of the Financing of Terrorism, and United Nations Convention against Corruption. These treaties require States to develop specific prescriptive jurisdiction.[6]

In addition, States started to use elaborate mechanisms such as DPAs. While its legality may be debated in a strict term, as individuals and private entities cannot formally renounce sovereignty, such law enforcement activities are unlikely to lead to international conflict.[7]

2.2 International Cooperation through Non-Criminal Agreements

Part II followed international cooperation through non-criminal agreements. The critical development is that many States amended their national legislation to allow their counterparty foreign States to use information for criminal procedures. This book examines how human rights are protected in investigations in key areas of business law, namely competition law, securities fraud, and tax fraud.

In investigating violations of competition laws, major developed States and bodies, most notably the United States and the European Union, apply their competition laws to foreign corporations that affect their respective markets. The US effects doctrine, which previously gave rise to jurisdictional conflicts, is now widely accepted by many States. Mechanisms such as positive and negative comity agreements have become essential in minimizing conflicts and fostering mutual legal respect among competition authorities. A central issue in such cases is the right of defence. Safeguarding individuals and corporations from excessive or unjust prosecution in cross-border investigations is paramount. However, most States do not demand the same level of rigorousness in administrative investigations as in criminal procedural law. The European Union has been at the forefront of developing standards for fair proceedings.[8]

Jurisdictional conflicts among States have been less significant in securities fraud investigations, as States typically base their enforcement on transactions

5 Chapter 4, Section 4.
6 Chapter 2, Section 4.
7 Chapter 5, Section 3.
8 Chapter 6.

conducted within their stock exchanges. Efforts have been made to harmonize domestic laws, but limitations in judicial assistance under treaties have led financial regulatory authorities to develop informal cooperation mechanisms. In some countries, domestic authorizations support this shift by allowing financial authorities to share information with other States under more lenient conditions than those required for mutual legal assistance. The International Organization of Securities Commissions has played a key role in facilitating such informal exchanges of information. However, the protection of individual rights remains primarily confined to domestic laws, with limited international debate on these issues. Discussions have mainly focused on financial privacy and protecting fundamental rights through domestic civil and administrative procedures.[9]

Tax information collection across borders has distinct features characterized by the proliferation of offshore markets and the bank secrecy maintained in these jurisdictions. However, the scope of international cooperation has expanded through various tax agreements, including tax information exchange agreements. The use of tax information in criminal proceedings has also become increasingly common. The United States, in particular, has implemented various measures to obtain tax information from financial institutions, including the Foreign Account Tax Compliance Act, to enhance cross-border information collection. Meanwhile, international efforts, such as those within the Organisation for Economic Co-operation and Development (OECD) Global Forum, have further advanced mechanisms for cross-border cooperation. However, the protection of individual rights, including taxpayer rights and tax privacy, remains primarily addressed at the domestic level, with limited development at the international level.[10]

States increasingly utilize non-criminal agreements and mechanisms to gather information and evidence for addressing conventional transnational crimes such as foreign bribery and terrorism.

Significant efforts have been made to harmonize substantive laws in the context of foreign bribery, as exemplified by the OECD Anti-Bribery Convention. However, the enforcement of these laws remains limited due to practical challenges, particularly the difficulty in detecting such offences. States have established informal cooperation mechanisms among law enforcement authorities to address these issues. Additionally, some States have developed collaborative frameworks with corporations, including DPAs and measures that incentivize self-reporting.[11]

In the case of terrorism, counterterrorism intelligence operations have significantly evolved, particularly following the 9/11 terrorist attacks in the United States. The United States, for instance, began collecting terrorism screening information through administrative agreements, such as the Homeland Security

[9] Chapter 7.
[10] Chapter 8.
[11] Chapter 9.

Presidential Directive 6 Agreements and Preventing and Combating Serious Crime Agreements. Moreover, the exchange of airline passenger name records has been formalized through administrative agreements overseen by the International Civil Aviation Organization. States have also entered into administrative agreements to exchange biometric and biogenetic information to bolster counter-terrorism efforts.[12]

2.3 Direct Cooperation between Governments and Foreign Business Entities

Part III examined direct cooperation with the investigating government and a foreign private entity, namely financial institutions and communications service providers.

States have developed strict anti-money laundering and combating the financing of terrorism (AML/CFT) regulations, particularly in the aftermath of the 9/11 attacks in the United States in 2001. Data protection and privacy legislation can potentially conflict with AML/CFT regulations. However, jurisdictional clashes have largely been avoided because States assert jurisdictional authority because financial institutions operate within their territory. The focus has shifted from intergovernmental cooperation towards direct collaboration between governments and financial institutions. In recent years, private financial institutions have increasingly shared information among themselves. States actively encourage such exchanges and use AI to detect irregular transactions. This issue raises significant privacy concerns, which the European Union has partially addressed. However, there remains a lack of established international standards on the matter.[13]

States obtain information from foreign communication service providers based on a substantial connection between the State and the providers. Even without a physical presence within the State, the virtual provision of services is often considered sufficient to establish such a nexus. Significant challenges arise due to personal information protection and data protection legislation, which typically prohibit the transfer of user data to foreign authorities. Another contentious issue is the obligation placed on service providers to decrypt data. The conflicting approaches to privacy, particularly digital privacy and national security among States, further complicate efforts to harmonize standards. In response to these challenges, some like-minded countries have established data access agreements, enabling them to require service providers to submit the requested information directly. On the other hand, it is unlikely that States with differing political systems will agree on common digital privacy standards.[14]

[12] Chapter 10.
[13] Chapter 11.
[14] Chapter 12.

2.4 Implications of the Findings

This book's findings have several implications for the literature on transnational criminal law. First, previous scholarship in international law has primarily focused on the extent of States' obligations to suppress certain transnational crimes. This perspective has its value, as fostering criminal justice cooperation within the decentralized framework of the international community represents a significant achievement. However, States now rely on consent-based frameworks other than MLATs to collect information and evidence. There is less motivation for affected States to protest such informal measures.

The significance of this book lies in redirecting scholarly attention from an emphasis on criminal obligations to an examination of private rights in the context of transnational crime. This shift in perspective opens new avenues for research and deeper analysis of the multifaceted nature of cross-border criminal justice cooperation.

Second, the outcome of this research will be a new addition to the study of international human rights law. In response to globalization, recent years have seen a growing number of recommendations and arguments from international human rights organizations arguing for extending States' obligations to guarantee human rights beyond their territory or for States to provide remedies for human rights violations committed abroad. These debates have included whether human rights violations in one country can be addressed through civil proceedings in a third country or how corporations can be held accountable for human rights abuses. Over time, these debates have generated a significant volume of academic literature.

The consideration on the general principles of transnational crimes is part of this broader discourse. It explores the possibility of remedying extraterritorial human rights violations through criminal proceedings in the jurisdiction where the crime occurred. This publication aims to contribute to the ongoing debate in related fields by presenting these theories and examining their implementation. It seeks to shed light on the potential avenues for addressing extraterritorial human rights violations and to provide valuable insights for scholars and practitioners working in these areas.

While not a central focus of this book, an understanding of the potential impact on these marginalized groups is crucial for developing comprehensive and inclusive regulations that consider the diverse range of stakeholders affected by transnational crime. For instance, protecting victims of crime is a significant issue that requires attention. To illustrate, in cases where the country with jurisdiction over the crime in question differs from the country where the victim is located, the provision of adequate remedies necessitates the collaboration of both parties. This issue has been acknowledged as a matter of policy concern, yet the provisions of the relevant treaties addressing it remain limited in scope.

Furthermore, the financial burden of combating crime is ultimately borne by the citizens of a country and consumers in related industries. The impact of these regulations is particularly evident for individuals and groups who lack economic or political power. For instance, implementing rigorous regulations on financial institutions has resulted in more expensive account maintenance and transaction fees, which may present a challenge for individuals seeking to open accounts or transfer funds from their home country. Similarly, strict regulations on the financing of terrorism can prevent humanitarian non-governmental organizations from providing essential assistance by restricting their ability to transfer small amounts of money into areas controlled by terrorist organizations. This restriction can deprive local communities of much-needed assistance. It is necessary for each State to adopt comprehensive legislation to ensure that these people remain protected.

Third, the findings of this book highlight that the regulatory framework for each crime involves not only the State but also non-State actors, such as financial institutions and corporations, who seek to uphold international public values in their own capacity. The report provides a comprehensive account of the cooperation between these non-State actors and the State, particularly in the enforcement phase of information sharing and evidence gathering.

Cooperation between governments and financial institutions emerges as a crucial element in collecting financial information relating to various crimes, including violations of economic sanctions, securities crimes, tax crimes, and terrorist financing. While excluding non-State actors from the realm of international legal actors is a recognized issue in other areas of law, its significance in the context of international criminal law has rarely been explored. This book presents a fresh perspective on the issue, shedding light on the complex dynamics between State and non-State actors and their contributions to the regulatory landscape of transnational crime.

Fourth, the analysis in this book reveals the diversification of international law in international criminal law. The book emphasizes that while certain information can only be obtained through mutual assistance treaties, informal methods are used due to the availability of information through alternative channels.

Previous studies have highlighted the problematic nature of a State-centric approach, the limitations of the distinction between international and national law, the blurred boundaries between public and private law, civil and criminal law, and the expanding area of soft law. It is noteworthy, however, that these discussions have often neglected the interface with international criminal law. This book tried to break with this trend by demonstrating that general principles of international law apply to the international regulation of transnational crimes, transcending these conventional distinctions. It emphasizes the interconnectedness and relevance of broader international legal theories to the specific regulation of transnational crimes, challenging the notion that these distinctions should be taken for granted.

3. Ways Forward—Necessary Legal Development

3.1 The Remaining Problems

The remaining questions arise about the fairness of data practices and how individual rights are protected in the digital age. The protection of due process, the right to a fair trial, and privacy are paramount. This issue has been addressed in each chapter of this book. The conclusion is that there is no established, coherent rule of international law to protect human rights in the context of cross-border investigations.

However, the lack of harmonized international regulations and rapid technological change pose significant obstacles. It is necessary to build a foundation of trust between individuals and institutions based on transparency, accountability, and the rule of law to address these challenges. By upholding these principles, society can ensure that the benefits of digital technologies are realized while mitigating potential risks. With this regard, fostering a global dialogue prioritizing protecting individual rights and the responsible use of digital technologies is imperative.

The ongoing debate on the fundamental principles of international criminal law aims to address these limitations and challenges. Efforts are being made to increase the transparency of information-gathering procedures, strengthen the rights of private parties to object, and promote impartiality in the legal framework. These objectives are pursued through individual criminal provisions in the hope that they will strengthen rules and protect private individuals' rights.

In addition, this publication highlights that collecting evidence and information through the international regulation of transnational crimes may potentially conflict with each country's criminal procedure principles. These conflicts may involve due process guarantees, the exclusionary rule concerning illegally obtained evidence, and the risk of double jeopardy. While remedies for such disputes may be available under the domestic law of the forum State, there is no international coordination on the criteria for addressing these issues. Even if a violation of these principles were found, it would not necessarily invalidate the effectiveness of the assistance provided.

The possibility of legal challenges against the authorities of the requested State remains, at least to some extent. While previous scholarship has suggested that once a State has agreed to provide mutual legal assistance, private individuals cannot bring legal claims against it; this publication challenges the accuracy of this State-centric understanding of international law, particularly concerning substantive law. The debate on general principles of cross-border criminal law aims to overcome existing limitations. There is the possibility that defendants bring litigation against law enforcement authorities, either in their home State or in the international forum, such as regional human rights courts.

3.2 Legality and Due Process of the Investigation

As discussed throughout this book, criminal procedure must align with the established principles of international human rights law, encompassing due process and the right to privacy. In the context of cross-border investigations of transnational crimes, these rules and standards should be adapted to meet the demands of the digital era and be harmonized at an international level. In particular, the following gaps concerning substantive law should be addressed.

First, States should develop international standards for cross-border investigations that uphold due process and the right to a fair trial as central principles. States should adopt common standards aligned with international human rights law to ensure individuals are afforded equitable protections, regardless of jurisdiction.

Second, States should establish protocols to ensure due process, including the right to legal representation, transparent communication of charges, and access to evidence. They should avoid procedural inconsistencies when the procedure takes place in more than one jurisdiction so that they can maintain the integrity of the investigation.

Third, States should implement strict international guidelines to protect privacy rights while exchanging personal and digital data in cross-border investigations. Measures should comply with the OECD Guidelines on the Protection of Privacy and Transborder Flows of Personal Data of 2023, including limiting data collection to what is strictly necessary, ensuring secure data transfer, and prohibiting unauthorized use or sharing of personal information across borders.

Fourth, States should promote uniform rights to fair trial standards across jurisdictions involved in cross-border criminal investigations. It should include impartial judicial bodies, evidence disclosure, and timely proceedings, ensuring defendants are not disadvantaged by varying national standards.

The principle of due process is critically dependent on the procedural aspect of the investigation. Transparency and accountability in law enforcement measures are necessary to build and maintain citizens' trust in their governments and companies that use their personal information. Policies should be documented and accessible to courts and relevant parties to ensure oversight and compliance with substantive human rights standards. Agencies must be accountable for their actions, which would prevent abuses of power and provide avenues for redress when violations occur. Such trust is fundamental to the legitimacy of investigations, including data-sharing practices. Ultimately, these principles will strengthen the rule of law.

3.3 Forms of Norm Creation

The characteristics of investigating transnational crimes necessitate a flexible approach to norm creation. While essential, the conclusion of treaties, such as MLATs or conventions regulating specific crimes, is not the sole avenue for developing effective investigative frameworks. It can also occur through alternative frameworks, including informal agreements, harmonized procedural guidelines, and evolving cooperation among international organizations. Combined with the consent-based framework of information exchange, they can have a meaningful impact on cross-border cooperation.

Cooperation within and among international organizations plays a significant role in fostering these norms. Intergovernmental bodies, such as the OECD and the Financial Action Task Force, can influence rules and standards by setting informal norms, which the member States voluntarily adopt. Such informal norms can enhance efficiencies because such standards can reflect technical development more rapidly. Peer-review mechanisms, which employ 'naming and shaming' strategies for non-compliant States, can be effective, as they risk damaging the reputation of these States and their enterprises within global markets and networks.

National legislation further contributes to norm creation through extraterritorial effects. In addition to the United States, the European Union has a strong voice concerning the protection of human rights, where their regulatory standards extend beyond the EU borders, influencing foreign jurisdictions to adopt similar norms. Norm creation in this context can take various forms, including harmonization, norm diffusion, and dissemination. These processes effectively create norms that support principles necessary for investigating transnational crimes.

4. Concluding Remarks

International criminal jurisprudence has engaged with diverse frameworks to address crime and mitigate the decentralized structure of the international community. Regulating cross-border crime remains a critical aspect of this effort, yet its complexity surpasses the scope commonly depicted in studies on criminal mutual assistance. This complexity arises from the pressing need to address the disparities in wealth and information that globalization intensifies. This publication illustrates how establishing international cooperation on cross-border crime entails gradually delineating cooperative boundaries and carefully weighing values deeply embedded in the policies, economies, and cultures of the nations involved.

It endeavours to harmonize the imperative of crime control with the principle of national sovereignty.

To fully comprehend the construction of this intricate legal framework, it is essential to analyse the nature and legal functions of State practice. Only through such efforts can international criminal jurisprudence offer meaningful insights to address the complex challenges of globalization. If this publication has in any way contributed to advancing this effort, it has fulfilled its purpose of promoting the study of international law and the investigation of transnational crimes.

Selected Bibliography

Aaronson E and Shaffer G, 'The Transnational Legal Ordering of Criminal Justice' in Gregory Shaffer and Ely Aaronson (eds), *Transnational Legal Ordering of Criminal Justice* (CUP 2021)

Abbell M, 'Obtaining Evidence in the U.S. in Criminal Cases through Use of Compulsory Process' in Richard D Atkins (ed), *The Alleged Transnational Criminal: The Second Biennial International Criminal Law Seminar* (Martinus Nijhoff Publishers 1995)

Abbell M, *Obtaining Evidence Abroad in Criminal Cases 2010* (Brill 2010)

Aiolfi G and Bauer H-P, 'The Wolfsberg Group' in Mark Pieth (ed), *Collective Action: Innovative Strategies to Prevent Corruption* (Dike Verlag 2012)

Akehurst M, 'Jurisdiction in International Law' (1972) 46 British Year Book of International Law 145

Allen S, 'Enforcing Criminal Jurisdiction in The Clouds and International Law's Enduring Commitment to Territoriality' in Stephen Allen and others (eds), *Oxford Handbook of Jurisdiction in International Law* (OUP 2019)

Allum F and Gilmour S (eds), *The Routledge Handbook of Transnational Organized Crime* (2nd edn, Routledge 2022)

Andō T, *Kokusai Terorizumu Ni Taisuru Hōteki Kisei No Kōzō: Terorizumu Bōshi Kanren Shojōyaku Ni Okeru Saiban Kankatsuken No Kentō* [*The Structure of Legal Control of International Terrorism*] (Shohan, Kokusai Shoin 2020)

Antoine RMB, *Confidentiality in Offshore Financial Law* (2nd edn, OUP 2014)

Avi-Yonah RS, *International Tax as International Law: An Analysis of the International Tax Regime* (CUP 2006)

Avi-Yonah RS, *Advanced Introduction to International Tax Law* (3rd edn, Routledge 2021)

Baisini J, 'The Taking of Evidence for Foreign Courts' in International Law Association (ed), *Report of the Fifteenth Conference Held at Genoa, October 5th-10th, 1892* (Wyman and Sons, Ltd 1892)

Baker P, *Double Taxation Conventions and International Tax Law: A Manual on the OECD Model Tax Convention on Income and on Capital of 1992* (2nd edn, Sweet & Maxwell 1994)

Baker P, 'Some Thoughts on Jurisdiction and Nexus' in Guglielmo Maisto (ed), *Current Tax Treaty Issues. 50th Anniversary of the International Tax Group* (IBFD Publications 2020)

Baker S, 'The Taking of Evidence for Foreign Tribunals' in International Law Association (ed), *Report of the Eighth Annual Conference, held at Berne, August 24th–27th, 1880* (William Clowes and Sons, Ltd 1880)

Barbezat D, 'Cooperation and Rivalry in the International Steel Cartel, 1926–1933' (1989) 49 Journal of Economic History 435

Basedow J, *Limits and Control of Competition with a View to International Harmonization* (Kluwer 2002)

Basedow J, 'Antitrust or Competition Law, International' in Rüdiger Wolfrum (ed), *Max Planck Encyclopedia of Public Internation Law* (online edn, OUP 2014)

Bassiouni MC, 'An Appraisal of the Growth and Developing Trends of International Criminal Law' (1974) 45 Revue International de Droit Penal 405

Bassiouni MC, 'Mixed Model of The International Criminal Justice' in M Cherif Bassiouni (ed), *International Criminal Law, Volume 3: International Enforcement* (Martinus Nijhoff 2008)

Bassiouni MC, 'The Modalities of International Cooperation in Penal Matters' in M Cherif Bassiouni (ed), *International Criminal Law, Volume 2: Multilateral and Bilateral Enforcement Mechanisms* (Brill 2008)

Bassiouni MC, *Introduction to International Criminal Law* (Martinus Nijhoff Publishers 2012)

Basu S, *Global Perspectives on E-Commerce Taxation Law* (Ashgate 2007)

Baumbach A, Hopt K, and Hanno Merkt, *Handelgesetzbuch: Mit GmbH & Co., Handelsklauseln, Bank- Und Börsenrecht, Transportrecht (Ohne Seerecht)* (CH Beck 1982)

Bay NC, 'Executive Power and the War on Terror' (2005) 83 Denver University Law Review 335

Beare ME, *Critical Reflections on Transnational Organized Crime, Money Laundering and Corruption* (University of Toronto Press 2003)

Beare ME, *Encyclopedia of Transnational Crime and Justice* (Sage Publishing 2012)

Beaton-Wells C, 'Substance and Process in Competition Law and Enforcement: Why We Should Care If It's Not Fair' in Paul Nihoul and Tadeusz Skoczny (eds), *Procedural Fairness in Competition Proceedings* (Elgar 2015)

Berghoff H, '"Organised Irresponsibility"? The Siemens Corruption Scandal of the 1990s and 2000s' (2018) 60 Business History 423

Beyea G, 'Morrison v. National Australia Bank and the Future of Extraterritorial Application of the US Securities Laws' (2011) 72 Ohio State Law Journal 537

Blakesley CL, 'National Reports: United States of America' in Albin Eser, Otto Lagodny, and Christopher L Blakesley (eds), *The Individual as Subject of International Cooperation in Criminal Matters* (Nomos 2002)

Blas J and Farchy J, *The World for Sale: Money, Power, and the Traders Who Barter the Earth's Resources* (OUP 2021)

Blum J, 'The Regulation of Insider Trading in Germany: Who's Afraid of Self-Restraint' (1986) 7 Northwestern Journal of International Law & Business 507

Boister N, 'Human Rights Protection in the Suppression Conventions' (2002) 2 Human Rights Law Review 199

Boister N, *An Introduction to Transnational Criminal Law* (OUP 2012)

Boister N, 'Further Reflections on the Concept of Transnational Criminal Law' (2015) 6 Transnational Legal Theory 9

Boister N, 'The UN Convention against Transnational Organised Crime 2000' in Pierre Hauck and Sven Peterke (eds), *International Law and Transnational Organised Crime* (OUP 2016)

Boister N, 'Law Enforcement Cooperation between New Zealand and the United States: Serving the Internet "Pirate" Kim Dotcom Up on a "Silver Platter"?' in Saskia Hufnagel and Carole McCarthy (eds), *Trust in International Police and Justice Cooperation* (Hart Publishing 2017)

Boister N, *An Introduction to Transnational Criminal Law* (OUP 2018)

Boister N and Currie RJ, *Routledge Handbook of Transnational Criminal Law* (Routledge 2015)

Boister N, Gless S, and Jessberger F, 'Introduction' in Neil Boister, Sabine Gless, and Florian Jeßberger (eds), *Histories of Transnational Criminal Law* (OUP 2021)

Böse M, 'Judicial Protection in International and EU Law' in Martin Böse, Maria Bröcker, and Anne Schneider (eds), *Judicial Protection in Transnational Criminal Proceedings* (Springer 2021)

Böse M, Bröcker M, and Schneider A, *Judicial Protection in Transnational Criminal Proceedings* (Springer 2021)

Bowett DW, 'Jurisdiction: Changing Patterns of Authority over Activities and Resources' (1983) 53 British Year Book of International Law 1

Boyd V, 'Financial Privacy in the United States and the European Union: A Path to Transatlantic Regulatory Harmonization' (2006) 24 Berkeley Journal of International Law 939

Bradford A, *The Brussels Effect: How the European Union Rules the World* (OUP 2020)

Bradford A, *Digital Empires: The Global Battle to Regulate Technology* (OUP 2023)

Bregeault J, *De l'audition En Matière Criminelle Des Témoins Résidant En Pays Étranger* (E Thorin 1878)

Brilmayer L, 'The New Extraterritoriality: Morrison v. National Australia Bank, Legislative Supremacy, and the Presumption against Extraterritorial Application of American Law' (2010) 40 Southwestern Law Review 655

Brown D, 'Extraterritorial Ambit through Offence Definitions, Technology and Economic Power' in Micheál Ó Floinn and others (eds), *Transformations in Criminal Jurisdiction* (Hart Publishing 2023)

Brownlie I, *Principles of Public International Law* (2008)

Brunnée J and Toope SJ, *Legitimacy and Legality in International Law: An Interactional Account* (CUP 2010)
Buxbaum HL, 'Territory, Territoriality, and the Resolution of Jurisdictional Conflict' (2009) 57 The American Journal of Comparative Law 631
Buxbaum HL and Ralf M, 'Reasonableness as a Limitation on the Extraterritorial Application of U.S. Law: From 403 to 405 (via 404)' in Paul B Stephan and Sarah H Cleveland (eds), *The Restatement and Beyond* (OUP 2020)
Bygrave LA, *Data Privacy Law* (OUP 2014)
Canenbley C, *Enforcing Antitrust against Foreign Enterprises: Procedural Problems in the Extraterritorial Application of Antitrust Laws* (Kluwer 1981)
Cate FH, *Privacy in the Information Age* (Jessica Kingsley Publishers 1997)
Cate FH and Dempsey JX, *Bulk Collection: Systematic Government Access to Private-Sector Data* (1st end, OUP 2017)
Cavers DF, 'A Critique of the Choice-of-Law Problem' (1933) 47 Harvard Law Review 173
Chaikin DA, *Corruption and Money Laundering: A Symbiotic Relationship* (Palgrave Macmillan 2009)
Chaikin DA, 'The Impact of Swiss Principles of Mutual Assistance on Financial and Fiscal Crimes' (2006) 16 Revenue Law Journal 192
Chander A and Lê UP, 'Data Nationalism' (2014) 64 Emory Law Journal 677
Chandler HS, 'Searches South of the Border Admission of Evidence Seized by Foreign Officials' (1967) 53 Cornell Law Review 886
Chehtman A, 'The Presumption against Extraterritorial Criminal Jurisdiction' in Micheál Ó Floinn and others (eds), *Transformations in Criminal Jurisdiction: Extraterritoriality and Enforcement* (Hart Publishing 2023)
Chiu IHY, *Regulatory Convergence in EU Securities Regulation* (Wolters Kluwer Law & Business 2008)
Christensen MJ and Boister N, 'New Perspectives on the Structure of Transnational Criminal Justice' in Mikkel Jarle Christensen and Neil Boister (eds), *New Perspectives on the Structure of Transnational Criminal Justice* (Brill 2018)
Clarke E, *A Treatise upon the Law of Extradition* (Stevens and Haynes 1888)
Cleveland SH and Stephan PB, 'Introduction: The Roles of the Restatements in US Foreign Relations Law' in Paul B Stephan and Sarah H Cleveland (eds), *The Restatement and Beyond: The Past, Present, and Future of US Foreign Relations Law* (OUP 2020)
Cockayne J, 'Counterterrorism and Transnational Crime' in Jacob Katz Cogan, Ian Hurd, and Ian Johnstone (eds), *Oxford Handbook of International Organizations* (OUP 2017)
Cockfield AJ, 'The Rise of the OECD as Informal World Tax Organization through National Responses to E-Commerce Tax Challenges' (2005) 8 Yale Journal of Law and Technology 136
Cockfield AJ, 'A Comparative Analysis of Canadian and Foreign Private Sector Privacy Laws' in Elia Zureik (ed), *Surveillance, Privacy, and the Globalization of Personal Information* (McGill-Queens UP 2009)
Cockfield AJ, 'Protecting Taxpayer Privacy Rights under Enhanced Cross-Border Tax Information Exchange: Toward a Multilateral Taxpayer Bill of Rights' (2010) 42 University of British Columbia Law Review 420
Cohen FS, 'Transcendental Nonsense and the Functional Approach' (1935) 35 Columbia Law Review 809
Collins L, 'Provisional and Protective Measures in International Litigation' (1992) 234 Recueil des Cours 9
Cox D, *Handbook of Anti-Money Laundering* (Wiley 2014)
Crawford J, *Chance, Order, Change: The Course of International Law* (Martinus Nijhoff 2014)
Cruver DR, *Complying with the Foreign Corrupt Practices Act: A Guide for U.S. Firms Doing Business in the International Marketplace* (American Bar Association 1994)
Currie B, 'The Constitution and the Choice of Law: Governmental Interests and the Judicial Function' (1958) 26 The University of Chicago Law Review 9

Currie RJ, 'The Protection of Human Rights and the Suppression of Transnational Crime' in Neil Boister and Robert J Currie (eds), *Routledge Handbook of Transnational Criminal Law* (Routledge 2015)
Currie RJ, 'Cross-Border Evidence Gathering in Transnational Criminal Investigation: Is the Microsoft Ireland Case the "Next Frontier"?' (2016) 54 Canadian Yearbook of International Law 63
Dabbah MM and Hawk BE (eds), *Anti-Cartel Enforcement Worldwide* (CUP 2009)
Daskal J, 'Borders and Bits' (2017) 71 Vanderbilt Law Review 179
Daskal J, 'Microsoft Ireland, the CLOUD Act, and International Law Making 2.0' (2018) 71 Stanford Law Review 9
Davis K, *Between Impunity and Imperialism: The Regulation of Transnational Bribery* (OUP 2019)
Donnedieu de Vabres H, *Introduction à l'étude Du Droit Pénal International: Essai d'histoire et de Critique Sur La Compétence Criminelle Dans Les Rapports Avec l'étranger* (Sirey 1922)
Donnedieu de Vabres H, 'De La Reciprocité En Matière d'extradition d'après La Loi Francais Du 10 Mars 1927 et Le Nouveau Projet Allemand' (1928) 35 Revue générale de droit international public 333
Donnedieu de Vabres H, *Les Principes Modernes Du Droit Pénal International* (Librairie du Recueil Sirey 1928)
Dugard J and van den Wyngaert C, 'Reconciling Extradition with Human Rights' (1998) 92 American Journal of International Law 187
Dworkin RM, 'The Model of Rules' (1967) 35 The University of Chicago Law Review 14
Edwards CD, *Economic and Political Aspects of International Cartels* (Arno Press 1944)
Eser A, 'Common Goals and Different Ways in International Criminal Law: Reflections from a European Perspective' (1990) 31 Harvard International Law Journal 117
Eser A, 'Basic Issues' in Edward Martin Wise (ed), *Criminal Science in a Global Society: Essays in Honor of Gerhard O.W. Mueller* (FB Rothman 1994)
Eser A, 'Collection and Evaluation of Evidence in Comparative Perspective' (1997) 31 Israel Law Review 429
Farahany NA, *The Battle for Your Brain: Defending the Right to Think Freely in the Age of Neurotechnology* (1st edn, St Martin's Press 2023)
Faure MG and Zhang X, 'Towards an Extraterritorial Application of the Chinese Anti-Monopoly Law That Avoids Trade Conflicts' (2013) 45 George Washington Internation Law Review 101
Fedders JM, 'Policing Trans-Border Fraud in the United States Securities Markets: The Waiver by Conduct Concept—A Possible Alternative or a Starting Point for Discussions' (1985) 11 Brooklyn Journal of International Law 477
Fedders JM and others, 'Waiver by Conduct—A Possible Response to the Internationalization of the Securities Markets' (1984) 6 Journal of Comparative Business and Capital Market Law 1
Feuerbach PJA, *Lehrbuch Des Gemeinen in Deutschland Gültigen Peinlichen Rechts* (GF Heyer 1812)
Fijnaut C, 'Transnational Organized Crime and Institutional Reform in the European Union: The Case of Judicial Cooperation' in Phil Williams and Dimitri Vlassis (eds), *Combating Transnational Crime: Concepts, Activities and Responses* (Frank Cass Publisher 2001)
Finder LD, McConnell RD, and Mitchell SL, 'Betting the Corporation: Compliance or Defiance?' (2009) 28 Corporate Counsel Review 1
Findley MG, Nielson DL, and Sharman JC, *Global Shell Games: Experiments in Transnational Relations, Crime, and Terrorism* (CUP 2014)
Fjeld J and others, 'Principled Artificial Intelligence: Mapping Consensus in Ethical and Rights-Based Approaches to Principles for AI' (15 January 2020) Berkman Klein Center Research Publication No 2020-1 <http://dx.doi.org/10.2139/ssrn.3518482>
Fleischer AJ, 'Extra-Territorial Application of United States Securities Law' in Cecil J Olmstead (ed), *Extra-territorial Application of Laws and Responses Thereto* (OUP 1989)
Floinn MÓ and others, 'Introduction' in Micheál Ó Floinn and others (eds), *Transformations in Criminal Jurisdiction* (Hart Publishing 2023)

Forlati S and United Nations Office on Drugs and Crime, 'The United Nations Convention against Transnational Organized Crime and International Human Rights Law' (2022) UNODC Issue Paper <https://www.unodc.org/documents/organized-crime/tools_and_publications/21-01901_Human_Rights_eBook.pdf>
Franck TM, *The Power of Legitimacy among Nations* (OUP 1990)
Franck TM and Lockwood Jr BB, 'Preliminary Thoughts towards an International Convention on Terrorism' (1974) 68 American Journal of International Law 69
Franssen V and Ligeti K, 'Current Challenges in Economic and Financial Criminal Law in Europe and the US' in Katalin Ligeti and Vanessa Franssen (eds), *Challenges in the Field of Economic and Financial Crime in Europe and the US* (Hart Publishing 2017)
Freyer TA, *Antitrust and Global Capitalism, 1930–2004* (CUP 2006)
Friedman FB, Jacobs E, and Macel SC, 'Taking Stock of Information Sharing in Securities Matters' (2003) 10 Journal of Financial Crime 37
Friedman M, 'The Euro-Dollar Market: Some First Principles' [1969] Morgan Guaranty Survey 4
Friedmann W, *The Changing Structure of International Law* (Stevens 1964)
Takeshi Fujitani, 'Kazei mokuteki no jōhō kōkan seido no gurōbaruka to kokunai saibansho no yakuwari' [Globalisation of Information Exchange Systems for Taxation Purposes and the Role of National Courts] (2018) 69(1) Shakai Kagaku Kenkyu 39
Furukawa T, 'Punishment' in Yasuaki Ōnuma (ed), *A Normative Approach to War: Peace, War and Justice in Hugo Grotius* (Clarendon Press 1993)
Gallant K, *International Criminal Jurisdiction* (OUP 2022)
Gane C and Mackarel M, 'Admissibility of Evidence Obtained from Abroad into Criminal Proceedings: The Interpretation of Mutual Legal Assistance Treaties and Use of Evidence Irregularly Obtained' (1996) 4 European Journal of Crime Criminal Law and Criminal Justice 98
Garrett BL, 'Structural Reform Prosecution' (2007) 93 Virginia Law Review 853
Garrett BL, 'Globalized Corporate Prosecutions' (2011) 97 Virginia Law Review 1775
Garrett BL, *Too Big to Jail: How Prosecutors Compromise with Corporations* (Harvard UP 2016)
Gilmore WC, *Mutual Assistance in Criminal and Business Regulatory Matters* (CUP 1995)
Gilmore WC, *Dirty Money: The Evolution of International Measures to Counter Money Laundering and the Financing of Terrorism* (Council of Europe Publication 2004)
Gless S, 'Transnational Cooperation in Criminal Matters and the Guarantee of a Fair Trial: Approaches to a General Principle' (2013) 9 Utrecht Law Review 90
Gless S, 'Bird's-Eye View and Worm's-Eye View: Towards a Defendant-Based Approach in Transnational Criminal Law' (2015) 6 Transnational Legal Theory 117
Gless S and Richter T, 'Introduction' in Sabine Gless and Thomas Richter (eds), *Do Exclusionary Rules Ensure a Fair Trial?* (Springer 2019)
Gless S and Vervaele JAE, 'Law Should Govern: Aspiring General Principles for Transnational Criminal Justice' (2013) 9 Utrecht Law Review 1
Goeldner DM, 'France: Ordinance Creating a Stock Exchange Commission' (1968) 7 International Legal Materials 1063
Goelzer DL and Sullivan A, 'Obtaining Evidence for the International Enforcement of the United States Securities Laws' (1990) 16 Brooklyn Journal of International Law 145
Gray DC, Cooper M, and McAloon D, 'The Supreme Court's Contemporary Silver Platter Doctrine' (2012) 91 Texas Law Review 7
Greenleaf G, *Asian Data Privacy Laws* (OUP 2014)
Greenleaf G, 'Asia's Data Privacy Dilemmas: 2014–2019' (2019) 4 Revista Uruguaya de Protección de Datos Personales 49
Guerrin M and Kyriazis G, 'Cartels: Proof and Procedural Issues' (1992) 16 Fordham International Law Journal 266
Hachigian N, 'Essential Mutual Assistance in International Antitrust Enforcement' (1995) 29 International Lawyer 117
Hague Conference on Private Law, 'Report of the U.S. Delegation to the Eleventh Session of the Hague Conference on Private International Law' (1969) 8 International Legal Materials 785

Hall WE, *A Treatise on International Law* (Clarendon Press 1884)
Harari M and Jobin D, 'International Co-Operation' in Mark Pieth, Lucinda A Low, and Nicola Bonucci (eds), *The OECD Convention on Bribery* (2nd edn, CUP 2013)
Harfield C, *Covert Investigation* (OUP 2008)
Harris L, *Mutual Assistance in Criminal Matters: International Co-Operation in the Investigation and Prosecution of Crime* (Sweet & Maxwell 2000)
Härter K, 'Norms, Procedures and Practices of Transnational Criminal Law in 18th and Early 19th-Century Europe' in Neil Boister, Sabine Gless, and Florian Jeßberger (eds), *Histories of Transnational Criminal Law* (1st edn, OUP 2021)
Harth L and Chen Y, Chasing Fox Hunt: Tracing the PRC's Forced Return Operations around the Globe (Safeguard Defenders 2022)
Harvey D, *A Brief History of Neoliberalism* (OUP 2005)
Hawley JG, *The Law and Practice of International Extradition between the United States and Those Foreign Countries with Which It Has Treaties of Extradition* (Callaghan and Company 1893)
Hedlund G and Dunning JH, *Organization of Transnational Corporations* (Routledge 1993)
Heffernan WC, 'The Fourth Amendment Exclusionary Rule as a Constitutional Remedy' (2000) 29 Annual Review of Criminal Procedure 799
Helleiner E, *States and the Reemergence of Global Finance: From Bretton Woods to the 1990s* (Cornell UP 1994)
Herzog BE, 'The 1980 French Law on Documents and Information' (1981) 75 American Journal of International Law 382
Higgins R, *International Trade Law and the Avoidance, Containment and Resolution of Disputes: General Course on Public International Law* (Martinus Nijhoff 1991)
Hinterseer K, 'The Wolfsberg Anti-Money Laundering Principles' (2001) 5 Journal of Money Laundering Control 25 <https://www.emerald.com/insight/content/doi/10.1108/eb027291/full/html>
Hirsch Ballin MFH, *Anticipative Criminal Investigation: Theory and Counterterrorism Practice in the Netherlands and the United States* (TMC Asser Press 2012)
Honegger PC, 'Swiss Banking Secrecy' [1990] Butterworths Journal of International Banking and Financial Law 344
Hopt K, 'Insider Trading on the Continent' (1982) 4 Journal of Comparative Corporate Law and Securities Regulations 379
Hörnle J, *Internet Jurisdiction Law and Practice* (OUP 2021)
Hostetter V, 'Turning Insider Trading Insider out in the European Union' (1999) 30 California Western International Law Journal 175
Hufnagel S, 'Policing and Prosecution of Transnational Crime' in Valsamis Mitsilegas, Saskia Hufnagel, and Anton Moiseienko (eds), *Research Handbook on Transnational Crime* (Edward Elgar Publishing 2019)
Hufnagel S and McCartney C, 'Police Cooperation against Transnational Criminals' in Neil Boister and Robert J Currie (eds), *Routledge Handbook of Transnational Criminal Law* (Routledge 2014)
Hufnagel S and McCartney C, 'Introduction' in Saskia Hufnagel and Carole McCartney (eds), *Trust in International Police and Justice Cooperation* (Hart Publishing 2017)
Ishii Y, 'On Law Enforcement through Agreements between the US Regulatory Authorities and Foreign Corporations' in Dominik Brodowski and others (eds), *Regulating Corporate Criminal Liability* (Springer 2014)
Ishii Y, 'Keiji Sosa Ni Okeru Gaikoku Jigyosha Karano Tsushin Joho Shutoku' (2023) 12 Tokyo Journal of International Law 137
Ishii Y, 'Information Sharing with the Private Sector under Anti-Money Laundering and Countering the Financing of Terrorism Regulations' (Research Institute of Economy, Trade and Industry 2024) 24-E-010 <https://www.rieti.go.jp/en/publications/summary/24010014.html>
Ishii Y, 'Limits of State Jurisdiction in Cyberspace: The Legality of the Cross-Border Remote Access and the Use of Policeware' (2025) 67 Japanese Yearbook of International Law 26

Ivory R and Søreide T, 'The International Endorsement of Corporate Settlements in Foreign Bribery Cases' (2020) 69 International and Comparative Law Quarterly 945

Iwasawa Y, *International Law, Human Rights, and Japanese Law* (Clarendon Press 1998)

Jahae JIMG and others, 'Criminal Evidence Obtained Abroad—How to Assess the Legality of Obtaining It' in CM Breur and others (eds), *New Trends in Criminal Investigation and Evidence* (Intersentia 2000)

Jencken HD, 'The Taking of Evidence for Foreign Courts' in International Law Association (ed), *Report of the Sixth Annual Conference Held at Frankfort-on-the-Main, 20-23 August, 1878* (William Clowes and Sons, Ltd 1878)

Jennings R and Watts A, *Oppenheim's International Law* (9th edn, Longman 1992)

Jennings RY, 'Extraterritorial Jurisdiction and the United States Antitrust Laws' (1957) 33 British Year Book of International Law 146

Jessup PC, *A Modern Law of Nations: An Introduction* (Macmillan Company 1948)

Jessup PC, *Transnational Law* (Yale UP 1956)

Jimenez P, 'International Securities Enforcement Cooperation Act and Memoranda of Understanding' (1990) 31 Harvard International Law Journal 295

Johson V, *As I See It: How Cayman Became a Leading Financial Centre* (Book Guild Ltd 2001)

Jones A, *Jones and Doobay on Extradition and Mutual Assistance* (Anand Doobay and Alun Jones eds, Sweet & Maxwell 2005)

Joubert C, *Judicial Control of Foreign Evidence in Comparative Perspective* (Rozenberg Publishers 2005)

Keefe PR, 'Privatized Spying: The Emerging Intelligence Industry' in Loch K Johnson (ed), *The Oxford Handbook of National Security Intelligence* (1st edn, OUP 2010)

Keegan LE, 'The 1991 US/EC Competition Agreement: A Glimpse of the Future through the United States v. Microsoft Corp. Window' (1996) 2 Journal of International Legal Studies 149

Keith KJ, 'The International Court of Justice and Criminal Justice' (2010) 59 International and Comparative Law Quarterly 895

Keohane RO and Nye JS, *Transnational Relations and World Politics* (Harvard UP 1972)

Kerzner DS and Chodikoff DW, *International Tax Evasion in the Global Information Age* (Palgrave Macmillan 2016)

Kingsbury B, Krisch N, and Stewart RB, 'The Emergence of Global Administrative Law' (2005) 68 Law and Contemporary Problems 15

Kiriazis G, 'Jurisdiction and Cooperation Issues in the Investigation of International Cartels' (2001) 2 ABA Advanced International Cartel Workshop 6

Kleiner B, Schwob R, and Winzeler C, 'Art. 47' in Daniel Bodmer, Beat Kleiner, and Benno Lutz (eds), *Kommentar zum Bundesgesetz über die Banken und Sparkassen vom 8. November 1934 sowie zu der Verordnung vom 17. Mai 1972 und der Vollziehungsverordnung vom 30. August 1961* (Schulthess Verlag 2014)

Knittel MB, 'Articles 25, 26 and 27 Administrative Cooperation' in Thomas Ecker and Gernot Ressler (eds), *History of Tax Treaties: The Relevance of the OECD Documents for the Interpretation of Tax Treaties* (Linde 2011)

Koops B-J and Goodwin M, 'Cyberspace, the Cloud, and Cross-Border Criminal Investigation: The Limits and Possibilities of International Law' (2016) 5 Tilburg Law School Research Paper 1

Krauskopf L, 'Comments on Switzerland's Insider Trading, Money Laundering, and Banking Secrecy Laws' (1991) 9 International Tax and Business Law 277

Krisch N, 'Jurisdiction Unbound: (Extra)Territorial Regulation as Global Governance' (2022) 33 European Journal of International Law 481

Kropf JW and Cohen N, *Guide to U.S. Government Practice on Global Sharing of Personal Information* (2nd edn, American Bar Association, Section of Science & Technology Law 2015)

Kuner C, *Transborder Data Flows and Data Privacy Law* (OUP 2013)

Kuner C and OECD, 'Regulation of Transborder Data Flows under Data Protection and Privacy Law: Past, Present and Future' (2011) OECD Digital Economy Papers No 187 <https://www.oecd.org/content/dam/oecd/en/publications/reports/2011/12/regulation-of-transborder-data-flows-under-data-protection-and-privacy-law_g17a2074/5kg0s2fk315f-en.pdf>

Lagodny O, 'Comparative Study' in Albin Eser, Otto Lagodny, and Christopher L Blakesley (eds), *The Individual as Subject of International Cooperation in Criminal Matters: A Comparative Study* (Nomos Verlagsgesellschaft 2002)

Lasagni G, *Banking Supervision and Criminal Investigation*, vol 1 (Springer International Publishing 2019)

Laufer WS, *Corporate Bodies and Guilty Minds: The Failure of Corporate Criminal Liability* (University of Chicago Press 2006)

Lee P, 'Law and Practice with Respect to Insider Trading and Trading on Market Information in the United Kingdom' (1982) 4 Journal of Comparative Corporate Law and Securities Regulation 389

Lowe AV, *Extraterritorial Jurisdiction: An Annotated Collection of Legal Materials* (Grotius Publications 1983)

Lowenfeld AF, *Public Law in the International Arena: Conflict of Laws, International Law, and Some Suggestions for Their Interaction* (Martinus Nijhoff 1979)

Lowenfeld AF, 'Sovereignty, Jurisdiction, and Reasonableness: A Reply to AV Lowe' (1981) 75 American Journal of International Law 629

Luif P and Trauner F, 'The Prüm Process: The Effects of Enhanced Cooperation within Europe and with the United States in Combating Serious Crime' in Ronald L Holzhacker and Paul Luif (eds), *Freedom, Security and Justice in the European Union* (Springer New York 2014) 101-117

Lupsha P, 'Transnational Organized Crime versus the Nation-State' (1996) 2 Transnational Organized Crime 21

Lynch GE, 'The Role of Criminal Law in Policing Corporate Misconduct' (1997) 60 Law and Contemporary Problems 23

Madsen FG, 'The Historical Evolution of the International Cooperation against Transnational Organised Crime: An Overview' in Pierre Hauck and Sven Peterke (eds), *International Law and Transnational Organised Crime* (OUP 2016)

Madsen FG, 'Policing Transnational Organised Crime—The International Perspective' in Pierre Hauck and Sven Peterke (eds), *International Law and Transnational Organised Crime* (OUP 2016)

Maier HG, 'Extraterritorial Jurisdiction at a Crossroads: An Intersection between Public and Private International Law' (1982) 76 American Journal of International Law 280

Maier HG, 'Interest Balancing and Extraterritorial Jurisdiction' (1983) 31 American Journal of Comparative Law 579

Mallinak B, 'The Revenue Rule: A Common Law Doctrine for the Twenty-First Century' (2006) 16 Duke Journal of Comparative and International Law 79

Mann FA, 'The Doctrine of Jurisdiction in International Law' (1964) 111 Recueil des Cours 1

Mann FA, 'The Doctrine of International Jurisdiction Revisited after Twenty Years' (1984) 186 Recueil des Cours 9

Mann MD and Barry WP, 'Developments in the Internationalization of Securities Enforcement' (2005) 39 International Law 667

Mann MD, Mari JG, and Lavdas G, 'Developments in International Securities Law Enforcement and Regulation' (1995) 29 International Lawyer 729

Mann MD, Mari JG, and Lavdas G, 'International Agreements and Understandings for the Production of Information and Other Mutual Assistance' (1995) 29 International Lawyer 780

Markert K, 'Merger Control in Western Europe: National and International Aspects' in Oscar Schachter and Robert Hellawell (eds), *Competition in International Business: Law and Policy on Restrictive Practices* (Columbia UP 1981)

Martitz FV, *Internationale Rechtshilfe in Strafsachen: Beiträge Zur Theorie Des Positiven Völkerrechts Der Gegenwart*, vol 2 (H Haessel 1897)

Masui Y, 'Sozeijoyaku Ni Motozuku Joho Kokan' (2011) 30 *Kinyu Kenkyu* 253

Masui Y, 'Kazei Jōhō No Kōkan to Ōshū Jinken Jōyaku [Exchange of Tax Information and Human Rights Treaties]' (2017) 123 *Hogaku Shinpo* 333

Maxwell WJ, 'Systematic Government Access to Private-Sector Data in France' in Fred H Cate and James X Dempsey (eds), *Bulk Collection: Systematic Government Access to Private-Sector Data* (1st edn, OUP 2017)

Maynard PD, 'Offshore Banking Secrecy: Myth or Reality?' (1998) 1 Journal of Money Laundering Control 316

McCartney C, 'Forensic Data Exchange: Ensuring Integrity' (2015) 47 Australian Journal of Forensic Sciences 36

McCartney C, Granja R, and Töpfer E, 'Biometric Forensic Identity Databases in Europe: Precariously Balanced or Faulty Scales?' in Andrew Roberts, Joe Purshouse, and Jason Bosland (eds), *Privacy, Technology, and the Criminal Process* (Routledge 2024)

McClean JD, *Transnational Organized Crime: A Commentary on the UN Convention and Its Protocol* (OUP 2007)

McClean JD, *International Co-Operation in Civil and Criminal Matters* (OUP 2012)

McDougal MS, 'International Law, Power, and Policy: A Contemporary Conception' (1953) 82 Recueil des Cours 133

McGoogan C, 'Case Comment: Global Securities Corp. v. British Columbia (Securities Commission)' (2003) 61 University of Toronto Faculty of Law Review 219

Meier HB, Marthinsen JE, and Gantenbein PA, *Swiss Banking Secrecy* (John Wiley & Sons, Inc 2012)

Meili F, *Lehrbuch Des Internationalen Strafrechts Und Strafprozessrechts* (Art Institut O Füssli 1910)

Mejía-Lemos D, 'Advisory Opinion OC-22/16' (2017) 111 American Journal of International Law 1000

Mendez M, 'Passenger Name Record Agreement and European Court of Justice' (2007) 3 European Constitutional Law Review 127

Mettgenberg W, 'Die Reziprozität Im Deutschen Auslieferungsrecht' (1909) 25 Archiv für öffentliches Recht 1

Meyer BF, 'Swiss Banking Secrecy and Its Legal Implications in the United States' (1978) 14 New England Law Review 18

Meyer HH, 'Banking Secret and Economic Espionage in Switzerland' (1954) 23 George Washington Law Review 284

Milanovic M, *Extraterritorial Application of Human Rights Treaties: Law, Principles, and Policy* (OUP 2013)

Milanovic M, Gammeltoft-Hansen T, and Vedsted-Hansen J, 'Extraterritoriality and Human Rights: Prospects and Challenges' in Thomas Gammeltoft-Hansen and Jens Vedsted-Hansen (eds), *Human Rights and the Dark Side of Globalisation* (1st edn, Routledge 2016)

Mills JL, *Privacy: The Lost Rights* (OUP 2008)

Mitsilegas V, 'Transnational Criminal Law and the Global Rule of Law' in Giuliana Ziccardi Capaldo (ed), *The Global Community Yearbook of International Law and Jurisprudence 2016* (OUP 2017)

Mongillo V, 'The Jurisdictional Reach of Corporate Criminal Offences in a Globalised Economy: Effectiveness and Guarantees "Taken Seriously"' in Micheál Ó Floinn and others (eds), *Transformations in Criminal Jurisdiction* (Hart Publishing 2023)

Monier F, *Des Commissions Rogatoires En Droit International* (Impr H Jouve 1909)

Montague GH, 'Limitation of What UN Can Do Successfully: The Proposed UN Program on Restrictive Business Practices' (1955) 1 Antitrust Bulletin 441

Moohr GS, 'Prosecutorial Power in an Adversarial System: Lessons from Current White Collar Cases and the Inquisitorial Model' (2004) 8 Buffalo Criminal Law Review 165

Morishita T, 'Technical Description of DLT for Conflicts Lawyers' in Andrea Bonomi, Matthias Lehmann, and Shaheeza Lalani (eds), *Blockchain and Private International Law* (Brill 2023)

Morita A, 'Theoretical Analysis of Conflicting Approaches on State Jurisdiction—Focusing on "Liberté" and "Basic Positions"' (2024) 67 Japanese Yearbook of International Law 126

Mueller GOW, 'Transnational Crime: Definitions and Concepts' in Dimitri Vlassis and Phil Williams (eds), *Combating Transnational Crime: Concepts, Activities and Responses* (Routledge 2001)

Murschetz V, *European Police Cooperation in the Future Legal Framework of the European Union* (Brill 2010)

Nadelmann KH, 'Joseph Story's Contribution to American Conflicts Law: A Comment' (1961) 5 The American Journal of Legal History 230

Nakagawa J, *International Harmonization of Economic Regulation* (OUP 2011)

Nakasaki R, *Hanzai Shūeki Iten Bōshi Hō* (Indendently published, 8th edn, 2025)

Nakatani K, 'Terorizumu Ni Taisuru Sho Taiō to Kokusaihō' in Atsushi Yamaguchi and Kazuhiro Nakatani (eds), *Anzen Hoshō to Kokusai Hanzai* (Tokyo UP 2005)

Nanda VP, 'Corporate Criminal Liability in the United States' in Mark Pieth and Radha Ivory (eds), *Corporate Criminal Liability: Emergence, Convergence, and Risk* (2011)

Natarajan M, 'Gerhard Mueller's Role in Developing the Concept of Transnational Crime for the United Nations' in Neil Boister, Sabine Gless, and Florian Jeßberger (eds), *Histories of Transnational Criminal Law* (1st edn, OUP 2021)

Nelson BL, 'Insider Trading Originating Abroad and "Waiver-by-Conduct"' (1985) 19 The International Lawyer 817

Neo D, 'A Conceptual Overview of Bank Secrecy,' in Booysen S and Neo D (eds), *Can Banks Still Keep a Secret?* (CUP 2017) 3–30

Nishimura Institute of Advanced Legal Studies, 'Report by the CLOUD Act Study Group Ver. 2.0: Legal Analysis and Proposals On Criminal Investigations Obtaining Data Held by Companies' (2023) <https://www.nishimura.com/en/knowledge/publications/92692>

Nobel P and Braendli B, 'Switzerland' in Booysen S and Neo D (eds), *Can Banks Still Keep a Secret?: Bank Secrecy in Financial Centres around the World* (CUP 2017) 308–336

Noble RK, 'A New Anti-Crime Framework for the World: Merging the Objective and Subjective Models for Fighting Money Laundering' (1997) 30 NYU Journal of International Law and Policy 79

Obokata T, *Transnational Organised Crime in International Law* (Hart Publisher 2010)

O'Brien J, *Conflict of Laws* (Taylor & Francis 1999)

Odudu O and Bailey D, 'The Single Economic Entity Doctrine in EU Competition Law' (2014) 51 Common Market Law Review 1721

O'Keefe R, 'Cooperative National Regulation to Secure Transnational Public Goods: A Reply to Nico Krisch' (2022) 33 European Journal of International Law 515

Okuwaki N, 'Kokusaihō Kara Mita Kokusai Keiji Kyōryoku No Gendaiteki Tenkai' (2003) 278 Hogaku Kyoushitsu 4

ONUMA Yasuaki, *International Law in a Transcivilizational World* (CUP 2017)

Oppenheim L, *International Law: A Treatise* (Longmans, Green and Co 1905)

Oppenheim L, 'The Science of International Law: Its Task and Method' (1908) 2 American Journal of International Law 313

O'Sullivan JR, 'How Prosecutors Apply the "Federal Prosecutions of Corporations" Charging Policy in the Era of Deferred Prosecutions and What That Means for the Purposes of the Federal Criminal Sanction' (2014) 51 American Criminal Law Review 29

Palan R, 'Tax Havens and the Commercialization of State Sovereignty' (2002) 56 International Organization 151

Palan R, *Tax Havens: How Globalization Really Works* (Richard Murphy and Christian Chavagneux eds, Cornell UP 2010)

Papadopulos A, 'Bilateral Enforcement Cooperation Agreements' in Philip Marsden (ed), *Handbook of Research in Trans-Atlantic Antitrust* (Edward Elgar 2011)

Parlett K, *The Individual in the International Legal System: Continuity and Change in International Law* (CUP 2011)

Passas N, 'Globalization, Criminogenic Asymmetries, and Economic Crime' (1999) 1 European Journal of Law Reform 399

Paul JR, 'The Transformation of International Comity' (2008) 71 Law & Contemporary Problems 19
Pauwelyn J, Wessel R, and Wouters J, 'When Structures Become Shackles: Stagnation and Dynamics in International Lawmaking' (2014) 25 European Journal of International Law 733
Pauwelyn J, Wessel RA, and Wouters J, *Informal International Lawmaking* (OUP 2013)
Petrig A, 'The Expansion of Swiss Criminal Jurisdiction in Light of International Law' (2013) 9 Utrecht Law Review 34
Phillimore R, *Commentaries upon International Law*, vol 1 (T & JW Johnson 1854)
Picciotto S, *International Business Taxation: A Study in the Internationalization of Business Regulation* (Quorum Books 1992)
Pieth M, 'Introduction' in Mark Pieth, Lucinda A Low, and Nicola Bonucci (eds), *The OECD Convention on Bribery* (2nd edn, CUP 2013)
Pieth M and Aiolfi G, *A Comparative Guide to Anti-Money Laundering: A Critical Analysis of Systems in Singapore, Switzerland, the UK and the USA* (Edward Elgar Publishing 2004)
Piggott FT, *Extradition: A Treatise on the Law Relating to Fugitive Offenders* (Butterworth 1910)
Podgor ES, *White Collar Crime* (Nancy J King, Jerold H Israel, and Peter J Henning eds, West 2013)
Posadas A, 'Combating Corruption under International Law' (1999) 10 Duke Journal of Comparative and International Law 345
Privacy International, 'Responsible Use and Sharing of Biometric Data in Counter-Terrorism' (17 July 2020) <https://privacyinternational.org/advocacy/4064/briefing-responsible-use-and-sharing-biometric-data-counter-terrorism>
Public Prosecution Service of Canada, 'Deskbook, Guideline of the Director Issued under Section 3(3)(c) of the Director of Public Prosecutions Act' (2020) <https://www.ppsc-sppc.gc.ca/eng/pub/fpsd-sfpg/fps-sfp/tpd/p3/ch21.html>
Raible L, *Human Rights Unbound: A Theory of Extraterritoriality* (1st edn, OUP 2020)
Raustiala K, 'The Architecture of International Cooperation: Transgovernmental Networks and the Future of International Law' (2002) 43 Virginia Journal of International Law 1
Razzano FC, 'American Money Laundering Statutes: The Case for a Worldwide System of Banking Compliance Programs' (1994) 3 Journal of International Law and Practice 277
Reisman WM, *Folded Lies: Bribery, Crusades, and Reforms* (Free Press 1979)
Reuters, 'China Has Closed Unofficial "Police Stations" in Britain, UK Minister Says' *The Guardian* (7 June 2023) https://www.theguardian.com/world/2023/jun/07/china-has-closed-unofficial-police-stations-in-britain-uk-minister-says
Robinson D, Vasiliev S, Sliedregt E & Oosterveld V, *An Introduction to International Criminal Law and Procedure* (5th edn, CUP 2024)
Robinson PL, 'The Commonwealth Scheme Relating to the Rendition of Fugitive Offenders: A Critical Appraisal of Some Essential Elements' (1984) 33 International and Comparative Law Quarterly 614
Rosenne S, *League of Nations Committee of Experts for the Progressive Codification of International Law (1925–1928)*, vol 2 (Oceana Publications 1972)
Rosenzweig P, 'Civil Liberty and the Response to Terrorism' (2003) 42 Duquesne Law Review 663
Rotman E, *Regulating Fraud Across Borders: Internationalised Criminal Law Protection of Capital Markets* (Hart Publishing 2021)
Ruggeri S, *Transnational Inquiries and the Protection of Fundamental Rights in Criminal Proceedings: A Study in Memory of Vittorio Grevi and Giovanni Tranchina* (Springer 2012)
Ruggiero E, 'The Regulation of Insider Trading in Italy' (1996) 22 Brooklyn Journal of International Law 157
Ryngaert C, *Jurisdiction in International Law* (OUP 2015)
Ryngaert C, 'Jurisdiction' in Jean D'Aspremont and Sahib Singh (eds), *Concepts for International Law* (Edward Elgar Publishing 2019)
Ryngaert C, 'International Jurisdiction Law' in Austen Parrish and Cedric Ryngaert (eds), *Research Handbook on Extraterritoriality in International Law* (Edward Elgar Publishing 2023)

Saltzburg SA, 'The Reach of the Bill of Rights Beyond the Terra Firma of the United States' (1979) 20 Virginia Journal of International Law 742

Samaha J, *Criminal Procedure* (West 2010)

Satzger H, *International and European Criminal Law* (Hart Publishing 2012)

Saul B, *Defining Terrorism in International Law* (OUP 2006)

Schenk-Geers T, *International Exchange of Information and the Protection of Taxpayers* (Kluwer Law International 2009)

Schlosser P, *Der Justizkonflikt Zwischen Den USA Und Europa* (De Gruyter 1985)

Schlosser P, 'Jurisdiction and International Judicial and Administrative Co-Operation' (2000) 284 Recueil des Cours 9

Schmid AP, 'The Links between Transnational Organized Crime and Terrorist Crimes' (1996) 2 Transnational organized crime 40

Schroth PW, 'The United States and the International Bribery Conventions' (2002) 50 American Journal of Comparative Law 593

Schulhofer SJ, *The Enemy Within: Intelligence Gathering, Law Enforcement, and Civil Liberties in the Wake of September 11* (Century Foundation Press 2002)

Schwartz P, 'Legal Access to the Global Cloud' (2018) 118 Columbia Law Review 1681

Schwartz PM, 'Systematic Government Access to Private-Sector Data in Germany' in Fred H Cate and James X Dempsey (eds), *Bulk Collection: Systematic Government Access to Private-Sector Data* (1st edn, OUP 2017)

Scott J, 'Extraterritoriality and Territorial Extension in EU Law' (2014) 62 American Journal of Comparative Law 87

Seligman ERA, *Double Taxation and International Fiscal Cooperation* (Macmillan 1928)

Shaffer G, 'Globalization and Social Protection: The Impact of EU and International Rules in the Ratcheting Up of US Data Privacy Standards' (2000) 25 Yale Journal of International Law 1

Shaffer G, 'Transnational Legal Ordering and State Change' in Gregory C Shaffer (ed), *Transnational Legal Ordering and State Change* (1st edn, CUP 2012)

Shalchi A, 'Unexplained Wealth Orders' (14 April 2022) <https://commonslibrary.parliament.uk/research-briefings/cbp-9098/>

Shany Y, 'Digital Rights and the Outer Limits of International Human Rights Law' (2023) 24 German Law Journal 461

Sharman JC, *Havens in a Storm: The Struggle for Global Tax Regulation* (Cornell UP 2006)

Shearer IA, *Extradition in International Law* (Manchester UP 1971)

Sieber U and Neubert C-W, 'Transnational Criminal Investigations in Cyberspace: Challenges to National Sovereignty' (2017) 20 Max Planck Yearbook of United Nations Law 241

Simma B, 'Reciprocity' in Rüdiger Wolfrum (ed), *Max Planck Encyclopedia of Public Internation Law* (online edn, OUP 2008)

Simon RMM, 'Transnational Crime, Local Denial' (2007) 34 Social Justice 111

Smith CF and Parling BD, '"American Imperialism": A Practitioner's Experience with Extraterritorial Enforcement of the FCPA' (2012) 2012 University of Chicago Legal Forum 237

Snowden E, *Permanent Record: A Memoir of a Reluctant Whistleblower* (Macmillan 2019)

Solove DJ, 'Privacy and Power: Computer Databases and the Metaphors for Information Privacy' (2000) 53 Stanford Law Review 1393

Stadler A, *Der Schutz Des Unternehmensgeheimnisses Im Deutschen Und U.S.-Amerikanischen Zivilprozeß Und Im Rechtshilfeverfahren*, vol Bd. 3 (Mohr 1989)

Stein E, 'International Integration and Democracy: No Love at First Sight' (2001) 95 American Journal of International Law 489

Stessens G, *Money Laundering: A New International Law Enforcement Model* (CUP 2000)

Stiefel EC, Stürner R, and Stadler A, 'The Enforceability of Excessive US Punitive Damage Awards in Germany' (1991) 39 The American Journal of Comparative Law 779

Stone R, *The Interstate Commerce Commission and the Railroad Industry: A History of Regulatory Policy* (Praeger 1991)

Story J, *Commentaries on the Conflict of Laws, Foreign and Domestic* (Little Brown 1834)

Strobel K, *Organized Crime and International Criminal Law: History, Lex Lata, and Developments de Lege Ferenda* (Brill/Nijhoff 2021)

Stürner R, 'Die Gerichte Und Behörden Der U.S.A. Und Die Beweisaufnahme in Deutschland' (1982) 81 Zeitschrift für Vergleichende Rechtswissenschaft 159

Stürner R, 'Der Justizkonflikt Zwischen U.S.A. Und Europa' in Walther J Habscheid, Rolf Stürner, and Dieter G Lange (eds), *Der Justizkonflikt mit den Vereinigten Staaten von Amerika* (Gieseking-Verlag 1986)

Sutherland EH, *White Collar Crime* (Dryden Press 1949)

Sutherland PF, 'The Use of the Letter of Request (or Letter Rogatory) for the Purpose of Obtaining Evidence for Proceedings in England and Abroad' (1982) 31 International and Comparative Law Quarterly 784

Swan, Winifred, 'The 1988 Japanese Insider Trading Amendments: Will Japan See Results From These Tougher Laws' (1991) 12 University of Pennsylvania Journal of International Business Law 275

Swiss Bank Corporation, *The Truth about Swiss Banking* (Swiss Bank Corporation 1972)

Takeuchi M, 'Asian Experience with Extraterritoriality' in Austen Parrish and Cedric Ryngaert (eds), *Research Handbook on Extraterritoriality in International Law* (Edward Elgar Publishing 2023)

Tallman DA, 'Financial Institutions and the Safe Harbor Agreement: Securing Cross-Border Financial Data Flows' (2002) 34 Law and Policy in International Business 747

Taracouzio TA, 'International Cooperation of the USSR in Legal Matters' (1937) 31 American Journal of International Law 55

Taylor M, *Transatlantic Jurisdictional Conflicts in Data Protection Law: Fundamental Rights, Privacy and Extraterritoriality* (CUP 2023)

Teleki C, *Due Process and Fair Trial in EU Competition Law: The Impact of Article 6 of the European Convention on Human Rights* (Brill/Nijhoff 2021)

Thaman SC, 'Report on USA' in Stefano Ruggeri (ed), *Transnational Inquiries and the Protection of Fundamental Rights in Criminal Proceedings* (2012)

Thaman SC (ed), *Exclusionary Rules in Comparative Law* (Springer 2013)

Tiedemann K, *Wirtschaftsstrafrecht. Einführung Und Allgemeiner Teil Mit Wichtisten Rechtstexten* (Verlag Franz Vahlen 2014)

Tittle MB, *The Integrated 2006 United States Model Income Tax Treaty* (Reuven S Avi-Yonah ed, Vandeplas Publishing 2008)

Travers M, *Le Droit Pénal International et Sa Mise En Œuvre En Temps de Paix et En Temps de Guerre*, vol 4 (Sirey 1920)

Travers M, *L'entr'aide Répressive Internationale et La Loi Française Du 10 Mars 1927* (Librairie du Recueil Sirey 1928)

Umhoefer C and Pietrancosta A, 'Le Delit d'Initie: Insider Trading Law in France' (1992) 30 Columbia Journal of Transnational Law 89

Van Cleynenbreugel P, 'Effectiveness through Fairness? "Due Process" as an Institutional Precondition for Effective Decentralized EU Competition Law Enforcement' in Paul Nihoul and Tadeusz Skoczny (eds), *Procedural Fairness in Competition Proceedings* (Edward Elgar Publishing 2015)

Van Hoek AAH and Luchtman MJJP, 'Transnational Cooperation in Criminal Matters and the Safeguarding of Human Rights' (2005) 1 Utrecht Law Review 1

Van Uytsel S, 'The Original Leniency Programme of Japan' in Steven Van Uytsel, Mark Fenwick, and Yoshiteru Uemura (eds), *Leniency in Asian Competition Law* (CUP 2022)

Van Uytsel S and Uemura Y, 'Negotiated Leniency in Japan Embedded in Ever-Increasing Sanctions' in Steven Van Uytsel, Mark Fenwick, and Yoshiteru Uemura (eds), *Leniency in Asian Competition Law* (CUP 2022)

Vesque von Püttlingen J, *Handbuch Des in Österreich-Ungarn Geltenden Internationalen Privatrechtes Mit Besonderer Berücksichtigung Des Staats- Und Völkerrechtes* (W Braumüller 1878)

Vogel K, 'Double Tax Treaties and Their Interpretation' (1986) 4 International Tax and Business Law 1

Vogel K, *Klaus Vogel on Double Taxation Conventions: A Commentary to the OECD-, UN-, and US Model Conventions for the Avoidance of Double Taxation on Income and Capital, with Particular Reference to German Treaty Practice* (Kluwer Law International 1997)

Von Roenne CF, 'The Very Beginning—The First Tax Treaties' in Thomas Ecker and Gernot Ressler (eds), *History of Tax Treaties: The Relevance of the OECD Documents for the Interpretation of Tax Treaties* (Linde 2011)

Wang Z, 'Systematic Government Access to Private Sector Data in China,' in Cate FH and Dempsey JX (eds), *Bulk Collection: Systematic Government Access to Private-Sector Data* (OUP 2017) 241

Webb A, *The Big Nine: How the Tech Titans and Their Thinking Machines Could Warp Humanity* (Public Affairs 2020)

Thomas Weigend, 'Defense Rights in European Legal Systems under the Influence of the European Court of Human Rights,' in Darryl K Brown, Jenia Iontcheva Turner, Bettina Weisser (eds), *The Oxford Handbook of Criminal Process* (OUP 2019) 164

Westlake J, *International Law* (CUP 1910)

Wharton F, *A Treatise on the Conflict of Laws, or, Private International Law Including a Comparative View of Anglo-American, Roman, German, and French Jurisprudence* (Kay and Brothers 1872)

Whelan A, *Reciprocity in Public International Law* (CUP 2023)

Wiater P, 'Fundamental Rights of Corporations as International Human Rights: The Perspective of Regional Economic Courts' (2023) 23 Human Rights Law Review

Witterick CL, 'Regulation of Competition in the Canada/US Context—Extraterritorial Reach of US Antitrust Law—A Canadian Perspective' (1998) 24 Canada–United States Law Journal 299

World Conference on New Trends in Criminal Investigation and Evidence, *New Trends in Criminal Investigation and Evidence* (CM Breur and others eds, Intersentia 2000)

Wrage A and Richardson A, 'Siemens AG: Violations of the Foreign Corrupt Practices Act' (2009) 48 International Legal Materials 232

Zagaris B, *International White Collar Crime: Cases and Materials* (CUP 2010)

Zagaris B, 'U.S. Court Authorizes First Use of John Doe Summonses on Behalf of Foreign Government' (2013) 29(10) International Law Enforcement Reporter 1

Zagaris B, *International White Collar Crime* (2nd edn, CUP 2015)

Zagaris B and Gordon RA, *International Exchange of Tax Information: Recent Developments* (Practising Law Institute 1985)

Zanettin B, *Cooperation between Antitrust Agencies at the International Level* (Hart Publishing 2002)

Index

For the benefit of digital users, indexed terms that span two pages (e.g., 52–53) may, on occasion, appear on only one of those pages.

Editorial note: Country specific laws, policies and organizations are basically listed in the respective names of the countries. The country name in parentheses following each company's name indicates the country of incorporation at the time of the incident or case discussed in this book.